TIME FOR ACTION

THE WEST INDIAN COMMISSION

Patron: H.E. Dame Nita Barrow

Chairman: Sir Shridath Ramphal
Vice-Chairman: Sir Alister McIntyre

Mr. A. Leonard Archer
Mr. William Demas
Dr. Howard Fergus
Dr. Marshall Hall
Rev. Allan Kirton
Dr. Vaughan Lewis
Ms. Sandra Mason
Ms. Gillian Nanton
Mr. Philip Nassief
Prof. Rex Nettleford
Mr. Roderick Rainford
Mr. Frank Rampersad
Dr. Neville Trotz

Report Of The West Indian Commission

Time For Action

Second Edition

With a Postscript by Sir Shridath Ramphal

The Press–University of the West Indies
Kingston Jamaica

Originally published by
The West Indian Commission
© 1992 The West Indian Commission

The Press–University of the West Indies,
Mona, Kingston 7, Jamaica

© 1993 by *The Press*–University of the West Indies
All rights reserved.
Published 1993. Second Edition 1993.
Printed in Jamaica.

Cataloguing in Publication Data

West Indian Commission
    Time for Action: report of the West Indian
Commission / with a postscript by Sir
Shridath Ramphal.—2nd ed.

        p. cm.
    Includes bibliographical references.
    ISBN 976-41-0044-9
        1. Caribbean, English-speaking—Economic
integration. 2. Regionalism—Caribbean, English-speaking.
I. Ramphal, Shridath S. II. Title.

F2131.W467 1993
972.9—dc20

Cover design by Karen Holloway, Jamaica
Electronic page layout by BusinessPrint, Guyana
Printed by Lithomedia Printers Limited, Jamaica

CONTENTS

List of Acronyms and Note on Sources	xvi
Map of the Caribbean Basin	xx
Chairman's Preface	xxi
Postscript by Sir Shridath Ramphal	xxix

PART I: ASSESSMENT

CHAPTER 1: INTRODUCTION

1. Mandate and Proceedings 3
Origins
Mandate
Extensions of the Mandate
Establishing the Commission
Proceedings
Documentation
Studies and Occasional Papers
The Progress Report
Good Offices
Bibliography

2. Introducing the Report 18
Range of Issues
Beyond Chaguaramas
The Pressure of External Events
The Urgency of the People's Needs
Solving Problems through Integration
What Kind of Integration?
No Return to Federalism
The Wider Caribbean Family
The West Indian Diaspora
Improving Education – The Vital Task
Meeting Youth's Aspirations
Implementation is the Key

3. The Commission's Goals 29

CHAPTER II: THE CARICOM EXPERIENCE

1. Reviewing the Record — 34

2. Technical Successes — 35
Our Common Economic Space
Functional Cooperation
External Relations
Administrative Tenacity

3. Falling Short Strategically — 46
The Deficit in Ambition
Strategic Timidity
Community Marginalised
Failing to Follow Through

4. The Potential of Community — 56

5. The West Indies Today — 57
A Statistical Profile
Regional Organisations

CHAPTER III: CONTEXT AND PERSPECTIVES

1. International and Regional Imperatives — 60
International Developments
Regional Prospects

2. The Human Condition: Constraints and Resources — 68
Constraints
Resources
A West Indian Model

3. Preparing for the Twenty-first Century — 88

PART II: CHALLENGES AND OPPORTUNITIES

CHAPTER IV: DEVELOPMENT

1. New Emphases in Development — 93
The Global Setting
An Export Propelled Strategy
Small Business Development and Self-Employment
Economic Growth and Human Development
Correcting Imbalances in Wealth and Income
The Role of Governments
The Labour Movement

Recommendations — 103

2. Towards A Single Market and Economy — 104
What is Involved
Integration and the Less Developed Countries

Recommendations — 109

3. Common Currency Arrangements — 109

Recommendations — 115

4. Investment, Savings and Financial Institutions — 115
A Higher Rate of Investment
Higher Rate of National Savings Required
The Importance of Sound Economic Policies
New Instruments to Mobilise Savings
The Caribbean Development Bank
Reducing Capital Flight
Savings in the Diaspora
Institutional Strengthening
Debt Relief
The Allocation of Capital
Avoiding Crowding Out
Instruments to Improve the Allocation of Savings
Management Development

Recommendations — 132

5. Ease of Travel and Freedom of Movement   133
    Separateness the Challenge, Togetherness the Ambition
    Problems and Opportunities
    Implementing Our Aspirations

    Recommendations   142

CHAPTER V: ECONOMIC ISSUES

1. Export-led Growth   143
    Trade Performance
    Promoting Export-led Growth
    Trading Houses
    Mobility of Labour
    Reducing Anti-Export Bias
    Expanding CARICOM Trade
    Extra-Regional Trade
    Manufacturing and Diversification
    Niche Markets
    Development Financing
    Credit
    The Regional Stock Market

    Recommendations   159

2. Agriculture   160
    Place of Agriculture
    Regional Agricultural Planning
    Agricultural Marketing
    Improving Agricultural Performance
    Bananas
    Sugar
    The Rum Industry
    Other Important Agricultural Resources
    Marine Resources

    Recommendations   183

3. Mining   187
    Minerals Available

Contribution to the Economy
Prospects for the Mining Industry
Policies

Recommendations 190

4. Tourism and Services 191
Tourism In The Region
Challenges Facing Tourism
Human Resource Development in Tourism
The Attitude of Resident Populations
Tourism and the West Indian Diaspora
Intra-CARICOM Tourism
Tourism and Diversification
Services in CARICOM
The Major Service Areas
The Collective Potential of CARICOM Services
Niches in The Market For Services
Supporting Measures

Recommendations 201

5. Air and Sea Transportation 202
Global Trends
Regional Demand
Issues and Challenges
Policy Options
Necessary Responses
Regional Cooperation

Recommendations 216

6. Environment 216
Global Awareness
Caribbean Issues
CARICOM Responses
A Wider Response
Looking Ahead

Recommendations 231

CHAPTER VI: HUMAN RESOURCES DEVELOPMENT

1. The Background — 234
Selected Aspects of the Issue
A Single Market for Human Resources

2. Education — 236
Educational Attainments
Supply Gaps
Resource Needs and Financing
Efficiency and Management
Imperatives for Regional Cooperation
A Regional Agenda for Reform
Learning to Earn: An Over-arching Concept
Tertiary and University Reform and Development
Mobilising Caribbean Expertise in the Diaspora
The Disabled

3. Research and Development — 253
Existing Capability
Policy Formulation and Infrastructure
New Technologies
Developing Appropriate Human Resources
Intellectual Property
Involvement of the Private Sector and the Diaspora
Proposals

4. Entrepreneurship — 261
Sourcing Outside Skills and Knowledge

Recommendations — 263

CHAPTER VII: THE CULTURAL DIMENSION

1. Overview — 265
A Distinctive Cultural Expression
Language
Religion
The Arts
Regional Cultural Initiatives
The Enterprise Dimension

Releasing Creative Energy
The Racial Mix

2. Responses Needed for Integration 291
Regional Cultural Action
Artistic Culture for Employment
Cultural Penetration and the Media
Art and Education

Recommendations 305

CHAPTER VIII: COMMUNICATIONS AND SPORT

1. Communication for Community 308
Cultivating Common Ground
Exploring Common Ground through Language
Contracting Common Ground through Telecommunications
Nurturing Common Ground through Information
Circulating on Common Ground through the Media
Alternative Communication
Training
Community is about Communication

Recommendations 325

2. Sport — Connecting at the Grass Roots 326
Overview
Cricket
Seeking Success in Other Sports

Recommendations 331

CHAPTER IX: SOCIAL CONCERNS

1. Gender Issues 334
Education
Employment
Health
Women and the Law
Economic Adjustment Programmes
Response

Recommendations 342

2. Illegal Drugs   343
    Overview
    Regional Incidence of Drug Abuse
    Measures to Combat Drug Abuse
    Drugs and Youth
    The Money Cost
    The Threat to Sovereignty
    Coordinating Regional Action
    Measures To Be Taken Urgently

Recommendations   354

3. Health and Housing   355
    Health: An Overview
    Health Management Systems
    Training and Retention of Medical Personnel
    Regional Pooling of Health Resources
    Health Education
    Financing Health Services
    A Regional Health Service
    Procurement
    The Problem of Housing
    Disturbing Trends
    Housing by Self-Help
    Incentives

Recommendations   371

4. The Concerns of Youth   372
    Health
    Labour Market/Education
    Housing
    Illegal Drugs
    Recreation
    Powerlessness
    Youth's Responsibilities, Society's Expectations

Recommendations   381

CHAPTER X: SPECIAL ISSUES

1. Our Original Peoples — 383
Memory
Presence and Condition
An Identity to Protect
An Autonomy to Assist
An Inheritance to Preserve
Tomorrow

Recommendations — 399

2. Concerns About Remoteness — 400
Belize and The Bahamas: Their Special Situation
Shared Characteristics, Significant Differences
Geography
The Immigrant Problem
Education
Conclusion

Recommendations — 407

3. Diaspora - Commitment and Potential — 408
An Expanded Concept of Community
A Readiness to Respond

Recommendations — 414

CHAPTER XI: SHAPING EXTERNAL RELATIONS

1. Creation and Conduct of Common Policies — 416

2. CARICOM, The Wider Caribbean and Latin America — 426
Relations With The Wider Caribbean
Relations with Central and South America

3. International Relations Toward the Metropoles: EEC and NAFTA — 436

4. Relationships in Other Areas — 442

5. Compulsions for Widening Integration ... 443
   What Caribbean
   CARICOM, The 'Inner Core'
   An Association of Caribbean States
   Windows on the World

Recommendations ... 457

PART III: TIME FOR ACTION

CHAPTER XII: DEFINING A STRONG COMMUNITY

1. The Deepening of CARICOM ... 461
   Commitment to CARICOM
   Implementation: the 'Achilles Heel'
   New Machinery For Action
   A Community of Sovereign States
   Making a Reality of Community
   Leaving Space for Unity Within
   A Place for Small States
   Security

2. Structures of Unity ... 473
   The Council of Ministers
   The CARICOM Commission
   A Method of Financing
   The CARICOM Assembly
   A CARICOM Charter of Civil Society
   Disaffection with Governance
   The CARICOM Supreme Court
   The CARICOM Secretariat
   The Mills Report

Recommendations ... 506

3. The Public Service ... 509

4. Transitional Arrangements ... 517

5. Forward: The Only Way ... 517

APPENDICES

"A" The Declaration of Grand Anse 525

"B" The West Indian Commission 529

"C" Meetings and Workshops 534

"D" Itinerary and Consultations 536

"E" Submissions to the Commission 541

"F" Commission Publications 554

"G" Select Bibliography 558

"H" Regional Organisations 576

LIST OF ACRONYMS

ACP	African, Caribbean and Pacific Group of Countries
ACTI	Association of Caribbean Tertiary Institutions
AMP	Agricultural Marketing Protocol
AOSIS	Alliance of Small Island States
BECO	Banana Export Company Limited
BVI	The British Virgin Islands
BWIA	British West Indian Airways International
CAD/CAM	Computer-aided design/Computer-aided manufacturing
CANA	Caribbean News Agency Limited
CAREC	Caribbean Epidemiology Centre
CARDI	Caribbean Agricultural Research and Development Institute
CARIBCAN	Caribbean and Canada Trade Agreement
CARICAD	Caribbean Centre for Development Administration
CARICARGO	Caribbean Air Cargo Company Limited
CARICOM	Caribbean Community and Common Market
CARIFESTA	Caribbean Festival of Creative Arts
CARIFTA	Caribbean Free Trade Area
CARISAF	Caribbean Stabilisation and Adjustment Facility
CARIAD	Caribbean Institute on Alcohol and Other Drugs
CARIRI	Caribbean Industrial Research Institute
CAST	College of Arts, Science and Technology
CATCO	Caribbean Agricultural Trading Company Limited
CBI	Caribbean Basin Initiative
CBU	Caribbean Broadcasting Union
CCA	Caribbean Conservation Association
CCC	Caribbean Conference of Churches
CCCRIS	Consultative Committee on Caribbean Regional Information Systems
CCPAD	Caribbean Community Programme for Agricultural Development
CCST	Caribbean Council for Science and Technology
CDB	Caribbean Development Bank
CDCC	Caribbean Development and Cooperation Committee
CEDP	CARICOM Export Development Project
CEHI	Caribbean Environmental Health Institute
CER	CARICOM Enterprise Regime
CERMES	Centre of Resource Management and Environmental Studies

CET	Common External Tariff
CFC	Caribbean Food Corporation
CFTC	Commonwealth Fund for Technical Cooperation
CHA	Caribbean Hotel Association
CICAD	Caribbean Institute on Control of Alcohol and Other Drugs
CIDA	Canadian International Development Agency
CMCF	CARICOM Multilateral Clearing Facility
CMO	Caribbean Meteorology Organisation
COIP	Caribbean Organisation of Indigenous Peoples
CSC	Commonwealth Science Council
CTC	Cultural Training Centre
CTO	Caribbean Tourism Organization
CTU	Caribbean Telecommunications Union
CXC	Caribbean Examinations Council
DAWN	Development of Alternatives for Women in a New Era
EAI	Enterprise for the Americas Initiative
EC$	Eastern Caribbean Dollar
ECCA	East Caribbean Currency Authority
ECCB	East Caribbean Central Bank
EEC or EC	European (Economic) Community
EEZ	Exclusive Economic Zone
EFTA	European Free Trade Association
ESAF	Enhanced Structural Adjustment Facility
ESOP	Employees Stock Ownership Plans
FAO	Food and Agriculture Organisation of the United Nations
GATT	General Agreement on Tariffs and Trade
GDP	Gross Domestic Product
GMS	Guaranteed Marketing Scheme
HFI	Harmonisation of Fiscal Incentives Scheme
IAST	Institute of Applied Science and Technology
ICAO	International Civil Aviation Organisation
ILO	International Labour Organisation
IMA	Institute of Marine Affairs
IMF	International Monetary Fund
INTELSAT	International Telecommunications Satellite Consortium
INTERPOL	International Criminal Police Organisation
IDB	Inter-Amercan Development Bank
IOJ	Institute of Jamaica
ISER	Institute of Social and Economic Research
ITF	International Tennis Federation
ITU	International Telecommunications Union

LDCs	Less Developed Countries of the Caribbean Community and Common Market
LIAT	Leeward Islands Air Transport (1974) Limited
MDCs	More Developed Countries of the Caribbean Community and Common Market
MERCOSUR	Mercado Comun del Sur
NAFTA	North American Free Trade Agreement
NIC	Newly Industrialised Countries
NDF	National Development Foundation
NFI	Non-Bank Financial Institutions
NGO	Non-Governmental Organization
OAS	Organisation of American States
ODA	Overseas Development Agency
OECD	Organization for Economic Cooperation and Development
OECS	Organization of Eastern Caribbean States
OECS/NRMU	Natural Resources Management Unit of the Organisation of Eastern Caribbean States
PAHO	Pan American Health Organisation
PSE	Producer Subsidy Equivalent
RCC	Regional Cultural Committee
R&D	Research and Development
REAP	Regional Energy Action Programme
RFP	Regional Food Plan
S&T	Science and Technology
SAF	Structural Adjustment Facility
SCME	Standing Committee of Ministers of Education
SCMFA	Standing Committee of Ministers of Foreign Affairs
SELA	Sistema Economico Latinoamericano
TCI	The Turks and Caicos Islands
TIE	Theatre Information Exchange
WAND	Women and Development Unit (UWI)
WID	Women in Development Unit (UWI)
WINBAN	The Windward Islands Banana Association
WISCO	West Indies Shipping Corporation
UG	University of Guyana
UK	United Kingdom
UN	United Nations
UNCED	United Nations Conference on Environment and Development
UNCTAD	United Nations Conference on Trade and Development

UNDCP	United Nations Drug Control Programme
UNDP	United Nations Development Programme
UNDP TOKTEN	Transfer of Knowledge through Expatriate Nationals Programme of the United Nations Development Programme
UNECLAC	United Nations Economic Commission for Latin America and the Caribbean
UNEP	United Nations Environment Programme
UNESCO	United Nations Educational, Scientific and Cultural Organisation
UNICEF	United Nations Children's Fund
USA	United States of America
USAID	United States Agency for International Development
UWI	University of the West Indies
UWIDITE	University of the West Indies Distance Teaching System

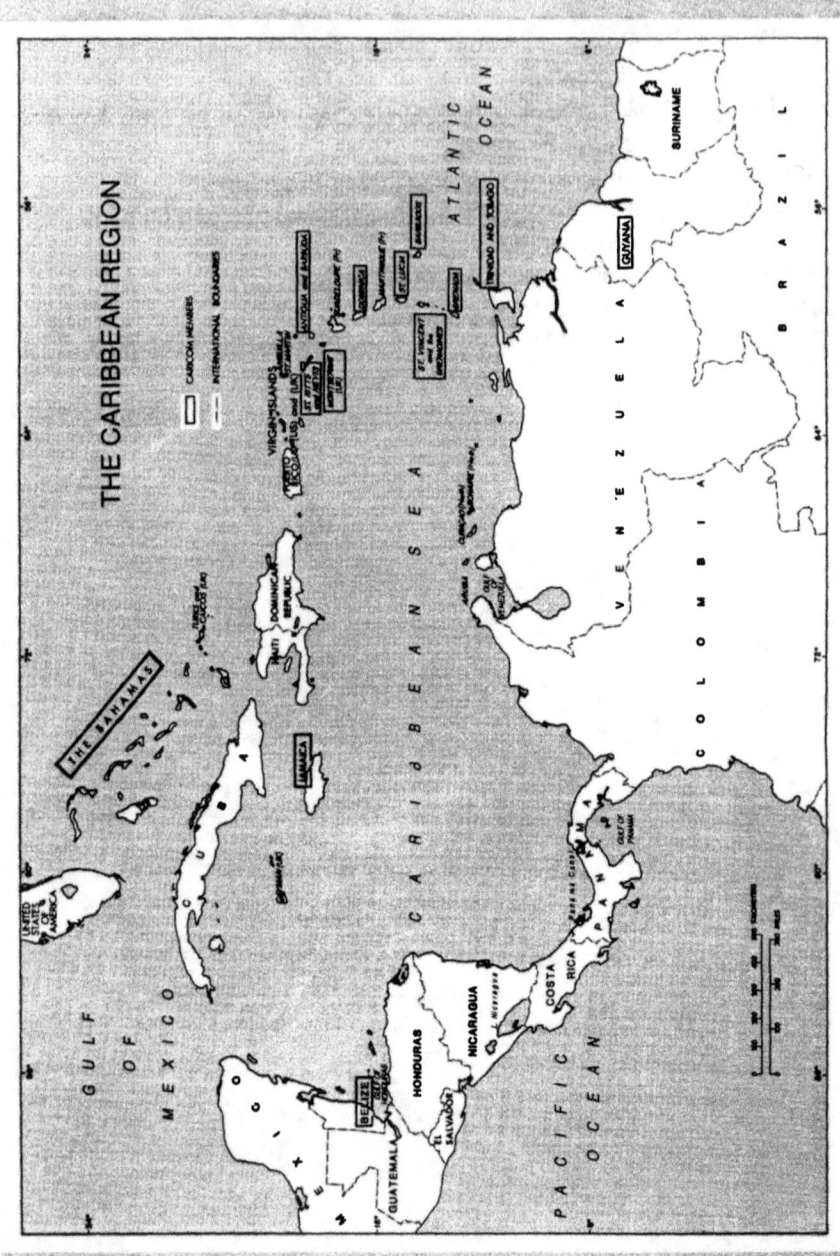

CHAIRMAN'S PREFACE

Why waste lines on Achille, a shade on the sea floor?
Because strong as self-healing coral, a quiet culture
is branching from the white ribs of each ancestor,

deeper than it seems on the surface; slowly but sure,
it will change us with the fluent sculpture of Time.

Derek Walcott, *OMEROS*

That fluent sculpture of time has already changed us; we the diverse people of scattered islands and mainland countries plucked from far continents by cruel history, drawing strength from our variety of race and culture and place of origin, but reaching beyond them for other strengths from uniting elements. Historical forces and the Caribbean Sea have divided us; yet unfolding history and that same Sea, through long centuries of struggle against uneven odds, have been steadily making us one. Now West Indians have emerged with an identity clearly recognisable not only to ourselves and our wider Caribbean but also in the world beyond the Caribbean Sea.

I am the fourth generation of my family's anguished transplantation. Other West Indians have been here over a longer period, and through systems of greater anguish; yet it was natural for me to remind an audience during the Commission's consultations that "I am a Guyanese before I am an Indian; I am a West Indian before I am a Guyanese". Oneness had replaced separateness in four generations. So it is for most of the people of our CARICOM Region. That oneness is the basic reality of our West Indian condition.

It is also the central message of this Report. For the West Indian Commission that proposition is not the bottom line of integration, it is its starting point: awareness of belonging to a West Indian home of many mansions. In the Report, we recall the impact made on us by a slogan in Belize displayed prominently outside the Prime Minister's office: 'All ah we mek Belize'. So it is with us regionally: CARICOM is not something apart; it is all of us; 'is we'! Everything in the Report derives from that reality, and everything responds to it. It is the credo of integration, and the ethos of the Commission's work.

When I was invited by CARICOM Heads of Government to chair the West Indian Commission I was reassured by the fact that Alister McIntyre, UWI's dynamic Vice-Chancellor, would be with me as Vice-Chairman and Roderick Rainford and Vaughan Lewis *ex officio* members as Secretary-General of CARICOM and Director-General of the OECS respectively. But I could not know at Grand Anse in 1989 how handsomely we would together be supported by the team of Commissioners yet to be assembled. It has been support of a truly superlative order, and I pay tribute to my colleagues for their impressive blend of skills and for their many splendoured qualities: of professionalism with a common touch; of humanism with a West Indian bias; of intellectual rigour not constrained by ideology; of staying a rugged course with steadying good humour. In the end, chairing the Commission was not a task but a great privilege to have shared such an exciting experience with so worthy a team.

But there was more to that privilege than our own interaction as Commissioners. For all of us, our consultations with the people of the Region rank among the most stimulating and rewarding experiences of our lives. We have tried in our Report to convey the flavour of these 'groundings' with fellow West Indians. I hope we have succeeded, because the richness of those encounters needs to be shared with all West Indians. The fact that our compatriots came forward in such numbers, no less than their written submissions to us; the frankness, often passion, sometimes anger, that characterised their presentations; the good humour that was ever present, the element of 'picong' directed to the Commission; and, always, the underlying message that they cared about their West Indianness, about their Caribbeanness, as some preferred — cared enough to come forward to 'tell it to the Commission': all this was for us not just an unforgettable personal experience, but a process of enduring value in our evolving regionalism.

Each of us will have high points in our recollection of these consultations — with people and with Governments; in CARICOM, in the wider Caribbean and with West Indians abroad. For me, a few recollections help to make the point of their unique significance:

Chairman's Preface

- a poignant moment in Georgetown's City Hall with a young woman of Guyana's Amerindian community speaking plaintively, but scoldingly, of the needs and hopes of the first peoples of CARICOM;

- our meeting in Barrouallie, a fishing village in St. Vincent, in a dimly lit school hall, and the people, pleased that we had come to talk with them, telling us of their concerns: about unemployment, about teenage pregnancies, about the falling off of fishing catches and production of their famed 'black oil' (of aphrodisiac quality) that was their speciality;

- our public meeting in the Titchfield High School on a bluff overlooking one of the lovely bays of Jamaica's east coast; a school established 200 years ago where all kinds of linkages confirmed for us our oneness. One Commissioner had been trained nearby at a Methodist seminary and had married a teacher of the school. The Principal had been at the University of the West Indies with at least three other Commissioners; there were eight Guyanese teachers on the staff; one of the ladies in the audience had married an Antiguan, she yearned aloud for the return of the 'Federal ships' so that she might travel through the Region;

- our meeting with sixth formers in Port-of-Spain when young people spoke with us about their anxieties, including anxieties about the re-emergence of ethnicity as a factor in national life — and our dialogue with them on the value of a transcendent regionalism that subordinates ethnic origin to an overarching West Indian identity;

- the Saturday morning I spent with Rex Nettleford and Allan Kirton talking with Rastafarians and others in Temple Yard in Barbados, as we reached out to them to hear at first hand of their grievances and to witness their industry and determination to overcome;

- the throbbing West Indianness of our meeting in Birmingham in the English midlands when the diaspora spoke with us of their sense of being forgotten and neglected and their worry that their homeland — they were in no doubt that they were all West Indians there from a West Indian homeland — was falling behind in responding to contemporary needs;

- a night in Cuba which the Commission shared with Fidel Castro: his

Time for Action

view the present economic problems that Cuba faced and his resolve that the Cuban people would overcome them; and the chance it gave us to explore our own ideas of a wider Caribbean ultimately embracing all the countries of the Caribbean Basin;

- the irony of a visit to Carriacou when 'an old timer' asked us — not mockingly, but in serious vein — what was 'in it' for Carriacou "joining up with all those poor people in Jamaica and Guyana and even Trinidad": recalling to our minds an earlier time at Montego Bay in 1947 when those same sentiments were aired but with the countries reversed. Carriacou was then among the 'pauperised' — as it seemed from Jamaica, 45 years ago.

There were messages for us in all those encounters — as in all the consultations everywhere. Messages of 'today for you, tomorrow for me'; of ignoring only at our grave cost that integration is about people and their everyday concerns which go beyond such matters as trade regimes and rules of origin; of being mindful of how much we have to grow beyond our English speaking communities into the wider multilingual Caribbean; and many, many more messages.

Our Report is about those messages; and about our ideas of how we must respond to them. I do not need to dwell on them here in this Preface. We hope the Report will be widely read. It is addressed to the people of the West Indies everywhere — including, of course, their Governments; and we have tried to write it in that way. The Report is something of a regional manifesto for the nineties and beyond; one we were specifically asked to provide by the Grand Anse Declaration. If our ideas are sound, it is support for them from the people of CARICOM that will both justify and compel action.

As the Commission faced the many problems that are at hand and the others that lie ahead, we reminded ourselves constantly of the strengths and achievements of the West Indies. They lie principally with our people. We have produced in this generation alone a Nobel prize winner, a Judge of the International Court of Justice, two under-Secretaries-General of the United Nations (one of them a woman), an Assistant-Secretary-General of the UN, a Secretary-General of the ACP — and one of the Commonwealth. Our political leaders have won the respect of their peers in the world community: at the level of the UN, at Commonwealth Summits and in Third World encounters, the world beyond has glimpsed Caribbean excellence. Caribbean achievements at diplomatic levels — from negotiating the Lomé Convention to achieving Zimbabwe's freedom widely acclaimed. Our writers and musicians are among those that twentieth century history will acknowledge as being among the most brilliant and creative. We have produced academics of sterling quality who are in the front line of research and teaching in universities abroad, and increasingly at home. Our women, of whom our patron, Dame Nita Barrow, is such a shining example, have commanded respect for their leadership all around the world and not only in advancing the just cause of women. As a nation of five and a half million we are contributing beyond our numbers in the wider world.

But our achievements have not only been on the world stage; they would not be enough if they were. The overall story of governance in the post-war period has been one that brings credit to West Indian Governments. Despite reverses experienced recently, we have increased significantly over the last fifty years basic levels of literacy; we have cut infant mortality rates; we have improved life-expectancy and advanced health care in significant ways. Democracy is fashionable now, but our Region's political culture held fast to democratic traditions through all those years. There have been lapses, it is true, and we have spoken out about them and expressed our hope that, where they still remain to be remedied, such aberrations will soon be behind us.

In sport, we have made a most dramatic impact; on track and field our small countries have mounted the medal winners podium at successive Olympic Games; indeed, we were told that in per capita terms West Indians hold the foremost place among the winners of Olympic medals in the post-war years. All our achievements seem to come together in cricket, which remains the living example of the successes we can achieve and sustain when we act together as one. There is much more besides; overall, this is a substantial record of achievement. We are a great little nation. At the centre of this Report is our conviction that we can translate these qualities more widely across the board of regional life as the West Indies enters a new period, with new challenges, and with many new opportunities.

What we must not do is to run out of steam. The Moyne Commission's report 50 years ago led to many changes; to an input of capital for social development, to new possibilities for local autonomy and eventually for full freedom. We received help in substantial order; and, for the greater part, we turned it to good account for the benefit of West Indians. Now, we face a new time of threat to those achievements; new social concerns that we could be falling back; new economic problems like shortages of foreign exchange which had not been a part of past experience. And with all our gains for democracy over the years there are deep anxieties about the quality of governance now — indeed, of disaffection with the entire political process. And on top of it all we face the menace of the drug problem.

We need to recapture some of the strengths of yesteryear and they must come from new generations. When, at our public meeting in Washington, a West Indian professor of Political Science called, in the best tradition of 'the University of Woodford Square', for an end to 'heirloom politics' in CARICOM, we knew what he was urging — basic change in our political processes. Yet we are learning to change without being pushed. When Michael Manley stepped down recently from the Prime Ministership of Jamaica he was setting an important example. What we have to do now is to ensure that we blend experience with change; that we draw on all the political talents of our Region as we move into this new time; finding roles for all who have roles to play; learning how to use political talents even when they may be for the time being on the other side. In some of the structures of unity we propose in this Report, there are opportunities of this kind.

As we came to the end of our work, we were conscious that there is unlikely to be another Commission of this kind for many a year, perhaps for many a decade. That awareness seemed to enlarge our responsibilities; but we were encouraged as well that a process of change had begun. When CARICOM leaders accepted our interim proposals to ease up on the 'hassle' of travel in the Region, to create a single line at airports for 'residents and CARICOM nationals'; when they accepted that graduates of the University of the West Indies and other skilled West Indians, as well as West Indian media personnel, should be the start of a process of freeing up the right of West Indians to live and work anywhere in the Region; when they agreed to establish the

Caribbean Investment Fund and to take steps towards a common currency — in addition to quickening progress towards their goal of a Single Market and Economy — something had begun to happen in our Region.

So, we have a great potential to do much better in future. There is enough that is positive in our domestic, regional and external circumstances to make us feel hopeful. But there is much to be done, and time is not on our side. The global system is becoming more competitive and many nations are making great efforts to be more efficient in economic organisation and in resource, product and services markets. We must not be left behind; we believe our recommendations offer the means to go forward. But we must go forward in unity. Regionalism, integration, are at the heart of getting our act together.

As we move to what we hope will be the early adoption and implementation of our central recommendations, that process will acquire momentum and will help to give faith to the people of the Region that the end years of this century and the advent of a new millennium could be a period of hope, not of hopelessness. I underline only one aspect of that process, to which we have given emphasis in the Report, namely, that we must not proceed at the pace of the slowest; that those who are ready to move must do so — reserving a place for the others when they are ready. That was how the integration process started. The CARIFTA Agreement at Dickenson Bay was between three countries. We would not be where we are today, with the prospect of going further forward, had they not had the courage to begin and to lead.

It follows that CARICOM must always leave space — under the CARICOM roof — for even closer integration among some of its members. However, the proviso of not diluting commitment to CARICOM in the process is, as we stress in the Report, an absolutely crucial one. The integration cup must always be more than half full. CARICOM cannot be true to itself if it becomes a group of groups held together by string, each doing its own thing..

My final word in this Preface, therefore, is about action. We have called the Report "Time for Action"; we have done so to dramatise how necessary it is for us to speed up the process of integration — of acting together in a systematic way. Whether we are dealing with Europe or North America, Latin America or the Caribbean Basin, or with deepening our own integration in meaningful ways, we have to act now. And we have to enlarge our capacity for action. That is why establishment of the CARICOM Commission is at the centre of our recommendations. Many of our own policy and programme recommendations will require a good deal of working out and of negotiation within CARICOM and with others; what we cannot postpone is putting in place an effective process for doing so.

We have called for the CARICOM Commission to be established by 1 January 1993. That is not a moment too soon. If we are to achieve it, we have to act with a sense of urgency appropriate to this moment of challenge. With the Commission in place — giving regional leadership on a day to day basis within the framework of CARICOM as a Community of sovereign states — we have a chance to implement the manifesto of change. Without that process, if we merely titivate with our separateness and forego the opportunity we have at this moment to act collectively in those areas that demand a shared response, we are in danger of drifting along — only now towards rapids and waterfalls, drifting separately but towards a single desperate fate. Even in error, our destinies are linked. "We must save ourselves together, or together we will disappear", warned Jose Martí over a century ago in a Caribbean context. His warning has resonance for us as we look to the twenty-first century.

To the Governments of CARICOM who invited us to undertake this mission, we record our gratitude for their confidence in us; but, even more so for their vision in setting in process the task itself. To the people who have shared their hopes and fears with us and strengthened our resolve by their robust and refreshing West Indianness, we record our thanks; their talking with us was confirmation that our mission was a valid one.

We have completed that mission. Now it is TIME FOR ACTION.

Barbados
25 May 1992   S. S. R

Postscript
by Sir Shridath Ramphal

Time For Action was completed at a Meeting of the West Indian Commission ending in the early hours of 14 May 1992. At that moment, there was a strong sense of fulfilment among Commissioners—normal to the completion of any major task, particularly a collective one. We believed we had done as CARICOM Heads had asked. We had tried to "prepare West Indians for the twenty-first century"; to "let all ideas contend—political, economic, social and cultural; to "let unity of all kinds be appraised, no less than the prospects of disunity"; to "let the outpouring of the creative talents of our peoples in the Region stimulate a process by which our Region becomes a public forum on the future" (see "Grand Anse Resolution on Preparing the Peoples of the West Indies for the 21st Century", Grenada, 1989).

Yet, that morning in the conference room of the Divi Southwinds Hotel in Barbados, we knew that even for us as Commissioners it was merely the end of one stage of a longer journey. This *Postscript* is about the stage that followed immediately—down to the Special Summit of CARICOM Heads in October 1992 that considered the Report, and the final winding down of the Commission by the end of the year. Other stages will follow, and there will be other guides; but the West Indian people will be a continuum. This record of events aims to assist their further journeying.

The Grand Anse Declaration had looked to the completion of the Report in time for the July 1992 CARICOM Summit.[1] The timing was important. In Grenada in 1989, the quincentennial overtones of

---

[1] The annual summit is normally held from 4 July each year and this was contemplated in the Grand Anse Declaration where the Commission's target was fixed. However, because of a clash of dates with the Seville Quincentennial Ceremonies (which some CARICOM Heads attended), the CARICOM Summit (Port-of-Spain 1992) was advanced by a few days and in fact began on 30 June. Hereafter, therefore, reference to this Summit dates the month as June.

1992 ("this background of historic change and historical appraisal") had seemed to require of us as a people a response to the legacy of those 500 years and to the challenge of the time ahead. Long before we found a title for our Report, 1992 was seen as a time for action. We were keen to meet that expectation; if our Report was to provide the basis for those timely responses, the obligation to produce it on target was compelling. We would have wished a second round of public consultations to share our conclusions with the people—as we had planned and promised; but that would have meant failing to produce the Report on time. We had to content ourselves, instead, with using radio and television as extensively, and intensively, as we could to convey to West Indians the nature of our analysis and recommendations.

Even so, completing the Report in mid-May 1992 and getting it out to Governments and the public before the June meeting called for heroic efforts by our small Secretariat and those who turned our text into electronic type and print. That this work was accomplished with high quality and on time was further confirmation of the commitment and talent that lie within our Region yearning to be acknowledged and ready to be used in a wider context than our separate communities. With their help we were able to present the Report to Governments in the week beginning 15 June 1992. I did so personally to most Heads of Government, explaining our principal findings and recommendations. Simultaneously, other Commissioners did the same with other Heads.

In fact, CARICOM Heads had received earlier intimations of the Commission's thinking. We had talked with all Heads of Government and most Cabinets. At the June 1991 Summit at Basseterre, we had presented a Progress Report, "Towards a Vision of the Future", calling for a "programme of immediate action" and pointing the way to further change—especially with a view to strengthening decision-making and implementation in CARICOM. In February 1992, at the Inter-Sessional Summit in Kingston, I had briefed Heads on behalf of the Commission on the nature of our thinking and our likely principal recommendations both for strengthening CARICOM and widening the regional integration process. Our Report held no surprises; in fact, in February 1992, I

Postscript

had urged Heads to begin to think of responses to the Commission's proposals for early action against the background of the substantial public support we had found for making the process of regional integration dynamic and effective.

Simultaneously with the release of the Report, the Commission published and distributed widely in the Region an *Overview of the Report...*—which was essentially a shorter version—as well as a "Synopsis of the Report" in the nature of a briefing note. The latter was issued mainly to Governments, the media and regional organisations.

At the Port-of-Spain Summit, on 30 June the Commission presented the Report to Heads of Government collectively, outlining the principal recommendations and the Commission's thinking, with special emphasis on the need for timely action. Among the concluding words of the presentation were these:

> History has a few moments for every community when what we do or fail to do changes the future in decisive ways. In presenting our Report to you, the West Indian Commission believes we are at such a time. To the bold who grasp the baton and move—go the medals. But the fate of communities, our people, is also involved: not for them the virtues of "Quintus Fabius Maximus Cunctator". CARICOM Heads of Government sensed all this in 1989. In the Grand Anse Declaration and related documents you acknowledged as much. That is why you asked us to work. We have worked, talking to the people as we did so; and we have confirmed your worst fears—but confirmed as well that there are opportunities, and hope if we seize them. One way or another, this moment, these months, your decisions, will irrevocably change our regional lives—and by necessary extension, our national lives as well ["Time for Action". Address by WIC Chairman to the 13th CARICOM Heads of Government Conference presenting the Report of the West Indian Commission, pp.10-11].

In their response in June, CARICOM Heads noted "the central recommendations in the Commission's Report concerning basic and fundamental changes in the structural arrangement for decision-making and implementation processes in CARICOM, as well as the many wide-ranging recommendations on numerous sectoral and policy issues affecting the life of the Community", acknowledged that once again, as at the Chaguaramas Summit in 1973, CARICOM was at "a defining moment" in its evolution, and agreed that it was "time for action". They decided to meet again in a Special Session on 28 October 1992 to consider the Commission's Report and to determine the action to be taken on its recommendations.

In the four months from July to October 1992, there was much activity. The Report was widely disseminated both in the Region and among the West Indian diaspora abroad and much discussed. To facilitate consideration of the Report at the Special Summit in October, the Commission prepared a Working Paper ["Working Paper by the Commission". HGC(SPEC)92/1/4] highlighting a limited number of recommendations for priority decision. Additionally, the Commission held a special meeting with the regional media in Jamaica in the first week of September at which Commissioners briefed regional journalists extensively on the Report and encouraged wide-ranging discussion of the recommendations. Following that regional encounter, the Commission accepted the invitation of the Inter-American Development Bank, whose President, Dr Enrique Iglesias, had been a special guest at CARICOM at its June Summit at Port-of-Spain, to a Symposium on the Report at the IDB Offices in Washington. This was attended by a group of eminent persons from the Hemisphere, including representatives of the principal multilateral institutions. It was clear from the discussions that the Hemisphere believed that CARICOM was, indeed, at a defining moment and that it was ready to help once the basic political decisions were taken within the Region itself. As we approached the Special Summit at the end of October, we felt that as a Commission we had done all in our power to discharge the mandate placed upon us by CARICOM Heads three years earlier in the Grand Anse Declaration.

In September 1992 the Report was also discussed in the Parliaments of Jamaica and Barbados and the Commission was invited to a two-day symposium with parliamentarians in Trinidad and Tobago. It is outside the purview of this *Postscript* to give an account of the parliamentary debates in Jamaica and Barbados, but it became clear from both that the spirit of resolution that had been so evident at Grand Anse in 1989, at Basseterre in 1991, and at Kingston and Port-of-Spain earlier in 1992, was unlikely to translate into political will at the Special Summit. That in fact was precisely what West Indians had predicted during the Commission's public consultations. At the opening of the Port-of-Spain Special Summit, I explained this to Heads of Government in the following terms:

> ... but it is a symptom of what ails our regional processes that the most pervasive mood we have encountered among West Indian people is disbelief that anything—anything serious, anything effective, anything lasting, anything fundamentally different, anything that can anchor ambition in a West Indian future—will come out of our efforts and yours. They have grown enured to high flown declarations, they have grown cynical about bureaucratic delays, they have grown disdainful of the instinct to protect small areas of turf leaving the wide West Indian pasture fallow. They will not be surprised if in this time for action you do not act, if at this moment of decision you differ and defer.
>
> I must say this in all candour, because you have asked us to consult the people; and we have done so—imperfectly perhaps, but as best we could and in larger measure than they have been consulted for fifty years. You have asked us to help to prepare our Region for the twenty-first century. Everything in that preparation turns on the faith of West Indian people in our regional processes. This is therefore not only a time for decision; it is a moment of affirmation. If regionalism falters now, it will not easily recover. That might sound stark, even alarmist; but after three years as West Indians working together, looking towards the future, we believe it is a simple truth ["Time to Act". Address by WIC Chairman at the Opening Session of the Special CARICOM Summit to consider the Report of the West Indian Commission, Port-of-Spain, 28 October 1992].

In the Working Paper that the Commission offered to the Special Summit, the recommendations proposed for priority decision came down (as we explained) to a small cluster, namely:

> a regional process that goes forward as a Community of Sovereign States; the deepening of CARICOM through the Single Market and Economy (on which you have already agreed) being made a reality; the widening of our vision of the Caribbean by encompassing not just our enclave of English-speaking countries, but the wider Caribbean Basin which needs to be reclaimed—not a lake that is Spanish, or English, or French, or Dutch, or American—but, at last, 500 years later, a Caribbean lake; and, to make all this happen in practical ways and with a qualitative flavour that touches West Indian lives, a CARICOM Commission that can energise the process of regionalism and the CARICOM Charter of Civil Society that can help to keep us on course for enrichment beyond the economics of regionalism...[ibid.].

That was a handful of decisions. They were not small decisions; but the Commission believed they were the ones that had to be taken urgently if as West Indians we were to answer the summons of history in the context posed by the Grand Anse Declaration—a summons addressed to our generation, but one to which we could not defer an answer without defaulting on our obligations not only to present but also to future generations.

In presenting the Report to the Summit, the Commission urged three basic propositions as follows:

> The first is that the idea of an integrated Caribbean Basin—or, more realistically, of first approaches toward it—can only be consummated if espoused and promoted and developed by CARICOM.
>
> Our second proposition is that CARICOM can only have an effective outreach to perform that role if it first gets its sub-regional act together. CARICOM coherence, conviction, intellectual strength and political drive are preconditions of CARICOM's widening role. We have to be together before we can bring the wider Caribbean together. With CARICOM apart, we will all remain apart. We will be back to the era of Columbus. We have to deepen our own integration as we try to widen the integration process to the greater Caribbean. So we must move on to our Single Market and Economy. We must enlarge our functional cooperation. We must tackle our social issues together. We must make our own people aware that all this means better governance at home: hence the Charter of Civil Society. We must have credibility at home if we are to build a larger Caribbean home. And, of course, we must do all this for our own sake—as a duty to ourselves.
>
> Our third proposition is that we can do nothing effective if we lack the capability to mobilise your political authority and translate it through organisational strength into practical action: political and organisational capacities overreaching CARICOM's parts and giving tangible form and credibility to CARICOM's wholeness. At the apex is CARICOM's political leadership without whose commitment to this enterprise nothing can happen. But at the heart of the pyramid is the CARICOM Commission as proposed in "Time for Action". It is the CARICOM Commission that must develop, facilitate, negotiate, bring to realisation the dream of CARICOM as a Community of sovereign civil societies, CARICOM as a Single Market and Economy, CARICOM as the catalyst of the Association of Caribbean States. Without the Commission working for all this on a full-time basis, a shadow we fear will fall between the vision and the reality, between the dream and its fulfilment: the shadow of inertia [Address by WIC Chairman to 13th CARICOM Summit, op. cit.].

Postscript

In taking stock of the Port-of-Spain Summit, it is pertinent that the Working Paper prepared by the Commission, and used by the Chairman in recording the Summit's conclusions, invited initial decisions on just 19 of the Commission's 200-plus recommendations, and acceptance of one overall proposition. This proposition was that the CARICOM Heads "approve the broad thrust of the West Indian Commission's Report". They did not adopt that language. The Port-of-Spain Protocol says that the Conference considers the Report "as a landmark document in charting the course of Caribbean integration and accepts the challenge that it is 'time for action' " (see "Conclusions of the Special Meeting of the Conference of Heads of Government of the Caribbean Community", Port-of-Spain, 28 October 1992).

The Heads of Government accepted some of the 19 recommendations; but the exceptions were critical ones. The three recommendations for the CARICOM Commission were not accepted. The recommendation for a Charter of Civil Society was agreed to "in principle" and the reference to "greater public access to information" was dropped. The recommendation for the CARICOM Supreme Court with original jurisdiction was "noted" and mention made of the "need for careful study". The Record of Conclusions states that the recommendations for the Court and the Charter "would be further studied and developed for consideration at the next regular meeting of the Conference" [ibid.].

On the recommendation for joint representation overseas, the Heads accepted "the principle"; however, in respect of "London, Washington, Brussels, Caracas, Ottawa, New York and Geneva", they accepted only "maximum cooperation" [ibid.].

Of the ten recommendations on "Strengthening Integration" included in the Working Paper, the Heads can be said to have accepted three of them at this stage: the need for a revised Treaty of Chaguaramas, the concept of CARICOM as a Community of Sovereign States and the proposal for a Council of Ministers comprising Ministers for CARICOM Affairs.

Eight of the other nine recommendations related to widening Caribbean integration. They were, of course, predicated on the strengthening of CARICOM. Despite accepting only a few of the recommendations on "strengthening", the Heads adopted all eight of the "widening" recommendations with only a few modifications. CARICOM "unstrengthened" is therefore committed to the widening process we proposed—involving negotiating the Association of Caribbean States and evolving its character in ways that must try to sustain a lead role for CARICOM. It is committed as well to joint negotiations for entry into NAFTA, to keeping open CARICOM's windows on the wider world and to developing the "special relationship" with Canada.

The remaining recommendation related to transitional matters, principally arrangements for establishing the CARICOM Commission and revising the Treaty of Chaguaramas in due course. It envisaged, among other things, the establishment of an Inter-governmental Task Force to work with the Commission on the revision of the Treaty. The Heads accepted the proposals for a Task Force.

So much for the 19 recommendations in the Commission's Working Paper. In place of the recommendations not accepted, the Heads established a Bureau arrangement of rotating Heads, agreed to give the CARICOM Secretary-General executive powers and to enlarge the Secretariat's establishment.

These are the conclusions of the October meeting. What the outturn will be, how the decisions taken (and not taken) will affect the lives of West Indian people, are matters for the future. If the Commission's analysis is even partly right, that future will be for our Region an excessively difficult one. If CARICOM is seen by decision-makers (including others besides Heads of Government) as an occasionally convenient but mainly peripheral facility, not as a central, creative, energising force for development, it will forever fall short of the highest hopes for regionalism that we found among West Indian people. At the end of the Commission's experience, this must be the lingering fear: that while everyone will buy the concept of CARICOM as a "Community of Sovereign States", for people the emphasis will be on community, but for the political and bureaucratic establishment the emphasis could be on sovereignty and turf in general. Governments were inevitably in the forefront at Port-of-Spain; their conclusions, however, were actually the preferred options of the CARICOM Secretariat on the one hand, and those opposed to the very notion of genuine integration on the other. Such are the contrarieties of our time and circumstance.

We signalled these fears at Port-of-Spain when we complained that *Time For Action* fell victim to "insularity and insecurity". We were not being personal; we were echoing much that Arthur Lewis had written 30 years before in *The Agony of the Eight*. If, 500 years after Columbus, we are unable to overcome these ancestral urges or at least hold them in check, balanced against the contemporary claims of realism and rationality, we are in deep trouble. Regionalism itself may be questioned next; "marginalisation" (foretold in the Grand Anse Declaration) could then come to be rationalised as the virtue of "subsidiarity"— copying once more the trimmings of European fashion while the Europeans themselves move on—not allowing their own insularities and even insecurities to override reason and realism as they prepare for the twenty-first century.

Where does all that leave us? Certainly not in abject depression. We have expressed our disappointment that the October meeting did not accept some of the recommendations the Commission regarded as most critical to Caribbean progress. But as Commissioners we do not feel our efforts have been wasted. We believe, rather, that the Heads will be proved right in their assertion that the Report is a "landmark document"—in that it may ultimately make a firmer mark on West Indian affairs than the October conclusions suggest at the moment. I had an opportunity in November 1992 to touch briefly on these wider issues at the University of the West Indies Graduation Ceremony at the St Augustine Campus at which Prime Minister Manning was the Graduation Speaker. What I said then—after calling for an end to separateness within some of our countries—was this:

> In our Caribbean homeland, it is no different; we are one people too from Belize to Guyana, and beyond CARICOM from Cuba to Suriname; we have to give meaning to that oneness in tangible ways. Sometimes our West Indian contrariness gets in the way; but despite disappointments neither vexation nor opting out is a valid response. In Guyana we have a saying: "na mine how bird vex, he caan vex wid tree". The Caribbean is our tree;

for us it will ever bloom. Attachment, commitment, hope, effort must ever be sustained as well. When we stumble and seem about to collapse we have to recall that that, after all, is how on the whole we play our West Indian cricket; disaster is ever imminent, glorious recovery is almost always round the corner.

But adventurism is one thing, recklessness is another. We cannot make a habit of coming to watersheds and failing to cross over, of being at defining moments and opting for the old terms. In the new world that is upon us we cannot count on second chances. If our countries are to respond to the character and environment of the new age, we have to jettison smallness and meanness and preoccupation with self, and find ways of not being held to the pace of the most inert among us ["The Compass of Knowledge". Graduation Address by the Chancellor to the UWI Graduation Ceremony, St Augustine, Trinidad & Tobago, 28 November 1992].

Prime Minister Manning wrote Commissioners from Georgetown, as he chaired the first meeting of the new Bureau in December 1992 (see Letter from Prime Minister Manning to WIC Chairman, 15 December 1992). It was a letter of much encouragement in which he assured us that the "firm determination" of CARICOM Heads of Government was to "continue to give most serious consideration to all aspects of the Report"; and it is the case that for both meetings of the Bureau and of CARICOM Heads generally, the recommendations of *Time For Action* have been a dominant theme. The West Indian Commission is now part of Caribbean history; but *Time For Action* is a living force in West Indian affairs. Ideas wil continue to contend; the future is nothing if not in continuous creation. The Commission's work is a continuing factor in that process.

The West Indian Commission's Secretariat at Black Rock in Barbados, generously given by the Government of Barbados to support our work, formally closed on 31 December 1992. The substantial archives of the Commission—covering records of our public consultations in the Region and beyond it, papers commissioned from experts, memoranda received from the public as well as minutes of the Commission's own deliberations (including some audio-visual materials)—have all been deposited with the University of the West Indies and are housed in the Institute of Social and Economic Research at the Cave Hill Campus.

Postscript

Towards the end of the Commission's presentation to Heads of Government at the Special Summit in October 1992 were these reminders of the challenge facing the Region:

> Something is wrong structurally with CARICOM; not just with CARICOM policy. That is the West Indian Commission's basic finding. If the structure remains defective, enlarging the workload will only hasten the time when it falls down. We will deceive ourselves and not be true to future generations if our response to the challenges everyone knows we face is more of the same: the same fumbling that 18 years after we signed the Treaty of Chaguaramas still finds us far short of the reality of a Common Market; the same lack of coherence that 10 years after we agreed to establish a Common External Tariff finds us convening yet another Heads of Government Meeting to achieve it—the same inadequate structures of unity. They are our structures, and we can improve them; as everyone else is doing in these changing times; changes which enlarge our own need for change.
>
> ... We are powerless in many matters; but we are not powerless to improve our prospects through improving CARICOM's structures of unity. We need only conviction and will. The Commission has tried to provide the former; only you can provide the latter ["Time to Act", op. cit., pp.15-16].

In the context of the future, that reference to "you" must now be taken as a reference to all West Indians.

KINGSTON
24 MARCH 1993

PART I

ASSESSMENT

CHAPTER I

INTRODUCTION

1. MANDATE AND PROCEEDINGS

Origins

The origins of the West Indian Commission lie in the Grand Anse Declaration with which leaders of the Caribbean Community (CARICOM) concluded their Grenada Summit Meeting in July 1989. (Appendix "A"). In a deeper sense, they lie in the evolution of West Indian affairs since the dissolution of the Federation of The West Indies in 1962 and the processes of both separation and unity which marked the progress of the region since then: through independence, CARIFTA, CARICOM, the OECS and multiple regional endeavours at the level of our Governments and people. In a more proximate sense the Grand Anse Declaration was regional acceptance of a Trinidad and Tobago proposal based on a paper presented by the then Prime Minister A.N.R. Robinson, entitled "The West Indies Beyond 1992".

"The West Indies Beyond 1992" pointed out that across the world the central reality is that restructuring of a fundamental nature is in progress. It drew particular attention to the (already) historic changes in the Soviet Union, the far-reaching implications of the formation of a Single European Market in 1992, and the birth of a Free Trade Area between Canada and the United States of America. The paper concluded that:

> against this background of historic change and historic appraisal, the Caribbean could be in danger of becoming a backwater, separated from the main current of human advance into the twenty-first century...

It also summoned attention to the dramatic changes in the international environment and their implications for the Caribbean. It stressed that:

Assessment

> the period since political independence has been one of continuous awareness of the common identity which distinguishes the Caribbean people, and the structural constraints imposed upon them as small units in the international community.

Accordingly, it was in a context of recognition both of the important changes occurring internationally and the heightened sense amongst West Indians that they shared a common identity that the paper called on the people to:

> prepare for the future... to consider how best to bring about real betterment in their condition of life, to achieve their full potential as free people responsible for their own destiny, and to improve their Region's place in the community of nations,

and proposed that a West Indian Commission be established by the CARICOM Heads of Government to help the people of the West Indies to prepare for the twenty-first century.

Mandate

In adopting this proposal CARICOM Heads of Government specifically mandated that

- the Commission should be an independent body;
- the Commission should report to Heads of Government prior to their meeting in July 1992;
- the Commission should formulate proposals for advancing the goals of the Treaty of Chaguaramas which established the Caribbean Community and Common Market (CARICOM) in 1973.

The Commission's mandate therefore takes its starting point from the Treaty of Chaguaramas. But the Treaty of Chaguaramas was itself a beginning in the process of Caribbean integration, a new beginning through the Community and Common Market. That beginning was made possible by the political decision reached earlier in 1973 after negotiations that culminated in the Georgetown Accord. The aims elaborated in that Accord and in the Treaty have a continuing life and validity and have remained a point of reference throughout our work. Common to both was the primary 'determination [of CARICOM's Founding Fathers] to consolidate and strengthen the bonds which have historically existed among their peoples'.

Extensions of the Mandate

Since the Grand Anse Declaration of 1989 containing, *inter alia*, the substantive mandate of the West Indian Commission, successive meetings of the Conference of CARICOM Heads of Government have taken note of the work of the Commission and have taken decisions extending the original mandate.

At their Second Inter-Sessional Meeting in Port-of-Spain in February 1991, CARICOM Heads of Government reiterated the decision taken at the Eleventh Meeting in Kingston, Jamaica, 1990, that issues of a long-term nature in the report of the Review Team, chaired by Professor Gladstone Mills, should be taken into account by the West Indian Commission in the execution of its mandate.

In addressing the concerns of Belize and The Bahamas regarding a perceived remoteness from the Community, that same meeting noted that the West Indian Commission would be taking the opportunity of addressing that issue in its work during the course of conducting hearings in those countries.

With regard to the perceived need for fostering greater public awareness of CARICOM and the integration process, the Conference noted that the West Indian Commission would most likely be formulating important recommendations in this area and looked forward to the submission of those recommendations.

In relation to the possible widening of CARICOM, Heads of Government recognised that this was a matter which occupied a central place in the work programme of the West Indian Commission and decided to await the report of the Commission which they felt should facilitate further consideration of this matter. At that same CARICOM Summit in Kingston, a decision was taken to request the West Indian Commission to examine the application by the Dominican Republic for membership of CARICOM.

Assessment

The February 1991 Meeting of the CARICOM Heads of Government Conference also agreed that further consideration of the issue of decision-making in the Community would await the report of the West Indian Commission, since this matter overlapped with some aspects of the work of the Commission. Similarly, in the matter of the role of the Secretary-General and the Secretariat in the functioning of the Community, Heads of Government recognised that the issues arising in this area also overlapped with the work programme of the West Indian Commission, which had identified the question of Structures of Unity as one area for major study. The Heads accordingly looked forward to the input of the Commission in the further consideration of this matter by the Conference.

In considering the proposals to establish a CARICOM Commissioner, Heads of Government noted that this would be addressed within the study on Structures of Unity and agreed further that the proposal for establishment of a CARICOM Commissioner should be deferred until it could be considered in the context of the report of the West Indian Commission.

Establishing the Commission

At the Grenada Summit the Heads of Government appointed Sir Shridath Ramphal (Chairman) and Sir Alister McIntyre (Vice-Chairman) to lead the West Indian Commission; they also decided that the Secretary-General of CARICOM and the Director-General of the OECS Secretariat should be ex-officio members of the Commission.

The Chairman and Vice-Chairman, after conferring widely in the Region and consulting with Heads of Government, invited the following to join them as Commissioners:

> Mr. Leonard Archer
> Dame Nita Barrow
> Mr. William Demas
> Dr. Howard Fergus
> Dr. Marshall Hall
> Reverend Allan Kirton
> Dr. Vaughan Lewis (ex-officio)
> Ms. Gillian Nanton

Mr. Phillip Nassief
Professor Rex Nettleford
Mr. Roderick Rainford (ex-officio)
Mr. Frank Rampersad
Dr. Neville Trotz

On her appointment as Governor-General of Barbados, Dame Nita Barrow resigned her appointment as a Commissioner but graciously agreed to continue her contribution by becoming Patron of the Commission. Ms. Sandra Mason was invited to join the Commission in Dame Nita's place.

The Commission's Secretariat was established in a building at Black Rock, St. Michael, Barbados, made available by the Government of Barbados, and inaugurated in a ceremony held on 8th October, 1990. The Commission's work would not have been possible without this generous provision of office accommodation by Barbados and we record our gratitude for that generosity, as well as for the many acts of assistance rendered to the Commission by the authorities in Barbados.

The Honourable Don Brice was formally appointed Director-General of the Secretariat on 1st August, 1990 and a small staff was recruited to assist the Commission in its work and to undertake administrative and accounting duties. We express our particular appreciation to Prime Minister Michael Manley of Jamaica for facilitating Mr Brice's release from the Public Service of Jamaica, where he was head of the Prime Minister's Office. The Commission places on record its deepest appreciation for the dedicated and untiring service given to the Commission, and the Region as a whole, by the Director-General and his staff. Without service of that quality and commitment we simply could not have managed.

Appendix "B" contains the list of Commissioners, with brief background notes, together with a list of the Commission's advisers and staff.

The Commission held its first meeting on 9th–11th April, 1990 and in the course of its deliberations held 13 full meetings (Appendix "C") in addition to the numerous meetings held between teams of Commissioners and advisory staff.

Assessment

Pursuing the mandate from Heads of Government that the Commission should be independent, the Commission decided to seek, to the maximum extent possible, independent sources of finance to carry out its work. The Commission expresses its deep appreciation to the following for the financial contributions which funded the activities of the Commission, the studies undertaken on behalf of the Commission, and the Commission's publications including the Progress and Final Reports:

- Canadian International Development Agency
- Caribbean Development Bank
- Commonwealth Fund for Technical Cooperation
- Government of the Netherlands
- Government of Norway
- Government of the United Kingdom
- Inter-American Development Bank
- Swedish International Development Authority
- United Nations Development Programme.

The Commission expresses its gratitude for this support which made it possible for the Commission to discharge its mandate from CARICOM Heads of Government on the basis of independence and widespread consultation which they envisaged.

The Commission is also grateful for the contributions of the CARICOM Secretariat towards the work of the Commission through the particular assistance it rendered in providing rapporteurs for all the public and private sessions of the Commission, its contributions to the overheads of the Chairman's office and its constant support for the Commission's professional and administrative work.

That CARICOM Secretariat contribution was of fundamental importance to the Commission's work. It was provided at the highest level with the Secretary-General's personal involvement as a member of the Commission, and through the back-up support of his professional, technical and administrative staff, including the staff of the CARICOM Export Development Project (CEDP) in Barbados, all of whom worked with us on a basis of generous cooperation and absolute commitment to our objectives.

The same is true of the University of the West Indies. With the Chancellor and Vice-Chancellor as Chairman and Vice-Chairman respectively, and two of our other members drawn from the institution, the direct contribution of the University was clearly substantial. This was augmented, however, by support from the Bursar's Office and by the School of Continuing Studies through its Directors and staff in Member countries acting as co-ordinators of the Commission's consultations. The same was true of the University of Guyana in relation to our consultations there. We are deeply appreciative of these several contributions.

The Government of Trinidad and Tobago made a special financial contribution at a crucial stage in the Commission's work in 1991.

The Commission expresses deep and special appreciation to the regional air carriers, BWIA and LIAT, for their ready, generous and extremely valuable assistance in facilitating the extensive travels of the Commission in the course of its consultations.

A rather special and much appreciated service was provided to the Commission by the High Commissioners, Ambassadors, Consuls-General and their staff in Britain, Canada and the United States in relation to our visits to the large West Indian communities in those countries.

There are, in addition, a large number of individuals who gave freely of their time, skill and experience in helping the Commission at various stages of its work and in a number of different ways. To all of them, motivated only by a desire to contribute to a process they saw as having an historic dimension, the Commission expresses deep appreciation. We owe a special word of thanks to those who facilitated the publication of this Report through tireless effort and a high quality of professionalism. To Gordon Forte of BusinessPrint of Guyana and Carl Forde of Cole's Printery of Barbados we extend our particular appreciation.

Beyond these, no aspect of the work of the Commission has been a charge on the resources of the region.

Proceedings

The Commission's basic method of work followed closely the process of public consultations envisaged in the Trinidad and Tobago paper presented at the Grenada Summit and enhanced by the

Assessment

Grand Anse Declaration:

> ... consultations with the governments, political parties, trade unions, the private sector, religious bodies, professional groups, academics, the average West Indian, be held on the future of the West Indies.
>
> In that process, let all ideas contend — political, economic, social and cultural: let unity of all kinds be appraised, no less than the prospects of disunity. Let the outpouring of creative talent of our peoples in the region ... stimulate ... a process by which our Region becomes a public forum on the future.

We have sought to make a reality of this expectation. After our first Commission meeting in Barbados we addressed 'a communication to the people of the Caribbean Community' which included the following:

> We will travel to each Member State of CARICOM to engage in a process of meaningful consultation. No one who is interested in speaking to us will be excluded from the public forums which will be mounted in every part of our Caribbean Community. It is our hope that through your representative organisations such as political parties, private sector institutions, trade unions, youth groups, women's groups, professional associations and church groups, you will submit memoranda to us. But our consultations will not be limited only to such submissions; a vital part of our consultations will be with individuals in public hearings. We urge you to respond in great numbers, and share with us your concerns, your fears, your hopes and your aspirations for the future of our community of West Indian peoples.

We have gone far in engaging the talent, professional expertise and creative ability of a wide range of West Indians in the task of considering afresh the major challenges facing us. LET ALL IDEAS CONTEND has throughout been the watchword of the Commission's work.

Consultations

We have not taken our task of consultation lightly or informally. We traversed all 13 countries of CARICOM, as well as the two Associate Members, some of them more than once. We visited West Indians in London and Birmingham in the United Kingdom; in Montreal, Ottawa and Toronto in Canada; and in New York and Washington in the United States. In our extensive travels in the region we heard evidence in 36 centres — in rural areas and district towns as well as in the capital cities. The British Virgin Islands (BVI) and the Turks and Caicos Islands (TCI) were also visited. In addition, Commissioners visited Cuba, Curaçao, the Dominican Republic, Martinique, Puerto Rico, Suriname, the US Virgin Islands and Venezuela. Through these and other opportunities, we have discussed our mandate with President Aristide of Haiti, President Carlos Andres Perez of Venezuela and President Fidel Castro of Cuba, with Prime Minister Maria Liberia-Peters of the Netherlands Antilles, Governor Alexander Farelly of the US Virgin Islands, and Secretary of State Antonio Colorado of Puerto Rico.

Within CARICOM, we have met with every Head of Government as a Commission, and often with Cabinets.

We held sessions with Government and Opposition Parties and other politicians everywhere. We heard the views of, and discussed them with, groups representing the widest possible cross-section of professional bodies, interest groups, and non-governmental organisations: trade unions, representatives of all the religions, businessmen, farmers, representatives of the main industries and of small business, the media including the press, radio, television and the news services, teachers, academics, students, doctors and nurses and health-care workers, archivists and National Trust representatives, representatives of all the arts, sportsmen, groups representing the aboriginal people of the Region, architects, lawyers, Rotary Clubs and Chambers of Commerce, associations and individuals speaking for the disabled, groups and people deeply concerned about unemployment, crime, drugs and illiteracy. Everywhere we met with groups particularly concerned to express the problems and needs of women and youth.

The Commission held meetings with, and heard evidence from,

Assessment

the widest possible range of groups and individuals during the course of its consultations. Quite separately, 40 open public sessions were held. These were attended by people of all ages and from all walks of life.

In the course of these consultations and public sessions we cannot think of any theme or issue, concern or problem, that was not aired. The problems and prospects of regional integration were widely discussed but so too were a full range of issues that concern West Indians in their separate homelands — and overseas. Nor were individuals slow in voicing their complaints both general and personal. To some the Commission seemed a sort of court of last resort to which they felt able to bring their grievances and frustrations. Many distinguished older citizens were good enough to come out to give us the benefit of their knowledge and long years of experience and wish us well in our work. Young people got up to voice their hopes and fears. One young girl introduced herself as a future Prime Minister and we were glad to note that her vision was West Indian-wide!

Members of the Commission attended six workshops held to discuss in-depth most of the main issues with which we were confronted and joined in a Symposium especially organised in Caracas in cooperation with the Sistema Economico Latinoamericano (SELA) to discuss relations between CARICOM, the wider Caribbean, and Latin America. (See Appendix "C".) The intensive debates at these important sessions, attended by a wide cross-section of experts prominent in their fields, added greatly to our depth of understanding of the issues covered.

Documentation

A detailed itinerary of the Commission's visits and the list of organisations, representative groups and individuals with whom the Commission met, both inside and outside the West Indies, are given in Appendix "D".

Quite apart from those who delivered their views orally, in every West Indian accent, and on occasion with memorable force and imagination, a great many more took the opportunity of making submissions taking the form of letters, memoranda on specific subjects, full-scale briefs on a range of concerns, sometimes simple cries from the heart. At the time of writing the Commission had received over 350 separate written submissions. These have all been acknowledged and their authors will receive copies of our Report. A full list of written submissions is given in Appendix "E".

Minutes have been taken of all the consultations, the submissions have been carefully reviewed by staff and members of the Commission. These papers will have a value beyond assisting the Commission in formulating its conclusions. Together they will form a valuable archive for future West Indian scholars. So far as the Commission is concerned, the considerable documentation has assisted greatly in identifying major themes and issues. Our Report reflects the principal concerns of the Region's people not only as formally organised in their many representative groups but also, and prominently so, at the grass-roots.

Studies and Occasional Papers

To assist us in coming to grips with our task, we commissioned a number of major studies on issues and concerns requiring analysis in-depth and rigorous examination of options for action. These Studies have contributed significantly to our work. We recruited, from a wide range of West Indian expertise and experience, scholars of West Indian affairs. In some cases, the Studies in draft have served as source documents at Workshops organised by the Commission and attended by a cross-section of West Indians prominent in the field in question. These Studies were then refined in the form of final documents for the Commission's use.

The Commission intends to publish a number of these Studies as a contribution to the further study of the issues and concerns which they address. They should be valuable both to specialists in the fields covered and to others seeking knowledge about crucial issues facing the Region today.

The Studies commissioned and their authors are given in Appendix "F".

In the process of stimulating discussion on the issues, the Commission has published a number of Occasional Papers. These Papers reflect the views of their authors. They have been widely distributed during our consultations and we believe will be of continuing interest to all concerned with West Indian affairs.

Assessment

The Occasional Papers published by the Commission are also given in Appendix "F".

The Progress Report

After its first year of discussions and extensive consultations, the Commission believed it would be valuable and timely to present a progress report on its work to date. In particular, the Commission considered there were a number of specific matters which needed to be dealt with at once. These matters were grouped under six heads: Travelling in the Region; Free Movement of Skills; Towards a Common Currency; Enlarging Investment; Creating the CARICOM Single Market; and Mobilising for International Negotiations.

The Commission's Progress Report, entitled "Towards a Vision of the Future", was presented to CARICOM governments and people in June, 1991, and considered by Heads of Government at their Summit Meeting held in Basseterre in July, 1991.

The six recommendations for immediate action identified in the Progress Report can be summarised as follows:

1. Permit West Indians to travel in their Region with the freedom and ease due to them as citizens of a nation common to all — and encourage exchange visits, especially among young people.

2. Allow West Indian graduates of UWI (and other institutions to be identified) and media people to work and live freely anywhere in the Region as a first step to permitting the free movement of skilled people within the Region.

3. Take the first concrete steps — which the Progress Report defined — towards establishing an independent Caribbean Monetary Authority and a common currency.

4. Launch a Caribbean Investment Fund of US$50–70 million to invest in the Region's stock markets. The Progress Report set out a specific proposal for launching the Fund.

5. Complete as a matter of urgency — and setting aside all delaying argument — the CARICOM Single Market with its three principal instruments: the Common

External Tariff, the Harmonised Scheme of Fiscal Incentives, and the Rules of Origin.

6. Mobilise CARICOM to have a single negotiating posture and a single voice for international negotiations vital to our common interests.

In making these recommendations for immediate action the Commission recognised that its own credibility could be at stake but knew as well that good gains were possible. In our initial consultations scepticism about the determination of those leading the Community not simply to consult but to act was widespread. If the proposals were accepted and if nothing happened, scepticism would seem justified. On the other hand, purposeful action towards implementing these six urgent recommendations would provide a great morale boost to the integration movement and set the stage for further progress.

In the event, after initial delay, progress has now been made and the machinery set up to ensure more rapid progress has gone some way to producing significant results.

The six recommendations remain on the agenda and are repeated and refined in the body of this Final Report. They represent essential tasks to complete on the way towards closer regional integration. And we have been made aware in these concluding months of our work that West Indians are paying particular attention to judge whether, and how rapidly, these first sowings of the Commission bear fruit.

Beyond the action taken to start implementing the six recommendations, two useful lessons emerged.

The first lesson is that the full and whole-hearted involvement of civil servants at the national level is essential if decisions taken even at summit are to issue in action where it matters, that is, at ground level. Commissions, even Heads of Government, may propose but civil servants in the end dispose. This is a universal truth which the existing decision-making machinery in CARICOM does not fully accommodate. An imperial ukase to introduce hassle-free travel, for instance, will not yield results at the Immigration and Customs barriers unless employees of Immigration and Customs departments from top to bottom are not only instructed, but are

Assessment

enlisted in the cause over a sustained period of time. We are convinced that this is a fundamental truth which will have application to every single recommendation we make in this Report.

Secondly, taking our lead from a suggestion made by Prime Minister Sandiford in his speech at the 1990 Kingston Summit, we recommended that, as a transition until more permanent coordinating machinery is established, individual Heads of Government take on one each of the six areas in which we were recommending immediate action and, assisted by CARICOM Secretariat and technical back-up, become the implementor of the decisions taken.

This was agreed and individual Heads thus became responsible to colleagues, and to the West Indian people, for the implementation of the decisions adopted at the Summit. We feel that pending the establishment of formal machinery to allow decisions to be implemented more efficiently, it was essential that interim informal mechanisms be put in place to quicken the processes of implementation when decisions are approved at the highest level. Experience with the programme of 'immediate action' has confirmed our view that there really is no substitute for a central implementing authority — a matter with which we deal more fully in Chapter XII.

Good Offices

Beyond the Progress Report, the Commission used its 'good offices' to contribute to:
- a resolution of outstanding problems between Grenada and Cuba, resulting in the latter's recognition of the Government of Grenada and facilitating Cuba's membership of the Caribbean Tourism Organisation;
- a coming together of the regional private sector with CARICOM Heads of Government collectively in informed and productive dialogue;
- joint meetings of the security forces of the Region — both Military and Police.

Bibliography of West Indian Studies

There is a voluminous archive of writing about the West Indies. Indeed, some have said that we are more adept at analysing problems on paper than solving them in practice, more experienced at expertly showing the way forward than actually taking it. Certainly there is an extremely impressive library of books, reports, studies, pamphlets and articles written about the state of the West Indies in all aspects. There is also a considerable, and growing, literature about West Indian integration.

This work compiled by a long line of West Indian authors, academics, and specialists, built up over the years, is essential in examining the record, debating the issues, and attempting to draw conclusions about how the future should unfold. The archive also represents an important part of the single heritage of West Indian scholarship which is rapidly accumulating.

The Commission had prepared for it an exhaustive Bibliography of works on the West Indian condition. From this considerable volume we have derived a Select Bibliography, attached as Appendix "G", which can be used for reference, should more detailed information on specific subjects dealt with in the Report be required as background.

The volume of evidence to evaluate — the documentation already on the record, the Studies arising from the Commission's work, the first-hand views expressed and memoranda submitted "hot off the press" by West Indian people in every walk of life during the last 2 years — is considerable, even daunting. As was to be expected, the evidence is sometimes contradictory — West Indian experts as well as ordinary people are known to have differing views on every subject under the sun — and its very profusion places a high priority on clarity of thought in analysing it.

The richness of the documentation, the quality of the work of our West Indian scholars and experts, and the remarkably vivid and exuberantly up-to-date evidence produced by grass-root West Indians, has illuminated many an issue for us and has incalculably helped us in our task. We can claim that our conclusions and recommendations flow from what we as West Indians have made of quintessentially West Indian material forthcoming from every corner of the West Indies and from West Indians of every degree in and beyond the Region.

Assessment

2. INTRODUCING THE REPORT

Numerous Commissions or individuals have been mandated to report on the state of the West Indies in one way or another. We believe, however, that our mandate has required us to examine and make recommendations on a wider range of subjects and concerns than previous reports have encompassed.

The *West Indian Royal Commission*, 1896/7, and the *Olivier-Semple Enquiry*, 1929/30, both concerned themselves with sugar. The *Moyne Commission*, 1938/39, comprehensive though it was, was concerned principally "to investigate social and economic conditions". And, to take the examples of two excellent recently commissioned reports, the *Bourne Report*, 1988, investigated "Caribbean Development to the year 2000", and the *Mills Report*, 1990, was concerned to examine successes and setbacks in "regional programmes and organisations".

Range of Issues

The range of our concerns go beyond any of these reports. Governance and politics; regional institutions and the mechanisms of integration; economic conditions; finance, trade and industry; education from primary to tertiary level and the overall development of human resources; social conditions including the state of health in the Region, the incidence of crime and unemployment and the special problems of youth; gender issues; communications in every sense of the word; culture in all its aspects; sport; security considerations; the shaping of external policies to meet the challenges of international and regional developments; the special situation and needs of the aboriginal peoples of the Region; the place and influence of trade unions, religious bodies, professional associations and non-governmental organisations as a whole — these and more have been the subject of study by the Commission. How best to meet the challenges that lie ahead in the 1990s in all these areas necessarily finds a place in our Final Report; though each could be the subject of a definitive process of enquiry and report.

Particularly in this context, we consider the most important feature of our work is the emphasis we put on finding solutions, and meeting challenges, on the basis that a more integrated West Indian response best serves the purpose of improving conditions in whatever area of concern. In many areas solutions are not ready to hand; their evolution lies in processes without which the solutions themselves could be forever elusive. Similarly, responses to many challenges lie in machinery for implementation without which we simply delude ourselves that decisions represent progress. The concentration of our findings into the over-riding purpose of securing better lives for West Indian peoples through a more integrated, and therefore stronger, West Indian nation is another aspect of the Report which above all else, we believe, gives it a special place in the long line of reports and studies which have been undertaken on the West Indian condition.

Beyond Chaguaramas

The immense changes which have taken place externally, the entirely new challenges pressing upon us from the world outside our small domain, combined with the cumulative changes which have taken place in the Community for almost 20 years, deeply affecting every aspect of West Indian life in ways it was not possible to foresee, make it natural to re-examine the validity of the terms of the Treaty of Chaguaramas whose goals our mandate requires us to advance through our proposals.

The Treaty of Chaguaramas is a landmark in the history of West Indian people. And our mandate has made it the starting point in the work of the Commission. But implicit in the mandate is the inquiry whether the Treaty of Chaguaramas is adequate to the achievement of its own stated aims, and whether the stated aims are adequate to the aspirations of the West Indian people as we look in a new time to a new era. Indeed, Caribbean leaders have already answered some of those questions in such decisions as those embodied in the Grand Anse Declaration "to work towards the establishment, in the shortest possible time, of a Single Market and Economy for the Caribbean Community". We have concluded that the time is ripe to venture beyond the Treaty and break new ground. The terms of the Treaty are not so much outdated as in

Assessment

need of renewal and expansion. New imperatives require new responses and a new framework in which they can be accommodated. The logic of the work our mandate has led us into signals the need to open a new chapter in our West Indian story. Twenty years on it is time to formulate the terms of a successor Treaty to meet the challenges of the new century.

The Pressure of External Events

The time for taking a hard new look at the situation in the West Indies and making an appraisal of the best way forward for its peoples is well chosen. The last decade of a century might in any case be thought a suitable time to undertake such an exercise. But it is, of course, much more than the urge to take a grand *fin de siècle* view of the Region's affairs that has inspired the work of this Commission.

The Trinidad and Tobago paper, "The West Indies Beyond 1992", noted the real danger of the Caribbean becoming a backwater at a time of historic change when the central reality in international affairs lay in the fundamental restructuring which was taking place in the world. Since 1989, the continuing rush of events, and the restructuring which has proceeded apace, have amply confirmed the crucial, even historic, need to undertake a full-scale analysis of the West Indian condition and prospects for the future. That 1992 is the 500th anniversary of Columbus's first — and undoubtedly historically significant — encounter with the lands which have become homeland to us all may be seen as putting an appropriate, symbolic seal on the timing of this Commission's Final Report. But that encounter was full of negative implications for the first peoples of the Americas and, in particular, for our West Indian ancestors. The Quincentennial occasion could be a time of foreboding too unless we make deliberate efforts to respond to its challenges in bold and purposeful ways — together.

Extraordinary changes in the world enforce the need to act together with urgency. Change was fast enough before but in the short time since the Grand Anse Declaration the international context has been utterly transformed. Communism has been seen to fail, command economies are being discarded everywhere, the adoption of market mechanisms is increasingly seen as the litmus test of how to run economies properly. The Soviet Union has disintegrated, the Cold War has ended and it is now a world of one, not two, military super-powers with all that implies for the shaping of a new world order. The EEC has taken crucial steps towards establishing a Common Currency and Single Market and achieving closer political integration, and the EEC and EFTA propose coming together in 1993 to create an even wider consolidated market of 400 million. The Uruguay Round of GATT talks continue with no sure benefits, and holding a number of serious potential threats, for countries like our own.

The USA has gone rapidly beyond the Free Trade Agreement with Canada to begin negotiating a similar accord with Mexico in the context of a proposed hemispheric Free Trade Area in which our place as yet is uncertain to say the least. Canada, meanwhile, is engaged in debate on constitutional change, the outcome of which could have significance for the Caribbean Community. On the other side of the world — but in these days that phrase means infinitely less than it did not long ago — Japan continues its march towards economic and financial pre-eminence.

In our immediate neighbourhood change, including the prospect of even more rapid change, is the order of the day. Almost every month, it seems, we observe new initiatives towards closer cooperation. We have had the establishment of the Group of Three, involving trade co-operation between Colombia, Mexico and Venezuela; the launching of MERCOSUR, a grouping of the Southern Cone countries of Latin America; and the commitment of the Andean Pact countries to consolidate their grouping into a Single Market by 1995.

In the immediate CARICOM context, closer economic and trade relations with Latin American countries are being developed. Venezuela has offered one-way free trade to the Community and has joined the Dominican Republic in applying to join CARICOM. In Guyana the road being constructed between Georgetown and Brazil signals an era of closer connections between that great Latin American country and ourselves. Guatemala's recognition of Belize opens up new possibilities of constructive relations between CARICOM and Central America.

Assessment

Within the Region itself new challenges proliferate. In Haiti, the impasse after the ousting of President Aristide leaves the Region with a grave unsolved problem from which the West Indies in particular cannot turn aside. Cuba, its economic life dislocated and threatened by the breakdown in its links with Eastern Europe and the former Soviet Union, but with its ten million well-educated people, advanced technology in many areas, and unlimited tourist potential, offers a huge new challenge to enlightened statesmanship and entrepreneurial skills in the Community. At the same time, memories of the colonial experience are fading and links with metropolitan countries are seen much more in the cold light of what economic advantages might issue from such a connection. The consequences of this change in mind-set, especially for autonomous but non-independent countries in the Region, are likely to be a further complicating factor in plotting our course as a Community.

These far-reaching international and regional developments, and their implications for the West Indies, are analysed in-depth in the course of this Report. The conclusions we draw form the basis of an important part of our Report and recommendations. It is sufficient to say at this stage that a common factor in this turmoil of change is the need rapidly to expand our collective capacity to respond rationally to new developments as they arise, almost daily it sometimes seems, to challenge us. There are few who would not agree, certainly very few among the people of the West Indies, that clinging to ancient fiefdoms at this time in our history is a strategy we shall have to discard.

The Urgency of the People's Needs

However, it is by no means only the pressure and urgency of external events that have made the time ripe for a close examination of West Indian prospects and plans. The pressures and urgency of the people's needs call as insistently for such a review. In the course of our work over two years, in our visits and consultations in all 13 countries, we found deep concern, and even bitterness, about economic and social conditions in the Region and profound disquiet about the future.

No doubt the concern and the disquiet derive part of their force from the fact that people are in much closer contact with the external world than they have ever been. This has two effects: it brings tantalisingly near the over-glamourised attractions of living in a richer world and raises hopes unattainably high that the same might be provided here; and it brings home with vivid immediacy how fast events are moving and how easily small players in the game can be cast aside or overwhelmed by developments that have nothing to do with them. As a result, West Indians, much more acutely than even a short time ago, both feel they deserve to be offered much more and sense that they are in danger of receiving much less in a dangerous world. In the circumstances, the feelings of ambivalence and uncertainty among West Indians are now understandable.

This new, more acute and sophisticated, awareness makes the job of fulfilling expectations much harder than it otherwise would be. All the same, the needs are not simply derived from media-heightened expectations and fears. The needs are real and immediate. Unemployment, poverty, deteriorating health services, severe shortcomings in educational systems, a huge rise in crime, the new menace of the evil trade in narcotics, a serious lowering of standards of behaviour and discipline, the continued desperately disadvantaged state of most women bringing up children alone, were all scourges deeply disturbing West Indians throughout the Region. We are sure these concerns are real and must not be neglected.

Solving Problems through Integration

A great number of the West Indians we met looked upon the Commission as a suitable forum in which to ventilate their fears, concerns, and even sometimes their anger, and just as many looked upon the Commission also as a possible means of assisting in the solution or alleviation of the problems they or their communities were experiencing. The people, we found, were interested in closer integration, yes very definitely, but more as a means to improve the condition of their and their children's lives than in integration as an end in itself. This deeply impressed us and set the tone for many of our deliberations. *"Han' stronger than finger"*, Louise Bennett told us in Toronto, and *"One finger kyan ketch flea"*, and we listened.

Assessment

What Kind of Integration?

The people desired closer integration but within this general aspiration there were almost as many views as there were persons to express them about what form integration should take. The great majority of people seemed to despair that they would see full-scale West Indian political unity in their lifetimes. In the smaller ambit of the OECS a different situation and different expectations were subjects of keen, ongoing debate during our consultations. The peoples of those islands have important decisions to make about what is in fact the possibility of a special relationship within the larger framework of West Indian integration. What progress they make could be of the greatest possible consequence — by example and in practice — for the rest of the Region. The Commission is well aware of this extremely important dimension in our political affairs. In the meanwhile, the goal of general West Indian unity at the political level remains for our people, it is clear, a sort of Holy Grail shining on the edge of a distance too far away to matter for the time being.

Between the general desire to be closer and the general feeling that political unity is out of reach, we found any number of part-way stations, base-camps, so to say, on the way to the mountain summit. The waste, lack of focus, and dilution of influence which 13 full-scale governments and their separate apparatuses represent were almost unanimously deplored and, short of single government solutions, suggestions flowed for finding ways and means to co-ordinate administrations, bureaucracies, services, embassies and policy-making organs as far as possible so as to eliminate the perceived waste and duplication and provide the focus and force needed if we are to be seriously considered as at least a nation in embryo.

Common to all the suggestions — many ingenious, some impracticable, all welcome as showing us hearts in the right place — was a considerable element of integration at practical levels affecting everyday lives. Even those most protective of individual national identity or cultural difference put forward views which included regional institutions for achieving closer economic, financial and trading integration and for presenting a united front to the wider world.

Introducing the Report

We have had to pick our way carefully among these many views pressed upon us, not to mention the varied formulations of experts in the field, but at least we have been strengthened by what we clearly perceive as the general wish that the machinery and procedures for achieving closer integration should be revitalised and reformed.

No Return to Federalism

In giving form to this in our Report we have made the decision not to revisit the Federation of 1958–1962. We feel, and we believe that the people also feel, that that enterprise was an honourable episode in our progress as a people, but that it must be allowed to settle in its niche in history. There are lessons to be learned from the experience but those lessons have to be applied in our much changed context in radically new ways. It is a question of finding where there is real community of interest, the right measure of exercising practical powers jointly without over-balancing into the kind of centralised authority which is foreign to West Indian thinking at the present time, which people will not accept, and which in a democratic society cannot be imposed. Amalgamation of power in one single centre is not practical at this time; the joint exercise of sovereignty in a whole range of operational matters is, we believe, perfectly feasible. We believe the recommendations we make will suit the West Indian people and will bring us closer together in those important realms where everyday life is organised and lived and where we face the world. But they will involve change, particularly in how we see ourselves.

The Wider Caribbean Family

Our recommendations confront another unavoidable question, namely that of creating a closely integrated West Indies which will have as one of its principal aims — held in common as an article of faith and as a matter of priority — extending and tightening our links with the rest of the Caribbean family.

In our consultations we were often questioned about the appropriateness of the term "West Indies" in the title of the Commission. The question arose not only because people felt that Columbus's error and legacy did not deserve to be perpetuated (they forget perhaps how much we would miss the "West Indies" in our cricket team!), but also because many felt that "Caribbean" would better define a true remit for the work of the Commission. The term "West Indian" is appropriate in defining the present basis of our nationhood but, as we were always at pains to point out, it in no way precludes us venturing upon a larger enterprise, not only in our search for additional protection against the storms of change, but also in order to realise what is a natural regional bonding arising out of common historical roots. Reflected in the conclusions and recommendations of the Report is our deeply felt instinct that the West Indies lies at the core of a larger Caribbean Community which has a common destiny which in the end we must seek together.

The West Indian Diaspora

As we will not neglect our Caribbean neighbours, we must not take for granted the vast number of West Indians in the diaspora, the great majority of whom, including generations beyond the first emigration, retain a love of homeland and a preparedness to contribute "back home" to which we must respond more positively than we have done in the past. The Commission made a point of going to Britain, Canada, and the United States to meet with a large cross-section of West Indians in all the centres we visited. Throughout, it was a heartening experience. The interest in what the Commission was set up to do, the satisfaction at being consulted, the strong desire to assist in West Indian nation-building and in lobbying for West Indian causes, convinced us that here we have voices and talents and interests and resources which we must find organised ways, and devise systematic preferential arrangements, to involve in our work and lives back home.

And, *quid pro quo*, lest it be thought that our interest in the diaspora is purely mercenary, we must also find better organised, more systematic, ways of involving ourselves in the problems they face in their new homes. In particular, the racism which many have experienced, and which many more are likely to experience as the voice of extreme chauvinism becomes shriller in metropolitan countries, must be considered our problem too. We must represent our interest in the well-being of "our people" at the highest official levels and whenever required. We must treat these men and women and children of the diaspora as West Indians all, far from home but close at heart.

Improving Education — The Vital Task

Nothing has come through clearer in our consultations — and we believe nothing will be more clearly reflected in this Report — than the vital need to improve educational infrastructure in the Region and multiply many times over educational and training opportunities for all West Indians.

How we make our way in the world is the heart of the matter. In the early hours of 12 October, 1492, a lookout on the *"Pinta"* shouted in excitement to his captain and fellow seamen *"Tierra! Tierra!"* The answering chorus from below decks, it seems, was *"¡Albricias!"* That is to say, in Arabic-Spanish, "Rewards!" Five hundred years later it is no longer the world's perception that the Region is endowed with the wealth of all the Indies. That may be a good thing in one way — think only of the untold misery flowing out of that original perception — but it also indicates that here we provide no longer the sort of natural magnet which might allow us to earn an easy living in the world. It will take well-organised leadership and hard, disciplined work but, more than that, it will require well-trained minds and skilled hands to do the job for us. Today men still shout "Rewards!" and gather round the lure of rich natural resources — and we must take full advantage of those our countries still possess. But the future belongs much more certainly to the land which possesses an educated, well-trained, entrepreneurially-minded population. That is the true, modern equivalent to the wealth of the Indies. And it is a treasure, moreover, which we more than anyone can exploit.

Meeting Youth's Aspirations

Education — youth: the twin pillars of a nation in the building. It is the young whose eyes were brightest with all the questions. And it is the young whose questions we must be most alert to answer. How could it be otherwise? They are the future. If they lose faith

Assessment

the future is lost and our work will come to nothing. They have not lost faith but we have found them — and in many cases their elders on their behalf — on the edge of deep distress — about conditions which belittle and sometimes devastate their family and individual lives, about lack of opportunities in employment that leaves them idle and frustrated and tempts them down dangerous cul-de-sacs, about prospects often so unpromising that they have no alternative but to yearn for shipping out to greener pastures, about what the especially ambitious and patriotic perceive as lack of firm guidance from the political leadership, lack of plans that inspire long-term hope, lack of vision.

That is not the whole story, it may paint too gloomy a picture, since everywhere we went we found evidence of the sort of determination, resilience, and hope to inspire our belief that the younger generation is willing and able to help in improving their own lives and advancing the cause of West Indian integration. But it remains true that there is quite enough frustration, quite enough resentment about conditions, quite enough concern about future prospects in education and employment, and quite enough doubt that advancement in life can best be assured while remaining in the West Indies, to make it necessary for the Commission to urge with considerable fervour that its Report and its conclusions be read as if no time was left at all to meet the aspirations of young West Indians. This Report has been written with them in mind, in the knowledge that it is principally their future which is at stake, and with the certainty that little will come of our efforts if we do not succeed in inspiring their full participation in the immense tasks of the 1990s.

Implementation is the Key

TIME FOR ACTION must be the motto of the decade. It is clear to the Commission that the people of the West Indies desire to integrate the management of their affairs more closely. Doubts, hesitations, have been expressed, but the overwhelming consensus — with the possible exception of The Bahamas, whose problems of remoteness, along with those of Belize, we examine as a special issue of concern in the Report — is that West Indians as a whole believe that their economic, social, cultural and diplomatic future lies in achieving a single market, a common currency, a single force in international affairs, and a community within which their diversity is preserved but through which their voice is strengthened, their fortunes improved and their creativity recognised.

This central conviction lies at the heart of the Report. It is, we repeat, the people's conviction not merely the Commission's. The recommendations in the Report, in the many fields of activity and areas of concern to which our attention has been directed, will cohere around this central certainty.

But conviction without the power to implement, recommendations without the determination and means to act, are words on a page soon consigned to the archive. That is why, perhaps foremost among our concerns, has been the question of how to establish Community machinery which will enable important decisions to be more readily taken and, when taken, implemented without delay or dilution. This problem, expressed in one form or another in every West Indian accent in our consultations, has occupied much of our attention. Our recommendations on this score, therefore, figure prominently in the main body of the Report. Without acceptance of our argument in this area, and without rapid movement to act on our proposals, agreement in other respects is likely to be vitiated as so many important findings and initiatives have been vitiated in the past.

The basis of our work has been to listen to the people. The kernel of what they have reported is that their lives will be better if steps are taken to hasten integration. How best to clothe their hopes, and our conviction, with action will become the crux of this Report.

3. THE COMMISSION'S GOALS

The objective of our work is the improvement of the lives of all West Indians. Our conviction is that this can best be achieved through closer West Indian integration in every sphere of activity.

Deeper integration of the 13 Member States (accompanied by an

Assessment

intensive exploration of wider Caribbean co-operation) must be decisively and immediately accelerated. The aim must be to pursue initiatives, conclude agreements, and establish institutions of implementation with a sense of such urgency that by the end of the decade of the 1990s the West Indies, by whatever name — but still with some six million people — is near enough an integrated union of states as will make no difference in a world which by then will have no self-respecting place for anything less.

The intent of all our recommendations will be to achieve the above objectives. The micro-issues on which we might express opinions and advocate action are virtually endless and would not be outside the terms of reference which we have been given. Indeed, many of the studies we have commissioned and the research and discussions these have produced should contribute importantly to identifying, and then solving, a host of problems which beset the Region and which need urgent attention. We believe this will be a valuable fall-out from our work. But we cannot, in such short order, hope to be a super-Commission of Enquiry into the problems of health, crime, education, employment, trade, transportation, communications, culture, security, foreign relations and all the rest of the sectoral problems that exist in the Region.

We must set a limit on our ambitions in this Report. Our intention will be to focus clearly on those aspects of these matters for which the integration process has the most powerful and immediate impact. The Report will deal with those issues where the needs of the people, and the contribution deeper integration might make to meeting those needs, come together in a way where action becomes not merely advisable but, at this juncture in our affairs, imperative. When implemented, our recommendations are designed to build, well before the end of the decade, structures of unity within which West Indians can live more freely and openly together and, in common, operate their affairs with increased dynamism, competitiveness and creative energy.

On December 18, 1787, Alexander Hamilton explained why it was necessary to form a union of the American States:

> The principal purposes to be answered by union are these — the common defence of the members; the

The Commission's Goals

preservation of the public peace, as well against internal convulsions as external attacks; the regulation of commerce with other nations and between the States; the superintendence of our intercourse, political and commercial, with foreign countries.

We do not pretend to be undertaking the same sort of task as Hamilton and his peers were undertaking at that historic time, but the purposes for which he saw a union of states answering most importantly are easily recognisable, and certainly appropriate, in our West Indian context today. As we visited St Kitts and Nevis and looked on the plaque that commemorates his years there we could not fail to reflect on how much the strength — even the very reality — of the United States owed to his wisdom.

Our recommendations for action to integrate our affairs more closely are definite and far-reaching. We have not, however, except in those cases where immediate action is clearly appropriate, suggested a precise timetable. We have been wary of suggesting deadlines, with good reason. The history of deadlines set for achieving objectives in CARICOM is replete with repeated postponements and outright failure. Suspicion of all decision-making in the Community has, therefore, become ingrained among the public and the expression of this disillusion has been one of the phenomena of our consultations.

That is why in the first order of business the Report recommends new and more effective machinery for implementing centrally agreed decisions. If this can be achieved, then the establishment of a carefully worked-out timetable makes sense. A timetable in these circumstances could be useful in concentrating official efforts to meet deadlines under sanction and also in attracting public interest and support.

It will be for the Heads of Government, advised by their teams of officials, and exhorted by the people of the region, to decide a precise timetable within which our recommendations, if agreed, are to be achieved. If our package of recommendations is accepted, the achievement of a Single Market within which people, capital and trade move unimpeded, the establishment of a common currency with a central monetary authority, and the adoption of streamlined formal machinery for conducting external negotiations in common will rank high in the list of objectives to be met. Our recommendations will also point to the creation of a West Indies bound closer together not only through radically improved air and sea transport, but also through the introduction of a network of commercial and media linkages making full use of up-to-date communications technology. Our recommendations will lay stress on the absolute need to make a quantum leap in the delivery of improved educational opportunities at every level and strengthen the presence and expand the activities of the UWI throughout the community. Before this decade is much older these fundamental moves to closer integration and to nation-building must be made.

Measured in terms of the 1970s and 1980s such far-reaching steps to be taken in so short a timeframe may seem precipitate. But those times were static compared with now. Think back only 36 months and the argument for dramatic, decisive action to match fast-moving events becomes self-evident. The aim must be to have in place well before the end of the decade the essential mechanisms of an integrated Community so that, entering the 21st Century, we will have become accustomed to working them and living with them naturally.

There are, of course, some paths we do not seek to pursue: our vision does not include a monolithic, heavily centralised West Indian state seeking uniformity in all things. Far from it. Such a construct would offend the West Indian instinct for individuality and appreciation of diversity and would by no means be practicable. Nor would it come near how we conceive the future of West Indian nationality. It is a matter of building, out of a sense of belonging which already exists, institutions for practical action where there is a community of interests in acting together in a society where the values and the processes of democracy are secure. This would be a nationalism which derives strength, not weakness, from cultural differences within that shared community of interests. It would be a nationalism totally unaggressive in its external ambitions and insisting not at all on conformity within. It could indeed be a nationalism which sets an example to the rest of the world by providing a "West Indian model" of how various peoples, holding democracy sacrosanct, can live and work together successfully and in amity.

Lord Acton wrote, "the theory of nationalism is a retrograde step in history" — but he had in mind a nationalism of force and blood and race. This, indeed, has caused, and is causing now, misery and anger in the world. That is not the path we tread. We do not need, and should not desire, to create a West Indian chauvinism. Historically, we are too experienced for that. C.L.R. James wrote, "The West Indies is a microcosm of world civilisation.... We are not dominated by the past civilisations. We are in a most unique situation." That is an inheritance we need to cherish and build upon, not reject through concentration on single-state theories. The central institutions of a West Indian state should serve and improve, not dominate, the lives of our various peoples.

We come back to what the people want. In meeting with us everywhere people have been concerned that what the Commission does should result in a better life for themselves and, very importantly, the prospect of a better life and improved opportunities for their children. They believe that these ends can be advanced most effectively through accelerated CARICOM integration and closer co-operation with sister CARICOM countries.

On this basis people have supported the Commission with an extraordinary unanimity. However, almost as unanimously, they do not believe we can deliver the goods. They foresee that whatever our Report says, whatever it recommends, will be lost on a shelf, as they see it, along with so many other reports and recommendations.

This is the sticking point. The Report, we believe, is founded upon unimpeachable evidence derived from clear and expert examination of the facts available. It also has the support of the masses of West Indian people. And the urgency with which the Report's recommendations should be accepted and implemented is dictated by history itself now moving at breakneck pace. But the question remains large as to whether and how quickly action will issue from the Report and its recommendations. This is indeed the question, the answer to which will make or break the real usefulness of this Report and the work which has gone into addressing the concerns — and the vision — of those who gave the Commission its mandate.

CHAPTER II

THE CARICOM EXPERIENCE

1. REVIEWING THE RECORD

It may be that confidence was lacking. Perhaps it was too soon after the trauma of Federation's failure to be anything but cautious in setting goals. With the fear of a second, fatal, failure dominating the psyche of West Indian leadership, the gradualist approach may have seemed, and may well have been, the right one at the time. The aim was softly, softly, to get the monkey of Federation failure off the backs of the West Indian people. And only judgement by hindsight can question the validity of that self-limiting approach.

In the event, the cautious goals, the gradualist approach, has not matched the people's growing expectations. More and more they have seen progress as too limited. Increasingly they have become impatient to advance at a faster pace to a more exciting drumbeat. In such a mood even success has been brushed aside as too little too late and failure has fostered a disproportionate cynicism.

The terms of the Treaty of Chaguaramas setting out CARICOM's objectives are not written into the everyday record by which people judge progress or lack of it. It is more than likely that the West Indian people have come to believe that the Treaty incorporates more ambitious goals, and the matching mechanisms to achieve them, than in fact it does. This may explain why the great mass of people believe that CARICOM has been much more a failure than a success.

A balance sheet could no doubt be drawn up recording in terms of the Treaty a hundred technical successes, a hundred limited objectives achieved, a hundred administrative battles won, a hundred shopping list items ticked. And it is important that such a balance sheet exists and continues steadily to be supplemented on the credit side. It is important that the work has continued to be done, that the Treaty has been treated seriously and every effort made to ensure that its objectives are kept in focus whatever the delays and frustrations, that horses continue to be tugged towards the water even if they cannot in the end be forced to drink. There is an underestimated success story of unremitting toil and dedicated service to be told in this continuing, decades-long, effort to achieve the listed goals of CARICOM.

But in the end the peoples' instinct has been right. In the sense of achieving an integration which deeply matters in their lives, which allows their children more ample prospects, which gives the lands in which they live greater stature and a safer niche in a world of turmoil, the real balance sheet, the true bottom line, shows us falling well short of potential.

It will be useful to describe in outline both the successes which have attended the effort to further the objectives of the Treaty of Chaguaramas and the extent to which this effort has fallen short of matching the deeper purposes of West Indian integration. An overall assessment shows, we believe, a West Indian community in transition, with some important preparatory work done but ready now to match in actual product the much greater potential which the mass of people feel lies waiting in the concept and the ideal which inspired the original Treaty.

2. TECHNICAL SUCCESSES

The explicit goals of CARICOM have been pursued with skill and zeal over the years. A wide range of projects and programmes have been undertaken, usually out of the headlines but important in organising the affairs of West Indians jointly to their advantage. It has been a laborious business but slowly the elements of a common market are being pulled together. There have been signal successes in facing the world together in unity. It is an honourable record of dedicated West Indian public service, laying the groundwork if not yet starting to raise the shining city.

Our Common Economic Space

The Treaty of Chaguaramas envisaged the complete integration of individual markets into one enlarged market of over five million people. Progress has been desperately slow and halting. However, even if not completed, credible efforts have been maintained over the years to dismantle trade barriers as the intra-CARICOM market has enlarged. In 1967 intra-regional trade accounted for about 5 per cent or EC$95.7 million of the region's total trade. By 1981 the ratio had grown to about 10 per cent or EC$1.6 billion. In 1982-86 a severe bout of intra-CARICOM protectionism reduced the level of intra-CARICOM trade to less than half what it was in 1981. Intra-regional trade growth resumed in 1987 and by 1991 had reached EC$1.3 billion or 81 per cent of the 1981 level. It has been progress at a staggering and ungainly pace but the race at least is still being run and in the new mood of determination the finishing line may at last be in sight.

Slow and interrupted progress has marked the development of key common market instruments. The agreement to establish a Common External Tariff by 1983 never came remotely near achievement. Indeed, not until late 1986 did Member States start to make a serious effort to harmonise tariff rates. Since then, a sustained effort has been made to achieve the CET throughout the region. A package was agreed for implementation by 1st January, 1991, but to date has only been introduced by 8 Member States. In terms of population, however, these do account for 92% of the Common Market.

There has been greater success in establishing Rules of Origin for Common Market trade. The rules introduced in 1981 were a considerable improvement on the pre-existing initial rudimentary rules. Further improvements were developed to go into effect on 1st January, 1991. There have been delays in implementation but to date 10 of the 12 Common Market Member States have introduced the latest rules. The overall result has been a substantial improvement in the framework which facilitates intra-CARICOM production processes.

To advance the process of developing a common West Indian economic space the Treaty of Chaguaramas called for freedom of payments on current account, consultation on monetary and exchange rate policies, exchange by Member States of each other's notes and coins at par, and the establishment of a clearing mechanism in the Common Market. There have been successes in the important area of increasing economic solidarity in the Community but these have been disappointingly spasmodic and limited. From the late 1970s to the early 1980s the Multilateral Clearing Facility, co-ordinated by the Central Bank of Trinidad and Tobago, was strikingly successful in helping to conserve hard currency reserves and stimulate intra-CARICOM trade. However, lack of discipline in applying rules relating to credit limits and to the retiring of obligations led to a small number of participating countries including Guyana, the major debtor, nearly exhausting all credit in the scheme by 1982 and the facility collapsed. The initial success remains as an example of what can be achieved technically in bringing the region together economically and financially for the benefit of all.

Also in the late 1970s CARICOM Travellers' Cheques were introduced, primarily to conserve foreign exchange. There have been problems in the operation of this facility and lack of confidence in its use arising from doubts about the underlying strength of the Trinidad and Tobago dollar in which the instrument is designated. However, this instrument achieved some success and the concept remains valid for use until there is a common currency or Member States' currencies can be traded freely in intra-regional transactions.

The Agricultural Marketing Protocol and the Oils and Fats Agreement have been two regimes that provide identified products with more profitable access than they would enjoy under free trade conditions. The AMP lasted until 1983 and, along with the associated arrangement, the Guaranteed Marketing Scheme, gave special status and benefits to 22 primary agricultural products from the LDCs. The Oils and Fats Agreement has considerably benefitted the coconut-producing LDCs. Coconut farmers and processors in the Eastern Caribbean depend to a large extent on this agreement for their livelihood. However, the non-implementation of obligations now threatens to upset this agreement and the benefits it has brought. In a similar way, the LDCs have benefitted under Article 56 of the Common Market Annex to the Treaty which protects fledgling industries in the LDCs from MDC competition. This encouragement of industrial development in many of the small CARICOM countries has shown how the spirit of Community can be applied in a practical way to assist its more vulnerable members.

Overall, progress in developing a CARICOM economic space has been depressingly slow, coming to a complete halt for long periods and suffering reverses all too often. Probably more than anything, this lack of dynamism and commitment in pressing forward towards the attainment of this basic goal of the Treaty has led to the spread of cynicism in the region about ever achieving practical implementation of Community objectives. Yet there have been limited successes, and endeavour at least has never ceased.

This is important. The maintenance, and slow enlargement, of a market in which CARICOM products and manufactures have an edge holds an importance which has been generally underestimated. As one example, in Jamaica in the 1980s about 10,000 jobs — providing a livelihood for 30,000 people — were generated by exports of manufactures from Jamaica to other CARICOM countries. And for LDC countries in particular, the CARICOM market remains of great importance to economic success: in 1990, for example, Antigua and Barbuda sent 66 per cent of its exports to other CARICOM countries, St. Vincent and the Grenadines 32 per cent and Saint Lucia 18 per cent. Even for the larger economies, though CARICOM exports are a small proportion of their total trade, the regional market is very valuable for their manufacturing sectors; in recent years, for instance, manufactures have accounted for 65–78 per cent of total exports to CARICOM for Jamaica, 61–69 per cent for Trinidad and Tobago, 68–90 per cent for Barbados, and 34–77 per cent (in the first half of the 1980s) for Guyana. In the 1980s, also, few of the LDCs registered less than 50 per cent of their total manufacturing exports going to the CARICOM market; more often the percentage was well over 50 per cent and in some cases 75 per cent and over.

An objective assessment has to be that, through thick and more often thin, CARICOM has been maintained and developed to serve the role of a secure home market, a domestic learning ground for a significant part of the manufacturing operations of the region — an economic space which provides them with the opportunity of consolidating a base from which to launch into world markets.

Functional Cooperation

Significant technical successes in CARICOM have been registered in the promotion of functional co-operation in various important areas since the Treaty was established. By steady accretion cooperation among Member States has become a way of life in a number of fields. Even when there has been failure, the urge to act more closely together has not been allowed to die. Torches have not burnt out — they remain alight to be passed on to another, more ardent, generation.

Strengthening links between its sea-separated countries is an obvious priority for CARICOM. It has not been for want of trying that progress in this respect has been disappointing. After Federation collapsed, a Regional Shipping Council took over the operation of the "Federal Palm" and the "Federal Maple". In 1976 WISCO was established to serve as the vehicle for inter-governmental co-operation in shipping. Since then the Corporation has been plagued by problems — management shortcomings, operating deficits, subscription shortfalls, contradictory policy directives — and at the time of writing has ceased operations — temporarily, it is to be hoped. Yet WISCO has provided a scheduled service for moving goods around the region not otherwise available. Sustaining this basic service — and considerably improving it — whether in governmental or private hands, must remain a Community priority.

The strengthening of air transportation links is also a priority. In this respect, it is a little-praised achievement that all Member States of CARICOM, except The Bahamas and Belize, enjoy frequent, regular and reliable air services through the combined operations of BWIA and LIAT. It may be a major disappointment that one common air carrier has not emerged in the region, but the degree of co-operation achieved and the standards of service provided are not negligible. The latest move by BWIA and LIAT to "become one entity from a marketing perspective" is an example of how regionalisation slowly makes its way if the workmen stick resolutely to their lathes.

The University of the West Indies long predates CARICOM as an outstanding regional achievement. However, CARICOM processes have consolidated the achievement by assisting in co-ordinating

Assessment

further development among participating Governments and in mobilising support from external agencies. CARICOM can take its share of the credit for the 46,000 graduates with first degrees, certificates, diplomas, and higher degrees who have passed through the UWI to date. CARICOM has also had a considerable success in establishing the CXC system of regional examinations. CXC came into existence formally in 1972 and in 1979 the first examinations were held — 30,000 candidates registering in 61,000 entries spanning five subjects. In 1991, 80,000 candidates registered in 300,000 entries spanning 33 subjects. The establishment of the UWI as a regional institution with world-class credentials, the gradually expanding system of regional examinations, and the sponsorship and organisation of an increasing variety of human resource development programmes regionally — these represent a continuing CARICOM achievement of immense significance for the Community in the long term.

CARICOM activity in the health field, identified in the Treaty as an important area for regional co-operation, has been fruitful. With the help of PAHO an impressive number of regional institutions have been established, bringing numerous benefits to all Member States. During the 1980s the Caribbean Environmental Health Institute (CEHI), hosted in Saint Lucia, came into being and is helping to co-ordinate a number of environmental projects supported by donor agencies. The Caribbean Epidemiology Centre, hosted in Trinidad and Tobago, co-ordinates epidemiological surveillance throughout the region. Under the Caribbean Co-operation in Health Initiative, in the second half of the 1980s regional programmes dealing with AIDS, health protection, and maternal and child health have been introduced. The Caribbean Regional Drug Testing Laboratory, established in Jamaica, provides another common service aiming to secure the safety and efficacy of pharmaceuticals consumed within the region. Thus, by slow degrees, a practical network of regional health facilities is being extended.

CARICOM sponsors and facilitates regional co-operation in a growing variety of other activities. Population and housing censuses are co-ordinated collectively and the results processed and analysed centrally, yielding uniform data vital for social and economic planning across the region. The Caribbean Meteorology Organisation is responsible for a severe weather watch-and-warning system operated through an interlocking regional network of personnel and equipment and relating with other systems in the wider region and the hemisphere. Through the Caribbean Uniform Building Code (CUBIC), building codes setting our minimum standards relevant to conditions and hazards in the region have become available to Member States for adaptation and use. Also of considerable practical value has been the development of regional Disaster Preparedness and Response mechanisms, leading to the recent establishment of the Caribbean Disaster Emergency Response Agency, located in Barbados, aimed at further strengthening and streamlining the organisation and delivery of intra-CARICOM relief in time of disaster. Through the Caribbean Agricultural Research and Development Institute (CARDI), located in Trinidad and Tobago, programmes have been extended throughout the region assisting agricultural development. And, though slow to take root, the Caribbean Food Corporation (CFC), which mobilises resources for investment in commercial agriculture, has begun to assist a number of useful projects designed to reduce the region's huge food import bill.

CARICOM's "common service" function has been especially useful also in developing legislative models which individual countries then adapt and incorporate into national law. Member States, for instance, have been drawing on model legislation developed by CARICOM in the complex and important areas of Copyright, Maritime, and Company Law.

The work of co-ordinating regional endeavours, sponsoring and supporting Community institutions, and providing common services across the region continues to be pursued through all the vicissitudes of the CARICOM experience. If failure has often been in the headlines, progress continues to be made in the fine print. In any major enterprise the steady and regular accumulation of small successes is of the utmost value. It lays the groundwork for major advances in the end. All has not been lost in the various grievous disappointments CARICOM has experienced. The work continues and, almost imperceptibly it must sometimes seem, the Community presence is made more widely known and impinges on West Indian lives.

External Relations

Absolutely crucial in the integration movement is the need to create the capacity and the commitment to face the wider world as one. We have frequently fallen short in meeting this fundamental West Indian goal. We remain far from matching fully the potential for representing ourselves as a single resolute Community negotiating in unity. However, we have done enough acting together to whet West Indian appetites for more of the same and make us wonder why we do not, as a matter of course, seek West Indian solutions to difficult problems which have international dimensions.

The Community, acting together, played a leading role in establishing the ACP group and in conceiving, designing, and negotiating the Lomé Convention which has become by far the most important conduit of benefits from the EEC to a large part of the developing world. That achievement alone might have taught us both the value of negotiating jointly and our outstanding capacity to do so. Working closely together, CARICOM representatives also played a vital part in shaping the Sugar Protocol which has yielded immense benefits to the sugar industries of sugar-exporting ACP countries, including those in the Community.

CARICOM responded in unison to the United States' Caribbean Basin Initiative so as to obtain maximum benefits for the region as a whole. And, acting collectively, CARICOM representatives assisted importantly in negotiating improvements which were incorporated in CBI II. CARIBCAN, also, the special trading relationship with Canada, is an agreement worked out with Canada for CARICOM by CARICOM negotiating jointly. The plain fact is that CARICOM interests — whether relating to all or one — can be better protected when collective representations are made. It is a lesson which should be obvious but which we have not yet fully learnt. CARICOM solidarity prevented the substantial losses which the graduation of OECS countries from the concessionary resources of the World Bank would have caused. Let that stand as one instance of how collective diplomacy can count for us in a lonely world.

Part of the CARICOM rationale is to attempt the joint development of Member States. Over the years, a measure of success has been achieved in attracting external financing for joint regional projects in a wide range of sectors. In the 1980s, resources estimated at US$200 million have been mobilised for projects at the regional level and this does not include the resources raised by the Caribbean Development Bank. Joint CARICOM endeavours have yielded considerable funding over and above what Member States would ordinarily have mobilised on their own.

CARICOM also enjoyed a signal success when it got the International Civil Aviation Organisation (ICAO) to change it rules and adapt the "community of interest" principle. This has enabled Eastern Caribbean countries to designate BWIA as their national carrier to a number of destinations in the USA, Canada, and Europe and has been of immense practical importance to the region's airline and tourist industries — a good example of the regional movement working well.

Similarly, the CARICOM factor adds weight to representations made in key international organisations. With disappointing frequency we fail to combine our disparate voices when it would be appropriate to do so, yet we have had sufficient success when acting and negotiating together in these bodies to encourage us to make a habit of the process. We have had encouraging success, for instance, in identifying and jointly sponsoring candidates from the region for places in key international organisations. It is certainly true that the outside world is developing a sense of having to deal with a unified sub-region rather than with separate nations. Often now, when a non-CARICOM country approaches a CARICOM Member State about an issue, the approach is made as if to CARICOM as a whole and not simply to the individual country.

Where it mattered greatly, in protecting the territorial integrity of Guyana and Belize and in assisting Belize to achieve independence, CARICOM solidarity has not been found wanting. The Community also campaigned successfully as one in gaining admission for Guyana and Belize to the Organisation of American States. In the case of Haiti, it has not been easy to agree to a CARICOM policy at all times, but the CARICOM presence as CARICOM was an important one, and was recognised as such, in assisting the democratic process leading to free and fair elections in December, 1990. As the tragedy in Haiti continues to unfold, it is vital that CARICOM

Assessment

acts as one in helping to resolve the impasse. In the case of South Africa, CARICOM has campaigned resolutely together in the international effort to discredit and overthrow apartheid. Our strict maintenance of the cricketing boycott played a greater part than is generally realised in nailing the epithet 'outcast' on the South African regime over the years. Now that liberation and enfranchisement approach, the West Indian Community can be satisfied that it played a worthy role in the struggle.

Hemispheric pressures now lean especially hard upon us. The major new challenges presented in the Enterprise of the Americas Initiative and in the initiatives taken by Venezuela and other Latin American countries are best met through a collective response. To this end, CARICOM countries have signed a joint CARICOM-USA Framework agreement and are also negotiating together for one-way duty free access of CARICOM goods to the Venezuelan market. This pattern of collective and mutually supportive response, with negotiations focussed centrally, sets a valuable precedent for future Community conduct.

In the field of international diplomacy West Indian excellence is proven. All the more sensible, therefore, to multiply the benefits of virtuosity and magnify the effects of successful individual effort, by pooling resources region-wide and applying them as one in an international environment which grows increasingly harsh and daily more demanding of attention.

There are three considerations which make the case overwhelmingly for a collective diplomacy. In this field probably more than any other — if you leave out cricket — "we do it better when we do it together". Secondly, major actors internationally are growing bored at having to deal with a multiplicity of negotiating partners; they would welcome, and give priority to, reaching agreements with a Community united in its purposes and its policies.Thirdly, and perhaps most insistently, external challenges are proliferating at such a rate that it is quite impossible to deal with them as single units in CARICOM. It is only through cohesion that in many cases we will be able to react at all, much less with any realistic hope of success.

The time has come for a new clarity about how we approach our relations with the external world. Our various diplomatic successes to date, our proven negotiating capabilities, our fundamentally similar objectives, combined with the preference of our main negotiating partners and the requirements of a turbulent age, make the time ripe for organising more formal and considerably strengthened Community institutions and facilities for dealing with the region's external affairs.

Administrative Tenacity

By infinite, unremitting degrees the CARICOM administrative effort over the years has infiltrated official consciousness in every West Indian country. This is little remarked, but is a reality that is likely to have enduring value. Though it may seldom have prevailed so far the Community factor is increasingly likely to be introduced into countless governmental, departmental, political, and business debates around the region. The fact that nodding in the direction of Community ideals has become a virtually essential ritual — though too often little else thus far — in innumerable speeches, manifestos, discussions, seminars and conferences is itself implicit recognition that Community concepts and practices have been cumulatively and thoroughly inculcated in the West Indian public psyche.

This immense administrative effort, so often scoffed at as a waste of paper and a waste of energy and expertise, should not be so lightly dismissed. The thoroughly professional preparation, running, recording and servicing over nearly two decades of the stream of regional meetings from Heads of Government conferences and Ministerial meetings to technical groups deliberating on every conceivable subject have had effects which are important but are bound to be underestimated simply because it is so routine and regular a business and therefore taken for granted.

The commissioning and promulgation of regional studies, the compilation of regional reports and briefs, the recording of regional information and statistics and history, the feeding of regional considerations into Ministerial portfolios in every Member State, all have a sure and solid impact. The criss-crossing of the region by CARICOM officials, experts, envoys making Community inputs, urg-

Assessment

ing Community causes, arguing Community cases, representing Community views has brought the regional message home in official circles up and down the Member States.

A bureaucracy viewed as getting very little actually done, expertise perceived as going to waste in an ineffective machine whose wheels turn smoothly but go nowhere, a paper mill which produces words but few results — these have been seen as easy targets, especially since there is an element of truth in such perceptions. But that does not take into account the conversion which documenting the need for movement without immediately achieving it, making the policy point again and again, patient bureaucratic zeal at work, can effect over time by slow accretion. Administrative tenacity can outlive countless temporary setbacks finally to create a base from which progress suddenly seems easy.

3. FALLING SHORT STRATEGICALLY

CARICOM has endured. The show has been kept on the road. From time to time, even, new attractions have been added. There have been enough successes to make one wonder why there have not been many more. The rhetoric makes all the right points. But a sense that the movement is coming up short permeates the region. There is a feeling that well-intentioned people are tinkering with a machine that hardly moves. The disappointment with CARICOM goes deep. There are a number of elements in this disappointment.

The Deficit in Ambition

The Treaty of Chaguaramas was a cautiously crafted instrument, properly sensitive to what seemed feasible at the time. It was tempered to its age. What could the traffic bear? The race must be run to accommodate the pace of the most reluctant runners. Second-guessing the founders now is an idle exercise. Nevertheless, as time runs on and new imperatives demand new responses, and fresh generations leave behind old preoccupations, reassessment of goals and the means to achieve them becomes essential. In the regional movement now there is a deficit in ambition to be made up if the Community as a whole is to be given a new lease of life.

The Treaty was cautious in setting goals. Defensiveness was part and parcel of the drafting. A common market, for instance, should feature the free movement of capital — yet the Treaty contemplates only the "regulated movement of capital within the Common Market". And one would have thought that freedom of movement for all West Indians would have figured prominently in the aspirations of the Community's founders — yet Article 38 issues quite explicitly the sort of warning which makes it clear where Community ambitions must end: "Nothing in this Treaty shall be construed as requiring or imposing any obligation on a Member State to grant freedom of movement to persons into its territory whether or not such persons are nationals of other Member States". Thus was lofty aspiration put firmly in its place.

But such defensiveness could be remedied. In time, setting more ambitious goals would be a relatively easy matter. Much more fundamentally, however, the Treaty was virtually silent on how action was actually supposed to flow out of Community agreements. The temper of the times made the founders protective in the extreme of individual territorial sovereignty. Consensus yes, submission to majority no. Agreement yes, but with all the opportunity in the world for second thoughts. Co-operation and co-ordination yes, but only so far as it might suit the individual cause. Deadline yes, but no sanctions for slippage. Decision-making yes, but for decision-implementation only a grudging maybe. It would not matter, therefore, how far-reaching any new goals set might be. If the means to match them in practice were unavailable then the Treaty would remain a child of its times and the region would be stuck in the lower gear of a former era.

The intention of the Treaty was to press forward with economic integration, foreign policy co-ordination, and functional co-operation. To these ends substantial goals were announced and important decision-making powers gathered to the centre. However, the Treaty supplied an ultimate brake on what progress could be made by delegating implementation of decisions to Member States. The link between decision-taking and effective action could always be broken — and broken with impunity. Good Community intentions could in the after-event be ignored. There were no spurs in the machinery to prick action out of the laggard. A decision "binding upon each Member State" [Article 9(3)] might indeed be binding at the centre but, back on home territory, the knot was absolutely free to loosen.

Since 1973 the Treaty's goals have been substantially revised and important new goals added. The Grand Anse Declaration of 1989 redefines the objectives of integration to be a Single Market and Economy and not simply a common market. Financial integration and monetary union have joined economic integration as Community goals. In the political sphere, regional security and the protection of human rights (the Kingston Declaration of 1990) and the strengthening of democracy and social partnership (the Port-of-Spain Consensus of 1991) have joined co-ordination of external policies as Community goals. Preserving the cultural identity of the Caribbean, protection of the environment, the expansion of a telecommunications network, human resource development, joint management of the Exclusive Economic Zones (EEZs), and disaster preparedness and emergency response, have all been added as important new areas for the exercise of functional co-operation.

In setting goals, therefore, the original deficit in ambition has to a significant extent been made good. Further progress in defining the objectives of a Community able to respond to the sharp-edged challenges of a new age is essential and no doubt will be made with an appropriate sense of urgency. But that is not the heart of the matter. Declarations of intent can be crafted easily enough. Converting Community Declaration theory into Community practice is quite another matter. In this respect what the Treaty originally lacked has not been made good. A slow evolution of consensus-building techniques has taken place, but this is no substitute for putting in place institutions which enable the Community actually to function as one when agreement is reached to do so and respond together promptly when urgent challenges loom. The crucial deficit lies exactly in these continuing deficiencies — which, unfortunately, are deficiencies no Declaration can fix or Consensus cure.

Strategic Timidity

Often, CARICOM has had successes but failed, sometimes abjectly, to build on them. At other times there have been failures which need only have been temporary setbacks if some determination and imagination had been brought to bear. It is as if the regional movement had lacked the courage of its convictions, as if the spirit of Community had not been strongly enough embodied either to surmount obstacles or to take full advantage of gains. Great campaigns cannot be waged on a basis of such tentativeness. Instances abound of this tendency towards strategic timidity.

Take a simple, easily recognisable, example. The West Indian cricket team has been an outstanding success. We come together in joyful pride in their achievement and mourn together when the West Indies lose. Yet, even encouraged by that example, in no other sport have we seriously tried to come together to compete internationally as the West Indies — except in one. That one was Lawn Tennis, in the case of which we surrendered our West Indian status after 34 years with hardly a fight when we were instructed to break into our constituent parts.

The theme recurs. Consider, very importantly, the success of the CARICOM Multilateral Clearing Facility (CMCF) in the late 1970s and early 1980s. This was perhaps CARICOM's most productive period. Then the facility fell apart, principally through the failure of a major debtor country to fulfil its obligations. It was the sort of setback that should have prompted rapid reappraisal and prompt reactivation based on lessons learned and regulations reformulated. Instead, the facility, which had yielded such success, was never rescued. It is almost as if too many people were allowed to sit back and argue the case of "I told you so" and "We're not up to it". That way no great cause succeeds.

Consider, also, the vital area of sea and air transportation. WISCO, which provides an essential regional sea link, has been allowed to falter and fail. Five Governments have withdrawn as shareholders. There is a policy vacuum in regard to maritime transportation. No shared vision exists of the kind of regional shipping service required, with the result that the West Indies after all these years still suffers a damaging shortage of freight opportunities across the Region.

Assessment

Similarly, no overall coherence has been found to shape regional air transportation. There have been considerable successes — BWIA and LIAT provide regular services across most of the region, the "community of interest" principle won from ICAO has been mentioned — but a great deal more might have been achieved. Member States in the Eastern Caribbean have not been able to negotiate a single Multilateral Air Services Agreement with the UK, but have gone ahead and concluded separate bilateral agreements. Above all, after all this time, a single regional air carrier has not been achieved. The elusiveness of this clear and long-standing Community objective reflects a systemic weakness which these transformed times of urgent challenge will punish if not corrected.

There are too many other examples of opportunities gone a-begging for our comfort. CARICOM Travellers' Cheques were never more than a pallid, neglected success though they had, and still have, the potential to be a most useful instrument for conserving foreign exchange. In all the 19 years of CARICOM it has proved impossible to bring a regional industrial programming scheme into being. Nor has a CARICOM Enterprise Regime been brought into effect after years of fruitless endeavour. The important effort in the early 1980s to pool the procurement of pharmaceuticals on a region-wide basis failed, though happily the OECS has since introduced such a scheme successfully. The attempt to introduce nursing examinations on a regional basis failed — another opportunity lost to co-ordinate and therefore strengthen the development of Community human resources. In dealing with rapidly growing environmental challenges the Community has hardly gone beyond joint consultation when what is needed is the urgent forging of institutional arrangements to add force and decisiveness to regional responses and initiatives.

Perhaps strangest of all has been the failure to build on and extend the great diplomatic successes which the West Indies negotiating as one have achieved. Why have we not long ago formalised the ad hoc mechanisms of co-ordination and representation through which these successes have been achieved? Why have we not gone a long way down the road of joint West Indian diplomatic presences? Why have we not, to take one example of overwhelming recent relevance, pooled our expertise and our negotiating resources — and considered our mutual interests — to negotiate together, strong and weak side by side, with the IMF? Why have we been reluctant to play to one of our great strengths? What reason would Sobers have had to eschew his square cut or Kanhai his cover drive?

Too often in our success we have flattered to deceive or in our failures backed off too easily. It has seemed the movement lacked a commanding authority, to seize opportunities when they beckoned and make the most of them, to rally the forces when setbacks threatened and turn the tide. Too frequently the tiller has swung with the wind when a strong hand was needed to grasp it and give direction. Strategic thrust has been wanting at vital times. It has been a crucial weakness in the regional movement.

Community Marginalised

There is a strong sense of community in the Region. The people of the region, and indeed West Indians in the diaspora, would like to see this promoted and fostered. This sentiment should be an ally in all we do. It creates a climate of opinion out of which CARICOM itself grew and in which the regional movement gathers strength.

This instinctive sense of mutual belonging, however, cannot be indefinitely sustained unless out of it issues continuing evidence that its existence is advancing efforts to harmonise Community relations in a practical way. Attachment to an ideal inevitably weakens when the ideal remains forever no more than an ideal.

The sense of Community, the attachment to a West Indian ideal, will fade if it is suspected that the keepers of the keys of the kingdom are paying lip service only to the prevailing spirit. Should such a perception persist and grow it would constitute by far the greatest threat so far to constructing in time for the 21st Century a Community with many, if not by then all, of the practical attributes of a West Indian nation.

It is a danger that we clearly run. Throughout the history of CARICOM, a tension has existed between the yearning for a West Indian Community across national boundaries and a hesitancy about how far to go in actually dismantling those boundaries. Such hesitancy could easily become a positive disinclination to do any such thing if the spirit of Community was seen consistently to be honoured only in the breach.

It is a matter of grave concern, therefore, that over the years more progress has not been made in nurturing the intangible spirit of Community in the Region.

There has been only limited progress in spreading information about the Community, and the products of Community creativity throughout the Region. CARICOM's own information programmes — concentrated on disseminating inter-governmental data of a largely technical nature and circulating the journal *CARICOM Perspective* to a small readership four times a year — make no more than the most nominal of impacts. *Caribbean Affairs* and *Caribbean Contact* are virtually the only journals enjoying a circulation of more than a few scores across the Region. There has been little attempt to regionalise newspapers.

CANA and CBU are much more important contributors to the transmission and exchange of regional news and features, but so far still fall well short of what is required to supply regional needs. Private initiative is beginning to make a bigger impact — the increase in radio and television stations in Trinidad and Tobago and Jamaica eager to include programmes with a regional content in their transmissions, and the operations of Helen Television in Saint Lucia, give evidence of this important development. So far, however, there is more promise than achievement. If the sense of belonging to a single Community is to be fully served by the media, there needs to be an immense leap forward in developing new ways of regionalising information flows and in harnessing the most up-to-date telecommunications technology for widespread use in the Region.

Formally sponsored cultural exchanges in the Region are virtually non-existent. The Region's sense of cultural unity amidst diversity is nurtured by the efforts of individuals and groups who use their own initiative and resources to travel in the Region as best they can, bringing with them music, dance, theatre, poetry and art. It is a very ad hoc business. It is not enough. CARICOM's single cultural officer symbolises the inadequacy of Community efforts in this important field. In addition, the repeated postponements in holding

CARIFESTA makes the public wonder anew about whether concern for sharing creative activity in the Region is anything but completely superficial. The uncertainty over holding this festival deepens cynicism and shakes confidence that any real devotion exists to fostering a cultural sense of Community.

It is much the same with the effort to create Community symbols — apart, of course, from that supreme and long-established West Indian icon, our cricket team. Beyond the occasional use of the CARICOM logo and flag, the celebration of CARICOM Day in some Member States, and a CARICOM Scheme of Regional Honours which has only just come into force, nothing worthwhile has been done. It is a poor return for all the thought and the numerous studies devoted to the subject of how to forge and widely introduce symbols of West Indian unity and mutual participation in regional ceremony. It is a sad little store we have so far gathered. In two decades is this all that we can produce to fire the regional imagination? It hardly seems we can be serious.

Such failures of the imagination, however, may be insignificant when measured against the resentment felt by ordinary West Indians about the inconvenience, problems and even harassment they experience as they travel around the Region. Resentment becomes anger when West Indians encounter difficulties while foreigners travel in our home with a degree of freedom and ease never experienced by West Indian nationals. People know that being able to travel freely and easily within the Community — especially if some form of "favoured citizen" treatment could be offered — would help greatly to consolidate mutual awareness and understanding and would significantly enhance their sense of shared identity. This was long ago officially recognised, and repeated Declarations to act positively have been issued. The fact that the situation has only marginally and very recently improved has reinforced the feeling of ordinary West Indians that this "sense of Community" about which they have heard so many pronouncements and which, indeed, they do instinctively feel has become merely an outworn shibboleth.

The perception that at the practical level where it matters Community is being marginalised should be a matter of serious concern. The impression is given that fortifying Community in a spiritual/

cultural sense is a chore to which we give a low priority and that even in performing that chore we act most grudgingly. The time has come as we move on to bury that impression deep.

Failing to Follow Through

The sense that the regional movement is coming up short derives largely from the feeling that CARICOM leaders are good at rhetoric as an end in itself but not meant to be taken seriously, well versed in making decisions which stay on paper. Given the record, it is hard to maintain that such a perception is misguided. There is splendid rhetoric. There is too little action. Failing to follow through is, and is seen to be, a chronic CARICOM deficiency.

At least part of the reason for this, as we have seen, is that while the Treaty of Chaguaramas's limited goals could easily be expanded, and have been, its mechanisms for exercising central powers of implementation have remained what they always were, non-existent.

There is at present no institution which implements CARICOM laws, directives, decisions. Member States do this. As a result it is difficult to create a legal sphere specifically for the Community. The Conference or Council try to apply decisions by inter-governmental committees or working groups, assisted by the Secretariat. It is easy to imagine the propensity of such a process to breed bureaucracies in which further discussion is at a premium and additional problems all too easily come to light. And in the end implementing action still remains in the hands of Member State officials.

Moreover, these arrangements lack a direct democratic content. Parliaments do not play a role in integration processes and decisions, only Governments and bureaucracies do. Nor do CARICOM-wide political parties with CARICOM agendas exist. This means that the normal pressures of the democratic process are brought to bear second-hand, when the decisions get to the local level. There the context is likely to be very different and quite other forces may be, and often are, at play. When such pressures emerge it is all too easy for leaders, now in their role as politicians and not statesmen, to seek solutions in well-argued and loftily phrased delays.

However, the failure to follow through on decisions does not simply arise from an original flaw in the Treaty which has not been rectified. There is certainly more to it than that. We cannot suppose that CARICOM leaders over the years, when they have together reached agreement, have not done so in all sincerity, with genuine determination that their decisions should be implemented. Such sincerity and determination on their part must flow from the assumption that they have at their command the machinery, the resources, the personnel, and the expertise in their home bases to ensure that what they agree in solemn conference, what indeed they promise the West Indian people, actually will happen across the Region in good order and reasonably promptly. But it does not. So, granting their good faith, is their assumption correct? Here certainly is another key to why Community decisions are not followed through effectively: the lack of civil service implementing capability back at home. Such capability will, of course, vary from country to country but in general there is a substantial insufficiency across the Region.

Civil Service capacity to follow through Community decisions involves a number of vital elements: inclination to do the job — which relates to what priority the job is given; availability of personnel; availability of expertise; additional budget provisions; motivation. In all these areas the civil services of Member States are likely to be hard pressed to meet the requirements of Summit rhetoric. At home CARICOM decisions become an additional burden, no longer a priority. In any case, there are barely enough personnel to attend to local priorities. Expertise — for instance, in legislative drafting and fiscal applications — is sadly lacking. Budgets cut to the bone cannot accommodate further demands. And in these parlous times motivation to go the extra CARICOM mile is low. Overburdened civil servants, operating in often depleted establishments, with their eyes necessarily focussed on the local intray, are most unlikely to give CARICOM decisions passed down to them the sort of attention others out of the immediate firing line may believe these decisions deserve.

The absence of motivation to place a high priority on adapting and carrying out Community decisions when they are "repatriated", the rapidly growing local demands and pressures in a world of IMF conditionalities and any number of other challenges, the lack of capacity in depleted civil services to do the work — quite apart from the added quota of domestic political trouble that implementing CARICOM decisions may entail — together go a long way in explaining inertia in implementing CARICOM decisions and keeping to CARICOM deadlines. When these considerations are set beside the lack of implementing machinery in the battery of Community institutions, it is little wonder that the good intentions of Community are so seldom, or so slowly, brought to fruition.

4. THE POTENTIAL OF COMMUNITY

In terms of the Community that is envisaged in the Treaty of Chaguaramas, the enterprise we embarked on in another age has achieved a solid modicum of success — though even in those limited terms there have been failures of nerve and areas of neglect. The enterprise certainly cannot be counted a failure — there have been an impressive number of technical successes which not only have had a valuable practical impact throughout the region, but also have helped to keep the ideals of West Indian integration in a larger sense alive. The show has been kept on the road.

Nevertheless, there can be no doubt that the deeper potential which lies in the concept of West Indian community has not been released over the last two decades. A sense of hope unfulfilled is abroad in the Region. Given the terms of the Treaty by which integration has been guided so far, this feeling of inadequate response to a great opportunity may be unfair. But it is very real. The name CARICOM itself has come to seem peculiarly uninspiring. It has become associated with inordinate delay and indecisiveness, with bureaucracy, with meetings which generate rhetoric and paper but spur little action that makes a difference. The slow progress towards a common market has not exactly set the blood racing with excitement. Interminable skirmishing over CET and Rules of Origin has bored the people and has often seemed to lower the Community's sights to the level of a failed salesman's pitch. "If we called the West Indian cricket team the CARICOM cricket team we wouldn't beat Sri Lanka". The implication may be more than a little unfair — and too dismissive of Sri Lankan cricket these days — but the sentiment is clear and holds a truth we should not ignore.

Certainly in terms of impact on peoples' consciousness and day-to-day lives the "community" potential of CARICOM is still to be realised. Making such an impact will need all Member States to demonstrate singleness of purpose to the full and find a way of expressing this in central mechanisms of improved effectiveness. At the same time individual Governments and various powerful groups in the Region must sink narrow self-interest to allow regional singleness of purpose to take on flesh and content in the form of institutions and initiatives which reflect the "community" as a whole.

In the eyes of the people, and in our judgement also, what is needed is a new impulse towards integration which must be shaped within a new framework. What above all must be developed is decision-making and decision-implementing machinery which not only will ensure that centrally achieved consensus agreements are carried out on the ground, but also will enable decisions attracting a clear regional majority to issue in action applicable to the whole Region. Such machinery will entail an element of sanctions for backsliding. The test will be whether or not this Community of Member States has matured to a degree where it can accept temporary individual difficulty, and even pain, without drawing back, in order to move towards a Community of closer union for the larger and longer-term benefit of all.

5. THE WEST INDIES TODAY

A Statistical Profile

In the process of its work the Commission has compiled a detailed profile of the West Indies at this moment in history when the Commission is presenting its findings to Governments and people. A comprehensive survey, giving facts and figures for all the thirteen CARICOM countries, and (wherever feasible) the two Associate Members, has, therefore, been prepared and will be published as a companion to this book.

Assessment

Areas covered include: size, population, health indicators, labour force and unemployment, external debt, imports and exports, trade within the CARICOM Region, retail prices, Gross Domestic Product (GDP), the importance of agriculture, manufacturing, government services, other services in the GDP, interest rates, exchange rates, consumption, investment, saving, government revenue and expenditure, the proportion of government expenditure that is devoted to the social services, and the loans and deposits within the banking system.

We believe that this survey may be useful for those studying the Commission's findings and wanting to have a factual background easily available.

Quite apart from the intrinsic value of such a "snapshot" survey of the Community the exercise of preparing this material has served another useful purpose.

It has revealed gaps in the factual knowledge we have about our own circumstances and has shown up anomalies and differences that exist in data-preparation which makes the task of relating our various Member States to each other more difficult than it should be.

In many of our West Indian homelands there is a serious lack of fundamental statistics brought up-to-date and easily available. In too many columns, for too many years, N/A (Not Available) dominates. We are told, and it is indeed true, that this is the information age. How can we run our businesses and the public services, how can we keep the people properly and promptly informed, how can we be quick and decisive in response to information required when conducting external trade and political negotiations, how indeed can we govern effectively — if the basic factual data is missing or badly out of date?

If some effort is focussed on this problem we have no doubt, especially in this age of computer technology, that what weaknesses exist can be overcome. The growing need to have reliable and complete data promptly available for the purpose of well-informed decision-making should encourage all Governments not to neglect data collection and presentation as a basic requirement of good administration.

Regional Organisations

The number of regional organisations operating in the Community is impressive, numbering nearly 200 at last count. They range from the CARICOM Secretariat itself, whose year-long activities bind the Region, and the University of the West Indies, whose influence is of abiding value throughout the Community, to small-scale regional organisations functioning in every conceivable area of activity.

Large and small, the cumulative contribution of their work is of incalculable value in furthering the movement towards West Indian integration. Every day literally thousands of West Indians from all the Member States are working in a multitude of fields to develop a regional dimension to our lives. The impact of this steady work cannot be measured but over time will be a decisive factor in ensuring that the West Indian option is never forgotten. Together these organisations slowly weave the fabric of our future as one nation.

Appendix "H" contains a list of regional institutions, organisations and associations with their locations.

CHAPTER III

CONTEXT AND PERSPECTIVES

1. INTERNATIONAL AND REGIONAL IMPERATIVES

Any attempt exactly to predict the future in international, or indeed regional, affairs is likely to fail. One recalls how the French philosopher, the Marquis de Condorcet, confident of the "spirit of moderation and peace" which he saw as then prevailing in Europe, predicted in 1784 "fewer great changes, fewer great revolutions in the future than in the past," five years before the onset of the historic tumult in which, among other things, the unfortunate Marquis lost his head.

We are at least unlikely to repeat the Marquis's mistake, since our own predictions are of continuing changes so rapid that, between first draft and final printing, what we foresee is almost certain to be overtaken by events. To illustrate the rush of great events in which the Commission finds itself called upon to report, we need only mention a particular instance during our consultations. During a three-day period in Canada, while we were meeting West Indians in Montreal, Ottawa and Toronto, the following headlines tracked our movements. EEC leaders meeting in Maastricht were taking far-reaching discussions likely to lead to a common European currency and much closer political integration later this decade; the leaders of the Russian Republic, the Ukraine and Byelorussia were reported as declaring that the Soviet Union had "ceased to exist as a legal entity and geopolitical reality"; the Premiers of Quebec and Ontario were warning of a possible break-up of Canada; and the President of Mexico was reported as expressing a determination to bring his country into the North American Free Trade Area as a matter of urgency.

A world moving at such a pace is hardly likely to stay still long enough to be captured with any degree of certainty in a Report of this nature. If any conclusion survived it would most likely be that in such turbulent **times the need to** close ranks is the most urgent need of all. When white water threatens shrewd river men make sure the ropes that bind the logs are lashed secure to give the raft a better chance.

Difficult though it is to predict future developments with any assurance, it is still possible to discover patterns of transformation which should assist in identifying the policies and strategies most likely to earn ourselves respect and success as a new century approaches.

Earlier, we briefly noted some dramatic changes both international and regional, which have taken place recently. Looking back to the time of the Treaty of Chaguaramas, the transformations which have since then affected the world and the Region have entirely changed the context in which West Indians must make decisions about their future. Scientific, technological and environmental — no less than political, economic and social — changes have created a new set of circumstances which we need to take into account in making proposals for the course ahead.

International Developments

Political changes

A principal feature of the world scene for decades has disappeared. The Cold War has ended and with it the manoeuvering to gain advantage in the balancing of power between West and East. It no longer makes sense to play the game of appealing to Peter against Paul, and vice versa. And, without Paul, many of Peter's previous concerns have lost their relevance.

The part to be played by the nation state has also radically changed. Political systems, concepts about the management of economic and social forces, are still based on the nation state but supranational and transnational forces and organisations increasingly affect and lessen the ability of individual states to control events. No country can fail to take account of such a fundamental shift in how the relationship between nation states is coming to be viewed.

In addition, democratic movements and political pluralism are establishing themselves throughout the world, and especially so in our hemisphere. Repressive, undemocratic regimes are increasingly the subject of international sanctions. Sensitivity to such a development naturally becomes an element in all policy-making.

New Socio-Economic Pressures

The increases in population, and the pressures of rising expectations as modern communications technology shrinks the world, have led to a rapidly accelerating growth in social demands in developing countries. These are set out in the World Bank's 1990 *World Development Report*, focussing on poverty, and in the UNDP 1991 *Human Development Report*. Food, nutrition, basic health care, and educational demands have multiplied many times over and existing institutional arrangements — both at the national and international levels — have not been able to cope.

In the West Indies, though population pressures are not so intense and the basic social infrastructure is far better than in most parts of the developing world, we have by no means been immune from this explosive growth in social demands. Close proximity to conspicuous affluence in the north, brought closer every day by easier and easier access through television, has additionally served to concentrate and accentuate social demands in the Region.

At the same time, rural-urban migration has increased. Urbanisation has added immensely to the demands for housing, sanitation, transportation, and energy supplies. These proliferating urban needs and urban poverty are added to rural deprivation. And on top of these intractable problems, as if they were not enough, unemployment and under-employment are growing plagues that affect most of the West Indies endemically. How to respond to these immense new pressures, threatening as they do to tear the whole fabric of society apart, must be one of the gravest of all the concerns of any responsible government. Any attempt to respond standing alone is bound to be futile.

While these developments have been taking place, and infinitely complicating matters, environmental sustainability has been put firmly on the agenda of all countries. The need to stop, and reverse, environmental degradation is the responsibility of all countries irrespective of wealth, geography, or politics. But an additional problem turns out to be the attempt to put a quite disproportionate part of the burden of solving the problem on poor countries already facing immense developmental challenges. The West Indies will have to be in the forefront of those insisting on the predominant responsibility of the already developed world to act in restoring sustainability in the global eco-system.

The Transformation of International Business

World economic interdependence has been growing with astonishing rapidity. International financial transactions have become increasingly independent of the production and distribution of goods and services. Financial markets have caught up with, if not already outstripped, traditional markets in importance. These developments are not without considerable opportunities for developing countries but they require new strategies, policy adjustments, and new kinds of managers and professionals if most of us are not to be left struggling far in the wake of the main flotilla.

In addition, the content and direction of trade have altered significantly and in many ways. Japan, with its technological capacity, economic dynamism, and immense financial power, has become a major player in world trade and finance. International trade has shifted away from commodities towards high-technology services and manufactured products. There has been a broad shift, also, from import-substitution to export-oriented strategies of development. At the same time, powerful new regional trading blocs are emerging with breathtaking suddenness — in just a few years, for example, the huge EEC bloc has adopted all but a few of the 282 specific measures needed to bring into being the largest in the world.

These developments completely change the basis of how developing countries should plan their futures and organise their approach to international negotiations. And, while all this is proceeding, the status of the Uruguay Round of the GATT negotiations leaves it entirely unclear how best the essential requirements of developing countries are to be preserved in the hurly-burly of events in which no previous pattern of trade is set in stone nor market niche sacrosanct.

63

New Priorities in Aid and Investment

The context in which international assistance and investment is made available has changed radically. Developing countries like ours face the combined impact of "aid fatigue," the protracted and seemingly intractable debt crisis, the sudden needs and attractions of the former Soviet empire now freed and more than ready to call for help and investment, and the influence of all these developments on the direction of capital flows. At present the multilateral financial institutions are contributing very meagre net resources to countries like our own. And for the remainder of the decade developing countries are going to have to fight tooth and nail, and with drive and imagination, and with *quid pro quos* to offer, for direct private investment.

Such an assessment suggests that, compared with the past, the outlook for development finance is dim. Resources available through concessional or non-concessional channels in the 1990s will all too likely diminish in real terms and perhaps even in nominal per capita terms.

Faced with such thin prospects, this Report is bound to have as ever-running themes the need for fiscal prudence and discipline in every part of the Community, the need to coordinate our negotiating strengths, and the need to develop our entrepreneurial talents to attract what capital there is available.

Revolutionary Technological Change

Pervasive technological change dominates the international scene. There has been a general explosion of knowledge. Moreover, knowing that this knowledge is available, and that it holds the key to progress, has spread far and wide and fast. The whole psychology of how development can and should take place has been transformed. The emergence of entirely new technologies in fields such as bio-technology, micro-electronics and new materials increase opportunities but also create new threats. If we can attract the new technologies to our shores the prospect of leap-frogging to success in the development process opens up, yet if we are left behind in the race our brightest technical and business talents more than ever will not wait in frustration. If they are not assisted in bringing the action here, they will leave for where the action is.

Many of these new technologies are highly flexible and mobile and, as a result, are rapidly changing the way in which the international marketplace functions. Individuals, groups and nations actively participating in the generation and exchange of these new technologies will advance and prosper, those left behind will be increasingly marginalised. Moreover, in a time of such fast-moving technological change, in a Community of still loosely bound constituent parts, the tendency, the temptation, for front-runners in the technological race to seek their own individual advantage and benefit by tying up deals outside the Region which exclude the participation of sister states will grow and may quickly become a major threat to the integration process. We must act fast if we are to act as one in taking advantage of the opportunities and in avoiding the pitfalls of these technological developments.

The Marginalisation of Small Developing Countries

Amidst these transformations, the role and needs of developing countries have been consigned to the periphery of international attention and concern. Developing countries can no longer with any credibility make the collective demands they once did upon the global political economy. Their alignment for any purpose of bringing political/ideological pressure to bear, or to attract strategic interest or support, no longer makes sense. In particular, the old Cold War agenda which saw the Caribbean as a vital battleground in a global conflict has disappeared.

Developing countries, more particularly including our small and vulnerable West Indies, are on their own. Their, and our, salvation will reside simply in how successfully we can harness what assets we have and how skillfully we can deploy those assets in whichever sectors of the world we can best find a useful and acceptable place. It is for this reason — constrained as we are by considerations of history, geography and "special relationships" of long standing as well as by the magnitude of both opportunity and threat involved — that this Report will be addressing, in particular, our relations with the EEC in the context of the Single European Market and our relations with the Free Trade Area of the USA,

Assessment

Canada and Mexico which is in prospect. It is in getting these particular relationships to yield the maximum of advantage that our economic success most certainly lies in the 1990s. It will be our purpose to examine and propose how best to direct our resources to that end.

Regional Prospects

Such far-reaching international considerations lead us to focus on the Caribbean itself where we must muster our available resources, where we must shape our responses, to get the best deals we can.

CARICOM and the Wider Caribbean

At once we are confronted by a fundamental question: What Caribbean? It is a question we have been urged to answer on numerous occasions during our consultations. And the consensus during these consultations strongly advocates that CARICOM seek much closer cooperation with sister Caribbean countries in finding a place for ourselves in the new world order.

The conclusion we have reached is that the process of deepening CARICOM integration and the process of widening regional partnership are not irreconcilable strategies. We remain aware that a too rapid, or ill-considered, widening of CARICOM could adversely affect the integration process itself. But we recognise just as insistently that forging, and bringing to bear in world affairs, a wider Caribbean sphere of influence is essential both as a valid consummation in its own right and for enlarging the gains of our own deeper integration.

This dual track strategy we foresee, producing circles of partnership that start with our West Indian family, encompasses the extended family of the non-English speaking Caribbean islands, and involves a yet wider circle of closer relations with countries of the Caribbean Basin including South and Central American countries. With increased confidence in our own identity, we must be ready to take a lead in creating a Community of the entire Caribbean.

Enhancing Negotiating Capability

The importance of deeper CARICOM integration allied to closer

Caribbean cooperation arises also from the need to strengthen our negotiating hand. There is every indication that imaginative, cohesive and active diplomacy will be a resource of incalculable importance in the emerging new world order. We must cultivate this resource assiduously and give it as wide a scope as possible to operate.

The Community has built a tradition of diplomatic success. Our common diplomatic initiatives have, among a large number of achievements, promoted regional security, helped to preserve the territorial integrity of Guyana and Belize, enhanced our trade prospects by gaining preferential access for important exports to metropolitan countries, and promoted our economic interest by winning special status for small island developing countries in UNCTAD and in the Lomé Convention.

This is a diplomatic tradition which we need to build upon and extend. To do so it will be necessary to go beyond the *ad hoc* coordination of CARICOM foreign policies and common negotiating fronts which has yielded reasonably good results in the past but now needs to be superceded by more formal machinery as an integral part of reforming the processes of integration.

Responding to Latin America

Together with this, and in order to strengthen the diplomatic effort, CARICOM critically needs to attempt the engagement of an expanded Caribbean family of states. We must respond with alacrity and together to the many, sometimes even overlapping, initiatives being taken by our neighbours and friends in Latin America. We must play an active role in helping to resolvet the tragic situation in Haiti. We must increase contacts with Cuba, with the Dominican Republic and, paying due regard to its constitutional position, with Puerto Rico. We must respond positively to the Mexican desire to open new contacts with CARICOM. We must follow up the closer trading links being forged with Venezuela and the increased contacts with Central American countries. We have to seek as a priority to keep in touch with and where necessary take the lead in all regional developments related to NAFTA.

In diplomacy, as well as in other ways, widening Caribbean and

Assessment

regional cooperation must accompany the deepening of CARICOM integration. The larger the regional presence the major players confront in negotiations the more ready will they be to pay attention. In the past we might have hoped to promote that larger presence in the general international collective of developing countries. The realities of the present day necessitate a radically changed approach in which the construction of specifically regional and hemispheric joint diplomacy becomes our priority.

2. THE HUMAN CONDITION: CONSTRAINTS AND RESOURCES

What is the mood and mettle of the West Indian people in 1992? What developments make or mar their lives at this time? What restrains their ability to respond to the forces which the age has let loose in our society? What resources can they muster to confront the challenges? It is important to attempt an answer to such questions, make an assessment of West Indian weaknesses and strengths, so as to lay the basis for the conclusions we shall draw about how to move ahead in the decade leading up to the new century.

In an exercise such as this there is a tendency to define one's shortcomings rather than count one's blessings. It is the failings and failures in our societies and systems that we must spend most time considering. It is the nature of our task that we seek solutions to problems and improvements where there is breakdown rather than spend too much time declaring pride in what is working well, what has been achieved and created. It is better that we should be our most vigorous critics and bring to light our failings before time discovers them and a response is then in other hands as much as ours. Yet the blessings, the achievements, the success, the creativity must be recorded too to form the picture.

Constraints

There are a number of major concerns, failures and weaknesses which have been identified in the course of our work.

Vulnerability

No country is fully independent or self-sufficient in today's world village. But no one can doubt the special vulnerability of small states in international affairs. The peculiar fragility of small states standing alone is shown in the many fundamental ways in which they find themselves particularly exposed.

- The security of small states is especially at risk in the face of outside interference and criminal activity at international level.

- Control of the terms of trade is minimal. Very narrowly based economies — often depending on traditional commodity exports whose prices steadily decline in relation to the cost of manufactured imports — suffer severe disruption as the operation of economic forces in centres far from the small states' ken inexorably tend to swing their external accounts out of balance.

- Small states have no say whatsoever in deciding the level of interest rates in the world. The build-up and servicing of external debt is to this large extent at the mercy of others.

- Small states are wholly dependent on outside technology in every walk of life and in every aspect of their economies. And the micro-markets of small states standing alone often cannot attract up-to-date equipment and technology geared to much larger production runs and much wider applications.

- There is a strong tendency for small states to become dependent on external sources for information, entertainment, and cultural inspiration — especially via television which is an increasingly important fact of life in the West Indies now. The danger exists of having cultural values from outside overwhelm and degrade local cultural values.

- Small states in our location lose a vital proportion of their population to the rich countries whose appetite for skilled and experienced people is insatiable. It is a matter of great concern that we may be increasingly dependent on the strictness of other countries' immigration laws to keep our citizens at home.

Separateness

There is a sense that the Community suffers from a great failure to make more than faltering progress in solving the problem of our geographical separateness. There is a special urgency about this in Belize and The Bahamas where remoteness from the rest of CARICOM threatens to distance them almost to breaking point in many areas of life and work. But the sense of failure to overcome the separateness is universal.

Surely, it is said, if we were seriously committed West Indians this is one area above all where we would have been determined to succeed. And this failure is particularly ironic in an age in which technology is shrinking distances between countries and instantaneously linking people and business worlds apart. The irony is remarked. This is not an age of sail or even steam, it is not an age of crackling radios. Jets take a few hours to metropoles thousands of miles away but smaller Caribbean distances require overnight journeys. Goods rot for want of intra-CARICOM freight opportunities. Satellites orbit overhead and beam down the trial of William Kennedy Smith into our living rooms all day but we cannot all see Mandela arrive and speak live in the West Indies. We see — and, insidiously, more and more enjoy — the NBA and NFL all their seasons long but it was touch and go whether we would see the West Indies play live in the World Cup — and we do not all see as one our own first-class encounters in the Red Stripe and Geddes Grant tournaments.

Carefully explaining that it is all a matter of economics brings a glaze to the eyes of ordinary West Indians. They still cannot understand why a higher priority has not been placed on overcoming our separateness. And anyway they cannot believe that bringing us closer together will not have beneficial results in trade and business, quite apart from the advantages of getting to know each other better and sharing each other's achievements and even, indeed, each other's disasters.

Economies in the Doldrums

Perceptions of economic malaise and retrogression are widespread in the Caribbean. In fact, performance has been mixed; in many CARICOM countries growth rates in the decade of the 1980s exceeded those in developing countries on average, but output contracted in the larger countries. Even where there has been expansion and improvement in living standards, however, structural problems remain. Unemployment — affecting young people, women, and those in rural areas most of all — remains the most stubborn problem for the Region.

Several countries suffered economic deterioration in the past decade. Fiscal deficits frequently rose to unsustainable levels, trade balances worsened and foreign exchange reserves declined, as did domestic savings, and though the investment and savings ratios remain respectable by international standards, too little finance was allocated for investment that could increase productivity and enhance export competitiveness.

In the attempt to stabilise the economy, build up foreign exchange reserves and arrest inflation, countries affected have had to take strong corrective measures, often involving hardships for ordinary people. These hardships have come to be associated with the international financial institutions — and some of their recommendations have unquestionably been misguided — but in essence the economic hardships were mostly unavoidable. However, we should not lose sight of the fact that in some cases the most severe disruptions and declines in real expenditure on social services predated the involvement of the international financial institutions.

There are many lessons to be learned from the experiences of the 1980s. One is that sustained growth depends on increases in productivity. It is not enough that there should be investment; we must invest to lift productivity levels to a far greater extent than has occurred up to now. A second lesson is that governments must regain a medium to long term focus for macroeconomic policy, and in particular there must be a deliberate, well funded export development policy. A third lesson is that governments must give maximum scope to private enterprise to get economies going again while themselves concentrating on infrastructure improvement, human resource development, and the establishment of sound incentive regimes and regulatory frameworks. A fourth lesson is that extreme prudence in the management of public funds must be the order of the day. A fifth lesson is that renewed success will be

Assessment

largely dependent on developing entrepreneurial and technical talent for new businesses and new technologies.

And the final lesson is common to all: the Community together will have a much better chance of getting better results. Adjustment programmes designed and negotiated regionally would give all a stronger hand to play. A common currency and central monetary authority would lead more readily to prudent financing and more stable currencies. The Region acting together can much better provide the massive, coordinated, continuous investment of money and effort needed to develop human resources on the scale required. Aggregation of domestic markets in a context of regional industrial planning can better provide business opportunities for private entrepreneurs. And only businesses built on a regional basis can stand a better chance of growing rapidly and competing internationally.

Social Discontents

Hard on the heels of economic failure come social discontents. Depleted treasuries at once undermine the integrity and effectiveness of public servants. A significant proportion of what money exists is misspent in maladministration. Social services suffer. The provision of basic health and maternity care is disrupted. Educational systems deteriorate and teachers, underpaid, leave that most honourable of professions for want of prospects.

Inflation and unstable currencies destroy pensions and savings and hurt the most vulnerable — the young, women on their own, the old, the sick, the disadvantaged. Unemployment idles and frustrates youth, giving criminals and drug dealers the perfect opening to recruit young men and women into useless and violent lives. The whole harsh and cruel world of poverty expands.

At the same time, when compassion and honest concern for one's fellow citizens are most needed, contracting economic opportunities and less real money to go around make men selfish, protective of their own small parishes, keen-eyed for the main chance only, dismissive of even the desperate needs of others. It is sad to see this grow in any society, but in West Indian societies with our strong traditions of neighbourly concern and "looking out for Auntie

Jo", it seems an even more tragic development to see such cold-hearted practice begin to grow.

It is here, in the area of rapidly growing social discontents, that the idea of Community faces its greatest challenge. For, in an era when much has been made of CARICOM and the promise of regional integration, ordinary people see very clearly for themselves in their everyday lives that their circumstances are getting worse. What then can CARICOM mean to them? Indeed, it is perhaps surprising so much faith still seems to attach to the West Indian ideal. But it is certain that such faith will not hold up forever. The process of closer integration must be seen to coincide with an improvement in the lives of the people. The trouble for those who believe in the integration concept is that CARICOM and its institutions hardly at present make, or are seen to make, a direct impact on the everyday lives of people. It is national policies and programmes that do that. It is of the utmost importance that integration at the macro-level proceeds apace so that the beneficial effects at national level get down to the people quickly and they see why.

Women — Bearing the Most Strain

The exigencies of economic failure, adjustment programmes where they have had to be introduced, and social dislocations have fallen most harshly on women who increasingly, in any case, are heads of household and so bear heavier responsibilities. Women, especially women on their own with young children, are deeply and often desperately affected by the bitter realities of life in deteriorating economies and in countries where public services are contracting. Theirs is a daily struggle not only in trying to make ends just barely touch but also to obtain minimum health and educational services for the children and protect them from the temptations of societies increasingly inclined to cast young people into the pit.

They bear the most strain but women may also carry our best hope. Perhaps because they have had to grapple most intimately with the harsh problems of this era they are emerging with an independence, a maturity, and a determination which is putting them prominently in the vanguard of developing a creative response to the fearful new challenges of the time.

If there is one area which demands especially targeted action programmes, this is it. And regional planners and administrators must be closely involved to ensure as far as they can that Community arrangements bear fruit in better conditions, improved status, and an increased role and responsibility for women.

Environmental Stress

There is growing alarm that much too little is being done to address environmental issues. These issues affect the whole Community directly — global warming and sea level rise, marine pollution, poisonous substances traversing the Caribbean Sea — or they need a collective approach — protection of resources requiring co-operation or, for example, negotiations for a Climate Change Convention and involvement in projects for the Latin American and Caribbean Action Plan for the Environment. Such issues are vital to the Community's well-being. But there is a sense of helplessness abroad. To give only one example — if coastal erosion is not halted, if beaches are polluted by ships transiting through our seas (and, indeed by our own effluents), if coral reefs and marine life are endangered, if the sunshine ceases to be an attraction and becomes a liability because of the ozone layer's degradation, then the tourism industry will be much less sustainable in the future. Yet how do small countries begin to cope with this kind of vast, implacable problem? Where will they obtain the resources? It is a mood likely to grow. The realisation that standing alone makes no sense in a world of such problems takes on greater urgency.

The Educational Shortfall

We have been proud — but probably in an elitist sort of way — of our educational standards in the past. The facts are, however, that the deficiencies which most threaten our West Indian future are the deficiencies which pervade educational systems in the region at the present time. The achievement of universal literacy and numeracy at the primary level is dropping out of sight. Examination results at the secondary level are extremely disappointing nearly everywhere and in nearly every subject. The quality and frequency of the kind of education on offer throughout the systems simply do not measure up to what is required for a future in which we can compete. The deficiencies at tertiary level are of extreme and mounting concern.

Let the data from Jamaica tell a tale which is basically the same for the rest of the Region. The percentages of Jamaicans who can expect to attain education beyond the primary level is very low. Here are the truly alarming figures: Primary — 100 per cent; Secondary — 55 per cent; 4 CXC subjects — 4 per cent; A level — 3 per cent; Tertiary institution — 7 per cent; University — 2 per cent. If extrapolated across the Region, and into the future, that is a recipe for disaster.

Improved education and training does not only increase productive capabilities. It also substantially improves people's quality of life. There are correlations which are immutable between increased access to education and higher quality of education and training and the standards of living not only of direct beneficiaries but also of society as a whole.

Since technological innovation and the ability to master the techniques of entirely new businesses hold the key to our productive future, the enhancement of education and training at the technical level is of absolutely crucial importance. If we cannot respond quite dramatically to this need in the decade of the 1990s the often expressed fear by those who attended the consultations that their children would come to inherit a stagnant agricultural and industrial backwater will only too likely come to pass.

The Loss of Values

Economic failure, social discontent, distracted governments, divided families, declining education systems where discipline is a low priority, unemployed and frustrated people — the decay in standards of behaviour and performance is bound to have been rapid. And the decay in standards leaks back into every system multiplying failure, undermining achievement and lowering morale. The full circle is a vicious one.

The loss of "values" is of tremendous concern to every single community leader we encountered. The cult of pure materialism, the growing attractions of televised consumerism, the craving for the fast buck, the neglect of religion and the abandonment of moral values, the irresponsibility inherent in attitudes summed up in the conviction that only today matters and tomorrow must look after itself — welfare officers, headmasters and headmistresses, religious leaders in all the faiths, representatives of every possible community group in all the countries, political leaders themselves, have dwelt on these problems, particularly, of course, as they apply to youth. They see moral retrogression as the order of the day. They perceive the need for a great rescue operation to be mounted to restore to the younger generations of West Indians a sense of the values of hard work and discipline and honesty, a feeling for the benefits which sharing and teamwork bring, the satisfaction that comes from striving on behalf of others and for ends greater than personal gratification, a purpose in life beyond pure materialism and narrow career betterment. Most of these people who talked to us are hard-headed and practical men and women. But they sense that no matter how much success there is on that score something will be missing.

Here again, CARICOM stands by virtually helpless to make an immediate impact. Yet here again people and community leaders were looking to a West Indian Commission to make a difference.

We are not prophets come to judge all things, but such an appeal cannot be ignored. Somehow the ideal of Community and processes of integration must be made to count in addresssing these very basic concerns. Might it be then that, beyond the practicalities of helping create for people better lives in all the Region, the vision of a West Indian nation might itself inspire the youth of the Region as something larger than themselves for the achievement of which they can work and to which they might dedicate a part of their lives beyond the immediate and the material. It has happened in history. We are not so old and worn by the ways of the world to think that is a pointless hope to express or vision to impart.

Good Governance Under Threat

The West Indies have an enviably good record in governing

ourselves democratically. Guyana's blemished record was the exception and it is a matter of great relief that Guyana's recent electoral arrangements are on the way to returning that country to the democratic fold where all other West Indian countries have long been gathered.

But there is a clear, and clearly perceived, difference between "free and fair elections" regularly held and democracy in its truest sense. And here is the rub, because in the West Indies today there is considerable disquiet that threats to good governance are increasing fast. Parliament not functioning properly or meeting regularly, the media under governmental thumb, civil services and even judiciaries overawed by State power, corruption rampant in public life, the lack of rigour in public audits, the loss of faith in public integrity, the people ignored and unconsulted except at election time — the list is long and no country escapes some indictment. The disquiet is general enough to sound an alert. When conduct is measured against high standards then even venial sin is likely to seem quite close to mortal. But it is part of the best of us that we should continue to judge public behaviour by the highest standards. The disquiet abroad about governance falling short is a warning signal that cannot be ignored.

The Implementation Problem

Scepticism has become widespread about the political will to achieve real progress towards closer integration. Indeed, the near-despair about the ability of our processes of integration to deliver the fruits of consensus is probably the mood among the people which most needs changing.

There are three causes:

(1) The conviction that politicians are fundamentally not prepared to surrender the powers and privileges of their local positions in the cause of greater unity. Integration in peripheral activities may be secured but nothing important will be ceded.

(2) The failure to change the "unanimity rule" so as to achieve more rapid advances towards unified institutions and joint policies. It is true that this rule has not prevented many

important decisions being taken at central level and at Summit conferences in particular a remarkable degree of consensus has been reached. However, modification of the rule is seen as a crucial test of good faith in the integration ideal. It is an essential next step in a maturing society.

(3) Most importantly, perception has steadily grown that virtually no effective machinery exists to implement agreed decisions. The CARICOM Secretariat has administrative responsibilities and admirably facilitates the making of decisions. But decisions taken are then at the mercy of executive processes which belong to the 13 Member States.

At the local level, it is not appreciated that implementation of Summit decisions, in particular, far from being a surrender of sovereignty is instead the exercise of sovereignty held in common. That seems academic. Much more real are the countervailing pressures at the national level: the competing priorities of local interest groups, lobbying campaigns, inertia deriving from over-burdened administrations and lack of technical skills. These soon overwhelm consensus enthusiastically achieved at a higher, but distant and less vote-sensitive, level.

The lengthening list of unfulfilled agreements, declarations, and decisions entrenches scepticism. At its worst, political leaders are perceived as playing a game at Summits which they know will yield no result where and when it matters. As time goes by this mood of cynicism thickens and becomes harder to disperse.

We do not share this view; but the fact that it is widely held tells its own tale. It is, we believe, a tale of the futility of collective action without collective machinery for taking it. No enterprise, commercial or otherwise, could expect to succeed without executive management that gives day-round priority to implement policy agreed by the board of governance. Yet we expect CARICOM to achieve its goals by rolling up the policy board and the executive authority in the form of the Heads of Government Conference and have them meet for a few days each year. The CARICOM ship needs a captain — not only sailing orders. The CARICOM Secretariat provides a crew and the Secretary-General manages them.

But, gallant and skilful and committed as he may be, and as a succession of Secretaries-General have been, he and his colleagues cannot move the ship.

Community Contradicted

If scepticism about implementing agreed Community decisions is widespread, almost as widespread is the mood of disillusion, and even anger, at what is perceived as a betrayal of the ideals of community at elementary levels. As was emphasised in the Commission's Progress Report, the greatest resentment stems from harassment during travel, the hassle which too many West Indians encounter too often when visiting within their common home for business, holiday or family reasons. This clearly contradicts the often expressed commitment to give full expression in every practicable way to a sense of West Indian oneness from which the whole integration movement derives its force and historic purpose.

There are other contradictions. Work permit procedures constantly cause difficulties. The movement of skilled West Indians, unless they are required to fill specific vacancies, is by no means facilitated. Resentment, not welcome, seems to govern procedures when any hint of settlement surfaces in a West Indian travelling in the Region. The barriers which bureaucracies put in the way of qualified professionals, including UWI graduates, transferring home and work place are not only a contradiction of agreed integration principles but also a betrayal of the spirit of regionalism. Nor has anything been done to facilitate the easier movement of Community cultural products and artefacts among Member States though this has long been agreed.

In principle we open arms, in practice we close hearts. The mood of intra-CARICOM resentment and suspicion which this builds is potentially most damaging to our future. Attitudes must suffer a sea change through every level of administration.

Resources

The constraints are forbidding. To list them is to present a formidable bill of flawed goods. But of course it is not a full account. The credits add up also and when the sums are done let us see if

Assessment

the bias does not favour hope over despair, the promise of potential over what still keeps us back.

The first thing to be said is that many, perhaps most, countries and people would be glad to have a number of our serious problems. That is not to be complacent, but it will give perspective if we take due note that in many cases the gravity of our condition is relative to the basic good health we enjoy and much of the rest of the world does not. The second thing to notice is that often enough a problem can be turned into an opportunity, as we shall see, if we use enough initiative. The third thing to recall is that very point — initiative, energy and imagination are transforming factors: they can rapidly change the balance between loss and gain. And the final point is one we perhaps need not repeat since it is a general theme of this Report: how apparent it is that many of our problems are susceptible to relief at least, if not solution, if and when we act together. A hand, indeed, is stronger than its fingers.

Smallness Holds Its Own Truth

Small can indeed be vulnerable. But there is, of course, another saying with pleasanter implications for our Community of small states. "Small is beautiful" holds its own truth. We do not have the truly inhuman overcrowding, foetid pollution, and the miserably cluttered and high-pressure lives of many urban societies, even in the rich countries. We enjoy more of the uncorrupted joys of living than bigger and more powerful countries do, ridden as they are by furies that we do not know. When small is vulnerable we can band together to reduce the vulnerability. But where small is still beautiful we must act to preserve the amenities and advantages that flow from smallness.

Why should we not aim to get the best of both worlds — the benefits that accrue from adapting in closer community to the needs and pressures of the larger world and the advantages that derive from emphasising and preserving the traditions, the culture, the environment, and the pleasures of our small-scaled, really much more enjoyable and much friendlier countries?

Natural Resources

Relative to our combined population of five and a half million, we enjoy a treasure of natural resources which we have hardly begun to exploit. The immense, virtually untouched natural resources of Guyana and Belize alone give us a "frontier" to develop which few countries still possess.

At the same time, our newly acquired Exclusive Economic Zone of the sea has brought us an enormous enlargement of access to fishing and mineral resources — an expansion of sovereignty over riches the scope and value of which we have not yet even begun to grasp.

Nor have the resources currently being exploited run out of potential — oil, natural gas, bauxite, a varied agriculture including "niche" products with immense potential for export to the rich North and the attractions of sun and sea and sand (not to mention the pristine eco-systems of Guyana and Belize) on which one of the great expanding industries of the world is securely based.

These, together with our untapped resources, at the disposal of a few million people, is a more than sufficient inheritance. We do not lack the raw material wherewithal for economic success.

Human Resources

And yet, a greater potential resource could be our people taught to be entrepreneurial and skilled in commerce, industry, the new technologies and the burgeoning service industries. Abroad, West Indians have proved more than capable of rising to such challenges. Given the training and the minimum of opportunity they can certainly do so in their homeland.

That is why an immense new effort in education — a much larger investment in political energy, personnel and money than ever before — is essential. We possess the home traditions which place the highest value on education. We still enjoy an advantage that few developing countries possess, a basic literacy. School systems and the UWI network provide educational structures on which we could rapidly build. But we are losing our grip on the literacy advantage and beyond that, as we have seen, our current investment in education and training is wholly inadequate. It is not the basic capacity and adaptability of West Indians that is in doubt. That remains a fundamental strength.

An Overseas Resource

And those who have migrated in their hundreds of thousands, whom we have tended to identify with loss, drain, problems, weakness? It is becoming apparent that they may increasingly become a source of strength if we are imaginative enough to respond to their strong, continuing attachment for home. Our visits to consult with the diaspora in Britain, Canada and the USA were not only a revelation of the strengths, skills, resources, experience and energy in the keeping of our fellow West Indians living abroad but also a revelation of their continuing and enthusiastic commitment to help if given half a welcoming opportunity to do so.

That is a whole West Indian nation over there strategically placed in new homes but willing to be involved in constructing the future of a land they have not forgotten. Not entirely a drain then — perhaps a remarkable source of influence and assistance.

A Maturing Society

Adversity teaches, toughens, and matures a people. The last decade especially has weaned us roughly out of national adolescence. At last we have been removed far enough from the glory days of political independence to face the world without illusions. Hard times have shaken the innocence and naivete out of us. Great ideological ambitions, utopian concepts of how the world might be made to work, have had to be abandoned. We have a better chance now to act efficiently and responsibly in the interests of the ordinary people of the Region.

We know much better what needs to be done. Amidst the press of problems that at times and in places were made to seem insurmountable, there has been a healthy growth of realistic thinking. As we have gone around we have found leaders in every field — business, the trade unions, the professions, the University, the media, and politics also —who are aware as never before that nobody, especially nobody outside the Region, owes them a single cent of their living.

The Human Condition

When men have great tasks to perform, and especially when performance has lately been below expectations, the surest sign that recovery may be in prospect is when they recognise and openly declare that the fault lies not in the world, but ultimately in themselves. In our situation, to recognise and declare anything else is tacitly to admit that we were never serious about independence, never realised what cutting the umbilical cord that tied us to colonial supervision and traditions really meant. There is a sense abroad among echelons in charge, and near to being in charge, that we absolutely cannot contract out of the full responsibility for our own destiny which being in a world without any godfathers implies. Nothing is unfair in such a world except to be unfair to ourselves and to our capabilities.

Even more significantly, we believe there is a groundswell of the same feeling among the people at large. It is as if people have decided that the time has come to get at least some of the public things done for themselves and not leave them all to someone else in charge whose job it is "to run things" and who can, of course, be blamed when anything goes wrong. Once it might have been colonial administrators, then it may have been charismatic leaders of their own, but all the same it was some *deus ex machina* in a house upon a hill. The dependency syndrome is hard to break.

If the realisation that a large part of the solutions must be in the people's own hands is indeed gaining ground, as we believe it is, that is a development of great consequence. Interesting evidence of this comes in the surge of interest among people to form and operate non-governmental organisations of all kinds and of increasing vigour. It is a mood and a movement to be encouraged at every level. It could be the basis of a new kind of relationship between Governments and populations in which the greater participation of people in policy-making and decision-taking (and then in implementation as a natural corollary) is organised in fresh and imaginative ways.

The phrase "empowerment of the people" has become a sort of catch-word. In our case what it means is that our societies are rapidly maturing and people at the grass-roots are confident that they have something to contribute and therefore want, and deserve, a role beyond inscribing a mark on a ballot paper every few years.

Assessment

We must find a way to accommodate this new maturity.

An Ethos of Democracy

Problems are perceived of good governance under threat. The assumption made that good governance is in place defines one of the strengths of the Community. Despite the problems, and more or less serious irregularities, which this Report addresses with serious concern, we enjoy a rare degree of democracy and freedom. There has been one major deviation and particular examples of the people's rights invaded have surfaced during the course of the Commission's work. These are departures from a norm. They cannot be ignored. We must keep strictly in place what is one of the strengths, indeed one of the most attractive human features, of our Community: its societies are open, practising democracies based on the rule of law and the protection of human rights. We must not risk losing any part of that lest the very essence of what we are is diluted.

Location as Resource

Look at the map and our geographical advantages are clear. We rest at the junction of the Americas, North and South and Central. As well as the USA, great countries of the future, Brazil and Venezuela and Mexico, are our close neighbours. We are at the centre of a potential hive of business, investment, communications, banking and trade activity. Combined, our attractiveness as a tourist area is second to none in the world. Real though the threat of degradation is, our environment remains basically unspoiled, unpillaged, unpolluted, a haven of natural beauty, and we can keep it so if we act vigorously together.

Our fishing grounds and ocean mineral resources are superbly placed for sensible exploitation. In Guyana, one of the earth's last, great, untouched tropical forests has the potential to become in a few years an area which leads the world in scientific investigation of how best to manage and use one of humanity's great assets.

Look at us as one nation. Our location is superb. We are no longer by fate destined to be a strategic cockpit. What we have in prospect is to become a peaceful meeting ground of people doing business, finding and creating wealth, active in the arts and sciences, and enjoying themselves. It is a place for generations of the young to be. The phrase "backwater" to denote our possible fate describes a most unlikely consummation — if we enter the mainstream together.

The Favours of History

It is true, nobody owes us a living or a treaty. What we earn and what we win are going to have to be earned and won by the sweat of our brows, or more appositely, the humming of our brain cells. However, history has conferred upon us a number of advantages. In terms of trade and investment and influence and friendly support they add up to a priceless patrimony.

Over time the West Indies has become the beneficiary of a number of well-founded special relationships. The links with Britain, and with Europe when Britain entered the EEC, are strong and are now enshrined in the Lomé Convention. Canada specifically acknowledges the "special relationship" it enjoys with the West Indies and that has given us CARIBCAN and a continuing, active interest in the well-being of the Region. The USA also has long historical links with the West Indies. These are currently reflected in the CBI arrangements and the advantages for us in the Enterprise of the Americas Initiative and provide a secure base from which to negotiate favourable terms within the proposed hemispheric free trade area.

These relationships have opened up for our business and trade a spread of preferential markets which are unexampled in their potential value. Such markets, such preferential opportunities, are as much a natural resource as a string of oil fields ready to be drilled or cluster of gold fields to be mined. It is up to us to exploit them to the full.

In addition to these strong linkages, the West Indies enjoys important contacts with the hemisphere through membership of the Organisation of American States (OAS) and throughout the world through membership of the Commonwealth and the African, Caribbean and Pacific (ACP) group of countries. Furthermore our knowledge of and participation in the United Nations and its important network of institutions and worldwide activities have deepened

Assessment

through practice and eloquence into an asset that accompanies us wherever we visit for business or negotiate in the world.

This multiplicity of entry points in to the great worlds of diplomacy, politics, international institutions, trade, business, and investment represents one of the most valuable achievements built up by skilled and creative West Indians over the decades. It is a tribute to the exercise of experienced and imaginative diplomacy and hard work in international affairs. This has been one of the strengths of our people since they entered independently on to the world scene. That strength remains and is currently in evidence in a score of arenas. It is a strength we must be careful to conserve and expand since it is going to be needed more than ever in the years to come. And, this Report will hardly need to stress, it is a strength which is multiplied when we combine and negotiate and act in the closest concert.

"More Talent Per Square Foot than Ancient Greece"

That may have been a slightly dramatic way of putting it and perhaps on the fulsome side. But it makes a general point we need not forget. The immeasurable ingredient in our mix of resources is West Indian creativity. It has gone far afield and made its mark in a multitude of ways. Relative to population, what country, what developing country in particular, possesses the Caribbean Community's record of achievement? Famously in literature and the arts and music and sport and international diplomacy — but outstandingly also in the professions and academia and international administration and in the internal affairs of their new homelands — West Indian creativity makes an astonishing contribution in the Region and the wide world. Does a month pass without some signal evidence in the world of West Indian prowess? Walcott and Naipaul revered in the world's literary pages, Richards at the Oval receiving all the cricket world's adulation, Arthur Lewis and Patterson setting the academic world alight, Minshall at Barcelona. These are a few that represent the many just below the headlines. This is remarkable. In one field only has this creativity still to flower fully — the field of business, entrepreneurship, commerce, the new profit-makers. But there is no reason to believe it will not flourish there too if we make the climate right. Creativity has no boundaries. If our critical mass is community the fuse that sets the process going will be the individual genius and creativity of West Indians.

A West Indian Model

Problems are not in short supply. Our special vulnerabilities are clear. Difficulties abound and make life grindingly hard for too many. West Indians are more aware than anyone that in many areas we have fallen behind the front-runners in preparing for the future. And they have been eloquent in describing these problems, these difficulties, these vulnerabilities and in letting us know how far they think we have slipped in the race.

They have not seemed so certain of their advantages, their own strengths, their own unique capabilities. Perhaps it is for us to assure West Indians that they possess natural advantages and opportunities for advancement quite sufficient to make their way confidently in the world and bring resources of talent and creativity to their tasks ample enough to make their mark again in history.

Some of these advantages and opportunities, some of the special creativity, we have set out above to balance the formidable list of problems and constraints. But, as West Indians themselves who take care in examining the record will realise, the list is not exhaustive. All our peoples have a record of individual and collective achievements which defies full catalogue.

Much has been written — and indeed we have heard a lot in the course of our consultations — about a dominant American image, the new Europe, the Japanese example, the Singapore model.

These are useful as well as fashionable reference points in appraising our future. But we know our own worth. We have our own singular potential. We will find that we will not be ashamed, if we can get it right this decade, of proposing our own West Indian model for the 21st Century.

It must, first of all, be a community which has learned enough about industrial and business efficiency to generate the sort of economic dynamism which will yield the material sufficiency which people expect and deserve. That sufficiency of material return must not simply be numbers in an index of averages concealing great disparities in the distribution of goods and social services. The institutions of government, intervening as little as possible in the processes of wealth generation, must be alert and efficient in ensuring that people at every level share in the basic goods, essential services, and educational and employment opportunities which the economy produces.

Clearly, this is not all. These are the lineaments of any properly functioning economy and well-run society at the end of the Twentieth Century. But there are dimensions of achievement where the West Indies can be seen to make a special contribution. Basic to this is the example of smoothly working democratic institutions where the full range of basic human rights is protected as a matter of course. The world at large does not take such an achievement for granted. It is a special West Indian strength which we must be at pains to preserve.

And within that framework we may offer what is uniquely our creation. It is rare, especially in the still developing world — and it may become rarer yet as the decade advances — that a people of many nationalities, many races, many faiths, and different cultural heritages stay together, and indeed grow closer, in a single community. It is an example that is likely to be valuable in the world. The talents which have emerged from our amalgam of peoples have already made a telling and universal mark. This creativity, multiplied through the greater opportunities conferred by closer union, will add stature and a special vibrancy to the example we can expect to offer to our hemisphere and to the world as the new century dawns.

3. PREPARING FOR THE TWENTY-FIRST CENTURY

The West Indian Commission was established in 1989 because even then it was clear that the Region was experiencing a time of such universal change, and faced challenges so formidable, that a special effort was needed to survey and assess the scene, analyse prospects, and propose what might best be done to enable the people of the West Indies to prepare for the 21st Century. In the time which has elapsed since 1989 the pace of change has quickened, the challenges have grown more pressing and immediate, and the need now is no longer for proposals but for urgent action.

West Indians — the people and their leaders — must now make a number of decisive moves to secure their common future. We are convinced that the moves we advocate will provide the means to "bring about real betterment in their condition of life, achieve their full potential as free people responsible for their own destiny, and improve their Region's place in the community of nations".

In the pages which follow we deal with the issues in a number of broad areas including: decision-making and structures of unity; governance and securing civil society; education and the development of human resources; economic development; the establishment of a common currency and the strengthening of financial institutions; agriculture; trade, industry, and transportation; the environment; issues of particular social concern; gender issues; regional communications in the widest sense; cultural issues; the formulation and conduct of regional and international policies and relationships. We have also considered special issues concerning the aboriginal peoples of the Region, the problems of remoteness affecting The Bahamas and Belize, and bringing the Community into closer touch with the diaspora.

We will seek to make our proposals in a common form relating to the various matters covered. In each case the challenges presented will be analysed and the response we suggest will then be set out with specific recommendations for what action needs to be taken.

In many of the areas, venturing to suggest solutions to the multitudinous problems that pertain to individual countries would make this report many-volumed and unwieldy. Our particular concern here will be to consider how best the process of closer integration can be applied in responding to the identified challenges.

The sentiment we expressed in concluding the Commission's Progress Report, "Towards a Vision of the Future", has remained the touchstone of our work:

We have seen ourselves as challenged to find a common strength in our diversity. In our work we have indeed found great diversity; but we found great commonalities also, and we have been heartened by the vigour with which this identity within variety has been expressed — particularly because it is so remarkably underpinned by a belief in the possibility and the need for a common West Indian future. The flame of such a belief is flickering here and there; but the light of unity has by no means gone out. This is not a small thing. It must continue to illumine our regional labours. We have to face the challenges of our remarkable diversity — that the Caribbean Sea which unites us also divides us, and that history has done its separatist part as well; but we must accept that diversity and use it, and we must refine and build the institutions to accommodate it.

If there is one undeniable truth deriving from the total West Indian historical experience, it is that, whatever the task, we do it better if we do it together. West Indian cricket, and the University of the West Indies are outstanding examples of the Region achieving levels of excellence and international renown that would have been simply unattainable separately. There are others, less dramatic in their impact, but confirmation nonetheless that togetherness is our West Indian 'critical mass'.

Our faith in this credo remains undiminished and has inspired the conclusions we have drawn from our work over the past two years. These conclusions and the recommendations that flow from them are contained in the chapters that follow. The time is due to settle the conundrum Derek Walcott once posed for all West Indians: "and either I'm nobody or I am a nation".

PART II

CHALLENGES AND OPPORTUNITIES

CHAPTER IV

DEVELOPMENT

1. NEW EMPHASES IN DEVELOPMENT

We do not propose in this Chapter to undertake an exhaustive examination of the development situation and prospects of the Region. They have already been covered in a number of recent reports. Instead, we focus on certain selected items which merit greater emphasis in development policies or which involve a change of direction in development strategies. However, we are not unmindful that the successful execution of these strategies presupposes a measure of success in the implementation of stabilisation and adjustment programmes and in the servicing of the external debt.

The Global Setting

In Chapters III and XI, we draw attention to a number of fundamental changes which have been occurring in the world, and to policy developments that will impinge upon the development prospects of the Region and its external economic relations. It is important to underline the point that these changes require a thoroughgoing shift in perspective from an import-substitution economy to one of export-propelled growth. However, this is not to deny the importance of efficient import substitution in areas such as food production, nor the role of sectors such as construction in sustaining high levels of activity and employment.

CARICOM Countries have to lift their sights towards increasing participation in a global economy which is unfolding in ways that affect both traditional and new types of production, and in the conditions under which foreign trade takes place. We mention here only four of these changes.

First, shifts in the geographical patterns and product composition of world trade. The world economy is becoming more multipolar with the emergence of new leaders in world trade. Japan's ascendancy has already been mentioned. More recent is that of the six Asian Newly Industrialised Countries (NICS) — Hong Kong, Republic of Korea, Singapore, Taiwan, Malaysia and Thailand — which in 1991 had a combined value of world exports and imports greater than Japan, and a considerably strengthened balance of payments position. Among individual countries, Taiwan now holds the largest foreign exchange reserves in the world.

Related to this is the shift in product composition favouring knowledge-intensive products, notably in the machinery and equipment category. Here, the market shares of the NICS have been growing, reflecting their increasing technological sophistication and the sustained investment in human resource development which preceded and has been accompanying that increase. Related, too, is the growth in world trade in services, especially producer services, in which some of the NICS are also beginning to emerge.

Second, is the transformation that is taking place in international business organisation, evidenced by the increasing emergence of the network rather than the international company as the unit of production and trade. In many instances the vertically structured international company is transforming itself into a number of independent or quasi-independent profit centres, or organising its production in alliances with subsidiaries, affiliates, partners, sub-contractors, licencees and franchises — to quote just a few examples.

Companies are now sourcing their components and services worldwide, thereby creating new opportunities for component and specialty production, as well as niche marketing. It is believed that new players stand a better chance of penetrating these networks than has been the case with the vertically integrated enterprise.

Third, two contending policy developments are taking place in international trade. On the one hand, are efforts to promote the worldwide liberalisation of trade through the Uruguay Round. These negotiations are still to be completed. It is therefore difficult to assess what benefits will eventually accrue to the CARICOM Countries from them.

At the same time, efforts are being made to strengthen existing regional groupings or to establish new ones within which trade liberalisation is also taking place. It is possible that we are witnessing new patterns of regionalisation in the world economy. The CARICOM countries have therefore to retain the capacity to respond flexibly to both of these policy currents, so that they can secure the best possible openings for expanding their export earnings.

Fourth, are the important changes taking place in the pattern of financial flows. Commercial lending to developing countries has diminished. There is increased competition for limited world savings. Major increases in official flows to the Eastern European countries and the former Soviet Republics are likely to put pressure on such flows to developing countries.

Gross flows from the multilateral development banks have been increasing, but on a net basis they remain very small. Cross-border private flows are expanding, and new instruments are developing to facilitate such flows and meet changing needs. Only a small number of developing countries are benefitting from this expansion.

While CARICOM countries must continue to seek ways of increasing total inflows of finance, it is to private flows and, particularly, direct and portfolio investment they must seek increased access. Investment geared to increasing exports is a particular need. Investment policy in the Region must seek to ensure improved access to foreign finance. The development and regionalisation of capital markets in CARICOM countries could increase the attractiveness of the area to overseas lenders and investors.

One central message emerges: in order to make progress in the conditions of today's world the CARICOM countries have to summon their determination to increase their adaptability, resilience, innovation, and international competitiveness. This will require more concerted and sustained efforts to improve production than have so far been made. It means more concentrated attention to critical constraints such as human resource development, on which the region's production and export prospects will increasingly depend.

What the new trends in the world economy show is that new players can find space in that economy, if they can demonstrate the necessary drive and competitiveness. It represents a challenge to which the countries of the Region can respond positively, and by that means move ahead in the years and decades to come.

An Export Propelled Strategy

CARICOM has the opportunity for self-sustained growth, based on a strong orientation towards exports of goods and services in the context of the changing global environment. The export thrust must be fully supported by Government initiatives following the example of the successful East Asian exporters. Development will be based on increased competitiveness, innovation, the use of information services and the exploitation of CARICOM's good educational base and natural resources. Exports of goods and services will have to be of high quality. Many will be in the service areas, in tourism and in the new information services to which CARICOM has access through modern telecommunications facilities. Investment will also be directed to reducing costs and increasing productivity in traditional export items, to ensure that they command competitive niches in a dynamic export market.

The development strategy involves the mobilisation of capital, labour and skills throughout the CARICOM Region. Firms must combine and form strategic alliances so as to achieve the range of skills and the diversity needed to be competitive players in export markets. CARICOM needs to achieve a minimum cadre of exporters in order to gain advantages of synergy from export activities. Individual countries will find it difficult to achieve that level of activity on their own but as a Region the prospects are favourable.

Firms producing export goods and services must develop a strong information base and the capability to shift production in a strategic fashion in response to market changes.

The export-oriented development strategy will be complemented by the evolution of domestic goods and services that are ancillary to the export activities. In this context education should emphasise self-confidence and entrepreneurship to encourage many of those entering the labour force to exploit opportunities for self employment and for providing personalised services to the foreign exchange sectors.

This development strategy opens the promise of flexible, resilient and diversified foreign exchange earnings sectors for the CARICOM family. Development will be self-sustainable to the extent that CARICOM adapts continuously to a changing world, modifying goods and services to avoid obsolescence and organising to exploit new opportunities.

For countries with good natural resources for mineral, agricultural and forest products, increased efficiency and innovativeness must be pursued in order to maintain or expand production. The large agricultural resources of some countries e.g., Guyana and Belize, could be used to ensure food self-sufficiency in the Region and to develop new large scale exports.

There is much scope also for expanding mineral production and forestry extraction on a sustainable basis. In some cases export industries could be relocated within the Region according to changing comparative advantage.

The development strategy will also enable us to absorb the unemployed labour force. Many will find jobs in the successful growing export sectors — both goods and services. The employment creation will be on a comparatively large scale because the firms which are needed must be large enough to address the international market. While we expect they will be small by international standards, they will be quite sizeable by the measures usually employed in CARICOM. Moreover, the success of exporting firms will create a demand which should see the growth of small firms supplying ancillary goods and services to the export sector. A vibrant small enterprise sector supporting the traded sectors should serve to mop up the remaining unemployed.

Small Business Development and Self-Employment

Accordingly, we see the promotion of small businesses and self-employment as important means of generating employment and advancing economic development. Family farms and firms absorb family labour, promote self-reliance, provide scope for flexible remuneration, nurture entrepreneurship and afford opportunities for utilising scientific methods of production, thereby yielding high incomes to farmers. New technologies are giving increased scope to small businesses, and there is much scope for these businesses in the expanding services sector, including the provision of services to larger firms. Family farms, suitably modernised and having adequate access to land, have a crucial role to play in helping the Region to meet an expanding proportion of its food requirements, as well as contributing to increased traditional and non-traditional agricultural exports.

Recent developments have confirmed the ability of the informal sector to be responsive to business opportunities. Informal activities are not a temporary economic phenomenon, but could be important in low-cost production of goods and services and as a means of business mobility and a source of entrepreneurship. With suitable assistance to help the shift from trading to production activities, with training, concessional credit, the provision of work space and other common services, this sector could make a substantial contribution to the generation of employment and production.

CARICOM Governments have begun to give attention to the promotion of self-employment and small businesses. However, much more could be done to provide incentives and support. Comparative regional experience could be a good guide in the further development of policies.

Economic Growth and Human Development

Economic development is first and foremost about people and the quality of their lives. The search for self-sustained growth is a quest for resources with which to enhance the lifestyles of all Caribbean peoples. The emphasis on export oriented growth reflects the fact that we can offer our people a diversified range of necessities and quality products only by importing either final products or the fuels and raw materials from which to produce them. Exporting is not an end in itself; it is the means of enriching the lifestyles of all Caribbean peoples. The development strategy must therefore ensure that export promotion is accompanied by policies which develop the potential of the individual and give both incentives and access for citizens to improve their standard of living. Moreover, development must be sustainable in the sense that it is supportive, not destructive, of the physical environment.

Correcting Imbalances in Wealth and Income

A recurring concern throughout the Region, and even in the

diaspora, is the perceived inequalities in wealth and income distribution. This manifests itself in terms like 'the big man' and 'the capitalist' and obviously remains a major issue in the growth and developmental process.

The Commission recognises also that the very necessary stabilisation and structural adjustment programmes, with their emphasis on direct tax reduction and greater reliance on indirect taxation, mean that inequalities in income and wealth distribution are likely to be exacerbated rather than improved. That is why in Chapter VI the Commission stresses the need for greater expenditure not only on human resource development but also on programmes that give individuals the tools to develop themselves — developing entrepreneurship, learning to earn, small business programmes, appropriate research in agriculture, are all parts of the required investment in our human resources.

In our discussion on agriculture, we also draw attention to the role that greater access to land can play in alleviating wealth and income imbalances. To this must be added better rural infrastructure, including improvements in the quality of housing.

We must also work continuously to reduce the barriers to entry for the new businessman, the new farmer, the new entrepreneur. New here does not mean only the poor and small; it means also the professional turned businessman, the returning immigrant hoping to start a substantial business, the sucessful small firm striving to diversify and to grow. How to access capital, when to establish a joint venture, when and how to invest in the securities market, must be common knowledge.

Another concern is with the ownership and control of the key institutions which garner the nations savings, viz., the insurance companies, commercial banks, near banks and pension funds. These institutions determine where funds should be invested, and while we do not wish them to become wild risk takers we recommend that they be encouraged to give more attention to investment in the productive sector, especially export-oriented activities.

Who owns and controls these financial institutions is also important. We recommend the widening of the shareholder base and the promotion of Employee Share Ownership Plans (ESOPs) as a means of ensuring that these institutions become very much "people owned".

We do not recommend that attempts be made to restrict the size and growth of these institutions. Our "big" banks and "gigantic" insurance companies are still small on the world stage and we need big blocks of capital to undertake large investment projects.

The Role of Governments

CARICOM Governments now accept that in the light of their own experiences, and of the changing international environment, their role in the economy has to be modified.

It is generally acknowledged that the private sector must constitute a driving force in the productive process. We have indicated before that Governments should become less and less involved in the direct production of goods and services, and should increasingly concentrate on catalytic, facilitating, supportive, and regulatory functions. This means different government. It does not mean no government.

Although the role of government has been the subject of recent reports, it is worth emphasising that Governments have to be active in ensuring that the overall framework is conducive to the achievement and sustenance of high levels of investment and economic activity. This should include an appropriate medium to long term focus pointing towards the strategic directions which the economy can follow, and areas in which comparative advantages can be developed. Governments have also to ensure the removal of biases and obstacles to export growth. Furthermore, they have to work assiduously to create adequate incentives for human effort and risk-taking . Additionally, they have to be active in the area of human resource development: more and better education and training at all levels, greater research, more support for local entrepreneurship.

In the field of regulation, Governments have to ensure the effective maintenance of rules for competition so that any barriers to the entry of new businesses are removed. In addition they have to establish standards both for production and for work, in order to protect the interests of consumers and workers respectively.

Under contemporary conditions, it is also expected that Governments will pay specific attention to socially disadvantaged and marginalised groups. Public resources should be deployed to create a social safety net for the poor, and to deal specifically with the problems of youth, women, the elderly and the disabled. Further, in the provision of social services, the development of community-based structures of delivery should be encouraged. Governments need to underpin these efforts by contributing resources, technical assistance, and appropriate policy frameworks.

To summarise, Governments have a major and dynamic role to play in the new policy situation. This involves efforts not merely to streamline the public sector, but also to upgrade it, so that it would effectively fulfil these essential roles.

In so doing, Governments should view themselves as the nexus of a new alliance with the social partners, so that the community as a whole can go forward in a harmonious and mutually supportive manner. This will call for greater and more continuous interaction with the social partners, as well as more transparency in the operations of governments.

The Labour Movement

We touch finally on the role of the labour movement in the changing economies of the Region. We were very impressed by the positive interventions made by the Trade Union representatives at several of our public consultations and in our direct encounters with them everywhere we went. We benefitted also from written memoranda. In the course of these contacts we became aware that the Trade Unions themselves are engaged in a series of reflections about how they should respond to the changing economic environment. We mention here just a few directions in which we believe thinking should proceed on this subject.

There is no question that Trade Unions continue to have an important role to play in ensuring good working conditions for the labour force and levels of remuneration consistent with productivity and international competitiveness. In an export economy, unions and management must be continuously sensitive to the need for good industrial relations and for continuous upgrading and training of the labour force. In this context, we encourage the unions to take a larger hand in the development of human resources and support directly the education and training of their members and their families. We think, for example, that the time has come for the Trade Union movement to seek to mobilise more resources for bursaries and scholarships tenable at Universities and tertiary educational institutions.

We believe also that the unions have a critical role to play in the tripartite dialogue with Governments and the private sector in identifying new development opportunities and the steps required to take advantage of them. This will demand a much greater fact-finding and analytical capability among the unions in monitoring trends in both the regional economy and in the outside world. It is, therefore, gratifying to note the establishment of institutions such as the Joint Trade Union Development and Research Centre in Jamaica which is intended to undertake these precise tasks.

There would, of course, be difficult issues with which the Unions will have to grapple alongside the other social partners. These have to do with the adjustments that are indispensable during the process of structural adjustment, involving greater mobility of labour, retraining of retrenched workers, and so on. Again, this calls for greater preparedness on the part of both Union leadership and the rank and file to take the long view and to participate actively in finding mutually satisfactory solutions to these problems.

The labour movement has been for most of this century the flagbearer of regionalism in the Caribbean. In all our consultations, whether with Trade Unions at the national level or with the regional representatives of the movement, we have been impressed by the degree to which the labour movement has kept faith with regionalism. Their early pioneering role has obviously changed as the first fruits of their efforts developed with the independence of Caribbean countries. But they remain attentive to the need for regional action by way of solutions to the problems that confront West Indian people today. We encourage them to sustain this faith. The Treaty of Chaguaramas acknowledges the importance of labour in the process of integration. There are important responsibilities to be discharged by the labour movement as we go forward. Our consultations with them have been an encouragement to us. We encourage them in turn to seize the opportunities that are at hand and to play the roles which are uniquely theirs.

Recommendations

1. that Governments become less involved in the direct production of goods and services and concentrate on catalytic, facilitating, supportive and regulatory functions;

2. that all parties ensure the removal of biases against and obstacles to export-led growth;

3. that Governments and the private sector emphasise human resource development with particular attention to programmes in learning to earn, entrepreneurship, and technical skills;

4. that programmes be introduced to remove barriers to the entry of new farmers and new businessmen (small, medium and large) into the commercial arena;

5. that throughout the Region enterprises providing export goods and services develop a strong information base to support their activities;

6. that savings institutions — commercial banks, insurance companies, pension funds, etc. — be encouraged to give more support to investment in the productive sector especially export-oriented activities;

7. that every effort be made to widen the shareholder base of financial institutions in particular through the use of ESOPs and other appropriate mechanisms;

8. that Governments encourage the growth of local financial institutions to meet the need for large blocks of capital to undertake major investment projects.

9. that the Trade Union movement give increasing attention to its new role in a changing economy, particularly enhanced contributions to human resource development and the tripartite discussion on the economic situation and prospects.

2. TOWARDS A SINGLE MARKET AND ECONOMY

In Chapter II we examined the evolution of CARICOM and assessed to what extent CARICOM has achieved success or fallen short of expectations. We gave a picture of where the Community now stands in the development of its institutions.

Now we must turn to examine the future as the Community sets course towards becoming a Single Market and Economy.

At their Meeting in Grand Anse, Grenada, in July 1989 the Heads of Government of the Caribbean Community declared their intention to work towards the creation of a Single Market and Economy for the Caribbean Community in as short a time as possible. In terms of scheduling, the 1990 Kingston Declaration could be interpreted to have fixed 1993 as the date for establishing the Single Market and Economy. Subsequently, several Heads of Government have repeatedly referred to 1994 as the target date for the Single Market and Economy. Additionally, in 1990 at their Meeting in Kingston, Jamaica, CARICOM Heads of Government called (in the Kingston Declaration) for monetary integration.

What is Involved

Technically, a Single Market involves a market structured and functioning to a large extent as if it were within the borders of a single country. There must, therefore, be freedom of movement of goods, services, labour and capital, and supportive fiscal and monetary measures and administrative arrangements. The Single Economy must be a regional economy closely approximating a national economy, incorporating measures to achieve a balance in the distribution of costs and benefits. While many policy functions may be carried out at the national level, these should be conducted within a coordinated policy framework at the regional level.

It has been suggested that because the vast majority of the exports of the individual countries which make up CARICOM are extra-regional, the Single CARICOM Market is unimportant in the Region's developmental thrust. While conceding the relative importance of extra-regional trade now and for the future we must fully recognise the benefits to production and development that will flow from the advent of a genuine Single Market.

First and foremost is the increase in the size of the home market which will allow for significant cooperation in production, transport and marketing. Firms would not have to worry about governmental or bureaucratic obstacles in other CARICOM countries and could safely introduce technology consistent with a market of five and a half million and not the 100,000 typical of most OECS countries. Region-wide marketing firms would emerge and they in turn would almost automatically focus on the wider Caribbean and, of course, the world beyond the Region. The success of beer exports by more than one CARICOM firm first nationally, then regionally and ultimately extra-regionally is typical of what can be expected. Beer producers now have both a regional and extra-regional production and marketing network.

A second area of importance is the development of certain key services and professions allowing for a size of firm capable initially of servicing the entire Region but ultimately developing sales to the wider Caribbean and outside the Region. Examples of the professions are accounting, architecture, engineering, actuarial science and general business and agricultural consultancies. These professions can grow and prosper in a five and a half million market. Some cannot even exist in a 100,000 market, thus condemning some of the brightest Caribbean peoples to work and live outside the Region or to eschew totally certain professions. The development of these professions will of course mean the creation of additional jobs. In services the financial sector is one example of a sector that can benefit from the Single Market and already regional insurance companies and commercial banks are beginning to appear.

A third major possibility lies in the development of genuine Caribbean franchise-type operations in areas such as restaurants, merchandising, specialist foods, travel agencies, hotels/motels, etc. The expanded home markets permit the investment and development of systems for more than one country. If it works in Port-of-Spain and Kingston it can work in Miami, Toronto, New York and London. The creation of the Single Market will change the mindset which is a necessary condition for genuine export-led growth. It will allow for joint ventures, licensing and other forms of business endeavour.

We must not, however, be under any illusions as to what is required for the creation of a Single CARICOM Market and Economy and point out that it involves the following:

1. Free movement of goods and services, implying:
   - elimination of all tariffs, quantitative restrictions and other non-tariff barriers on intra-regional trade;
   - appropriate rules of origin;
   - uniform customs laws and simplification and harmonisation of customs documentation and procedures;
   - elimination of legal and administrative procedures affecting the unrestricted flow of goods and services throughout the Single Market;
   - harmonisation of standards for goods and services;
   - the introduction of rules applicable throughout the Single Market to ensure genuine intra-regional competition;
   - once an imported good or service enters a customs entry port and has fulfilled all entry requirements, it can circulate freely in the Region without further restriction.

2. An effective CET must be structured so as to reflect both the trade and production situation of the Region. It must encourage production and consumption of regionally produced goods at appropriate levels of competition. It must also be reserved as a bargaining instrument for trade negotiations between CARICOM and other countries and entities.

    The Heads of Government decided to introduce a truly Common External Tariff with effect from 1st January, 1991.

    There has been some criticism that, in those countries where the introduction of the CET will lead to an average increase in import tariffs, trade diversion is likely to take place. This means that expenditure in the countries concerned will be diverted towards high-cost goods produced within CARICOM and away from lower-cost goods imported from outside. It is argued that this will increase the cost of living.

    As shown in our Peport any such costs have to be set against the benefits accruing to those countries in the larger context of the Common Market arrangements as a whole. Moreover, critics rarely point to the benefits of CARICOM producers 'learning by doing' and thereby increasing productivity and lowering costs in the longer term.

Having regard to all the considerations involved, the CET should, in our view, be implemented speedily by all CARICOM countries.

Notwithstanding the implementation of the CET, CARICOM countries must also be cognisant of the trade liberalisation processes taking place internationally as well as within the South/Central American sub-region. Such trade policy reforms would imply that if CARICOM countries are to continue to exploit their comparative advantages, increase competitiveness, as well as attract investment into the Region, they would have, as a group, to be ready to undertake tariff reductions in a phased and systematic manner. However this may also imply the retention of certain restrictions for the protection of certain "sensitive" items — such as food for the local and regional markets.

3. Common Trade Policies *vis a vis* third countries and provision for joint representation in international economic negotiations.

4. Free Movement of Capital, facilitated by:
   - abolition of intra-regional exchange controls and the introduction of a common regime of exchange controls and practices with respect to transactions with third countries;
   - *either* an agreed level of exchange rates and free convertibility as between regional currencies *or* a single currency;
   - coordination of monetary and fiscal policies with a view to encouraging intra-regional capital mobility, avoiding major payment imbalances among Member States and promoting the development of a regional capital market including a Stock Exchange;
   - negotiation of intra-regional Double Taxation Treaties.

5. Free Movement of Labour, facilitated by:
   - removal of impediments to intra-regional travel;
   - mechanisms for accreditation and equivalency certification for professional and technical workers;

- provision for transfer of remittances and pensions;
- harmonization of social security measures so that they can be transferred when a person leaves one country to work in another.

6. Other measures, including:
   - concerted policy efforts by Member States to achieve balanced development among themselves with specified support for less developed parts of the Region;
   - harmonisation of fiscal incentives for extra-regional exports of non-traditional agricultural and manufactured products;
   - common policies towards foreign investment — both direct and portfolio;
   - regular consultations with the social partners on a sustained basis to ensure that all sectors in the Community are involved in the integration process.

If a further step is taken to establish monetary union this would involve a single currency and related arrangements for managing the supply of money and credit. This is dealt with further in the section that follows.

The Single Market and Economy would in effect mean completing the development of the Common Market. We believe this to be the right and necessary path for CARICOM. It will involve intra-regional cooperation in production, including production integration — that is, the use of resources on a regional basis to produce goods and services not only for the Common Market but also for extra-regional markets. It will require significant levels of policy integration as well as closer cooperation between the Government and private sectors and between national private sectors themselves.

Integration and the Less Developed Countries (the OECS and Belize)

In nearly all integration groupings among both developed and developing countries special regimes for the relatively less developed participant countries or areas have been established. These include a number of special concessions in the fields of trade and development finance. CARICOM has been no exception to this general pattern.

We wish to emphasise that the various elements of the Single Market should not be accepted on a piecemeal basis, but as a package. Member States must all jointly work assiduously to honour their implementing obligations. Only by these means can the balance of advantages for each Member State be secured.

Recommendations

1. that CARICOM Governments which have not implemented the CET should do so speedily;

2. that Governments and the private sector recognise all the dimensions of the Single Market and Economy and the benefits that could flow from them;

3. that they further recognise that the creation of a Single Market and Economy is an evolutionary process and that the full benefits will be derived therefrom when the whole package of measures is implemented;

4. that, consistent with that understanding, Governments ensure that national policy takes full cognisance of the requirements and obligations of a Single Market and Economy.

3. COMMON CURRENCY ARRANGEMENTS

In our Progress Report, we referred to public concern over the great disparity in exchange rates of national currencies within the Community; and we return to this matter in this Report in a number of places — including our analysis of the requirements of the Single Market and Economy earlier in this Chapter. Those concerns derive both from practical experience of inconvenience in travelling through the Region and severe impediments to the functioning of economic integration. There are examples of exchange rate stability in the

Region which show that it should not be beyond the reach of the Region as a whole. Fiscal discipline is a cardinal factor in currency stability and institutional arrangements for a common currency can place very strict limits on the extent to which Governments can borrow from the established Monetary Authority, if at all. This has been the key feature in the success of the EC dollar and of the relatively better economic performance of the OECS countries as against other Member States of CARICOM.

These lessons have not been lost on regional Governments. As we have seen the Grand Anse Declaration and Work Programme for the Advancement of the Integration Movement has already pointed the direction towards common currency arrangements for the Region. In expressing their 'determination to work towards the establishment, in the shortest possible time, of a Single Market and Economy for the Caribbean Community', they agreed on important steps being taken including 'arrangements for intensifying consultation and cooperation on monetary, financial and exchange rate policies by July 1990 and the removal of all barriers to trade by July 1991'. These targets have already slipped; but *the direction* is clear — as is the acknowledged sense of urgency.

In 1990, CARICOM leaders went further. In their Kingston Declaration they specifically "mandated the Governors of the Central Banks of the Region to commence a study as soon as possible for consideration by the Heads of Government to transform our Common Market into a monetary union... and to work towards the coordination of the establishment of a monetary union."

In our consultations throughout the Region, the question of a common Caribbean currency has arisen insistently, and from many quarters. This is not surprising. A common currency in the Region would be an important condition for the successful establishment of a single CARICOM market. With free movement of goods and services within the Region, a common currency would serve to eliminate transaction costs of national currency conversions as well as exchange rate uncertainties in trade and investment decisions. This in turn should serve to facilitate expansion of regional trade and investment and deepen Caribbean integration. It would bring into being a regional capital market, with free capital flows on a regional basis deterring capital flight from the Region and encouraging more efficient use of regional capital.

Convertibility of existing currencies, which we recommend in our chapter on Economic Issues as a necessary step (Chapter V) and which would itself require important institutional arrangements within the Region, would achieve some, but not all, of these objectives.

And beyond economic considerations, a common Caribbean currency would be extremely important for Caribbean unity in a symbolic and political sense.

With these considerations in mind, the Commission believes that immediate steps should be taken towards the goal of a common Caribbean currency — a goal to be attained on a phased basis and under arrangements which take account of existing exchange rate differentials. Full and free convertibility should perhaps be the first step on the way to a common currency. Some suggestions for such a scheme are offered below. We commend these arrangements, starting with the early establishment of an independent regional Caribbean Monetary Authority which will issue and manage the new Caribbean currency.

There are various forms that common currency arrangements can take. At one extreme is a single common currency as exists in the OECS states at present. At the other is a parallel common currency usable for restricted transactions only. In between lie other arrangements where both the national currencies and the common currency are circulating freely, with the value of national currencies either fixed or broadly-fixed against the common currency or floating against it. While all forms of common currency arrangements would facilitate regional trade and investment, a single currency or arrangements where national currencies are fixed and convertible into a common currency, can provide a much needed framework for national, fiscal and monetary discipline and consequently also for the expansion of investment and stable economic growth nationally as well as regionally.

Because of the differing economic circumstances in the CARICOM Region, however, it would not be possible to replace national currencies with a single Caribbean currency immediately in all the countries. An approach is therefore recommended which accommodates different country circumstances, but with a goal of a single currency for the whole Region, and with specified policies to bring it about within a short time-frame — about five years. Countries that are not able to move to the Caribbean dollar immediately would specify a time-frame not exceeding five years in which their monetary and fiscal policies would bring this about.

If the Caribbean currency is to be attractive and fulfil its proper role, it must have a stable US dollar value. The Caribbean dollar should be preferred to making the US dollar legal tender, because the introduction of the Caribbean dollar would mean that CARICOM countries will be freely exercising an area of their sovereignty on a joint basis in the interest of stimulating intra-regional trade and investment. The Region would also gain seigniorage from the issuance of its own currency and economise on the use of its scarce foreign exchange earnings.

While monetary union could be achieved without external support, its speedy achievement to enhance the integration process could be greatly helped by lines of credit and stabilisation loans. Short-term lines of credit, if necessary, from leading central banks with close relations with the Caribbean could help underpin the Caribbean currency to a stable US dollar value in the initial phase. In this context it is of interest to note that, at Poland's request, donor countries established a $1 billion currency stabilisation fund to support the Polish currency after the introduction of internal convertibility. Stabilisation loans can permit orderly and speedy movement towards a single currency by those countries unable to do so immediately. Movement at a good pace towards a single region-wide currency in an environment free of trade and exchange restrictions and a single market for goods and services could be greatly facilitated by the establishment, perhaps within the CDB, of a Caribbean Stabilisation and Adjustment Facility (CARISAF) with providing support from the World Bank, the Inter-American Development Bank and bilateral donors amongst others. Its main concerns would be with providing support for trade adjustment and currency stabilisation. The evolution of such a facility would be an important element of the common currency arrangements recommended, and the process may be started by the convertibility of regional currencies at the earliest possible stage as recommended in Chapter V.

The following is an outline of the recommended scheme:

1. The establishment under appropriate legal arrangements of an independent regional Caribbean Monetary Authority (CMA) which will issue the new Caribbean currency. The CMA would be under the control of an independent board of directors (free from political interference), appointed by CARICOM Heads from suitably qualified and experienced candidates from the public and private sectors. They would serve on a rotating basis. In addition, the CMA would be required to prepare and monitor fiscal, monetary and borrowing policies for members in Categories A and B as identified below. It could prepare forecasts and policy advice for all member Governments and it would supply public information on regional economic developments. Member countries would also agree on a common regulatory framework for financial institutions which would be superintended by the CMA.

2. All countries of CARICOM would accede to the CMA in one of two categories:

   a. Countries with a good record on stable exchange reserves (Category A countries) would be able to convert their national currencies into Caribbean dollars at a fixed rate and transfer their hard currency reserves to the CMA. A good record could be defined as maintenance of:
      - a stable US dollar value of the currency for 36 consecutive months, in a climate free of significant exchange restrictions;
      - a level of reserves equivalent to three months of imports for twelve consecutive months, without resort to significant abnormal external borrowing and indebtedness;
      - a level of projected debt service which does not rise above 15 per cent of exports.

OECS countries, because of their current single currency arrangement, could join *en bloc* into the new arrangement. The Caribbean dollar would be issued as soon as a minimum of 3 existing currency units, including either Jamaica or Trinidad and Tobago, meet the eligibility criteria.

    b. Other countries (Category B countries) would be required to introduce the Caribbean dollar for use in all regional transactions without restrictions. Financial institutions in these countries would be able to denominate deposit accounts and other financial assets in Caribbean dollars provided they were funded in Caribbean dollars or in hard currencies. They would have access to travellers cheques denominated in Caribbean dollars. Because of their deep-seated problems, these countries could adopt in a phased and targeted manner stricter monetary and fiscal policies. This would bring about step by step convertibility of their national currencies into the Caribbean dollar with eventual conversion to the single currency.

3. To achieve a stable US dollar value of the Caribbean currency, there would need to be strict limits on the power of the CMA to issue fiduciary money and to lend to Governments and Government institutions. Lending to financial institutions would be only via marketable securities and there could be no bail-out of bankrupt institutions. Members would undertake to abide by CMA advice on external borrowings. Such advice would be in the public domain and available to potential foreign lenders.

4. The existing CARICOM Conference of Central Banks, which meets twice yearly, should be institutionalised into a CARICOM System of Central Banks, (CSCB), to monitor progress towards achievement of performance targets for access to the CMA and to plan the establishment of the CMA.

Recommendations

1. that CARICOM Governments reiterate their intention to establish a common currency, as an essential part of the Single Market and Economy;

2. that such a common currency be introduced by those Member Countries which satisfy prescribed criteria, leaving the door open for others to join within a defined time period;

3. that a broadly based technical committee be appointed, including representatives from the private sector, to develop the detailed arrangements for the introduction of the common currency;

4. that the establishment of an independent Monetary Authority be an integral part of the process of launching the common currency;

5. that convertibility of regional currencies be secured at the earliest possible stage.

4. INVESTMENT, SAVINGS AND FINANCIAL INSTITUTIONS

Closer economic integration among the Member States of CARICOM, and the widening of economic and political cooperation between CARICOM and countries in the wider Caribbean, will create new opportunities for economic advancement for the cooperating states and enable them to achieve synergies in the mobilisation of financial resources. However, these benefits will be achieved only if the states, individually and collectively, take steps in both the real and financial sectors, to convert the considerable potential into a reality by undertaking an enlarged and more efficient investment effort directed towards diversifying the production base and increasing their capacity to compete in the evolving international market place. In this section, we discuss some of the issues in the mobilisation and allocation of savings which the countries and the Region will wish to address in order to enlarge the gains which integration and cooperation make possible.

A Higher Rate of Investment

Given the diseconomies of size, the occurrences of natural disasters and the large requirements for infrastructure investments, especially to open the potential for development which exists in Belize and Guyana, CARICOM countries need high gross investment rates, perhaps of the order of 25-30 per cent of the Gross Domestic Product or even more, and the diversion of a greater proportion of investment into the tradeable goods and services sectors, if a significant impact is to be made in reducing the high levels of unemployment and relaxing the foreign exchange bottleneck.

Other developing countries have achieved earnings and investment ratios of this order of magnitude as the data given below show:

	Gross National Savings / Gross National Product	Gross Investment / Gross National Product
	Averages 1975–1985 Per Cent	
High Growth Countries >7 per cent per year (7 countries)	28.0	28.6
Medium Growth Countries, 3–7 per cent per year (51 countries)	23.2	26.1
Low Growth Countries <3 per cent per year (22 countries)	19.0	19.0

(Source: World Development Report 1989)

Based on estimates prepared by the multilateral financial institutions, CARICOM countries have achieved savings ratios in excess of 20 per cent in recent years so that the target rate of savings and investment of 25-30 per cent GDP is reachable provided that public sector savings show a reasonable increase.

The Region has been able in the past to record an investment ratio larger than its savings ratio because it has received inflows of investment funds from the multilateral financial institutions, bilateral aid and direct private foreign investment. However, these sources of support, especially support from the multi-national financial institutions, have been declining. Finance from the major multilateral financial institutions (the World Bank, the International Monetary Fund, the Inter-American Development Bank) has not provided the Region with massive support even though the potential for a much greater contribution does exist. In fact, the participation of these institutions in recent years, when looked at in relation to their net transfers, has been negative; and even though, in the aggregate, the proportions to GDP are not massive, for some countries, e.g. Guyana and Jamaica, the negative flows are quite large. The negative flow was approximately US$246 million in 1987, US$131 million in 1988 and US$119 million in 1989. The reversal of these negative flows of net transfers requires, in the first place, a higher rate of net purchases or net disbursements which, in turn, depends on giving much greater attention to the preparation and execution of public investment programmes; and, in the second place, debt relief from the multilateral financial institutions. The latter encounters strong institutional resistance that CARICOM countries must collectively address. With regard to private flows, the Region as a whole has received net foreign direct investment flows, but the quantum in recent years has not been of significant size.

Higher Rate of National Savings Required

The point to be emphasised in relation to domestic and external financing is that all the countries are required to increase their investment ratios and direct more of this investment into the production of tradeable goods and services particularly for export. Three approaches are necessary. First, they must, without crowding out private sector investment, achieve a substantial increase in the rate of public sector savings in order to establish the basis for private sector development; second, establish the institutions and policies which will stimulate the use of private sector savings into more efficient production both regionally and locally; and, third, adopt policies which will raise the inflow of external capital to substantially higher levels than those recently achieved. In short, public sectors need to become more self-reliant, private sectors need to be more export-oriented in the use of investible resources, and the Region should become more self-assertive in the mobilisation and use of external resources.

The Importance of Sound Economic Policies

As the data suggest, the rates of private sector investment and private sector savings are not low by international standards. Yet there is an absence of dynamism in private sector businesses, particularly in relation to export growth. In general, it is the development of this internal business dynamism that has the greatest potential for promoting employment, exports and economic development. The design and implementation of policies to secure this private sector dynamism is a mammoth task. Private sectors in the Region are small; they lack the stimulus of internal competitiveness and tend instead towards collusive arrangements. Traditional production functions have limited stages in production processes and therefore limited access to the wider international markets. Diversification of production activities, either for internal consumption or for the external markets for intermediate and final products, is not readily achieved. The flexibility for private sector dynamism to move from loss-making areas to profitable alternatives is inhibited by a lack of profitable domestic alternatives. The education and training systems are still heavily influenced by classical and metropolitan imperatives rather than by domestic production options. Labour costs and other input costs are not generally sufficiently attractive to lure private direct foreign investment that is not associated with local capital. At the present time, the portfolio type of investment inflow is similarly inhibited.

These difficulties cannot be addressed by the conventional economic policies that are at present applied to the larger developing economies like Indonesia and Malaysia with already varied production systems. The policies which West Indian Governments must therefore adopt should demonstrate a commitment to maintaining a stable parity for the currency and should convince the population that such stability in the exchange rate is, and will remain, an important objective of national, and coordinated regional policy.

These policies relating to the stability of the exchange rate are also an essential underpinning of the movement towards a common currency. One aim of the associated price stability objective should be to provide an anchor from which labour productivity can be raised over both the short and the long term.

All of this requires that the tax systems be revamped to reduce inflationary biases; at the same time the fiscal systems must be strengthened to eliminate the money creation propensities inherent in Government borrowing from the Central Banks. The reduction of inflation and the strengthening of fiscal systems will underpin exchange rate policy. Improvement in revenues collected will allow Governments to invest in the human resources necessary for efficient production and to provide the surpluses for financing infrastructure that is evidently everywhere in need of improvement.

It needs to be reiterated that the centre-piece of these macroeconomic policies is a strengthened fiscal policy which must
- support a very tight exchange rate policy;
- finance the upgrading of manpower training;
- enhance physical infrastructure.

All these are to be achieved with an external tariff regime that reduces protection and stimulates competition from external sources to place some limit on the strong domestic tendencies to business collusion. Fiscal policy needs to be accompanied by a policy on wages that is performance related. Wages policy should be designed to allow wages to lag behind increases in productivity and allow increases in corporate savings for reinvestment. The combination of these economic policies will redirect private sector savings to the diversification and growth of production with an export orientation, and the resulting dynamism can impact favourably on external flows, particularly foreign direct investment and equity and venture capital funds, and produce a reversal of capital flight.

New Instruments to Mobilise Savings

Over and above the pursuit of sound macroeconomic policies which will increase public sector savings, Governments need to take other steps to encourage a larger national savings effort. In this connection, the Governments may wish to consider enlarging the scope and importance of collective savings efforts such as expanded social security schemes which have proven to be important contributors to the pool of national savings in countries in Asia. These devices should supplement other measures which countries in the Region have already adopted to encourage private savings — for example, Credit Unions, assistance towards home ownership, the discouragement of conspicuous consumption, especially of imported consumer durables, and enlarging share ownership in public companies in the Region. But the countries of the Region also have an obligation to mobilise foreign savings to increase domestic investment.

In order to tap into the international pool of savings, Governments of the Region are advised to re-examine the legislation relating to private foreign investment in order to ensure that the Region is not at a disadvantage in attracting private investment flows. But they may also wish to go beyond this and establish Equity and Venture Capital Funds in order to attract portfolio investment to, and from within, the Region. At their Intersessional Meeting in Kingston in 1992, the Heads of Government accepted the proposal for the operation of the Caribbean Investment Fund which had been proposed in the Commission's *Progress Report* to the Conference of Heads of Government at its Meeting in Basseterre, St. Kitts and Nevis in 1991. Urgent efforts should be made to get the Fund established, including the enactment of legislation for its operation.

The Caribbean Development Bank

High priority should be attached to effecting a substantial increase in the capacity of the Caribbean Development Bank (CDB) to enable that institution to raise capital in the international financial centres for on-lending to support national and regional projects, to upgrade human resources and enlarge the production and export base. We are glad to see that the CDB has arranged its first private placement in New York with an AAA rating.

The CDB has satisfied the criteria required of a soundly based development finance institution. It has provided professional economic analysis of the development issues which the countries of the Region must confront; given sound technical advice on the strategies which the individual countries of the Region and the Region as a whole should realistically adopt; demonstrated sensitivity and professionalism in shaping, financing and supervising the investments which it has made; and adhered to the canons of sound development finance practices.

The membership of the Bank has been broadened to include, in addition to the CARICOM Member States, the UK and Canada, three countries in Latin America (Venezuela, Colombia and Mexico) and three countries in Europe (France, Italy and Germany). The Bank has guided the borrowing Member Countries in satisfying the requirements of project lending financed largely by loan funds, and the quality of its portfolio of loans meets the stringent criteria which institutions of its kind must satisfy.

However, the capital base of the Bank is still relatively small and this acts as an obstacle to any effort it might make to access fully the international capital markets and so become the premier long term lending institution in the Region.

A stronger CDB, being closely acquainted with the shape, form and functions of the Region's production infrastructure (assets which the global and hemispheric institutions do not possess) is likely to impose conditions on its lending which will elicit the required positive response from the production system and better promote the growth and diversification of the economies of the Region on which their long term viability will rest. For these reasons, we advocate an enhanced role for the CDB in policy lending.

Reducing Capital Flight

It is our view that if the measures which we have outlined above are applied — and they are illustrative rather than exhaustive — the countries of the Region will be better able to cope with the phenomenon of capital flight. For the widening and unification of the regional market, the relaxation of exchange control regimes which will attend the creation of a single market, the fiscal discipline, the commitment to exchange rate stabilisation and the greater economic viability of the regional economy will assuage the concerns of those actors involved in capital flight and diminish the leakage which derives from this source. This form of additional strength will receive further buttressing from cooperation between CARICOM and the other states in the Caribbean Sea and its littoral. The stemming of capital flight must therefore attract positive action from the Governments of the Region.

In this connection, we draw attention to the positive net transfer of resources which was experienced by several Latin American countries in 1991, a year in which there was an unprecedented decline in the world production of goods and services. Inflows of productive capital into that region trebled in 1991, reaching a level of US$40 billion, compared with US$13.4 billion in 1990 and only US$4 billion in 1989. Much of the influx represented the return of flight capital sent abroad in the 1970s and 1980s. There is a lesson in this for the CARICOM countries which would involve giving special attention to attracting back flight capital and making the investment environment more conducive for nationals living abroad.

Savings in the Diaspora

Equally, on the other hand, since it is unrealistic to attempt to insulate the Region from the wider world, especially in today's telecommunications revolution, the Region could derive benefit from promoting a reverse flow of funds through adopting special devices for the purpose, which would attract portfolio investments and other forms of foreign exchange flows from the rest of the world. The creation of Equity and Venture Capital Funds, which we have mentioned earlier, is one of these devices. But there is one further source into which CARICOM countries can tap; this is the diaspora. The consultations which we have had with West Indians in the diaspora, in the United Kingdom, in Canada and in the United States, have impressed upon us that there is potential capital for investment to be mobilised in these countries through the opening of branch banks and facilities for the retailing of commercial and Government securities in the principal concentrations of West Indians in the diaspora. Indeed, the several people in the diaspora who appeared before us, or who presented papers on West Indian economic integration, stressed the imperative that Governments in the Region should define the integration movement in two dimensions: the first is the geographical dimension, involving the islands and countries in the Caribbean Sea and its littoral; the second is the demographic dimension, that is, the additional economic space and opportunity which have been created by the existence of a large concentration of West Indians who have created new lives and livelihoods for themselves and their families in foreign lands, but who maintain a deep and abiding interest in the growth and development of the unified Region. We are convinced that the adoption of specific steps to mobilise for the development of the Region the creative skills and the financial capital which residents in the diaspora possess will materially enhance the investment and production effort which the countries of the Region, and the Region as a collective unit, can mount in the years ahead.

It may well be the case that the establishment of appropriate institutions in the diaspora to harness the savings and investment potential which resides there may require the collective efforts of several of the regional financial institutions and the active support of the Governments. We can see no good reason why such cooperation should not be encouraged. Indeed, since two of the important watchwords for future economic planning for the countries of the Region are "cooperation" and an "outward-looking orientation", this kind of activity holds the potential of an acceptable return for the effort.

Institutional Strengthening

Capital Markets Development

Capital markets are a principal source of investment capital in the industrialised and in the fast-growing developing countries; they also act as a spur to management to strive after rising levels of production, productivity and profitability. In the light of the imperative to increase the pool of investible funds in the Region and to become and remain competitive in international markets, the countries should attach high priority to developing their capital markets to mobilise savings from small and large investors; for these markets satisfy the small investor's need for investment and liquidity. Employees' Stock Ownership Plans (ESOPs) which have been introduced in a few firms in the Region are more likely to be acceptable to workers if a market for such securities is available. We note that legislation to introduce ESOPs is being considered in Trinidad and Tobago.

By and large, capital markets in the Caribbean are narrow and poorly developed. A market for securities exists in only a few countries of the Region and only a handful of companies have their securities listed on the exchange. Trading is therefore limited and the thinness of the market gives rise to concerns about insider trading. Economic information and financial analyses of the performance and prospects of business in general, and of the quoted companies in particular, are sparse. In 1991 cross trading in securities was introduced among the exchanges in Barbados, Jamaica and Trinidad and Tobago, but the volume has been severely restricted because of balance of payments constraints. Governments, however, must recognise that there is a symbiosis between capital market development and increasing sophistication in the organisation and transaction of business. Such sophistication is an essential prerequisite for achieving and sustaining competitiveness in the international market place which holds the key to economic survival of the countries of the Region and the Region as a whole.

As pointed out above, as well, capital markets offer an additional mechanism for increasing the pool of savings and for democratising business enterprises. It behoves the Governments therefore to take steps to foster the growth of such markets.

Perhaps the most important requirement in this regard which the Governments can satisfy is the establishment of a proper legal institutional framework. This, along with closer monitoring, achieved through the requirement of quarterly and half-yearly accounts, containing adequate disclosure of the quoted firms, is necessary to increase investor confidence. The stockbrokers and analysts should also see a need to publish, for general public information, professional analyses of the performance of listed enterprises and of business generally. A relaxation of exchange control would increase portfolio investment and allow a linkage between CARICOM and the diaspora, and this should be pursued.

Finally, we believe that there is merit in the suggestion advanced during the Workshops that Governments should at least equalise tax rates between interest on savings deposits and earnings from securities.

In the light of the financial scandals which have occurred in the capital markets in some industrialised countries, there is clearly justification for advancing in this area with circumspection. But circumspection does not mean inaction in the area of developing the capital markets of the Region which do provide important supplementary assistance in enlarging the savings pool.

Supervising and Regulating Deposit-Taking Institutions

The commercial banks, with their networks of branch banks located strategically in the different geographical areas, have dominated the deposit collection function in the countries of the Region. They have all but replaced the traditional forms of savings, i.e. the sou-sou, the money-lenders and the Friendly Societies which still, however, assume importance for the small saver. The commercial banks collect deposits, maintain their liquidity through a judicious blending of short-term lending largely on a revolving basis, and provide a limited range of financial advice to their clients.

More recently, new types of financial institutions have risen to some degree of prominence on the landscape. These are the Non-Bank Financial Institutions (NFIs), Savings and Loan Associations (which have been significant in Jamaica for a long time) and Unit Trust Corporations. These institutions provide an array of assets distinguishable from the commercial banks in terms of liquidity, safety and returns and cater for the ever-changing needs of the saver.

Studies in CARICOM have shown that these institutions have deflected some savings from the traditional commercial banks; but they have also increased the savings rates especially among small savers. Further, because the deposits which these institutions collect are usually longer term than those in the commercial banks, they are able to offer long term facilities to borrowers and hence, facilitate long-term fixed investment.

The insurance companies, both long-term and general, have long been associated with long-term investment. However, their participation in the capital market has largely been in the area of fixed interest-bearing securities, since the legislation regulating the activities of these institutions has limited the extent of their participation in the equity market. During our consultations, the case was presented for a review of the traditional criteria governing the administration of these entities, particularly in the light of the demonstrable need for companies with enlarged bases who have the financial depth and strength to enter the export market.

During the last fifteen years or so, the credit unions have begun to assume an increasingly prominent role among the deposit collecting institutions, and they receive the active support of the Governments of the Region. Indeed, in the Southern Caribbean, some credit unions now exceed the financial strength of the smaller commercial banks, a development which has brought to the fore the imperative of proper management structures in the credit unions and more effective supervision of their lending activities in order to give greater assurance to depositors in these institutions.

In considering the question of depositor protection, it is important to take note of the following:

- Several Savings and Loan Associations in industrialised countries have become insolvent, with the attendant costs on the depositor and the taxpayer;
- Bank failures in the Caribbean, although not widespread, have been known to happen;
- Economic and financial planning in the Region has to face up to the reality that the investor/management class, although growing, is still relatively thin, so that there is a considerable amount of crisscrossing in the ownership and management of business enterprises;

These and other characteristics of the financial market would indicate a need for close supervision of the financial institutions in order to give reasonable protection to the depositor and hence reinforce the savings ethic. At the same time, it is necessary to allow adequate flexibility to the financial institutions to enable them to respond creatively to the changing demands of savers and borrowers alike. In the case of commercial banks, the Savings and Loans Associations and the other Non-Bank Financial Institutions, there is a strong case to be argued that compulsory deposit insurance schemes should be instituted, and that inspection should be carried out, not so much to ensure that the institutions comply with the regulations which Governments impose from time to time, but mainly to assure the superintending bodies that the management is efficient and following prudent financial practices and is keeping the population adequately informed.

In view of the growth in the number and size of credit unions, it appears necessary to review the legislation relating to supervision and management and prescribe guidelines for the distribution of their lending and loan recovery practices.

In the case of the insurance companies, in the light of the need to enlarge the corporate sector and of the significant role which these companies play in mobilising long term savings, Governments should examine carefully ways of prudently enlarging the role of insurance companies in the ownership of equity in publicly owned companies.

As a general principle, we believe that savers/depositors should be prepared to strike a balance between risk and returns, and that the regulations relating to the protection of depositors should also reflect this choice.

Debt Relief

But it is unrealistic to expect that the national pool of freely disposable savings will be adequate to sustain the desired level of capital investment as long as the countries of the Region continue to be overburdened by the heavy weight of international debt. Many countries of the Region now have to commit in excess of 30 per cent of their export earnings, and a higher proportion of Government revenues, just to service their official and guaranteed foreign public debt; this is taking place in a context in which the countries have to import a large proportion of the technology which their production systems require and many of the essential services which they need; for example, insurance, transportation, and certain areas of higher education have to be purchased from abroad.

Over and above this, the countries must finance a significant outflow of funds in the form of dividends and management fees to foreign firms. The Governments of the Region must therefore collectively press for an adequate measure of debt relief, at least to change the present situation where outflows to the multilateral institutions and the international commercial banks exceed inflows by a sizeable margin. The negotiation of debt relief, including debt to the multilateral institutions, must therefore remain high on the regional agenda if the essential underpinnings of integration — freedom of movement of capital, goods and labour, the establishment of a common currency, and a unified regional regime in trade and payments with the rest of the world, are to have a fair chance of producing their beneficial effects.

A significant proportion of the Region's external debt is owed to the Multilateral Financial Institutions and to bilateral lenders including the export credit agencies to these countries. We recommend that the Region should continue to mobilise efforts to persuade the MFIs to grant significant debt relief in respect of debt owed to them by small developing countries. In the interim, efforts should be directed to securing an increase in net disbursements by the MFIs to the Region to a level higher than the one half of one per cent of GDP which CARICOM countries now receive. In addition, the IMF should be asked to expand the coverage of the Structural Adjustment Facility (SAF) and the Enhanced Structural Adjustment Facility (ESAF) to include small lower-middle income countries whose debt service profiles are similar to those of the low-income countries which are now eligible under these facilities. Finally, the Region should collectively request bilateral lenders to follow the example of Canada and write off a significant proportion of the official debt and export credits which all Member States now owe to them.

The Allocation of Capital

The transformation of the economies of the Region requires a substantial and sustained infusion of long term capital into industrial and commercial enterprises oriented towards the export market. Government policy must promote this infusion. In this connection, a number of obstacles have to be overcome; some of these are listed below.

Historically, most of the countries, being largely appendages of a metropolitan economy, have produced what they do not consume and conversely consume what they do not produce; there is a large import content even in basic foods which the population consumes. This pattern of production and consumption has had its mirror effect in the orientation of the financing practices evident in the countries of the Region. The production of staples and minerals geared to export markets has been financed by externally based financial institutions; the local financial sector has been concerned largely with providing funds for imported consumer goods and has, in consequence, developed only very weak linkages with the production sector.

The fall-out of the historical development has also been that the commercial banks, the principal source of financing, have become risk averse and are more comfortable with short-term financing. Few of the banking institutions have developed an in-house capability to appraise and analyse investment projects in manufacturing or large scale agriculture, or even in the important service sector such as Tourism. This makes development and transformation excessively dependent, for both ideas and finance, on external sources, increasingly the multilateral financial agencies — which often incorporate assumptions not directly in tune with the mores and culture of the recipient country.

Avoiding Crowding Out

The risk aversion which the local financial sector displays also results in an excessive preoccupation with the security for, rather than the economic viability of, the loan or the contribution which it can make to the development process. In consequence, even where the institutions are prepared to lend on a long term basis, they show a marked preference for Government securities. Private enterprises are, therefore, either crowded out or are forced to make use of revolving credit which entrenches a short term planning horizon. However, in one country in the Region, arrangements have been concluded between the development banks and the commercial banks which allow the latter to engage in long-term lending. That experiment deserves careful study by the other countries in the Region.

Instruments to Improve the Allocation of Savings

We have already drawn attention to the need for Governments to pursue sound macroeconomic policies which ensure that they do not preempt an excessively large proportion of the available savings. But a case has been repeatedly argued before us during the consultations, that the Governments should go beyond this and adopt policies which direct the available credit into productive activity with an emphasis on manufacturing industry and services with an export orientation.

However, in this area of the central direction of credit, the traditional policy instrument, i.e. selective credit controls, has not been very effective in CARICOM countries. The experience has been that greater success is achievable through direct interest subsidies, improving the institutional framework and human resource development.

In the area of interest subsidies, the evidence is that favourable discount rates for loans to preferred activities and for pre- and post-export shipments have produced positive results. More generally, there is a consensus that exporters in developing countries should not be required to bear effective interest rates which are higher than those which their competitors in the importing countries have to shoulder, and this fact should inform Government policy. It is, in many respects, a source of concern that the current trend of policy in this area of interest rates is in the reverse direction; this trend will not assist in the transformation of the Region's economies.

In dealing with the improvement of the institutional framework, Governments in the Region would wish to direct attention to three separate, but related issues. The first is the establishment of institutions which will provide the range of financial services which modern business requires; this varies depending on the type of business and the stage of development of particular enterprises in the sector. The second is the scale of operations. It may well transpire that the volume of localised business which is available may not be adequate to enable institutions to operate profitably at an economic cost to the user of the service; Governments of the Region must therefore be prepared to facilitate the establishment of Region-wide business enterprises providing financial and related consultant services to producing enterprises. The third, which derives from the second, is the harmonisation of rules and regulations across the Region, to which institutions providing financial advice and other services must comply.

Management Development

At the end of the day, however, whatever the institutional framework and the set of rules which may be prescribed, it is the quality of the human agent in both the doing and the regulating agency which matters. If the Region intends to establish the financial infrastructure which an expanding production system requires, then it must be able to call upon the requisite expertise to manage it. Most of the Governments of CARICOM have embarked upon programmes of localisation of the principal financial institutions and this, while producing certain gains, has removed the experienced technical back-up which supported the local activities of the institutions which were transferred, by a sale of shares, to local hands. But there is no substitute for experience, and this can only be acquired in real life situations; it cannot be acquired through formal teaching.

The financial infrastructure of the individual countries of the Region, and the Region as a whole, will not be able to play its full role in mobilising and allocating financial savings in a commercially optimal manner unless it is operated by personnel with the required blend of formal training, commitment to nation building and regional development, and experience in the intricacies of financial management. This has been an important gap in the approach to development which the countries have adopted — as a general rule they have not made extensive use of the processes by which qualified nationals have been attached to large institutions abroad where they could learn the 'tricks of the trade'. The experience of the fast growing countries of Asia indicates that this is a productive course of action to pursue. We believe that the Governments of CARICOM should follow this course of action.

In general, policy and action in the Region in the future must be guided by the reality that finance is the lifeblood of the complex economic systems which characterise the modern day world economy. The institutions through which finance flows constitute an indispensable part of a healthy economic system and these institutions link umbilically the domestic and regional economy to the rest of the world. The maintenance of growth in Caribbean economies therefore requires efficiently functioning financial institutions which will sustain confidence and which, as a result, will optimise the savings pool available to the country and the Region and allocate the pool in the manner which will optimise national and regional welfare over the long term. Governments of the Region have the obligation to put in place the rules by which the financial system will function but, at the same time, they must allow adequate flexibility in its operation in order to enhance benefits for savers and borrowers alike. The improvement of the quality of the human agents involved in operating the financial system must be accorded as much weight as legislative provisions which are designed to entrench sound financial practices by the institutions.

Recommendations

1. that CARICOM Governments set as their target the achievement of an investment ratio of 25–30 per cent of the Gross Domestic Product;

2. that Governments take steps to ensure that the regime for attracting private foreign investment is competitive with those which other developing and developed countries have introduced;

3. that Governments enter into negotiations to reverse the present net transfer of funds to the multilateral financial institutions;

4. that Governments pursue sound overall policies which generate current account surpluses, avoid borrowing from the Central Banks, curb the rate of inflation to levels no higher than those prevailing in their principal trading partners, advance systematically towards stabilising a common currency and demonstrate an unmistakable commitment to the maintenance of parity of the currency;

5. that all sectors of the society make greater efforts to increase national savings. In that context, Governments should

adopt new policies which could include enlarging collective savings schemes, such as enhanced National Insurance Systems. Additionally, they should encourage the establishment of Equity and Venture Capital Funds and enact the legislation relating to the Caribbean Investment Fund;

6. that Governments strengthen the surveillance machinery over existing deposit collecting institutions and require adequate deposit insurance;

7. that Governments take steps to increase the capital of the Caribbean Development Bank and thereby strengthen the capability to raise funds on the international market for on-lending in the Region;

8. that Governments provide the necessary support to financial institutions to establish facilities for mobilising savings of West Indians living abroad;

9. that Governments, together with the private sector, establish the legal, institutional and information infrastructure to enable modern development of the capital markets;

10. that Governments, collectively and in concert with other like-minded countries, press for significant debt relief from the multilateral institutions, bilateral donors and the official export credit agencies; and for the IMF to enlarge the coverage of the SAF and the ESAF to include small middle income countries whose debt service profiles are similar to those of countries which are now eligible.

5. EASE OF TRAVEL AND FREEDOM OF MOVEMENT

Fundamental to both the potential and the problems of the Caribbean are its geographical location and disposition.

The Member States of CARICOM extend in an arc from Belize on the Central American mainland, through the Bahamas, to the north-westernmost end of the archipelago of Caribbean islands, to Trinidad and Tobago in the south-east, and are finally anchored on the South American mainland by Guyana. On the positive side, this Region constitutes a natural link between North and South America, enjoys the distinct advantage of proximity to the world's largest and still growing market and most substantial source of investment, capital and technology; and straddles both the air routes and sea lanes through which a preponderance of the world's traffic in both people and goods circulates.

Separateness the Challenge, Togetherness the Ambition

Endowed as the Caribbean is with all the attributes of a successful destination for tourism, the world's fastest growing industry, with undoubted agricultural and mineral resources, and with a people rich and resilient in its cultural diversity, it is increasingly clear that in order to establish advantageous relationships with the wider world what now needs to be recognised and nurtured is a regional identity to which that wider world can sensibly relate at a time when political and economic groupings of meaningful proportions are increasingly the prerequisites for survival and growth.

On the negative side is the reality that, given the increasing costs and inherent difficulties of intra-regional travel and communications, the Caribbean Sea unfortunately still divides the countries of the Region at least as much as it unites them. Historically, this reality has given rise to what has been, for want of a better term, labelled as an 'island mentality'; a mentality which has sometimes fostered rank ignorance to the extent that until relatively recently some West Indians would refer to Guyana as a "small island" — this notwithstanding the fact that in terms of land area Guyana is several times larger than Jamaica.

When the definition of the Region is extended to encompass the wider Caribbean equally divisive forces of linguistic differences and of colonial history are added to those which bedevil the English-speaking Caribbean. However, the Commission is in no doubt that these latter forces are to some extent mitigated by the fact that the countries of the wider Caribbean share a common cultural bedrock in much the same way as they are geologically anchored on a common continental shelf. During consultations with the people of the CARICOM Member States and with West Indians in the diaspora, one view that has been consistently and sometimes vociferously expressed is a recognition that "we are one people". The Calypsonian Black Stalin struck a responsive chord which had resonance throughout the Region some years ago in his "Caribbean Man" in which he reminded the people of the West Indies that from the early beginnings of Caribbean society "we made the same trip on the same ship".

This is no doubt an oversimplification of sorts, but the underlying message is nonetheless clear. At the beginning of the final decade of the 20th Century the people of the West Indies have repeatedly and consistently told the West Indian Commission that the logic of, and the need for, much closer togetherness and a more tightly knit family relationship are impatient of debate. Caught as CARICOM is today between rapidly deepening social and economic stresses and strains within the Region and the ever-increasing pressures from external developments and realities, West Indians have a clear sense that in order to survive the Region had better get its act together, and quickly, as time is certainly not on its side.

In putting the case to the Commission only a few had articulated the extent, form, or structure of the closer unity being called for and fewer still have proposed that the federal experiment be revisited. Instead all that the Commission has heard from the people is designed to fit within a contextual framework of the collective exercise of sovereignty. The desirable and acceptable degree of structures of unity raise fundamental and weighty issues of both concept and substance which are addressed elsewhere in this Report.

Problems and Opportunities

It is in this framework that we attempt to address the widely perceived and expressed need for greater ease of travel throughout the Region and greater freedom of movement for the people who ultimately constitute a key factor of production. What is being dealt with here is the repeatedly voiced insistence of the people all over the Region on the elimination of all the hassle and humbug that appears to be reserved for West Indians moving from place to place within what they regard as their regional homeland.

In virtually every CARICOM Member State there have been expressions of deep resentment at the multiplicity of forms and documentation which CARICOM nationals are called upon to produce in moving around the Region. This situation stands out in bolder relief in a tourism-oriented Region in which travellers of extra-regional origin are generally welcomed and accorded fast-track treatment at the same Caribbean ports of entry and more often than not with a minimum of required documentation. Unfortunately, what are regarded as anachronistic regulations have over time tended to encourage negative attitudes on the part of the immigration personnel in exercising their authority at the ports of entry. The result is as often as not a chicken-and-egg situation in which the CARICOM traveller arrives at a port of entry anticipating discriminatory treatment and the immigration officer is programmed to ensure that the visitor is not disappointed in his or her expectations.

The resultant resentment and frustration is exacerbated by the need to obtain and travel with a multiplicity of currencies, including the United States dollar which is seen as the most acceptable currency in the absence of a common currency for, or convertibility of currencies in, the Region.

The problems of intra-regional travel are of course still further compounded by what the people regard as the relatively exorbitant cost of such travel and the weakening sea and air links within the Region in certain respects over the past three decades. West Indians find it difficult to understand why it is often less expensive to fly from some point in the Region to the northern metropolitan centres than it is to fly between the capitals of the Caribbean countries. They are duly regaled in advertisements on satellite television with intercontinental and transcontinental airfares which are less than intra-regional fares relating to substantially reduced distances.

The older generations of West Indians recall with nostalgia the days of the 'Federal Palm' and the 'Federal Maple' when they not only had an affordable, rewarding and enriching opportunity of getting to know the places and people of the West Indies at first hand but also often forged friendships which have endured over the years. In a very special way the intra-regional travellers of the '50s and '60s have come to regard the two Federal boats, alas now defunct, as second only to the University of the West Indies as vehicles for overcoming the sense of separateness which has been the legacy of the Region to this day.

The business community and others who find it necessary to move up and down the Region recall with equal nostalgia that in the sixties it was possible to fly nonstop from Kingston to Port-of-Spain on the 'CARIFTA Clipper' in two and a half hours, or from Jamaica to Haiti or the Dominican Republic in approximately one hour. In the days of CARIFTA the people of Belize could make their southbound connections in Jamaica, obviating the irksome and often problematic necessity to travel through Miami with its own brand of hassle, not the least being the need to apply for a United States visa in order to move from one point of the Caribbean to another — a situation which obtains today. In the more recent past there was a scheduled thrice weekly nonstop flight between Barbados and Jamaica which meant that travel between those two countries was reduced to a little over two hours' flying time. Alas, this rapid air link has now gone the way of its predecessors.

All over the Region the young people deeply lament the difficulties in the way of getting to know each other better, and the steady increase in intra-regional airfares is a factor making travel well nigh impossible for sporting, social or touring teams and groups, and putting student exchange visits well beyond the reach of the majority of young West Indians. The same unfortunately holds good for intra-regional travel as it relates to women's associations, religious groups, non-governmental organisations and cultural groups, and indeed for West Indians who simply wish to spend their vacation getting to know their Region better.

As a result of the consistently strong feelings expressed by the people of the Region throughout the Commission's series of consultations, the matter of travelling in the Region was one of the six areas recommended by the West Indian Commission to CARICOM Heads of Government at their meeting in July 1991 for immediate action. At the Summit Meeting in Basseterre, St. Kitts and Nevis,

CARICOM Heads accepted the urgent need to facilitate 'hassle-free' travel and freedom of movement of CARICOM nationals within the Region, and expressed recognition of the fact that due attention should be paid to the needs of hucksters and higglers who account for an important part of intra-regional trade.

Implementing Our Aspirations

The Third Inter-sessional Meeting of CARICOM Heads of Government held in Kingston, Jamaica, in February 1992, noted marked progress in efforts to facilitate intra-regional travel. The Governments of Belize, Grenada, Guyana, Jamaica, Montserrat, St. Kitts and Nevis, Saint Lucia and Trinidad and Tobago were able to report that legislation and other administrative measures had either been implemented or were in train to facilitate ease of travel. Those CARICOM Member Governments which had not at that time taken action undertook to do so before the CARICOM Heads of Government Meeting scheduled for July 1992. At the time of finalising this Report (mid-May, 1992) much remains undone.

In addition, by May 1992 Belize, Grenada, Guyana, Jamaica, St. Kitts and Nevis, Saint Lucia and Trinidad and Tobago had introduced a separate line at ports of entry designated "Citizens, Residents and CARICOM Nationals" or were in the process of introducing such a facility. Again, those countries which had not yet done so gave an undertaking to take similar action before July 1992.

It has also been agreed that throughout the Region there would be orientation programmes for Immigration and other relevant officials to familiarise them with the new policies and arrangements designed to ease intra-regional travel. Looking to the immediate future, with the participation of the regional private sector, arrangements would be developed to encourage exchange visits within the Community with an emphasis on exchanges between secondary school students and for the purpose of facilitating cultural and other sporting events. These latter arrangements are essentially for the second phase of the programme and should in no way be permitted to delay immediate implementation of the first phase scheduled for completion by July 1992.

The West Indian Commission would be lacking in its duty if it did not give due recognition here to the leadership role of the Government of Grenada, which initiated action towards achieving greater ease of travel within the Region simultaneously at the level of the Organisation of East Caribbean States (OECS) and of CARICOM as a whole. Nevertheless, care has to be taken to ensure that the Governments of the Region do not relax their efforts and fall into the trap of settling for immediate perception rather than dealing with the longer term realities. Such progress as has been achieved in making intra-regional travel easier for CARICOM nationals, while undoubtedly laudable in itself, is but the beginning of a far more significant and meaningful process.

In recognition of this fact the West Indian Commission in its Progress Report to CARICOM Heads of Government in July 1991 also recommended that a start be made with the free movement of CARICOM nationals beginning with all graduates of the University of the West Indies (UWI) and other recognised institutions and duly accredited media workers. This latter category was included in response to the Commission's view that 'communications' is essential to community and that the right of West Indian journalists to be assigned anywhere within the Region will significantly enlarge the capacity to improve communication and advance the realisation of the aims of the Community.

The logic of freedom of movement for all categories of West Indian professionals, skilled personnel and workers generally, and entrepreneurs including higglers and hucksters, will have to be permitted to work itself through the system. In much the same way as the manufacturers and producers of the Region have come to regard the Caribbean Common Market as a widened domestic market, the people of the Region are now pressing for a wider field for ambition without necessarily having to seek their fortune beyond its boundaries. West Indians are now signalling their desire to be able to practice their professions and make their skills available throughout the length and breadth of CARICOM. In our Chapter on Economic Issues (Chapter V) we elaborate on this matter and make some specific suggestions.

It is therefore important to take note of the fact that CARICOM Heads of Government are now committed, as an important part of the regional response to recent international trends and developments, to the establishment of a Single Market and Economy by 1994. Such a commitment must in the final analysis assume the free movement of all the factors of production throughout the Region. The free movement of goods assumes the removal of all remaining barriers to intra-regional trade; a significant start has been made towards increasingly free movement of capital by the introduction of cross-trading of securities on the stock exchanges of Barbados, Trinidad & Tobago and Jamaica; and free movement of people, the labour force, cannot be allowed to lag behind.

In terms of decisions and actions taken by CARICOM Governments since July 1991, the Government of Guyana in February 1992 informed the Inter-sessional Meeting of CARICOM Heads of Government of its decision to allow CARICOM nationals who are graduates of the UWI and the UG to travel freely, practice their vocation and, if necessary, settle in Guyana, with effect from March 31, 1992. Legislation to that effect has since been enacted. That Meeting was also informed of approval by the Government of Jamaica for graduates of the UWI and UG to travel freely and work in Jamaica. The Governments of Barbados, Grenada, and St. Kitts and Nevis indicated approval in principle of these measures and undertook to take steps to implement the necessary arrangements at the earliest opportunity. In the meantime, the matter of free movement of skills continues to be addressed by an Inter-Ministerial Committee led by Guyana and comprising representatives from Dominica, Grenada, Guyana and Trinidad & Tobago. We are making progress in an area of fundamental importance to the reality of 'Community'.

Studies relating to future survival strategies for CARICOM point to the fact that the key for the Region lies in its human resources and the pooling of those resources. Freedom of movement within the Region for CARICOM nationals is therefore a central strategy for achieving this goal and freedom of movement is not new within the Commonwealth Caribbean Region as, particularly within the Eastern Caribbean, there is a history of movement of primarily male unskilled labour to destinations offering employment and economic opportunity. Additionally, there has also been a movement of professional and quasi-professional personnel throughout the Region dating as far back as the colonial civil service. What is clear is that Caribbean migrants moving within the Region do not move randomly. Migrants move to destinations which offer employment and educational opportunities and where a support network exists. Where employment opportunities contract, migrants tend to waste no time in moving to other destinations.

Beyond all these short-term horizons, however, the Region now has to anticipate greater movement of hucksters or traders and perhaps just as importantly, a new surge in intra-CARICOM tourism which is increasingly being seen by the regional tourist industry as possessing considerable potential for complementarity to the seasonal extra-regional tourist market.

Among the outstanding matters now requiring attention, the Commission lists elimination of the necessity for work permits for CARICOM nationals; the elimination of anomalies in immigration and citizenship legislation governing spouses and children of nationals; the active encouragement by both public and private sector of exchange programmes and travel among farmers, school children and community leaders, and among other groups.

Within the context of the emerging Single Market and Economy the Commission is satisfied that the old bogies of invasion of peoples from other territories are not only anachronistic but are indeed ill-founded. Few West Indians, if any, will be leaving their corner of the West Indian homeland to relocate elsewhere unless the free play of market forces and the law of supply and demand indicate that it is prudent for them so to do. Those inclined to take the plunge out of desperation are far more likely to go for broke in terms of migrating to the more traditional metropolitan destinations. In the move from Community and Common Market to Community, Single Market and Economy, it is inevitable that greater ease of travel by CARICOM nationals throughout the Region should be accompanied by increasingly greater freedom of movement of such nationals wishing to work in parts of the Region other than the country of their birth. That will remain an important goal for us to reach as we deepen the process of integration.

In summary, the fundamental recommendation is that CARICOM Governments, in recognition of the imperatives of the Single Market and Economy to which they are already committed, and the urgent need to achieve both critical mass and mobility in respect of the region's greatest asset, its human resources, should proceed systematically with the amendment of legislation and regulatory instruments which may be required to clear the way towards achieving the implementation of decisions already taken by CARICOM Heads of Government.

Recommendations

1. that there be the earliest implementation throughout CARICOM of recommendations, already adopted, for ensuring:

    - 'hassle free' travel for West Indians within the Region;

    - a single line at airports for "Citizens, Residents and CARICOM Nationals"

    - that West Indian graduates of UWI and other designated Universities and media personnel should have the right to live and work anywhere in the Region — as a start in the process towards mobility of people within the CARICOM Single Market.

2. that the implementation of the measures listed above be seen as the initial steps towards the full freedom of movement of people, an essential pillar for the establishment of the Single Market and Economy, on which the Heads of Government have already agreed.

CHAPTER V

ECONOMIC ISSUES

1. EXPORT-LED GROWTH

In this section we briefly review the trade performance of CARICOM countries over the recent past; define the conditions for promoting export-led growth; comment on the benefits to CARICOM of intra-CARICOM, intra-Caribbean and extra-regional trade; identify for development and growth the manufacturing, service and agri-business sectors as the sectors to promote growth; identify the pathways to the development financing needed in the Region, and conclude with a set of recommendations.

These matters have engaged our attention as a Commission from the outset, and they influence much that we have to say in this chapter on economic issues. They focus very largely on the role of the productive sector and, therefore, of the business community, but we make it clear at the outset that these private sector roles do not wholly displace responsibilities that Governments must acknowledge and fulfil.

Decisions to increase exports, to diversify their product composition and market destinations are essentially medium- to long-term strategic decisions requiring the full involvement of both Governments and the private sector. Through a continuing process of interaction and confidence building, the government/private sector dialogue and the policy action that will flow from it can create an environment in which exports can flourish. Although decisions to increase exports or to diversify them are implemented at the level of the individual firm, it is necessary that Governments get the business environment right in terms of putting into place the mix of incentives and support measures that would favour achievement of agreed goals.

Trade Performance

The deteriorating export performance of CARICOM economies over the past twenty years must be a cause of great concern to the Governments and policy makers of the Region. Exports from CARICOM to third countries are concentrated in the agricultural and mining sectors. Within those sectors, the exports of most CARICOM countries are dominated by one or two commodities. Bananas, for example, account for almost 50 per cent of the total exports of the Windward Islands, and in Trinidad and Tobago petroleum accounts for more than 60 per cent of total exports. In Jamaica and Guyana, bauxite and alumina exports accounted for 34 per cent and 37 per cent respectively of merchandise exports in 1990.

This failure to diversify is unfortunately not a function of outstanding performance by the one or two commodities emphasised by each country. In fact, the reverse is true. Over the period 1979 to 1988, the average annual rate of growth for merchandise exports of the 'four" were as shown in the table below:

Average Annual Merchandise Export GrowthRates
1979 to 1988(Current US Dollar Equivalent)

Country	Annual Average Growth Rate
Barbados	+ 1.0
Guyana	− 1.0
Jamaica	− 1.9
Trinidad and Tobago	− 4.2

These four countries, over the same period, also experienced a deterioration in their terms of trade and, except for Trinidad and Tobago, their already small manufacturing sectors experienced negative growth rates greater than that for all of their merchandise exports. In other words, while exports generally declined, the export of manufactured products declined even more.

The rate of growth of merchandise exports for the OECS countries on the other hand was approximately 10 per cent over the period 1985 to 1989, but, despite this growth rate, imports continued to exceed exports and the negative balance of visible trade worsened from EC$1,027 million in 1985 to EC$1,861 million in 1989. In other words, imports continued to play a much greater role than exports. A part of the increase, however, can be attributed to the expansion of tourism.

This overall poor performance is even more disturbing when it is realised that both bananas and sugar benefit significantly from special preferential treatment under the Lomé Convention. Whatever the prospects for continued benefits in the short-term, there is concern that the CARICOM Region could experience a reduction in the Lomé benefits over the longer term following the integration of the European Community into a single market in 1993.

The Region was also supposed to have benefitted from the Caribbean Basin Initiative (CBI) as well as CARIBCAN. The performance described above suggests that such benefits have been less than expected. Not surprisingly, it has forced the Region to rethink and redesign the strategies necessary to increase intra-regional trade and exports from the Region. This has led to a general consensus on the importance of promoting export-led growth.

Promoting Export-led Growth

Because of the small size of the Region and the small size of our firms it is especially important that no obstacles be placed in the way of firms mobilising capital for investment which will earn foreign exchange. Put differently, there must be *mobility of capital* within CARICOM. This free movement of capital is necessary to allow the firms of the Region to undertake joint ventures in production as well as marketing and so obtain the benefits of economies of scale that will flow from such investment.

Mobility of capital requires, at the minimum, currency convertibility within CARICOM, and we urge CARICOM Governments to take urgently the necessary steps to ensure that their respective currencies are freely convertible with each other. This step is not as bold as it sounds when we note the relatively small proportion (less than 10 per cent of total exports) of intra-regional trade to total trade. Elsewhere, we have advocated convertibility as a stipulation towards the introduction of a common currency. While we regard a common currency as the ideal, we stress that without at

least free convertibility on the way towards it the firms of the Region will be unable to:
- freely come together to produce the larger blocks of capital necessary for undertaking particular investments;
- freely and quickly purchase inputs for their exports from within the Region;
- develop the markets of the Region with the full assurance that they will be paid promptly, particularly in situations where currencies are undergoing significant devaluation.

Trading Houses

From time to time, a number of commentators have urged on the Region the development of major trading houses similar for example, to those of Japan. These provide services of a wide range for small producers — bulk procurement of inputs, consolidation of export volumes, financing, quality-control and marketing. In our Region, trading houses like these cannot be created by administrative fiat. It is the mobility of capital which will allow the trading houses of the Region to flower and undertake the branding and marketing of products from a diverse range of small manufacturers and producers. Already, a small number of CARICOM companies are striving to increase their exports by purchasing, for marketing under their own brand, a range of products from small manufacturers and farmers.

A common currency or full currency convertibility within the Region will allow these and other firms to establish the contacts and build the trading houses that are absolutely necessary for export-led growth. But free convertibility among regional currencies or a common currency must ultimately mean free convertibility both within and beyond the Region. CARICOM Governments must set their sights firmly on that broader goal if full mobility of capital is to be obtained.

Mobility of Labour

Mobility of labour, the other over-arching requirement for export-led growth, is of current concern. We had earlier proposed in our progress report that steps be taken towards the creation of a

Single CARICOM Market for human resources, starting with UWI graduates.

We further propose that both the public and private sectors of the Region be encouraged to recruit their employees freely within CARICOM and that work permits be automatically available for such CARICOM nationals and their spouses. In addition, once a CARICOM citizen has been working continuously in a country for a specified period, say five years, he or she should, at the minimum, be granted permanent status for themselves and their immediate families.

In our consultations, neither the business community nor anyone else were asking that all CARICOM countries immediately throw their doors open to allow labour from one country to seek employment in another. They are merely urging that, when a firm identifies an individual from the Region for employment, whether he or she be a university graduate or not, the granting of a work permit with no time limit attached should be automatic.

Firms cannot be asked to manufacture throughout the Region without the right to place personnel of their own choosing, drawn albeit from citizens of the Region, in their establishments. Firms, which know very well that making a profit is necessary for survival, are not likely to abuse this privilege in a context where the relocation costs for moving personnel throughout the Region are significant.

Reducing Anti-Export Bias

A major requirement for export-led growth is to ensure the removal of all the biases against exports. In a special study done for the Commission, it has been noted that:

> A significant correlation was found to exist between countries with a strong export performance and trade neutral or bias-free incentive structures. The empirical studies of the foremost successful Far Eastern economies — Hong Kong, South Korea, Taiwan and Singapore — indicated that these countries were closer to neutrality than to substantive bias for or against export. It is on this basis that an export-promoting trade strategy is defined as one where there are neutral incentives between export

> promoting and import substituting activities. Neutral status means that a country's exports must be able to compete with its foreign competitors on equal footing. To achieve neutral status requires that there is duty free status for imports used in export production.
>
> [Arnold McIntyre]

In other words, the anti-export legislation and practices of the 1970s and before, when import substitution was the order of the day, must be removed and neutrality must exist between import substitution and export promotion. It is also important to note that full neutrality requires that there be no advantages given to foreign competitors by the imposition of, for example, duties on the imported inputs of the exporters or an exchange rate regime that discourages borrowing in foreign exchange when, at the same time, local interest rates are well above foreign interest rates.

The development of neutrality or, at the least, preventing an anti-export bias presupposes the existence of a number of factors.

Based on the East Asian experience, the study mentioned above identified the following factors required to facilitate the goal of export-led growth:

- realistic exchange rates;
- free input and output trade;
- ready access to export finance;
- access to primary and non-trading inputs at undistorted prices;
- adequate institutional infrastructure for trade.

We will not here attempt to debate or analyse the relative importance of each of these factors, save to recommend that each CARICOM country should, as a matter of urgency, undertake an analysis of all of the factors affecting trade and particularly those mentioned above, to ensure that any implicit or explicit anti-export biases are removed. This exercise should not be treated as a one-off affair. We recommend that annually there should be an audit, with inputs from the private sector, to ensure that, at least, neutrality as between export and import is maintained.

Expanding CARICOM Trade

Many commentators look at the small size of the CARICOM market and the fact that extra-regional trade is vastly greater than intra-regional trade and conclude that the concern for fostering intra-CARICOM trade is over emphasised. This view is not shared by most of the manufacturers and producers in the Region, who point out that not only is the amount of intra-regional trade significant in itself — EC$1.6 billion in 1981 (the best year to date) when it grew to 10 per cent of total CARICOM trade, but it has a substantial impact on employment. In Jamaica alone, it has been estimated that exports to CARICOM account for some 10,000 jobs.

As CARICOM countries adopt exports as the linchpin of their growth strategy, it will be instructive to distinguish between the benefits that flow from intra-CARICOM trade, integration with the wider Caribbean and extra-regional trade. It is the opportunity of intra-regional trade that allows CARICOM firms to interact and eventually to develop joint ventures and make plans for the assault on extra-regional markets. Five and a half million people is small as a market place, but it is certainly far larger than the 100,000 or less which is the typical size of an OECS country, or even the two and one half million of Jamaica. The regional market of five and a half million allows individual firms in each country to contemplate a home market where total control of the market is not a necessity. At present, only producers in Jamaica and Trinidad and Tobago can envisage a home market of any reasonable size.

CARICOM Heads have long recognised the benefits of CARICOM trade and have sought to foster it through, for example, the Common External Tariff (CET) and the establishment of the CARICOM Enterprise Regime. We have proposed in the preceding Chapter that all CARICOM countries should immediately implement the CET.

A major concern expressed during our public meetings throughout the Region was frustration at the failure of some Governments to implement decisions taken by the Heads of Governments collectively. We deal with this in Chapter XII. We recommend that, on decisions relating to CARICOM trade, the unanimity rule should be replaced by a two-thirds majority decision.

It was also recommended that there should be provision for enforcing sanctions against Member States which fail to implement decisions taken by Heads of Government.

The market links with the wider Caribbean would, of course, mean a larger market. Two-way trade between CARICOM and the wider Caribbean/Latin American region is not insignificant. It amounted in 1988 to US$1,046 million. The trade balance was, however, heavily skewed in favour of the non CARICOM countries with CARICOM imports amounting to US$794 million, while exports totalled merely US$252 million.

These links are caught up in the issues that relate to the deepening and widening of CARICOM. The benefits that flow from widening the common market are obvious, provided that there is free mobility of capital and labour. But free mobility of capital and labour for a wider Caribbean are worthy goals that are unlikely to be achieved in the immediate future. There are, however, significant benefits to be obtained by undertaking measures which allow for freer trade within the wider Caribbean.

Joint shipping in the area of extra-regional trade is one such feature as the European Community single market takes effect. Banana-exporting countries like Jamaica and Belize, whose volumes are still relatively small, must ensure that whatever bananas they send to Europe are shipped as economically as possible. This may very well require those countries to develop joint shipping arrangements with Caribbean producers — say, Honduras or Costa Rica.

Similar benefits may be available to the Windward Islands from closer association with Martinique and Guadeloupe and possibly Suriname. These benefits need not be confined to banana exports alone, but would allow other produce, as well as manufactured items, to have a weekly and cost-effective shipping service to Europe. Already, the major Caribbean markets for CARICOM goods are Suriname, Martinique and French Guiana which in 1988 accounted for 51 per cent of CARICOM exports to the wider region.

Diversification requires regular inexpensive shipping to both Europe and North America and, to achieve this, links with the wider Caribbean will be necessary. If the export trading houses are to develop to the size and breadth that the Region demands, they too will have to source and manufacture from and for the wider Caribbean. Already a few of the larger companies within CARICOM are sourcing in the wider Caribbean. The decision by Geest, the sole importer of Windward Islands bananas into the United Kingdom, to develop 6,000 hectares of bananas in Costa Rica, is indicative of the need to forge closer links with all of the countries washed by the Caribbean Sea.

Extra-Regional Trade

Given our relative proximity to North America and the importance of the North American market, CARICOM must ensure that the emergence of the North American Free Trade Agreement (NAFTA) does not destroy the benefits that were supposed to flow from the Caribbean Basin Initiative (CBI) and CARIBCAN.

For most firms within CARICOM, the requirements of the United States and Canadian market-place mean investments in new plant and machinery. Given the small size of our market and the small size of our firms, these decisions are not made lightly. They require feasibility studies, market studies and negotiations for finance. Even after the plant is developed, there is often a gestation and learning period for the firms. The prospects of a NAFTA embracing the United States, Canada and Mexico with benefits for companies within NAFTA not available to those outside is enough to discourage CARICOM and foreign firms from even undertaking the feasibility studies, let alone making the investments.

As a Region, we must negotiate with North America, Canada and Mexico. We must convince NAFTA negotiators that not only must the benefits of the CBI and CARIBCAN be maintained, but that parity of treatment must be available to us in CARICOM when NAFTA is implemented. This kind of negotiation can only proceed on a CARICOM basis if we are to maintain the benefits of our Common Market for ourselves and not descend into "beggar my neighbour" type diplomacy.

We were reminded of how complex the NAFTA negotiations were when a senior trade representative of the United States pointed out to us that over 300 negotiators from Canada, the USA and Mexico were involved in the NAFTA negotiations, and that we needed to make our voice heard in a number of different NAFTA committees. Some sources are projecting a date for concluding the negotiation in 1992 and the entering into force of the Treaty in 1993. Our NAFTA team must be put in place now. The aim should be to secure parity of treatment regarding access within NAFTA and a continuation of the non-reciprocal arrangements established under CBI and CARIBCAN. Other aspects of the NAFTA issue are discussed elsewhere in this Report, particularly in Chapter XI.

We recommend, therefore, that the approach to NAFTA be regional. CARICOM Governments need to make a strong and coordinated effort in securing favourable terms and conditions under NAFTA. In principle, we recommend that the Region seek the same concessions as those given to Mexico under NAFTA, but without reciprocity. It is critically important that the machinery to achieve this, instructed by CARICOM, be established without delay.

Problems under the Lomé Convention will be documented in the Agriculture section of this Chapter, but it should be noted here that the Caribbean banana exporting countries, including Martinique, Guadeloupe and Suriname, as well as the Windward Islands, Jamaica and Belize, were forced to operate as a unit to put their position before the European Commission in Brussels. It is, of course, clearly instructive to recall that CARICOM countries found it absolutely necessary to coordinate their efforts in relation to the negotiation of the Lomé Convention itself and that since then they have had to work together in the current discussions on sugar and bananas arising out of the establishment of a Single Market within the European Community.

Manufacturing and Diversification

In both our public meetings and those with the business community, we were constantly urged to stress in our Report the need for a CARICOM approach to the region's industrial development. The, by now, time honoured suggestions of an aluminum industry based on Trinidad and Tobago's oil and Guyana's and Jamaica's bauxite, and self-sufficiency in food based on agricultural developments in Belize and Guyana were often mentioned. We believe that if capital and labour could move freely, these and other projects would receive from the private sector the careful assessment that they deserve. What is clear to us is that export-led growth is itself, for the Region, a movement towards diversification. It is a movement that should be dictated by market signals and not by government fiat. Given the uncertainties which attend the prospects for traditional exports such as sugar, bananas, bauxite and aluminum, a compelling case exists for focussing export-led growth on the development of the manufacturing, agri-business and service sectors.

Manufacturing has the major share of our small intra-CARICOM trade, accounting, in many years, for over 50 per cent of the CARICOM exports of Barbados, Guyana, Jamaica and Trinidad and Tobago. For exports outside of CARICOM, the manufacturing base of the Region is weak and currently focuses on our low wage advantage in the "footloose" industries of garments, electronic and other assembly-type operations. Given the ease with which "footloose" industries can move, it would be difficult for us to fashion a diversification strategy based on those industries. We recognise, however, that for the immediate and medium term, these industries must be supported. We propose, therefore, that tripartite committees of Government, labour and the private sector continuously examine this sector both to ensure that we maintain our viability and reduce unemployment, and make certain that our labour laws are honoured and implemented.

New industries require time to select and train their new workers, particularly during the first two years in operation. It is important that regional trade unions try to find a tripartite arrangement for an adjustment period during the critical selection and training period when the company is not making a profit and the workers are benefitting from some measure of skills training and industrial discipline.

There are a number of incentives to industry under the regional Harmonisation of Fiscal Incentives (HFI) Scheme, which was designed to encourage new manufacturing enterprises and reduce competition between CARICOM States for foreign investment. Because of the "footloose" nature of many labour intensive export industries, the export allowance for extra-regional exports after the expiration of the tax holiday should be reviewed and liberalised. If this is not done, we fear that these labour intensive "enclave" industries will continue to move to other countries where they can get new generous tax incentives, particularly in some Free Zones within the Caribbean Basin where there is no time limit on the export tax allowance.

In its efforts to promote exports, establish labour intensive industries and generate foreign exchange earnings, the Region should endeavour to provide a comparable level of incentives to those offered by most countries in the Caribbean Basin.

We recognise, of course, the concern that exists over working conditions in Free Zone enterprises. They were forcefully put to us, particularly in the context of their implications for women. Such concerns should be be addressed and the tripartite committee is a useful vehicle for doing so.

Permanent diversification, however, should not be based entirely on seeking to expand and maintain these "footloose" industries. Accordingly, we must focus on areas where we can build on our comparative advantages and, if necessary, educate ourselves into acquiring the necessary advantages. The medium- and long-term focus for manufacturing should therefore emphasise the development of a skilled work force (as in furniture making) and, where possible, build on our tourist base in areas such as custom-made clothes and other locally made products. In addition to manufacturing, however, we must look to other sectors, in particular the service and agri-business sectors.

Elsewhere we have focussed on manufacturing for exports. In stressing the importance of the Single Market we have identified its role in facilitating "learning" before firms face the full rigour of international competition. As we have mentioned before, however, we must not forget the vital role that import substitution can play in saving foreign exchange and developing greater self-sufficiency. This is particularly true in the area of food and still remains true in certain aspects of manufacturing. The service sector, which is a vital sector of export-led growth, is dealt with in another section.

Niche Markets

On a more general level, CARICOM countries must identify the markets in which they have gained or could develop an advantage.

These markets are best identified and developed by the individual business firm; and we restate the requirements of currency convertibility, mobility of labour and the removal of anti-export bias in incentives as a necessary condition before firms begin to identify the niches and develop the exports.

We share the conclusion reached in the study to which we referred earlier, namely:

> The integration movement will need to be restructured to assist in the implementation of a regional export development strategy aimed at developing skill intensive manufactured exports and service exports. The new export areas will rely heavily on the quality of the Region's human resource and new technical institutions will need to be developed on a regional basis to generate the skilled labour. Therefore, new approaches to regional human resource development will be a critical aspect of co-operation in the development of exports.
>
> [Arnold McIntyre].

Whether it is the service sector or agri-business sector, our size requires that we focus on niche markets. There is strong evidence that this is already beginning to happen. Sales of certain manufactured food items, such as beer in Europe and North America, non-traditional fresh produce, sauces, fruit-based drinks, etc., point to what is possible.

But we are merely scratching the surface. The experience to date does confirm, however, that, except where a firm is large, as in the manufacture of rum and beer, the development of trading houses could be vital for the securing of niche markets.

In our discussions throughout the Region, we had explained to us over and over again how difficult it is to sell extra-regionally, even when one is satisfied that the product being marketed is a good one and that a market exists for the product.

We have heard all this directly from many a frustrated producer or manufacturer. Quite often the reasons for failure were the shortcomings in the major developmental requirements mentioned earlier — realistic exchange rates, ready access to export financing, access to primary and non-trading inputs at undistorted prices and an adequate institutional infrastructure for trade.

In addition to all these factors, however, the inability to guarantee reliability of supply and products of high quality were major concerns of the importers outside of the Region. They would not even consider assessing a product if they were not satisfied that adequate supply and quality arrangements were in place.

Importers outside the Region often pointed to the high cost of shelf space in, say, supermarkets, and were simply not prepared to undertake the development cost of selling a product only to discover that the potential supplier was unable to fill a reasonably sized order on time and had little or no quality assurance programme. The private sector also confirmed that in new product development, losses for one, two or three years, were normal and pointed to the inability of many firms in the Region to withstand these losses.

All of the above highlights the need for the development of relatively large firms with a regional capacity to undertake the marketing of the products in which we have a comparative advantage.

Development Financing

Adequate financing, both development and pre-shipment financing, are vital if export-led growth is to succeed. In several of our hearings, the view was expressed that small and medium level borrowers and new entrants in general faced severe difficulties in accessing loan funds from commercial banks or other traditional lending institutions.

Development Banks, on the other hand, have in the past attempted to provide loans at modestly concessional rates and exhibited a greater willingness to take on riskier projects. The Multilateral Financial Institutions (MFIs), however, are now strongly insistent that interest rates charged should be at market levels and concessions, if any, should be reflected only in a longer payout period.

Indeed, the private sector arms of institutions like the World Bank and the IDB offer interest rates to the private sector on no better terms than would be available from commercial banks. The CDB, as well as the MFIs, tend to operate only at the larger end of the spectrum and their resources are thus not available to most

CARICOM firms.

The investors' insistence, however, on loans with significant concessional interest rates suggest that the way forward may be for Development Banks and other institutions to provide a mix of equity and loan funds so as to reduce the overall interest burden on the newly emerging companies.

Investors in CARICOM traditionally shy away from joint venture partners and, in particular, institutional type joint venture partners, such as Development Banks. There is, therefore, a need to educate the investors on the virtues of joint venture equity financing, and at the same time, there is a need to fashion instruments that will allow investors to take out the Development Bank venture partner when the private sector owners are able to do so.

The increased use of venture capital funds requires the identification of appropriate funds and the understanding by the investor of the role of the venture partner and the conditions under which he or she would be allowed to buy out the venture partner's stake. The institutional venture partner could also provide sorely needed "extension services" in the areas of finance and financial management for new businessmen.

The National Development Foundations (NDFs), which operate in almost all CARICOM countries have provided small and medium size business firms with "extension services," and many small companies in the Region testify to the benefits received from NDF participation.

Accordingly, we recommend wider use of venture capital funding and the recognition by Development Banks, both large and small, that many of their clients need financial "extension services".

Credit

Pre- and post-shipment credit guarantees and rediscount facilities need to be readily available and easily accessible. The general feeling of the exporters in the larger CARICOM countries is that bureaucratic delays and the lack of concessional interest rates reduce the usefulness of these facilities when they are available.

A more fundamental concern, however, is that these facilities are available only to firms deemed to be nationals of the particular country offering pre- and post-shipment financing.

If, as argued earlier, the export thrust requires 'regional' type firms, then regional type financing will have to be made available to them. We believe the Caribbean Development Bank should take the lead in developing this kind of facility. Some trade credit is available in the wider Caribbean to CARICOM countries, particularly from Mexico, Colombia and Venezuela, but invariably this credit is under-utilised due mainly to unawareness about trade possibilities in the Region. If trade is to be expanded to the wider Caribbean, information on these trade credits will have to be widely disseminated to the private sector. It is also worth noting that until recently CARICOM and Latin American investors have not sought to attract each other to their respective countries.

Very few investment promotion or protection treaties exist between CARICOM and the wider Caribbean and if we are to make the goal of widening CARICOM a reality, programmes designed to foster investment by the private sector in each other's countries will have to be developed.

The Regional Stock Market

The common listing and sale of shares listed on all three stock markets of CARICOM have not yet contributed to the provision of capital for new investments. There has been some purchase of existing shares, but the information and market understanding necessary to fund the equity offerings of a new company are unavailable. The stock brokers of the Region should be urged to provide better information on the companies listed on their Exchanges and develop programmes for small purchasers to enable them to understand the implications of buying shares in another country.

Because of the small number of public companies in the OECS, it has been suggested that the OECS should join the Barbados Stock Exchange. This joint effort could be the nucleus for further cooperation between Barbados and the OECS economies.

Indeed, the whole matter of share purchases in the Region is still the preserve of a minority, albeit a growing minority. We recommend that stock exchanges and brokerage firms develop programmes to enable the small investor to feel comfortable in the purchase of shares, both within his country and in CARICOM.

The experience of Jamaica in relation to the divestment of the Government's profitable firms suggests that there is a pool of untapped capital from households and small firms that could significantly contribute to the capital formation of the Region.

In a general sense, we have made some progress in the transition to an indigenous environment in respect of investment, finance and trade. If we are to maximise the gains of integration, however, we must make the further transition to a more broadly-based enterprise culture.

Recommendations
1. that CARICOM Governments, as a matter of urgency, take the necessary steps to make their currencies freely convertible with each other and allow for the free mobility of capital within the Region;
2. that the private sector and the Governments of the Region be allowed to recruit CARICOM citizens freely within CARICOM. Work permits should be automatic both for applicant and spouse and should not depend only on the educational status of the employee;
3. that each CARICOM country undertake an analysis of all the factors affecting trade, with a view to removing all implicit and explicit anti-export biases;
4. that CARICOM Heads of Governments insist that all Member States immediately introduce the agreed CET and seek to prevent States from modifying the general rules for certain commodities or to suit certain circumstances;
5. that negotiations with NAFTA be conducted on a regional basis and continued with urgency, and that every effort be made to ensure that the Region obtains the same concessions as Mexico but without reciprocity;
6. that tripartite committees of Government, labour and the private sector be set up to maintain the Region's viability in the "footloose" industries of garments, electronics,and other labour-intensive export industries;

7. that Development Banks provide more long-term financing to the private sector and the CDB be urged to make much greater use of "equity" funding and to recognize that, in the area of exports, most firms need a degree of financial, marketing and management type "extension services";

8. that every facility be put in place to promote and encourage the development of regional Trading Houses

9. that every effort be made to enlarge and integrate the Region's stock exchanges, and widen transactions in the shares of companies owned by nationals of the Region.

2. AGRICULTURE

The Treaty of Chaguaramas contains a number of provisions for a framework of policies to rationalise the agricultural sector within the Common Market; the stated goal was to promote complementarity in the agricultural programmes for the cooperating states and enhance the contribution which the sector could make to national and regional economic development.

The framework of policies, while having due regard to the potential and prospects of the individual Member States and to the demands of the evolving international market place, provided a basis and rationale for agricultural programming and institution building within the Community. Pursuant to these provisions, the Community Secretariat and national agricultural administrations have undertaken in-depth analyses of this sector and instituted arrangements and programmes which, prima facie, would respond to the perceived underlying needs of the farmers in the Region in order to accelerate the increase in the incomes which they could earn. However, the pace of regional and national agricultural development has been far slower than was envisaged and below the expectations of the planners.

There have been several exhaustive analyses of the agricultural sector over the past twenty to twenty-five years. Many of these are available in published form. It is therefore proposed to deal only briefly with this important sector of the regional economy. We will discuss first the place which agriculture occupies in the economies of the countries of the Community. Then we will describe in summary form the efforts which have been made in the area of regional agricultural programming. The special needs of domestic agriculture will then be discussed. Sugar and bananas occupy a central place in Caribbean agriculture and we will present a brief review of some of the principal issues involved. Fisheries development in the Region can receive a major boost as a result of the Exclusive Economic Zones and a brief description of some of the issues is therefore presented. Finally, the principal recommendations will be summarised.

Place of Agriculture

In seven member states of CARICOM, agricultural commodities contributed the largest single share of merchandise exports in 1988 (Belize: sugar, almost 80 per cent; St. Kitts and Nevis: sugar, 62 per cent; Saint Lucia: bananas, almost 50 per cent; St. Vincent and the Grenadines: bananas, almost 50 per cent; Dominica: bananas, more than 60 per cent; Grenada: nutmeg and mace, more than 34 per cent; Barbados: sugar, 30 per cent). In Guyana, bauxite contributed the largest share of merchandise exports (38 per cent) but sugar and rice together accounted for 54 per cent of merchandise exports. Agricultural exports, although extremely important in Jamaica and Trinidad and Tobago, contributed only a small proportion of their total merchandise exports; and agricultural exports were relatively insignificant in the other Member States.

With respect to the contribution to the Gross Domestic Product in 1990, agriculture's share ranged from 2.6 per cent in Trinidad and Tobago to 28 per cent in Guyana, with 9 per cent in St. Kitts and Nevis, 23 per cent in Belize, 26 per cent in Dominica and 17 per cent in Grenada. Agriculture is however a significant provider of employment in all CARICOM States. The share of the labour force contributed by agriculture in 1988 ranged from a low of 13 per cent in Trinidad and Tobago to 23–37 per cent in the other Member States (Belize, 37 per cent; St. Lucia, 30 per cent; Grenada, 29 per cent; Jamaica, 28 per cent; and Guyana, 23 per cent).

Historically, Caribbean agriculture was organised to meet the demands of the metropolitan countries; by and large, the countries of the

Region produced what they did not consume and consumed what they did not produce. The efforts at agricultural programming (which are described later) were designed in part, to establish production and marketing systems which would allow the region's agriculture to play a somewhat larger role in satisfying the regional food needs and in providing for a minimum of food security.

If we use food imports as a measure of the success of the policy of import displacement, then the results indicate that the policy has not yet yielded significant success. Intra-regional food imports have hovered between US $85 million in 1988 and US $120 million in 1990. However, the region's food import bill from extra regional sources, which was about US $700 million in 1988, rose to almost US $900 million in 1990. A part of the increase in the food import bill is doubtlessly associated with the significant rise in the number of tourist arrivals to Member States; population increase in these states will also account for about 5 per cent of the increase in imports over the last three years. However, it is difficult to resist the conclusion that the region's agriculture has not responded effectively to the efforts at transformation which were intended to derive more of the dynamism and growth from internal developments; the sector has continued to depend on the export market which is coming under increasing threat by the pressures to vitiate the preferential marketing arrangements which have assisted Caribbean agriculture.

There is validity in the argument which has been advanced as an explanation of the lacklustre performance of regional agriculture in providing greater regional food security, that the heavy subsidisation of agriculture in the industrialised countries — estimated at US $299 billion in 1990 — makes it difficult for the region's agriculture to compete in its own market against imported food. This inability to compete could grow in future as the multilateral financial institutions insist on the removal of agricultural supports as part of their Structural Adjustment Loans, while ignoring the effect on the region's agriculture of the heavy subsidisation of agriculture in North America and Europe. The extent of the subsidisation of agriculture in the advanced countries is shown in the Table opposite.

Agriculture

NET PRODUCER SUBSIDY EQUIVALENTS (a) FOR SELECTED COMMODITIES AND COUNTRIES, 1979-1990

Commodity	1979-86	1987	1989	1990	1979-86	1987	1989	1990	1979-86	1987	1989	1990
	Australia				*Austria*				*Canada*			
Wheat	10	14	11	17	32	73	38	62	26	54	26	43
Coarse Grains	7	9	7	7	26	61	34	31	27	49	23	28
Rice	25	29	23	25	...	...	...	...	...	...	...	...
Oilseeds	8	12	16	12	...	...	...	...	20	30	23	21
Sugar	9	19	15	16	58	73	65	61	25	39	17	17
Milk	31	36	25	31	47	60	48	61	66	81	73	79
Beef	10	9	9	9	43	49	50	51	32	49	35	36
Pork	5	5	4	4	9	33	11	22	12	11	24	16
Poultry	5	4	4	4	14	2	52	49	28	45	37	40
	EEC (b)				*Finland*				*Japan*			
Wheat	32	60	27	46	62	82	77	81	96	103	95	99
Coarse Grains	34	68	35	52	58	90	80	82	97	102	94	96
Rice	46	62	51	60	...	...	...	...	79	94	86	87
Oilseeds	45	70	60	69	64	90	80	96	82	79	67	69
Sugar	55	78	49	57	70	86	62	76	68	75	63	62
Milk	55	67	59	69	66	87	74	77	83	91	83	85
Beef	47	46	55	54	57	63	63	62	62	60	59	54
Pork	6	6	6	6	36	48	53	55	42	46	54	37
Poultry	20	22	26	28	46	56	52	56	17	13	13	13
	New Zealand				*Norway*				*Sweden*			
Wheat	9	25	14	10	63	78	76	79	35	65	41	73
Coarse Grains	10	5	5	3	77	83	86	92	29	48	53	73
Rice	...	...	...	...	...	...	...	...	...	...	...	...
Oilseeds	...	...	...	...	...	...	...	...	36	42	61	68
Sugar	...	...	...	...	...	...	...	...	54	62	35	60
Milk	23	14	3	3	79	83	79	82	66	71	67	71
Beef	14	12	4	3	68	67	72	70	44	46	49	42
Pork	16	4	1	0	48	56	47	46	22	41	25	12
Poultry	29	47	49	57	56	64	65	59	26	36	38	29
	Switzerland				*United States*							
Wheat	72	85	76	81	28	64	25	44				
Coarse Grains	74	91	84	89	21	46	30	24				
Rice	...	...	...	...	31	50	40	49				
Oilseeds	83	95	93	98	8	10	9	7				
Sugar	75	86	83	85	46	71	46	47				
Milk	73	85	76	84	63	70	55	62				
Beef	76	78	84	84	34	37	32	31				
Pork	45	62	38	44	7	7	7	6				
Poultry	80	83	82	81	8	35	10	10				

Extracted from *UNCTAD Trade and Development Report 1991*. Source: *OECD Agricultural policies, markets and trade: Monitoring and outlook 1991*, Paris, 1991. (Figures for 1979-86 are estimates, those for 1990 are provisional.)

(a) Total assistance for a given commodity as a percentage of the total value of receipts from sales of the commodity. PSE thus measures the value of transfers to farmers generated by agricultural policy.

(b) Excluding Portugal and Spain in 1979-85.

One of the success stories of Caribbean agriculture has been the extent to which the Windwards have responded to the incentives of adequate pricing arrangements, predictable transportation facilities and a sufficient flow of research and other support services and have enlarged their production base. In consequence, the Region which started the decade of the 1980s with a deficit on its export/import trade in agriculture — largely due to the decline of sugar — is expected to show a positive export/import ratio in 1991 and 1992. However, it must also be noted that this positive ratio does not derive from the region's competitive strength in international markets in the principal agricultural exports — sugar, bananas, and, to a lesser extent, cocoa, coffee and nutmegs — but rather from the preferential position which exports from the Region of sugar and bananas enjoy in Europe and, to a lesser extent, in the United States (for sugar). Some of the issues which will have to be addressed in the question of preferential markets are discussed later.

Regional Agricultural Planning

The efforts in the planning of regional agriculture have focussed on three principal areas: first, the establishment of marketing arrangements within the region to ensure that regional supply of certain non export commodities occupied a preferred position in satisfying regional demand or, conversely, that regional demand made its first call on regional supply; second, on promoting the development of relevant agricultural research to support regional agriculture; and thirdly, in developing facilities to improve the marketing of agricultural commodities both within and outside the Region. The CARICOM Secretariat and the Standing Committee of Ministers of Agriculture have also played a very active role in prolonging the life, and improving the export conditions, of the special arrangements under which sugar and bananas are exported to the United States and to Europe.

Agricultural Marketing

Several efforts have been made to organise the Region's agricultural production in order to enable it to make a larger contribution to income.

The Agricultural Marketing Protocol (AMP), patterned after the Regional Oils and Fats Agreement, was included as part of the CARIFTA arrangements. This Protocol, which operated on a system of declared surpluses and deficits among Member States, covered trade in twenty-two agricultural commodities and accorded a preferential position to the LDCs. However, it did not provide a sufficiently durable basis for planning regional production, especially in those areas where the LDCs were presumed to have a comparative advantage.

The CARICOM Oils and Fats Protocol itself worked effectively for several years when the world market price for coconut oil was high. However, since the unsubstantiated claim that coconut oil could give rise to health problems, and the establishment of soya bean processing plants in some parts of the Region, the Oils and Fats Protocol has become ineffective. This has resulted in the decline of the coconut industry in some parts of the Region.

The AMP was subsequently modified in the Guaranteed Marketing Scheme (GMS) under which the MDCs were required to purchase specified quantities of selected agricultural commodities from the LDCs each year at predetermined prices.

Neither the AMP nor the GMS yielded their expected benefits in terms of an increase in regional agricultural production and intra-regional trade in agricultural commodities. Subsequent analysis has shown that marketing schemes, per se, are unequal to the task of promoting agricultural production and increasing intra-regional agricultural trade. The constraints to agricultural production in the Region appear to be more deep seated and reflect the economic and political legacy of the Region which assigned minimum importance to agricultural production outside the export sector.

The Regional Food Plan (RFP) was the next stage in the evolution of an agricultural planning strategy which sought to combine the Region's agricultural resources for the satisfaction of the Region's agricultural needs. The RFP, which also set out the framework for the establishment of the Caribbean Food Corporation, addressed the following principal issues:

(i) the unequal distribution of regional resources for agricultural development and the consequent need to move investment into areas offering good potential for growth in food production;

ii) the imperative to improve land utilisation and employment opportunities in agriculture; and

(iii) the need to ensure an acceptable distribution of the gains from increased agricultural production in the Region.

However, economic conditions were generally unpropitious for Caribbean countries during the late 1970s and most of the decade of the 1980s. Most of the Member States were beset by serious balance of payments difficulties and a consequent inability to mobilise the finances for the infrastructural investments which the agricultural sector required, particularly in the area of water management and an adequate marketing and transportation infrastructure. Besides the Region as a whole made little effort to improve land tenure systems and to address the question of praedial larceny. Finally, the movement towards freeing intra-regional trade suffered severe set-backs during the decade of the 1980s, as the countries sought to wrestle with the problems of severe balance of payments difficulties and burdensome debt service obligations.

More generally it appears, in retrospect, that the policies which individual national Governments, and the Region as a whole, sought to introduce in the agricultural sector did not reflect the required ordering of priorities. The policies — as reflected in their preoccupation with organised marketing arrangements — sought to import into the sector as a whole arrangements which have been successfully pursued in the export agriculture sector, that is, to establish marketing systems and assume that the investment and production needs would follow automatically.

Over the years export agriculture has enjoyed a well developed infrastructure including water management, access roads, research facilities, land tenure systems, income protection through negotiated pricing arrangements favourable to the grower, freedom from the forays of subsidised agricultural imports from the more developed countries, farmer training and protection against loss of income through praedial larceny. However, the same has not been true for the rest of the sector producing food for the domestic market and certain non-traditional exports.

In 1986, the Standing Committee of Ministers responsible for Agriculture decided to modify the approach to development of the Region's agriculture and formulated the Caribbean Community Programme for Agricultural Development (CCPAD).

The CCPAD was formulated with the following five objectives in mind:

(i) to foster the revitalisation of regional agriculture through enlarging trade opportunities within the Caribbean Community;

(ii) to strengthen regional institutions which provide, directly and indirectly, certain of the support services such as technology development and adaptation, investment, training, and joint marketing;

(iii) to mobilise funds and technical assistance for agricultural development, particularly with respect to non-traditional agriculture;

(iv) to encourage an enlarged flow of investment funds into viable agricultural projects; and

(v) to coordinate national and regional investment projects in order to ensure that they would benefit from the synergies inherent in the regional cooperation movement.

It is yet too early to make an assessment of the effectiveness of this new regional initiative. It is however encouraging to note that the four principal regional institutions which are active in supporting the Region's agriculture — the University of the West Indies, CARDI, the Caribbean Food Cooperation and its marketing affiliate CATCO, and the CDB — are all actively supportive of the objectives which comprise the mandate of CCPAD.

Improving Agricultural Performance

We deal later with the specific problems and prospects of sugar and bananas, the Region's principal agricultural export commodities.

While, therefore, in this section we concentrate attention on the other areas of agriculture, in an important sense, we must also have adequate regard to the imperatives which must derive from any restructuring of the agricultural export sector which may ensue from the progressive reduction of the special marketing arrangements which currently obtain for the two principal export crops.

Perhaps the most important requirement facing Caribbean Governments nationally and regionally is to develop a holistic concept of the role which they expect agriculture to play in the development of the individual economies. A decision on the kind of role which agriculture is to play must address at least the following issues:

(i) the degree of protection which the Region's agriculture can expect in the face of the highly subsidised exports of agricultural products from North America and Europe. Anti-dumping legislation, the enforcement of unified phytosanitary regulations and a tariff policy which will mirror that of the industrialised countries under which the tariff escalates with the degree of processing, must be put high on the agenda of the decision makers;

(ii) there is need for a more focussed and concerted policy to integrate agriculture with manufacturing and tourism. This will not only assist the farmers of the Region but also reduce the leakages associated with tourism and manufacturing.

(iii) the countries of the Region must adhere to the rules of regional free trade. The Caribbean must strive towards a single market in agricultural and other trade and this must enjoin on all, within the framework of a unified anti-dumping regime *vis-à-vis* the rest of the world, the obligation to eliminate barriers to intra-regional trade and allow comparative advantage to determine the location of production. One of the important requirements in this regard is the introduction of assurances of prompt payment for exports within the Region. These are all matters which have been addressed by the Common Market Council; the problem is one of implementation;

(iv) there is a need for larger investment in the agricultural sector. This has two dimensions. First, countries with surplus agricultural land, particularly Belize and Guyana, need to attract more regional and international capital into their agricultural sectors. All countries of the Region have expressed interest in attracting foreign investment. But while a general announcement of policies to welcome capital is useful, the reality is that the inflow of such capital investment requires the concomitant investment in the infrastructure needed to support agriculture — water management systems, access roads, training and research;

(v) CARICOM Governments need to take positive steps to upgrade the technical capability of the regional farmer. The Region has not been delinquent in the provision of training facilities for its would-be farmers, at both the professional and technical levels. However, for the most part, these trained personnel have occupied niches in agricultural services and advice rather than function in the area of being farm owners/managers. This bias in the distribution of the employment of the qualified agriculturists is not solely the product of chance. For a very long time, CARICOM Governments have tended to view agricultural development, and in particular agricultural settlements, not as an economic venture but rather as mechanisms for the distribution of social benefit;

(vi) perhaps the most important requirement for the resuscitation of Caribbean agriculture is an assault on the land tenure system which will both provide land holdings adequate to warrant the use of technological aids in farming and ensure adequate security for borrowing. Certainly, with the inevitable demise of the plantation system which buttressed the present non-viable agricultural economy of the countries of the Region, Governments must decide early on the kind of landholding pattern which will sustain the Region's agricultural thrust. The broad consensus of professional opinion in the Region is that there is a need for a greater proportion of the arable agricultural land to be held in farms in the 30–50 acre range rather than in the one to two and a half acres which appear to predominate outside the plantations. CARICOM Governments must take measures to ensure that small scale farmers also have access to technological aids in order to enlarge their incomes;

(vii) the Region's research and development capability needs to be assessed; the present structure is not suited to a situation where the Region's agricultural system will be reorganised, as it needs to be, to operate on the basis of comparative advantage and the free movement of labour, capital and goods. We believe that the Region could, with profit, examine a structural change in the agricultural research institutions taking into account a satisfactory division of responsibilities between regional and national bodies, but more especially determining the priority areas on which the Region's research capability should be directed. One important priority in this regard should be the identification of inputs and techniques to increase local value added. In bananas, for example, almost one third of the value of the banana before it leaves our shores is imported;

(viii) finally, the Region's non-traditional export agriculture could derive benefit through a greater concentration on the particular problems which the farmers of the Region confront in their day-to-day living. Some of these special requirements have been mentioned before — land tenure systems, adequate physical infrastructure, marketing systems, a satisfactory regime to protect against dumping of the subsidised agricultural crops from industrialised countries and a close integration between agriculture, tourism and manufacturing.

But there are other areas where farmers require policy attention. High priority must be accorded to protecting the incomes of farmers through effective control measures against praedial larceny, a condition which is prevalent under Caribbean conditions of high urban unemployment. Further, whatever the international institutions may propose, the reality of the matter is that farmers cannot plan their affairs when interest rates reach the astronomical levels which are now being prescribed; there is a danger that farm investment will grind to a halt and farmers, being unable to meet their debt obligations, will simply abandon their farms. CARICOM Governments must determine their priorities; if they attach importance to a dynamic domestic agricultural system which will assure them a minimum of food security, stem the rural/urban drift and reduce the strains on the balance of payments, they must assure themselves that the basic preconditions are right. The continuous devaluation of the currency, which is the stock in trade of the proponents of the new international economic system, is not a solution which we advocate for CARICOM Governments. Rather, our perception is that these Governments should ensure that their farmers are given conditions which will enable them to provide the Region with a minimum of food security, keep inflation in check and enlarge the contribution which the national agricultural systems can make to employment and national welfare.

We now turn to the two principal export crops of the Region and we discuss these in the light of the evolving international market situation which initially triggered the expansion of these two subsectors of the Region's industry — bananas and sugar.

Bananas

Bananas are the major export crop for a number of CARICOM countries, as well as Suriname, Martinique, Guadeloupe and, of course, the Dollar banana countries of the Caribbean — i.e., Honduras, Costa Rica, Panama, Nicaragua, Guatemala and Colombia. The Commission fully recognised the importance of bananas and not only saw at first hand the loading process in the Windward Islands, but discussed the single European market banana issues with CARICOM and UK Government officials in London.

Because of the greater export potential of the Dollar countries, bananas are seen as a divisive force in the Region, with ACP and Community countries — i.e. the Windward Islands, Jamaica, Belize, Suriname, Martinique and Guadeloupe — seeking to maintain the preference they have in the European Community and the Dollar countries seeking to remove preference with the advent of the single European market in 1993.

Within CARICOM, the importance of bananas as a foreign exchange earner cannot be over-stated. In 1988, for example, bananas constituted 47 per cent of the foreign exchange earnings of the Windward Islands and reached a peak of 64.2 per cent for Dominica.

While occupying a lower percentage of total exports in Jamaica and Belize, it is of vital importance to these countries, providing both sorely needed foreign exchange and significant employment.

Because of the preferential benefits enjoyed under Lomé, CARICOM bananas, sold almost exclusively in the United Kingdom, yield prices to the growers significantly above those now earned by the growers in Dollar countries. Bananas and tourism dominate the economies of the OECS countries and every effort must be made to maintain the viability of these industries over the next several years.

The producers are accepting the challenge of the quality requirements of the United Kingdom and the European markets and, throughout the Region, great strides have been made in improving the quality of bananas exported from CARICOM. The Region must, however, continue to improve its quality and strive to increase the export yield per acre. It is, however, expected that prices will fall if preference is reduced.

Every effort must therefore be made to purchase the imported inputs for the banana industry as cheaply as possible, and the banana-controlling companies within the Windward Islands, Jamaica, Belize and Suriname must address the possibility of joint purchase for a number of key inputs and, where possible, as in the case of Belize and Jamaica, joint shipping arrangements.

There are good signs that existing preferences will continue for some time in the future. However, if there is a significant loss of preference because of developments in the single European market, for entities like WINBAN in the Windward Islands and BECO in Jamaica, their Governments will not have the resources to cushion the decline in returns to the growers.

These are the cold economic realities. The social costs could be staggering — particularly for small farmers in the Windwards. For this reason CARICOM must continue to work together to safeguard its collective interests. Such joint efforts have had their first success in the single market context of avoiding bananas being taken into the General Agreement on Tariffs and Trade (GATT). Vigilance is still necessary, however, as too large a quota for Dollar fruit could erode the benefits guaranteed under Lomé. This experience holds many basic lessons for us; but none more telling than that success at this first hurdle was possible for Jamaica and Belize, only because the Windwards were also involved; and was possible for the Windwards only because Jamaica and Belize were with them. We shall continue to need each other for survival in these ways in the harsh economic environment of the end of the century and beyond.

Sugar

The sugar industry has a crucial place in the economic and social lives of Community countries — in Jamaica and Trinidad and Tobago it plays an important role and in Barbados, Belize, Guyana and St. Kitts and Nevis an exceptionally vital one. The industry contributes in a variety of ways: earning foreign exchange (US$270 million for the Community under the Sugar Protocol alone), little of which is exported; self-generating most of its own energy; generating employment; spreading services in health care, housing, welfare, and sporting facilities; providing educational and training opportunities in a wide range of industrial and agricultural skills; creating good business for suppliers of materials and services throughout the communities in which they exist; and supplying the by-products which form the basis of other important and lucrative existing enterprises and perhaps, as technology progresses, for future enterprises as well.

Nevertheless the reality is that the Member States of CARICOM have been reducing their dependence on the sugar industry. This is reflected in the production data for sugar which show that, whereas in 1980 CARICOM production of sugar was in excess of 900,000 metric tonnes, by 1991, production levels had fallen by almost 25 per cent to reach just under 700,000 metric tonnes.

The following table gives sugar production in CARICOM Countries in the years since 1980:

TABLE I
Sugar Production in CARICOM Countries – Tonnes (Raw Value)

YEAR	BARBADOS	BELIZE	GUYANA	JAMAICA	ST. KITTS	TRINIDAD	TOTAL
1980	135,493	108,363	286,230	236,389	35,609	113,580	915,664
1981	96,867	103,645	320,168	204,010	33,135	93,317	851,142
1982	88,378	113,628	304,853	198,050	36,876	78,685	820,480
1983	85,837	120,323	265,481	202,295	27,594	79,020	780,550
1984	97,688	108,576	256,481	187,778	30,612	66,504	747,639
1985	101,414	109,520	257,688	209,125	27,455	83,337	788,539
1986	112,633	104,704	260,547	198,771	28,491	94,732	799,878
1987	83,868	87,761	233,515	189,435	25,256	88,046	707,881
1988	81,033	88,846	178,307	221,715	25,815	94,275	689,991
1989	67,044	93,949	170,496	204,973	24,769	100,440	661,671
1990	69,311	108,146	136,185	215,000	15,632	122,264	656,538
1991	65,681	106,929	162,573	237,343	18,889	103,663	695,073

Source: Sugar Association of the Caribbean

This compares with the following table of immediate marketing outlets (quite apart from the world market) available.

TABLE 2
CARICOM SUGAR MARKETS — TONNES (Raw Value)

COUNTRY	EEC QUOTA	US QUOTA 1991/92	DOMESTIC CONSUMPTION 1990	TOTAL
Barbados	54,687	9,249	12,238	76,174
Belize	43,857	14,535	8,680	67,072
Guyana	173,272	15,856	28,560	217,688
Jamaica	129,017	14,535	114,121	257,673
St. Kitts-Nevis	16,947	7,258	1,600	25,805
Trinidad and Tobago	47,555	9,249	62,403	119,207
Other CARICOM	-	-	20,000(est.)	20,000
TOTAL	465,335	70,682	247,602	783,619

Source: Sugar Association of the Caribbean

CARICOM sugar is marketed under preferential arrangements in the United States and in the European Community. The quota in the US is just under 71,000 metric tonnes while that in the European Community is just over 465,000 metric tonnes. Domestic consumption in the region is estimated at about 250,000 metric tonnes so that the protected market is roughly 785,000 metric tonnes. Production in the Region's industry has fallen to a level which is inadequate to satisfy its preferential and domestic markets.

The price in the US market is approximately US $450.00 per tonne; that in the EC market is approximately US $600.00 per tonne; these prices are to be compared with the world market price which currently is approximately US $200.00 per tonne.

There are two issues which must be addressed. The first is that even though prices in the protected markets are higher than world market prices, a number of sugar companies in the Region are producing at a loss which has to be financed by their treasuries.

The second problem derives from the uncertainty over how long the preferential marketing arrangements in the US and Europe will last. Certainly, the US has, for several years, been reducing the quota which it grants to the sugar importers; and in the European Community, prices have been kept stable since 1986; indeed, in 1989/90 the Community reduced the price by 2 per cent.

It is claimed that sugar's preferential markets in the USA and, particularly, in the EEC, now only have a medium to short life-span. We do not believe that this is necessarily so. But even if the most likely prospect is for preference to diminish substantially in, say, the next 10 years, that is no reason to neglect the valuable asset we currently possess in our sugar industries and their historic and assured marketing outlets. It rather gives reason to seek to retain preferences for as long as possible by showing how essential they are in the Region, to parley with them, if it comes to that, for equivalent support in other forms, and meanwhile put in hand, where this is profitable, the investment necessary to rationalise, modernise, and strengthen the industry so that it can compete world-wide if ever the playing field is actually levelled.

The high production costs, and the consequent financial losses, which most of the CARICOM sugar industry now experiences, derive in part from the steep declines in production levels (Jamaica and Belize excepted) during the decade of the 1980s. However, in the consultations which we held, there was also strong support for the view that state ownership is impeding the introduction of the structural changes which are necessary to make the lands on which sugar cane is now grown more productive and profitable.

One thing emerges with clarity. The industry cannot remain in its present form and shape. It must be given a new dynamism directed either to an expansion at reduced unit cost of production, capable of competing in the international market; or to its replacement by other, more profitable, uses of the resources now employed in sugar. The specific course of action will be determined by the particular circumstances, including cost structures, prevailing in each country; but transformation in the ownership of the lands would appear to be an essential ingredient whatever the final objective of policy decided upon.

EEC Market

In respect of the vital EEC market, which provides the Region's sugar with a stable and high-priced outlet, there are two points we wish to stress.

- Current access — guaranteed under the Sugar Protocol indefinitely into the future — must be preserved inviolate. We appreciate that the Protocol specifies the allocation of individual country quotas but we believe that, as the Community integrates more closely, negotiations should be pursued for a joint regional quota within the ACP so that, in any particular year, shortfalls within the Region are taken up regionally in the first place, before wider re-allocation among ACP countries.

  When Portugal, basically a cane refining country, becomes a full member of the EEC in 1993, the opportunity for additional access for ACP sugar at the guaranteed prices becomes available. The case for this valuable additional access — amounting to as much as 225,000 tonnes per annum over and above the 75,000 tonnes currently supplied to Portugal by 4 African states under a previous transitional arrangement — must continue to be pressed hard. It is commendable that CARICOM'S share of such additional access, if it can be negotiated, will be allocated under an arrangement which allows reallocation of shortfalls within CARICOM.

- There has been no increase in the EEC price since 1986 and there was a reduction of 2 per cent in 1989/90 in respect of which the EEC agreed to provide assistance to ACP sugar industries amounting to 10 million ECUs! (£ 7.2 million) per annum for three years. Further price reductions — arising out of cuts in EEC farm support — could very well result in the future, and no mechanism or fund at present exists after 1992/93 for continuing compensation to ACP sugar producers for such price cuts — in contrast to the assistance in prospect for European beet farmers under the European Agricultural Guidance and Guarantee Fund. This is unacceptable and contrary to the whole spirit of Lomé and the Protocol, designed to stabilise export earnings; it is especially unacceptable inasmuch as it is continually asserted and promised that ACP cane sugar producers are to be treated on par with European beet sugar producers. The collective case against erosion of valuable foreign exchange earnings from the Region's sugar must continue to be made with all possible vigour and conviction.

U.S. Market

The availability of sugar quotas in the US market is a substantial benefit. Efforts therefore to retain regional quotas, at least at the minimum level of 71,000 metric tonnes where they now stand, should be vigorously pursued through joint governmental representation and through the CBI sugar group in which CARICOM sugar industry representatives play an important part.

GATT

As they stand at present, the GATT negotiations hold serious dangers for the Region's sugar producers, since a reduction in the internal EEC sugar price will entail a reduction in the prices which ACP producers receive. A reduction of 20 per cent in internal support in the sugar sector, as proposed in the Dunkel compromise paper, would lead to a fall of 7-8 per cent in the EEC sugar price; and the conversion of import levies into their tariff equivalents and subsequent reductions in tariffs would bring about much deeper price cuts.

Further, notwithstanding statements made in certain quarters that the "freeing up" of the sugar market could cause world prices to rise, studies undertaken on the matter show that that outcome is highly uncertain at the very best. Such "freeing up" would in no way compensate for the loss of foreign exchange earnings through the reductions in current guaranteed prices which the GATT proposals will entail.

The Punta Del Este Declaration recognised the need to avoid disruptive effects in the trade of less developed countries and agreed on the principle that a balanced outcome to the GATT negotiations be achieved. It is essential, therefore, that CARICOM negotiators should press hard to ensure that adequate safeguards to protect the income generated by current sugar arrangements, and particularly by the Sugar Protocol, be written into a general GATT agreement.

The CARICOM Domestic Sugar Market

In respect of CARICOM's domestic requirements for sugar, a substantial market clearly exists — within the realised concept of a common market — for which revitalised sugar industries in CARICOM can and should be able to compete in future. It is estimated that not less than 75,000 tonnes of sugar are currently imported from countries outside the Community. Much of this is refined sugar to meet requirements for which capacity does not currently exist in CARICOM. Entrepreneurs, both in sugar and in industries outside of sugar, should be encouraged to undertake investments necessary to exploit these opportunities.

The Rum Industry

The sugar industry provides basic inputs for many other industries which are in commercial production, and more for which the technology is in an advanced stage of development, e.g., pharmaceuticals, animal feeds and construction materials. Rum is the best known of the derivatives of the sugar industry, and Caribbean rum is one of the better known products coming out of the Region. The expansion of the Region's rum industry can therefore enhance the viability of its sugar industry. However, growth in the industry has been severely curtailed by the application of restrictive quotas in the European market; and, within the Caribbean, CARICOM rum exporters are placed at a disadvantage *vis-à-vis* Puerto Rican and US Virgin Island rum because the US rebates to Puerto Rico and the Virgin Islands the duties and levies charged not only on the rum exported by these countries to the US market, but also on rums exported by other Caribbean countries; this allows producers in Puerto Rico and the Virgin Islands to pre-empt the US market through the larger promotion campaigns they are able to mount. We believe that it is more than time that the playing-field for this important Caribbean product should be levelled, that CARICOM rum should be treated equitably in the US market, and that rum should be allowed fair competition with other alcoholic beverages in Europe.

Other Important Agricultural Resources

We have considered in some detail those resources which the Region has developed yielding benefits which collectively we must seek to preserve in the face of particularly intense international pressure. We have not attempted to report on the many other agricultural enterprises which are being developed in the Region. Each of these is important and would, were there the space, merit detailed study in its own right. We take note that the farmers, entrepreneurs and agricultural experts who explained their various businesses to us left an impression of variety, enthusiasm and optimism in the agricultural field greater than we had expected.

Here we call attention to two which are of particular importance in a regional context:
- the cultivation of rice, particularly in Belize and in Guyana where the present recovery in that industry renews the prospect of Guyana one day supplying a market-integrated Region with the main part of its requirement for this staple as well as taking advantage of the available outlet in the EEC under Lomé;

- citrus is becoming of increasing significance and importance to certain countries in the Region, notably Belize, Jamaica and Trinidad and Tobago, where the industry has recently embarked on a growth and diversification programme. The inexorable international trend towards trade liberalisation could expose the industry not only to increasing competition within CARICOM from producers in Latin America, but also to the importation of new pests and diseases. In order to sustain the ongoing expansion, phyto-sanitary protection of the Region's agriculture generally, and of citrus in particular,' needs to be strengthened and long term development finance on concessional terms made available to the industry in order to improve its competitiveness in the market. The individual Governments, the Region's development financial institutions, and the Region as a whole must address these imperatives as a matter of urgency.

Marine Resources

It is one of the paradoxes of history that the Member States of CARICOM, although being completely, or almost completely, surrounded by the seas with an abundant supply of fish have, up to recently, been extensively dependent on imports of fish in dried, smoked, canned and pickled form from the temperate countries. Imports of fish have comprised a significant share of the food import bill in all CARICOM States; and the development of the human and physical capability to harvest the resources of the territorial seas has not occupied a significant place in the development plans which these States have drawn up.

The waters of the Caribbean Sea contain substantial quantities of fish and shellfish; this has been confirmed by surveys which have been undertaken by the FAO and UNDP and that fact receives further corroboration by the presence in the area of large numbers of fishing vessels from Taiwan, Korea and Japan. The marine area over which individual States in the Region exercise economic jurisdiction has been extended up to two hundred miles with the international acceptance of the concept of the Exclusive Economic Zone. The acceptance of this international agreement puts a vastly enlarged potential income source in the hands of the States of the Region. The questions which they have to address are how to protect the wholesomeness of this marine area, control the activities of the large number of predators from outside the Region who have been operating illegally in Caribbean waters and optimise the benefits they can derive. In particular they must examine the following:

- what options are available to them to optimise the income they can receive from the known fisheries resources and the potential resources which exist on the sea-bed;
- what role can they play in preventing the transportation of illegal drugs over their sea space.

These questions have to be addressed against the background of the reality that the member States of CARICOM have not yet developed adequate experience to cope with the demands of deep sea fishing; nor have they set in place adequate surveillance machinery to control the illegal discharge of ships' waste in the sea, or, worse still, the discharge in the Caribbean Sea of urban waste from North Amerian cities, some of which is reported to contain toxic substances.

We note that CARICOM States, acting with the assistance of the Commonwealth Secretariat and the Government of India, have begun the mapping of the resources which potentially exist in this area. But this is only a very early beginning to a necesary task which will take a long time to complete. We do, however, urge that this exercise be continued and, if possible, extended to include other countries in the Caribbean Sea and its littoral.

But what emerges from all of this is that it will take a very long time for the individual States in the Region, especially the small island States of the Eastern Caribbean, to develop the nautical and other capability to provide effective surveillance over their territorial sea and ensure that their populations derive commensurate benefit from the exploitation of the resources which exist in it. It is clear that special arrangements have to be devised to meet the problem.

Opportunity for Cooperation

The Caribbean Sea is one area which offers a unique opportunity for the nations of the Caribbean to engage in effective functional cooperation for the long-term benefit of all. As yet, it is not seriously embroiled in issues of sovereignty and national pride. All the countries washed by the Caribbean Sea have an interest in safeguarding its wholesomeness and in ensuring that it is not used for illegal purposes. Effective cooperation among the States involved can therefore unlock the door to other forms of collaboration and expanded trade.

In the eighteenth century, the nations of Europe used the Caribbean Sea to divide up the Caribbean area and keep the countries apart. The present-day nations in the Caribbean should, in our view, use the Caribbean Sea as an agent of closer collaboration.

We believe therefore that CARICOM States should work with the other countries of the Caribbean Region to develop a Convention which will provide initially, at least, for three things:

- effective surveillance of the Caribbean Sea to prevent pollution and reduce the transportation of illegal drugs by sea;
- the establishment of standards to avoid pollution from the land area affecting the sea; and
- the exchange of information derived from the mapping of the sea-bed.

Fishing Rights

The question of the exploitation of the fisheries resources is likely to present more difficulty. Some countries have worked out bilateral arrangements between themselves, notably Venezuela and Trinidad and Tobago and Barbados and Trinidad and Tobago; but these have not always proved to be very durable. One way forward might lie in an agreement on fishing in the Exclusive Economic Zones among the countries of the Eastern Caribbean and Guyana; this group of countries can then engage in bilateral negotiations on fishing with other countries of the Region.

Parallel with these steps, we believe that the Governments of the

Agriculture

Region should recognise that the Exclusive Economic Zones provide them with a new opportunity for economic growth and should begin to take the steps internally to exploit it. These steps must include training the population in the requirements of deep sea fishing and installing the onshore facilities needed to increase the value added from the resources which the enlarged territorial sea could provide.

Recommendations

Improving Agricultural Performance

1. that domestic agriculture be accorded adequate protection against subsidised exports from the industrialised countries over and above that provided by anti-dumping legislation, and that those safeguard policies be focussed, targetted and time-bound;

2. that agriculture, manufacturing and tourism be developed on a symbiotic basis;

3. that the Region develops and applies a common set of phytosanitary regulations to safeguard the regional agricultural sector;

4. that, in accordance with the decisions already taken to create a Single Market and Economy, the barriers to intra-regional trade in agriculture be removed;

5. that steps be taken to increase investment in agriculture with local and foreign private investment; that adequate infrastructure be put in place; disincentives such as praedial larceny removed; land tenure systems reformed; farmers given training, other support and opportunities available in the manufacturing and service sectors; and the development financial institutions provide finance on concessional terms to develop the infrastructure and to satisfy the special needs of tree-crop agriculture;

6. that regional and national research capability programmes

be made more mutually supportive, economical and focussed on specific priority areas;

7. that Governments adopt policies which would maintain stability, keep inflation under control and so restrain increases in interest rates which act as disincentives to investment and long-term planning in agriculture;

Bananas

8. that producers of the Region continue to regard increased yields per acre and quality improvement as fundamental necessities for their staying in the industry.

9. that banana-growing entities in CARICOM explore joint purchasing of key inputs, insurance and shipping arrangements, so as to minimise expenses;

10. that, given the serious implications of a reduction in preference on the incomes of the banana growers, the industry should work to hold the position both with respect to access and to price;

Sugar

11. that since many of the sugar companies are incurring losses which their national treasuries are unable to sustain, each CARICOM sugar producer must take and implement a firm decision on whether:

    (a) the industry should continue — in which case the modernisation and research must be undertaken in order to enable the industry to grow and become competitive internationally; or

    (b) the industry should be phased out over a specified period of time;

    whatever the final outcome, the transfer of ownership of the land to medium and small farmers would, in some cases, appear to be an essential ingredient in the transformation of the industry;

12. that regional research efforts in the sugar industry be extended to cover the wider economic uses of sugar cane and its derivatives. (International funding for such additional research is likely to be obtainable);

13. that, in respect of the EEC market:

    - current access under the Sugar Protocol be preserved as a matter absolutely vital to the industry and the Region;
    - as integration proceeds, efforts be pursued to achieve a joint CARICOM quota within the ACP;
    - the ACP case for obtaining additional access to the EEC sugar market when Portugal becomes a full member of the Sugar Protocol be wholeheartedly supported, with CARICOM's share of such additional access allocated under an arrangement which allows reallocation for shortfalls within CARICOM;
    - in concert with our ACP colleagues, every effort be made to stabilise sugar earnings obtained under the Sugar Protocol. In particular, the case must be pressed for making sure that if Sugar Protocol price cuts arise because of cuts in EEC farm support, compensatory arrangements are made to protect against losses of foreign exchange earnings;

14. that every effort continue to retain regional sugar quotas in the US at least at the minimum level of 71,000 tonnes at which they now stand;

15. that, in respect of the ongoing GATT negotiations, given the danger of a serious reduction in sugar prices received by the ACP, including CARICOM producers, the case be pressed to ensure adequate safeguards to protect the income generated by current sugar arrangements, and particularly by the Sugar Protocol, and these be written into any general GATT agreement;

16. that steps be taken to enlarge facilities in the Region to satisfy its requirements for refined sugar and in general for the Region's sugar producers to meet the Region's domestic sugar needs;

Rum

17. that CARICOM Governments join in pressing the case in the EEC and Canada, countries which have granted non-reciprocal trade preferences to the Region, to follow the practice of the US by granting to the exporting countries rebates on duties collected on rum imported from CARICOM countries in order to assist these countries to enlarge their production efforts; and that the US be requested to grant to CARICOM rum exporters the rebates of duties levied on those exports to the US;

18. that CARICOM Countries press for the removal of quotas on the importation of rum by EEC countries;

19. that CARICOM rum producers enlarge the area of cooperation to modernise the industry and increase their efforts to promote CARICOM rums;

Marine Resources

20. that CARICOM States begin to develop a Convention with the other nations in the Caribbean Sea and the littoral to provide for effective surveillance over the Sea, the establishment of standards to reduce sea pollution from the land, and to exchange technical data derived from mapping the sea-bed;

21. that the Member States in the Eastern Caribbean work out an agreement among themselves on fishing in the Exclusive Economic Zones and, as a group, negotiate similar arrangements with other countries in the Region; and

22. that individual CARICOM Member States enlarge their training opportunities for deep sea fishing and install the on-shore facilities necessary in order to optimise the value of the resources which the sea will provide.

3. MINING

Minerals Available

CARICOM countries own a significant array of mineral resources. Those with the greatest value are bauxite, crude oil/natural gas and gold. But there are also many other materials available which are of importance to industry, although, in terms of value, they are of less significance than those mentioned before: they include, for example, limestone, porcellanite, kaolin, gypsum, silica sand, aragonite and natural asphalt.

In the case of bauxite, now produced in Jamaica and Guyana (Suriname, Haiti and the Dominican Republic also have reserves in commercial quantities), the Caribbean was a significant world supplier during the 1970s. However, the share declined sharply during the 1980s in the wake of the major expansion taking place in Australia and Africa and the reducing competitiveness in the Caribbean bauxite industry as a whole. Guyana's share of world production was 5.5 per cent in 1975 and 1.2 per cent in 1991, while Jamaica's share of world production fell from 16.6 per cent in 1975 to 10.3 per cent in 1991.

CARICOM countries have never been important players on the world petroleum stage although the industry is critically important in Trinidad and Tobago. In this country, an important shift is taking place in the output composition of the industry. Crude petroleum (and the associated refining facilities) has been in steady decline since 1978 and crude oil production is now somewhat below 150,000 barrels per day — some 30 per cent below the 1978 peak; on the other hand, natural gas has been growing in importance and, with proven and probable reserves of natural gas being in the region of 16 trillion cubic feet, this segment of the industry, along with the associated condensate production, seems likely to displace crude petroleum. Barbados' production of crude oil and natural gas, although important in that economy, is very small.

The search for additional reserves of minerals, especially hydrocarbons, has been accelerating in the Region during the last few years. In Guyana, exploration activity is concentrated on the land

and the foreshore area; while in Trinidad and Tobago, exploration activity is probing the potential of the deeper horizons on both land and sea. There has not yet been any significant exploration effort in the Exclusive Economic Zones (EEZs) where experienced observers believe that valuable mineral resources are likely to exist — although, with known technology, they could be expensive to produce.

Contribution to the Economy

The mining industry (and its associated processing activity) has been of critical importance in Jamaica, Guyana and Trinidad and Tobago. It is the largest earner of foreign exchange in these countries and an important contributor to national output. It is highly capital-intensive and therefore employs only a small proportion of the labour force directly. In Jamaica and Guyana, bauxite and alumina exports comprised 34 per cent and 37 per cent respectively of merchandise exports in 1990 and the bauxite industry contributed 7 per cent and 27 per cent respectively of the Gross Domestic Product in the same year. In the case of Trinidad and Tobago, the hydrocarbon industry contributed 68 per cent of total merchandise exports in 1990, and 27 per cent of the GDP in that year. The rest of the mining industry made relatively insignificant contributions to exports and output both in the three countries in which mining was a significant activity, as well as in other CARICOM States where it was not.

Prospects for the Mining Industry

The prospects facing the mining industry must take into account the probability of finding new reserves of producible material, as well as the evolving international market situation.

Both Guyana and Jamaica have large reserves of bauxite so that, for these countries, the future of that industry depends on the international demand for primary produced aluminium. In the case of hydrocarbons, while, as pointed out above, the proven and probable reserves of natural gas are relatively large, those for crude petroleum depend critically on the results of on-going exploration efforts. While it is hazardous to speculate on the outcomes of these efforts, the situation is reported to be reasonably optimistic. With regard to prices, there is no indication of any significant increase over the medium-term.

With regard to markets, the situation for bauxite is clouded by the very large new operations in Australia and Africa, the growing importance of secondary production of aluminium, the projected decline in the demand for the metal, and the increasing international cartelisation of the industry, which is concentrating markets within the domain controlled by the majors. Prices could therefore be depressed for a considerable period of time.

The other industrial minerals depend mainly on activity in the construction industry which, in turn, is a function of macroeconomic management and performance in the individual economies. Gold production is, however, subject to special price considerations.

Policies

In the face of these prospects, the policies which the individual countries, and the Region as a whole, can pursue can only be concerned with optimising the income which can be derived through the exploitation of the known resources and, though exploration, increasing the quantum of producible reserves available. To this end, the following measures should be pursued —

- combining the resources available in the Region to increase the value added. To some extent this is already taking place, as Jamaican gypsum is being combined in Trinidad with limestone and other inputs to produce cement. But the list may be extended to combine Guyana's silica sand and Trinidad's natural gas to produce glass and computer components. The situation of combining resources could reach a high level of development if the on-going talks on establishing a regional aluminium smelter make progress — although, given the market situation, the participation of one of the majors in the industry would appear to be necessary to bring this project to fruition;
- developing a capability in industrial design to make better use of the valuable clay resources which exist in Guyana and elsewhere and which can support a ceramics industry;

- introducing new arrangements to encourage an enlarged exploration effort to identify exploitable resources. This may entail the introduction of new fiscal incentives to local and foreign enterprises. But, especially in the exploration of the seabed in the EEZs, there are significant economies to be achieved by dealing with large blocks as exploration areas rather than restricting the scope of individual country efforts to the EEZ falling under the jurisdiction of individual Member States. A start has already been in this direction in the recent CSC/India project of mapping the sea and the seabed in the EEZs of CARICOM States. We urge that the Governments of the Region give careful attention to devising the most efficient mechanism for undertaking this exercise and, in this regard, suggest that the establishment of a multinational authority should be considered.

Recommendations

1. that the mining sector develop programmes to maximise value added by combining minerals from different countries, if necessary, to produce final products, e.g., aluminium from bauxite and petroleum or cement from gypsum and limestone;

2. that the mining sector develop the capability to use the clay resources of the Region to promote a ceramics industry;

3. that the mining sector, jointly with foreign private investment, undertake enlarged exploration efforts including exploration of the seabed. Seabed exploration in a single joint effort could encompass all the EEZs falling under the jurisdiction of Member States. Governments should provide fiscal incentives to support this effort.

4. TOURISM AND SERVICES

Tourism in the Region

Tourism is the dominant economic sector in many CARICOM countries; it is of growing importance in all. There used to be a time when one could speak of the tourism economies and the non-tourism countries of CARICOM. We are on the verge of a new era when that distinction will disappear. Even the one or two CARICOM countries which not many years ago embraced a policy of caution towards tourism development are now openly committed to nurturing in their economies a tourism sector geared to their particular endowments.

This is a well advised change of heart, for, in a regional and world environment in which temporary short-term shifts are often confused with underlying long-term structural change, the world tourism industry is one area of global economic activity that has settled down for the long haul, and is destined to expand. Countries in the Region cannot, however, assume that their share of world tourism is assured merely on account of the current level of performance of their tourism sectors, and because world tourism is projected to continue growing well into the foreseeable future; they have to work hard at promoting growth in the industry.

The tourism industry within CARICOM is a substantial part of the Caribbean-wide tourism industry, providing approximately 120,000 jobs. Within CARICOM, the ratio of estimated tourism income to GDP in 1989 ranged from a low of about 2.0 per cent in Trinidad and Tobago to a high of some 78.0 per cent in Antigua and Barbuda, and the industry was the major source of foreign exchange earnings for many countries in the Region.

Tourism has clearly emerged in CARICOM and the wider Caribbean not only as a leading sector in terms of the level of activity generated in the linked bundle of activities that constitute the sector (air, sea and ground transportation, boating, hotel accommodation, entertainment, restaurants, tourist attractions), but also on account of the momentum it imparts, or has the potential of imparting, to other key sectors of the regional economy — agriculture, manufacturing, construction, banking and finance and other services. Through powerful backward linkages that can be fostered between tourism and these other sectors, the industry can be an engine for boosting growth in their output because it expands the demand for their products. Out of the tourist industry radiates stimuli for a wide range of industries producing goods and services; this is the concept of tourism as an axial product. Viewed in this light, the tourism sector can play an important role in the diversification and transformation of the Region.

We welcome the fact that there has been in recent times a marked and discernible increase in public and official recognition of the strategic position that tourism has come to occupy in the Region. It is a matter of considerable encouragement that this recognition is shared by the public and private sectors throughout the Caribbean, a recognition that was impressively demonstrated by the highly successful initiative of Prime Minister Michael Manley of Jamaica in convening a CARICOM Tourism Summit in Kingston in February 1992, in which tourism interests from throughout the wider Caribbean were involved.

Challenges Facing Tourism

But what of the challenges facing the tourism sector in CARICOM and the Caribbean today? All the important challenges relate to one central and overriding issue: that of retaining, and possibly increasing, the Region's market share in world tourism. We have already pointed out that the Region cannot complacently assume that its market share is assured merely on account of the present level of performance of its tourism sector, and simply because world tourism is growing, and is projected to continue growing, well into the future. The Region must work consciously and continuously to defend and increase its market share. That translates into the need for both national and regional action on various levels and in a number of directions.

In this context, we wish to highlight a few key issues and challenges. One is the question of exploiting the potential that exists for enhancing joint development in the Region through stronger linkages between tourism and other sectors. There is considerable untapped potential for increasing regional supplies to the tourism sector in CARICOM, and this can be encouraged in various ways through the right mix of public sector policies and cooperation with the private sector, without necessarily doing anything that compromises the principle of competitiveness with extra-regional supplies.

The agricultural sector is one example of this and so is entertainment where there is much scope for the Region's pool of talented performers to move around freely to provide entertainment services both for local audiences and for visiting tourists.

We anticipate that with the coming into being of a Single Market and Economy in CARICOM, an environment will emerge which will foster stronger linkages of the tourism sector in the Region with other areas of production and services. But that, by itself, may not be sufficient. Along with the enabling environment of the Single Market arrangements, it will be necessary to actively promote greater information exchange between procurement personnel in the tourist industry and operators in other industries and promote greater consciousness of the possibilities for competitive procurement within the Region.

There is of course one particular regional industry with which the tourism sector already has a strong linkage, and that is the regional air transportation industry.

The vital challenge for regional air transportation, as it relates to tourism, is not the issue of linkage as such, but rather, as we have indicated in another part of our Report, that of finding a strategy for survival in the current global air transportation environment, and thus of preserving that assured service on which the maintenance of the regional tourist industry itself may depend at critical moments when extra-regional carriers suspend their services, sometimes with hardly any notice at all.

This will be of strategic significance to defending and increasing market share in world tourism. Other issues are similarly of strategic significance.

Tourists worldwide are becoming more exacting and sophisticated in their demands, and more conscious of value for money. The tourism market is also becoming increasingly segmented, catering for different kinds of tastes and interests; and the emergence, in recent times, in response to this, of eco-tourism and adventure travel, health tourism and sports tourism, constitutes an important addition to the traditional sun-sea-and-sand tourism, and are playing a part in the growth of world tourism.

CARICOM countries, individually and collectively, must keep themselves fully informed of world trends in tourism product development, so that they are seized at all times of what their competitors are doing, and adapt their tourism product appropriately, without slavish imitation, to changing demands and changing international standards. The product development and adaptation that must be pursued embrace a wide range of matters, including the design and furnishing of hotel properties, the quality of personal services in hotels and elsewhere at the tourist destination, the general attitude of local residents to visitors, the ease, efficiency and degree of pleasantness in obtaining ingress and egress at ports of entry, organised facilities for exposing interested visitors to the history, culture, and natural attractions of the tourist destination, and the organisation of multi-destination packages within the Region that offer the holiday. As indicated earlier, the tourism consultations in Kingston in February 1992 led to the adoption of a comprehensive package of resolutions and the subject of product development features prominently in this package.

Human Resource Development in Tourism

It is evident, from the foregoing, that to undertake all the things that have to be done to protect and expand the Region's market share in world tourism, it will be necessary to sustain and promote human resource development comprehensively within the tourism sector. As a Region, we must hone our human resources in tourism at the level of entrepreneurship, at the level of public sector planning and coordination, in the areas of marketing and promotion and of overall hotel management, and in all the specific roles that go together to keep hotel plants functioning — food and beverage management, housekeeping, portering, reception, grounds maintenance. This cannot be left to chance. The matter calls for the conscious establishment of strategic objectives, and for purposive planning and execution of programmes to achieve these objectives.

Very importantly, it is quite feasible for us in CARICOM to pursue human resource development in tourism, not only for the necessary purpose of sustaining the efficient operation of the sector, but also with a view to transforming our Community into a world centre of excellence in the area of expertise in tourism development and management. Already, considerable indigenisation of entrepreneurship and ownership in the tourism sector has taken place within some CARICOM countries, principally Jamaica, and this entrepreneurial talent is being invited to assist tourism development in other parts of the Caribbean. We believe the development of skills at other levels in regional tourism can be pursued to the point where we are able to cater to our own needs within CARICOM and will be able at the same time to sell tourism management and operational services outside the Region.

The Attitude of Resident Populations

We would also call attention to the attitude of the resident populations at our tourist destinations. Regrettably, even with increasing recognition of the importance of tourism, there is still some lingering ambiguity in the attitude of sections of the resident population towards tourism and tourists. The marked difference in pigmentation between the majority of tourists on the one hand, and the predominant number of the populations in CARICOM destinations on the other, sometimes brings back deep-seated historic memories of servitude, exploitation, and alienation, and this has, on one occasion, threatened to affect the climate for tourism adversely. This is a problem which must be overcome urgently if CARICOM is to protect and increase its market share in world tourism. It will be necessary to inculcate in West Indians an outlook in which tourism is accepted as one of the Region's legitimate business sectors in which careers can be pursued with dignity at all levels of the industry.

Tourism and the West Indian Diaspora

We have examined, in another section of our Report, the unused potential of the West Indian diaspora. Encouraging more visits back home from West Indian nationals abroad is certainly one way of utilising the potential of the diaspora for contributing to the development of the West Indian homeland. The estimated 3.5 million West Indians now living abroad in Canada, the United Kingdom and the United States — to say nothing of West Indians living in other parts of the world — constituting as they do vibrant communities of professionals and other workers, and sharing in the enjoyment of the average income levels of their adopted countries, comprise a market from which a greater contribution could be made to the flow of visitors to the Region.

We are of course, fully conscious of the fact that West Indians abroad do visit the Region, particularly to maintain contact with families and with the original local communities from which they hail. What we are suggesting is that the volume of these visits could be substantially increased, and that the West Indian national abroad should be encouraged to go on holiday not only in his home country but in other CARICOM countries as well.

Intra-CARICOM Tourism

Equally important is the need to exploit more fully the potential for intra-CARICOM tourism. This should neither be seen as being anything out of the ordinary, nor should it be approached — as some appear inclined at times to do — on the basis of an 'either/or' mentality of CARICOM tourists versus non-CARICOM tourists. In many places in the world — the UK, USA, Canada — domestic tourism constitutes an important part of the national tourist industry. This should be no different in the context of a CARICOM Region conceived as a unified community; and we hope that with the coming of the Single Market in CARICOM and the advent of arrangements to facilitate hassle-free travel within the Community, intra-CARICOM tourism will be greatly enlarged.

It is, of course, hardly necessary for us to point to the benefits to be derived from expanded intra-CARICOM tourism. It would help to increase the size and the output of the industry, with all that that entails for expansion of employment and of the demand for goods and services from other sectors. Very importantly, greater intra-CARICOM tourism would have the effect of conserving scarce foreign exchange resources within the Region, which would then be available to help diversify and broaden the productive base of the regional economy. Moreover, it would provide an opportunity for us to get to know ourselves better as West Indians and to discover at first hand particular aspects of our shared culture and the natural environment with which we have been endowed.

Tourism and Diversification

We wish, finally, to emphasise one critically important issue in relation to tourism. It is that even if there were to be full implementation of all our recommendations and the resolutions emerging out of the Kingston consultations, the Governments and peoples of the Region would still need to be conscious of the critical importance of channelling surpluses generated in tourism, as a leading sector, into building up other diversified areas of income generation. This would be a very relevant concern even if, as a result of sound measures to preserve the natural attractions of regional holiday resorts, tourism, unlike the mining sector, for instance, does not turn out to be a wasting asset. The relevance of this concern is, therefore, even more pressing when it is considered that we cannot assume automatic victory in our battle against environmental degradation of our tourist destinations in the Region.

Services in CARICOM

Services as an area of economic activity have always been of considerable importance, but nevertheless have not been a subject of serious and consistent policy-making in CARICOM countries, or indeed, in developing countries as a whole. A change in attitudes is now taking place. This has been fuelled in part by the decisive push by the industrialised countries, led by the United States, to use the Uruguay Round of international trade negotiations to bring international trade in services under the disciplines of the GATT. It seems also to be propelled in part by the growing awareness in many developing countries that in an era of rapidly changing technology, and of transformation of production structures, the prospects are not very bright in the unfolding world economy for many of the staple commodity exports on which developing countries such as our own have traditionally relied for their export earnings.

CARICOM countries, therefore, no less than many parts of the developing world, now find themselves at a critical crossroads where they must seek to achieve a more balanced product mix in their economies, as between commodities and services, for sale both in regional and domestic markets and for export to extra-regional markets. Preoccupation with the issue has been fully reflected in the study, *CARICOM to the Year 2000*, and in a number of regional technical workshops on the subject convened by the CARICOM Secretariat.

The Major Service Areas

Other than tourism, major areas of services of interest to CARICOM countries are financial services, telecommunication services, professional services, transportation services and cultural and information services. Each of these, in turn, breaks down into several specific services, all of which present different prospects and challenges in terms of the critical interests which the Region must pursue. Space does not permit detailed treatment in our Report of each specific sub-area. We propose only to address some general issues and principles which are of particular importance to the development of the services sector in CARICOM.

As the Uruguay Round moves to a conclusion, generating agreed measures for the conduct of world trade which for the first time will include rules governing international trade in services, CARICOM Governments have to be concerned with securing adequate breathing space to allow the Region to develop its own production and trade in services to the point where regional performance can hold its own in domestic and external markets.

The Collective Potential of CARICOM Services

We believe very strongly that trade in services is one of those areas in which CARICOM countries are better served if they deal with the outside world as a group rather than individually. In practical terms, this means that CARICOM countries should move expeditiously to establish free trade in services within the Community, and pursue this positively as a key component of the

CARICOM Single Market.

We believe that such a course would enhance the individual and collective potential of CARICOM Member States to benefit from the services sector. The Governments and people of the Region must get into the habit of thinking of each area of the services sector as an area of economic activity — no less than the case of the production of physical commodities — with the potential for creating value added, for income generation, for the saving and earning of foreign exchange, for generating employment, and for developing a regional pool of skills, not only for sustaining the development of the particular service area.

Niches in the Market for Services

CARICOM countries must start positioning themselves to secure viable niches in emerging international markets for services. We expect that even if CARICOM countries, along with other like-minded developing countries, succeed in securing a breathing space to allow for consolidation of sensitised areas in their services sector, our regional economy will nevertheless be constrained, overall, to operate in a more liberalised system of international trade in services.

Already, there are interesting indicators in various parts of CARICOM of the kind of possibilities that beckon us. We understand, for instance, that there are dentists in some CARICOM countries who remain based in the Region, but commute periodically to metropolitan centres to provide dental services. Again, some highly qualified engineers in the Region, instead of migrating overseas, are seeking ways and means of selling engineering design services abroad without leaving their countries. In some parts of the Region, the capability of the construction industry, in housing and in a wide range of civil works, has reached a level where efforts can be, and are being, made to make competitive bids for building contracts abroad; and in the field of data processing, modern breakthroughs in communications and computer technology make it possible for persons with the requisite skills to provide data entry services for a wide range of companies abroad.

Supporting Measures

We have already emphasised the importance, as a basic point of departure, of free trade in services being established among CARICOM member countries. This would be reinforced by appropriate supporting measures, one of which would be to move from national to regional systems of registration and other regulations for key groups such as medical, engineering, accounting, and legal professionals. We believe that this kind of development should be pursued within the context of the Community's programme of harmonisation of laws, regulations, and standards, and that the necessary technical task forces should be established early to start working on these matters.

We must also draw attention to the importance of human resource development in the strengthening of the services sector. Education and training in certain traditional professions such as law, medicine, engineering, and accounting have been relatively well established over the years, even if these traditional areas of training have come under some pressure in recent times. CARICOM faces human resource development challenges in the services sector, however, that go considerably beyond this.

In the context of being able to hold our own in services for regional and extra-regional markets, we must consciously target the creation of cadres of high-level professionals in the new technologies in computer science, telecommunications, informatics, international finance, and with a capacity to understand and operate in an increasingly complex and sophisticated international market place. As in other areas, this perhaps points to new demands that must be placed on our tertiary education system in the Region. The policies and strategies for human resource development, which we have discussed more extensively elsewhere in our Report, will need to address these particular needs.

We mention briefly other supporting measures for the services sector which should be given serious consideration in the Region. As is the case with the industrial sector, we believe that urgent study should be given to the question of a harmonised regional system of incentives for the services sector, or for strategic components thereof, particularly for the encouragement of the export of services by CARICOM countries. We are mindful that in the case of commodities, much effort within the Region in recent years has gone into the development and implementation of schemes to provide pre- and post-shipment financing for the export of goods and to provide insurance coverage for export risks. We believe that similar facilities should now be considered for the services sector, and recommend that the Community should give this matter early attention.

In all this we think it particularly important to be conscious of those circumstances in which West Indian communities abroad provide rich potential markets for which CARICOM entrepreneurs can provide certain services. Already, enterprising business groups from within the Region are establishing commercial banks in metropolitan centres where there are concentrations of West Indians. We believe that, once it can be demonstrated that these operations function in a manner that produces real and tangible developmental benefits for the Region, appropriate incentives should be devised to encourage these initiatives, including encouraging the West Indians in the diaspora to avail themselves of the services provided.

Recommendations

Tourism

1. that CARICOM Governments and the concerned regional institutions give special attention to the implementation of the programme implicit in the conclusions that emerged from the Regional Tourism Summit in February 1992;

2. that CARICOM Governments use every opportunity to encourage the joint marketing of the Caribbean, as a whole, as a tourist destination;

3. that a conscious effort be made to institutionalise the consultation process at regional levels in the tourism sector, between Governments and private sector interests;

4. that Governments and private sector organisations involved in tourism intensify their efforts to strengthen the backward

linkages of the tourism sector with other sectors within the Region;

5. that national and regional institutions in tourism, in collaboration with regional airlines and the hotels sector, and with the support of regional Governments, develop and implement programmes and strategies to expand intra-CARICOM tourism;

Services

6. that CARICOM Governments, in their strategic planning, address explicitly the development of services for the regional market and for export;

7. that CARICOM Governments harmonise their regulations regarding the accreditation and registration of professionals in fields such as accounting, engineering and law;

8. that CARICOM Governments examine closely the matter of extending appropriate incentives to the services sector.

5. AIR AND SEA TRANSPORTATION

It has been asserted in this Report and elsewhere that vision and political will must furnish the driving force propelling West Indian peoples into closer unity. But tangible results will flow from this vision and political will only if they are matched by the necessary enabling instruments that embody the fact of unity. Closer integration is manifested *par excellence* by the volume and intensity of the movement of goods and people among the countries comprising the integration grouping. Countries, even if in close geographical proximity, that do not engage in mutual commercial and social interchange do not make an integrated group. Adequate means for the movement of goods and people are therefore a *sine qua non* for integration among any regional grouping of countries seeking to enter into closer unity.

In the particular circumstances of CARICOM's five and a half million people, scattered over the Community's thirteen Member States and two Associate Member States, stretching in an arc measuring some 4,000 kilometers from Belize in the west through the eastern Caribbean, to Trinidad and Tobago and Guyana in the south east, and with no contiguous boundaries between any of them — this means that sea and air transportation are of strategic significance for sustaining the momentum of integration. West Indian integration would wither on the vine and die without adequate sea and air transportation services, whether they are furnished by the chance play of commercial forces, or whether they are ensured by conscious Community policy and programmes in one form or another. Indeed, this is precisely one of the issues for clear determination within the Caribbean Community: to leave the provision of sea and air transportation, which sustains the life of the integration process, wholly to commercial chance — and we hasten to insist that this has no necessary bearing on the issue of privatisation — or to define and apply a holistic Community policy in the matter, aimed at the provision of assured services, including services provided through private operators.

We believe that there is a role for conscious Community policy. Indeed, the history of developments in the Region affecting sea and air transportation reveals intermittent and fitful efforts to grope towards a Community policy in this area. CARICOM has long passed the stage where these efforts should have purposively led to a clear regional programme and strategy to guide the development of air and sea transportation services. A definitive Community policy is necessary, not only to ensure fulfillment of the requirements for intra-regional movement of goods and people, but also on account of the need for air and sea links with extraregional destinations to facilitate tourism and non-tourism travel and the exchange of goods with the outside world.

Global Trends

The policy, programme and strategy which the Caribbean Community needs to pursue in the matter of regional air and sea transportation must of necessity be defined in the context of global trends in air and sea transportation.

In air transportation, quantitatively, airlines of the member states of the International Civil Aviation Organisation (ICAO) are reported to have carried on scheduled domestic and international services in 1989 an estimated 1099 million passengers, an increase of 1.7 per cent over the 1988 estimate and 47.0 per cent over the 1980 estimate. Of these estimated carryings in 1989, it is believed that tourist travel accounted for more than 400 million, an increase of 3.0 per cent over the 1988 estimate and 42.0 per cent over the 1980 level. It is clear that, globally, people are increasingly on the move by air, both for tourism travel and otherwise.

Structurally, the global air transportation industry is undergoing profound change. Accompanying a process of persistent growth in the volume of traffic, the global industry is being transformed from one traditionally characterised by high levels of regulation of pricing, of market entry, and of capacity, and by a point-to-point route structure and considerable Government ownership, to one characterised by deregulation, privatisation of ownership (with some forty airlines world-wide passing out of Government ownership in recent years), and globalisation through acquisition, complex equity swaps, and market alliances, and a hub-and-spoke type of route structure in which traffic is concentrated at major airports for onward carriage to final destinations.

In the United States alone there were fifty-one airline mergers and acquisitions between 1979 and 1988, and the United States experience is being replicated in greater or lesser measure in other regions of the world. In 1987 the world's top ten airlines carried a total of 306 million scheduled passengers. Generally, airline companies have become more global and concentrated, with a consequent trend towards less competition due to the increased market dominance of a few expanding mega-carriers.

An integral part of this trend has been the increase in the control that major airline conglomerates exercise over critical airport infrastructure such as access to gates, landing slots and terminal facilities at important international and domestic ports of entry, and over the operation of feeder services and of the major computer reservation systems, which are often manipulated to crowd out competing and less powerful carriers.

In contrast with the global air transportation industry, sea transportation world-wide has not been characterised by the same pace and intensity of concentration among carriers. This is probably so because a key factor which drives the process of mergers and market alliances among airlines, namely the joint exploitation of air route rights, is not matched by any similar phenomenon in the field of maritime transportation. There is no system of sea route rights. In order to operate a service a shipping line basically needs to have only adequate capital and equipment capacity, and the requisite agency arrangement in each port, along with the necessary promotion and marketing effort.

Other interesting features characterise the global shipping industry. The volume of international sea-borne trade has been growing and has registered increases over the last five consecutive years, reaching a level of some four billion freight tonnes. Effective control of about fifty per cent of the world merchant fleet remains concentrated in the five major maritime countries of Greece, Japan, Norway, the United States and the former USSR. Developing countries as a whole own just 21.0 per cent of the world fleet, and 70.0 per cent of this is concentrated in ten countries. It is to be noted that, in contrast with their 21.0 per cent share, measured in dead-weight, of the ownership of the world fleet, developing countries as a whole generate nearly 37.0 per cent of the volume of world trade.

Of particular significance is the fact that the ratio of the element of freight to the full c.i.f. value of imports is invariably higher for developing countries compared to developed countries — customarily twice as high, with the figure for countries in Africa and Oceania being almost three times greater.

Regional Demand

The regional demand for air and sea transportation comprises, as would be expected, the two basic components of the demand for movement of goods and people intra-regionally on the one hand, and between the Region and extra-regional destinations on the other. Total international passenger arrivals by air in CARICOM countries in recent times have been at the level of about ten million, some 45.0 per cent above the level registered in 1980. North America continues to account for the dominant share, at over 70.0 per cent, of these arrivals, though its relative share has been declining, while that accounted for by Europe has been showing an upward trend.

Intra-regionally, over ninety per cent of passenger travel is undertaken by air transportation, and this has been showing significant growth in recent years. The performance of Leeward Islands Air Transport (LIAT), an important intra-regional air carrier of CARICOM, provides a good indicator of the trends in intra-regional air travel. LIAT carried just under 500 thousand passengers during its financial year 1984-1985. This rose steadily to 806,000, or by 63.2 per cent, by 1988-89, and by a further 2.0 per cent to 821,000 the following year.

Of course, an important part of the regional demand for air transportation to extra-regional destinations is connected with regional tourism. This component of demand depends very much therefore on the health and performance of the tourism sector. As Caribbean tourism is an industry affected by high income elasticity of demand, and is sensitive to price trends and product quality at the Region's tourist destinations relative to alternative destinations, an important part of the demand for air travel between the Caribbean and North America and Europe is determined ultimately by economic buoyancy in the developed countries and by the maintenance of price competitiveness of the tourism product in the Region, including, of course, competitiveness of air fares.

The regional demand for sea transportation is mainly in connection with the movement of goods. There is indeed a certain amount of movement of cargo by air, but just as it is the case that over ninety per cent of intra-regional passenger travel is by air, it is also the case that a roughly similar proportion of the intra-regional movement of goods is by sea. The issue has often been examined in the Region of the greater movement of goods by air and also, apart from cruise ship travel, the provision of more and better facilities for movement of people by sea. It is recognised, however, that, for the foreseeable future, all feasible adjustments or shifts that may take place in the mode of movement of people and goods will still leave air transportation as the dominant means of intra-regional passenger travel, and sea transportation as the dominant means for the intra-regional movement of goods.

Issues and Challenges

Regional Governments are yet to formalise a conscious CARICOM policy and programme on regional air and sea transportation. We urge more expeditious action on this matter. We reiterate that the justification for such a conscious policy and programme lies in the fact that the matter is, in the most profound and fundamental sense, at the very heart of the integration process itself. This is so in various mutually reinforcing ways. It is so in terms of facilitating the integration of production and trade in the Community. It is so in terms of buttressing the performance of the vital tourism sector in CARICOM and supporting its integration in the Region. Most critically, it is so in terms of helping to foster among West Indian people a sense of community in a West Indian homeland.

But there is one other consideration that enters into this justification. It is the fact that regional air and sea transportation constitute a sector of economic activity in its own right, with the potential for providing direct and indirect employment, for adding to the regional skills pool, for income generation, for contributing to regional Gross Domestic Product, for earning and saving foreign exchange for the Region, and thus for enhancing the overall regional net foreign exchange position.

All these considerations make it abundantly clear why, in a prevailing international policy climate of liberalisation, the Community must at all costs avoid abdicating responsibility for providing leadership in ensuring the availability of reliable regional air and sea transportation. The provision of these services must not become wholly a matter of chance, depending on calculations and decisions made elsewhere in response to considerations far removed from the goals and the objectives of West Indian integration.

Policy Options

In these terms, important issues and challenges arise for attention in regional transportation. A first issue is what choice is to be made from the strategic policy options open to the Community for determining its basic orientation to regional transportation. Basically, four such options present themselves, with respect to both air and sea transportation.

One of these is for the Community to seek to operate in each sector an inter-governmentally owned entity or entities which would be mandated to provide air or sea transportation comprehensively among the Member States, regardless of the internal financial viability of these operations. The critical implementation of this approach, of course, is that the concerned Governments would have to be prepared to provide subsidies for such operations almost indefinitely. This option is clearly not an acceptable one, since CARICOM Governments are neither able to mobilise the capital resources to establish such operations properly, nor do they dispose of the financial resources necessary to finance the deficits of the operations.

A second possible scenario for each sector would be one involving an inter-governmentally owned entity or entities providing regional transportation services on the basis of a clear mandate to operate on a commercially viable basis. While this approach would avoid the problem of Governments having to provide subsidies, it would still suffer from the drawback of Governments not being in a position to marshall the investment capital needed to place and keep regional transportation entities on a viable footing. It is therefore not an approach that recommends itself for the long term future.

A third strategic option for determining the Community's basic posture towards regional air and sea transportation would be one in which matters are left entirely in the hands of the regional and international private sector in a completely 'laissez faire' environment, and in an atmosphere of Governmental disengagement from regulatory or policy involvement in regional air and sea transportation. The implications of this option would be that regional transportation services could not be assumed to be available on an assured basis; that regionally based services could be crowded out by competition from large externally based mega-carriers; and that there would be a danger of the Region not enjoying a reasonable share of the employment, skills generation, and income produced by the regional transportation sector.

A fourth strategic option for the Community's approach is one in which privately-owned or joint Government and privately-owned operations provide regional transportation services within an operational framework established by regional Governments collectively, including a facilitating and enabling inter-Governmental regime to support the functioning of the entity or entities. This fourth option is the preferred option, as it allows the overall goals and interests of the Region to be pursued and protected while harnessing private sector energies and resources, including extraregional private sector access to markets, capital, technology and management skills, to the operation of viable air and sea transportation services based in the Region.

Whichever of these options is ultimately chosen, there is a further consideration that needs to be addressed. The provision of air and sea transportation services linking all parts of the Community, and the Community with the rest of the world, must address not only the question of the operating equipment which provides services, such as ships and aircraft, but also the land-based infrastructure which is necessary — port facilities, airports, air-control facilities and handling equipment. All of these make a substantial claim on the resources which the countries of the Region, and the Region as a whole can mobilise for the purpose of assuring itself of the quality and scale of the services it requires to promote development. Note must also be taken of the reality that the international requirements being stipulated for the safe operation of these facilities are resulting in much higher cost.

While it has been traditional for these facilities to be provided by the public sector, there could be other policy options. There are already several examples in CARICOM countries where on-land facilities servicing at least maritime trade are owned and operated by private enterprise with the Government providing regulatory and other control services in the area. In terms of international air traffic, there is one airport which is operated by private enterprise, but for the most part this facility is provided by the State.

Necessary Responses

In working towards this dispensation, regional Governments need to respond, or continue responding, to a range of other critical issues and challenges. These issues and challenges appear on two levels. At the higher and more ambitious level are issues and challenges relating to commercial consolidation of the structure and operation of regional air and sea transportation services.

Air Transportation

In air transportation, five principal airlines owned within CARICOM currently provide services within the Region and between the Region and extra-regional destinations. They are the Trinidad and Tobago-based British West Indian Airways (BWIA); Leeward Islands Air Transport (LIAT); Air Jamaica; Guyana Airways; and Bahamasair. A sixth airline owned within the Region, the Barbados-based Caribbean Airways, succumbed in recent years to the typical ailment that affects small airlines around the world, namely, an unsupportable accumulation of operating losses, and very recently a seventh — CARICARGO — based in Barbados — has suffered the same fate. Of the five in operation, Air Jamaica, Guyana Airways and Bahamasair ply only between their respective national bases and extra-regional destinations, with Air Jamaica and Bahamasair being principal carriers for their respective tourism industries. BWIA provides a service linking all CARICOM countries which possess jet airports except Belize and The Bahamas, as well as a service from various points in CARICOM to various non-CARICOM Caribbean destinations and to extraregional destinations in North America, Europe, and South America. LIAT at present provides a service to all CARICOM countries except The Bahamas, Belize and Jamaica, as well as to the Associate Member State of the British Virgin Islands, and to a number of non-CARICOM Caribbean destinations.

All these airlines are Government owned. CARICARGO was owned jointly by Barbados and Trinidad and Tobago, and LIAT is owned collectively by all CARICOM Governments except The Bahamas and Belize, the result of a regional response to a threat of closure of the airline in 1974 by its then parent company, Court Line of Britain. The other four airlines are owned by their respective national Governments, with BWIA being acquired in 1961 by the Trinidad and Tobago Government in face of the threat by its then parent company, BOAC, to close it down, and following the collapse of an attempt by the West Indian Federal Government to take it over jointly with other West Indian Governments, along with continued BOAC share-holding.

With the exception of Guyana Airways, which makes a modest profit on its international service (due mainly to the fact that it operates on selected routes on which there is strong demand and no direct competition), the regional airlines customarily incur losses each year on their operations. These losses have had to be made good by the treasuries of the shareholder Governments, a burden that is becoming unsustainable in an era of structural adjustment-linked pressures to reduce public sector expenditure and to eliminate subsidies.

We believe that the current situation calls for urgent identification and implementation of strategies that would improve the operating results of the regional air transportation industry and at the same time provide scope for the Region to maintain and participate in the provision of assured services. In this context we welcome the studies and discussions that have been taking place in the Region on the issue of merger and privatisation of regional airlines, with the aim of having the resulting entity or entities retain a regional character.

Privatisation

Interestingly, this is not a new preoccupation. It is all reminiscent of the very valid search in the late 1960s for a strategy to rationalise the operations of regional airlines around the concept of a regional carrier. At that time, West Indian Governments had agreed to the strategy of establishing a West Indian Air Corporation, owned jointly by regional Governments, based on BWIA and providing service on extra-regional routes, and a West Indian National Airline Company owned by the Corporation and other interests, based on LIAT, and providing service intra-regionally. It is perhaps one of the grave misfortunes of West Indian integration that this bold and well-conceived resolution is numbered among other important regional commitments which were never brought to the point of implementation.

With the current resurgence of the issue of commercial rationalisation, which was triggered by a proposal from the late Prime Minister Errol Barrow of Barbados in 1987 for the establishment of a Single Multinational Air Carrier for the Eastern Caribbean, the current focus of attention for immediate action is the idea of linking BWIA and LIAT, though general hopes persist of the rationalisation net being cast more widely in due course, to incorporate other airlines in CARICOM.

In recent years the shareholder Governments of BWIA and LIAT have arrived at firm decisions that these two airlines should be privatised, and since August 1990 the BWIA/LIAT linkage issue has been before a Committee chaired by the Prime Minister of St. Vincent and the Grenadines, charged with preparing recommendations to the Community on whether BWIA and LIAT should pursue separate paths to privatisation and to finding a joint venture partner, or whether the two airlines should merge into one entity which would then privatise and find a joint venture partner in a manner which will not jeopardise the integrity of the route rights which the airlines now enjoy.

We have found a large measure of sympathy in the Region for the latter option and we identify with that sentiment. We understand and share the fears that exist that if BWIA and LIAT were to go their separate ways with separate foreign joint venture partners, this could open the way to damaging and wasteful rivalry for the regional air transport market which could be inimical to the interest of West Indian integration. On the other hand, the pooling of the air transportation assets that exist in the Region in terms of equipment, maintenance bases, aviation industry skills, goodwill painfully built up over many years, and the often ignored bundle of air route rights attaching to regional Governments, would put the Region in a strong negotiating position to secure the kind of privatisation and joint venture arrangements that would serve the best interest of regional air transportation.

We recommend most strongly that the Region moves to this position in the shortest possible time; and we are reinforced in our recommendation by the fact that, even in advance of any final Community determination on the matter, the two airlines have embarked in recent times upon a positive programme of collaboration, such as the rationalisation of their flight schedules and reciprocal arrangements for handling each other's ground services where circumstances warrant. We also support the view, already put forward by Civil Aviation Ministers of CARICOM, that in approaching the establishment of a single carrier in the Eastern Caribbean with regional private sector participation and a foreign joint venture partner, the ownership structure should reflect a majority stake held by the combined regional and extra-regional private sector share-holding, while at the same time regional share-holding — Government and private sector — should reflect a majority over non-regional share-holding.

Sea Transportation

On the maritime side, the situation with regionally owned sea carriers is at present in disarray. The premier regionally based sea carrier for some three decades has been the inter-Governmentally-owned West Indies Shipping Corporation (WISCO), whose history has been marked by a persistent lack of profitability and dependence on subventions from its shareholder Governments, which have provided an accumulated US$20 million for the financing of deficits. The other dominant feature of regionally owned shipping is the presence of a fleet of some two hundred privately-owned small vessels, defined as having a capacity of less than 500 tons deadweight, registered and plying in the Eastern Caribbean, including Guyana, Trinidad and Tobago and Barbados.

The present situation in regional shipping is one of crisis in the face of good potential for a well-organised regionally-owned and operated shipping service. WISCO, which was originally owned by all CARICOM Governments except The Bahamas, now has a reduced number of participating Governments following the withdrawal, in a mood of disillusionment over the performance of the Corporation, of Belize, Dominica, St. Kitts and Nevis and St. Vincent and the Grenadines. Among the remaining participating Governments, Montserrat is also threatening to withdraw. More recently WISCO has had to cease operations entirely, as creditors moved to have its vessels detained for non-payment of debts. At the same time, the small vessels fleet of the Eastern Caribbean urgently require refurbishing and upgrading to meet minimum safety standards, and introduction of greater order into their schedules.

We believe that the establishment of an orderly and profitable regionally-owned and -operated shipping service is not beyond the combined capacity of West Indian Governments and the regional private sector. To achieve this, attention will need to be addressed equally to the ailing, debt-ridden WISCO and to the small vessels fleet.

The shareholder Governments of WISCO, after many years of struggle to put the operations of the Corporation on a satisfactory footing, have now rightly decided that it should be divested. The Corporation must be prepared, however, for any proper divestment, and this involves, among other things, shareholder Governments discharging their accrued financial obligations to the Company. We urge Governments to discharge these obligations. As for the future, it remains a desirable objective to have a regionally controlled shipping service operating within and beyond the Community and in this connection we recommend that Governments examine what facilitative regime it might be possible to implement to encourage the establishment and operation of such a service.

With respect to the small vessels fleet, whose importance is underlined by the fact that the fleet carries an estimated fifty per cent of sea-borne trade in the Eastern Caribbean, we recommend that Governments collectively, through the CARICOM and OECS Secretariats, seek to secure the development and implementation of a comprehensive regional project aimed at upgrading the vessels in the fleet. Such a project could be designed to provide technical assistance and loan finance to the owners of the fleet for the purpose of refurbishing their vessels to meet basic safety standards, and to install facilities, such as refrigeration, to permit better cargo handling. It could be stipulated that the owners who would benefit would be those who are prepared to operate within guidelines established by the Region concerning basic standards.

Regional Cooperation

In the foregoing, we dealt with some selected key issues on the level of commercial consolidation and rationalisation of the operations of regionally owned air and sea transportation entities. The Region must also respond, or continue responding, to issues and challenges on the level of functional cooperation in sea and air transportation among Governments and among the operating entities themselves.

Indeed, while commercial rationalisation and consolidation in regional air and sea transportation have been difficult to achieve over the years, there have been some gains during this time at the level of functional cooperation. It is of the utmost importance that the efforts of Governments at this level be maintained and intensified, for functional cooperation in air and sea transportation helps to shape the kind of environment that is conducive to the successful operation of the commercial entities in the industry.

Over the years, regional Governments have advanced functional cooperation in regional transportation through the work of High Level Committees on Sea and Air Transportation, and through the decisions of CARICOM Ministers responsible for Civil Aviation and for Maritime Transportation and of CARICOM Heads of Government.

In air transportation, effective joint action by CARICOM countries in the forum of the International Civil Aviation Organisation (ICAO) secured the establishment of the Community of Interest principle, by virtue of which a country in a regional integration grouping which has no national airline of its own is able to designate the national airline of another Member of the grouping to exercise its route rights in bilateral air services agreements that it concludes with third countries. We welcome the fact that many Eastern Caribbean countries have been able, under this principle, to designate BWIA as their carrier under their bilateral air services agreements with North American, European and other countries, and we think that it is of enormous positive value that Eastern Caribbean countries are engaged in an effort to push the use of the Community of Interest principle even further, through their effort to negotiate a single collective multilateral air services agreement with the United Kingdom. We urge the countries involved to sustain their efforts to overcome the obstacles that have arisen in this quest, and proceed to conclude the contemplated agreement with the UK.

We commend equally strongly other functional cooperation efforts in air transportation: the efforts at harmonisation of civil aviation legislation; at improving communication and air safety facilities; licensing of pilots and aircraft; and promotion of training in the sector. We recommend that the concerned regional bodies active in this area maintain the momentum of these efforts. In this connection we note with encouragement the conclusion in 1984 of an Inter-Governmental Agreement for Cooperation in Air Transportation which provides an excellent framework for pursuing many aspects of functional cooperation among Governments as well as directly among the airlines. It is a matter of regret, of course, that this facility has not been invoked as fully and as often as was contemplated and as circumstances have warranted, and we urge regional Governments and the regional airlines to use the Agreement more fully.

Functional cooperation in regional sea transportation has included efforts towards modernisation and harmonisation of maritime legislation, the promotion of maritime safety, the development of training of maritime transportation cadres, and cooperation in port development. The Region must continue using the inter-Governmental process to advance these efforts.

Recommendations

1. that CARICOM Governments develop a regional policy aimed at ensuring that the Community is adequately provided with air and sea transportation services;

2. that in air transportation the efforts that have been mounted to rationalise and restructure air lines in the Eastern Caribbean be vigorously pursued to a satisfactory conclusion;

3. that the decision already taken by the shareholder Governments to privatise WISCO be implemented at an early date;

4. that CARICOM Governments, through the CARICOM and OECS Secretariats, examine the feasibility of a comprehensive regional project aimed at upgrading and refurbishing the small vessels fleet in the Eastern Caribbean;

5. that active steps be taken to explore the possibilities for functional cooperation and commercial rationalisation in air and sea transportation within the wider Caribbean Basin;

6. that the Regional policy on transportation services encourage regional private sector ownership with appropriate regulation and (in the case of air services) while safeguarding regional air transport rights.

6. ENVIRONMENT

As in so many areas of regional life where CARICOM is not immune from the problems that beset the world, we are today as imperilled as anyone else by the global environmental crisis. We have contributed little to such major elements of environmental degradation as ozone shield depletion or global warming. Still, we are not for that reason absolved of responsibility for caring for our local environments, and the truth is that we have been careless about them in several respects. At both the global and regional levels, therefore, the crisis of environment, linked directly for us to development issues, is a frontline problem as we look to the twenty-first Century.

Global Awareness

The increase in knowledge and scientific understanding of the functioning of the natural systems of the Earth led to the Stockholm Conference on the Human Environment in 1972. It resulted in bringing the global community together to delineate the rights of the human family to a healthy and productive environment. It provided a point of reference which has sustained the ongoing search for a more harmonious relationship between humans and their environment.

The past decade in particular has seen a dramatic upsurge in international concern about environmental degradation and significant changes have occurred in perceptions of the problem. Advances in scientific knowledge have exposed grave dangers that over-consumption by a few and the poverty of many now pose for all people. A better understanding of ecology has also led to greater awareness of the irreversible damage that has been done to some of Earth's life support systems. Conventional notions about economic growth and development are increasingly being questioned as environmental awareness grows.

In 1980, the first World Conservation Strategy provided guidelines for action by governments and societies towards conserving the natural and biological resources of the earth and in harmonising human activities with its ecological systems. The report of the World Commission on Environment and Development (the Bruntland Commission) served to accelerate the building of universal consciousness about the links between environment and development, leading to the current emphasis on the need to study environmental problems in the context of natural resources management and economic planning.

At a global level the relationships between environment and development are now being addressed directly and the UN Conference on Environment and Development (UNCED) will have been held in

Rio de Janeiro by the time this Report is published.

Allied to UNCED, there is a multiplicity of other initiatives which seek to promote the overall course of environmental protection and which are targeted to specific phenomena or resources. Of note among them are the intergovernmental negotiations for a Climate Change Convention, a Convention on Biodiversity, a Declaration of principles concerning protection of forests, a framework agreement on desertification, and the already concluded Montreal Protocol for the Protection of the Ozone Layer. All these signify the increasing recognition that many of the issues inherent in environment and development concerns require international cooperation, globally and within geographical regions, for their resolution.

While conceptually the world is now quite advanced in its understanding of the relationship between environment and development, methodology for their harmonisation, formulation of conducive economic instruments, approaches to intersectoral planning, appropriate social organisation and public administration models, meaningful public participation in decision-making about management of resources, mechanisms to deal with the international dimensions are all in their infancy.

Caribbean Issues

As we said at the outset, the Caribbean has not been immune from these global developments. The tourist brochures portray one view of the Caribbean, the squatters on the hillside around many capital cities convey another, and the banana farmers in the Windward Islands yet a third. These and many other situations make up the Caribbean which we know today. All are interconnected and all are under threat.

Our Region consists essentially of small island and low-lying coastal developing states which have unique ecological and environmental characteristics that make them particularly susceptible to environmental problems. There is a cluster of issues that affect us with particular severity. It includes:

- the predicted rise in sea level due to climate change;
- the greater demands on coastal zone management;
- the fragility of water resources and the risk of contamination, including salt water intrusion;

- risk from the movement of hazardous waste;
- problems of managing the impacts of tourism;
- sustainable utilisation and monitoring of the EEZ;
- controlling waste management;
- population pressures resulting from limited land space (not in the coastal countries);
- the destructive potential of increased frequency and severity of hurricanes and tropical storms.

Tourism

As we have underlined earlier in this Report, tourism is a major industry in several Caribbean countries and it is estimated that between 1970 and 1987 international tourist arrivals in the Region had doubled to almost 10 million per year. Generally tourism has yielded beneficial economic results, but produced mixed social and environmental impacts. The Caribbean has been blessed with natural assets of sun, sand, sea, rich flora and fauna, and appealing landscapes. It is proper that these assets be used to further national development goals. But there is cause for serious concern over pollution problems in relation to Caribbean beaches and hotel development, dating back to when environmental concerns were not on the development agenda. There is no such excuse now. It would be foolhardy if the development which results from the tourism sector undermines its very base, to the point of unsustainability of tourism itself.

Several initiatives have been taken by Governments and within regional programmes as a result of the increasing appreciation of the role and potential of the Caribbean Sea in the economic viability of the ocean. These activities are however too sporadic and inadequate when the full range of benefits, threats and required management actions are considered. What is required is an integrated approach by the Community that seeks to optimise the benefits of the Caribbean Sea while protecting it from misuse and abuse, and ensuring that its resource base is used in a sustainable manner.

Coastal Zones

The coastal zones of all CARICOM States is the scene of intense development pressure. The coastal strips of the islands and mainland countries of CARICOM accommodate the majority of the population as well as the most vital aspects of their economic activities and services. In Guyana, 90 per cent of the population live within 5 km of the coast, while in Barbados 60 per cent of the population live within 2 km of the coast. Because of the small size of the countries, especially the islands, other inland activities (such as agriculture and mining) directly contribute to the ecological stress of the nearshore marine environment.

The impact from these development actions has been identified as follows:

- disposal of a wide range of wastes into the sea;
- agrochemical leachates;
- soil erosion;
- oil pollution from land and sea;
- coastal engineering works including land reclamation, construction, marine outfalls, port facilities and artificial reefs.

These land-based sources of pollution, coupled with the Region's shipping and maritime activities, pose serious threats to the marine environment. The problems of coastal deterioration in general, and beach erosion in particular, have become increasingly severe in recent times and evidence suggests that rapid, poorly controlled physical development is a major contributing factor.

Unplanned physical development is still the norm in many countries, and this exposes them to several adverse environmental impacts. These include soil erosion, reduced land availability for cultivation, siltation of water bodies, death of sensitive marine and fresh water resources and destruction of watersheds. Therefore, it is important that decisions about the utilisation of land resources are derived from consciously articulated land use policies and based on a sound environmental approach. In response, some Governments have introduced Land Conservation Boards and others have introduced or are about to introduce Systems Plans for Parks and Protected Areas. Environmental Impact Assessments are now emerging as an integral part of the decision-making process in most of the countries; but a great deal more needs to be done at the national and regional levels to improve the management of land resources.

Agriculture

CARICOM agriculture is a dominant sectoral activity in most countries, creating particular problems for the environment. In many of the countries less than 20% of the total land area is suitable for agriculture and this results in an attempt to maximise output through a process of intensification of existing land use that involves large inputs of fertilisers and pesticides. Though this has led to an improvement in food quality and production, it has also created environmental problems with serious effects on human health (pesticide residues) and ecosystem integrity (agricultural leachates).

Generally the institutional response to the problem posed by the agriculture/environmental interface is far from adequate. Some countries have specific legislation addressing the management of pesticides but do not appear to have implementing regulations.

Industry

The industrial sector constitutes a major component of the economies of most Caribbean countries and includes a large number of diverse industrial processes which generate wastes that can affect human health and the environment in many ways. Many of the industries in the Region were established during a period of lax environmental controls in the pre-1980 period. The result is that in setting up these industries, due concern was not paid to such priorities as thoughtful site selection, use of pollution control mechanisms, introduction of effluent guidelines and standards, rigid inplant monitoring and control regimes, and adherence to sound occupational health and safety practice. This has meant that some industrial activity has had adverse impacts on the environment and the health of the Region's people.

There is now a growing awareness of the need to address this problem on the part of the community, Governments and public and private sector industrial corporations, and some attempts are being made to address them. The major difficulty now is to set up the infrastructure that makes planning, operation, surveillance and quality control effective and routine and to avoid tempting shortcuts which may appear economic in the short run, but which may carry high costs of environmental and health damage and clean up and restoration in the long term.

Wastes

The problem of solid, liquid and hazardous waste disposal inevitably emerges in any treatment of environmental problems confronting the Region. The publication, *Caribbean Environmental Programming Strategy* (CIDA,1988) summarises the situation as follows:

> ... Growth in urban population, industrial activity and tourism have outstripped infrastructural capacities to handle waste. In the absence of adequate sewage collection systems, waste treatment has in many instances been undertaken in an adhoc and insanitary fashion. Septic tank effluent is sometimes disposed of in storm drains, and in some instances directly into coastal waters; where sewage treatment systems have been installed, there are deficiencies in plant capacity and less than adequate plant operation, maintenance and monitoring practices...

These realities have had a range of negative impacts on the natural environment such as river, beach and marine pollution as evidenced by high faecal coliform counts, eutrophication effects in coastal waters from untreated wastes, resulting ultimately in the death of coral and other marine life, and contamination of surface and ground water supplies from leachate emanating from crude solid waste dump sites.

A number of factors impede the ability of countries to effectively manage waste. These include institutional capacity, industrial policy, low public awareness and lack of financial resources. The absence of inhouse capacity to conduct systematic monitoring has been particularly constraining. But more fundamentally it is the lack of knowledge of the waste itself. For example, there is little knowledge on: the process by which waste is generated; the physical forms of the waste under the climate conditions of its location, i.e., liquid, sludge, solid; and constituents of the waste which are considered potentially hazardous to human health and the health of the environment.

Fresh Water

Another resource of importance to the Region and under constant threat from environmental factors is its fresh water resources. Poor land use planning, deforestation, insensitive farming practices, mining and quarrying activities all affect the production and distribution, as well as the quality, of fresh water. Deforestation is the major cause of the problem as it triggers off a range of adverse environmental impacts, notably soil erosion, silting rivers and clogging water intakes.

Ground water pollution from nutrient and pesticide leaching landfills and unsewered sanitation in urbanised and semi-urbanised areas poses a serious threat to health.

Forests

The Region's forests are a vast resource and a most important ecosystem in maintaining ecological balance and sustaining economic activity. Forest resources are of major significance in the mainland territories of Belize and Guyana, where exploitation to date has not led to any significant degradation of the resource base. Despite the presence of legislation dating as far back as the 1940s in many countries however, deforestation and degradation of forests are major threats to their preservation and to the continued availability of the resources which they offer.

The major causes for such deforestation are:

- migratory agriculture;
- expansion of the country's agricultural base through forest clearing;
- resettlement programmes and unregulated building and settlement;
- unregulated commercial forestry.

Major international focus is now being given to the management of tropical forests which have taken on a new significance in the ongoing global debate of the role of these forests in controlling the carbon dioxide balance in the atmosphere. Over and above this, however, Caribbean countries are aware of the great benefits to be reaped through prudent management of their forest resources and are all addressing the problem of sustainable management and utilisation of their forest resources.

With the exception of mineral extraction, all primary producing sectors depend heavily on a continuing and plentiful supply of biological resources. The conservation of biodiversity, especially genetic diversity within species, is the foundation for the Region's food security, since it is genetic diversity which enables improved fresh water species, improved crop production, horticulture, animal husbandry, forestry and aquaculture. Human health and welfare also benefit from the use of wild plants and animals for pharmaceutical products. Biological diversity in marine ecosystems is also necessary for the natural and ecological functions which they perform, while soil organisms play an important role in maintaining fertility of soil for agriculture.

These biological resources are under stress internally through bad environmental practices which have led to habitat degradation in areas of high biodiversity such as coral reefs and forest ecosystems. At another level, exploitation of these resources by the industrialised countries has led to hardly any benefits being derived by the suppliers of these resources. The question of adequate compensation for their use and for the indigenous knowledge associated with their husbandry was one of the major debates being addressed at the preparatory meetings leading up to UNCED. It has relevance for all of us in the Region.

Conservation of these resources is a prerequisite to harvesting the benefits to be derived from their sustainable utilisation. In this respect the Guyana/Commonwealth Forestry Programme offers an excellent opportunity for the Region to participate in and build a regional capability in areas related to the conservation and sustainable use and management of biodiversity. The programme provides for a pilot project on approximately 900,000 acres of pristine tropical rainforest, designed to develop and demonstrate sustainable management techniques. There is also now a Belizean conservation programme involving 122,000 acres of tropical forest.

Energy

One of the predicted consequences of the present global pattern of energy consumption is sea level rise, leading to the flooding of low-lying and coastal areas, destroying beaches and coastal structures and salinising fresh water supplies. As a region made up mainly of small island states, the Caribbean is very vulnerable to this threat. While to date the Region has contributed hardly at all to this prospect of climate change and sea-level rise, it has responsibilities in relation to future patterns of energy use. Energy is, of course, an important input necessary for the Region's future development, and energy consumption will inevitably rise with development. However, this increase in energy use can and should be accompanied by increased energy efficiency and reduced pollution. The Regional Energy Action Plan (REAP) which was developed in 1983 could form the basis for a regional position on energy, but it would necessarily need to be adjusted to reflect the realities of the present and future decades. This would also provide a link with possible renewable energy resources, such as solar energy.

The introduction of environmentally sound, energy efficient technologies (whether renewable or nonrenewable) would impose significant incremental capital cost to the Region. It is clear that additional resources will be necessary to enable countries of the Region to incorporate energy efficient and low pollution technologies in the production and use of energy.

CARICOM Responses

The Region has been responding to the needs to deal with the multiple problems and challenges of environment protection and management by setting in place various national and regional institutions. Regionally environmental matters are discussed at the Meeting of Ministers responsible for the Environment. Institutions such as the Centre for Resource Management and Environmental Studies at Cave Hill, the Institute of Marine Affairs in Trinidad and Tobago, and the Caribbean Environmental Health Institute in Saint Lucia have the potential to deal effectively with many of the environmental problems facing the Region. The Natural Resource Management Unit of the Organisation of Eastern Caribbean States(OECS/NRMU) manages and promotes the required policy, legislation and programme activities for the sustainable utilisation of the natural resource base of the OECS. However, despite the complex of existent national, regional, international and nongovernmental organisations, there is great need to coordinate, rationalise and focus their activities in such a way that the Region's environmental problems are effectively addressed. Further, these institutions need strengthening through increasing the human capacity and upgrading of their physical facilities.

A major strength of CARICOM in the area of the environment is the emergence of an NGO community that is playing an increasingly effective role in calling attention to environmental wrongs and influencing corrective policies. It includes environmental NGOs such as the Caribbean Conservation Association (CCA), but it also include the concern with the environment that is part of the agenda of other NGOs, such as the Caribbean Network for Integrated Rural Development, the Association of Caribbean Economists, and Development Alternatives for Women in a New Era (DAWN). The contribution of NGOs to the discussion on environmental issues during the Regional Economic Conference in February 1991 was a convincing argument for the whole process of dialogue between the social partners. As CARICOM increasingly comes to grips with the serious environmental problems on the Region's door step, the non-governmental community will have major contribution to make. It should be encouraged and facilitated in making it.

There is clear need for strengthening the regional institutional framework in relation to environmental issues. The overall need is to facilitate the development of policy, the formulation of programmes, the allocation of financial and human resources, the monitoring function and, as important as anything else, the raising of public awareness for, and participation in, remedial environmental action. It is easy to recognise that all this will be best facilitated through regional effort. Indeed, it may not happen at all in any adequate way, if it does not happen on a shared regional basis.

But we have to lift our sights beyond CARICOM itself and be aware of the need to develop a wide perspective of the environment. Later in this Report, we recommend the creation of an Association of Caribbean States (ACS). Functional Cooperation will be a central dimension of that new integration process. Cooperation in the area of the environment could be a major mandate of the ACS.

It is not too fanciful an idea, for example, for CARICOM to promote within the wider Caribbean context, the vision of a Caribbean Region that is a zone of environmental protection. The world is in need of a regional effort of this kind, and the Caribbean environment provides a range of opportunities for demonstrating human capacity to develop while living in harmony with nature. The Caribbean as a role model of sustainable development is an enterprise which would attract significant international support, and we commend it as part of our vision of the future. That effort could begin with the initiation by CARICOM of a Convention on Environment and Development among the countries of the wider Caribbean in order to provide a political and legal framework in which decisions and action could be coordinated for the protection, conservation and sustainable management of the Caribbean environment.

Some of the institutional support that we envisage must come from the Universities, and we believe the Region should give particular support to the new initiative at the University of the West Indies which has resulted in the establishment of a Chair for Sustainable Development. We would like to see an Institute of Sustainable Development evolve from this beginning, providing the focus for the much needed research and intellectual work that has to be undertaken quickly. Supplementary contributions will come from the Centre of Resource Management and Environmental Studies (CERMES) at the UWI Cave Hill Campus, and the Regional Forestry Institute to be established at the University of Guyana, along with the International Centre for Forestry Research being established under the aegis of the Guyana\Commonwealth Programme on Sustainable Forestry, the Institute of Marine Affairs in Trinidad and Tobago as the Region's specialised agency on the marine environment, the Caribbean Environmental Health Institute (CEHI) in Saint Luica, the Natural Resources Management Unit of the OECS and the Fisheries Unit in St. Vincent and the Grenadines.

Additionally, we would expect the CARICOM Commission, the establishment of which we propose in Chapter XII, to pay particular attention to the need for leadership and coordinated regional action in environmental matters. And there will be need to strengthen the Secretariat's technical capability to support such leadership and action. It is that leadership, most of all, and commitment to respect for environmental protection, that must underpin all the Region's efforts. With commitment, much will be attained that may now seem beyond our grasp.

The First CARICOM Ministerial Conference on the Environment held in 1989 issued a set of declarations which were recorded in the Port of Spain Accord on the Management and Conservation of the Caribbean Environment. The main institutional feature of the Port of Spain accord was the creation of the CARICOM Consultative Forum on the Environment as a mechanism for consultation among a wide range of entities in order to achieve coherence, coordination and better use of resources devoted to environmental matters in the CARICOM. The functions envisaged for the Forum were seen to be vital to any regional approach or consolidated programme and must become an integral part of the regional institutional matrix, with systematic links with the lead national institutions and departments. The responsibility for convening the Forum was allocated to the CARICOM Secretariat.

The Second Ministerial Conference on the Environment which was held in Kingston in 1990 appointed a Task Force to define a regional position on all the relevant issues being discussed at UNCED. This Task Force has met and has coordinated a regional approach to the major UNCED issues affecting the Caribbean. At the Heads of Government in Basseterre the President of Guyana was designated CARICOM's spokesman at the Earth Summit — a good symbol of a unified approach to critical issues.

A Wider Response

CARICOM countries are involved in significant numbers among the 36 countries that have joined forces under the "Alliance of Small Island States" (AOSIS) to highlight the special dangers which the twin crises of environment and development possess for the small and the weak. We must be vigorous within such groupings, contributing at many levels: to the scientific research, to the diplomacy, and to the wider intellectual work involved — all of which we will do better if we work on a regional basis.

Amazonia is part of the environmental heritage of CARICOM through Guyana's rainforest. When the Earth Summit took place in Rio, Latin America and the Caribbean contributed substantially to its underpinning. But the people of CARICOM are hardly aware of these contributions, as if they concern esoteric issues removed from their daily lives. Nothing could be more untrue. Both these contributions and the wider issues as they impinge on our Region should be at the centre of regional thoughts.

"Development and Environment: Our Own Agenda" was one of the first regional reports highlighting developing-country views — including Caribbean views — on the issues before Rio. "Amazonia: Without Myths" has been another. Both were sponsored by the IDB and UNDP in a laudable effort to ensure that Latin American and Caribbean interests were not neglected in a debate that acutely concerns our people. The Commission, through its Chairman, was involved in both reports, and another of its members with the Amazonia report. In 1991 the World Resources Institute sponsored another hemispheric study "Compact for a New World," to which prominent Caribbean voices contributed. The point is that, in these now critical areas of environment and development, there is need for us to rise out of our island or other territorial isolations and articulate our needs through enlarged perception of our condition.

That condition, as we have seen, is fraught with danger: whether climate change and sea level rise, which threatens our coasts and their economy; or ozone layer depletion, which could make exposure to sun and sand and sea not what tourists come for but from which they turn aside in fear; or global warming with its implication of fiercer hurricanes and storm surges; or dying coral reefs that deplete the ecological capital of our coastal waters; or solid wastes, both of our own making, as we absorb the consumption culture of the industrial world, or industrial country wastes dumped in our waters by cruise ships or in even more deliberate ways despoiling the purity of the Caribbean Sea to accomodate other people's lifestyles; or, perhaps most destabilising of all, the pollution of poverty which an unpropitious global economic environment threatens to make endemic in parts of our Region.

Looking Ahead

There is, perhaps, no greater danger that we face as we look to the 21st Century than the implications of the crisis of environment and development. It is no comfort that it is a global crisis. Our capacities, the absence of resilience in our economies, the overall vulnerability of our condition: all make it imperative that we come together in the face of these threats. They concern specifically the question of what kind of Caribbean we leave for future generations — those already with us and others to come. This hemisphere's encounter with Europeans 500 years ago was to produce an indescribably savage onslaught on nature, including that on the first people of the hemisphere. Today's onslaught is less physical and overt; much of it comes from within the hemisphere; but the processes of industrialisation — only minimally our own processes — are visiting on the region an onslaught of another kind, of which nature and Caribbean peoples are again the victims.

In an introduction written for the Report "Amazonia: Without Myths", the celebrated writer of our wider Caribbean region, Gabriel Garcia Marquez, summed up the Amazonian predicament as follows:

> ... More than twenty million people live in this enclave of age-old myths and fantastic illusions which, over time, have become intermixed with reality. This, in the world's imagination, is the Earth's ultimate paradise. It is, however, a paradise on the verge of extinction. Its slow and silent agony poses one of the most dramatic threats to human survival. The common belief has been that the world would end in a Biblical cataclysm. But reality is more disturbing than that: the world began to die many years ago, at the hand and disgrace of environmental degradation....
>
> However, an analysis of the deterioration in the Amazon cannot ignore the false ethic of the industrialised countries which limits the world's ecological disaster to the deterioration of the tropical forests. In reality, the most serious causes originate in these same countries: the contamination of the air and the waters with all types of waste, global warming, the ozone layer depletion, the threat of a nuclear holocaust. And the most unpunished of all: social injustice and chronic poverty, which inflict destruction and ruin the length and breadth of the continent and, in the final analysis, affect all marginal areas of the industrialised countries themselves. In this regard, the salvation of Amazonia must become not merely a heroic feat of its natural trustees but a crusade that all humankind no longer can defer.

This is a voice of our wider Caribbean. It has a message of import, beyond the issues of the forests, for the primary challenge we face in the areas of environment and development as we prepare for the twenty-first Century.

Recommendations:

1. that at the national level all Member States of CARICOM ensure that environmental considerations are incorporated into national development planning;

2. that the Task Force be given the responsibility of guiding the region's actions in response to the outcome of UNCED (e.g., Agenda 21);

3. that in the longer term Governments consolidate the Forum as originally conceived in the Port of Spain Accord, supporting it fully with the resources needed to effectively carry out its mandate;

4. that at the national level, all Member States of CARICOM establish arrangements that would present an integrated approach to environmental management at the political, technical and administrative levels, and that such arrangements include designated focal points which would relate in a coherent manner to the regional and international levels;

5. that having regard to the significance of the Caribbean Sea as a regional resource and asset, and as an international waterway, CARICOM Member States agree to develop the Institute of Marine Affairs in Trinidad and Tobago as the regional specialised entity for conducting research and acting as an information centre on the marine environment of the Caribbean and adjacent regions, to study their resource potential, to advise on policy options in marine affairs and to undertake appropriate activities;

6. that the Caribbean Environmental Health Institute (CEHI) be further strengthened and continue to be supported as the Region's specialised institution for providing scientific monitoring, information, training and laboratory services, and as a centre for networking the technical services and co-operation with other national, regional and extra-regional entities required to guide and support the regional programme in environmental monitoring;

7. that full support be given to the new initiative at UWI, Mona which has resulted in the establishment of a Chair in Sustainable Development so that this activity can provide the context in which much of the research and intellectual work required to promote and realise the concept of sustainable development could be undertaken. This should lead to a Sustainable Development Programme at UWI Mona and links should be established with the CERMES programme at Cave Hill;

8. that regional Governments consolidate the foundations for tertiary multidisciplinary training in resource management established by the CERMES programme at the University of the West Indies, Cave Hill, and provide more substantive support for its continuance;

(9) that the University of Guyana expand the present Diploma in Forestry programme into a full degree programme as part of the activities of a Regional Forestry Institute to be established at that University. This will develop in close collaboration with the proposed International Centre for Forestry Research now being established under the aegis of the Guyana/Commonwealth Secretariat Programme on Sustainable Forestry. Regional support should be given to the full realisation of the implementation of the Guyana/Commonwealth programme on Sustainable Forestry;

10. that, to enhance the quality of full public participation in the region's environmental programmes, the Region arrange for the systematic incorporation of environment and development issues into curricula at all levels of the education system including continuing education curricula. Vigorous attempts should be made to incorporate all the social partners — women, nongovernmental organisations, private sector entities — in activities related to environmental management and protection;

11. that regional Governments utilise the well-articulated Regional Energy Action Programme (REAP) as a basis for developing a regional strategy for providing for the energy needs of the

Region in the future, consistent with the requirements for environmental protection;

12 that CARICOM encourage and facilitate the constructive contributions of the regional NGO movement in relation to environment issues; and

13 that CARICOM take the initiative at regional, Caribbean-wide and international levels for establishing the Caribbean Basin as a Zone of Environmental Protection in the context of an appropriate Convention on Environment and Development among the countries of the wider Caribbean.

CHAPTER VI

HUMAN RESOURCES DEVELOPMENT

1. THE BACKGROUND

It is widely recognised that development of human resources can be conceived of as being both a cause and an effect of economic development. Education, skills, the knowledge-base, and entrepreneurship, constitute together the human input into the production process. Study after study has confirmed the central role of these elements in the economic growth of both advanced and developing countries. Their role has been vastly enhanced in the contemporary period with the emergence of new technologies in fields such as biotechnology, telecommunications, robotics, new materials, computers and software. Computers themselves have underpinned most of these developments. They have also been transforming the services sector, permitting a whole range of services to become internationally tradeable items, where hitherto they have been largely confined within national boundaries.

Countries of very different situations and levels of development are making strenuous efforts to adapt to this new situation by developing a larger stock of knowledge for use in both their traditional and new industries. The Caribbean can be no exception to this trend. More than ever before greater skills, more Research and Development (R & D), more vigorous entrepreneurship, are needed to maintain and strengthen the international competitiveness of sectors such as export agriculture, involving both unprocessed and processed products; manufacturing; tourism and other services. Moreover, the Region's capacity to attract new investment will very much depend upon our relative endowment with these inputs.

In other words, the prospects for economic recovery and development will hinge very largely upon the performance of the knowledge sector. Among other things, this calls for comprehensive modernisation and restructuring of the educational system; unprecedented initiatives to build up R & D capacities in a wide range of activities; and deliberate and sustained efforts to promote widespread development and diffusion of entrepreneurial skills. In many ways, this represents the most formidable aspect of the development challenge facing the CARICOM Region today.

Selected Aspects of the Issue

It was not the Commission's function to go into all aspects of the human resources problem. We have focussed essentially on those issues and suggestions which emerged in the course of our consultations. Besides, there is already voluminous documentation on many topics. We wish to draw attention to some matters requiring urgent action, and to suggest areas where a regional approach is indicated.

A Single Market for Human Resources

We start with the proposition that the CARICOM countries have reached a stage in relation to their individual development needs and prospects, and the furthering of the integration process, to take deliberate steps towards the establishment of a single market for human resources, served by a common pool of workers of all levels of skills.

In our Progress Report, we took the stance that the process of creating such a market should commence with the freer movement of professional and skilled people, starting with UWI graduates. We are glad to see that some Governments are beginning to implement our proposal, and urge those that are not already doing so, to act expeditiously in the matter.

The process of a single market, as it relates to human resources, does not however only involve the removal of impediments to the movement of people. It also entails concerted action to develop the quality of the Region's human resources through undertaking common and joint projects; pooling educational and research capabilities; attracting back West Indian expertise in the diaspora, and adopting common policies towards the sourcing of extra-regional knowledge and skills. Accordingly, the analysis and commentary that follow are cast within this overall perspective.

2. EDUCATION

Complaints about the deficiencies of the educational system are legion. During the course of our public consultations, oral and written submissions were made which lamented the poor performance of students at both the primary and secondary levels; the inappropriateness of curricula and teaching methods, including very few linkages between the world of study and that of work; the critical shortages of teachers, school books, and other instructional materials; the poor physical state of schools reflecting, in the main, inadequate maintenance and security; the over-centralisation of decision-making which confines local communities to a largely peripheral role in the management of schools, and open the door for the politicisation of matters such as teaching appointments and scholarship awards.

It is not our purpose to engage in an exhaustive analysis of the validity or otherwise of these claims. Suffice it to say that some educators have pointed to the achievements registered in primary and secondary education over the past three or four decades, reflected in a remarkable increase in enrolments, and in the number of trained teachers. Several experiments are taking place with new curricula and teaching methods, even if the experience with them has not yet been widely disseminated. Certain Governments are also making efforts to decentralise schools management, and to discourage political patronage. Nevertheless, even if it were only a crisis of perception, the issue of educational reform needs to be addressed urgently.

Educational Attainments

The Table on the following page, prepared by the World Bank, tells its own tale about the skewed pattern of educational attainment. It shows that all West Indian children have a chance of entering primary school, and a very high percentage of them stand a chance of completing. Nonetheless, other data suggest that large numbers of students graduate from primary school without the numerical or cognitive skills needed to secure a job in the modern sector of the economy.

Education

PROBABILITIES OF DIFFERENT LEVELS OF EDUCATIONAL ATTAINMENT ACROSS ENGLISH SPEAKING COUNTRIES

	Antigua	Barbados	Belize	Dominica	Grenada	Guyana	Jamaica	St. Kitts	St. Lucia	St. Vincent	Trinidad
Enter Primary 1	100	100	100	100	100	100	100	100	100	100	100
Complete Primary	98	100	59	93	95	80	85	97	93	98	100
Enter Post Primary	43	4	..	..	48	54	32	4	50	39	23
Enter Secondary	55	96	35	25	45	26	53	95	23	39	70
Complete Secondary	...	...	21	...	38	26	53	...	21	...	65
CXC Stream	55	...	21	25	...	26	32	43	21	35	65
CXC English	28	...	8	7	12	3	8	18	9	13	(24)
CXC Maths	18	...	6	7	8	3	7	15	7	11	(19)
4 + CXC	4	8	2	2	3	2	3	4	2	4	5
Take 'A' Levels	...	5	2	3	5	...	3	5	2	6	7
Pass 2 + 'A' Levels	...	...	1	1	1	...	...	2	1	1	2
Enter other Tertiary	...	42	5	3	3	6	7	9	4	4	10
Enter Caribbean University	1.5	3	0.25	0.25	1	2	2	2	1	0.5	3

Notes:
1. The probabilities are based on each 100 primary students
2. .. indicates a data gap
3. ... indicates not applicable
4. CXC is Caribbean Examinations Council
5. 'A' Level is General Certificate of Education Advanced Level which is required for entry to UWI.

The probability of moving further up the educational ladder drops sharply at the secondary level, and even more sharply at the tertiary and University stages. In several countries, the probability of entering secondary school is about 50 per cent or less. More serious, apart from Barbados, there is only about a 2 per cent to 5 per cent probability of securing four or more CXCs. Not surprisingly, this is reflected in very low probabilities of entering tertiary and university education — in the case of the latter, the best cases are 2 per cent to 3 per cent.

Commentators have drawn attention to the low tertiary enrolment ratios in the Region which compare very unfavourably with those of other middle income developing countries, where the average ratio is about 16 per cent to 17 per cent. The gap is particularly wide in science and technology where a country like Singapore, with a total population not too dissimilar in size to Jamaica, has ten times the number of students enrolled at the tertiary level in science and technology.

It is by and large the tertiary system which provides the skilled, supervisory, and management personnel required to run the economy. It provides, too, the quality teachers to secure high success rates and, correspondingly, high intakes at the various levels of the system. In parenthesis, it should be noted that the educational system ought to be viewed as a whole, with appropriate attention being given to inter-linkages between different parts of the system.

Supply Gaps

Data on the skill attainments of the labour force are limited. However, available information points towards major deficiencies in the supply of technologists/technicians, and skilled manual workers. It appears that technician level graduates account for only a minute proportion of the labour force. At current levels of the output of graduates it would, in the best case, take five years, in the worst, over 30 years, to achieve a one per cent increase in the proportion of technicians and technologists in the labour force.

The supply gaps at the University level are now being documented. Surveys done of the projected private sector demand for graduates over the period 1991/1996, indicate demand levels in the range of 4,800 to 7,200 per annum over the period. At the present time, the UWI produces about 2,600 graduates per year. The rest of the tertiary system about 1,400, while some 1,600 emigrate. In other words, net current output is about one-half to one-third of projected private sector needs. When to that is added the requirements of the public sector, it is clear that the Region faces very major shortfalls in high-level personnel in the immediate period ahead.

It is true that part of the supply of university graduates is trained abroad. Up-to-date information is not available, but it is possible that there are around 8,000 full-time West Indian students doing university degrees overseas. How many of these will return to the Region can only be a matter for speculation. At the same time, the large increases that have been taking place in the fees charged to overseas students in Britain and North America, might deter many students from going abroad in the future.

At the current time in this Region, a large number of working persons have not had the opportunity of effective secondary education at either the narrowly 'academic' or the technical levels. Yet responsibility for quality work in the industrial system and for maintenance of existing equipment depends on them.

Emphasis needs to be placed on mechanisms to meet the educational requirements of these persons who constitute a large part of the work force. Efforts should therefore be made in conjunction with the private sector (local and foreign investors) to support systems of instruction emphasising (a) continuing education and (b) training and upgrading of skills at the workplace.

Resource Needs And Financing

To put the entire education problem in a nutshell, very considerable resources are needed to achieve desired quality improvements in the primary and secondary systems, and a substantial expansion of access at the tertiary level. In its 10-Year Development Plan, the UWI has proposed a target of doubling the tertiary enrolment ratio from its present level of 5 per cent to 10 per cent by the year 2000.

It is, therefore, a matter of the utmost urgency that Governments, in full consultation with their communities, set specific targets for educational improvements, estimate the financial requirements involved, and set about resolutely to mobilise the necessary resources both at home and abroad.

In so doing, countries have to examine carefully how the costs of educational reform can be shared between Governments, and the non-governmental communities. It is a hard reality that West Indian Governments are already devoting a share of their national budgets, and of their Gross National Products, which compare well with those of many other developing countries, and even of developed countries. For instance, the latest figures show that most CARICOM countries are allocating between 17 per cent to 24 per cent of their budgets to recurrent expenditure on education. This compares with a range for other developing regions of 13 per cent to 25 per cent. A similar picture emerges with GDP shares, CARICOM countries being in the range of 3 per cent to 5 per cent, and other regions in the range of 2 per cent to 4 per cent.

In the foreseeable future, economic growth is unlikely to provide very substantial increments to the resources available to education. Most projections suggest that over the next several years, the economies of the Region are unlikely to grow by more than about 3 per cent per annum. At the same time, there is only limited scope for increasing the share of education in national budgets by cutting back on other sectors. It follows from this that, if the countries of the Region do not wish to be left behind in the race towards knowledge development, the non-governmental parts of the community have to commit vastly wider resources to education than they have done up to now.

There is a tendency in some quarters to argue that education is a right, which makes its provision the exclusive responsibility of governments. Although this has some validity at the primary level where a 100 per cent coverage is being provided, it is less so as one progresses up the educational ladder. For example, it is difficult to argue that University education is a right for the 2 per cent to 3 per cent of the student population receiving it, without considering the claims of the remaining 97 per cent to 98 per cent.

The reality is dawning that the introduction of cost recovery schemes might be a necessary condition for securing the resources required for educational reform. Such schemes will have to be designed to ensure that they do not inhibit access, especially for qualified students coming from low income households. In this latter connection, it must continue to be borne in mind that the purpose of education is not only to provide people with skills. In the Caribbean, as in many other parts of the developing world, education is a, if not the, principal vehicle for achieving greater social mobility and equilibrium in the society. This over-riding objective has therefore to condition approaches to the financing of education.

There is a menu of options available for financing which need not affect increased access. These include: tuition fee schemes with means testing; student loans on affordable terms; cost reimbursement arrangements, whereby students pay back a part of the cost of their education after graduation, with repayments linked to their income. One possibility is to link the terms of repayment to supply scarcities in different occupations. For example, graduates going into teaching may be given special concessional terms for repayment.

We propose later the undertaking of specific work to bring the issue of cost recovery to the stage of policy decision and implementation.

Efficiency and Management

More money is not the only route towards achieving educational reform. Perhaps of equivalent importance is the attainment of greater cost effectiveness, to ensure that as far as possible full value is received for every dollar spent. Although there might be substantial differences between countries, and among institutions in each country, impressions of waste in the education system are widespread. Examples include cost over-runs in school construction, and in the procurement of teaching materials; poor maintenance of buildings and equipment; high rates of absenteeism and turnover among teachers, partly associated with the phenomenon of teachers looking elsewhere for supplementing their income or for new career opportunities; imbalances in the allocation of school places leading to severe over-crowding in some schools, co-existing with significant under-utilisation of space in others.

There is a general belief that many of these problems can be alleviated by greater decentralisation towards a community-based system of schools management. As already mentioned, educational systems in the Region tend to be highly centralised. Resources are controlled by Ministries of Education, along with responsibilities for policy, planning, curriculum development, materials production and procurement, maintenance of facilities, and the recruitment and appointment of staff. Several people appearing before the Commission expressed the view that Ministries of Education are overstretched, many of them suffering from staff shortages, and insufficient acquaintance with the situation at local community levels, to run schools efficiently. It was represented to us that Ministries should increasingly confine themselves to policy determination, and monitoring, leaving the day-to-day operations of the schools systems to local Boards. In some CARICOM countries, such as Barbados, elements of a decentralised system along these lines are already in place.

There is also a dearth of adequately trained school administrators. Until quite recently, administrators were generally expected to learn on the job. Appointments to positions of school principal have tended to be based upon length of service and seniority as a teacher. The situation is beginning to change, but it still remains the case that the number of principals with formal training in modern methods of management are in the minority. As suggested later, a major initiative is required to upgrade school administrators through a scheme of in-service training.

Imperatives for Regional Cooperation

In the course of our public consultations, and during our own examination of the issues, it became increasingly apparent that most of the problems which beset the educational system are common in greater or lesser degree to all of the countries in the Region. It is also evident that several countries lack critical minimum size by way of expertise to tackle issues such as curriculum development, the use of new technologies in teaching, the measurement of student and school performance, even the achievement of sufficient depth in teaching across disciplines. In a fairly typical situation, the numbers of teachers in a particular discipline may be so small that teaching programmes can be easily disrupted because of absences or emigration. Given the urgent challenges that they confront, the countries of the Region need to pool their resources in many areas if they are to make a significant dent on the educational problem.

The Standing Committee of the Ministries of Education in CARICOM, together with its Advisory Task Force, has substantially prepared the ground for some of the regional initiatives being proposed below. The report of the OECS Education Reform Working Group is also an impressive document that sets out very constructive strategies for reform. What is being suggested seeks to reinforce, and in some cases amplify, ideas for reform that are already before Governments.

A Regional Agenda for Reform

In the light of the above considerations, we consider that there are five inter-related areas for immediate regional action in reforming and restructuring the primary and secondary schools systems. They are:

- Curriculum Reform
- Teacher Education
- Schools Management
- Finance
- A sustained capability for policy research, analysis and monitoring.

Curriculum Reform

Starting with curriculum reform, we propose that steps be taken immediately to initiate a comprehensive review of curricula, the aim of which should be to create a common curriculum framework that would involve the establishment of regional standards, and a core of learning goals for all levels of basic education. It would also involve joint action to investigate appropriate ways of applying the new educational technologies, so that relevant computer software can be developed, as well as high-quality audio and visual programming, to support revised curricula. Also envisaged are improvements in testing and measurement, by the creation of new regional testing services, or arrangements for back-stopping and monitoring the quality of national testing.

It must be emphasised that the adoption of regional approaches to curriculum reform is not intended to create a straitjacket of curriculum regulations, with each Member State complying, but rather a framework of agreed minimum objectives for various levels, and a pool of process-oriented learning activities and evaluatory methods. Within this framework there would be opportunities for each Member State to put emphasis on its particular concerns and issues. In any case, the translation of the curriculum framework into the teaching-learning reality in the classroom always demands the use of local examples familiar to the students and the infusion of related material of local concern. In short, the proposal is not for rigid standardisation region-wide, but for a harmonisation within which there can be a response to local and national interests, issues and demands, reflecting the social, cultural, environmental and economic variation that abounds in the Community.

Teacher Education

The second area of teacher education is no less vital. Despite the very long established schemes of teacher training at the College and University levels, we see a need for substantive upgrading and enlargement of the teaching corps, especially in basic subjects such as English, Mathematics, and the Sciences; across-the-board improvements in the quality of teacher education involving more focussed staff development at all levels; greater networking and more teacher and student exchanges among training colleges; as well as fundamental re-thinking of the balance between substantive content and pedagogy in the training of teachers.

It is unlikely that the quality of teachers will improve unless definite efforts are made to increase the attractiveness of teaching as a career. Fundamental to this are improvements in compensation and working conditions. It is no accident that the best performing school systems are in those CARICOM countries where teachers are comparatively well paid. Concomitant efforts have to be made to restore the status of teachers in communities, through various forms of recognition and encouragement.

Schools Management

The third area of schools management calls both for more and improved training of educational administrators. It also necessitates far-reaching changes in the institutional arrangements for the management of schools. As to the former, we encourage the UWI, among the many areas where it needs to do further work, to overhaul its existing programmes in educational administration. There needs to be a much closer integration and cross-fertilisation of the management disciplines with the traditional subject matter in this field. Administrators need hands-on exposure to matters such as budget management, the maintenance of physical plant, inventory control, procurement, fund-raising, and the earning of income by schools in providing cost-recoverable services to the community. The basic aim should be to develop a new cadre of entrepreneurial school administrators.

At the institutional level, Governments need to take a basic policy decision to withdraw on a phased basis from the direct management of schools, by developing and/or encouraging the emergence of strong community-based structures for their management. As previously observed, the future task of Ministries of Education should essentially be to determine overall strategies and policies, to allocate public funds, and to monitor the performance of schools and the use of resources. Community-based school boards should be left to manage individual schools or clusters of them, taking direct responsibility for day-to-day operational matters, such as the appointment and disciplining of teachers. Naturally, there will be safeguards to prevent abuses of power by the Boards. It is here that the monitoring responsibility of Ministries will assume critical importance.

Financing

The issue of financing is probably one of the most complex problems with which Governments have to contend. As already discussed, it affects all levels of the system, and its relevance increases as one progresses up the educational ladder. Given the burgeoning needs of education, and the critical shortages of public resources for it, Governments should not delay in 'biting the bullet' on this matter. It could be mutually advantageous if regional Governments were to agree on a common set of guidelines for financing, so that all countries would be proceeding along the same basic lines. Indeed, Heads of Government might ask the Ministers of Education and Finance to hold a joint meeting for the purpose of adopting such a common set of guidelines. There is enough information and analysis now available to facilitate the early convening of such a regional ministerial meeting.

Technical Leadership

Finally, there is an immediate need to pull together the technical leadership in education, with a new mandate to work as a team in addressing all of the major policy issues. There are several highly trained and motivated individuals dispersed throughout the regional Universities, the rest of the educational system, the Ministries of Education, and other public agencies, and even in the private sector. A mechanism should be found for mobilising the best available brains to work on educational reform, drawing wherever possible on West Indian and other expertise outside the Region.

What is needed is not so much a new institution as a mechanism — without a large bureaucracy — but with resources to facilitate collaboration and teamwork among the leading educators in producing policy advice for Governments on major issues, and in arranging for the preparation of new approaches, techniques and materials for the different levels of the system.

We suggest that Heads of Government establish a CARICOM Network for Educational Policy, the members of which will be appointed in their personal capacities. The UWI could be asked, in cooperation with the University of Guyana, to serve as the secretariat for the Network. The work programmes to be undertaken by the Network will be approved by the CARICOM Standing Committee of Ministers responsible for Education, and would be funded by regional Governments, supplemented by any support which external donors can provide.

The Network would work closely with Ministries of Education and would function as a 'Think Tank', and as a source of technical backstopping for them on policy issues. It would itself undertake, or commission, major studies, reports and reviews on issues of common importance. It could also function as a focal point for linkages with work going on outside of the Region.

Learning to Earn: An Over-arching Concept

There is one over-arching concept which is germane to the fundamentals of educational reform. It has to do with the insertion at all levels of the system of links between the world of study and that of work. However, it has particular relevance at the tertiary level, where this is one area of reform being strongly advocated by many sectors of opinion.

If the Region is to hold its own in the highly competitive world of today, it is necessary to take comprehensive steps as a matter of urgency to achieve far-reaching improvements in work attitudes and habits, discipline, team work, and capacities for leadership, innovation, and creativity.

From the earliest ages, children should be exposed to values which place a premium on hard work, the achievement of excellence, and the exercise of social responsibility at the level of the family, the workplace, the community, and the nation.

Work study programmes are being adopted by many tertiary institutions. In Jamaica, the West Indies College, as well as CAST, are good examples of this. In Trinidad and Tobago, the SERVOL programme is achieving interesting results. Given the high cost of tertiary education, and the urgent need to expand access at that level, modular work study courses (elsewhere called co-op or sandwich courses) are likely to assume increasing importance in the programmes offered by tertiary institutions.

There are indications of a large unsatisfied demand throughout the Region for tertiary and higher education on the part of people who cannot afford to take up full-time study. In any event, alternating periods of work and study could provide graduates with hands-on experience and practical approaches to their work, which should serve to improve their quality and employability.

CAST prescribes now a minimum number of hours of work as a pre-requisite for graduation. We believe that all of the tertiary institutions, including the regional universities, should adopt this practice. There is a whole range of community projects and activities to which students can contribute to mutual benefit.

At the primary and secondary levels, activities like school gardens, savings clubs, micro enterprises, and the encouragement of vacation employment, are among the possibilities that deserve greater attention.

There is also the question of tailoring the school year to correspond more closely to seasonal variations in production and economic activity. For example, it has long been the practice in some European countries to have vacations during peak periods of planting and harvesting — and, in the case of some tourist countries, during the height of the tourist season. Typically, students help firms in their localities during those periods and, thereby, develop a sense of involvement in the economic life of their community. Although there are differences in the prevailing situation in Europe as compared to the Caribbean, the feasibility of this idea is deserving of study.

One aspect of learning to earn is the establishment of incentives for achievement at all levels of the educational system, and outside of it. The awards, honours, and recognition available for achievement in fields such as scientific, technological, or institutional innovation, and success in management, need to be increased and accorded higher standing. Information on role models of success in business and community leadership should be widely disseminated. The entire development communications effort should be targeted to emphasise self-help, initiative, and team work. We return to this theme later in some comments about entrepreneurship.

Finally, we emphasise the place of the concept of 'Learning to Earn' in the Region's correctional institutions — particularly in relation to young people who are now so large a percentage of their inmates and who need to be prepared for new lives.

Tertiary and University Reform and Development

The tertiary institutions and the Universities themselves also need to take a hard look at the standards and viability of their academic programmes; the efficiency of their delivery; and the costs of their operations. We focus here particularly on the opportunities for cooperating for quality among the universities and the tertiary institutions.

Given the unswerving support of Governments for the retention and strengthening of the University of the West Indies (UWI) as a regional institution, UWI needs to grasp fully the opportunities that regionalism provides. Special attention is required to ensure that benefits are grasped in areas such as achieving critical minimum size in teaching and research, through processes that facilitate staff and student mobility, and entrench habits of cooperation among the campuses, and between them and cooperating tertiary institutions.

In the period 1990-2000, UWI plans a 50 per cent increase in its enrolments, with a good part of the increment originating from off-campus enrolments. This is a commendable effort to build up outreach programmes through distance education, and through a network of links with other tertiary institutions. We are glad to note the support that Governments are already giving to the implementation of UWI's Development Plan, including its outreach elements.

In pursuing these initiatives, care should be taken to discourage excessive duplication of programmes and courses. Greater standardisation of these should be encouraged, if only to facilitate the easy movement of students from one institution to the other. It is also very costly to offer courses which are being provided for only a small number of students.

The small size of the higher education plant, combined with the high cost of tertiary education in this Region, suggests that while there can be an increase in numbers attending the tertiary institutions, many persons will not be able to do so. Governments need to emphasise therefore the necessity for facilitating the implementation of systems of distance education. We commend the initiatives of our Governments who participated in the establishment of the Commonwealth of Learning, and would hope that full use will be made of its facilities, and assistance sought towards the establishment of distance education systems in and across these countries.

Governments should also give strong support to the Association of Caribbean Tertiary Institutions (ACTI), which was recently established. ACTI can become an important vehicle for cross-institutional cooperation and collaboration. Already, its Standing Committees are addressing issues that include accreditation and equivalence as well as programme development. In the period ahead, ACTI could also facilitate the development of teacher exchanges, as well as programmes and courses organised on a joint or consortium basis, and regular student mobility. All of these can contribute towards the consolidation and strengthening of the regional educational effort.

In the field of research, UWI should, as far as possible, encourage team work among the staff at its different campuses, while at the same time leaving room for the efforts of individual scholars. UWI can enhance its research reputation especially in inter-disciplinary and multi-disciplinary fields, if it can succeed in mobilising its best talents for research on an inter-departmental, inter-faculty and inter-campus basis. In these endeavours, UWI should also seek to draw upon research skills available in other educational institutions, and in the public and private sectors.

We are also gratified to learn that UWI is endeavouring to be more cost effective: looking at possibilities for increasing student/staff ratios and the contact hours of staff; streamlining and upgrading support services; introducing modern management methods throughout its administration. The days are long past when quality Universities can be run with amateurish methods of work. The rigorous application of modern management methods, the institution of quality controls, and the provision of productivity incentives, are now as essential to Universities as they are to other organisations.

Increases in productivity and cost effectiveness are a *sine qua non* for receiving and sustaining public support for the increases in staff salaries which UWI needs badly if it is to remain a quality institution able to recruit staff on a competitive basis.

One of the matters deserving review is the current system of financing UWI. The system of campus-based financing introduced in the 1985 restructuring, together with the economic cost per student formula, have given rise to many anomalies, including problems of equivalent access for students coming to campuses from different contributing countries. It has also complicated the task of financial management, since the institution has lost many of the advantages that accrue from pooling resources. We join our voice to that of the recent World Bank Report on education in the Region, in suggesting that Governments review the financing formula in the interest of strengthening the regional University. We assume that such a review would also be accompanied by the introduction of a new system of cost recovery.

The University of Guyana (UG) has tried hard to maintain its academic work in the face of many handicaps. The demands made upon it for delivering a variety of programmes, especially during a long period of chronic resource shortages, has inevitably tended to weaken the institution. Some commentators have argued that UG should be encouraged to rationalise and streamline its programmes, especially the more costly ones such as Medicine, where there is a dearth of the necessary academic and physical infrastructure. Despite the useful outside assistance that UG has received, and some good staff that it has managed to retain, we are deeply concerned about its academic viability. The losers in the end are, of course, the young deprived of an effective university education and marketable qualifications.

We come out in support of those who argue that UG's best chance of regaining academic and institutional strength would be through a process of integration with UWI, notwithstanding the immediate financial, administrative, and even academic difficulties that such a shift might entail. We believe that a commitment in principle to the idea, by the governing bodies of both institutions, could provide a basis for joint medium- and long-term planning to achieve this objective. Accordingly, we urge the two institutions, as well as their contributing Governments, to take a decision along these lines.

Mobilising Caribbean Expertise in the Diaspora

We have already adverted to the large numbers of West Indians who are studying abroad and to the numbers of highly skilled and professional people who emigrate each year. It is possible that in several fields, the numbers of West Indian specialists abroad exceed those who are at home. For example, in the field of medicine, it is reported that in the United States alone the number of West Indians working at the consultancy level run into several hundreds, with the majority of them having been trained at UWI. As for the UWI alumni themselves, although precise and up-to-date information is not available, there are indications that the numbers in North America are in the thousands.

In our discussions in both North America and the United Kingdom, we found a great readiness on the part of professionals and other trained people to help in appropriate ways. Although most of them have become citizens of their country of residence and might not wish to relocate to the West Indies on a permanent basis, we consider that large numbers of them might respond very positively to opportunities for short and fixed-term assignments. We feel that in several cases they might possibly do so without expecting the levels of remuneration that they are receiving abroad.

We think it urgent that the countries of the Region move decisively to organise a scheme for attracting West Indians back. One scheme which is already having positive results is the UNDP TOKTEN arrangements, under which the services of expatriate nationals are provided to their countries of origin for short periods of time. We would like to see a very substantial West Indian scheme established along these lines, to which both regional Governments and external donors could contribute.

In developing such a scheme, we feel that CARICOM Governments should have no hesitation in urging on Britain, Canada and the United States in particular the reasonableness of their giving positive and material support to such a system. The repatriation of skills from among West Indian communities who are contributing so significantly to their new societies beyond the Region, should not need advocacy. We have had many complaints from these communities abroad of their inability to contribute through ongoing technical programmes either because they are specifically excluded by virtue of their connection with the Region, or simply because they do not occupy an inside track in the consultancy system on which so much of 'aid' money is spent. The time has come, we feel, to look at these matters anew with those external agencies genuinely committed to helping the development of CARICOM countries and the process of regional integration.

We suggest that Heads of Government set up immediately a high level working group to prepare the details of a scheme, and to engage in preparatory discussions with Governments and prospective donors. It would be timely if such a scheme could be launched within the course of 1993.

The Disabled

We reserve a special word for the disabled. In more than one of our public consultations disabled persons have spoken out. They have spoken with dignity but in complaint. They share a feeling of being on the margins of society by virtue of their disability but, even moreso, by the relative indifference they sense from the rest of their communities. They have looked to us to carry this message to CARICOM in all its manifestations, and we do so without hesitation. But we do more; we raise our voice in reinforcement of their complaint that the disabled are too often the forgotten and so the neglected as well. It takes resources, it is true, to provide services; but it takes only awareness and compassion and a proper sense of obligation for us to reach out to the disabled in many of the ways that they regard as important. And we believe that in so reaching out the Region will find it easier than in an uncaring society to mobilise the resources for these basic services that the disabled deserve as a matter of right, not of charity. Meeting these needs must form a part of the human resource development programmes of the Region in a purposeful way. And Governments of the Member States should make a special effort to pass relevant legislation — along the lines of the U.K's Disabled Persons Act, suitably adapted — to improve the context in which these too often forgotten citizens live and work.

3. RESEARCH AND DEVELOPMENT

Existing Capability

In regard to research and development, our comments are confined to the field of science and technology, which from many standpoints represent the critical part of the problem.

Notwithstanding significant individual achievements over the years, the research and development capability of the Region is still at a rather rudimentary stage. Most countries are spending only an extremely minute proportion of their GDP on research and development. For instance, in the field of science and technology, it is reported that Jamaica's expenditure is probably equivalent to one-fifth of 1 per cent of GDP. This compares with figures of 3 per cent to 5 per cent for some of the newly industrialised countries.

The Bourne report points out that the Region will have to explore the specialist/high quality end of the markets (particularly for exports) as against mass market requirements which we cannot satisfy given the way we organise our production at present. To pursue this, the Region will need a cadre of highly trained technicians to help manage the new technologies, and re-orient our production techniques or even to maintain our obsolete plants. The report further notes that the Region has to adopt a new attitude to the other areas of its production and its productivity and to examine what we produce, how efficiently we produce it, how competitive we are in the producer market place, and what is the likely demand for those goods.

Some of the weaknesses in the productive sector have been highlighted in this Report. In the manufacturing sector for instance, it has been observed that there are inadequate technical and management skills, poor equipment maintenance and concomitant high incidences of down-time, energy and production inefficiencies, quality control insufficient to challenge international competition, and inadequate capacity for product engineering, design and development expertise. The fact is that if the Region is to be competitive in its productive sector, particularly given the present emphasis on export-led growth, heavy reliance will have to be placed on "knowledge-based activities" and this in turn demands a highly trained workforce more oriented to the utilisation of modern technological tools in the workplace.

Despite the heavy emigration of professional people that has taken place, the Region still has a good nucleus of highly trained scientists and technologists. However, they are scattered through numerous countries and institutions in the Region, and their individual efforts separately do not have the desired impact on the regional scene. What is needed is a rationalisation of the present installed institutional capability so as to develop regional centres of excellence in certain selected areas, development of better infrastructure in the form of well-trained support staff; upgrading of equipment; material and other incentives for scientific and technological work; and links with the private sector that could, among other things, provide funding for projects, as well as facilitate the dissemination and commercialisation of research. Advantage should also be taken of modern telecommunications technology to develop an effective network of institutions and expertise in science and technology in the Region.

At the regional level, some attempts have been made to address the issue of regional cooperation in science and technology through a Standing CARICOM Committee of Ministers. Since its inception, this Committee has commissioned the preparation of a regional policy and plan in science and technology for the CARICOM Region. This policy document, which was approved by the CARICOM Heads of Government in 1988, focuses on initiatives that can be taken at the regional level while recognising the need for national policies and plans.

Preparation of the regional policy document was coordinated by the Caribbean Council for Science and Technology (CCST), another regional body which became operational in 1981, based on the decision by the Caribbean Development and Cooperation Committee (CDCC) which is an advisory body to the United Nations Economic Commission for Latin America and the Caribbean (UN ECLAC). Among the objectives of CCST is the promotion of the establishment and strengthening of appropriate national and Caribbean organs and mechanisms for science and technology development and application. CCST is made up of thirteen member countries including Cuba, Suriname, and Haiti, but it has never realised its full potential as a regional coordinating mechanism for science and technology. It still operates out of a temporary Secretariat provided by ECLAC, and most members have not been able to meet subscription fees.

Policy Formulation and Infrastructure

Throughout the Region, attempts at science and technology policy formulation vary widely, and the results of these attempts are equally varied. There has been a definite awareness at the level of Governments of — at minimum — the need to keep a "watching brief" on the area of science and technology. At this time, there is at least one official in the public service of every territory who includes science and technology in his or her portfolio of responsibilities. Formulation and parliamentary approval of a documented policy for science and technology has been accomplished in Guyana and Jamaica, but only the latter has translated this policy document into a Five-Year Development Plan. Generally speaking, there is a total lack of integration of science and technology into national development plans, hence the negligible allocation of resources to the development of that sector in the Region.

The R & D infrastructure that exists in the Region is evidence of the laudable efforts made by some individual territories to respond to the evident need for an indigenous S & T capability. Except in agriculture and at the University of the West Indies, however, there have been no attempts at creating a regional capability. Industrial research institutions have been established throughout the Region — the Institute of Applied Science and Technology (IAST) in Guyana, the Caribbean Industrial Research Institute (CARIRI) in Trinidad and Tobago, the Scientific Research Council (SRC) in Jamaica. These, together with the produce chemists laboratories located in some of the OECS countries, carry out R & D and provide some services to the industrial sector. Some countries have well established Bureaux of Standards capable of providing quality control services to the entire Region. Ministries such as Agriculture, Mining, Industry and Commerce and Tourism engage in some sponsoring of R & D work. There are also certain commodity-oriented research facilities — rice, bauxite, sugar, bananas. Regional agricultural research programmes are executed by the Caribbean Agricultural Research and Development Institute (CARDI) and to a lesser extent UWI. The regional tertiary institutions such as UG, UWI and CAST, have a great potential for contributing to the regional R & D capability through both coordinated research and training of specialised manpower. Other specialist institutions such as the Caribbean Environmental Health Institute (CEHI) in Saint Lucia and the Institute of Marine Affairs (IMA) in Trinidad and Tobago also contribute to the regional pool of resources.

Although there exists in the Region such a wide range of institutions, they have not made a significant impact on the economies of the countries in which they are situated. One reason for this is that several of the institutions are understaffed and ill-equipped. To that must be added the fact that there is seldom any coordination of their activities at the national much less at the regional level. Further, many operate without links to the productive sector, so that much of the work being carried out is not demand-led. We believe especially that networking and the complementary development of R & D capacities among countries in the Region could yield very positive results.

New Technologies

In this information age, competitive advantage in the production of goods and services is almost entirely technology based. Investors seeking to enhance competitiveness, establish their businesses in close proximity to knowledge pools rather than labour pools, since the cost of labour in today's world provides a relatively small advantage compared to the cost of information. The emerging trends in technology, however, hold very good prospects for small states. The new technologies have created a comparative economic advantage for small-scale decentralised production over a wide range of goods and services. Flexible manufacturing techniques are revolutionising the concepts of economies of scale. New industries like electronic data entry services, desktop publishing, and software engineering, are giving the small business sector an increasing role in modern electronic growth, contributing to employment and export development.

These opportunities would be open to small Caribbean states when we produce entrepreneurs and knowledge workers in our labour force. Identification of the S & T development needs to realise these opportunities is the first prerequisite to moving forward.

Several suggestions were canvassed with us. Priorities proposed were areas such as biotechnology, especially plant tissue culture; natural products; aqua- and mari-culture, and the general resources of the sea bed; new and renewable sources of energy; health and environmental problems; remote sensing and mathematical modelling — all constitute fields in which the Region has some initial capacity with good prospects for development.

Developing Appropriate Human Resources

Technological developments will impact on Caribbean states at an ever increasing pace. To avoid becoming marginalised, Caribbean societies have to achieve the ability to adjust and thrive in such a changing world environment where science and technology play a role of prime movers. The key to developing that ability is education and training, that is, the correct orientation of the human resource. Effective utilisation of science and technology will not be possible until the human resources are developed which are able to utilise the technology.

In this respect, the University of the West Indies is already taking steps to look into the feasibility of establishing Science Parks, or Innovation Centres, which could undertake commissioned R & D work for the private and public sectors. Attention is also being given to improving the staffing situation in science, and to establishing collaboration arrangements with overseas centres of high repute.

The recruitment and retention of high-level professional staff, as well as technicians, has become an acute problem in all countries. Efforts are being made to improve remuneration packages and career prospects for such staff. These need to be intensified insofar as regional cooperation can open up opportunities for greater intellectual interchange, team work, and career mobility. It should also help to stem the outflow of scientists and technologists.

Ultimately, the development of research and development capacity, and a vibrant scientific environment, need to be underpinned by greater scientific and technological sophistication on the part of the population as a whole. In this respect, the formation of professional groups, e.g. Associations of Engineers, Scientists, Technicians, engaged in the application of S & T to development, need to be actively supported. Continuing public education and a greater input of S & T into the school curricula are indispensable to developing such awareness. Once again this is a matter where the Universities can give important leadership.

Intellectual Property

Finally, the countries of the Region need to pay greater attention to questions of intellectual property. The laws governing patents and copyrights are woefully out of date. If greater encouragement is to be given to developing the stock of local knowledge, adequate legal protection must be provided for that stock. We also need to give greater visibility to our innovators, and reward them for their skills through conferring national or regional honours or significant monetary awards.

Involvement of the Private Sector and The Diaspora

In developing this regional capability in S & T, mechanisms must be found to ensure the participation and full support of the private sector, which, given the new emphasis on private sector-led growth, will be a major beneficiary. During our consultations with professionals in the diaspora, it was evident that Caribbean nationals had developed a wide range of relevant skills in S & T which could be accessed from time to time to boost our own capability in areas considered vital for development. The Commission was heartened by the willingness of many of our overseas nationals to participate in this process once the way has been cleared for them to do so.

Proposals

To effectively address the issue of S & T development in the Region, the Commission recommends that:-

- At the regional level, a mechanism must be established for coordinating S & T activities. The present arrangement for coordinating regional science and technology activities through the CARICOM Secretariat needs to be overhauled and strengthened. Some definite decision has to be made about the future role of the Caribbean Council for Science and Technology (CCST) taking into consideration that its membership includes Suriname, Haiti and Cuba.
- At the national level more attention needs to be paid to the integration of S & T into national development plans, so that the S & T needs of every sector are clearly identified and budgeted for.
- As a matter of urgency the Region should develop endogenous capability in certain key technologies — microelectronics, biotechnology, computerisation, telecommunications, mathematical modelling, remote sensing, computer-aided design and computer-aided manufacturing (CAD/CAM) — if it is to remain competitive in a market-oriented economy and if it is to cope

with the prudent management of the Region's environment and natural resources.

- In developing the regional capability, efforts should be made to develop regional centres of excellence in particular technologies, and to establish regional networks of scientists/technologists with specific skills. The effectiveness of these networks can be enhanced by use of advanced telecommunications technology. These regional centres and regional networks will provide the critical mass of resources and skills needed to effectively address major S & T issues relevant to Caribbean development.

- A major regional effort should be made to address the shortage of specialised skills in the science and technology sector. Based on an analysis of the human resource needs in the major productive sectors, a major initiative should be supported to provide the necessary training in the regional tertiary institutions.

- The same effort is required to boost the regional stock of technicians of all types and middle level technical management personnel. Full utilisation of the Region's installed training capacity in both public and private sector organisations is envisaged. Some effort too is required to ensure parity of certification among the different countries, and to build in career mobility opportunities for technicians comparable to those available for their administrative counterparts.

- As an interim measure, special incentives should be built into the conditions of service of highly skilled technical personnel, particularly those operating in public sector organisations.

- A scheme of significant regional awards, including monetary awards, should be introduced on an annual basis, for the best innovations which have led to creation of new productive activity in the Region.

- Policies and incentives geared to attract private sector participation and investment in the development of a regional S & T capability should be introduced. Also mechanisms for utilising the know-how of our highly skilled professionals in the diaspora should be developed.

- In an effort to raise the S & T temper of the entire society, regional curricula for S & T should be developed for primary, secondary, and continuing education programmes. A higher S & T content in the news media including television should be actively encouraged, along with such events as science fairs and science museums.

4. ENTREPRENEURSHIP

There is widespread acknowledgement of the importance of developing local entrepreneurship. This has been underlined by the leading role which the private sector is now being called upon to play as the principal engine of economic growth. Accordingly, Governments and the private sector are engaged in sponsoring or supporting a variety of initiatives. These include expanding and upgrading tertiary and University programmes in business administration; the establishment of incubator services which can help the potential entrepreneur to transform an idea into a bankable project; and venture capital/investment funds to contribute towards equity financing of new business or the expansion of existing ones.

There is now greater support for the development of small business and micro enterprises. For example, training courses and technical assistance are now being offered to informal commercial importers (higglers, hucksters and traders), designed to upgrade their business skills, and to encourage them to go beyond commerce and enter the field of production. There are many examples of the emergence in the Region of small-scale specialty production in non-traditional fields such as the cultivation and processing of exotic foods and vegetables; horticulture; aquaculture; up-market garments; textiles; furniture; telecommunications; medical equipment; boat and yacht construction — to name just a few examples.

The view has been expressed on several occasions that the Region can find a whole range of opportunities for specialty production and niche marketing. These tend, however, to be knowledge-intensive, which serves to reinforce the observations made earlier about enlarging and diversifying the Region's stock of skills and technology.

Sourcing Outside Skills and Knowledge

Our discussion of human resources would not be complete if we did not make reference to the need for countries in the Region to adopt more aggressive and outward-looking policies towards the sourcing of extra-regional knowledge and skills. We have already dealt with the issue of the freer movement of skilled and professional persons among Member States.

In the period immediately following Independence, it was understandable that Governments should give priority to nationals occupying the key positions in society and to developing local sources of knowledge and expertise. All of these are still very much needed. The proposals that we have made earlier are intended to build-up enhanced knowledge capabilities at the national and regional levels.

At the same time, given the growing interdependence of the world and the increasing need to compete on an international scale in practically every field of endeavour, we need to develop less restrictive policies to highly trained outsiders wishing to work in the Region. This applies particularly at the managerial, supervisory, and technical levels, where serious personnel shortages are holding back development.

In the race towards export-propelled growth, some of the most advanced and rapidly growing countries in the world are liberalising their immigration requirements for professional and skilled people. In the case of the CARICOM countries, we are still locked into work permit policies more reflective of strategies of national import substitution than of regional integration and export-led growth.

We propose that regional governments develop a common package of measures designed to liberalise work permit regulations in areas of serious skills shortage, and put into place incentives to encourage very highly skilled people to establish knowledge-based activities in the Region, either on a company or on an individual basis. For example, we believe that if Governments were to encourage explicitly the establishment of research and research and development activities in the Region, this, combined with the other measures that we have outlined, could serve to strengthen the image of the Region as a knowledge centre in the world. A whole range of benefits could flow from such a development in the form of the establishment of new lines of economic activity and the strengthening of existing ones.

To return to the overall requirements for human resources development, it is necessary to recognise the important social and cultural advantages associated with such development. Knowledge is empowerment and, therefore, supportive of greater people participation in the development process. If the CARICOM countries can 'get their act together' in this very vital field, a large part of the battle for development can be won.

Recommendations:

1. that deliberate steps be taken to work towards the creation of a single CARICOM market for human resources;

2. that regional action be pursued in five areas to reform and strengthen the primary and secondary schools system:
   - Curriculum Reform
   - Teacher Education
   - Schools Management
   - Financing
   - Research and analytical capability

3. that at all levels of the educational system, starting at an early age, arrangements and orientations towards learning to earn should be established;

4. that there be more systematic networking between the regional Universities and the other tertiary institutions, and strong support of ACTI;

5. that there be quality improvements at both the academic and administrative levels at UWI and UG;

6. that a commitment be made to integrate UWI and UG;

7. that a regional scheme for attracting back West Indian expertise in the diaspora be developed;

8. that the disabled be recognised as an element of the Region's human resources with special needs, and that in this context CARICOM Member States agree to enact relevant legislation — along the lines of the U.K's Disabled Persons Act, suitably adapted — to improve the context in which these too often forgotten CARICOM citizens live and work;

9. that a number of new measures be adopted to strengthen the institutional framework for science and technology; to determine a regional programme of priorities in this field; introduce incentives for innovation; and provide for the creation of greater scientific and technological awareness;

10. that there be some regional support for the creation of Science Parks, Innovation Centres, and other facilities for R & D;

11. that vigorous encouragement should be given to local entrepreneurship through training and support schemes of various kinds;

12. that there be systematic liberalisation of policies and work permit regulations applicable to highly skilled and professional people coming from outside of the Region.

CHAPTER VII

THE CULTURAL DIMENSION

1. OVERVIEW

A Distinctive Cultural Expression

Whatever else West Indian society may be, it has long regarded itself, as others have regarded it, as a distinctive "cultural expression". Arthur Lewis, the Region's first Nobel Laureate and a renowned economist writing on 'being a West Indian', had this to say: "A society without the creative arts is a cultural desert. I would commend to our statesmen that they put a lot more money into the creative arts departments of our secondary schools". His acknowledgement of the importance of artistic culture to West Indian development and identity found unequivocal endorsement from an earlier passage in his essay, which reads: "Music, Literature and Art are as important a part of the heritage of mankind as are science and morals. They differ from science in that they do not represent what is, but are products of the creative imagination. They have, therefore, infinite scope for variation. And yet they tend to be distinctively national in character... This", he concludes, "is the essential and most valuable sense in which West Indians must be different to other people".

If this was, as we suspect, the intuitive view of the people at large, it still took some time to take root in political consciousness. Today, however, there are many Ministers of Culture, served by Directors of Culture, charged with implementing cultural policies focusing primarily on the encouragement of the arts for national and human resource development. A Standing Committee of Ministers of Education and Culture at the CARICOM level is an echo of this commitment on the part of member Governments of the Community. The structures are being put in place.

The Caribbean's genesis, development and general character over the past half a millennium have been determined in large measure by common cultural responses to a variety of shared experiences:

- aboriginal decimation following on the early settlement by European explorers, adventurers and planters;
- the institution of slavery involving the involuntary migration of millions of West Africans to be used as chattels in the production of sugar, followed by the further migration, albeit semi-voluntary, of hundreds of thousands of Asians (East Indians and Chinese) into indentureship to replace the Africans once slavery was abolished;
- the crucible of plantation life in which was forged patterns of human interaction, fuelled by racial discrimination, labour exploitation, dehumanisation, cultural resistance, a struggle for liberty and equality, and a sense and sensibility which accommodates diversity without personal psychic or social disintegration; and
- colonialism which deepened the sense of economic and political powerlessness even while it reinforced the inheritance of struggle against injustice and the yearning after self determination.

The establishment in 1979 of a Cultural Desk in the CARICOM Secretariat, and the introduction since 1972 to the Region's cultural agenda of Carifesta (Caribbean Festival of Arts) are seen, at best. as modest institutional acknowledgements of the cultural imperative. The role of the University of the West Indies as a major agent of cultural cooperation, if not full blown integration, since its founding in 1948 is undoubtedly of inestimable value preceding, as it did, both the aborted West Indian Federation of 1958 and the signing of the Treaty of Chaguaramas in 1973. It has, after all, spawned an entire generation of West Indians who are well steeped in the history and socio-economic realities of the still developing region, as well as in its agricultural, engineering and environmental potential. Yet, the over-arching integrative influence of cricket notwithstanding, not everyone is agreed that the potential of the Region as a distinct geo-cultural zone has been sufficiently explored in the interest of regional unity and development.

We have a common history whose fabric, woven of many strands, now stretches back 500 years. These strands are tightly interwoven now and, though each can be identified (and pointed out as having pride of place in the eye of the beholder), none can be unpicked from the other. One strand, first on the loom, is Amerindian and we do not forget in this 500th anniversary of the arrival of Columbus in the Americas itsessential place in the pattern, holding an original distinction.

By now we have securely 'placed ourselves in history'. "I have long believed," C.L.R. James wrote, "that there is something in the West Indian past, something in the West Indian development, which compels the West Indian intellectual when he gets involved with subjects of this kind, to deal with them from a fundamental point of view, to place ourselves in history". This was written in the course of paying tribute to J.J. Thomas's famous *Froudacity*. And it is appropriate to notice that James went on to remind us that Thomas himself, when he broached the subject of "West Indian Confederation", sought to explain "why there should be a confederation of the various *types* of people, the various classes, the various *races* in the West Indies".

We have assimilated each others' histories. We have experienced the European arrival and colonisation, the Amerindian decimation, slavery, indenture, the struggles for freedom and freedom itself and they are in our historical consciousness. We have inherited, adapted, Caribbeanised, European institutions. "The West Indies is a microcosm of world civilisation", James wrote. "The great problems are posed *in such a way that everything can be seen*". That is well and profoundly put.

Against the background of its peculiar history and continuing existence, the CARICOM Region demonstrates a certain uniqueness of cultural reality, manifest in those indices that are the measure of the internal logic and integrity of any civilisation, and of the self-esteem of its individual inhabitants. These are the factors of language, religion, kinship patterns, ethnicity, artistic manifestations and attitudes to authority, as well as the decisions consciously taken with respect to production, distribution and exchange of material goods and services.

Underlying all of this are the values that make possible the distillation of form out of the disparate elements of social living and of order out of the noise of contention and conflict. This is the nature of the cultural imperative which is likely to realise itself the more commonalities exist among a set of territories sharing a similar history as in the case of CARICOM's archipelago and its mainland members.

Language

One of the things West Indians have in common is language: the English language inherited and adapted to our various uses and to describe our varied experiences. The opportunity to debate, argue, explain, refute, intellectualise, clarify — communication at a fundamental level — is basic to the grounding of the nation. Our histories, ethnicities, customs, religions, cultures, myths, legends and lore have a shared accessibility in the language we use both in our everyday life and in our greatest literary creations. West Indian cultural and intellectual activities, in all their variety and astonishing creativity, are expressed in one basic language which no West Indian is excluded from understanding. But to describe CARICOM categorically as English-speaking is not, of course, to tell the whole story.

Language, a prime product of the exercise of the creative intellect and imagination of a people anywhere, was to be forged by the mass of the population into genuinely creole (i.e. native-born and native-bred) forms over a period of at least three centuries. So in the CARICOM Region alone there are at least two well developed creole languages — Jamaica Talk and kweyol (créole) — as well as variations of linguistic expression closely related to Standard English. Their relation to other such creole tongues as *Papiamento* (of The Netherlands Antilles) and *Srnan Tonga* (of Suriname) as well as their internal consistency as manifestations of the creolisation process have been the subject of serious academic investigation for four decades at least.

The Region's linguistic diversity and complexity are after all rooted in 500 years of a history of imperialist rivalry, migrations and cultural interaction. Probably less than 10 per cent of the populations of Dominica and Saint Lucia are monolingual English-speakers for instance. Guyana has nine indigenous pre-Columbian languages in addition to some residual East Indian dialect; and a 1974 study showed that 46 per cent of Trinidadian students were exposed to Bhojpuri. Most of Jamaica's 2.4 million speak Jamaica Talk most of the time, reserving Standard English for formal discourse.

Side by side with the linguistic diversity is a commonality expressed through the widespread use of "creole" languages and mass vernaculars. Some of these are intelligible across geographical boundaries. For example (French) patois or "creole" (as it is called in Haiti) is a shared tool of communication in Cayenne, Dominica, Guadeloupe, Haiti, Martinique and Saint Lucia. This commonality can be positively exploited in the quest for ease of communication between the peoples of the Region. Indeed, we can recall with some gratification that it generally facilitated the delivery of CARICOM's assistance to the organisation and conduct of the first genuinely democratic elections in Haiti in December 1990.

But let us not be misunderstood. The basic commonality of language is English, and while we must not let it extinguish our other cultural forms of expression and communication we must not lose, or forfeit by default, its inestimable value to us as we look to the wider world and our interaction with it. Our cultural development is enriched by Caribbean vernacular; our economic development, our access to mere knowledge, our openness to advances in science and technology, quite apart from other gains, are enhanced and facilitated by our proficiency in the leading international language. No one expressed better our good fortune in this dual inheritance than the Jamaican writer V. S. Reid. His counsel is ours too; it is counsel our Region must heed.

> In our search for the tap root, let us never sever the nourishing laterals. ... We who talk, and talk quite sensibly too, of working and playing and trading with the world, must be able to communicate with the world. We are heirs to a heritage bought by our blood-sweat-and-tears. We are heirs to the English language. A good bit of luck. It is the closest approximation to an international tongue that has ever existed. Millions in the world would give anything to be able to speak it. Maybe it is the only plus salvaged from savage slavery, much of whose residual we had to be quit of; but desuetude here is self-defeating.

Communication is critical in the process of human resource development and even democratic decision-making. A shared language and the empowerment it gives is necessary for full participation in the political, social and cultural activity of a people. The need to develop proficiency in a common language is necessary as the basis for a common identity and common action.

In our primary school classrooms much more attention should be devoted to giving our children a love of reading and an early facility in using language. In our secondary schools, the teaching of language and literature must find a more prominent place. The imagination of our young people must be fired early by the infinite potential and universal outreach of our common language and the immense achievements, not least West Indian, of its literature. If there is a shortfall in quality or quantity or teachers of English in the schools, let us realise that we are short-changing our children in a most fundamental way and undermining the bedrock on which the building of a nation depends.

The fact that the University of the West Indies, as well as business firms, find it necessary to provide courses in remedial English at post secondary school level is profoundly disturbing.

In the University, English Departments, ultimate custodians of our own developing literary traditions and leading facilitators of teaching the language, should hold an important place in the mainstream of University research and activity. Research and teaching in English at the highest level in our various societies is not an expendable option.

The widening of Caribbean integration to take in Spanish-speaking, French-speaking and the Dutch-speaking Caribbean inhabitants poses the challenge of linguistic pluralism. With the advancement of the technology of simultaneous translation, regional discourse on matters of moment could proceed apace without undue difficulties. But when all this is conceded, there remains the issue of deepening the core-CARICOM which, though officially English-speaking, has a plethora of creole Caribbean languages whose marginalisation continues to jerk out of proper perspective the quite practical use of Standard English as the Region's instrument of formal discourse.

Creole languages in which many CARICOM citizens converse must be given the dignity and recognition they deserve. It is clear from studies done into the sociolinguistics of the Region that the denigration of popular forms of language communication will serve to alienate many elements of the population, creating a barrier to the sense of community that is vital to national unity and regional integration. The kweyol that links the ordinary people of Dominica and Saint Lucia with Haitians and Martiniquans and Guadeloupians already finds a place in the communication process between decision-makers and the mass of the population.

There has to be open and national recognition of the importance of creole language as a reservoir of a dynamic aspect of national culture. It is bound up with people's sense of self and serves cognitive, expressive and interactional functions. It should not be linked with deprivation. This recognition is critical for human resource development. Such a recognition does not vitiate the mastery of official English or entail a threat to it.

There is need for a facility to promote and co-ordinate language learning and teaching in the Anglophone Caribbean. This can be based in the UWI School of Education and can draw on the experiences of a similar ECLAC project, "Removal of Language Barriers in the Caribbean", which proposed the setting up of a Language Institute in Curacao.

CARICOM Governments should therefore give support to language training at all levels of the educational system in the same way that due emphasis is being placed on science and technology.

The Lexicography Project at the Cave Hill Campus of the University of the West Indies should be facilitated in its work on Caribbean English.

Religion

As with language, religion was forged by Caribbean peoples in their response to oppression. When the worship of African gods was forbidden in a Christian dispensation, the God of the oppressor was duly adopted for veneration with appropriate variations in the quest for the best of all possible worlds. West Indian cultural history is replete with examples of creolised forms emerging from the creative energies of the people of the Caribbean — from pukkumina (pocomania) in Jamaica through the generic evangelical revivalism to be found throughout the entire Region, to Shango in Trinidad. Were Cuba, Haiti and Brazil to join CARICOM, the mass of the population in each of these territories would find kindred souls (and spirits) through the respective religious expressions of santeria, voodoo and candomble each of them would bring to the Region's religious plurality.

They would of course bring, as well, the orthodoxies that came with the European branch of the Caribbean family. Christian orthodoxies abound — Protestant, non-conformist and Catholic (Roman and Anglo, high and low). The majority of the inhabitants of the CARICOM countries are be Christian by adherence, and the ethos of the society is certainly shaped by a strong Euro-Christian value-system.

However, in two Member States, Trinidad and Tobago and Guyana, the Hindu and Muslim religions are the faiths of a major part of the population. These great religions not only inspire the lives of hundreds of thousands of CARICOM citizens but also spread their influence widely in the cultural life of society. To these must be added the more recent Bahá'í faith, as well as variants of latter-day American evangelism fueled by the influence of North American televangelical and pentecostal proselytizers.

Religion has had a pervasive influence on the lives of the Caribbean peoples throughout the past 500 years. It made sense that, over the past three decades, it should serve as an integrative force in welding together Caribbean peoples of similar faith and, within a particular faith, of different denominations.

The emergence of the Caribbean Conference of Churches and CADEC, its development arm, attest to this, as did the West Indianisation of church administration in the different dispensations. There is an Anglican Archbishop for the entire province of the West Indies, and an Episocopal Conference for the Roman Catholics. The Methodist Conference, from the time of its founder John Wesley, whose influence on the Region started in the journey to the Leewards in the 19th century, has long brought together churchmen, both clerical and lay, periodically from all over the Region. The Seventh Day Adventists and the Salvation Army are also forces of regional co-operation, especially the former, through its programmes of educational development at the tertiary level, region-wide. Quakers, Assemblies of Brethren, other lesser-known Christian communions and members of the Bahá'í faith have long maintained a Caribbean link.

On the evidence gathered by the Commission, Caribbean religious organisations do not regard a diversity of faiths and creeds as an insurmountable barrier to unity. But unity does not necessarily mean uniformity, and there is probably as much evidence of the divisive potential of religion as there is of its great integrative powers. The covert and overt discrimination against indigenous religious expressions like the Rastafarian faith, of which we heard much complaint in our consultations, is evidence of this divisive force; and the deep historical hold of a Christian world-view on Caribbean citizens was cause for expressed concern among those CARICOM citizens who are not of Christian faiths. The Caribbeanisation of Christianity is a claim that would be made by many of that faith who have been involved in creolising the liturgy, vestments, and symbols, if not the theology. Such creolisation presents challenges for non-Christian faiths as well as for newly arrived religious groups, like the Mormons, whose expansion throughout the Region through emphasis on community development presents a new phenomenon.

Nearly all the religious groups are critical Non-Governmental Organisations (NGOs) whose constituents are identical with those of the civil government. They are engaged in important social and educational work and in the moulding of moral and spiritual values — all vital ingredients for the proper working of civil society. Caribbean peoples are a captive and, in some ways, a compliant audience for moral messages and spiritual injunctions from the pulpit, as much as from political platform and lecturer's podium. In short, the Church, synagogue, mosque and temple are critical media of social communication and education. They remain important agents of regional integration. Some national governments have in fact taken the laudable step of appointing Advisory Committees on religious affairs — a step worthy of imitation on the regional level.

If the importance of religion to Caribbean history, contemporary life and the life of the future is to be taken seriously, the integration movement must find appropriate response to the challenge of the depth and intensity of religious commitment evident among millions of Caribbean citizens. The Christian Church, not only in terms of the witness of its conscientious, committed members but even more so as a formally structured community, has been an active *de facto* social partner in governance in CARICOM Member States. Despite the diversity of faiths, there is the common thread of belief in the concept of brotherhood and sisterhood of man and woman as well as of mutual service. What better basis for forging the idea of a regional citizenship and a sense of community?

The Caribbean Conference of Churches (CCC) has succeeded in promoting over two decades a measure of harmony among a number of Christian churches. It has also commendably focussed attention on the need to practise faith both as a matter of personal and community piety as well as an informative for social responsibilities. It has therefore pursued a social and political mandate of the Church particularly in its concern for the plight of the poor and the oppressed. It has also been a moving spirit in raising the consciousness of Caribbean citizens to take into account regional objectives.

There is, nevertheless, a need for a more comprehensive body to address the issue of inter-faith harmony and to mobilise the members of all religious groups for social action. This may well be a parallel functional body to address all inter-faith concerns including ecumenicity in the broadest sense. This would embrace non-Christian traditions and guarantee to newer movements a place in the inter-faith dialogue concerned with social issues and the underlying principles of Caribbean civil society.

Where discrimination is practised against minority faiths, (e.g. the Rastafarians) this should cease. Equally in keeping with the rule of law, members of such groups are expected to obey the law of the land and to fulfil their civic duties. This is more than a call for religious tolerance. Caribbean governments must give a lead in abolishing religious prejudices.

Each religion will always wish to protect its particular doctrinal turf and its brand of inherited traditions in beliefs and practices. Any effort to deny them such specificity would be unnatural to human experience and be in defiance of the texture that is the Caribbean reality. But some element of liberation from this preoccupation with diversity at the expense of functional unity is necessary if religion is to remain responsive to the social imperatives of contemporary life in the Region.

Those religious bodies which have attempted to indigenise their liturgies utilising the creativity of Caribbean people in dance, music and poetry have long found sustained enthusiasm among their congregations.

The Arts

In no respect has our shared history and continuing commonalities had more influence than in the artistic manifestations of Caribbean culture. Whether in literature, the performing arts (especially music, dance, drama and more recently video), the visual arts (painting, sculpture), the domestic crafts (ceramics, jewelcraft, basket weaving, etc), architecture, Festival arts (and related crafts like wirebending, metal sculpture, etc) and that most West Indian of all performing arts, the sport of cricket, the Region has built up an enviable track record of world-class achievement.

Cricket has been a major cultural force in forging a sense of community among West Indians. It carries with it an historical pedigree dating back to the twenties and flourishes today as foremost among the Region's agents of cultural integration, embracing the enthusiasm and interest of all West Indians irrespective of class, race, gender, political affiliation or creed. The achievements have served to foster a sense of regional identity and unity-in-diversity with far-reaching implications not only for an integrated future but for coping with a new century that will demand of ordinary mortals the capacity to make sense of difference and complexity in their everyday living. In the long run, the deep concern with which other CARICOM citizens reacted to the boycott of the Test Match in Barbados earlier this year may be of more significance than the boycott itself.

Such is the potential of a cultural reality that has given the Region as a whole the benefits of the collective genius of its population and the treasured creativity of gifted individuals in the creative arts. Rich oral literatures are the patrimony of the Region, thanks to the richness of the creole languages created by the people as a whole.

The folktales with the wistful impish Anancy as hero are matched by the "*contes*" tradition of the kweyol-speaking territories of the Eastern Caribbean. And everywhere the collective wisdom of forbears survives in the proverbs which condense the profoundest of philosophical notions which prove to be universal in their application across creole linguistic barriers and geographical boundaries in the physically and still politically fragmented Caribbean. Without this collective legacy the Region might never have had the experience of the poetic genius of Louise Bennett and her epigones, the dub poets of more recent vintage, or of Paul Keens-Douglas and the brilliant calypso lyricists who use the language of the people with the same verbal dexterity that once guaranteed survival to forbears in bondage. Only now, it serves to give people a sense of continuity and identity, the natural basis for regional integration. Neither Louise Bennett nor Paul Keens-Douglas is likely to be a stranger to CARICOM citizens, whatever their racial origin, perceived class position, gender, religious persuasion, or territory of residence.

Festival Arts

Caribbean festival arts provide yet another manifestation of a historically sustained cultural commonality among the people of the CARICOM Region. Starting with the Christmas masquerades of the middle-slavery period, the pre-Lenten representation of this (which blossomed into the Trinidad Carnival) followed at end-of-slavery and persisted up to contemporary times with increasing vigour and expansiveness. These were to be later joined by the East Indian-derived Hosay which flourishes to this day in Trinidad, Jamaica and, to a lesser extent, in Guyana. They are all three distinctive, creolised, cross-fertilised, genuine Caribbean cultural expressions engaging the participation of a wide cross-section of West Indian citizens by bridging the ethnic and religious divide shaped by the differences of ethnic origin. Masquerade, known severally as Jonkonnu in Jamaica, Belize and the Bahamas, and as Gombay in Bermuda, still thrives in varying degrees of intensity at Christmastime in all these places, as well as in Guyana and the Leeward Islands. The characters in the masked revelry are to be found in varying versions throughout the Region from Pitchy Patchy, the vegetal spirit of the Forest, through

Mother Lundi to the Devil, King, Queen and Horsehead, among others. They share the common historical provenance of three days of respite from the hazards of plantation labour; and the masqueraders seized the opportunity to pass judgement through wit and humour, mime and make-believe on a cruel society and the hapless perpetrators of that cruelty. The masquerades continue to serve as a source of energy for contemporary theatre, for ribald humour and social commentary up and down the Region.

This genre of popular artistic/cultural expression found a variant form during the early nineteenth century in the pre-Lenten carnival, concentrated in Trinidad with its strong Catholic and Latin (Spanish and French) antecedents, despite the official presence of Anglo-Saxon political overlordship. It was to develop characters of its own, though sharing with older Jonkonnu from the northern Caribbean some others, with marked similarities in characterisation, movement and costuming. Like its sister festival art to the north, it has served as point of reference for contemporary theatre. But more than masquerade/jonkonnu, the Carnival has provided a means for cultural sustenance and a point of reconnexion with home for the hundreds of thousands in the Caribbean diaspora shaped by the migration since the fifties of hordes of West Indians seeking better opportunities for material well-being denied them in their homeland. There are today celebrations of Caribbean Carnival (Trinidad-style) in Notting Hill (London), Toronto, Brooklyn (New York), Miami (Florida) and Boston. It is West Indian in its content, orientation and in its expansiveness; it commands the adherence of diasporic West Indians from every part of the Region.

Within the Region itself the Carnival has caught the imagination of the people of nearly all the CARICOM territories. Some use it as a form of tourist attraction (as in Antigua, the Bahamians re-stage their Jonkonnu in the "winter season" and call it Gombay), while others follow the pre-Lenten tradition as a natural historical necessity as in Dominica and Saint Lucia, which has its own La Rose and Marguerite festivals, West Indian creolised representations of the English Wars of the Roses. Jamaica, which resisted the Trinidad Carnival for decades, finally succumbed at the beginning of the current decade despite its own Government- sponsored Independence Festival which has recovered from earlier panic brought on by a fear that the "imported" Trinidad Carnival would render the Jamaica celebrations superfluous. The Barbados Crop Over Festival has long freed itself of any such panic, though the influence of the Trinidad Carnival on the modem of streetdancing and other forms of merrymaking in this Barbadian innovation (also Government-sponsored) are clearly evident. The Trinidad Carnival is no longer exclusively a Trinidadian enterprise. It has become a Caribbean-wide exercise embracing the talents of a wide cross section of Caribbean people wherever the festival is celebrated in the Region; and Cuba, Haiti and the Dominican Republic would be no strangers to this genre of Caribbean popular mass expression were they to find themselves membership on a level with us in a cordial integration process.

Hosay, without the genealogical pedigree of Jonkonnu/Masquerade or Carnival, is nowhere as widespread in the Region. Only where East Indians have settled since Emancipation in substantial numbers is the festival art to be found. But wherever it is to be found it betrays all the characteristics of the product of a process of adaptation, adjustment and innovation from its original dominant source(s). Christian West Indians of African ancestry are to be found playing the tassa drums in all three of the territories where Hosay is to be found and the two otherwise differentiated ethnic groups can be caught in collaborative endeavours through this particular festival art. Here the Caribbean cultural imperative works, albeit on a temporary basis, to foster harmony between two distinctive and potentially combative ethnic groups.

These festivals also serve as vehicles for other artforms that have come to be regarded as the common stock and capital of all West Indians, irrespective of origin. East Indians sing calypsos as Trinidadians, and the most popular soca band is one led by a West Indian of Jamaican/Chinese stock. The Tassa drumming is now regarded as a West Indian ingredient of West Indian-music and no longer exclusively "Indian" by the likes of individual artists like Bugsy Sharpe, the creator of exploratory West Indian jazz, and Peter Minshall, the revolutionary designer of successful, if highly controversial, Carnival bands, the one of African, the other of European ancestry.

Music

But it is the steelband, arguably the only acoustic instrument to be invented in the 20th century (and by West Indians), that has had the greatest single impact on a major stream of Caribbean music over the past 50 years. It spread beyond its place of origin even before Carnival, its great frame of reference, did. "Brute Force" of Antigua was known throughout the CARICOM region in the Fifties alongside such great contemporaries in homeland Trinidad as "Invaders" led by Ellie Mannette, "Desperadoes" and the Trinidad All Steel Percussion Orchestra (TASPO) which toured Britain in 1951 under N. Joseph Griffith, who helped to train the Antiguan band. And though the Jamaica School of Music, which serves as a regional facility, is yet to develop an active enough passion for the instrument in its curriculum, there are enough converts to the steelband in Jamaica to make it an urgent proposition in the musical life of this one Caribbean country which itself is a major exporter of yet another original Caribbean music-form to the rest of the Region.

The reference is to reggae and later its controversial offspring, dancehall. It is, however, important to recall that preceding all of this was the Trinidad calypso which was so powerful as to be used by the outside world generically to describe all forms of folk music coming from the English-speaking Caribbean in the forties and fifties. The calypso had its impact on the music inside the Caribbean and outside it and came to be considered a Caribbean staple for radio stations all over the Region. Soca, its offspring, has had even more impact since the late seventies making someone like Arrow, the calypsonian from Montserrat, a major concert artist of the Region, following in the footsteps of the Mighty Sparrow who is credited with definitively changing the style of calypso in the mid-fifties, as well as of his mentor,, Lord Kitchener, who was well known in Jamaica during the forties and who came to be a truly Caribbean musical icon in his assaults from the United Kingdom, where he went to live for a while.

By the mid-sixties popular musical innovation in the Region seemed to have shifted to Jamaica where, in keeping with the tradition of popular self-assertion via protest, it manifested itself through the exercise of the creative imagination. The intellect had expended energy on the cause for self-government and Independence which was by then a fact. The imagination of the mass of the population were activated to produce in quick succession a particular form of protest-music rich in social commentary and drawing on the inheritance of cultural history. The "ska" was followed in rapid succession by the "rock-steady" which quickly blossomed into the reggae. That was to become the music of West Indian youth from the late seventies as it did of young people all over the world. The names of Bob Marley, Jimmy Cliff, Peter Tosh, to name just three genuine creators, are as Caribbean as they are Jamaican though some would say they are no less 'citizens of the world'. The important thing is that, like Sparrow, Arrow and Kitchener of the southern Caribbean, the reggae musicians are prime agents of cultural identity, the products of a process that draws on the historical experience and existential reality of the CARICOM Caribbean. So Zouk, the popular music of all of the Francophone Caribbean, has ancestral links with cadence, itself rooted in the traditional music of the former French-occupied islands of Dominica and Saintt Lucia. The organic links are unmistakable and the opportunity for widespread Caribbean acceptance guaranteed.

The same can be said of the choral theatre genre of the Region, with groups of singers of traditional Caribbean music sharing selections from each other's repertoire. The songs are indeed the common stock and capital of all Caribbean countries. Whether it is the University Singers on the Mona campus or the Cavite Chorale at Cave Hill, the Jamaican Folksingers or the NDTC Singers of Jamaica, the Police Male Voice and Woodside Choirs of Guyana, the Olive Walke La Petite Musicale of Trinidad, or the Hewanorra Singers of Saint Lucia, the National Chorale of Dominica, the Kingstown Chorale of St Vincent, the Emerald Community Singers of Montserrat, or the Renaissance Singers of The Bahamas, there are to be found commonalities of tone, pitch and timbre which make them all the variants of a common West Indian choral theatre tradition. The point of reference is in all cases the collective experience of the Region's ordinary men and women over time, distilled into song.

That the discoveries here have served to enrich Caribbean musical theatre, from the Jamaican pantomime to the musical dramas written by Caribbean playwrights, is now common knowledge. And the Church, through the efforts of the Caribbean Conference of Churches and CADEC, has ensured that this musical heritage is incorporated into the liturgy and hymnodic innovations of Caribbean Christian orthodoxy.

Literature

The literary artists are themselves at their most "Caribbean", without being any less "universal" for that, when organic connection with Caribbean social reality is made. This is as true of Vidia Naipaul whose *A House for Mr Biswas* and *Miguel Street* are considered great classics among his body of works by the cognoscenti both within the Region and outside it. Never mind that it is the Region's undoubted folly, its blatant shortcomings at working civil society, its weaknesses and political immaturity that have fueled the literary genius of Naipaul's later work, and that many take issue with his vision of Caribbean social and political reality. Derek Walcott who stayed at home (living in Saint Lucia, Jamaica and Trinidad) to maturity could have come from nowhere other than a Region like the Caribbean with its congenital turbulence, creative chaos, and hope-in-despair syndrome. His most recent masterwork, *Omeros*, like so many of the others before, brings the physical landscape of the Region to poetic stanzas he crafts so artlessly; and his dramatic writings explore the multi-faceted character of the Caribbean persona with the wit, even in-the-midst of tragedy, that underpins a sensitive and accurate reading of the contradictory omens that Edward Kamau Brathwaite, that other major home-bred (Barbados-Saint Lucia-Jamaica) Caribbean literary artist and historian, said were the dynamic of the Region's dialectical existence.

Walcott's poignant passage in his essay "The Use of History" puts in perspective such contradictory omens.

> But the tribe in bondage learned to fortify itself by cunning assimilation of the religion of the old world. What seemed to be surrender was redemption. What seemed the loss of tradition was its renewal. What seemed the death of faith was its rebirth.

Before Walcott and Brathwaite were writers like George Lamming, Samuel Selvon, Vic Reid and others whose celebration of the Caribbean sensibility provided a change of cultural certitude getting within the grasp of succeeding generations of Caribbean citizens just as earlier members of "the tribe", like Edgar Mittelholzer and Roger Mais, laid the ground for continuing exploration of the Region's rich and textured literary imagination.

Men of letters like Philip Sherlock (operating from as strategic a regional institutional base as the UWI) played guide and mentor to many in underpinning the march to self-government with the rhythm of artistic culture. Creative intellectual activity simultaneously served the cause of regional cultural unity without undue self-indulgence, as is evident in the seminal works of C.L.R. James (historian, man of letters, thinker and social commentator), Eric Williams (as historian and regional public servant), Elsa Goveia (as historian and teacher), M.G. Smith (as social anthropologist and academic animateur) and Arthur Lewis (as economist, pioneer thinker in the field of Third World development economics and adviser to several territorial governments in the Region). Their heirs have been many, not least of them the New World Group of social scientists targeting Caribbean economic integration in the Sixties through painstaking research, creative analysis and polemical advocacy.

A healthy climate for West Indian publishing has attempted to respond to the dynamism in the region's exercise of literary and intellectual creativity. The ancestral cultural journals are undoubtedly *Bim*, edited in the early years by Frank Collymore of Barbados, *Kyk-over-al*, edited by A.J. Seymour of Guyana, and *Caribbean Quarterly* first edited by Philip Sherlock, out of the UWI. Today there are as well Paria Press (Trinidad), Cole's (Barbados), Kingston Publishers, Sangsters and Sandberry (Jamaica) and Demerara Publishers (Guyana). Such overseas Publishing houses as MacMillan, Longmans, and Oxford have found it necessary to establish Caribbean divisions in response to a growing and profitable readership ready for the work of Caribbean scholars, poets, novelists, and essayists. The University of the West Indies now has in its Ten Year Plan to the year 2000 the establishment of a UWI Press to bring greater institutional rationality to existing facilities that now produce a number of academic journals out of the Faculty and Schools of Law, the Faculties of Social Sciences, Medical Studies and Education as well as from the Institute of Social and Economic Studies and the School of Continuing Studies. They all now produce journals of regional interest. Newspapers like the Trinidad *Express* and the Jamaica *Daily Gleaner* also publish material of regional interest from their publication houses. *Caribbean Affairs* is establishing itself as a serious regional journal.

The Performing Arts

Dance

Like the literary arts, the performing arts can indeed claim a tradition of an integrated Caribbean "vision" in terms of both production and the scope of their appeal. Music comes quickly to mind. The records of the eighteenth and nineteenth centuries are replete with comments by European travellers about the "natural" talents of West Indians in the performing arts, especially music and dance. Needless to say, many of these were dismissed as 'uncivilised' even if exotically intriguing to the observers.

Like music, the Caribbean dance emerged out of the setting of religious rituals, secular festivals and village recreational play. They have served to inform a budding Caribbean dance-theatre which is distinct and distinctive in its techniques, vocabulary and style. Beryl McBurnie, with her pioneer Little Carib Theatre in Trinidad and Tobago of the forties, was the first to claim form and purpose for this artform. She was successful enough to be regarded as an icon of regional unity by such avowed regionalists as Eric Williams, Norman Manley and Albert Gomes in the fifties. The vision of cultural integration through exploration of the common heritage of Caribbean dance-forms found favour with Ivy Baxter in Jamaica where the internationally acclaimed National Dance Theatre Company came to be established in 1962, with the express objective of developing and codifying a Caribbean theatre-dance art form. Further institutionalisation through a School of Dance open to students from the entire Region was to result in the replication of the Trinidadian and Jamaican experiences in Barbados, Guyana, Dominica, and

Belize with short-lived experiments in The Bahamas and Antigua — thanks to the early assistance given by the regional UWI in its annual Summer schools in the fifties. Exchanges with Haiti and Cuba were commonplace in the fifties and sixties and continue to this day.

Drama

Similar "schools" were held in drama all over the Region presided over by Staff Tutors in Drama attached to the Department of Extra Mural Studies of the UWI. The Department at St Augustine was to continue the work, with full-fledged year-round programmes now offered by a Creative Arts Centre on the St Augustine campus paralleling the Centre established in the sixties on the Mona campus in Jamaica. So important was the cultural dimension of development to the student-body in the heady days of hope for revolutionary change that the Centre at Mona was the target of 'occupation' in 1970 by students advocating greater emphasis on cultural relevance in the creative arts programmes offered by the University.

The organic links with the collective cultural genius of the forbears of the region came to be seen as investing artistic/cultural output with a certain legitimacy that is likely to be denied the output of West Indian artists, who may be of undoubted competence in reproducing the art of others, but who lack the ancestral Caribbean link as creators. The perceptions persist despite continuing respect for artistic products of excellence (and sometimes of less than excellence) from elsewhere. But clearly what is of West Indian cultural significance remains that which is mediated by West Indian social reality, and attracts identification and empathy from Caribbean-wide audiences.

Such products await a greater show of courage, foresight and daring among private impresarios, entrepreneurs, television and radio stations in the Region by way of programming policy and production assistance and market planning. The consumer, region-wide will respond with enthusiasm as would sponsors from the private sector. Such regionally produced programmes as "Caribbean Eye", "Caribscope" and "Oliver at Large" were repeatedly cited by many who appeared before the Commission as the sort of television fare desired and appreciated by all throughout the Region.

Radio and television drama has a ready source of inspiration in the long tradition of live theatre which dates back to the early nineteenth century in some territories of the region. The twentieth century was to spawn in several other territories theatre activity ranging from vaudeville to so-called serious drama drawing on the life and experience of the Caribbean people. As elsewhere, the theatre reflects the reality of the human condition. Concerns of decolonisation drove West Indian playwrights to self-exploration and social analysis. The results in a series of plays had no difficulty appealing to CARICOM citizens. Playwrights of the ilk of Derek Walcott, Trevor Rhone, Roderick Walcott, Dennis Scott, Errol Hill, Errol John, not only wrote plays of regional appeal and relevance but also worked in different parts of the Region as did directors like Noel Vaz, Errol Hill, (as Staff Tutors with the UWI), and later Ken Corsbie, Alwyn Bully, David Edgecombe and Earl Warner.

The vitality of drama in Barbados, Guyana, Trinidad and Jamaica at different times over the past fifty years afforded some exchange of fare and individual talent, but with nothing of the frequency and scope that many feel Caribbean drama deserves. Initiatives by enterprising playwrights, actors and directors to coordinate regional drama activity and codify vocabulary and technique as in the case of TIE (Theatre Information Exchange) are yet to flourish, deprived, as they have been, of financial resources and access to inexpensive travel around the Region. Some of the dramatic literature, like the novels and poetry of Caribbean writers, are now to be found on the curriculum in schools and on the school-leaving CXC examination question papers, ensuring that a future generation of Caribbean citizens will be knowledgeable in the literature of their Region as a former generation undoubtedly was in the literature of Europe (e.g., Shakespeare, Dickens, Wordsworth and Coleridge).

Painting and Sculpture

Output in the arts of painting and sculpture in individual CARICOM countries since the thirties has commanded regional attention especially through displays at Carifestas or exhibitions in metropolitan centres where there are large concentrations of Caribbean nationals living. Among the CARICOM artistic community at home, the names of Edna Manley, Broodhagen and George Gabb (sculptors), of Carlisle Chang, Aubrey Williams, Barrington Watson and Karl Parboosingh (painters), among others are well known. The 'school' of Jamaican intuitives carrying such acclaimed practitioners as John Dunkley and Kapo (Mallica Reynolds) finds kindred souls in parallel "schools" to be found in Cuba and Haiti. Yet scores of painters and sculptors continue to work in isolation away from fellow-artists, without the opportunity of regular contact.

Many in the Region's current generation of visual artists will have had opportunity to meet through study at the Jamaica School of Art (later the Edna Manley School of Visual Art) which is a constituent part of the Cultural Training Centre (CTC) established in 1976 in Jamaica in time for the second Caribbean Festival of Arts. The Jamaican government, following the tradition of the regional University, threw the facilities open to the entire CARICOM Caribbean. The Organisation of American States (OAS) was later to declare the Centre a regional Centre and, along with UNESCO, funded scholarships for students from the OECS in the fields of music, art, theatre and dance. For the CTC houses the Schools of Art, of Dance, of Drama and of Music as part of the prestigious Institute of Jamaica (IOJ), whose earlier regional cultural focus was through the West India Reference Library and the invaluable collection of Caribbean flora in its Natural History division.

Regional Cultural Initiatives

A regional Cultural Training Centre was therefore a natural development for the IOJ. More recent efforts to have the CTC's work articulated into that of the UWI and have it become a degree-granting institution speak further to the growing awareness among Caribbean educators and decision-takers of the importance of the cultural dimension of future regional development.

We attach so much importance to support for the cultural dimension of integration that we believe special efforts must be made to encourage and facilitate it. Governments cannot afford to do it all, particularly in the context of the other demands of development. The private sector has demonstrated both a desire and a capacity to help.

Indeed they have been among the most generous patrons of the arts in the Region. We are sure they can do more, and have a disposition to do more; but it would help to translate this into practical assistance if they were themselves encouraged to do so.

Tax relief with appropriate ceilings for assistance to the arts would be a particularly feasible way of providing that encouragement, and we recommend that Governments look seriously at this, preferably as a matter of regional policy. Our forms are increasingly regional in character — the cultural bedrock spans the Region. Policies of a regional nature are wholly appropriate. A very specific dimension of that encouragement to private sector assistance to the arts might well be support for CARIFESTA programmes and development of the CARICOM Foundation of Arts and Culture.

The Enterprise Dimension

To those concerned with the economic future of the Region there is enough to draw on in terms of the long-established search for profitable cultural enterprise via the route of what has been termed "cultural tourism". Tourists indeed expect to find excellent strawwork, good pottery, some metal sculpture, items in leather and shellcraft, woodcarving and much else that may be considered appropriate curios for the tourism market. How distinctively Caribbean are such objects may well be a matter for debate, but the School of Art in Jamaica has for years collaborated with the Things Jamaican Company on the matter of craft design in an effort to respond faithfully to the cultural realities of the Region and to the expectations of the market. Other territories are conscious of the need to take appropriate measures to ensure that their 'local' souvenirs are not made in Japan. Jewelcraft for the commercial market has received some emphasis as well; and with the Trinidad Carnival ambience as inspiration for costume designing, the art has developed in that country, as have metal sculpture and wire-bending. The use of Caribbean pottery in Caribbean hotels is evident. Whether it reaches the profitable commercial proportions that would guarantee economic sustenance to enough citizens in the exercise of the creative imagination remains a moot point. Craft development has been the target of intra-regional bilateral technical assistance (e.g. between

Jamaica and Grenada). The possibilities are supposedly great; however, the promise still awaits fulfillment.

Releasing Creative Energy

That fulfilment is deemed by many to be a function of investment in the creative potential of the Caribbean people. The importance given to self-confidence and self-awareness as desirable ends in any programme of human resource development derives from the evidence of the close connexion between the release of productive energy and the individual who is free of self-doubt and attendant psychic stress. Notions of self-worth nurtured from early life in family structures conducive to healthy upbringing are deemed to be important cultural factors in the character of a people. Caribbean citizens of African ancestry have shared the inherited unease of "illegitimate birth" which, apart from its long-standing reason for loss of "caste", has in the past relegated such offspring legally to disinheritance and socially to disabilities depriving them of the enjoyment of full citizenship.

The Status of Children Acts, which since 1976 (in Jamaica) have sought to rid hundreds of thousands of such disabilities, will undoubtedly release a future generation from such psychic and other concerns. But the cultural inheritance of social stigma has persisted with stubborn tenacity. Thanks to the continuing research by social scientists, there are now available for acceptance more creative and tolerable perceptions of the Region's plural family patterns ranging from the nuclear, through the single-parent and matriarchal to the extended family. This last pattern of family life is to be found among West Indians of East Indian and Chinese stock as well.

The ability to deal sensibly with such plurality of human reality may be seen as evidence of the Caribbean's capacity for tolerance, a value that should not be underestimated in the forging of a sense of community that treasures the equality of all regardless of circumstances of birth or mode of socialisation — i.e., whether one was fathered by one's mother, or has been the surrogate offspring of countless courtesy aunts and uncles, or whether one has had the pleasures of the company of siblings in the collaborative care of a mother and father bound by holy matrimony and living under the same roof.

"Circumstances of birth" apply as well to both gender and racial origin. On the matter of gender, the entire Region is the legatee of patriarchal world views dominant in Western civilisation. despite the matriarchal reality of family-patterns, socialisation processes and the responsibilities borne in practice by women for social development and breadwinning. Another section of this Report deals with gender issues appropriately but as part of the cultural profile of the Region, gender-specificity in the strict performance of roles has had a definite effect on such developmental imperatives as population regulation and family planning, manpower policy leading to misuse, abuse and underuse of valuable human resources, child-rearing practices reportedly leading to personality dysfunctions in the young adult, and structural adjustment strategies embarked on reportedly by male decision-takers at the expense of female cheap labour in the home *inter alia*.

The self-assertion of women since the seventies in claiming full recognition has in some territories brought some harmonisation between legal provisions for women's rights (with respect to maternity leave, claims of their children on the inheritance of their fathers, equal pay for equal work, access to positions of authority on the basis of skills and qualifications, etc.) and the reality of the actual position of women who form some 50 per cent of the CARICOM Caribbean population and are as qualified as, and at times better qualified than, men in many fields of endeavour. Women now outstrip men as graduates by 2 to 1 in some disciplines in the University of the West Indies.

The school system throughout the Region is revealing higher levels of achievement among female students at all levels. Men are, in defence, said to be "at risk". Yet the complaint persists on good grounds that men still dominate the corridors of power. Of the 13 CARICOM countries, only one has a female Prime Minister in 1992, and fewer women than men are to be found in the Cabinets of all the Governments. The ratio among the technocracy is however showing improvement in some places. But no woman has yet been able to accede to the chief executive officer's post in the CARICOM Secretariat itself, in the Caribbean Development Bank or the University of the West Indies, three great institutions of Caribbean integration.

The Racial Mix

The matter of racial origin also invites ongoing debate. CARICOM is inhabited by five or so million souls of African, European, Asian (East Indian and Chinese), Native American stock, plus persons of biological mixture between two or more of these. There can be no doubt that the overriding reality of racial pluralism with persons not only living side by side but cohabiting has forced on West Indians an understanding and broad acceptance of racial tolerance — yet another value of inestimable importance in sustaining civil society in the racist world of the twentieth century. Many West Indians could boast that they are part-African, part-Asian, part-European but totally Caribbean. The truth in this should not, however, blind the world at end-of-century to the creative tension that still exists in the Region in its urgent effort to come to terms with its polyethnicity.

Others besides ourselves have an interest in our success. In a world increasingly riven by a resurgence of ethnicity in the wake of new freedoms, the West Indies can revive hope for the triumph of oneness over otherness. To do so we must assert the values of cosmopolitan living that the process of creolisation, so long at work in our Region, has elevated to a West Indian ethic. Through the integrative force of our evolved West Indian culture an ethic of oneness arches over our own elements of otherness: not denying diversity, but making it a factor of enrichment. When the Commission visited Prime Minister George Price in Belmopan we were struck by the message of a small poster on the wall beyond his office which proclaimed: "ALL AH WE MEK BELIZE". All ah we mek Jamaica and Guyana and Barbados, we reflected — and every CARICOM country. But, even more to the point, 'ALL AH WE MEK CARICOM'. It was itself a reminder of our over-arching oneness and of its profound relevance to the integration process.

There is little doubt that cultural shifts on the part of all will be necessary down the decade into the tewnty-first century. An old-fashioned, unsophisticated, race-determined structure of socio-economic and political organisation is the antithesis of development and a deterrent to any kind of regional integration worthy of the name. The meaning of creolisation is a new sense and sensibility reflected in tolerance of diversity without personal psychic or social disintegration, as well as in a capacity to function on several levels of existence with the fullest understanding of complexity, contradictions and the cross-fertilisation process itself. The creative application of this cultural norm to all of Caribbean life may well be the primary challenge for the region in everything it plans to do for its development, integrated or otherwise, down the decade of the nineties and into the tewnty-first century.

2. RESPONSES NEEDED FOR INTEGRATION

What the above outline suggests is that responses to the various challenges for cultural action could be critical to regional integration. Certainly, this is the view, recently expressed, by a great many of those who appeared in towns and villages before the Commission.
These responses may be viewed severally:

- greater regional institutionalisation in the creative arts, whether government-sponsored or not;

- the promotion of artistic activity for employment as part of wider economic development strategies;

- the mobilisation of media (print and electronic) resources as an antidote to cultural penetration and as an instrument of promotion of regional identity;

- action in the area of language and communication to serve wider regional development;

- the promotion of religious ecumenicism;

- the enhancement of the cultural imperative in the regional educational system.

The first three responses concern practical programmes of cultural policy already evident in CARICOM Member States but now deserving of co-ordinated regional application. The remainder look to conditions necessary for their effective implementation, and we have dealt with some of them in dealing earlier with language and religion.

Regional Cultural Action

The rationalization and consolidation of mechanisms already on the CARICOM agenda with respect to cultural policy and action is a natural response in light of the importance of cultural activities as an instrument of integration.

Already in place are:

- the Meetings of CARICOM Ministers of Culture who work in tandem with the older Standing Committee of Ministers of Education (SCME) which at its Fifth meeting in 1984 approved recommendations for the establishment of two Regional Advisory Committees — a Carifesta Advisory Committee and a CARICOM Arts Awards Committee. The first meeting of the CARICOM Culture Ministers in 1985, however, decided that the Committees were so similar in terms of membership and objectives as to justify their amalgamation into

- a single broad-based Advisory Committee now known as the Regional Cultural Committee (RCC). The decision of the Culture Ministers was endorsed in 1986 by the Sixth Meeting of the SCME. The RCC met in inaugural session in June 1987 in Port of Spain. Such rationalisation of the institutional framework for regional cultural action should be an ongoing activity of CARICOM. The RCC comprises a maximum of 21 members, the core-group of which is formed by Directors of Culture, Chief Cultural Officers or Senior Cultural Affairs officials from Member States. Other members are selected by the CARICOM Secretariat, in consultation with Member Governments, taking into account the need for geographical representation and the maintenance of an adequate balance among cultural interests and artistic disciplines. It is to be hoped that able individuals with experience and proven expertise, but without formal government affiliations, would be allowed a place or a voice on the RCC.

The following terms of reference of the RCC approved in 1988 at the Seventh Meeting of the SCME in Georgetown, Guyana, make the broad-based composition of the RCC's membership more crucial. The RCC is "(a) to advise on and participate in the development, implementation and on-going review of a regional Cultural Policy; (b) to advise on the use of the Caribbean media in the promotion of cultural development with particular reference to its role in communicating the link between cultural variables and the development process; (c) to advise on the organisation, development and co-ordination of regional festivals; (d) to advise on and assist in the mobilisation and organisation of financial and technical resources for cultural development; and (e) to advise on matters pertaining to cultural development." All of these are to be co-ordinated by the executive officer occupying yet another CARICOM cultural mechanism;

- the Cultural Desk, the establishment of which was based on a decision taken at the Seventh Heads of Government conference held in October 1972. The decision was to have a Cultural Officer based at the CARICOM Secretariat to work in close liaison with the Education Desk in the promotion of cultural activities in the CARICOM Caribbean. The future suggests a strengthening of this facility to guarantee to the Region an effective facilitator for regional cultural initiatives in the person of the Cultural Officer. In 1979 Rex Nettleford in his book *Caribbean Cultural Identity: The Case of Jamaica* had this to say about the CARICOM mechanism:

    The development of guidelines to cultural planning working in collaboration with international agencies and the cultural institutions of Member States is still in the future. The compilation and analysis of cultural statistics for the Commonwealth Caribbean would be a welcome activity and the activation and the monitoring of certain joint projects (study of say the employment potential for artists, education for cultural action, management of cultural policy, economics of cultural action, cultural development policies in member states, etc.) await the support from CARICOM's Secretaries-General, Commonwealth Caribbean Governments and their Ministers of Culture and/or Education for further conceptualization and implementation, using

CARICOM as "co-ordinator and clearing-house". The need for this clearly still holds though some progress has been made over the past decade. The Culture Desk needs to be upgraded to a full-fledged unit within the Secretariat and not be seen as an appendage to "Education" as was originally conceived. As catalyst or fertiliser in the development process the subject-area needs to be strengthened to have full effect.

The Commission endorses these long standing observations of one who is now of our membership.

In addition to the above well-articulated institutional arrangements for regional cultural cooperation, a number of other activities point directions to future mechanisms of collaboration that could help deepen regional integration. The CARICOM Foundation for Art and Culture which is still in its embryonic stage should be developed so that systems of awards and recognition for cultural achievement can be rationally worked out.

The Caribbean Festival of Arts (CARIFESTA) has a longer history admittedly, but now needs a new policy-framework that will ensure greater certainty as to its occurrence, promotion and content in the future. There was a lapse of a decade between the fourth Carifesta held in Barbados in 1982 and the fifth scheduled for 1992 (August) in Trinidad and Tobago.

The intention to include in Carifesta V a symposium charged with making plans for the conduct of future Carifestas should lead to better articulation not only of policy but also of implementation of the Region's major show-case of artistic/cultural products. The decentralisation of the celebrations into periodical subject-area mini-festivals in between major Festivals probably every decade was in fact the recommendation that came out of the first meeting of the RCC in 1987. This view deserves re-visiting.

Yet another type of regional activity summoning CARICOM to continuing action and evaluation are the regional cultural projects funded by international agencies like UNESCO or the OAS. The current Regional Museum Development Project and the Caribbean Inter-Cultural Music Institute based in Port of Spain come to mind. There will no doubt be others in the future; we need to ensure their success and multiplier effect in the Region. Regional mechanisms for ensuring implementation, monitoring progress and appraising performance must be put in place.

Linkages with similar mechanisms, cultural institutions and initiatives in Latin America are also needed. A loose colloquy of Culture Ministers of Latin America and the Caribbean has had at least four meetings in Latin America. CARICOM, which was invited for the second meeting, should follow through with the request by the Latin Americans for the CARICOM Caribbean to help determine the possible benefits to be derived from, the objectives to be targetted and the strategies to be adopted through, participation in such a forum.

Outside of the Caribbean and Latin America, there will be further room for regular cultural participation on a regional (CARICOM) basis. The three seats originally earmarked for the Independent Caribbean on the Executive Board of UNESCO were lost entirely to Latin America with which the Caribbean is linked as a bloc in UNESCO (i.e. as the Group of Latin American and Caribbean countries — GRULAC). With the Caribbean regaining a seat on the Executive Board as of November 1991, it is important that CARICOM acts regionally where necessary through the representative who was elected with the help of the concerted efforts of CARICOM Member States. Joint CARICOM diplomatic representation to UNESCO here suggests itself as a matter of urgency.

Back in the Region, the facilitating of the non-governmental initiatives taken by voluntary cultural organisations should be given in CARICOM cultural policy. The Caribbean Film Federation which was recently established is one such initiative, but others are likely to come on stream in the foreseeable future as they did in the past requiring the advice and facilitative care of the CARICOM Secretariat.

Such bona fide organisations and individual artists should be able to benefit, *inter alia*, from regional support by way of freedom of movement for performing and visual artists and exemptions from work permits for those engaged in intra-regional cultural exchanges. On the question of cultural exchanges the RCC in 1987 had developed a set of recommendations on the movement of goods and services (expertise) throughout the Region on the basis of some degree of Member State reciprocity where possible. Since these were later endorsed by the SCME at its Seventh Meeting in Georgetown in 1988, it is important that these recommendations be reviewed with a view to implementation.

Effective rationalisation of regional cultural action is predicated on the assumption that each Member State has a cultural policy with clearly stated aims and objectives as well as plans of action. Where these do not exist, the CARICOM Secretariat should endeavour to assist in the formulation of such policies and in the designing of related plans of action. Learning from the experience of other Member States which already have such policies should be facilitated by the CARICOM Secretariat, working through the RCC and the Standing Committee of Ministers of Culture and/or Education. There is no shortage of issues awaiting both national and regional attention for incorporation into a cultural policy which could form the basis for cultural development.

On the matter of a regional cultural policy the Regional Committee on Culture should vigorously pursue its own expressed aim to examine the possibility of proposing the outlines of a regional policy for study and endorsement by the Standing Committee of Ministers of both Education and Culture, with a view to achieving greater unity and focus for national efforts. Not least among the objectives should be the provision of minimal cultural infrastructural facilities in each CARICOM Member State to facilitate intra-regional exchange of artists and the development of greater artistic activity.

Artistic Culture for Employment

It is also clear that Governments and the wider communities in CARICOM need to respond to the potential for employment-creation in the field of the creative arts. Caribbean creative artists certainly do not see their activity as belonging to the "non-productive sector". On the contrary, the exercise of the creative imagination has led to the tremendous increase in earning power of a number of the Region's performing, visual and literary artists who are able to attract hard currency to a region which is already badly starved of foreign exchange earnings. A number of income-generating, employment-creating occupations in the cultural industry sector therefore suggest themselves and await support mechanisms facilitated by the Region for their development.

The recording industry comes first to mind. Whatever can be done to attract investment (local and foreign) into the area of the music recording industry would be welcome. There are already world-class recording studios to be found in Jamaica, Barbados and, until recently, Montserrat. They attract foreign recording artists as well as provide facilities for the production of discs and audiotapes by West Indian musicians (calypsonians, reggae and dance-hall artists). That they are able to compete on an international basis is already demonstrated. They should have no difficulty operating in a market-driven economy. Besides the artists themselves, there is room for the employment of producers, sound engineers, mixers and a range of workers whose duties are related to the maintenance and operation of such recording studios.

Cultural tourism offers as wide a range of occupations dictating official regional attention in any structured employment policy CARICOM might wish to adopt. The entertainment industry offers employment for armies of singers, dancers, special acts performers, instrumentalists, producers, choreographers, etc., for hotel and cabaret presentations. It also offers professional cadres of persons involved in the otherwise voluntary festival arts such as Carnival and Jonkonnu (offered as Goombay in The Bahamas) which are already strong visitor attractions. Crop Over in Barbados does the same. Associated with some of these Festivals are some craft-manufactures sold as curios by wire-benders, doll-makers, as well as metal sculptures, tie-dye fabric and the like.

Craft stands on its own in any case ranging from straw goods (basket, floor-mats, place-mats, etc.) to ceramics, costume jewelry (sea shells, dried seeds) leather-craft and wood-carvings. There are excellent outlets for own-account dealers to be found all over the Region. Design and marketing admittedly need far greater improvement than exists in most territories. But generally, greater entrepreneurial attention needs to be paid to these. The same goes for what is termed in some places "culinary arts" — jams and jellies made from local fruits and condiments.

The facilitating of publishing houses should also be seen as a possible investment area providing income/employment for writers, book illustrators, editors, etc.

Graphic arts which are related to publishing find more direct outlet in commercial advertising, which is vital to private sector activity throughout the Region. The opportunity for employment in the above field would make more sense for the training programmes already on stream, as well as for those yet to be developed in schools, training colleges and specialist arts schools like the Burrowes School of Art in Guyana and the Cultural Training Centre in Jamaica.

CARICOM Governments should extend to all artists not already enjoying it, the opportunity for absorption in both the educational system and community development programmes as teachers, cultural agents, animateurs and cultural administrators. The CXC examination system should therefore add drama and dance to music and art, which are already offered. And the University of the West Indies should take on board the preparation of artists in its programme.

Yet another area of absorption of people trained in the creative arts is the media (especially radio and television) which, if they are serious about becoming the antidote to the penetration from the North Atlantic, could provide gainful employment for the skills prepared in the production and transmission of Caribbean cultural programmes.

All of the above would naturally have to take place within an enabling context of intra-regional cultural exchanges facilitated by the lifting of work permits, by the encouragement of free movement of artists, media workers and sportsmen and the interchange of cultural programmes between media houses in the Region. The creative arts are therefore to be encouraged and promoted, not only as an aspect of national cultural policy or as means to greater cultural integration of the region but also as an added vital means of income-generation and employment-creation, especially among the young.

Cultural Penetration and the Media

Cultural penetration through US satellite and cable television has undoubtedly had a telling impact on Caribbean societies. Two dangers are often cited: it dulls the edge of creativity and reduces participation in community activities; it also distorts authentic Caribbean culture. It, however, poses challenges that can be transformed into creative opportunities. Cricket for instance, can be deemed an "imperialist" game but it has been absorbed into the culture of the Commonwealth Caribbean to the point where the region excels at it, surpassing the metropolitan country in performance. In any case, the penetration via satellite is so pervasive and the social influence so great that banning would be ineffectual and pointless. It is not beyond the creativity of Caribbean people to devise positive alternatives and counter-measures.

Governments, with the assistance of cultural specialists and workers, should develop programmes to promote awareness of the richness and diversity of the Caribbean cultural patrimony and deepen an appreciation of it. This is bound up with developing a positive self-image. CARICOM Governments should collectively seek to establish a regional television and radio project to produce and share indigenous programmes. The embryo exists in CARIBSCOPE. The Caribbean Broadcasting Union, national television stations and a number of private producers have done valuable pioneering work, but something much more ambitious should be attempted and would benefit from satellite facility. This might mean utilising existing satellite signals for a fee. Artistic culture is an area which requires and justifies national and regional investment. We return to this matter in the following Chapter on Communication.

There should be television awareness training and appreciation both for children and adults. Hopefully, persons will develop discriminating tastes as they seek to select a mix of programmes to suit their particular needs from among local as well as imported programmes. Indeed, informed and intelligent interest in the work of international artists as displayed on television may well stimulate the production and development of indigenous programmes. Caribbean alternative programmes need not always be perceived as being at variance with imported ones.

The Caribbean media houses should strive to present to the Region's citizens an identity of an emerging Region of free people, contributing uniquely to the liberation of the human spirit and the development of their own creative potential. This is necessary for attaining self-confidence and for escaping the syndrome which regards what is foreign as synonymous with what is best.

The business of building national and regional cultural consciousness can be enhanced by a new focus on the Region's history of struggle and survival and our multi-faceted achievements. As part of this thrust, the media should be used more extensively to propagate knowledge of eminent Caribbean personalities and their accomplishments — liberators, politicians, opinion leaders, thinkers, poets, playwrights, musicians, cricketers, artists, scholars, scientists, as well as the successful small farmers, technicians and fishermen.

Part of the solution to cultural penetration lies in the development of popular theatre, coupled with a progressive media policy. It is recommended that:

- the policy and infrastructure be established which allows regional radio and television link-up around major cultural and sporting events in the various Caribbean countries — carnivals, CARIFESTA, Christmas festivals, Crop Over, Divali, Hosay, cricket and football tournaments;
- annual cultural and sporting festivals be promoted.

As part of the policy to conserve our cultural wealth and patrimony, museums should be established where they do not now exist and, where they do, they should be strengthened by, among other things, the acquisition of trained staff to give quality service. There remains much work to be done in sorting, organising, cataloguing and storing the facts and fruits of ancestral memories. Our flora, fauna and scientific inventions should also be organised for exhibition. Museums should, however, be operated as educational instruments rather than showcases of dead artefacts. Adequate legislation should be enacted to protect and secure artefacts from local and foreign pirates, and in particular to prevent them from being exported.

Protection of Caribbean cultural and artistic property should be extended to music, works of art and literature. This calls for adequate copyright laws and their proper articulation with international conventions.

Thought should be given to the establishment of a Caribbean Film Institute as part of the infra-structure for a film industry. This has obvious implications for indigenous television and it can be one means of integrating a number of artistic disciplines including photography, dance, music, theatre and creative writing.

Caribbean writers themselves need to be given greater national and regional recognition and support. There is call for more conferences and workshops for writers and for prizes for literature in the manner of the Guyana Prize for Literature.

The call for a Caribbean Publishing House is over a decade old. It may not seem as urgent now with the proliferation of mini printing and publishing firms using 'desktop publishing' facilities. But regional facilities to handle bulk publishing and distribution, aided by economies of scale, is still a current imperative.

The thrust of the recommended responses above is that the peoples of the Region must provide themselves with indigenous alternatives to the persistent fare of US cultural programmes that assault the Caribbean consciousness particularly through the electronic media.

What the Region should not do is attempt to impose any embargo on imported television or radio fare, no more than it should impose restrictions on print material (books, journals, magazines, newspapers). Caribbean people are a people of options in any case. The Region should educate its citizens far more than it does now in its history, cultural realities, artistic innovations of importance to Caribbean development, and in such a way that they will choose local programmes as a matter of course and with enthusiasm. Responses to such programmes as exist give cause for optimism.

Art and Education

This limited survey together with our folklore and folk art reveal a rich artistic patrimony which has to be mainlined into school curricula and impact on the programmes of relevant tertiary institutions. And let us not undervalue folk art. Since these predated European intervention, they harbour a pristine energy and authenticity which make them critical to the process of self-definition. Art in education should transcend the mere passive passing on of the artistic heritage; it must be the basis for engagement and it must generate further creativity. The present generation must add the product of its creative intellect to the artistic capital of the Region.

The arts are not really new to Caribbean education. Drawing, reciting, dance, acting, choral singing and crafts were on the time table of every primary school. Scenes from Shakespeare and plays from Moliere and more recently Caribbean plays were staged as part of Speech Day exercises. Some of these have proved fertile nurseries for the development of stagecraft, and teachers of the old school have taught drawing to great effect. Craft, too, in the form of book binding, needlework and straw work, have had some carry-over albeit in a small way, into industry.

The flowering of the arts over the past three decades, their links with the entertainment industry, their economic potential, recognition of their central role in defining the identity of Caribbean peoples, and the CARIFESTA experience have all served to enhance the importance of the cultural arts in the popular mind. Consultation with the people of the Region indicated a new and growing awareness of the pivotal role of the arts in development and something of the implications for education. Moreover a central place for the arts in education is amply justifiable on educational and social grounds, even when education is perceived as predominantly concerned with the development of intellectual skills.

A number of reputable educationists recognise aesthetics among the disciplines which develop rationality. And aesthetics for them include sub-disciplines such as music, visual arts, the arts of movement, the fine arts and literature. But even so the tradition that generates this thinking has tended to emphasise the contemplative rather than the expressive and productive dimension. Crafts and dance, for instance, would fit uncomfortably in their knowledge criteria. This needs to change.

Clearly, there is ample evidence of the worthwhileness of the arts as knowledge, and of their fundamental educative nature both in an intrinsic and in instrumental terms. Caribbean people are ready to accept this. Indeed, they are ready to accept that the cultural arts must necessarily inform any distinctive Caribbean world-view that emerges. It follows then that there are educational implications for schools and colleges and for institution building.

The Caribbean Examinations Council (CXC) has so far made impressive forays into the Caribbeanisation of educational content. It currently offers Arts and Crafts as an examination subject. It should consider going further and devise a syllabus in the performing arts (dance, drama and music), and the literature syllabus might carry a creative component even if this were initially optional. A programme in the performing arts leading to the CXC certificate may need 'piloting' in those schools with appropriate facilities, with a view to gradually implementing it in all.

A new era in arts education will naturally manifest itself in teacher education policies. Special courses have to be mounted for arts and crafts teachers, and since ideally they must themselves be practitioners, attention will have to be given to the acquisition of aesthetic knowledge and skills as well as to the relevant pedagogy. For both aspects, it will be expedient to establish sub-regional and regional centres of excellence. The Jamaican Cultural Training Centre, which is to be designated a College, should be further resourced as one such regional centre; it is already serving students from several territories. Plans are in hand to make it a degree-granting institution in art, dance, drama and music in a few years. The Burrowes School of Art in Guyana which specialises in the fine arts can also become a regional resource if it is properly financed and developed. In fact the University of Guyana recently began a one-year 'top-up' programme for graduates of the Burrowes School of Art diploma programmes, leading to a BA in Art Education.

Similar institutions can be sited to take advantage of a particular artistic climate and community in other territories. Some teacher training colleges will work in tandem with Cultural Colleges by offering post-graduate courses in arts education. The Saint Lucia School of Music does something similar in its one-year Certificate in Music Education. As the arts come into their own in education, they should begin to impact on indigenous television programmes. The preparation and production of educational radio and television programmes in the visual and performing arts can be made a component of some teacher training courses.

In this business of arts education, there is an obvious role for the regional universities in the production of knowledge and scholars in the arts. Drama and Art are offered as minor programmes at the University of Guyana, and some campuses of the University of the West Indies are already moving to introduce the visual and performing arts into their curricula. This is enormously important. University courses should involve in-depth research by Caribbean artists/scholars in the rich cultural resources of the Region, including festivals and architecture. The aim will be to establish degree and higher degree courses in the arts at UWI. Some of the knowledge generated by the University will eventually find its way into school classrooms in suitable form.

It is important that our educational institutions contribute to the development of a regional aesthetic and an understanding of its implications for a regional identity and a general world-view. If there is a Caribbean way the arts have a role in determining it and that way, that dream or philosophy, rightly belongs to the educational encounter.

Recommendations

1. that CARICOM adopt, foster, and promote among its Member States the integration of cultural factors into macro-planning strategies for overall regional growth and development in the decades ahead. The fields of human resource development, education and employment-creation come readily to mind;

2. that CARICOM strengthen its Culture Desk, and increase its capability to: perform its functions of co-ordinating, facilitating, guidings and monitoring the formulation and implementation of cultural policies (national and sub-regional); administer efficiently and effectively the regular meetings of cultural agents through the Regional Cultural Committee, exchanges, symposia, conferences and training workshops; and help plan and stage regional festivals (e.g. CARIFESTA) and other such events that serve to mobilise collectively the creative energies of CARICOM citizens;

3. that CARICOM Governments, through public consultation and with private sector cooperation, review the mounting of the Caribbean Festival of Arts (CARIFESTA) with a view to

revising and re-organising the content, emphasis and the frequency with which the event can be held while guaranteeing to all CARICOM Member States the best possible opportunity for the fullest participation;

4. that CARICOM, through such newly strengthened cultural institutional frameworks as the strengthened Culture Desk, the proposed CARICOM Arts Foundation, and the Standing Committee of Ministers, itself formulate a regional cultural policy, matched by national cultural policies of Member States and designed to facilitate the growth and development of artistic culture rooted in Caribbean experience;

5. that the potential for employment-creation via the promotion of cultural industries be addressed by both the private sector and the Governments of CARICOM Member Countries as part of their strategies for attracting investment capital inflows; that there also be an analysis of the global environment for trade in cultural industry services;

6. that regional groupings of musicians, playwrights, actors and others within the entertainment sector be facilitated, e.g., by way of ease of travel within the Region and removal of work permit barriers; that artists themselves in the meantime take initiatives to combine and form professional associations and make themselves responsible for establishing professional standards, codes of ethics and training programmes;

7. that established cultural training institutions serving regional needs in CARICOM, such as the Cultural Training Centre in Jamaica, be strengthened and expanded wherever possible;

8. that CARICOM support and facilitate the adoption of common technical video standards by the Region's entertainment industry in the context of world-wide standards;

9. that CARICOM intensify its efforts to have Member States address such international legal issues as copyright and be in a position to bargain for reasonable tariffs for access to global satellite distribution systems;

10. that, with easier and ready access to global satellite distribution systems, CARICOM Governments and private sector media producers seek to address the urgent task of producing for regional transmission a wide range of programmes which draw on the social realities, history and rich cultural heritage of the Region;

11. that a progressive media policy be deliberately pursued throughout the Region to allow for regional radio and television link-up around such major cultural and sporting events in the various Member States and wider Caribbean territories as carnival, Carifesta, Christmas revelries, Crop Over, Divali, Hosay, cricket and football tournaments, as well as University convocations and religious celebrations;

12. that the CARICOM Region maximise the gains from its inheritance of English as an international language; and expand its language policy to support training in foreign languages, particularly those spoken widely in the Caribbean and Latin American region.

13. that concurrently, CARICOM as a cultural community acknowledge and support its creole language development, affording it appropriate status as a rich cultural heritage;

14. that in support of both 12 and 13 above, effective language policies in the various territories be buttressed by research in language learning and teaching in the regional tertiary institutions, with the Lexicography Unit at the Cave Hill Campus of the UWI being strengthened and maintained;

15. that a Caribbean Council of Religions, with national counterparts, be established to promote inter-faith dialogue and harmony as well as a broad ecumenicity which embraces established orthodox (Christian and non-Christian) creeds and creole religious expressions. The role of religious groups as social partners should be facilitated through their participation in designing, planning and implementing agreed social agenda;

16. that the performing and visual arts as well as the art-crafts be treated as curricular rather than as extra-curricular subjects in primary and secondary schools throughout the Region;

17. that regional tertiary institutions be made conscious of the need to promote a sense of "Caribbeanness" among its students through dynamic Caribbean Studies programmes;

18. that some mechanism be found to assist in the early development of regional facilities to handle bulk publishing and distribution.

CHAPTER VIII

COMMUNICATIONS AND SPORT

1. COMMUNICATION FOR COMMUNITY

Cultivating Common Ground

The Treaty of Chaguaramas is, among other things, a mandate for the creation of community among countries which have spent the greater part of their historical evolution in struggle of one kind or another; for emancipation, for freedom, for independence, for nationhood — pursuits that are not at odds with the Treaty's mandate but have generated tendencies towards separatism rather than unity. We consider that the major challenge of this hour is to weave out of both the benefits and the disadvantages of our past experiences the fabric of a better life for all of the people of our Caribbean continent of islands and territories. This will necessarily require that we claim and cultivate the common ground of our Caribbean existence. Celebration of the full harvest cannot be immediate; there are many acts of husbandry to perform. High among them are the search for, and the development of, our best skills, mechanisms and devices in communicating with each other.

As the Third Meeting of CARICOM Ministers responsible for Information agreed:

(i) the development of public communication systems and information services is an integral and essential element in the process of defining and implementing strategies to take the region into the Twenty-First Century;

(ii) the preservation of a Caribbean identity requires the promotion and protection of a Caribbean character, culture and Caribbean priorities, through the production, storage, dissemination and exchange of information, within and without the region.

Elsewhere in this report we discuss the movement of goods and of people, and the importance of air and sea transportation, as economic issues. In this Chapter we extend that discussion to the movement of information, whether as commodity or as idea, and the mechanisms by which information may be created and communicated. We will find that some of the barriers to the easy movement of information throughout the Eegion are the mental barriers from which "none but ourselves can free our minds", in the words of Bob Marley. But the process of liberation, of deconstruction, must have concrete structural and even legal underpinnings if it is to be effective and on-going. Caribbean peoples must be enabled, and indeed encouraged, not only to overleap barriers and cross boundaries but also, through active participation in the marketplace of information and ideas, to chase away shadows, explode stereotypes and touch each others' lives. That is what communication between peoples is about.

Exploring Common Ground through Language

Before looking at the structures, we must first touch on language beyond the issues we have touched on in the previous Chapter. In these most verbal/oral of societies language has worn many faces. It has been divider and unifier, liberator and oppressor; it has been a cultural resource and discriminatory tool. At the same time as it unites islands within linguistic sub-regions it fractures the region as a whole. This complex issue of language as vessel of communication (and as political reality) must be addressed on two levels.

Looking first at the West Indies as a sub-region the fact must be faced that native English speakers constitute a minority of the Caribbean population. It is also true that a far greater number of Spanish, French and Dutch speakers are conversant and even fluent in English than is the opposite case. Learning the other languages of the region must become a necessary and compulsory pursuit for all who would participate in and benefit from what a community, if that is what we want, has to offer. The 'if-you-want-to-talk-to-me-you-must-learn-to-speak-English!' attitude smacks of an arrogance which is no less reprehensible for having been inherited from our colonial masters — who have since, it should be noted, been made to address the folly of that particular conceit. While West Indian higglers and others in the informal commercial sector must be commended for having broken ground in venturing into markets of the non-anglophone Caribbean and by improvising their way through their various transactions, the relationships of the future must be built on a firmer linguistic base. The goal has to be that every person in the region be capable of conversing in at least one language other than his or her native tongue. The school systems of the Region must take account of this objective and begin addressing it at the primary level, where young minds are most receptive to new words and thought-patterns.

The second aspect of the language conundrum is more intractable. "If it is true," says Professor Mervyn Alleyne of the UWI, "that an ideally functioning communication system needs a homogeneous unambiguous code accessible to and understood by all the members of a society, then Caribbean societies do not have ideally functioning communication systems. Here we are dealing with language situations which result in severe disruptions of communication." The European languages used in Government, business and the educational system confer status on those who master them, or are associated with their use as the natural order of things. On the other hand the popular languages spoken in our homes; on the street, on the playing fields are still, while the subject of academic study in our universities, accorded far lower status in our countries. Almost exclusively, the print and the electronic media ply their trade in the European language, fully understood by a small minority of the population. The mass language, to the extent that it finds a place, is usually the vehicle for humour or anger.

Contracting Common Ground through Telecommunications

An International Telecommunications Union report of 1984 asks us to regard telecommunications "not simply as one technology among others, but as the neural system of a society." That metaphor of a neural system can be extended to apply even more appropriately to a region wanting to make itself into something greater than the sum of its separate parts. Communications in all its dimensions, whether by information technology (IT) or as plain old telephone services (POTS), is in our view a crucial prerequisite infrastructure for the development of closer Caribbean cooperation. The tremendous developments made over the past thirty years — during what we can properly call the independence period in the West Indies — through the convergence of the technologies of telecommunications and computer science, offer us a matrix on which to overcome the disadvantages of size and separation and develop shared approaches to common problems. In the process, as they have done in many other societies, the information technologies can create whole industries and thereby employment, wealth and growth.

As we look around the world we can see the building blocks of a post-industrial or information society being put in place by countries which in some cases are as small as our own. And from our experience of the industrial revolution we can know the cost of being left behind or, in the current word, marginalised. We must begin to seriously and consciously transform our societies to avoid a compounding of our present condition. As UWI Professor Gerald Lalor reminded us recently — and it has always been true: "a bleak future awaits the unskilled". Our societies must maximise the resources available to us, including and especially those of the information sciences, to increase the pool of skilled men and women who can shape and sustain the new technologies and apply them to the benefit of all. It is here that our inheritance of an international language is an immense regional asset; not enough in itself, but on no account to be discounted or, worse, dissipated. The human resource needs of the Region are dealt with at greater length elsewhere in this Report. Here we focus on what we see as the policies which must be examined and implemented over the next few years to re-shape those sectors of our societies concerned with communications.

The capacity for communications between the people of our Region at all levels is a vital prerequisite to the maintenance of a sense of West Indian identity. But beyond this crucial consideration, the means of everyday commercial and social contact, and government consultation, which is the fabric upon which integration is woven, require to be far better facilitated than they now are.

The facilities for telecommunications within the Region and their cost prohibit the transmission of television pictures within the Region. By the same token receiving foreign television programmes by satellite and transmitting them locally is relatively cheap. Thus, the images on West Indian television screens reflect not the culture or discourse of the West Indian family, but the culture and preoccupations of another society whose values and perceptions are necessarily different. This situation is, by itself, dangerous to the maintenance of the traditional West Indian value system since such high exposure draws audiences closer to the societies from which the television pictures emanate. But the situation is made worse by the fact that while West Indian television audiences are swamped by images of distant metropoles, they are denied the opportunity of exposure to the experiences of their neighbours in the West Indian family.

The severe financial constraints on West Indian television programming are replicated in regard to radio stations and newspapers in the region. The Caribbean News Agency (CANA) and the Caribbean Broadcasting Union (CBU) which originate radio broadcasts and wire services for newspapers are unable to find sufficient subscribers who can afford the costs of circuits except on an *ad hoc* basis.

The effect of limited media communications on the maintenance of close relations within the West Indian Community is worsened not only by the cost of telephone and facsimile links, but also by the shortage of circuits available for connecting the Region. The majority of circuits from each West Indian country are dedicated to North America and Britain. The volume of traffic on these routes and the foreign exchange which they earn justify the allocation of a high number of circuits to them, but the need for intra-Caribbean communication is also important to increasing commercial activity and promoting greater social contact within the area.

We are of the view that Governments should enter a dialogue with telecommunications companies in the Region to examine ways in which the number of intra-regional circuits for telephones or for other telecommunication linkages such as for distance teaching, cultural communications and news dissemination could be increased and the costs brought to a level of greater affordability, subject to the operating companies maintaining reasonable profitability.

Beyond the cost of telecommunications and the paucity of circuits within the Region, there is also the inadequacy of access to telephone service in the face of increasing demand in many of our countries. The international community has accepted that a satisfactory penetration rate for telephones (lines per 100 of population) should be in the order of 35 per cent. By this standard, CARICOM countries, except Barbados, lag woefully behind. For example, the penetration rate in Trinidad and Tobago and Grenada is less than 20 per cent; in Jamaica it is less than 10 per cent, and others are not yet in double digit percentages.

What these percentages reflect, at the height of the telecommunications revolution, is how far away the Region is from adequate telephone service. The revolution may not have passed our countries by; but it has certainly not yet touched the lives of the majority of the people. In practical terms, it means that the capacity for economic growth in large areas of the Region is restricted by poor telecommunications. Such areas are unattractive in terms of production whether at the level of business or manufacturing or marketing, and certainly in the whole area of services. And that means, of course, that there are diminished possibilities of generating new economic activity and enhancing employment opportunities.

We recognise an increasing demand for telephone services by the people of the Region and feel that telephone operating companies should be encouraged to significantly increase access. It should not be beyond the resources of the companies to put a telephone within reasonable walking distance of most West Indians by the end of the century.

We advocate a regional position on telecommunications matters, but the basis of a good negotiating position (on any issue) is information. The Region requires trained professionals who understand telecommunications to keep it informed on a timely basis and to advise them in negotiations with telecommunication companies on the provision of improved telecommunication service to meet domestic, regional and international needs. The basic mechanism for cooperation already exists in the Caribbean Telecommunications Union (CTU) with headquarters in Port-of-Spain. The CTU needs to be adequately staffed, with the calibre and numbers of professionals to enable it to assist Governments in formulating and implementing policies directed at improving telecommunications in the Region.

For such regional initiatives to be successful, however, changes need to be made within each country to improve the administrative and regulatory mechanisms. Responsibility for telecommunications, information services and media often resides in the portfolios of three different Ministries. We believe that Governments should examine their structures and operational realities with a view to bringing responsibility for these three internally related subjects under a coordinated structure.

Nurturing Common Ground through Information

We need to look at information as a sector — in the same way as tourism or manufacturing is routinely regarded as a sector — one in which information is no longer considered a "free good" but as a commodity and a resource to be managed. We need to consider the uses to which information can be put, and how Information Technology relates to development.

The information sector includes the processes for the production of data/information/knowledge; the data/information/ knowledge themselves; the systems for their organisation and management; their transmission by whatever communication means — radio, television, video, print, teletext, videotext, satellite, telecommunications; the services provided by such transmittal or communication; and the information products which emanate from these systems and services.

If all of the disciplines concerned with this industry (computers and related technologies, communications and telecommunications, publishing, printing and replication, libraries and library science, microform and miniaturisation technologies, statistics, information sciences, systems and management sciences, the information arts) coordinated to ensure interaction among them, the benefits to the society would be incalculable. Clearly a high level of training and retraining (already adverted to) is demanded for this sector to achieve the potential which it already shows as a means of diversifying the economic monoculture in which the Region has been mired for generations.

Despite the recent moves towards a more participatory and less authoritarian mode, the role of Governments in the development process is still a dominant one. Reorganisation, like charity, should begin at home, in this case with the need for the bureaucracies themselves to effectively manage their own information systems, applying information technology to areas of operation and not just to accounts and other financial operations.

At the regional level, CARICOM Member States have been asked to have national consultations on science and technology information policy, which may well serve, with very little adjustment, for the determination of national information policies. The Conference of Heads of Government agreed to the establishment of the Consultative Committee on Caribbean Regional Information Systems (CCCRIS) to monitor and coordinate the development of regional information systems. This Committee needs to be additionally empowered to execute advisory and coordinating programmes, and to evaluate information systems; additionally, it should have representational relationships with the Standing Committee of Ministers of Information and with the Committee of Statisticians.

But Governments are not the only players on the field. With regard to the several information disciplines mentioned above, there are regional associations of many of the professions — statistics, library sciences, radio, television, print and publishing, to name a few. But for the computer sciences there is only a national body in Jamaica, and a less formal grouping in Barbados; the linkages across the Region are personal and business ones. The regional private sector needs to take the information sciences more seriously than it presently does, not only as an occupational tool, but as a focal point for it's economic relationships with the rest of the world.

Out of the trauma of structural adjustment and devaluation a competitive advantage can be gained based on lower labour costs, high educational standards and proximity to large markets. The telecommunications infrastructure is improving, thanks in part to new capital injections over the past five or so years. The regulatory climate is becoming, albeit slowly, less restrictive and more supportive of entrepreneurship. In the post-industrial world, as in the present one, the real gains are to be made by the amount of value which can be added at each stage of a process. Our participation in the global information marketplace cannot be at the same level as that at which we presently function *vis à vis* agricultural and industrial products. The rules which will govern that marketplace are being made in several fora — most notably at the General Agreement on Tariffs and Trade (GATT), under which some countries are seeking to have the trade in information services subsumed. The Region needs to be alert to the implications of changes like that, as a Region, because the expertise and resources available to any one Government is nowhere sufficient to even keep track of conference proceedings, much less to make proper recommendations for action.

Circulating on Common Ground through the Media

If the information sciences provide the conceptual framework for regional communications, and telecommunications its neural system, then the media, taken collectively, form its face.

Every West Indian has the right to communicate, not just the professionals in the field. In fact, Article 19 of the Universal Declaration of Human Rights states: "Everyone has the right to freedom of opinion and expression; this right includes freedom to hold opinions without interference and to seek, receive and impart information and ideas through any media and regardless of frontiers." West Indians, even those unaware of its enshrinement, take that right to heart.

The West Indian is among the most articulate of the world's people. But while the Region has produced writers of world class the culture remains predominantly oral, with the calypsonian and dub artiste occupying a prominent place, and the radio and television being far more popular than books and newspapers, even among the most literate sectors of the population. Yet all hold the written or printed word in high regard. There is little doubt that the written language continues to be associated with the truth ('they would not have printed it if it were not true!', goes the rationale of first defence.)

Despite the tremendous democratisation in education which has taken place in the independence era, we find ourselves agreeing with Professor Alleyne that "it is not altogether certain that we can speak of the Caribbean as 'literate societies' as there seems to have been a passage from oral societies to electronic ones without experiencing the literate stage in any long and intense way." This perhaps explains, despite the reverence for the word-as-written, the popularity of the newer audio visual technologies — radio and television as mass media, but the audio cassette, the VCR and the satellite dish as well.

The electronic mass media, and especially radio, have long been a part of the landscape of West Indian society, playing no small role as an integrative factor in the Region, especially of late through the efforts of the Caribbean Broadcasting Union. It is arguable that West Indian cricket may not have survived as so vigorous a flower of regionalism had it not been for the radio linkups for Test matches and one-day Internationals; though we feel obliged to comment that cricket is one part of West Indian culture which could be more aggressively cultivated, in this case by the Board of Control when negotiating rights with foreign broadcasting entities. It is indefensible that West Indians should be prevented from watching their stars on their home television screens when the nationals of opposing countries can do so as a matter of course.

Earlier in this Chapter we drew attention to the "language dichotomy" operating in the societies at large and manifest in the media. Programming and, until very recently, music have been reflective of the opinions and tastes of the elite. It has even been argued, mainly by the print media, that the libel and slander laws throughout the Region, have been unnecessarily over-protective of the strong, and have served to reinforce their exclusivity of access. We need to search for a satisfactory formula which would protect the privacy of the individuals — whether public figures or not — while protecting the right of the public to criticise their leaders and others and to hold them accountable for their actions.

The Commission is encouraged that one of the recommendations in its Progress Report concerning the freedom of movement of media professionals for the practice of their craft has been accepted by CARICOM Heads of Government and is already being put into effect — although not yet everywhere. We believe this to be an important way of enlarging the media's capacity to contribute to the wider process of integration.

These journalists largely write for national media or are 'stringers' for international agencies, or both. Whatever their antecedents and avocation, their perspectives must match those of their employers. In our consultations, the particular need for press publications with a genuinely regional spread was highlighted. The CCC's *Caribbean Contact* newspaper, now in its twenty-first year of publication, and forced by economic factors to take a new look at its format, has been the only truly regional popular journal, regularly including articles in Spanish, French and Dutch. Commercial and other attempts at establishing other newspapers have, largely for economic reasons, proven short-lived. In the absence of a truly regional market-place the private sector is not encouraged to advertise in journals targeting a Caribbean readership.

A sub-regional marketplace functions in the eastern Caribbean, especially through radio stations, many of which can be heard in more than one island. The extremities of the CARICOM Region, Guyana, Belize, The Bahamas and even to some extent Jamaica, pose a particular problem, especially for FM transmission and for television by anything but satellite. This problem has been and is the subject of intensive study by groups from the CARICOM Secretariat, CBU, the ITU, the CTU and private groups, which appear to be working towards a consensus on the means whereby telecommunications can enable the creation of regional media.

We urge Governments to give the recommendations of these technocrats, when they are made, the most careful study. They are likely to involve financial commitments which may or may not be realistic *vis à vis* other priorities. But they will certainly also require supportive administrative action by regional Governments at INTELSAT and the ITU; that support should be extended to the fullest extent needed. If this opportunity to create truly regional media is lost, so too will be the dreams and ambitions of hundreds of media workers, and perhaps the last opportunity for us to really get to know each other as West Indians and, eventually, as Caribbean people.

Many of the building blocks for that sort of encounter are already in place. The CANA wire and radio services have made regional 'copy' available for several years but for reasons having to do with telecommunications costs many local media houses have been unable to afford access to this resource to an extent that does more than whet the appetite for more. Telecommunications as a factor in media costs has been on the regional political agenda from the earliest days of CARICOM. Governments must address the issue in a political manner that offers hope to our media houses.

Meanwhile, media houses make such arrangements as they can. Three radio stations which specialise in an all-Caribbean diet featuring regional information, music and sport, one each in Trinidad & Tobago, Barbados and Saint Lucia, conduct a three-hour link-up once a week. This transmission is jointly hosted and permits reasonable interchange.

The other very important institution which has become a standard part of every radio station's programming is the Call-in Programme which has virtually revolutionised communication by enhancing the potential for democratic participation. This popular device has also enabled the occasional linking-up of at least two radio stations widely separated by water. The Eastern Caribbean Television News Exchange and other programming broadcast by a Saint Lucian television station through a privately-owned uplink facility, have found a ready and faithful audience. The popularity of these programmes fuels the desire for more of these kinds of inspired, creative and courageous ventures.

The question of ownership of the media, especially the electronic media, is a very important and much-debated one in the Region. This is especially so where the radio and television stations are owned and operated by Governments which, in their turn, use regulatory or other devices to ensure that they retain a monopoly, or at least control. This is usually accomplished by using their licence-granting function to deter investors, or to impose upon would-be investors measures which would have the effect of maintaining the status quo.

The view was widely expressed in our consultations that, with respect to the electronic media, particularly in the Eastern Caribbean and Guyana, Governments have too much control. Some, among them opposition politicians alleging that they have been on the receiving end of injustice at the hands of an incumbent regime, have usually identified themselves with the calls for the privatisation of all the state-owned media houses. Traditionally, however, that zeal for reform seems to dissipate when the political tables turn and, with it, the power to effect change.

It is the case, however, that the ownership pattern is changing in terms of the balance between public (i.e. Government) and private ownership. There are more privately-owned radio stations (and television, if one counts cable systems) than there were in 1965 or even 1975. But that is balanced, some would say outweighed, by the continuing preponderance of Government-owned broadcast television stations.

It is clear that guidelines are needed for media ownership to deal with such questions as monopoly and the establishment of conglomerates which could dominate the industry. Unrestricted privatisation could have the undesirable effect of creating private monopolies to replace the government ones; on the other hand the so-called 'democratisation' espoused by some could have equally unacceptable consequences.

Television, which provided the means by which we were first able, at the level of general publics, to see ourselves, to reach beyond our islands and territories to the others in CARICOM, occupies a special place in national and regional media. But there is a pervasive perception that television has failed the people of the Region in some fundamental and deeply personal way. Popular wisdom has it that much of the convulsive change (particularly the negative and traumatic experiences with which we have difficulty coping) affecting the region may not be unrelated to the subliminal impact that television is making upon our culture, and the effect it is having on our self-image, behavioural patterns in family and other close relationships, and to our sense of commitment to ourselves and to our country and Region.

There is well-founded concern that while in the natural scheme of things (travel, tourism, emigration) there was always a process of acculturation at work making of us a polyglot people, the advent of television with its 'hi-tech' delivery and its user-friendliness, has improved the efficiency and increased the speed with which an external culture has made inroads into our own. Our size, our geographical position and our history have combined to render us particularly susceptible to foreign blandishments which subvert our values and peddle wares that define us largely as consumers of imported commodities. Even the religious community has not been untouched. Hence the notion of 'cultural penetration'.

There has been a well-sustained outcry against this trend; and some have suggested that governmental action be taken to prevent it. However much we share the basic anxiety we cannot agree with this prescription. In the first place, the most recent developments in media transmission would easily nullify the possibility of official intervention since the satellite dish is making it possible to receive such programmes directly from the satellite. But, in any event, we cannot close off exposure to the outside world without making a prison of our Region. Exclusion of external media cannot be the way for CARICOM. It is intrinsically wrong. It is also unworkable.

As the Third Meeting of Ministers responsible for Information within CARICOM observed, this phenomenon does not only constitute a threat, it also presents a challenge, for which we must invest resources. It is a challenge to the inventiveness which produced the steel pan; to the creativity which motivates Carnival; to the sense of humour which permeates our calypsos; and to the enterprise which has made reggae and dub music household names all over the world. The response to cultural penetration will lie in our ability to produce our own material that will fulfil the felt and expressed needs of the Caribbean audiences.

Advertisers, considering the ways in which to spend their money, consider local programmes too expensive to produce and sponsor. Stations and production houses therefore find them difficult to 'sell'. The solution obviously lies in productions which would command a regional and an international market, thereby spreading the unit cost over a larger number of buyers than is the case at present. This does not overcome a problem of start-up money which most regional producers face. There is no tradition here, as there is in larger countries, of bankers being willing to lend money for media projects as they do for other business ventures. This is one of the areas where, we feel, public money, perhaps the proceeds of media licence fees and advertising revenue, could be used to 'kick-start' certain types of projects, especially those with an educational or cultural bias.

Alternative Communications

But that is at the macro level, so to speak. Our people are also seeking their information and entertainment, not to mention livelihood, elsewhere than through the mainstream media, whether publicly or privately owned. There is now a large and evolving network of persons, groups and organisations involved in what is sometimes termed alternative communications, or informal media. Collectively they are categorised under the heading of Non-Governmental Organisations (NGOs) but they are as diverse as they are numerous, ranging from theatre groups to agricultural cooperatives to women's construction training groups and consumer education organisations.

These organisations and individuals make use of the latest media technology to communicate with each other on an interactive (though not necessarily real-time) basis and, most importantly, to teach what amounts to survival techniques for hard times to 'grass roots people (who) don't consider themselves very important', as one informant expressed it. They operate within and between countries, forming networks that criss-cross the Caribbean and extend beyond it.

Operating in the interstices of their societies, these members of the "Development community" are largely apolitical in the party sense. At one level the NGO community is self-contained. It is in a real sense its own medium and its own message. It holds its own seminars, workshops, creates its own publications and dramatisations of issues all toward the end of greater self-reliance and building "positive self-image" among Caribbean peoples.

In the interest of building, consolidating and defining community we feel that NGO's (Churches, Trade Unions, Professional and other people-based organisations) should be recognised as having an important role to play in communications generally, but specifically in the development of media which are relevant to the Region.

Training

Something must be said, however briefly, about an issue which bedevils all our activities in this region — training. The need for it is a constant refrain in discussions about our enormous potential and our less impressive achievements. There are several institutions which make training available in one or other area of the information field. Multilateral agencies such as UNESCO have also, over the years, been more than generous to the Region. The problems come afterward, when the earnest and rejuvenated trainees return from their university course or other attachment to their radio station or whatever — and are put back into the slot from whence they were plucked, or given an assignment that makes absolutely no call on their newly-acquired skills. The training, and the taxes of numerous people around the world, have been wasted; the possibility of new ideas, new techniques, new results, is lost. We plead with managers, in the public and private sectors, to place a value on training equal to that they would place on other capital investments — a new machine, a new building. A well-trained employee who knows he or she is valued for that training is an asset which appreciates.

Community is about Communication

We end this section as we began it, with a reminder that Community is about communication. Without effective communication between the people and the countries of CARICOM, the reality of Community cannot be sustained. In a world in which there is intense competition for our attention, we have to speak more directly and more constantly with each other. We have to do that consciously and, taking account of our smallness, promote that communication as a matter of policy. It cannot be merely left to the operation of market forces or the magnetism of metropoles. We have set out in this Chapter many pathways that such a deliberate policy of promoting communication in CARICOM should follow. There will be others that emerge as we proceed along those pathways. As part of our commitment to the concept of acting together in CARICOM, and through CARICOM, we have to communicate constantly — not just at the level of the actors, but of the people who must increasingly animate their actions.

We have attached so much importance to this matter from the outset that, in every CARICOM country we have visited, we began our consultations with a meeting with media representatives; not with a press conference, but a consultation with media workers as the professionals in communication. We were anxious to hear from them about the state of communication in CARICOM and we were pleased with their readiness to talk with us about it in a frank and constructive manner. The Region may not have the sophistication of the media in large countries; but the best of our print media, our radio, our television programming — in terms of local content — can hold their own in the wider world. We have the human resources in the Region, and it is increasingly a trained and skilled resource base qualified to make communication an effective tool of integration. We must nurture and support it.

The media, of course, must themselves deliver. They have an obligation to our societies that goes beyond selling newspapers or pulling in advertising revenue. We do not scoff at these needs, but we set alongside them some very real responsibilities. We have, for the greater part, a free press in the Region. It must remain so, and grow stronger with more freedom and less constraint. It will do so as media workers themselves make the media better by the quality of their professionalism. They have a special role to play in the process of communication in CARICOM. That they are playing that role with increasing awareness of their capacity to energise the integration movement, has been one of the more heartening aspects of our experience as a Commission.

We end our observations in this section with the recognition that if the various aspects of the communication and information challenge in the Region that we have reviewed are to be dealt with adequately, then there must be a clear collective policy consensus among regional Governments in this vital area of West Indian life. We note with much encouragement that CARICOM Information Ministers also registered this recognition in their call, at their Third Meeting in May 1991, for the preparation and adoption of a comprehensive Regional Information and Communication Policy which would serve as an authoritative signal of where Governments stand on the many vital issues affecting the development of communication and information systems in CARICOM. We welcome the fact that a panel of regional experts has been established to prepare a draft of the proposed Regional Policy, and that the result of their work will go before the Ministers at their next meeting.

Recommendations

1. that CARICOM Governments commit themselves to developing communication in the Region as a necessary element of integration, and to enlarging that process as CARICOM increasingly reaches out into the wider Caribbean;

2. that an essential element of that policy be the promotion of regional radio and television, and programmes designed to enhance communication within the Region;

3. that such policies be supported by collective CARICOM action at the international level to secure an equitable entitlement of CARICOM countries to space in the geo-synchronous orbit over the Caribbean with a view to enhancing CARICOM's capacity for negotiating access to satellite communications;

4. that in a context of increasing demand for telephone services for the people of the Region, telephone operating companies be encouraged to significantly increase access;

5. that utilising a well-staffed Caribbean Telecommunications Union, CARICOM Governments coordinate their telecommunications policies with special regard to:

   - national and regional infrastructural priorities;
   - incorporating this approach and unifying our regulatory structures in the provision of operating licences;
   - establishing special communications rates for press and other media purposes and for data transfers;
   - developing common positions on international telecommunications issues and joint representation at conferences;

6. that in relation to the electronic media, regional guidelines be developed, paying special attention to issues of monopoly ownership, whether by Governmants or by private individuals, and to the need to minimise opportunities for political interference in the media;

7. that Ministers of Education ensure that as many schools as possible participate from the very beginning in the computer science CXC curriculum when offered for examinations across the Region, bearing in mind that an information society cannot be created under present conditions without widespread computer literacy;

8. that arrangements be established in the Region for the general teaching of at least one of the other international languages spoken in the Region;

9. that CARICOM Governments seek expert advice on the feasibility of establishing a mechanism to support the production of Caribbean programmes, with special consideration given to programmes of an educational nature and those directed at young children;

10. that more effective information legislation be developed through regional effort designed to protect the right of privacy — in both a governmental and individual context — while safeguarding the public's right to information through discussions and enquiry;

11. that in the matter of training, administrators and media managers, in particular, maximise the benefits of existing training opportunities both in relation to training itself, as well as the utilisation of skills.

2. SPORT — CONNECTING AT THE GRASS ROOTS

Overview

Sport at the regional level in the West Indies has developed in a generally haphazard manner. While West Indian Governments have devoted much attention, in their separate territories, to the provision of sporting facilities, to coaching young people, and to some support for physical education, little effort has been made to follow the pattern of West Indian cricket and pursue the development of regional teams for participation in international competition in the varieties of other sports which West Indians play.

Of course sports — to some extent like culture — is *par excellence* an area for voluntary activity. Governments have largely concentrated on providing the infrastructure, leaving the organisation of sporting activities, and largely rightly so, to private individuals and groups.

Our concern is to encourage Governments to actively promote the development of regional teams. They should do what is required domestically, and in the international fora concerned with the management of sporting organisations, to facilitate over the next five to ten years the development of West Indian teams and their participation in the Olympics, the football World Cup and the Davis Cup, for example. This orientation should apply also to games which are not normally within the European sphere of sporting activities, but which, given our geographical location, are becoming prominent — for example, basketball.

In these pursuits, Governments should continue to encourage the systematic participation of the private sector. This sector has made a substantial contribution to inter-country competitions within the Region, providing in that way a reservoir of participants from which regional teams can be objectively chosen. Governments must persistently encourage these contributions.

It is important also, in order to encourage a firm and continuous pool of talent for the development of successful participation in regional and international competition, that Governments pay particular attention to the introduction of physical education in primary and secondary schools.

Cricket

In *Beyond a Boundary*, C.L.R. James described in a famous passage the importance of cricket in the West Indian psyche:

> What do they know of cricket who only cricket know?
> West Indians crowding to tests bring with them the whole
> past history and future hopes of the islands.

And he added:

> In the inevitable integration into a national Community, one of the most urgent needs, sport, and particularly cricket, has played and will play a great role.

When we lost a particularly vital World Cup match, a commentator tried to get a dismal, undedicated performance by the West Indies cricket team into what he thought might be the right perspective by saying: 'after all, it is just another game'. He made a fundamental mistake. To us it was not, it is not, 'just a game'.

No West Indian believer can afford to underestimate or neglect this game. It is an element in our heritage which binds us close and is seen as such both by ourselves and the outside world. When first Frank Worrell in that famous tour of Australia in 1960 and then later Clive Lloyd, followed by Viv Richards in the 1970s and 1980s, led the West Indies to a dominant position in world cricket, it built our stature as a people both in our own eyes and in the eyes of others. When we stood as one in the cricket boycott of South African apartheid it really mattered. And when we failed as a team in crucial games in the World Cup throughout the Region we felt ourselves indefinably but definitely diminished as a nation in those performances.

The performance of the West Indian team in their miracle win in the historic Test match against South Africa revalidated the supremacy of cricket in the West Indian psyche as an enduring source of inspiration and as demonstration of the fact that we do it better when we do it together.

It may be instructive that it was in a presentation made to the Commission on the sources of West Indian success in building a great cricket team in the late 1970s and 1980s that we heard what we thought was perhaps the most succinct recipe for success in all the endeavours we pursue as a community of nations acting together.

> We must develop confidence in ourselves, in our ability to beat the rest of the world, in our right to be an example to others.
>
> We must make a commitment to excellence. We must be prepared to learn from the best and then make that best

our own and put it into practice.

We must make a total commitment to doing the job we had to do very well indeed. And, in making that commitment, build a reward structure which made the commitment worthwhile in a practical as well as a psychological sense.

We must believe in frank and open communication at all times between those involved in the endeavour — and especially believe in this requirement at times of particular challenge or crisis.

We must know that serious discipline is involved, self-discipline, team-discipline, discipline for a profoundly important purpose, not just for selfish purposes but for others who depend on our success being achieved.

It was from those principles, we were told, that the greatness of the West Indies cricket team was built.

Seeking success in other sports

Cricket springs to the mind, but it is not only cricket among the sports that could serve the cause of closer West Indian integration. We take to heart the active role which the joint organisation of sporting activities has played in helping to bring the OECS countries closer together; it is an example ripe for wider application. As West Indians draw closer together in other respects, we cannot afford to neglect the tremendous emotional charge that can be derived from grass-roots identification with sporting teams and sporting competitions which embrace us all. When Trinidad played the USA for a place in the finals of the last Football World Cup the whole of the West Indies came together behind them. Such a feeling lies at the root of our Community.

Given the success and worldwide acclaim for the West Indian cricket team it is surprising that West Indians have not had more success in coming together in other sports to compete internationally. In some sports efforts have been made — in one of them over an extended period — but in no case have these efforts been either sustained or sufficiently successful to catch our own or the world's imagination.

In the Federal era, at the Pan Am Games in Chicago in 1959 and at the Olympic games in Rome in 1960, we participated as the West Indies. In the 1960 Olympics the West Indies won bronze medals in the 400 metres, 800 metres and, most significantly, the 4 x 400 metres relay. There is no doubt that we should strive as hard as we can in a new era of much closer integration to revisit that experience.

In Lawn Tennis the West Indies, under the auspices of the Commonwealth Caribbean Lawn Tennis Association, competed as a single team in the Davis Cup between 1953 and 1987, only then to be informed by the International Tennis Federation that West Indies would no longer be eligible to compete since, in the ITF's view, the West Indies was not a country. An attempt was made by some to protest this development. However, Jamaica entered a team on its own in 1988 and since then individual West Indian countries (the OECS as one) have competed separately, thus bringing to an end the most extensive effort, apart from cricket, to achieve West Indian participation in international sport.

There have been attempts to put together a West Indian challenge in a few other sports. For instance, in 1976 a West Indian Rugby team toured Britain. In 1959 a West Indian Football team toured England, playing 30 matches against 3rd and 4th Division teams but winning none — the effort was not repeated. In Rifle Shooting from 1950 to 1960 a West Indian team competed with other Commonwealth teams and since 1982 a West Indian rifle team has been entered in the triennial International Palma competition for Commonwealth and United States participants. West Indian netball teams have also competed internationally and made their mark.

All in all, the results have been disappointing and the regional sporting bodies in general appear to have been too easily discouraged. Perhaps they have not remembered clearly enough the decades West Indian cricket spent in the doldrums before its first successes. It is true that financial and organisational constraints present formidable obstacles to sustained West Indian participation. Yet it remains something of a mystery why the determination shown in organising cricket on a West Indian basis — though the problems of finance, organisation and initial lack of success must have been as great — has not been replicated in any other sport. Nor do we believe that constitutional impediments which may exist in the rules and regulations of international sporting bodies against single West Indian participation will not yield to persuasive effort.

As West Indian integration proceeds now at a faster and more urgent pace, fresh and determined initiatives must be taken by national bodies acting in concert to mount a West Indian challenge in sports other than cricket.

We lack the detailed expertise, and in any case do not desire, to try to indicate what steps might be taken to strengthen the regional content of the many sports which West Indians play with so much enthusiasm and talent. In respect of all sports, however, we would hope that associations in the Member Countries of the Community would make a renewed effort to co-ordinate their activities with a view to promoting much increased intra-Community competition and with a central objective being to field West Indian teams at an international level.

Regarding international competition, we believe it is especially important that efforts be directed to organising West Indian teams to compete in the Olympic Games, the Football World Cup, and in the Davis Cup. If approval can be given — as it has been — to the Commonwealth of Independent States to compete in the 1992 Olympics as one team, there is clearly no let or hindrance in principle to individual CARICOMcountries coming together in the various sports to compete internationally as "the West Indies."

In respect of cricket in particular we express our strong belief that, as a tried and true definer of our common identity, the West Indian cricket team, and the game back home which underlies the team's immense international success, need to be cherished. We fear the fact that familiarity with success breeds neglect of those who achieve it and we urge that this mistake not be made with cricket.

Recommendations

1. that the West Indies Cricket Board of Control be encouraged to prepare a comprehensive report on the state of cricket in the Community: suggesting means for strengthening the game in the Region and giving the West Indies the best possible chance to be competitive internationally. Problems of fi-

nance, the improvement and extension of facilities, the need to keep a larger number of our leading players performing and coaching within the Region, and increasing the popularity and playing of the game at school level should all be addressed;

2. that the televising of West Indian Cricket matches at the international level, on tour or at home, hold a high priority in regional broadcasting. A report should be sought from the CBU on the possibility of televising the annual intra-regional cricket competitions, the Red Stripe and Geddes Grant competitions;

3. that fresh initiative be taken by national bodies acting in concert to mount a West Indian challenge in sports other than cricket;

4. that there be a regional sports desk at the CARICOM Secretariat concerned with encouraging, organising, publicising and seeking finance for regional sport. The very successful OECS regional sports desk is an appropriate model;

5. that a CARICOM Sports Personality of the Year scheme be established through the Sports desk. The criteria for selection can be creatively developed based not simply upon success in international events, but also on performance and contribution to sport at the regional and local level;

6. that regional media be encouraged to provide more coverage of regional sporting events, even when they are not taking place in their locality. Regional sport writers and commentators should also be recognised by a regional award;

7. that greater attention be given to preserving and building up regional sports archives to foster a greater awareness of the traditions and importance of sports in the West Indies.;

8. that through the proposed Caricom sports desk, an attempt be made to provide cheaper travel for sportsmen and spectators as well as lower-cost accommodation structures;

9. that regional sports organisations seek to utilise teleconferencing facilities to hold more frequent and timely meetings as a way of breaking down an insularity which has meant that meetings are held only during tournaments and the regular contact needed to advance regional arrangements is therefore rarely achieved;

10. that in the spirit of promoting entrepreneurship and enterprise, efforts be made to establish in the Region a Cricket Academy to train persons in all aspects of the game of crocket. In this regard the services of available past and present West Indian cricket stars may be retained; it is also possible that similar ventures may be undertaken in areas of sport where there is internationally acknowledged West Indian expertise;

11. that linkages between tourism and sport be pursued and strengthened with a view to deriving the maximum benefit from the West Indian reputation for sporting excellence, linked to other aspects of the regional tourism product;

12. that a corps of well trained physical education instructors be established to undertake school programmes of physical education and sport — as a counter to some of the anti-social lifestyles threatening the youth of the Region.

CHAPTER IX

SOCIAL CONCERNS

1. GENDER ISSUES

Paramount among the matters which were consistently brought to the West Indian Commission as we conducted the consultations throughout the length and breadth of the Region was the situation of women in West Indian society today. The general feeling was that the Region still has far to go in correcting certain fundamental disadvantages which have for too long characterised the situation of women in the Region.

The changes which have taken place within the Region in the past fifteen or so years since the proclamation of the United Nations Decade for Women in 1975, have not been as dramatic as was, or could have been, expected. What has been achieved is recognition that gender is a key issue to be factored into the development thinking, policy and programmes. What has not been achieved to any significant extent is the translation of this recognition into adequately resourced programmes which genuinely improve the position of women in West Indian societies. As a result, there continues to persist a perception that West Indian women are strong, powerful matriarchs, reluctant or otherwise, who are perfectly capable of taking care of themselves and their families without assistance; that they are adequately represented in the work force and in civic activity; that they have benefitted significantly from the social and infrastructural provisions of successive Governments; and that there already exists formal equality between the sexes. It is therefore often said that there is no need for any special action for the women of the Region.

Closer and more critical examination of the relevant material, however, reveals that the situation is not as straightforward as these perceptions would seem to suggest. Rather, considerable variation exists among women across age, marital status, class and racial lines within individual territories and between territories of different levels of development. Further, the basic assumption about the matriarchal nature of these societies masks the essentially male-dominated nature of these societies and the substantive inequality in the position of women.

The time has therefore come for the correction of the asymmetry of gender relations so detrimental not only to women but also the wider society, since this asymmetry ignores that women are the prime focus in the reconstruction of the moral, social, cultural, economic and political fabric of the Region. The centrality of the position of women lies in the range of roles performed by and expected of women. Primary responsibility for child care and domestic labour within the family traditionally rests with the woman. But she is also expected to engage in income earning activity in order to enable her to carry out her roles as mother, mate and caregiver. As an expression of her own individuality and independence, she herself desires to engage in such activity. Over two-fifths of Caribbean households depend on the income of women for their survival. As economic conditions deteriorate this proportion is expected to increase even further. The question for the Region is thus not whether special policy action is necessary to improve the position of its women, but how the absence of such action will affect the stability of the Region's societies.

Up to the present time, commitment to women and development remains token and under-resourced. The setting up of a Bureau of Women's Affairs within a Government ministry, for example, serves only to acknowledge that adjustments are necessary, but without the necessary resources does little or nothing to effectively address the needs. A gender perspective aimed at the integration and mobilisation of women as full participants and beneficiaries in the development process of regional integration must be incorporated into all Government projects and programmes. In so doing, greater attention must be paid to the questions of equality before the law, access to skills and resources, maximisation of educational and training opportunities, availability of adequate health care and opportunity to participate in decision-making processes at all levels in all sectors.

The major element underlying this is the concept of empowerment, i.e., providing women with the opportunity and knowledge to decide what is best for them and to act accordingly, secure in the knowledge of an absence of discrimination, explicit as well as implicit. This approach emphasises organisation, mobilisation and a participatory work style. To be effective it requires critical assessment of the major institutions of society, willingness to accept change and commitment to the provision of the necessary resources.

Education

One of the most critical instruments for social and economic development is education, both formal and informal. Education is perhaps the main means through which a society perpetuates and spreads its culture, reinforces its values and maintains stability. In the present context, formal education has been a major strategy for perpetuating the male-biased gender ideology which has prevailed in these societies. Shifts towards an approach implying equality of opportunity for both sexes have indeed resulted in relatively equal access in terms of enrolment rates at the primary and secondary levels and attainment rates at the secondary level. However, at the tertiary level there is marked predominance of males over females, even though attainment rates for both are unacceptably low.

Performance rates are another matter. Over and over again it was brought to our attention that there appears to be emerging throughout the Region a trend towards non-performance among male students at the secondary and tertiary levels of education. Some commentators consider that the process starts with the Common Entrance Examination where in virtually every territory the cutoff mark for girls is higher than for the boys and the number of places available for girls is lower. It is felt that this encourages low achievement among the boys from the very start of their secondary school life and this self perpetuates throughout the rest of their education, with the concomitant increases in the incidence of male "dropouts" and associated deviant behaviour. Other commentators felt that the increasing self awareness of girls and their recognition of the opening up of opportunities not previously available to them may be an incentive to their better performance. Yet others felt that the rapidly changing socio-economic environment and the opportunities to acquire vast sums of money with little effort acts as a deterrent to scholastic performance. Whatever the reasons, the issue is a vital one which requires much more careful investigation since it has serious implications both for gender relations and the future social and economic development of the Region.

The apparently favourable situation for girls masks certain features of the system which still require reform if the objective of reducing gender inequities is to be attained. Studies of school text books, for example, have revealed that women are most often portrayed in stereotypical roles as wives or mothers, or occupying subordinate positions in employment. No or limited access for girls to technical and vocational training within the formal education system is another shortcoming of the system which is frequently cited as a factor contributing to a general stigmatising of vocational training, the restriction of employment options for girls and the increasing unemployability of young people generally and young women in particular. The absence of a gender perspective in the teacher training programmes throughout the Region is seen as a major constraint to the ability of those in the teaching service to act as agents for changing gender attitudes. The preponderance of males in the administration and management of schools and in the Ministries of Education is seen as an impediment preventing women from participating in the decision-making processes affecting the operation and evolution of the educational systems in the Region.

The emergence of non-formal educational programmes as a mechanism to compensate for the failure of the formal system was initially seen as a hopeful sign, since many of these programmes emphasised short term skills training aimed at equipping recipients for self-employment. Non-governmental organisations have played a leading role in this. However, with few exceptions, these programmes emphasised training for women in such areas as handicraft, dressmaking, food preservation and the like, thereby further entrenching women in the traditional female activities and pushing them out to the fringes of the development agenda.

The re-evaluation of the educational system in order to introduce changes beneficial to women was one of the tasks set for national Governments within the United Nations system subsequent to the Decade for Women. However, apart from the introduction of a programme of Women and Development Studies within the University of the West Indies, the extent to which individual Governments have taken up the challenge is not yet clear. Much still remains to make even this fledgling effort effective. This has to be seen within the context of the human resource needs of the Region.

Employment

Relatively equal access of women to education has not been translated into high levels of economic activity among women. Male worker rates exceed female rates in every territory in some cases by as much as three to one. Women are concentrated in a narrow range of occupations in which the level of wages is lower than the occupations in which men predominate. Despite indications of incipient changes in some sectors, this pattern of women's working force participation has remained virtually intact. Further, indicators of unemployment suggest similar disparities. In every territory female unemployment rates consistently exceed male rates at all ages and especially at ages under 30, precisely the time when their responsibility for young children is at its highest.

Available evidence for the decade of the eighties suggests that the female working population has been increasing, that women have been assuming an increasing proportion of the overall work force and that women have been moving away from agriculture into the more remunerative services and industrial sectors. However, closer examination reveals three important discriminatory aspects of these changes. First is the preponderance of women at the lower end of the occupational scale at both sectoral and overall levels. Second is the increasing involvement of women in the informal sector in activities which reflect not only an extension of their domestic responsibilities but also the occupational segregation of the formal sector. Thirdly, although female worker rates are rising they continue to be lower than male rates. Further, they are accompanied by rising female unemployment rates, which, in turn, continue to exceed male rates.

The perpetuation of gender inequity in employment is further evidenced by the lack, or limited availability, of financial and credit facilities to assist women's income earning efforts. Even in the face of evidence to the contrary, many financial systems disregard women's potential as good credit risks and successful managers of resources. Thus many women are excluded from credit opportunities which could enhance their propensity to be self-sufficient. There are a few non-government development agencies which do provide credit to women for specific projects, but these are few, scattered and not able to fill the unmet need. Further, these efforts while benefitting individual women in the projects have brought no major changes in the pattern of articulation of women within the overall economic system.

At the root of these examples of gender inequity is the fact that women undertake multiple activities many of which are not usually classified as economic activity. Domestic labour, work in the informal sector, voluntary social labour are all excluded from the count on the assumption that they have little or no exchange value. Yet it is precisely these activities which reflect the resilience, resourcefulness and self-reliance of our women — qualities greatly needed if the Region is to emerge from the ongoing crisis.

Health

Among the multiple activities undertaken by women is the provision of health care for themselves and those in their families and households. Recognition of women's major role in health whether as providers of health care in the home, workers in health care institutions or consumers of health care is fundamental to an understanding of the links between health and development. Women's health issues have tended to be relegated to and defined in terms of their reproductive capacities and the provision of family planning services and maternal and child health services. But there is a wide range of other health issues relevant to women which have to be taken into account. For example, development strategies based on export processing zones and the use of female labour have resulted in the exposure of women to a set of disorders to which they would not otherwise have been subject. The changing age distribution of several populations of the Region, in which a grater number of women are living longer, carries a number of implications for the organisation of the health services. The resurgence of certain communicable diseases thought to be under control, and the emergence of new diseases which not only affect women and men but also the capacity of the populations to reproduce themselves are other health issues which need to be tackled from the perspective of women. The rising incidence of mental ill health among women as a result of violence against women, substance abuse and the stressful economic situation is yet another example of the contemporary health problems facing women in the Region.

The important point here is that no regional development initiative which is concerned with increasing efficiency and raising productivity can be successful if issues of health care are ignored. And no health care proposals which ignore women's health issues can be effective.

Women and the Law

A widespread assumption in the Region is that women are equal to men in the eyes of the law. However, in spite of significant changes during and since the Decade, women continue to be at a disadvantage in this sphere as well. Traditional common law in many territories in the Region still perceives wives as property of their husbands. For example, in some territories the husband of a woman who commits adultery can bring legal charges against the defiler and user of his "property". No similar recourse is available to women. Several territories have taken steps to eradicate this and other areas of discrimination in the civil law, family law, citizenship law — an area crucial to the issue of regional integration — and criminal law, perhaps the most vexed area at this time of increased crimes of violence against women.

By the end of the eighties, some progress had been made. However, there still remain areas in which more can be done. For example, existing labour law, even in those territories which have attempted some reform, still provides inadequate legal protection to workers in industries involved with new forms of chemicals and technologies the bulk of whom are women. Some of the family law reforms have resulted in placing women at a greater financial disadvantage than before. There are still territories in which women holding certain occupations are liable to lose their jobs if they become pregnant.

Economic Adjustment Programmes

The economic adjustment programmes of the eighties have produced both positive and negative results for women. On the positive side, opportunities have been opened for women to develop their entrepreneurial and managerial skills. On the negative side, many women lost their jobs and were forced into the informal sector, into illegal and other anti-social activities, and into the exploitative free trade zones in search of income. Reduced access to social services and the rising cost of living, especially rising food prices, affected women's ability not only to earn an income, but also to meet their household responsibilities, take care of their own health and that of those in their care. The result has been a growing inability to do what society expects and demands of them, i.e., to be responsible mothers and caregivers, while at the same time there is increasing pressure on them to perform those roles.

Response

Most of these issues have been brought to national and regional attention by the unflagging efforts of a wide network of women's non-governmental organisations working with each other and in close collaboration with regional institutions notably the CARICOM Secretariat, through its Women's Desk, and the University of the West Indies, through several of its departments. Several of them have adopted an advocacy stance based on research and action. Many others have preferred to maintain a version of the traditional welfare approach by providing material assistance and training in income-earning skills. Yet others have attempted to combine the two approaches. The major concern of these organisations is to increase women's self reliance as a means of reducing gender inequities.

The means by which women's issues could be incorporated into development strategies have been indicated in a variety of international documents and instruments to which CARICOM Governments have subscribed. The biennial meetings of CARICOM Ministers of

Women's Affairs have regularly determined action plans for national Governments. Yet the rate at which the relevant recommendations are being put in place is agonisingly slow. The present economic crisis afflicting the Region has introduced a sense of urgency of the need to transform the rhetoric into action.

It is undoubtedly true that there are encouraging signs that the women of the Region are assuming positions of highest leadership and responsibility in political life, in the public and private sectors, in the judiciary and the diplomatic service, in a wide range of professions which were formerly the province of males, and in a growing number of development-oriented non-governmental organisations. However, the numbers remain relatively low, the opportunities few and the obstacles, visible and invisible, many. The success of the few, however, has served to show that equity of opportunity can enable women of the Region to exercise their true potential in the development process. The women of the Region are not asking for, nor are they expecting, a reverse imbalance in their favour. All they wish is a fair and equitable chance to participate in and contribute to the further development of their Region. For them this is not just a call for the improvement of their own status, it is rather a fundamental requirement for sustained social and economic progress for all.

Recommendations

1. that it be acknowledged on all sides that CARICOM still has far to go in correcting fundamental disadvantages that have too long characterised the situation of women in the Region;

2. that the ability of regional institutions to deal with women's issues be strengthened by:
    - This means providing adequate infrastructural support for the CARICOM Secretariat's Women's Desk;
    - establishing focal points for Women's Affairs in regional institutions which do not already have these;
    - according to a regional women's NGO access to the CARICOM Heads of Government Conference analogous to that granted to regional umbrella organisations of other social partners, e.g. CAIC, CCL, CCC;

3. that women be increasing involved in regional planning. Greater numbers of women should be involved in the identification, planning and implementation of regional programmes, e.g. the Regional Food Plan, in order to ensure that gender issues are adequately taken into account;

4. that a regional approach be adopted to the implementation of programmes specifically designed to eradicate gender inequities. In particular, this implies regional initiatives:
- to develop curricula in gender studies at all levels of the education;
- to harmonise legal reform geared towards eliminating gender discrimination;
- to promote and implement the teaching of a second language initially to development practitioners and women in development specialists;
- to develop a computerised, regional statistical data base on women;
- to undertake training programmes in gender analysis and planning for public sector planners, private sector project officers and administrators of all organisations included amongst the social partners.

2. ILLEGAL DRUGS

Overview

Nothing poses greater threats to civil society in CARICOM countries than the drug problem; and nothing exemplifies the powerlessness of regional Governments more. That is the magnitude of the danger that drug abuse and drug trafficking hold for our Community. It is a many layered danger. At base, is the human destruction implicit in drug addiction; but, implicit also, is the corruption of individuals and systems by the sheer enormity of the inducements of the illegal drug trade in relatively poor societies. On top of all this lie the implications for governance itself — at the hands of both external agencies engaged in international interdiction, and the drug barons themselves — the 'dons' of the modern Caribbean — who threaten governance from within.

In our consultations in country after country the anxiety of citizens about these dangers, all of them, have been raised consistently. There is acute awareness that in our small societies they spell disaster for people, for institutions, for values, for the fabric of society itself; and there is concern that the menace is steadily enlarging. Occasionally, there is a disposition not to talk about it; understandable, perhaps, because of the prevailing sense of helplessness in responding to it in any meaningful way. Sometimes, however, this silence is with a view to preserving the image that all is well in the tourist garden of the Caribbean. Such reticence, however, only compounds the problem; because it runs the risk of shading into acquiescence and making matters worse. We believe that the drug problem in our Region has to be acknowledged and confronted for the monstrous evil and the pernicious cancer that it is. We have been heartened that several CARICOM Governments have taken courageous steps in doing so, despite all the limitations that their circumstances place on their efforts. In the result, however, the situation today is worse than it was when the Commission began its work in 1990; and it threatens to undermine all the progress that our Report calls for in civil and political, no less than economic, social and cultural life.

Many of the problems of CARICOM countries in relation to the illicit trade in, and abuse of, narcotics are not different in type from the difficulties experienced elsewhere in the world. The essential difference is that, in smaller countries — which all CARICOM countries are in this context — the problems have a greater impact because populations are smaller and far fewer resources are available to meet the awesome challenge posed by the narcotics trade.

Experts now suggest that the trade in illicit drugs rivals world trade in arms or oil. Some have put a figure on it of US$500 billion a year. Since the early 1980s, a substantial portion of that trade has originated in three South American countries: Peru, Bolivia and Colombia which produce virtually all of the trafficked cocaine. Three-quarters of the United States drug market, worth in excess of US$100 billion annually, is fed by the production of these Latin American countries. The lucrative US market, and the increasing demand in Europe, for cocaine and cannabis from South America places the Caribbean in the centre of trans-shipment activities. At the bottom end of that market, some Caribbean countries find themselves as producers of marijuana: Jamaica, Belize and Guyana face this additional hazard.

Altogether, the trans-shipment of illegal drugs through the Caribbean en route to destinations in North America and Europe has resulted in several major problems for the Caribbean.

Regional Incidence of Drug Abuse

One of these is drug abuse — the inevitable side-effect of trafficking. Accurate statistics are not available on the number of people in CARICOM countries involved in drug abuse or the number of crimes which are drug related. There are a number of reasons for this. Among them is that the police record crimes for what they are on the surface, for example, 'break and entry'. No mention is made of the reason for the crime which may well be to secure cash for purchasing drugs. But it is known that trafficking in narcotic substances increased in the Region by over eighty times in the two years 1984-86, during which the amounts involved have been estimated to have increased from 8,250 kgs to 712,778 kgs. Also, the majority of drug users in CARICOM countries do not register with rehabilitation centres. Official figures, therefore, do not fully reflect the number of users. But, however inconclusive the figures are, they do reveal a rising spiral. In Trinidad and Tobago, for instance, the number of admissions to hospitals for treatment related to cocaine and marijuana addiction rose from 376 in 1983 to 1,041 in 1989, and arrests for cocaine possession/trafficking rose from 5 in 1980 to 625 in 1989. We drew attention to this rising trend in our very first publication in July 1990 ('Let All Ideas Contend') where we warned that the 'number of West Indians abusing drugs and addicted to them is escalating with dangers for the productive capacity of the country and the control of crime'.

The Region has had relatively little experience with combating money laundering and with seizure of drug-related assets. A number of CARICOM States have been introducing legislation to permit action by Governments in this area, and efforts must be made to maintain regional coordination on these initiatives. The UN Convention on this subject provides for the establishment of reciprocal legal assistance in investigations, prosecutions, and judicial proceedings and thus provides a framework for closer collaboration among states in this sector which regional States must put to greater use.

Measures to Combat Drug Abuse

Demand reduction strategies are a central feature of all national programmes. Indeed the mandate from the CARICOM Conference of Heads of Government in 1988 establishing the CARICOM Regional Programme for Drug Abuse Abatement and Control placed emphasis on this as a priority aspect for regional action. In collaboration with CICAD, the European Commission, PAHO and the United Nations Drug Control Programme (UNDCP), school curricula on the issue have been developed within the Family Life Education Programme which has been formulated for implementation in the Region. Simultaneously, though not to the same degree, public awareness programmes have also been developed and are being implemented around the Region.

In support of the demand reduction programmes, measures have been taken to include the establishment of surveillance procedures to assess the extent of abuse and the strengthening of the documentation storage and retrieval capability. Treatment and rehabilitation is also an integral part of the demand reduction programmes. In this regard, due attention should be given to conducting training within the context of the better established treatment facilities in the Region.

The training of several categories of personnel to support the planning and implementation of programmes also received attention over the past four years. This should be improved and intensified where possible, and we welcome in particular the considerable contribution that the Caribbean Institute for Alcohol and other Drugs (CARICAD) programme has made to the development of personnel by providing for basic training both at the regional and national levels.

What is evident, and acknowledged, is that the incidence of crime has increased throughout the Caribbean and a significant number of new convicted criminals have a drug problem. The increase in crime which flows from drug addiction not only places severe strain on the small, overworked and under-equipped law enforcement forces of these states, it also creates social unease which threatens to degenerate into social disintegration and political destabilisation.

Drugs and Youth

Drug trafficking has clearly resulted in the abuse of drugs by a growing number of young people. This debilitation of the youth of small countries — already short of skilled and qualified labour — must, over time, have an adverse effect on the country's productive capacity. Moreover, as the number of addicts increase, CARICOM countries will have to devote a grater portion of their scarce resources to rehabilitation. Alongside the increased cost of rehabilitation will be the attendant increase in the costs of law enforcement, given the increase in crime that drug addiction has brought with it. The tourist industry — the mainstay of many an economy — is also being hit. There are increasing reports of tourists being harassed on beaches by drug vendors, but, what is worse, there is an increase in the number of tourists being robbed by addicts seeking the means to buy their 'fix'. It does not take many of these incidents for tourism, always a fragile plant, to begin to wilt. Apart from the loss of income from economic activity, such as tourism, the diversion of scarce resources from the productive sector into law enforcement and rehabilitation can have both short and long-term effects on the economic development, social equilibrium and political stability.

The Money Cost

Inevitably, combating drug trafficking severely taxes the foreign exchange resources of CARICOM countries. Some of these countries face significant balance of trade deficits, and the three largest in population terms — Guyana, Jamaica and Trinidad and Tobago — also have overwhelming debt problems. Indeed, the IMF currently runs economic recovery programmes in all three States. But foreign exchange is vital in all of the CARICOM countries for the maintenance of their productive sectors which still fail to offer jobs to half the young people seeking employment. Faced with a choice between purchasing essential inputs for production or equipping the law enforcement agencies, CARICOM Governments not surprisingly often choose the former. In June 1990 a Conference of Bishops and Pastors from the Caribbean and Latin America, organised in Kingston by the Caribbean Conference of Churches, acknowledged the dilemma that the presence of drug related resources 'enables some of our countries to better resist the economic crisis as they generate employment, inject foreign exchange into dollar-starved economies and enable investment to be made in other productive areas; in short, temporarily to cushion the crisis'.

The Threat to Sovereignty

But that is not an end to the catalogue of problems deriving from the illegal drug trade. Governments are concerned about threats to their sovereign authority posed by the manner in which the United States Administration has sought to deal with the interdiction of drug traffickers and related money laundering in the Region. This was most strongly expressed in July 1988 when the CARICOM Heads of Government at their Ninth Conference wrote, through its Chairman, to US President Ronald Reagan 'on a matter which threatens to create discord and division between the friendly nations of the Region on the one hand and the United States on the other'.

The letter stated that among the concerns of CARICOM Governments were the 'attempts to extend domestic United States authority into the neighbouring countries of the Region without regard for the sovereignty and independent legal systems of those countries'. Among those attempts were the pursuit of suspected drug traffickers into CARICOM waters and their arrest by US authorities within the jurisdiction of CARICOM.

Since then Caribbean Governments have been subject to more than a little coercion by US agencies in such matters as 'hot pursuit', personnel for Drug Enforcement Units participating in planning and even directing their operations. Regional Governments have faced similar demands for the establishment of National Drug Councils to review the situation with respect to drugs and take appropriate action. The response of CARICOM countries has not been uniform. Some have cooperated fully. The Government of The Bahamas was the first to allow joint hot pursuit of suspected drug traffickers in its territory by US law enforcement agencies. Other Governments have set up Drug

Illegal Drugs

Councils but limited their powers. Cooperation is clearly desirable; but even in cooperation with external agencies, coordination should be essential.

The aquiescence by some Governments to US pressure has not gone unnoted by significant groups in the Region. The Conference of Bishops and Pastors already referred to concluded that the policies of CARICOM Governments to drug interdiction and banking secrecy 'are not derived from a Latin American and Caribbean diagnosis of the problem but from the United States approach to the topic'. And the Conference stated: 'We are once again faced with the imposition of unilateral policies and ideas whereby one country determines what others should do without taking into account their problems and real needs'. Such are the realities of power and powerlessness in our Region. Cooperation with the US, we repeat, is morally right and politically necessary; but cooperation is ultimately prejudiced by the imposition of authority.

Coordinating Regional Action

CARICOM Governments have not reached a uniform or even a coordinated policy on the drug problem in the Region. Some Governments appear to have a policy for dealing with the problem at a national level, others seem to have no policy at all. Many countries which have instituted concrete measures for addressing the drug problem have done so in collaboration with the US and the UK. These measures include small, under-manned and under-equipped Drug Enforcement Units, and cooperation with the US Coast Guard in stopping and searching vessels in Caribbean territorial waters. But, as a Jamaica Minister has pointed out, the measures taken by all the Caribbean countries individually "fall short of a regional response which will be necessary in the development of a sustained Caribbean initiative ... the Caribbean countries do not possess either the facilities or the resources to achieve this most important objective". Not surprisingly, CARICOM leaders have sought wider responses.

CARICOM bodies such as the Conference of Ministers responsible for Health, the CARICOM Law Ministers Forum, the CARICOM Committee of Foreign Ministers and the Conference of Heads of Government itself have all reflected the Region's concerns in their deliberations. In 1987, the Heads of Government agreed to the development and implementation of a regional programme designed to complement the efforts being made at national levels to control the traffic in and abuse of, narcotic substances. A Regional Ad Hoc High Level Group comprising Heads of national committees was set up as the principal institutional instrument of the regional programme. It has met only three times during the last four years. Since 1987 the Region has indeed seen some strengthening of national infrastructure to develop and implement national drug control programmes, using national resources and with the support of international donors; but the gains are small and progress disappointing.

At the international level the UN Convention on Drug Trafficking provides a framework for collaboration. CARICOM countries were among the first signatories to this Convention in 1988. Since then, CARICOM States have been developing legislation in accordance with the Convention but several have not yet ratified the document because the necessary legal provisions have not yet been made at the national level to facilitate this process. The Convention is a multinational treaty providing for cooperation in the area of trafficking that places on States obligations which would require the enactment of complex implementing legislation and the modification of administrative arrangements and structures before ratification.

Decisions were made at the First and Second Regional Conferences of Law Enforcement Agencies to coordinate the operations of these agencies both at national and regional levels. Plans have also been made for the establishment of systems to facilitate the coordination of surveillance. While some progress has been made in this area, there is still a great deal to be done to achieve the level of coordination necessary to disrupt the trafficking networks which exist. Encouraging support has been received from donor governments and agencies to strengthen the law enforcement sector and efforts are now being made to provide for basic level training in the Region as well as for the strengthening of forensic capability nationally and regionally. There is also a clear need to strengthen the legislative, judicial and enforcement process as it relates to the combating of drug trafficking and drug abuse.

In 1989, Prime Ministers Manley of Jamaica and Robinson of

Trinidad and Tobago put forward separate initiatives for the establishment of a 'multilateral force, under the aegis of the United Nations, which would provide assistance in particular situations requiring intelligence and interdiction capabilities beyond the resources of individual states', and Commissions of Inquiry and an International Criminal Court 'which would be capable of investigating and adjudicating on the criminal responsibility of persons engaged in offenses such as drug trafficking'. Basically, the problem with which both Prime Ministers were trying to grapple in their proposals is how to reconcile their fear of being swamped by the United States with their need for help in dealing with the drug problem. In other words, how to protect the sovereignty of CARICOM states from erosion while meeting US pressure for interdiction. These initiatives secured the endorsement of CARICOM Heads of Government collectively at their annual meeting in 1989.

The Government of Jamaica enjoyed some success in getting the United Nations General Assembly to accept a Resolution in January 1990 on a Global Programme of Action Against Illicit Narcotic Drugs, but it fell short of the original intentions of Prime Minister Manley for the establishment of a 'multilateral force under the aegis of the United Nations'. The General Assembly agreed to consider 'the feasibility' of such a United Nations facility.

We believe both the Jamaican and the Trinidad and Tobago proposals should be revisited. The world has changed a good deal since they were first put forward; so has the United Nations. The feasibility of U.N. anti-drug 'Blue Berets' in CARICOM countries at the express wish and request of CARICOM Governments is not a farfetched proposition. An international scheme which provides for such help in order to end the scourge of drug abuse and drug trafficking should now not be beyond the imaginationation or the capacity of the world community.

Measures to be taken urgently

The damage to the people, the economies, the systems of government — to democratic society itself — from the drug problem is as great a menace as any dictator's repression. Ten years ago the Independent Commission on International Security Issues (the Palme Commission) had proposed a system of security support for small countries who felt threatened by aggression. CARICOM countries are threatened today by an onslaught from illegal drugs as crushing as any military incursion. It is better for them to call for and receive genuine international help before they are either overwhelmed by the drug trade (and all that goes with it), or overborne by unilateral external power. Both the United States and Europe should help to put in place such a system of international security against illegal drugs which will both help to cleanse the Caribbean of this scourge and remove it as a source of illegal drugs entering the United States and European markets.

The same is true of the Robinson proposals; though their adoption may represent a second stage of international effort. They may well have seemed beyond attainment three years ago. Today when extradition has become a pseudonym for forceable removal and the basis of international sanctions, the usefulness of a genuinely international enquiry and adjudication process on drug related matters is not so *avant garde* an idea. It is better for us to go in the direction of enlarging genuine international law enforcement than allow its questionable imposition by the exercise of unilateral power.

At the heart of any effort to move in these or any directions is a policy framework on drug abuse and drug trafficking. We believe CARICOM, using the central facilities of the CARICOM Commission which we propose later (Chapter XII), should take the initiative in redeveloping these proposals and seeking a broad base of diplomatic support for them from both 'supply' and 'demand' countries before it all becomes too late.

But that centrally coordinated defence of CARICOM against illegal drugs cannot rest on such high profile initiatives alone. Writing in *Caribbean Affairs* in 1990 one regional commentator proposed the following as the elements of a sustained initiative:

- the ability to police Caribbean waters effectively, and particularly to pursue the arrest of vessels carrying illicit drugs;

- the capacity to police ports and airports to guard against the transit of illicit drugs;

- well-manned, well-financed, and well-equipped Narcotics Units;

- stringent and common legislation allowing not only for heavy fines and long terms of imprisonment, but also for confiscation of property and other assets of those convicted of drug offences;
- the capacity for sharing intelligence within the Caribbean and extra-regional territories;
- the maintenance of the sovereign authority of CARICOM States;
- bilateral extradition treaties with non-Caribbean states for the extradition of citizens and non-citizens from and to each other's jurisdiction;
- the continuous education of the entire population, by use of the mass media, the education system and inter-personal communications, about the dangers of drug use;
- a vigorous diplomatic process designed to mobilise the United States, Canada, European countries and international agencies into providing additional resources to the Caribbean dedicated to helping the Region to:
  – more forcefully interdict drug traffickers;
  – provide acceptable alternatives to the financial benefits of the drug trade; and
  – mount effective anti-drug education programmes throughout their communities.

[R. Sanders]

This clearly contains some of the essential elements of the strategy CARICOM needs to adopt; but we will require substantial and multi-source help in putting it in place. The countries whose populations provide the market for these drugs owe the Caribbean an obligation to help us rid our societies of the consequential evils that befall us from the drug trade as it reaches out to that market. But they have an interest as well in protecting their own societies from the menace of illegal drugs in assisting that multilateral process so that, whatever else is done in producer countries, the Caribbean is eliminated as a Region of trans-shipment. If it ceases to be such an entrepôt, we will have gone a good deal of the way in ridding ourselves of both the ills of drug abuse and the corruption of our societies. The role of the CARICOM Commission, therefore, in coordinating the elements of an effective regional strategy and securing the necessary multilateral support for it is absolutely crucial. In this, as in so many fields of endeavour, we shall act more effectively if we act together.

Recommendations

1. that greater priority be given to regional approaches to drug abuse and drug trafficking starting with the Regional Programme for Drug Abuse Abatement and Control established in 1987. The High Level Ad Hoc Group supervising the Programme should intensify its activities and the CARICOM Secretariat be strengthened to service the Programme;

2. that CARICOM should pursue the Jamaica and Trinidad and Tobago proposals for, respectively, an International Drug Control Force and International Criminal Court — refining them into a package which could be negotiated with the principal consumer countries and, finally, the United Nations;

3. that CARICOM pursue a collective strategy of enlarging external financial resources for combatting drug abuse and trafficking on a basis consistent with the sovereignty of the countries of the Region;

4. that rigorous efforts be made at national levels to curb the trend towards the emergence of drug related centres of economic and political power;

5. that CARICOM should promote an international effort to develop a multi-dimensional strategy and programmes — including health, formal education, public awareness, information, rehabilitation and law enforcement — with a view to ensuring effective responses to drug abuse and drug trafficking;

6. that priority be given to training of personnel to implement the multi-dimensional strategy;

7. that there be greater networking among security forces within CARICOM and the wider Caribbean Region, with information

processing and surveillance systems developed through INTERPOL and supportive drug enforcement agencies;

8. that the decision of Heads of Government in 1991 to establish a regional centre for the training of law enforcement officers be implemented; and the recommendation of the High Level Ad Hoc Group for the training of health personnel at the regional centres be adopted and implemented. In both cases we should aim to build on our existing institutions negotiating effectively through enlarged coordination;

9. that the Caribbean Institute on Alcohol and other Drugs (CARIAD) receive strengthened support in providing training on a regional basis for all categories of personnel;

10. that the Region commit itself to programmes that seek to create new development and employment options particularly for young people and in a community development context which should be developed within national drug control strategies.

3. HEALTH AND HOUSING

Health and housing, along with education, go to the very heart of most people's concerns about their welfare. This is no less the case with West Indians for whom there is the added dimension of wanting to know how regional integration in CARICOM can contribute solutions to their problems in these areas. In a sense, this is the *raison d'etre* of our entire Report: identifying the ways in which regional unity can be harnessed to enhance the overall prospects of West Indians in today's world. In this part of our Report, we seek to respond to this challenge as it relates to health and housing in CARICOM.

Health: An Overview

The people of CARICOM have arrived at a critical juncture in the development of their health status. The ushering in of a process of political and constitutional change in the Region some fifty years ago brought with it improvements in public health and public sanitation, better water supplies, and improved public and personal hygiene as an increasingly local political dispensation placed emphasis on meeting basic human needs. This produced over the years considerable advances in the health status of the people of the Region, as reflected by falling infant mortality and rising life expectancy.

It has been possible to build on that progress. Over the post-war period there has been steady decline in the infant mortality rates and in the mortality patterns of the 1-5 year olds in all CARICOM countries and this downward trend has been maintained in almost all of them. In all countries, also, life expectancy has increased steadily to reach an average of 72.4 years — among the highest in the Caribbean and Latin America. Throughout CARICOM, the prevalence of infectious and parasitic diseases has abated along with the incidence of such afflictions as poliomyelitis, measles, diphtheria and whooping cough.

These positive developments in the health status of the people of the Region have been specially important for infants and children. The gains in child health have stemmed largely from the maternal and child health and immunisation programmes that have been established and the emphasis on nutrition and primary health care.

Yet as we went around the Region the Commission was troubled by the danger signs that loom on the horizon. The hard-won gains achieved over the last fifty years in the health of the people of CARICOM are under threat. This arises from two distinct sources of pressure. One is the constraint that structural adjustment programmes have been placing on the social services of several Member Countries, including health care. In too many parts of the Region public expenditure on health, while remaining a significant part of the overall national budget, has been declining in both real and absolute terms. We are spending less on health services. Not surprisingly, under the impact of economic adjustment programmes of varying degrees of severity, clearly discernible pockets of deprivation are now emerging across the Region with potentially serious impacts on health. At the same time, any loss of ground already won leaves the

Region vulnerable to new epidemic scourges that threaten such as cholera.

Paradoxically, the other source of contemporary pressure on the health of the Region's population is the alarming increase in illnesses attributable to improvements in life styles both at the work place and socially. Hypertension and heart diseases are becoming a leading cause of death in the Region; some 12.0 per cent of the over-forty population suffer from diabetes mellitus; the pandemic of AIDS has inserted its frightening presence in the Region; alcohol and drug abuse are taking their particular toll; cancer of the lungs carries off many who indulge their appetite for tobacco; and accidents, mainly motor vehicle accidents, are among the five leading causes of death in CARICOM countries. These afflictions, which are preventable by appropriate changes in life styles, place a heavy demand both on personal family resources and on national resources.

The fundamental strategic issue in health, therefore, that faces CARICOM countries individually and collectively, is that of defending and preserving the real gains made over past decades in the health of the peoples of the Region. In doing so, the Region's approach must be guided at all times by principles of equity in the distribution and quality of services provided. Within the framework of these principles, we believe the challenge for the Region is to place relatively greater emphasis on health promotion and illness prevention, with the long-term aim of deferring the provision of curative health care, while recognising, of course, that there must always be adequate provision for it. In achieving this, there will be need for substantial further advances in the introduction of community health systems at the local level in all regional countries, and for the development of primary health care programmes.

Against this background, we highlight some selected strategic issues and challenges.

Health Management Systems

National and local health management systems, by definition, have to be implemented at national and local levels. They may appear, therefore, to be somewhat removed from those areas where there is scope to bring regional cooperation to bear on health issues.

But much has been done in the past, and more can be done in the future, to use cooperation at the regional level as an instrument for mobilising financial and expert resources, as well as to foster exchanges of experiences and information, to design and implement local health management systems in support of the effort at the national level. We believe that out of this process of regional collaboration a concept of the model health management system can be continuously refined as a collective regional product — one which individual countries can take and adapt to suit their local circumstances.

The major CARICOM/AID Basic Health Management Systems Project of the early 1980s was a significant contribution in this regard, and there has been subsequent maintenance of effort along these lines by PAHO in collaboration with regional Governments. Every encouragement should continue to be given to these initiatives. Already, the experience of Dominica, where sound local health management systems have been successfully introduced, is an indicator of the achievements that can be made with regional support in this area of major concern.

Training for the health sector — developing our human resources for it — is an abiding challenge to our Governments and our societies, including the private sector. Adequate systems of health management at national and local levels cannot be put in place without the requisite range of personnel to service the interlocking functions that comprise such systems. Such training in health must cater for personnel to undertake ongoing planning and analysis; personnel to carry out the administration of established policies and programmes; cadres, including professionals and allied personnel, to undertake delivery of health care at primary, secondary, and tertiary levels; and, of course, personnel to undertake research and training in order to deliver health education. There are major opportunities here for regional co-operation.

We face very fundamental challenges in our CARICOM Region in this matter of human resource development for safeguarding the health of our peoples. One of these challenges stems from the pressure currently being experienced on national budgets as a whole, and in particular the budgets for social services, including health. Appropriations for health remain a significant proportion of national budgets; but, as we said earlier, these appropriations have been declining in absolute terms in line with the absolute decline in overall national budgets. Since the overwhelming part of national health expenditures is personnel-related, the fall in the absolute levels of national health budgets is exerting widely felt pressures on the provision of personnel for the health sector.

Training and Retention of Medical Personnel

This combines with a separate concern to compound the problems currently faced by CARICOM health systems in securing and retaining adequate trained personnel for the health sector. The training of health personnel must emphasise health promotion and illness prevention, and the application of these within the strategy of primary health care and in the ambit of the local community health systems. The traditions of excellence of training in curative medicine must be maintained, but must be parallelled by similar standards of training for health promotion and illness prevention, and the related development of primary health care and community health systems.

CARICOM Governments and people, for this is a matter that involves the entire society, have to face up to difficult choices in the matter of training personnel for health care delivery, whether doctors or nurses or health workers of several categories. It is essentially a question of how to train our citizens in these skills, preserve the open societies that we cherish and retain an acceptable level of trained personnel. The question was posed directly in the study prepared for the Commission on health issues in the following way:

> The haemorrhage of trained personnel, particularly nurses, has made the issue of health manpower planning more critical as the Governments have recognised that they cannot continue indefinitely to produce trained personnel which are acceptable to markets in which there is a shortage and then complain of lack of staff. It is possible to contemplate training persons to fulfill specific local needs without reference to any mythical international standard with the knowledge that these persons cannot leave. One may also contemplate training excess and exporting that excess to those areas which wish to have them — thus treating skills

> like any other commodity. One may also examine with some care the pattern of health services to be developed and train the manpower mix appropriate for that pattern of care. Too many Caribbean countries refuse to take one or other decision and continue to train along traditional lines and bemoan the loss of the trained persons.
>
> [Alleyne/Sealey.]

We cannot avoid these questions. They are not susceptible of easy, much less doctrinal, answers but they have to be faced. We believe that a special effort needs to be made in the Region to confront them on the basis of the best professional and technical advice and assistance that we can muster. That will be a process that should involve not just Governments but the medical fraternity, universities and the social partners generally. It may even be a protracted process, but it is one that has to begin now and it is one that can only be effectively concluded if it proceeds on a regional basis. The CARICOM Commission, as we suggest later, in its functions regarding functional cooperation within the Community, can exercise leadership here in coordinating the work that has to begin on this matter: work that is so central to the health of the people of CARICOM countries.

Regional Pooling of Health Resources

CARICOM ccountries must be concerned with the issue of the mix of health personnel used to deliver health services by appropriate orientation and training. This is not an issue which can be addressed effectively through individual national effort alone. Obviously, there is much that can only be done at national level. But there is at the same time considerable scope for using collective regional initiatives to develop ideas on what the right mix of health service personnel should be, to maximise the results of new and innovative approaches to training (e.g. building on the very positive experiences already gained in collaborative regional training of allied health personnel), and to increase the benefits the Region can gain from its pool of health service cadres by allowing them to be freely deployed regionally instead of just within their respective national borders. In line with this, we urge that efforts be maintained to mobilise resources and expertise regionally to expand health systems research and promote consultation and exchange of information; to train the required cadres and nucleus of health professionals; and to reactivate past efforts to introduce, for appropriate categories of health professionals, systems of regional registration and/or arrangements for reciprocal recognition of national registration, in order to facilitate the free movement of health service professionals and workers within CARICOM.

Health Education

Another challenging issue is that of the promotion of general public health education and awareness. No system of health management at national or local levels, however perfectly designed, and especially where it is oriented to health promotion and preventative health care, will achieve its objectives unless it is firmly anchored in an environment of public awareness of and interest in health issues. We believe that the consciousness of West Indian populations in general has long reached the level where they wish to be informed about matters affecting their health. Health planners in CARICOM countries are therefore presented with a receptive audience for well conceived programmes of general public health education and for sustaining high levels of public health awareness. Much has been, and is being, done in the development and implementation of such programmes. We believe, however, that considerable scope still exists for improvement and for more systematic efforts, for exploiting the potential of regional cooperation in advancing the interests of the people of CARICOM in this area.

A related consideration is that the impact of soundly conceived programmes of public education on health issues would be reinforced by ensuring that the subject has a continuing place in the primary and secondary school curriculum. Already, very useful regional collaborative work has been done in developing a framework for promoting Family Life Education in the school systems. It should be our objective to sustain and broaden this effort to ensure an adequate continuing place for general health education for our young people in school.

Financing Health Services

We earlier discussed the relationship between the financial constraints on the health sector, on the one hand, and the issue of training for the sector, on the other. We suggested that one response to the current inadequate financing levels could be by way of restructuring the mix of health service personnel utilised in delivering health services, complemented by appropriate reorientation of the training of health sector professionals and other workers, as well as the adoption of measures which would facilitate regional use of the Community's pool of health cadres.

In face of the reality that there is not likely to be any meaningful increase in the foreseeable future in public expenditure on the health sector, there is urgent need for other responses to continuous financial constraints. Numerous studies and discussions have been undertaken within the Region on the question of alternative approaches to financing the provision of health care. No fundamental breakthroughs have been made, but the quest for answers must continue. Basically, of course, there can be no 'magical' creation of resources in society as a whole where there were none before. The issue is one of instrumentalities for allocating our available resources to achieve critically important objectives on which there is social and political consensus, and to innovative approaches to using the allocated resources more efficiently.

In this we must recognise that although some beneficiaries of certain health care services may not have been charged directly for these services, there is nevertheless no such thing, ultimately, as a free service. The resources available to, and in, our societies are drawn upon in one way or another — through taxes and otherwise — to pay for these services. The ultimate issue, therefore, in the search for new arrangements for health financing, is that of examining alternative routes and channels for drawing on these resources, so that the Region's overall goals in health can be adequately met within a framework of social equity.

It is clearly going to be necessary for 'cost recovery' ideas which are becoming increasingly current to receive serious attention. The many ideas under study in the Region relating to allocation of costs should be pursued more vigorously, but they must allow for some cushion for the most vulnerable sections of society. We also urge that greater attention be addressed through the collaborative efforts of the public and private sectors to expanding collective or group health insurance schemes at all levels, on the basis of reasonable and affordable premiums, and that, in particular, steps be taken to examine the feasibility of establishing group health insurance schemes on a regional basis, which should have the effect, in principle of reducing the premiums for membership of such schemes on account of the greater pooling of risks that regional coverage would bring.

A Regional Health Service

We believe that there are other positive prospects, through intensified joint action at the regional level, for countering the constraints of declining national budgets for the health sector. At the pinnacle of ambition would be the idea of one comprehensive and internally coherent regional health service, under the management of an integrated body of health service personnel deployed appropriately around the Region.

The Commission believes that this concept is technically, administratively, and operationally feasible. Indeed it should be recalled that in colonial times there was a unified and functioning regional public service. Certainly we urge that the concept be kept in mind as a long-term goal, and that, meanwhile, active steps be taken to identify carefully selected aspects of the health sector that could be organised regionally as common services for all or for appropriate sub-groupings of CARICOM Member Countries. An example of such possibilities put to us is the treatment of cancer of the cervix. The costs involved here in terms of sophisticated equipment and specialised professional attention are such as to make it unwarranted for some CARICOM countries, especially the smaller Member Countries, to contemplate setting up their own individual nationally dedicated facilities and staff to provide the required care. A pooling of efforts into a common service with appropriately located centres becomes the logical answer.

Procurement

Pooled procurement of supplies and equipment also beckons as an area of potentially fruitful regional cooperation in health. In the early part of 1980s CARICOM operated an embryonic scheme among some Member Countries for the pooled procurement of pharmaceuticals. A considerable amount of dialogue and studies took place on the issue of making the scheme more comprehensive and covering the whole Region. Regrettably, nothing came of this at the CARICOM level; but the OECS countries maintained the initiative among themselves and eventually established the Eastern Caribbean Drug Service; it has been able to achieve considerable savings for the participating countries in their outlays on drug supplies. The potential is still there for pooled procurement of pharmaceuticals to be organised on a CARICOM-wide basis, using the greater aggregate volume of orders to obtain lower unit prices and thus generate more savings. We hope the Region will reawaken to these opportunities, and proceed to exploit them in a coherent and purposive manner.

There is also fruitful potential for CARICOM Governments to act together in the procurement and registration of certain critical lines of equipment with a view to reducing the cost of maintenance to each country, including the cost of maintaining inventories of spare parts.

We believe that the cumulative impact of measured action on the range of selected issues we have outlined would help significantly to defend the Region's achievements in health against the pressures now being felt. The abiding challenge is that of ensuring that the possibilities on all levels are being pursued by well designed interventions. In this connection we welcome the original launching in 1986 and the continued development of the Caribbean Cooperation in Health (CCH) initiative, under which CARICOM and PAHO have jointly been pursuing a major effort in resource mobilisation for projects in the agreed priority areas of environmental protection including vector control, human resource development, chronic diseases, strengthening of health systems, food and nutrition, maternal and child health and AIDS. This exercise has already met with some encouraging success, and we urge that CARICOM Governments, individually and collectively, continue to accord it the importance and the attention that it clearly warrants.

But these ideas and initiatives will need to be underpinned by appropriate institutional arrangements. A regional institutional infrastructure has been developed and consolidated over the years, and it is available to be used intelligently and imaginatively to serve the common health interests of CARICOM peoples. The mobilising function ot the CARICOM Commission, that we propose later, in the area of functional cooperation can be the crucial factor making for operational success. The Conference of Ministers responsible for Health of the Caribbean Community, in collaboration with the Pan American Health Organisation, charts the main policy directions and approves the major joint regional projects and programmes, whose implementation is assisted by such other entities as the Caribbean Regional Epidemiological Centre, the Caribbean Food and Nutrition Institute, the Caribbean Regional Drug Testing Laboratory, the Caribbean Environmental Healh Institute, the Commonwealth Caribbean Medical Research Council and the UWI Medical Faculty. These institutional bodies and their functioning should be kept under continuous review with the aim of maximising their effectiveness in helping the peoples of CARICOM to defend the progress they have made over several decades in improving their health.

We would also urge that as the Region pursues these goals it should avoid the temptation to be inward looking within CARICOM, and be mindful of the scope that exists for establishing beneficial linkages with nearby non-CARICOM Caribbean countries whose health facilities and capacities can be drawn upon to support the health development goals of the people of CARICOM. Arrangements between the Eastern Caribbean countries and Martinique and Guadeloupe are illustrative of this.

In this connection, also, on our visit to Cuba we were greatly impressed by the quality of community health care achieved in this Caribbean island. Cuba's attainments in this field must have great significance for us.

The Problem of Housing

In a very profound sense the availability of adequate shelter forms a continuum with the issue of adequate standards of health care. They go together to provide both the sense and the reality of that personal well-being which is vital equally for individual human fulfilment and for general social peace and development.

So close is the continuum between good health and proper shelter that it is impossible to conceive of advances in the health status of a community outside the context of advances in proper housing. Lack of housing, or inadequate housing, negates good health and is a cause of disease. Programmes to promote proper housing are at the heart of strategies for health promotion and preventive health care.

Today, housing, like health in general, faces a crisis in many of our societies within CARICOM, as indeed in numerous other countries in the developing world. Although the problem has been a subject of perennial concern within CARICOM, the observance in 1987 of the International Year of Shelter for the Homeless has brought into sharper focus the urgent and pressing shelter needs of low-income households.

We spoke earlier of the gains made over the years in the health of the people of CARICOM which are now under threat from the prevailing economic and financial circumstances of the Region. A parallel situation obtains in the case of housing. During the period from emancipation to the onset of heavy rural-urban migration, the working people of the Region, in the face of great difficulties and harsh conditions, succeeded nevertheless in creating for themselves strategies — in many cases community based strategies — for supplying themselves with food and shelter. This era of self-reliance in shelter provision is receding fast as a result of changing social and cultural conditions and of the way in which economic change in our societies has unfolded over the years. We are convinced that one of the most critical and immediate challenges now facing our societies — at Governmental and non-Governmental levels — is the urgent need to restore this ethos of self-provision of shelter in the regional populace at large.

Disturbing Trends

The urgency we attach to this matter is justified by certain disturbing trends in the housing sector in the Region. First, there is invariably a persistent gap in practically all countries of the Region between housing demand and housing supply. Illustratively, this gap stands at some 760 units per annum, or 4.0 per cent of the housing stock, in St. Vincent and the Grenadines, with some 6,000 existing units requiring major repairs or replacement, to some 15,000 units per annum, or 3.0 per cent of the housing stock, in Jamaica.

A second clear trend is the declining capacity of Governments, despite their best efforts, to do anything meaningful to close the gap, as well as the reduced emphasis placed by major external funding agencies on supporting socially relevant housing development schemes such as site and services projects. Although housing provision in CARICOM has traditionally been through private self-help and private commercial initiative, there have usually been certain sections of society which relied on Government-sponsored housing projects for shelter. It is going to be of the utmost importance to find other strategies to fill the gap.

Another worrying trend in the regional housing situation is that of the rapidly escalating cost, in the commercial market context, of obtaining shelter, while at the same time real incomes are either stagnant or declining. Actual experience, of course, varies from country to country, but the prevailing situation overall is one of increasing lack of affordability of housing on the part of the majority of people. It has been estimated that the cost of financing housing has escalated over the past decade by some 600 per cent in the case of Jamaica, 500 per cent in the case of Trinidad and Tobago, 400 per cent in Barbados, and 2000 per cent in the case of Guyana. At the same time, incomes have not been growing at a commensurate rate, and the severity of the gap between need and affordability becomes greater.

These trends signal a crisis in the making of enormous proportions. The seriousness of the matter has been, and will from time to time continue to be, compounded by the impact of hurricanes and other disasters which wreak havoc on the housing stock — some of which is uninsured — of the various countries of the Region.

The general situation is made even more serious in the case of households headed by single females, since females often enjoy lower incomes and, at the same time, the female head of a household, unlike the male household head, usually does not have a helping partner.

The prevailing conditions in housing in the Region therefore call for urgent and timely responses of a kind that will help prevent the situation from declining to the point of absolute crisis. In seeking to shape these responses the countries of the Region must, as always, seek to optimise the impact of their efforts through joint action at the regional level wherever feasible.

The ultimate answer to the Region's housing problem is to secure a dramatic advance in economic conditions and enhancement of real incomes. In reality, however, it is not likely that the people of the Region would experience a neat sequential process of achieving increased economic performance and increased incomes followed by improved housing supply and acquisition. In the real world, the two things would proceed hand in hand, each mutually reinforcing the other. In any case, even if it were possible to have a neat sequential process it would still be important to urgently define and implement initiatives that could start the process of responding to the critical challenges in housing.

Housing by Self-Help

In this connection, various ideas have been explored within the Region in recent years, and some basic ideas suggest themselves. One such is that if Governments are going to have a reduced capacity to undertake housing development for the sections of the population that usually get this assistance, and if housing is becoming less affordable for increasing numbers of families, then specific action should be pursued to help equip increasingly larger numbers of people with the skills to build their own housing. This combined with the provision of access to land, which in many cases is still within the capacity of a number of Governments, and with the home builder's own effort at securing building materials, would in time provide some relief from the pressure on the housing situation in the Region.

Accordingly, the Governments and people of the Region should pursue a policy of ensuring that every child should leave school, whether at primary or secondary level, equipped with the basic skills and knowledge to engage in self-provision of housing. In terms of integration, this means the incorporation of this dimension in regional cooperation on curriculum development for the primary and secondary level. But, outside of schools, there are also groups of people in countries around the Region who we believe would readily make themselves available for training in this regard. These include women's groups who have been or could be organised for the purpose, and young people in rural areas who would like to make an effort to live and work outside the urban centres. There have been some actual initial experiences in the Region along these lines, mainly NGO-initiated, with one of the more notable being the Women's Construction Collective in Jamaica, which has trained some 200 women in basic construction since 1983. An effort should be made to identify, document, and disseminate these experiences around the Region so that successful innovations pioneered in one part of the Region could be made to benefit other parts of the Region.

It is also necessary to bring more focussed attention to bear on the identification of materials and on development of designs for economical construction of basic housing and to translate this into action for better housing provision. This should be a challenge for the Region's tertiary institutions.

Incentives

Critically, the issue of financial facilitation of housing acquisition by the people of the Region looms large. There are, indeed, positive schemes in operation around the Region, both in the public sector and within the NGO or cooperatives community.

The National Housing Trust of Jamaica and the Sou-Sou land project of Trinidad and Tobago are examples of such schemes. But they are inadequate to meet the needs. Governments need to review their fiscal policies with the conscious objective of providing the maximum possible encouragement to home acquisition, especially by young families, and to bring renewed efforts to bear on getting an increased flow of international concessionary financing into the housing sector. Here regional Governments, adopting the model of the CARICOM/PAHO Caribbean Cooperation in Health Initiative, should consider launching a joint demarche on appropriate sections of the international community to pursue this objective.

The housing crisis is so real and has so direct a bearing on social and economic stability in the Region that we believe a case exists for special incentives for enterprise that facilitates an effective response to these needs. Given the factor of benefit to the society as a whole in the provision of low cost housing, it would surely be appropriate for Governments to provide tax incentives, say, over a 10-year period, designed to accelerate private sector activity in home construction and mortgage financing for low cost housing. Fiscal policy should surely seek to direct investment to meeting low income housing needs rather than the construction of shopping malls or other investment opportunities however unobjectionable. If such an emergency programme of tax incentives provides low cost housing on a scale even remotely commensurate with needs, it will be a policy fully justified.

On the other side of the equation there may be room as well for incentives to assist prospective purchasers in acquiring these houses. An example of one such measure would be the possibility of relieving from tax interest on savings that is devoted to purchasing low cost housing. We may need special instruments to implement such a policy; but it is the policy itself that needs to be adopted. The instruments can be cleared once the basic policy of orientation exists. The point we make is that this is a matter of the utmost importance to the stability of CARICOM societies. We know that the Governments are acutely conscious of the level of human need, and of the implications of their remaining unmet. It will help if regionally developed policies provided an overall environment in which decisions can be facilitated at the national level.

Recommendations

Health

1. that CARICOM Governments, working in collaboration with PAHO/WHO, and with regional and national health institutions and NGOs intensify their efforts to pursue strategies that emphasize health promotion and preventative health care;

2. that Governments, in designing structural adjustment programmes, whether in negotiation with the World Bank and the IMF or otherwise, maintain the integrity of primary health care and community health programmes and of facilities and infrastructure that guarantee public health;

3. that Governments and people of the Region pursue more comprehensive and broad-based public health education programmes with greater attention being paid to the communication aspects of public health education and awareness. Member States should exploit the potential that exists for regional coordination of the content and preparation of materials for public health education. Curriculum development should incorporate public health education firmly in primary and secondary schools;

4. that CARICOM Governments undertake an early in-depth examination of the scope for creating common services for selected aspects of the health sector. Active steps should be taken to implement regionalisation where this is shown to be feasible;

5. that the studies and discussions which have been taking place within CARICOM on health manpower issues be given more focus and direction, leading to the design and implementation of complementary national and regional strategies to achieve the right mix of health service personnel appropriate to the emphasis on health promotion, preventative health care, and for advancing the local health systems concept;

6. that CARICOM Governments, and the relevant professional bodies concerned, make a special effort to confront and take

new initiatives in solving the extraoardinarily difficult and important issue of how best to train, and retain, doctors and nurses in our open society;

Housing

7. that Regional Governments and the NGO community promote strategies to equip large numbers of people in the Region to engage in self-provision of housing;

8. that regional programmes be devised under which innovative approaches to housing provision could be identified, documented and disseminated within the Community;

9. that school curricula incorporating the basics of home construction and modules for imparting construction skills to community groups be developed;

10. that a regional programme be designed and established under which suitable experts from within and without the Community would be brought together to pursue research to identify low cost materials for basic housing and to develop model designs for constructing such units in the most economical manner;

11. that special emergency programmes of tax incentives for prospective house-owners, and for private sector enterprises, be introduced to accelerate the financing and provision of low-cost housing.

4. THE CONCERNS OF YOUTH

Many of the concerns facing youth at this juncture of Caribbean development reflect the social problems and issues confronting the wider society. Youth, after all, represents a social group within the wider societal structure and as such are impacted on by those issues which confront the society as a whole. Nevertheless, because of their specific location within the social structure, youth experience of social problems will not necessarily be identical to that of other social groups and hence attempts at problem resolution must reflect this reality. We here briefly present a synoptic examination of the concerns of Caribbean youth. While acknowledging the society-wide nature of most of the issues raised here, we attempt an assessment of these concerns with respect to the particular social location of youth.

The concerns of youth which have been identified for discussion here are not necessarily reflective of a representation among young people in statistical terms, but rather in terms of the seriousness of their implications for the under-realisation of the potential of the youth involved, and hence of Caribbean societies at large — so that, while Caribbean youth involved in crime and drugs or infected with AIDS remain a minority, it is the the resources which must be diverted for their treatment and the loss of their creative potential and energies which make this minority national, and indeed regional, concerns.

Health

A most serious health issue facing contemporary Caribbean youth is identical to that facing the general population of the Region — AIDS. Young people who traditionally have been untroubled by any sense of their own mortality are now faced with a disease which has effectively shattered that illusion. The regional statistics on AIDS indicate young people as the main victims. Furthermore, given the relatively long incubation period for the virus, an even larger proportion of AIDS victims would have contracted the virus as young people.

The concerns surrounding AIDS obviously extend beyond issues of morbidity and mortality and this is particularly so for youth. The predominant mode of transmission in the Region — sexual intercourse — and the consequent exhortations to mutually faithfully monogamy as a mode of prevention have important psycho-sexual and social implications for youth in the socio-cultural context of the Caribbean. Such exhortations strike at the very heart of the processes of experimentation and discovery which are critical to the period of youth as learning to be adult.

Furthermore, given the relatively early initiation to sexual activity in the Region, and the generalised pattern of family life-cycle in the Caribbean from visiting relationship, to common-law union, to marital union, the social implications of AIDS in terms of the patterning of conjugal relationships are obvious. Caribbean people typically enter a number of sexual relationships in the course of their movement through the family life-cycle, and the stark option which now looms before Caribbean youth is immediate sexual behaviour modification or serious risk of mortality by AIDS.

The prospect of an extended period of illness characterised by dependence on others and loss of control over bodily functions and from which there is (currently) no hope of recovery is antithetical to the very nature of youth. The socio-psychological consequences of this prospect for Caribbean youth is exacerbated by a number of factors such as the small size and hence "face-to-face" nature of social life in the Caribbean, and the inaccessibility of adequate care due to poverty at the individual and national levels.

Labour Market/Education

A wide range of socio-economic concerns of Caribbean youth devolve on their inferior and deteriorating labour market status. Probably the most effective predictor of the unemployed person in the Caribbean is that he or she will be young. Unemployment rates among Caribbean youth are typically double or even triple the national rates, and higher still among some categories such as females.

Today's Caribbean youth are the unfortunate victims of a credentials-inflation spiral which consistently increases the qualification for employment. Whether this is explained at the theoretical level as a means of rationing jobs among increasing numbers of the labour force, or as a response to expanded educational opportunity means little to the young person who faces the prospect of up to a decade of unemployment and under-employment on leaving school.

Furthermore, youth articulation of this problem suggests an even more sinister expression of credentials-inflation — the experience requirement which is tagged to so many employment opportunities for which they otherwise qualify. From the perspective of youth, this amounts *de facto* to age-discrimination since a young person, technically qualified and seeking his first job cannot, by definition, have five years' working experience.

This concern is also replicated at the national level: one of the most pernicious consequences of stagnant Caribbean economies is the trend towards a growing gap between an increasingly well-educated labour force — particularly youth — and the number of job openings which can utilise its skills and qualifications. Many of the concerns being raised by Caribbean youth, therefore, derive from the frustration, alienation and marginalisation resulting from the disparity between educational attainment and appropriate job content. These expressions of discontent are only the harbingers of the potential for social disruption carried in this expectations gap.

Yet even in the face of educational expansion, inequality of educational opportunity and access to education remain major concerns of Caribbean youth. This was, in fact, the most consistent theme expressed by youth delegates at the UNICEF-sponsored Caribbean Summit for Children held in Barbados on November 15th, 1991. This forum which represents the clearest recent expression of the concerns of Caribbean youth raised such issues as the lack of access to secondary and tertiary education, the education of the handicapped, and the impact of the economic crisis on education such as the absenteeism of students and the emigration of teachers. Perhaps no concern was more forcibly expressed at the summit than the consensus that any action by Caribbean Governments which either directly or indirectly reduced access to tertiary education would constitute a retrogressive step. A number of students at all three campuses of the University of the West Indies have already indicated that any requirement of payment of a proportion of the economic cost of their education would effectively mean the end of University education for them, but this matter is increasingly a matter of debate, including among students themselves.

Another aspect of this multifaceted issue relates to the development of entrepreneurial talent in the Region. Doubtlessly many Caribbean youth have creative ideas for entrepreneurial activity. Unfortunately they suffer many of the same disabilities which have affected larger socio-economic and ethnic groups in the historical development of Caribbean society: they lack capitalisation, network support and training which are all critical for any successful commercial endeavour. Undercapitalised, untrained, yet determined in their pursuit of self-employment rather than "working for somebody", many such youths have become marginalised in informal sector activities. The fact that there is no significant structural integration of the informal sector with mainstream economic activity in the Caribbean means that such marginalisation represents — at the national level — a loss of precisely the talents which may be necessary to stimulate economic activity, and at the youth level, a future with little promise of realising the dream of creative self-actualisation.

Caribbean youth are concerned about the state of the regional economies. They are fully aware that the current economic difficulties will be translated into reduced opportunities for them in a wide range of social activity. They have also been affected by the sense of powerlessness which has gripped large sections of the Region's population. The Region's youth already stand to inherit per capita national debts which are among the highest in the world. Even if this is not currently being articulated as a concern, it certainly exists as one.

Housing

Access to housing represents another serious concern of Caribbean youth, particularly those in their late teens and early twenties. The increasing desire for autonomy and independence from parental authority and control has manifested itself in an earlier separation from family of origin and the consequent increased demand for housing. Here again, however, the socio-economic disabilities of youth make the realisation of this demand for housing problematic. The implications of inflationary housing and land costs, and rising mortgage rates, for young aspiring home-owners are obvious. Just as they did at the beginning of this century, squatting, slum-dwelling and inadequate shelter still face Caribbean people at the end of the century. Many of these are young people whose continued residence with their family of origin is too fraught with conflict and whose access to adequate housing is restricted by their depressed socio-economic status.

Illegal Drugs

Perhaps nowhere is the coincidence of national and youth concerns more clearly evident than with respect to the problems of crime — including drug trafficking and abuse, with which we have dealt at length earlier in this Chapter. According to available statistics the most typical criminal offender is the young, working-class male. A large proportion of victims of crime are also young — especially in certain categories of crime such as assault, wounding, and sexual offences. Violent criminal activity is nevertheless still a behaviour restricted to a minority of youth, and as such, represents a general concern of youth in the Caribbean. Caribbean societies like most other parts of the world have become more violent societies: today's young person is more likely to be attacked, robbed, sexually assaulted or murdered than his parents were at his age.

Paralleling, and perhaps even a causative factor in increasing violent crime, is increasing drug abuse. In their call for a safe and stable environment in which to grow and develop, delegates at the Caribbean Summit for Children identified crime and drugs as two factors which threaten such an environment. Young people constitute such a large proportion of drug users that any attempt to tackle the problem of drugs must focus on youth as a social group. Regional Governments are all too well aware of the losses (in potential) and the costs (in rehabilitation and treatment) of drug addicts. The relationship between drug use and certain types of criminal activity has also been identified by regional law-enforcement agencies.

Despite this awareness, these problems remain, seemingly intractable and impervious to efforts at their resolution. Many young people have said that the regional anti-drug campaigns have not been speaking to them or speaking their language. Perhaps a closer examination of the social environment of, and motivation for drug usage will go some way towards remedying the shortcomings. In the meantime, young people, despite their knowledge of the dangers and risks involved, continue to predominate in the abuse of illegal drugs.

Recreation

This introduces another concern of Caribbean youth. For while they are often directed to engage in creative recreational and leisure activity as a counter to antisocial activity such as crime and drug usage, Caribbean youth frequently find stumbling blocks in this regard. For instance, in relation to sporting activity, the prohibitive costs involved have prompted youth agencies and national sporting associations to lobby regional Governments for the removal or reduction of duties on a range of sporting equipment. Similar calls have been issued in relation to the provision of recreational facilities, sporting infrastructure, meeting places for youth groups, technical and logistical assistance with youth projects, etc. Many such requests are stymied by governmental financial incapacity. However, youth are legitimately concerned that the economistic orientation to development which seems to be a feature of regional Governments prevent their identification of such programmes as productive.

Many youth are therefore, disappointed over the apparent disjunction between, on the one hand, the rhetoric of political campaigning, manifestos and even national development plans and, the actions of regional Governments on the other. Recent events in electoral politics in the Caribbean have suggested strong feelings of political apathy, alienation, and disaffection among youth. To the extent that this is so, it seems likely that at least part of the explanation lies in the rhetoric/action disjunction of regional political directorates.

Powerlessness

A number of other, less tangible, concerns of youth relate to their position in the social structure and specifically to the wish of the young to secure the position and consideration in society to which they consider themselves entitled. This is observable throughout the range of social institutions in which youth interact — particularly those designed for young people but generally run by adults. This demand is often blocked by the adult world's tendency to consider that the young are not yet full members of society and cannot, before being admitted as such, claim to exercise many rights that are directly or indirectly denied them.

Yet herein lies the contradiction, for none of this prevents society from exacting contribution from youth when it is deemed appropriate. Youth generally have no power in the process of definition of norms and values which are used to guide social behaviour. Nor are they included in the process of judging or evaluating their behaviour. From the perspective of youth, it therefore appears unreasonable for shifting criteria to be employed in such judgement: for them to be required to undertake all the responsibilities associated with the rôle of a full member of their society without the simultaneous enjoyment of the rights which go with that rôle.

Many Caribbean youth therefore, feel powerless in a world dominated by adults in which they are not listened to and over which they have no control. They feel alienated from the normative patterns which are supposed to guide their behaviour and on the basis of which they are judged. Their call for a greater say in the decision-making process, especially as it relates to issues impacting directly on them, is one echoed by youth internationally. It is perhaps time that we went a step beyond platitudinous statements to the effect that youth represent the future of the Caribbean and let them do so.

Youth's Responsibilities, Society's Expectations

The fact that no human or civil rights exist without concomitant responsibilities is as true of youth as of any other social group. Caribbean youth in the 1990s must know that they have inherited a legacy, hewn out of the social history of these small societies through generations of struggle, sacrifice and commitment. It is still within the living experience of Caribbean people that life expectancy stood below 50 years at birth; that wage levels were generally below subsistence; that secondary, much less tertiary, education was accessible only to a narrow elite; that trade unions, political parties and other social institutions concerned with the preservation and improvement of the quality of life of Caribbean people were non-existent; that right to self-determination did not even exist as an ideal much less as a fundamental assertion of Caribbean people.

One of the foremost responsibilities of Caribbean youth then is to defend this legacy which they have inherited and, perhaps as importantly, to help to restructure the underlying social, economic and political institutions to respond to the needs of Caribbean society and Caribbean people in the world of the 21st century. The suggestion here is far from being a mere idealistic abstraction divorced from reality. For example, the demands on trade unions and political parties in contemporary Caribbean society are much different from those of a generation ago. Our youth, as significant (and eventually major) proportions of the electorate and the labour force, must ensure that these institutions respond to the challenges which now face the Caribbean. Young people, unfettered by the inertia and nostalgic romanticism of tradition, imbued with the energy and zest for change, and educated as to the critical role of such institutions, represent, perhaps, the only force for ensuring the continuing relevance of this legacy.

Just as Caribbean youth have a right to education, health and employment, they simultaneously have the responsibility to ensure that these rights are transformed into enhanced human resource capacity of which youth are a major constituent and reservoir. Ironically, the Caribbean, as a relatively poor Region, continues to subsidise the human resource development of nations already well endowed as thousands of healthy, skilled and educated Caribbean youth emigrate each year just at the point where the investment in their education and training is at the point of generating productive returns.

Caribbean societies reasonably expect a greater degree of commitment to regional development from its skilled youth, and they, in turn, have a responsibility to realise and honour that commitment. Of course, this is by no means a simple matter given the narrower scope for personal advancement in the Region, but even so in the modern world of technological innovation and information distribution there are a number of circumstances in which the physical location of Caribbean experts here is not necessary. What is necessary is a Caribbean agenda and commitment. For, after all, a number of the "experts" who now sell their services across the Region do so from their offices in North America and Europe and at no less prohibitive cost for their physical absence.

So that to say that the youth are the future of the Caribbean is an assertion which goes beyond the clichéd expression. For the Caribbean is, in developmental terms, much like the youth which is the focus of this paper: from a history of intense colonialism, most Caribbean societies are now in their second or third decade of independence. Despite their relatively small size and youth they have demonstrated their legitimacy as nation-states. Yet very serious challenges lie ahead in a global political economy of increasing polarisation and the accompanying marginalisation of the small and weak. However, the Caribbean from its genesis to its contemporary state has historically been confronted by challenges, some perhaps more daunting than those which it now faces. Herein lies the Region's expectations of its youth — that they will exhibit the response to these challenges which Caribbean people have traditionally demonstrated and which have brought us here.

Recommendations

1. that there should be a reorientation of programmes in educational and training institutions to include:

    - emphasis on problem-solving rather than on passive fact acquisition;
    - a wider infusion of practical and creative skills in the interest of self-employment and entrepreneurship;
    - consonance of curricula with economic trends and potentials;
    - realistic work experiences through attachments and voluntary national schemes where feasible;
    - avoidance of symbols, images, and ideas which inculcate gender, ethnic and other negative social biases; and promotion of positive values which underpin equality and mutual esteem among social groups
    - regional self-understanding through Caribbean studies;
    - issues relating to sexuality, family life and civic awareness; a system of youth exchange within the community established under combined sponsorship of private sector and organisations such as service clubs in the Region, with appropriate support from regional Governments;

2. that Youth Work Centres be established where youths can develop and invest their skills gainfully;

3. that Governments seek to promote the development of sports and recreation by:

    - assisting communities to establish sporting facilities;
    - making sports an integral part of the programme of primary and secondary education;
    - facilitating the acquisition of sports equipment by reducing or abolishing duties;

- requiring private housing construction firms to provide recreational areas in residential housing projects;
- providing organisational assistance for community efforts in popular theatre and similar artistic and cultural endeavours.

4. that National Youth Councils be set up throughout the Region to operate as independent and autonomous institutions; and that their deliberations and views be given serious consideration by Governments in the formulation of policy affecting youth national concerns in general;

5. that public figures in the Region increasingly see themselves as role models, avoiding double standards in personal and public behaviour;

6. that parents accept and discharge their basic responsibilities in the upbringing of children and in the inculcation of values and standards;

7. that immediate attention be given to statutory reform, especially with respect to domestic violence, including incest and sexual abuse of children as well as to the incidence of rape in all forms.

CHAPTER X

SPECIAL ISSUES

1. OUR ORIGINAL PEOPLES

Memory

In the year of the quincentenary of Columbus's first landfall in the hemisphere — from which such disastrous consequences for the inhabitants were to flow — it would be strange if any West Indian report failed to give special attention to the status and needs of the descendants of the original peoples of the Region. The West Indian Commission has never been in doubt that we should give careful consideration to the present situation of our aboriginal peoples and their future involvement in a stronger Community. We have been moved and stimulated by our meetings with them throughout the Region.

We state at once that we feel no quincentenary fervour. Far from it. That first landfall turned into a veritable holocaust for the original inhabitants of the Region. For their descendants we express at this time a special and solemn fellow-feeling. Let the words of the Dominican friar Antonio de Montesinos, in a sermon preached in Santo Domingo on the last Sunday of Advent, 1511, speak for us all:

> Tell me, by what right or justice do you hold these Indians in such a cruel and horrible servitude? On what authority have you waged such detestable wars against these peoples, who dwelt quietly and peacefully on their own land? Wars in which you have destroyed such infinite numbers of them by homicides and slaughters never before heard of? Why do you keep them so oppressed and exhausted, without giving them enough to eat or curing them of the sickness they incur from the excessive labour you give them? And they die, or rather, you kill them, in order to extract and acquire gold every day.

If part of our mandate were to recommend an appropriate acknowledgement of the quincentenary we would unhesitatingly echo the suggestion made by the Dominican economist and historian Bernardo Vega. We would advise that 1992 should be made memorable by Europe excusing all debt accumulated by the countries in the Caribbean and Latin America as partial compensation for the wealth extracted from the Region, starting in 1492. And yet this would be an infinitesimal atonement in the scale of historical justice. Nothing can compensate for the blood and the lost spirit of a people. The conquests and dispossession that brutally marked the period after 1492 saw the depletion of populations to the point of genocide through oppression and Old World disease, the deracination of a long established way of life over a great region of the earth, the sudden near extinction of cultures and civilisations which held their own worth and were nurtured into being through centuries of adaptation and creativity.

The world is becoming increasingly sensitive to the violation of human rights. Inevitably this changes how history is read: mankind now senses that first landfall as a tragedy in the making and sees the conquest that followed through the eyes of Las Casas rather than the conquistadores. As we confront, as best we can, the wrongs of the present, we know that nothing can be done to atone for these evils of the past. But we can bear the ancestral wound in all our memories. Greater in proportion now than their numbers must be the extent of our respect and concern for the future of our aboriginal peoples. It is the least we can offer as we discuss the place of the original peoples of the West Indies and consider their relations with the larger society in which we all now live.

Presence and Condition

There are communities of aboriginal peoples in five CARICOM countries — Belize, Dominica, Guyana, St. Vincent and the Grenadines and Trinidad and Tobago, as shown in the following table:

Approximate Number of Aboriginal Peoples

Country	Population	Aboriginal Population	Settlement Pattern	Numbers
Belize				
1980	146,000	Garifuna	85% urban,	12,000
		Maya Mopan	15% rural	10,000
		Maya Kekchi	10 villages	4,000
Dominica				
1981	73,795	Caribs	26 villages	3,000
Guyana				
1986	756,000	Caribs, Warau Arawak Akawaio, Arekuna, Patamona,	rural	20,000
		Macusi, Wapishana, Wai-Wai	rural	21,000
St. Vincent and the Grenadines				
1990	113,000	Caribs	rural	6,000
Trinidad and Tobago				
1990	1,234,000	Caribs	urban	400
Total				76,400

The island aboriginals intermixed with the incoming populations much more than the aboriginal peoples did in Guyana and Belize. The islanders were the first to succumb to the ravages of European contact and their survival has resulted from their extensive intermixture with Europeans and Africans over a long period; this is perhaps the most important distinction between the island and mainland aboriginal peoples in CARICOM.

But the aboriginal peoples in all the countries naturally have distinctive features of their own — in terms of origin, historical development, economic and social progress, contemporary living conditions, and present status in relation to the larger communities in which they live. We will do no more here than take a glimpse at the aboriginal communities as they have come to take their place in our larger Community.

Special Issues

Trinidad and Tobago

In Trinidad and Tobago the original peoples suffered the classic fate of those subjugated by the Spanish. Today their descendants are located mainly in Arima where they reflect the crucial role Spanish society and the Church played in who they have become. The Spanish mixture is noticeable in their surnames and physical features. Their succession of titular leaders, styled "Carib Queen," has played a vital role in representing the community and ensuring that traditional skills and knowledge are passed on from generation to generation.

In 1990 the Government proclaimed the Santa Rosa Carib community as representative of the Republic's indigenous Amerindians, agreed to make an annual subvention of $30,000, and assigned an Amerindian Project Committee to assist in its development programme. There is, however, no statutory structure of local government for these aboriginal people. Nor have they been given land as a Community. The Santa Rosa inhabitants insist that both the Government and Church have not returned to them land that is rightfully theirs. They have a standing request that 30 acres be restored to them for agriculture.

Dominica

Aboriginals in Dominica maintained their territory against European take-over for a long time. Eventually, in the Treaty of Paris in 1763, the Island was "allocated" to Britain. Before that, however, the aboriginals there had gone a long way in intermarrying with both French and British settlers and also with Africans who, taking advantage of the autonomous state of the island, fled there in large numbers. The descendants of the aboriginals had a long record of resistance to subjugation and clashed violently with the British, even after their final acquisition of the Island in 1763. By about 1800, however, the aboriginal people of Dominica had been put down, with rebellious elements shipped to Central America. The remaining aboriginals were given a land grant of 232 acres. This was extended to 3,700 acres in 1903.

Today in Dominica, 3,000 aboriginals are concentrated in the land which they call Carib Territory. Through good use of the land they have done as well as, or better than, other Dominican farmers. NGOs have assisted greatly in several development projects and the Government has provided paved roads, electricity and telephones.

At the level of local Government, the Dominican aboriginals have their Carib Council, which is basically a Village Council, but one which has more power than the other 32 Councils in the country.

In Dominica, the Carib Reserve Act of 1978 vests ownership to the 3,700 acre reserve in the Carib Council. The law states that no part of this land can be alienated without the Government's approval.

St. Vincent and the Grenadines

The aboriginals of St. Vincent, as in Dominica, fought hard to protect their territory and autonomy and their history closely follows that of the Dominican aboriginals up to the end of the eighteenth Century. In the case of St. Vincent, more African slaves fled to freedom there. They mixed with aboriginal women and adopted their language and culture; these were the progenitors of the Black Carib (or Garifuna) nation who clashed repeatedly with the British between 1769 and 1797. St. Vincent, like Dominica, had been ceded to Britain in 1763 and by 1800 the aboriginals there, as in Dominica, had either been shipped out to Central America or put down. The St. Vincent aboriginals, the Black Caribs, received 230 acres of land in the area of Morne Ronde in 1805.

Today, the St. Vincent aboriginals number about 6,000 living in six villages. There is uncertainty about the status of the 230 acres land grant extended by the British to the Black Caribs in the area of Rose Bank. Although there are more of their people living in the Sandy Bay area, these people have no land reservation, despite folk beliefs to the contrary. The same applies to the area adjoining Greggs. A potential increase to the limited lands in the Sandy Bay area from the government repossession of the adjoining Orange Hill Estate has not taken place; the aboriginal residents complain that the payment demanded is too high.

Belize

The Garifuna, Maya Kekchi, and Maya Mopan are the main aboriginal nations of Belize. There is a third nation of Maya called Yucatec who, fifty years ago, surpassed the other Maya in numbers. However, they have undergone extreme acculturation, their language hardly survives in Belize, and there is no movement to revitalise their presence.

The Garifuna, the hybrid progeny of maroon African slaves and island Caribs, coalesced into nationhood over 200 years from the early 1600s. Since the 1940s the Garifuna in Belize have migrated in large numbers and currently there are far more of them in the towns than in their traditional villages — and there are probably as many in US cities as in Belize. The villages they have left are depopulated and grossly underdeveloped. Wherever they have gone, the Garifuna have taken their cultural vitality. In the last decade their music has dominated popular dancing along the Atlantic coast of Central America from Belize to Nicaragua.

Unlike the Garifuna who originated partly in the Amazonian Forest tradition, the Maya are part of the Meso-American cultural tradition. They predominate in villages in southern Belize. They share many characteristics, but differ in language and their places of origin in Guatemala. However, they live in the same and adjoining villages. As a result many are bilingual and share close family ties.

The Maya are successful farmers. For years they have sold beans, pork, plantains and root crops widely and now produce half the rice the country consumes. However, the Mayan rice farmer is made to subsidise the urban consumer through government control of pricing and therefore remains on the borderline of poverty. It is not surprising that aboriginals — also suffering reduced social services as budgets are slashed in hard economic times — seek other forms of livelihood in urban areas, and even less surprising that their children see no future in what their parents do.

In regard to local government, there is the alcalde system whereby villages of aboriginals elect the headman and his assistants every two years. In regard to land rights, the Government allocated reservations to some older villages, but not to the tens of new ones forming along the Southern Highway to whom lease lands are made available. To the requests of the Toledo Maya Council that the Maya be given a 500,000 acre block as their homeland, the Government responded by suggesting the Council conduct a public referendum. The Council, faced with a split in opinion on the subject among the Maya themselves, has not done so. Meanwhile, the Government is offering plots of land to those aboriginals who want help to become more intensive farmers.

Guyana

The relatively high level of participation by Belize aboriginals in the mainstream of national life is not duplicated in Guyana. Guyana is a country with two societies, one coastal, where 90 per cent of the population live, and the other hinterland, where the inhabitants are mainly aboriginals. The hinterland, thus far, is undeveloped, lacks roads and public utilities, and is dependent on the coast for goods, including food and medicines. Currently the exploitation of the hinterland is being greatly hastened. It is a most appropriate time to re-evaluate the participation of the original inhabitants in this important national development.

Currently Guyana's aboriginal population probably numbers 40-45,000, in nine "nations" located in 90 settlements. It is impossible to be definitive, since these peoples remain migratory within the Guyanese hinterland and to and fro across national borders. Population changes may also have been affected by measles and malaria epidemics in recent years, the incursions of coastlanders and foreign mining companies on traditional aboriginal lands, and the steady out-migration of the young and able-bodied to explore job prospects far afield.

All share pursuits in common — agriculture, fishing, hunting, knowledge of the forest — but there are also differences — in farming patterns, the construction of houses, belief systems, body adornments. And a principal difference between these peoples is language difference. Each of the "nations" traditionally spoke its own language. Because of the longer European domination, those nearer to the coast — Arawak, Carib, Warau — have almost completely lost their language in favour of the Guyanese English vernacular. Although others still speak their languages, the task of encouraging facility in the original language is an immense one among all the nations.

In regard to local government, the structure in Guyana takes the form of a pyramid, starting at the bottom with the Village Council headed by the Captain and proceeding to the Regional Democratic Council, the supreme administrative institution for the ten regions.

Regarding aboriginal land rights in Guyana, a guide was laid down by the Amerindian Lands Commission of 1969. The procedure and recommendations of this Commission are a model other countries should study and emulate as far as possible. Aboriginal peoples not living in their home settlements were to be given titles wherever they were by a relevant date. "Amerindians who on the relevant date were lease holders of home lands should be given freehold titles for areas held under lease up to a maximum of 30 acres". Freehold titles should be given to Captains on behalf of Village Councils, stressing collective ownership; and allotments should fall around existing settlements "with an adequate allowance for population expansion, natural boundaries being used as much as possible".

This is a matter of sacred concern to the aboriginal peoples. All titles should be handed over immediately where delivery is still in default. Aboriginal people in Guyana are also demanding that they be given access to minerals below the surface in their land areas.

In recent times, the future of the physical environment — which not only sustains aboriginals in Guyana materially, but also provides the basis of their society, culture, and spirituality — has come under increasing threat. Much increased development, and a greater opening up of the hinterland, are immediately in prospect. As night follows day, environmental degradation — extensive felling of trees without reforestation, poisoning of rivers, soil stripping as part of mining — will follow. In dealing with this threat it is of the utmost importance that the aboriginal peoples — given their intimate local knowledge, their millennia of co-existence with the environment and their absolutely fundamental interest in the outcome — should be fully consulted and involved in the planning to be done and the decisions to be taken.

This limited survey represents no more than a superficial glimpse of the aboriginal peoples of the Community. Indeed, the knowledge which we currently posses about the aboriginal presence in the West Indian Member States forms an insufficient basis for proper planning and wise decisions regarding their future. There is a serious lack of basic data about our aboriginal peoples — their history, mores, sense of identity, economic conditions, social milieux, culture, myths and the nature of the pressures from the outside world. This lack needs to be remedied urgently.

The quincentenary year is an appropriate occasion for embarking on a major, multi-disciplinary study of aboriginal peoples in CARICOM. Such a study, with the goals of establishing the objective conditions of our aboriginal peoples, would be of inestimable value in assessing their needs and measuring the impact of decisions affecting their future. Development practitioners, social scientists, government officials in the field, interested NGOs, and international funding agencies would all benefit greatly from the results of such a study. The basis would be provided to permit effective planning, efficient and relevant delivery of services and assistance, and the establishment of the best possible means for the productive co-existence of our aboriginal peoples with others within our, and their, Community.

Such a study — employing the full array of modern techniques of research and assessment — would be a worthy task to undertake on the threshold of the twenty-first Century. As far as possible, also, the basic data should be gathered and the study assembled out of the work of local aboriginal peoples so that they become active participants in the project and not, as is too frequently the case, mere objects of scientific research.

The detailed information and more accurate and scholarly understanding arising from such a survey or surveys would form a solid basis for assisting aboriginal peoples in the Region to define precisely their own identity and status and pursue goals they themselves conceive as valid within the larger Community.

Pending the development of policies based on the results of the detailed survey which we are proposing, the outline of some principal objectives in which the aboriginal peoples of the Region hold a vital interest can readily be described and action taken to help fulfil them while the collection of more detailed data is proceeding.

An Identity to Protect

The distinctiveness of aboriginal peoples is prescribed in ILO Convention 169 of 1989 and it must be a prime objective of policy to fulfil this prescription. In so far as current policies seek assimilation, this runs contrary to the concern of aboriginal peoples to preserve their culture and is in contravention of the international consensus written into ILO Convention 169. Even enlightened administrative measures are good only in so far as they are cast within a policy designed around the initiatives of aboriginal peoples themselves to improve the quality of their lives.

In the case of aboriginal peoples in the Community, it is impossible to pinpoint identification criteria — cultural analysis, written or folk history, location of first origin, legal distinction — which apply across the board. The basic criterion must, therefore, be self-identification as prescribed in the ILO Convention. This, however, holds its own difficulties since many who possess aboriginal characteristics prefer to deny them because of the low rank associated with aboriginal peoples. If our society undervalues the status of aboriginal peoples, there is little incentive to ascribe oneself an aboriginal, however unmistakable one's characteristics and cultural background. It must be one of our aims so to foster a sense of self-worth in our original peoples that of their own volition they take care to protect and promote their identity as a people. Certainly, the fact that aboriginal peoples have undergone transformations since the European arrival does not detract from their capability to identify as a people. Like all Caribbean people, they have undergone a creolisation process but their self-identity, with biological and cultural roots predating Columbus, cannot be denied.

In fostering a sense of identity and self-worth there is, of course, much on which to build. St. Vincentian Caribs cherish their collective memory of defending the fatherland against the British. A centuries-old community solidarity is a source of unique Carib identity in Arima in Trinidad. In Dominica, aboriginal solidarity is bolstered by the collective ownership of 3,700 acres of land in their own right. In the wider spaces and forests of Belize, and especially Guyana, the cultural distinctiveness of the aboriginal nations confer clear and increasingly respected reference points in society at large. However, the relentless pressures of the larger societies within which aboriginals function, the social values which aboriginals have often come to share in those societies, and the miscegenation which continues to take place despite a frequently expressed preference for purity of descent, over time have tended to erode aboriginal self-confidence in their original and continuing distinctiveness.

Within this difficult context, with their identity in many respects under seige, the quest of our aboriginal peoples to conserve and retrieve their distinctive nationhood and sense of self-value within our larger Community must be the quest of us all. Within the major quincentenary study there needs to be a specially focussed project to establish the roots and substance of aboriginal identity in their communities. Such a project would employ a wide array of social science methods and disciplines — the compilation of oral histories, a detailed study of myths and folklore, linguistic studies, archaeological work and analysis are some of the fields in which we have only touched the surface in the search to authenticate and validate the aboriginal presence in our Community. As in the major study it is essential, as far as possible, that aboriginals themselves should participate fully in the work to be done.

One aim of this special project would be to alert aboriginals to the way in which many of the values of the larger communities in which they have their being conflict with their own traditional and cultural values so that they can more precisely judge for themselves their future course. The essence of what is needed is to preserve that precious sense of identity and self-esteem without which the aboriginal peoples cannot make the special contribution which they are perfectly capable of making in a Community in which diversity is recognised, valued, and protected.

An Autonomy to Assist

A deliberate policy of assimilating aboriginal peoples into their larger communities against their will is not acceptable and should not be pursued.

Aboriginals, of course, enjoy full rights as citizens of Member States and may opt if they will, for full participation as they desire in the mainstreams of national life in the Community. However, such individual choice is not incompatible with a general fostering of the substance and spirit of autonomy among the various groups of aboriginals in the Community. Any other approach would lead to further rapid deculturation and would gravely prejudice the future of the original peoples of the place.

In fact, of course, CARICOM Governments have already extended elements of autonomy to aboriginals in local government and in the use of reservations and conferral of land titles. Also, by default, aboriginal peoples have long maintained their subsistence systems with a minimum of outside intervention and thereby have maintained their economic autonomy. There is now the need to formalise the nature and advance the means of establishing and strengthening aboriginal autonomy in their various communities.

Thus, again within the larger quincentenary study, there should be a special project to ascertain, in collaboration with the aboriginal peoples themselves, how they conceive of their future autonomy and how it should be reinforced.

Meanwhile, we propose a programme which involves the following elements:

Governance

As citizens aboriginals have, and use, the vote in their larger communities. But this does not translate into power for them where it matters, and their representation at the highest levels of decision-taking is minimal. This should be addressed. At local government level the situation is better and there are statutory structures for local government among aboriginals in Dominica, Belize and Guyana — though there are criticisms, particularly in Guyana, that the representative bodies serve the interest of only a few and function in accordance with the exercise of government patronage.

Land Rights

To aboriginals, land is not only an age-old domain which should be theirs within definitive borders, it is also their main source of livelihood, it is their ecological niche, it is endowed with spiritual attributes which affect their moral behaviour as a people. Their concerns in respect of land rights should be sympathetically and urgently addressed.

Environment

Assisting the aboriginal peoples to maintain an independent way of life directly involves protecting the environment in which they live, in particular the rainforest which more than anyone they use for daily survival. The views, welfare, and interests of aboriginals should therefore be central to any plans formulated for environmental conservation.

Economy

Our aboriginal peoples inhabit in general the lower levels of poverty. Something can be done about this by recognising their special place in our societies. In Dominica, for instance, where their role and contribution are more clearly articulated (and it should be added, a sufficiency of land reserved) they do as well as, and even better than, other rural dwellers.

In all CARICOM countries where aboriginal peoples live major structural changes are taking place in the economies. In negotiating these changes the aboriginal peoples must be treated with special regard and closely consulted on their role in the strategies to be adopted. The unique contribution they could certainly make in any programme of sustainable development of the environment is an excellent example of how aboriginal peoples could be encouraged to play an active and independent part in national strategies of development.

Education

Amidst the general problems caused by the decline in the delivery of social services, the greatest threat to maintaining the autonomous role and valuable special contribution of aboriginal peoples in the Community is the decline in their own language skills within the general deterioration in educational standards. It must be a matter of special concern that the aboriginals' own languages are preserved as a medium in their education and development in society.

Trans-border Intermediaries

The special role, and needs, of the aboriginal peoples of Belize and Guyana in the border areas of their countries should be recognised. In the much improved relationships that have now developed between Belize and Guatemala and between Guyana and her neighbours the concerns and capacity of the aboriginal people to contribute must be given full weight. Their future is at stake in the increased dialogue and multiplied contacts taking place. Both countries have joined multilateral agreements with their neighbours which will ultimately involve interchange among their aboriginal peoples: Belize is a member of the Mundo Maya agreement including Mexico, Guatemala, Belize, Honduras, and El Salvador; Guyana is a signatory to the Treaty for Amazonian Co-operation along with Bolivia, Brazil, Colombia, Ecuador, Peru, Suriname and Venezuela. In pursuing the objectives of these trans-national pacts, the aboriginal peoples, sharing common traditions and contacts across borders, clearly have a valuable role to play which should not be neglected. There will be new opportunities for aboriginals to impress their special knowledge and make a valuable contribution in these multilateral relationships. Their welfare and rights must also be kept in mind. In this area, more than most, recognising the autonomy and special needs of the aboriginal peoples will make a valuable contribution to larger national policy.

An Inheritance to Preserve

Their unique inheritance must not die. We are privileged that the Community includes these special people, original to the place, to add to our diversity. They must be given space and opportunity to flourish and be proud. The world around us grows crowded and careless of customs, cultures and ceremonies such as theirs. We must resist such carelessness. The processes of modern commerce and industrialisation encroach on and endanger ways of life which hold a value we must not let go.

Lives that have co-existed so intimately with nature for so long express a heritage we simply cannot afford to lose. It is now the way of the world to focus on the threat to environment, to the earth's whole habitat, and we join as we must in the growing effort to confront this threat. But part of that habitat, the great rainforest, under such close scrutiny now, in our case is where an important group of our own people live and find their way of life itself endangered along with the environment whose fate we debate. Within the larger concern, that must be our special concern.

In every aspect of their lives and culture our people original to the place offer special contribution. The ways they use, adapt to, live with, the land, the forest, the rivers, the vegetation, the wild-life are important to preserve. Their houses and constructions, their adornments and furnishings, their implements and river craft and technology, their medicines and recipes, their age-old, intuitive knowledge of the seasons and the heavens and the earth as it turns and nurtures man are all living treasures. Their music and dance and art, their governance of themselves, their myths and legends and folklore, proverbs and story-telling, must not be allowed to fade into dim memories — they must live and be vital for other generations. Their languages, under increasing seige, must not be lost. They have contributed to our common vernacular — think of cassava, maize, hammock, tobacco, canoe, among many — and must not only be retrieved and recorded in permanent form but be given increasing scope to live in the aboriginal peoples' everyday education and lives. In the rainforests, their absolutely intricate identification with a habitat all mankind now knows is vital to the future of the world, is an inestimably valuable source of knowledge we dare not risk losing.

In seeking to preserve all this, the aboriginal people themselves must be the chief actors. Patronising their ways of life, mollycoddling their efforts but seeing in these efforts only a temporary delay in their gradual disappearance or assimilation, would be abhorrent. Aboriginals must secure their own future and what is needed in the larger Community is the imagination to open up the opportunities for them to do so.

It may be that hitherto there has been excessive reliance on non-aboriginal people, including foreigners, as project initiators and implementors. However, there is a record of grassroots movements formed to represent aboriginal interests — in Guyana, for instance, the Amerindian Peoples Association and the Guyana Organisation of Indigenous Peoples; in Belize the Carib Development Society and the National Garifuna Council as examples; in Dominica the Carib Peoples Organisation, the Carib Liberation Organisation, the Carib Independent Organisation and the Dominica Carib Movement among others; and in St. Vincent the Carib Development Organisation and the Community Council for the Development of Caribs — and these organisations can form the basis of strengthening aboriginal efforts to organise and help themselves and also to focus outside help in ways thought most appropriate by aboriginals themselves. Material assistance by itself is certainly not enough. Organisation building, leadership training, the teaching of group co-operation and solidarity are needs on which to concentrate. Weakness in all these areas has meant that only recently, for instance, has it been possible to lay the groundwork for establishing a regional organisation: the Caribbean Organisation of Indigenous Peoples (COIP) was formed with a Secretariat and Co-ordinator based in Belize since 1989. This has already had an impact by holding a regional conference, issuing a newsletter, and maintaining contact with counterpart aboriginal groups all around the world. More of this is to be encouraged with the objective of rapidly changing the parochial perspective that has prevailed too long among aboriginals in the Community.

NGOs have an important role to play in helping aboriginals to help themselves. The NGO focus should be on working not just for, but with, aboriginal groups and not only on short-term, small-scale projects but more on integrated and comprehensive programmes of sustained development and conservation. Indeed, we would recommend that NGOs interested in aboriginals in the Region take advantage of the spirit of 1992 to call a major conference to discuss these issues in detail. This would be a natural follow-up to the Regional NGO Consultation on 1992 Initiatives (Esprit 1991).

Tomorrow

A strong Community will involve, indeed encourage, diversity within an integration which steadily grows deeper. It is in this context that the identity of our original peoples needs to be protected and their autonomy in contributing to overall progress specially assisted. Their power to determine their own cultural development must not be allowed to diminish. The rich, multi-faceted heritage they bring to our Community is an ancient treasure that we should do all in our power to preserve and augment. In the quincentenary of Columbus' landfall — threatening, in its aftermath, the extinction of whole peoples and their cultures — we can appropriately begin to re-focus attention on how best to achieve in the West Indies the survival and success of the descendants of the original peoples of the Region.

Recommendations

1. that this quincentenary year be accepted as an appropriate time for embarking on a major multi-disciplinary study of aboriginal peoples in CARICOM with the overall objective of assessing the needs and measuring the impact of decisions affecting their future;

2. that within this major study, there be specially focussed objectives:
   - to establish the roots and substance of aboriginal identity in their communities;
   - to ascertain how aboriginals themselves conceive of their future autonomy and how it could be reinforced;

3. that in the meanwhile, aboriginal autonomy in the Region be assisted by a programme with the following elements:

   Governance
   - the institution of mechanisms to integrate representation by aboriginal peoples at the highest levels of government decision-taking;
   - countries should review and revitalise their current systems to make them fully responsive in carrying through representative aboriginal programmes;

   Land Rights
   - the historical basis of current aboriginal land rights should be examined and established within the wider quincentenary study in order to shine a clearer light on their status in today's legal systems;
   - aboriginal claims to land titles should be comprehensively and sympathetically reviewed. Existing promises to grant land titles should be honoured expeditiously;

   Environment
   The views, welfare and interest of aboriginals should be central to any plans formulated for environmental conservation;

Special Issues

Economy
Aboriginal peoples should be encouraged to play an active and independent part in national strategies of development;

Education
The aboriginals' own languages should be preserved as a medium in their education and development in society;

Transborder Intermediaries
In pursuing the objectives of the trans-national pacts now emerging, the special rights of aboriginals and the valuable contribution they could make should be fully recognised;

4. that great care be taken to preserve the special inheritance of the aboriginal peoples of the Region. In achieving this, the aboriginal peoples must be encouraged to become the chief actors. To this end their organisation, on a regional basis, should be actively encouraged with a view to changing, as rapidly as possible, parochial perspectives which have hitherto prevailed;

5. that the special role of NGOs in helping aboriginals to help themselves be recognised. Their focus should be on working with, not just for, aboriginals and not only on short-term, small-scale projects, but integrated and comprehensive programmes of sustained development and conservation.

2. CONCERNS ABOUT REMOTENESS

Belize and The Bahamas: Their Special Situation

In the first part of this Report, we noted that at their Second Inter-Sessional Meeting in Port-of-Spain in February 1991, CARICOM Heads of Government, in addressing the concerns of Belize and The Bahamas, regarding a perceived remoteness from the Community,

Concerns about Remoteness

agreed that the West Indian Commission could take the opportunity of specifically addressing that issue. The Commission conducted hearings in Belize and The Bahamas in June 1991, and did indeed find perceptions of remoteness from CARICOM and of CARICOM from them. If this matter is not seriously addressed, it could become a source of great concern in the Community.

Shared Characteristics, Significant Differences

The Bahamas and Belize share many of the social and cultural characteristics of the other West Indian countries. But, in some ways, they are uniquely different. One difference, of course, is in their geographical location at the Northern and Western extremes respectively of the CARICOM Region. This has clearly contributed to the perception of being isolated and remote from the rest of CARICOM. But it is not only distance from other CARICOM countries but proximity to the United States and Central America.

Particularly in the Eastern Caribbean, our territories enjoy a certain mutual closeness in various respects. There are relatively short distances between them, facilitating easy and frequent interchange of their peoples, and it is easy for nationals of one country to be aware of what is happening in a neighbouring country. Travel between the countries is regular and information flows informally and freely between them. Trading practices, both formal and informal, led to contacts on a daily basis, and a shared interest in sports, mainly cricket, produces a similarity in activities in neighbouring countries. For these nationals, there is a sense of belonging to a grouping of people who share a common experience and a similar destiny. And Jamaica, though somewhat further away from the Eastern Caribbean, is closer in many other ways.

There is no similar strong sense of belonging felt by the nationals of The Bahamas and Belize. The distances between these countries and their CARICOM neighbours, compounded by the absence of direct air and sea links, while not great in themselves, are great enough to isolate them from the mainstreams of West Indian life. There is no direct travel between these two countries and their CARICOM neighbours, and the only travel possible is through third countries, principally through Miami. This actually means in practice that Bahamians and Belizeans must receive US permission — and US visas — for them to travel within CARICOM. It is as clear as that.

Information does not flow freely and regularly between The Bahamas, Belize and the remaining CARICOM countries. Most nationals in these two countries are only remotely aware of what is happening in other CARICOM countries. It is not possible in The Bahamas and Belize, as it is in Grenada and Antigua, to use ordinary radio to hear broadcasts from neighbouring countries, and the media in The Bahamas and Belize have shown only a nominal interest in West Indian news. There is very little trade between The Bahamas, Belize and their CARICOM partners, and both countries are only marginally involved in one of the two greatest success stories of the West Indian society, the University of the West Indies and the West Indian cricket team.

Geography

The geographical location of The Bahamas and Belize has inevitably and understandably played a fundamental role in determining the outlook of their people. Because of its location just off the coast of Florida, historical, cultural and commercial ties, the orientation of Bahamians has been towards Florida, rather than to the West Indian countries to the South. Historically, the majority of its inhabitants came to The Bahamas from the Southern states of the United States of America and much later, some of them returned to settle in southern Florida. The development of tourism strengthened the links between Southern Florida and The Bahamas, since most tourists came to The Bahamas by way of Florida and most of the actual trade of The Bahamas was between The Bahamas and Florida. Florida media, particularly the electronic media, are more accessible to Bahamians than the national media, and American sports — basketball, football and baseball — are more important to Bahamians than cricket.

For much of its history, Bahamians were officially encouraged to see Florida as more of a natural partner than the West Indian countries to the South. It was argued that while Bahamians shared a common colonial experience with the other West Indian countries, they had more in common with Florida, and that the future of The

Concerns about Remoteness

Bahamas was linked to the development of Florida. It was probably considerations like these, which led The Bahamas to join the Caribbean Community, to continue to share in its experiences, but not to join the Common Market, so as not to disrupt its trading relations with Florida. It was argued then, and still is, that The Bahamas has little to gain by developing trading links with its CARICOM partners, and therefore there is little to gain by joining the Common Market.

The resulting ambivalence of The Bahamas towards CARICOM has contributed significantly towards the feeling of remoteness. The average Bahamian has the same feeling of kinship, though not as strong as is felt in Barbados or Jamaica, towards other West Indians, but he is deprived of the basic information which would allow the feeling of kinship to strengthen. It has never been explained to the Bahamian people why a particular type of relationship with CARICOM was chosen, or why The Bahamas almost invariably reserves its position on most CARICOM decisions. A sustained and imaginative campaign is necessary to overcome the feeling of remoteness perceived by Bahamians and to foster a stronger feeling of belonging to CARICOM.

We find, for example, almost total unawareness in The Bahamas of the degree to which access for Bahamian rum in the European market resulted from the CARICOM negotiations for rum from the Region to enter the European Community. There is a CARICOM story to be told in The Bahamas; the rest of us share some part of the blame if it is not being heard.

The decision that The Bahamas should be not only, as at present, a member of the Caribbean Community, but also a member of the Common Market (which it is not at present), is a decision essentially for The Bahamas. A warm welcome to Common Market membership is awaiting it. While some of the factors we have mentioned above may be impediments to that decision being taken, many of those elements of remoteness may come to be removed with the enhanced level of interaction that is then bound to develop between The Bahamas and the rest of the Caribbean in the context of the Common Market.

Geographical location is also an important element in understanding the relationships and feelings of the people of Belize to

CARICOM. Because it is a part of Central America, it is surrounded by countries whose language, culture and institutions are very different from its own, and even though for many years there was official hostility between Belize and one of its neighbours, the culture of Belize was being influenced and modified by the contact of the citizens of the two cultures. Because of this, many Belizeans see themselves as both West Indians and Central Americans at the same time, and they espouse the view that this orientation and experience will be useful to CARICOM as it seeks to meet the wider Caribbean cultures, most of which are very similar to Belize's neighbours.

Besides the shared historic experience of colonialism, and of sharing similar institutions and culture, the strong feelings of solidarity between Belize and CARICOM were forged in the struggle for its freedom, and through the assistance CARICOM provided in ensuring that Belize gained its independence, and continues to be at peace with its formerly hostile neighbours. The feeling of gratitude and warmth that Belizeans naturally have towards CARICOM could be dissipated, as its security is consolidated and new issues arise. As we have said, there is no direct link by air from Belize to any CARICOM country and there are no regular shipping lines for passengers and goods. There are extremely limited radio, television and newspaper links between Belize and the other CARICOM countries, and much of what is available in terms of information is often the negative, highly jaundiced view of journalists from third countries. Other than the deep-seated feeling that they belong to the Caribbean, there is very little of substance occurring on a daily basis to strengthen that feeling and cause it to grow.

The Immigrant Problem

Earlier, reference was made to some significant ways that distinguished The Bahamas and Belize from the other Caribbean countries. One such difference is that they both have to contend with a significantly large immigrant population, which has the capacity to put great strain on essential social services and development resources. In the case of Belize, the immigrants or refugees are Spanish speaking persons fleeing the economic and political turmoil that has existed in Central America for much of the last two decades. The refugees are estimated to number about 40,000 or about one quarter of the total population. In the case of The Bahamas, the illegal immigrants are French Creole-speaking Haitians fleeing the political oppression and the depressing economic situation that have characterised Haiti for the last four decades. The illegal immigrants are estimated to number about 60,000 or also about one quarter of the total population.

Belize and The Bahamas have chosen to deal with the illegal immigrants in vastly different ways. Belize has chosen to call its immigrants refugees, and has invited the United Nations High Commissioner for Refugees to assist it in dealing with the problem. It has begun a process of registration of the refugees, and the policy seems to be to absorb them, by allowing them to become productive farmers, using the vast land resources that the country possesses.

This pragmatic policy is probably influenced by the fact that Belize's relatively small English-speaking population shares its borders with Spanish-speaking countries, whose populations number in the millions. This policy, in addition to increasing Belize's productive capacity, helps to demonstrate Belize's friendliness towards its Central America neighbours, thus helping to safeguard its borders.

The Bahamas, on the other hand, calls its illegal immigrants aliens, and the official policy is that as many of these aliens as possible must be repatriated to Haiti. Attempts have been made to negotiate treaties with Haiti to deal with the orderly repatriation of the illegal Haitians, but these efforts have been thwarted by political instability in Haiti. The Bahamas has thus, so far, chosen to deal with its problem on a bilateral basis, since it appears that it is not the intention to treat the Haitians as refugees.

It is important for The Bahamas to find a solution to its Haitian problem because the presence of so many illegal immigrants in the country has become the source of social instability. Many of the immigrants have been in The Bahamas for over 30 years and have children who were born in The Bahamas and are therefore entitled to certain constitutional rights in regard to citizenship. It would also seem that any wholesale repatriation to Haiti will not be possible in the foreseeable future. Unless a practical solution is soon found, the present tensions are likely to broaden.

As CARICOM seeks to influence events in Haiti and to determine how Haiti best fits in CARICOM, the Haitians in The Bahamas could form the vital bridge between the English- and French-speaking peoples and their cultures. Many of the young Bahamians of Haitian parentage are bilingual and bicultural. In a sense they live in both worlds, the world of their parents and the world of their country and birth. They could supply the expertise and the sensitivity needed to successfully integrate Haiti into CARICOM.

Education

The feeling of remoteness and isolation also manifest itself in the educational policies followed by The Bahamas and Belize. In both countries, the University of the West Indies (UWI) is physically present, but the educational thrust suggests that both countries see the UWI as being marginal to their needs. It appears that both are determined to develop four-year degree granting institutions which are independent of UWI.

This attitude towards the UWI is not new, since for many years students from the two countries have opted to go to the United States for university education, citing the flexibility of the American University system, and the relative ease of entrance to the system, as the main reasons for doing so.

Many persons also question the inability of the government to provide adequate financial and human resources for a properly funded university system, and whether the small universities could be independent enough to guarantee their intellectual integrity.

Conclusion

To overcome the sense of remoteness and isolation that is so potentially destructive of the idea of The Bahamas and Belize as integral and important members of the CARICOM family, special efforts will have to be undertaken. Those efforts will fall to a substantial degree to the rest of us to remove the sources of irritation in the relationship between Belize, The Bahamas and the remaining CARICOM countries. Belize and The Bahamas must become convinced that they are the valued members of the family that they are;

and of course special efforts must be made in these countries to develop the vital sense of community and belonging which is essential to strengthening the weak but positive feeling that currently exists.

Recommendations

1. that overcoming remoteness, in the special context of The Bahamas and Belize (and more generally in the Community, for whatever reason) is a challenge to meet, not an issue to avoid; meeting it will require effort on all sides, but that effort will strengthen CARICOM;

2. that every encouragement be given to developing, in the shortest possible time, direct air links between The Bahamas, Belize and the remainder of the CARICOM countries;

3. that special efforts be made to encourage the citizens of Belize and The Bahamas and the citizens of the other CARICOM countries to see each others' countries as holiday destinations;

4. that radio and television be used to bring The Bahamas and Belize nearer to the people of the other CARICOM countries, and vice versa;

5. that the the University of the West Indies continue to expand the educational facilities it provides to both Belize and The Bahamas, using direct teaching facilities as well as the distance teaching systems provided through UWIDITE;

6. that the shipping lines that service the Region be encouraged to call in The Bahamas, Belize and other CARICOM ports on a regular basis;

7. that the schools of the Region, including The Bahamas and Belize, exchange teams in the major sports, and that similar encouragement be given to cultural exchanges.

Special Issues

3. THE DIASPORA: COMMITMENT AND POTENTIAL

From the very inception of its work the West Indian Commission took a decision to include in its series of consultations encounters with the considerable numbers of people of West Indian origin resident outside of the Caribbean. Indeed, once the establishment of the Commission and the nature of its mandate were made public, West Indians in Britain, the United States of America, and Canada wasted no time in conveying to the Commission their concern that their voices should be heard and in reminding the Commission that if all the West Indians resident in those countries were to return home *en masse* they could practically overnight double the population of the Region as geographically defined.

What was clearly demonstrated by this strong show of interest was the fact that "you can take the man (woman) out of the West Indies, but you can't take the West Indies out of the man (woman)". During several sessions with the diaspora many speakers assured the Commission that nothing could alter the fact that their "navel strings were still buried in some corner of the West Indies". Psychologically and emotionally the umbilical connection between West Indians at home and abroad is a real one.

In his essay "Towards West Indian Survival" prepared for the West Indian Commission, William Demas, in demonstrating that the case for regional integration is both simple and irrefutable, points to the fact that all the Member States of CARICOM, including the "bigger" countries, are so small that we need to achieve economies of scale and "critical mass" in markets, production, the mobilisation of regional capital for regional use, trained and professional manpower, export marketing, business management, university education, research and development, science and technology, sea and air transportation — to mention some areas.

The urgent need to look beyond the geographical confines of CARICOM has been reinforced by the recognition that as things now stand CARICOM constitutes a market of some five and one-half million people, not even remotely approaching the minimum critical mass required to achieve any of the objectives outlined above which in the final analysis are all essential for the improvement of the condition of the people of the Region. Logically, therefore, as proposed elsewhere in this Report, steps have to be taken to widen the Caribbean community of states even as we deepen the CARICOM relationship.

However, the visits to the West Indian diaspora beyond the geographical Caribbean have served to bring into sharper focus a concept which suggests redefinition of the Caribbean and alters significantly any assessment of the extent to which the Region may in fact be within reach of attaining the "critical mass" which is a *sine qua non* for economic viability and sustained development.

Consultations with the West Indian diaspora in Britain, Canada and the United States have highlighted the fact that the relatively small size of the Region's natural resource-dependent economies has limited the range of opportunities of the Region's people and forced them to be outward-looking. The result is that over the past three decades many thousands have left the Caribbean in search of what they perceive to be a better life. Ironically, however, in the course of this search West Indians have rediscovered their "oneness".

In the words of one eloquent presenter in the United States, "We came as Jamaicans, Barbadians, Trinidadians, and Guyanese, and became West Indians in America. This unifying experience in America has not lessened our appreciation for our own particular national heritage. Some of us may have come with small suitcases but we all came with a large cultural baggage. It is from this baggage that we draw sustenance from time to time, as we confront the challenges of assimilation into the host society. Our becoming West Indians in America has sharpened our appreciation for the common threads running through our individual heritages, such as our common history of the struggle for freedom and our common desire to excel in our endeavours. And from our continental perch we wonder how this unifying experience might be transmitted to a West Indies fragmented by sovereignty." This Caribbean-American perspective holds equally true for Caribbean people in Britain and Canada.

An Expanded Concept of Community

It is entirely arguable that the concept of regional unity and closer integration should not be limited to geographical space alone, because migration has made the Caribbean significantly larger than its geographical space. This larger Caribbean comprises a thriving expatriate community with considerable resources. This reality suggests that if Caribbean integration is predicated on economic and demographic space rather than on geographic space alone, the Region can immediately enlarge considerably the human and financial capital resources available to it.

An indication of the extent of these resources can be gained from the official statistics of the US Department of Commerce which reveal that in 1991 the estimated West Indian population in the US was 1,744,355, with almost 900,000 West Indians living in New York State alone and over 800,000 in New York City. Within the context of the wider Caribbean, the population of Caribbean immigrants in the US is estimated at 3.5 million, with over 1 million coming from the Spanish-speaking Caribbean; almost 2 million coming from the English-speaking Caribbean and the rest originating in the French-speaking and other areas of the Region.

What this suggests is that over the past 35 years the Region has built up, particularly in the United States of America, Canada and Britain, considerable human and financial resources, important skills and enduring goodwill, resources which in the past have only been called upon in times of natural disaster in various parts of the Region.

The experience of countries in other parts of the world serves to demonstrate that the systematic engagement and mobilisation of these resources can go a far way towards transforming the potential of the Region for accelerated economic growth and sustained social development while at the same time making more achievable the minimum critical mass required for real viability and growth.

Wherever the Commission has met with the West Indian diaspora we have been accorded a warm and positive reception. The general feeling among West Indians abroad is that for far too long has this rich reservoir of goodwill been allowed to remain untapped. Indeed, in some quarters, there have been expressions of cynicism and resentment as the people of this wider Caribbean have over the years grown to feel that they are only remembered in times of crisis or when political parties come seeking campaign funds and moral support. In between such occasions the diaspora could not even claim to be the subject of benign neglect. But beneath all this the connection remains intact and there is still time to develop a vibrant relationship between the expatriate Caribbean community and the Caribbean people at home.

By and large the attitude of CARICOM Governments towards the expatriate CARICOM community has in the past been, to say the least, ambivalent. While they have applauded the success of those who have won recognition abroad they have at the same time tended to treat the migration phenomenon with indifference. In more recent times, however, this attitude has begun to undergo some significant changes as GovernmentS increasingly come to recognise the importance of the large thriving, expatriate communities as a source of capital and skills as well as of emergency aid.

The fact is that the process of outward migration has expanded today's CARICOM beyond its geographical boundaries as substantial numbers of our people have moved to the United Kingdom and North America to improve their economic and social conditions. The phenomenon is that West Indians at home and abroad have remained connected with the Region by the objective of maximizing the welfare of the migrant's household. This linkage has contributed to the betterment of many CARICOM households, but at a more global level it has to be recognised that private transfers from West Indians abroad have been playing and can continue to play a critically important role in fostering long-term development of the Region. Private transfers (such as remittances from nationals living abroad and grants from overseas non-profit organisations (NGOs), but excluding labour income from workers with less-than-1-year contracts) currently constitute an important source of foreign savings for CARICOM countries. In 1989 these transfers amounted to some US$420 million or between 2 per cent and 13 per cent of CARICOM countries' gross output in 1989. While these transfers tend to fluctuate dependent upon the perceived needs of the recipient country (for example, during times of natural disasters) they clearly represent an important source of financial inflows into the economies of the Region from the large population of their nationals living abroad. Perhaps even more significant is the fact that these private transfers (migrant and worker remittances) account for only one-third of total private transfers to the Region. The other two-thirds originate from NGOs, pensions and insurance claims.

A Readiness to Respond

The West Indian community overseas has uniformly welcomed all the moves in the direction of closer integration and has consistently professed concern for and commitment to the future development of the Region.

West Indian businessmen in the United Kingdom see as one serious constraint to trade and investment in the Region the current fragmented state of the CARICOM market which requires potential investors or traders to secure a multiplicity of entry permits, work permits, exchange controls and other authorisations in respect of each of the relatively miniscule segments of the CARICOM Market, to say nothing of the varying regulations and requirements attendant on doing business in CARICOM. Many find it more profitable to look to other markets such as West Africa when their first choice would have been the West Indies. They welcome the decisions of CARICOM Governments to work towards a Single Market and Economy by 1993 as this development would for the first time permit the rational development of trade and investment proposals which the expatriate business community haS so far found it impossible to implement. For West Indian businessmen overseas, the CARICOM Single Market and Economy cannot materialise a moment too soon.

The consensus among the West Indian diaspora is that closer integration should have as a critically important component the mobilisation of financial and technical resources from the West Indian community abroad — that is, the fullest utilisation of the additional resources which would be afforded by the demographic space as defined earlier.

The view from the diaspora is that there is no mystery surrounding West Indians abroad. Most maintain direct contact with families and friends; take visits home on a regular basis; remain concerned and loyal to the lands of their birth; and have over the years nurtured a desire to contribute to and share in the opportunities for growth and development in the Region. The missing links which have retarded the process of full involvement of the diaspora have therefore neither been social nor personal.

What has been identified as the real missing link has been the absence of formal or institutional mechanisms connecting emigres with their homelands in a caring manner; institutional mechanisms which invite them to play a part in the process of development and which systematically seek them out as potential contributors to the process. This approach would be more effective if it is regional in scope rather than national, given the strong regional identity which West Indians abroad have developed.

Despite an accumulated perception of real or imagined indifference on the part of Governments and people at home, the citizens of the wider West Indies profess that, far from abandoning their homelands, they are more than willing to be partners in the Region's developmental process, if only the Region would make the appropriate overtures.

The first signal, succinctly put, would be the substitution of the "red carpet" for the more usual "red tape" that seems to be reserved for West Indians returning home or seeking to do business with the Region. The West Indian community overseas still nurses some resentment over what they perceive to be almost studied indifference on the part of both the Governments and people of the Region to any attempt on their part to become involved in any aspect of regional development. The diaspora, however, professes to remain constant in its commitment and to continue to be open to proposals for deeper involvement.

The view in North America is that the accumulated *per capita* spending power of West Indians outside the Region could be today approaching ten times that of their counterparts at home. This translates into financial resources for both deliberate and discretionary spending among the migrant community. The picture is not different in the areas of technology, skills and expertise. Given new technologies, the time is now ripe for accessing these resources to the benefit of the Region, without the need for relocation. This requires survey and analysis of the resources resident abroad, and the systematic inclusion of the concerns and hopes of the diaspora on the Region's agenda.

There is no doubt that a strong case has been made for the far greater involvement of the diaspora in the development of the Region. Other countries and regions of the world have successfully capitalised on the resources of their citizens resident beyond their geographical borders.

Accordingly, in the movement towards closer integration a conscious effort must be made to facilitate the participation of West Indians abroad in the social and economic development of the Region.

The recommendations that follow are by no means exhaustive, but their early implementation would have a catalytic effect on the reservoir of goodwill and resources which the West Indian Commission encountered among West Indians abroad, and would send a strong signal to the diaspora that they have a vital role to play in the future of the Region — indeed, that they *are* an important part of the Region.

In short, the "critical mass" of CARICOM or the anglophone Caribbean could immediately be significantly enlarged to reinforce the deepening process even as widening proceeds.

Recommendations:

1. that Governments of CARICOM Member States be more demonstrably aware of the critically important resource which the West Indian communities abroad represent;

2. that everything be done to facilitate trade, investment, social and cultural initiatives within the context of the greater demographic space offered by the full and active engagement of the West Indian diaspora;

3. that both the public and private sectors consciously seek to engage the West Indians overseas in all aspects of development in the Region;

4. that there be a process of continuous consultation with the diaspora, involving, as appropriate, joint action between Embassies, High Commissions and Consulates of CARICOM countries;

5. that credible mechanisms for the mobilisation and channelling of investment capital from the diaspora be put in place;

6. that there be encouragement and utilisation of increasingly significant West Indian lobbies in advancing the interests of the Region in the political processes of the metropoles;

7. that there be the establishment of a 'Skills Bank' and the identification and location of professional skills and technical expertise which could be harnessed by the Region on terms and conditions mutually advantageous to both donor and recipient;

8. that there be improvement of the channels of communication, both official and private sector, to facilitate far more effective two-way flows of information, and full utilisation of the media to this end;

9. that tourism advertising and promotion be targeted more specifically to the growing market which exists throughout the diaspora.

CHAPTER XI

SHAPING EXTERNAL RELATIONS

1. CREATION AND CONDUCT OF COMMON POLICIES

In the Preamble to the Treaty Establishing the Caribbean Community, the participating Governments recognised that the objectives which they set for themselves could be attained most effectively by, among other things, ensuring what they referred to as "a common front in relation to the external world."

In subsequent Articles of the Treaty they sought to give this prescription specificity in particular directions: by enjoining themselves to "seek a progressive coordination of their trade relations with third countries or groups of countries" (Art. 34.1); by asserting as a central objective "the coordination of the foreign policies of Member States" (Art. 4 (b)); and by pledging to "coordinate their positions and presentations at all international economic, financial and trade meetings at which they are represented" (Art. 39.1.(iii)).

These principles and objectives reflected not only the broad governmental post-independence sentiment that, even though constituted as separate sovereign states, it was necessary "to consolidate and strengthen the bonds which have historically existed among their peoples." But it reflected also that as recognisably small and even "micro" states, the West Indian territories would have to pool resources and identities in some measure if they were to establish a visibility in the international arena,and provide themselves with a reasonable and sustained capacity for international representation and negotiation.

From the vantage point of time since the establishment of the Community (1973), the principles and objectives indicated in the Treaty in respect of coordinated external relations might well appear limited. There is no suggestion of "joint" or "unified" positions, but the requirement only for "coordination". No specific objectives as to time are set which might indicate systematic institutional development in respect of "coordination". What is indicated is simply a "progressive" coordination of positions and relations.

These relatively limited objectives and measures might indeed have reflected recognition of the difficulties of harmonisation — especially institutionalised as against ad hoc harmonisation —for newly sovereign entities; particularly as initial attempts by some states at joint diplomatic representation in the immediate post-independence period had proven unsuccessful.

Yet even within this limited framework, some degree of successful, though perhaps ad hoc or one-time, harmonisation was achieved in a very visible way in the first decade of the Community's existence. This was particularly evident in the countries' attempts to maintain a common front *vis-à-vis* the European Community in negotiations towards the establishment of the First Lomé Convention. The impulse towards coordination was not essentially externally impelled —Europe was itself divided in a policy sense and the preference of the EEC then was to negotiate with single states rather than with cross-region groups or blocs of states. But the decision of the CARICOM Governments to pool diplomatic and technical resources into a single negotiating team to be kept in existence for a substantial period of time, did indicate the possibilities for what we are calling *institutionalised harmonisation*, once the political will to do so could be sustained and that political will was generated by our judgement that it was in our interest to work together: first as CARICOM, then as the ACP.

Such achievements were however few and far between. So much so that the *Group of Caribbean Experts* (the "Wise Men"), reporting in 1981 in *The Caribbean Community in the 1980s*, felt it necessary to remind Members States that certain provisions of the Treaty relating to the coordination of external relations and trade policies were "obligations" that were "mandatory"; and that "Governments should *obviously* (our emphasis) intensify their efforts to achieve coordination of their external trade relations with third countries and groups of third countries". The Group of Experts, undoubtedly already observing certain tendencies towards increasing diversity rather than harmony in CARICOM countries' external economic relations, felt it necessary too, to remind Governments of their own decision, taken in 1975, "to have consultations with their CARICOM partners before concluding trade, aid and complementarity agreements with third countries or groups of third countries, and not merely provide information after the event."

The period of the second half of the 1970s and the beginning of the 1980s was indeed largely one of diversity in regional external relations — partly induced by various Governments' ideological or populist orientations. Unilateral initiatives in extra-regional external relations tended to take precedence over consolidation of a process of harmonised intra-region relationships. The importance of sustaining a *regional* identity devised by internal consultation, balance and consensus among the constituent units was downplayed. The margins of flexibility for small countries in external relationships were perhaps over-emphasised, and the constraints of dependency for small, open economies, perhaps too little recognised.

Dependency as economic constraint, while much discussed by Caribbean economists and analysts in the 1970s, was seen as a factor which could be substantially minimised by changing domestic policy and by foreign policy initiatives designed to change the terms of trade between developed and developing countries. Today there is wider acceptance at both academic and policy-making levels of the view that dependency as economic constraint is a continuing attribute of these small and open CARICOM economies, and that foreign policy should substantially be devoted to both seeking to enlarge the small space for independent action and making continuous adjustments to external circumstances over whose dynamism we have little control. The straitened economic circumstances of many states in the Region had the effect of tilting the balance towards the latter posture.

In terms of the shaping of external relations, the conclusion to be drawn from such constraints on the real autonomy of CARICOM states is not that of paralysis of decision-making, or lack of capacity to make meaningful external relations decisions. Rather, there is a need to recognise that:

- external circumstances are major and continuing determinations of the resources available to our countries for domestic, economic or social policy-making (The objective of such policy-making is defined in the Treaty's Preamble as that of fulfilling "the hopes and aspirations of... peoples for full employment and improved standards of work and living");

- the openness of the CARICOM economies implies the existence of multiple relationships between those economies and the markets with which they trade and to which they are open;
- these conditions require the development of capabilities for adjusting to changes in these multiple and inter-connected relationships and for managing these ties if some domestic stability is to be maintained;
- some of these capabilities will need to be developed and sustained multinationally —that is, jointly between the local economies/systems and the (private) systems in the external marketplace;
- the limited and periodically reduced financial resources of one or other CARICOM economy suggests that national resources need in certain circumstances to be institutionally pooled (pooled over the long term) in order to develop and maintain the capabilities for adjustment that may be required. And, consequentially, that the use of *regional* capabilities may be necessary for the protection or adjustment of the *national* or local economy/system.

Current domestic and external policies of many CARICOM States suggest also that there is growing recognition by Governments of the necessity and importance of this orientation, and that this is partly due to the failure of alternative orientations and the limitations of economic resources.

It is, however, important to emphasise as well that the changing orientations of our Governments are due not only to changed domestic circumstances but also to substantially changed external circumstanceS since the establishment of the Caribbean Community.

First, it seemed to be an assumption of the external relations policy of many CARICOM States in the 1970s that the geopolitically and ideologically "bipolar" world that then existed provided possibilities for major "diversification" of external economic and political relationships. While this stance was characteristic of many Third World countries and led to the policy of non-alignment, in CARICOM it was also taken to suggest possibilities for reduction of dependency on the United States, the dominant state in the Hemisphere.

Two factors have come to militate against the sustenance of these assumptions and policies. The Soviet adoption and application of the principle of *glastnost* as the main thrust of its foreign policy progressively reduced the divide between the two superpowers, and consequently the space in which others could 'play' between them. The dissolution of the Soviet Union has now removed the space altogether.

Then, in the sphere of international economic relations, the decisive thrust by Third World countries, joined by some leading CARICOM States, to significantly change the terms of trade between themselves and the developed world by a series of initiatives exercised mainly through UNCTAD, met stiff resistance from the dominant Western economic powers and only lukewarm support from the socialist bloc. This has led to a loss of enthusiasm for pursuit of the initiatives by the Third World States, a virtual abandonment of them, and a loss of belief that the terms of international economic relations can be changed by international negotiation outside the framework of the GATT. Only the current debate on environment and development offers a modest, still uncertain, revival of earlier expectations of change through North-South dialogue.

The character of the external environment which was presumed to constitute the basis for the previously held policy has thus disappeared. CARICOM Governments have come to recognise new sets of external circumstances likely to affect their own orientations in the future — and a new, if largely unspoken, sense of powerlessness, in responding to them.

In effect, the disappearance of the bipolar world has reinforced for CARICOM the strength and dominance of the United States in our geopolitical sphere. This had already begun to be apparent during the era of the Reagan Presidency when the effects of American hostility to their initiatives negatively affected certain Governments.

But what has also been recognised, especially in the post-Reagan era of large budget deficits and economic recession in the United States, are the limits of US assistance to the CARICOM countries, except in special and strategic circumstances, given their relatively high (in Third World terms) levels of living, shifts in American priorities to other geopolitical spheres,and an inclination among US policy makers to limit foreign aid in the context of increasing national budgetary deficits. The essential neutralisation of externally supported socialist initiatives in the Region has reinforced this tendency. And CARICOM countries while characterised as being in the American sphere, find themselves, like other developing states, pushed in the direction of dependence on multilateral institutions for needed concessionary financial assistance.

The actual and potential significance of American-induced trade and investment into the Region does, however, sustain the closeness and asymmetry of the relationships as the United States itself seeks to respond to the changing nature of its international economic environment. As is now well recognised, the emergence of regional economic groupings in other parts of the Western world has prompted the United States to seek to consolidate an hemispheric economic zone in this area, through the North American Free Trade Area initiative (NAFTA) now encompassing Mexico, and the Enterprise for the Americas Initiative (EAI).

The CARICOM states have already acknowledged the necessity and urgency of responding to these initiatives and, in respect of the Enterprise for the Americas Initiative, have established with the US a Joint Council on Trade and Investment as an instrument of negotiation and probable incorporation. But the CARICOM Governments recognise too that this is not simply a special CBI-type initiative directed towards them and their special characteristics as small states in the Hemisphere. Rather it reflects one of the current US responses to the variety of trade and investment initiatives taking place in the global arena; and as such it has the potential for placing the Caribbean States in direct competition with other larger states of the Hemisphere.

The Enterprise for the Americas Initiative, as also the likely establishment of a Free Trade Area with Mexico, will certainly therefore also change the developing design for the types of relationships which the Caribbean Community has been hoping to establish with leading Latin American countries, and in particular those which exist on the rim of the Caribbean Basin. These countries have themselves been abandoning the notion of regional economic blocs based on cultural homogeneity and geographic proximity, and a level of economic protection, as instruments of their long-term economic development. They are turning to a conception of such blocs (integration groupings) as market spaces that are instruments for negotiation in yet larger liberalised economic (trading and investment) spaces. That they possess some substantial market space and actual or potential purchasing power is to them important in this conception and in their choice of participation in the emerging North/South (hemispheric) American economic space.

This North/South American economic context raises for the Caribbean Community the question of the relevance of its own economic space as a valid and viable participant in that arena. The seeming hostility of some multilateral institutions to the level of the Common External Tariff established for the Caribbean Common Market is indicative of the problem. The United States suggestion that the Enterprise for the Americas relates to, in our area, the CBI countries as a whole rather than to portions of it which can be dealt with bilaterally, is yet another indication. And it is constraining the CARICOM grouping, for the first time since its establishment, to seriously contemplate new strategies for negotiations and institutionalised relationships with the states of Central America. It should be recalled, in this connection, that the CBI did not have this effect.

What this means is that the Caribbean Community is finding itself gradually geopolitically and, more importantly, economically, redefined by external initiatives.

The strategic questions being posed, in this context, for the Community are (a) whether the continuous removal of trade and financial barriers and the effective merger of systems and negotiating teams with others in order to respond to the initiatives discussed above will lead to the creation of wider integration entities; and (b) whether, in the context of the wider economic arrangements seeming to emerge in the Hemisphere, the Community will be able to designate itself as an identifiable integration grouping in the hemispheric or international arena, and function meaningfully as one. These questions had in fact been posed in a limited way since the mid-to-late 1970s by the entreaties of the Dominican Republic and Haiti for some significant institutionalised participation in CARICOM. The relative insignificance of the two countries, however, either as trading partners or in terms of their diplomatic weight, had led for most of the time to a limited and peripheral treatment of the matter.

The North American initiatives are now bringing the question into fuller relief. But at the turn of the 1980s the European Community, through the process of the renegotiation of the Lomé Convention, had already implicitly posed the question of regional redefinition by accepting the possibility of membership for the Dominican Republic and Haiti in the ACP grouping, with the clear implication that they would form part of the Caribbean sub-section of that grouping. The widening of the European Community itself to include Spain and Portugal has in fact invigorated European interest in relationships with Hispano- and Lusophone America, and in 'original' areas of colonisation like Santo Domingo.

In the short run, the European willingness to see the widening of the Caribbean grouping as the relevant negotiating sub-section with which it deals in the ACP system, poses the question of appropriate ways and means of institutionalising the extended set of relationships, whether or not Haiti and the Dominican Republic actually form part of CARICOM. And this in turn poses the question of the coherence of CARICOM in that setting.

This takes us to another set of relevant questions implicitly suggested above in our discussion of the responses of South/Central American countries to the EAI and NAFTA initiative. These are whether the CARICOM grouping as currently constituted possesses, and will possess, sufficient coherence and strength as an economic space to be able in the future to sustain its integrity as an economic integration system —a common market with its identifiable tariff; whether the grouping will have sufficient assets (market power) to serve as an adequate negotiating instrument to achieve its goals in the emerging North/South American economic space; and whether the common market will be perceived by those with some weight to force some redefinition of the CARICOM system, as having relevance in that space as well as in the Region's relations with the European Community.

When the questions are posed in this way, they take us towards consideration, in this section on Context and Principles, of the broad categories of external relations within which the CARICOM countries are required to act. And for this purpose a first broad division between regional relations —that is, intra-CARICOM relations— and extra-regional relations —that is, extra-CARICOM relations— can be made.

The Caribbean Community as it currently exists can be said to have within it its own particular arena of inter-state and therefore international relations. The Treaty recognises that its members are (with one exception) sovereign states, and that the Treaty itself does not contain any institutional objective beyond inter-state cooperation. External relations objectives of the Member States acting as a Community presuppose a prior consensus within the Community arrived at on the basis of inter-state negotiation. For the consensus to be meaningful, that is, for the objectives of the consensus to be effectively implemented within or beyond the Community, requires a certain level of coherence at the level of the international relations within the Community itself.

Coherence means (a) willingness to implement at (or from) the national level such decisions as are pre-requisites to the effective implementation of objectives at the extra-Community level; and (b) willingness to observe, whether locally or extra-nationally, international obligations deriving from the implementation of agreed Community objectives. These constitute the essence of the regional relations of the Community which, therefore, have their own integrity and can be distinguished from the Community's international relations.

The point here is that the Community has, in the practice of its regional relations, been found wanting in the implementation of decisions agreed upon by Member States. In that context Member States, unlike those of, for example, the European Community, have not been willing to accept and subordinate themselves to a system of sanctions designed to ensure enforcement of decisions. And as a consequence the Community has appeared, particularly to extra-Community States, to lack coherence and effectiveness.

The final aspect of the changed external relations context of the Region relates to the now almost fully evolved implications of the adherence of the United Kingdom to the European Community, and the evolution of the European Common Market into a Single Market free of physical, financial and technical barriers to the factors of production and to commodities and services produced. As is well known, this has raised the question of the ACP countries' capacity to ensure that the EEC maintains its obligations, particularly in agricultural and agro-industrial trade, deriving from the terms of Britain's accession to Europe and from the ACP/EEC Lomé Convention. And what is now being posed is the strength and validity of these legal obligations in terms of their practical implementation within market determined processes and frameworks (as, for example, in the case of the banana regime).

In summary, the international relations environment in which the Caribbean Community States find themselves having to function has substantially changed since the period of the independence of the larger states. While, in the face of domestic difficulties, Member States have sought to undertake financial and structural adjustments, and have come to recognise the need to adapt to the changing environment, this adaptation process has been slow. The machinery for conducting the regional relations of the Community has not proven effective. And Member-States have also not been able to use it effectively to design strategies for relating to extra-Community states in the region or in the wider hemisphere and global environment whose initiatives and activities have increasingly been determining the context of the Community's own relations and decision-making. The danger of 'marginalisation,' of which the Grand Anse Declaration spoke, is now real indeed.

2. CARICOM, THE WIDER CARIBBEAN AND LATIN AMERICA

Situated as they largely are in Middle America, the orientations of the countries of the Caribbean Basin are inevitably likely to be multi-pronged within the North/South American geopolitical arena. That two Caribbean Community countries (Belize and Guyana) are actually on the mainland would serve to reinforce this orientation.

Official (colonial) relations had in some measure served to obscure this geographic reality, though the movements of Caribbean peoples to a diversity of countries in the hemisphere often ignored colonial and linguistic demarcations, particularly after the turn of the century. The onset of independence has quickly brought to the fore the question of the nature and intensity of relations between the English-speaking Caribbean and the non-English-speaking independent Caribbean and Latin American states. One Latin American state in particular, Venezuela, moved quickly to establish diplomatic presences in even the smaller Eastern Caribbean states.

Location has, of course, determined the extent and intensity of relationships. Such has been the case in the evolution of the Belize-Guatemala as well as the Guyana-Venezuela border controversies, the counter-balancing relationship between Guyana and Brazil, varying relationships between The Bahamas and Haiti, and The Bahamas and Cuba, and the inclination of some Member States to accept, perhaps more than others, the necessity for some kind of institutionalised relations between the Caribbean Community and Haiti and the Dominican Republic.

But given the small size of the CARICOM States, and even though diplomatic relations have been established particularly between the larger CARICOM Countries and many Latin American states, some emphasis has been placed in recent times on the Treaty requirement for coordination of foreign policy initiatives, particularly where these have related to economic groupings formed by the Latin American states.

Relations with the Wider Caribbean

It is appropriate, however, to deal first with CARICOM States' relations with the non-anglophone Caribbean states. These divide themselves into the independent states in the northern Antilles (Cuba, Haiti, the Dominican Republic), Suriname, and the non-independent entities, with varying degrees of autonomy, in the East and Southern Caribbean (French Overseas Departments, Puerto Rico, United States Virgin Islands, Netherlands Antilles).

The requests of Haiti, the Dominican Republic and Suriname for full, formal participation in CARICOM have been responded to by granting forms of institutional relationships somewhat short of this — through observer status on some of the more technical Standing Committees of the Community. There has been an obvious fear that full membership for these countries could disrupt the internal coherence of the Common Market or the Community with no, or few, attendant benefits by way of increasing substantially the level of trade within the system. The least cautious attitude in this respect has been taken to Suriname which has not been seen as being particularly competitive with the CARICOM States in terms of trade or the search for investment.

Recent initiatives have emphasised the imperative for the community to develop a dynamic set of relationships with these countries which will be durable and mutually beneficial.

As has been discussed in the first section of this Chapter, both the United States and the European Community have "redefined" Haiti and the Dominican Republic by including them in negotiating units with the other CARICOM States for the purpose of concluding arrangements in respect of the initiatives which they have taken towards the Caribbean. In terms of the EEC, the CARICOM response has been tentative, in the sense that the two states currently fall, for internal negotiating purposes, within the ambit of the Caribbean Forum, rather than that of the CARICOM Council. It may be that this in fact can provide an appropriate first step in the institutionalising of relations — as a learning and familiarisation system for all parties. The trade, aid and investment framework of the Lomé Convention is deemed to be an important instrument of the future development of the ACP countries. As such, it can, for the Caribbean states, provide a basis for developing a network of functional cooperation relating to the various development activities of these states. This possibility is already perceived in the area of tourism. We will return to this later.

A similar orientation can be adopted in examining the implications of the relationship intended to be established between the Caribbean states, the Central American states and the United States in respect of the Enterprise for the Americas Initiative. This would be so particularly to the extent that the CARICOM grouping would wish to see a structured relationship (similar to that of the ACP/EEC relationship) develop as a framework for such an arrangement in the hemisphere. CARICOM has, of course, already established a Council on Trade and Investment with the United States as a negotiating tool and, perhaps, as an incipient instrument for a more permanent institutional relationship.

The likelihood is, however, that the US will, for the purposes of the EAI, wish to function in an institutional framework that is somewhat wider than one constituted only of the CARICOM States, and that such an inclination will, again, provide an avenue for establishment of a more coherent set of relationships between the CARICOM group and the non-Anglophone sovereign Caribbean states.

The internal impulses towards closer contact or relationships — whether cordial or antagonistic —have stemmed from political changes towards non-authoritarian constitutional arrangements in Haiti; and, secondly, from the apparent desire of the Dominican Republic to induce and support the production and export of bananas to the single European market, placing itself in direct competition for the UK market, in particular, with certain of the CARICOM States.

While in fact the CARICOM countries do not have the level of resources required to assist a transition from authoritarianism in Haiti, the thrust towards characterising this problem as one susceptible to resolution at least partially within a hemispheric framework has provided the Region with a role as a technical partner in a cooperative hemispheric venture. Two reasons can be advanced for this: first, the CARICOM requirement that only a non-authoritarian Haiti can have any meaningful institutional relationship with

CARICOM; and secondly, that the extensive migration towards a CARICOM Member, The Bahamas, from Haiti as a result of worsening socio-political conditions, can induce disruptive conditions within one part of the regional system.

The potentially antagonistic relationship with the Dominican Republic, deriving from the banana issue, again draws the CARICOM system into establishing more systematic arrangements with that country, in order to ensure that that Government's initiative does not damage the interests of the relevant CARICOM countries. It is recognised that the problem arising here is not simply a state-to-state one; but that it has to be placed in the context of the play of a market characterised by a variety of multinational corporations involved in this particular industry.

The CARICOM States are therefore becoming drawn into a system of transnational relations involving both state and market activities and itself influenced by the impending "free market" system of the European Community. This requires a form of diplomacy for which the CARICOM system and the affected Member States are ill-prepared.

Finally it is recognised that the major global political changes that have recently occurred are inducing, and will further induce, changes in the international behaviour towards Cuba, drawing that State towards normalisation of its relationship with hemispheric states — a process that will be hastened by developments within Cuba itself. CARICOM countries, however, cannot simply be passive spectators. Despite our relative powerlessness, the four larger CARICOM Countries, first to independence, played a crucial principled role nearly twenty years ago, in ending the hemispheric embargo against Cuba. It was not a commentary on West Indian approbation of Cuba's domestic policies; it was a stand against the isolation of a member of the Caribbean family.

Today, in the Commission's view, there may well be other roles that CARICOM can play in assisting the process by which the physical trade embargo that continues to be maintained against Cuba is ended as a relic of an era that has passed. In matters of this kind, Governments can be assisted in overcoming political constraints by the strength of public opinion. There is evidence that this public opinion is stirring within CARICOM. Even as we were finalising our Report, the press in the Region were calling for a "New Policy on Cuba". We identify with the Editorial of the *Daily Nation* of Barbados of 23 April 1992, which ended on the following note:

> This is not an argument in favour of existing domestic policies of the Castro Government, with which we have our own reservations, including its human rights record.
> Rather, we seek to remind the government of a great democracy ... that it's time to replace its policy of aggression against a small Caribbean nation with dialogue aimed at promoting the kind of politics and policies with which it could be at ease.

The long-term significance of this for the CARICOM system lies largely in Cuba's increasing involvement in the emerging system of economic relationships and institutions involving the hemisphere as a whole into which, as we have suggested earlier, the Caribbean will most likely be drawn.

The people of CARICOM expect similarly from our Region a more forthright position in relation to the problems that flow from developments in Haiti. Again, our basic condition may be one of relative powerlessness; it is certainly not one of total incapacity or moral indifference. Certainly, we can define the CARICOM position with greater clarity and act within our limited capacities, including action on the diplomatic front.

We have been involved in that diplomatic activity in recent months arising from the overthrow of President Aristide's democratically elected Government; but we have been less than generous in relation to the issue of Haitian refugees.

There are questions of cost, of course; but even in this context there have been exceptions within the Region— Belize has led the way in accepting a quota of refugees; Jamaica has accommodated some who arrived. Surely, as a Region, we can do more, and perhaps take a lead, not only by example (which will inevitably cater for limited numbers) but but also by using that example as moral authority for demanding more effective responses to the Haitian problem from the international community — including recognition of the genuine refugee status of Haitians who are constrained to flee their country.

The point we make is that Caribbean people expect CARICOM to take positions on these matters. They are aware, sometimes more aware than the political leadership acknowledges, of the international pressures that bear on their countries; but they are ready, we believe, to support their Governments in taking a stand on these matters that raise such major principles of solidarity, of humanitarianism, and of morality.

In respect of relationships with the non-independent entities of the Region, two observations can be made. The first relates to, as in the early part of this century, the extensive migratory patterns occurring irrespective of linguistic division and juridical impediments to settlement. The extensive movement of peoples from some Eastern Caribbean states to the French Overseas Departments, and from these states also to the United States Virgin Islands is indicative of this. As these non-independent states seek to stretch the limits of autonomous action within their given juridical frameworks, while being at the same time the objects of economic development action from their respective metropoles, it will most likely be the case that interested CARICOM countries will be drawn to establish a network of economic and functional cooperation relationships with, for example the French Departments under the aegis of the aid, trade and investment framework of the European Community. It should be noted that the OECS States are currently negotiating with representatives of France and of the Overseas Departments towards the establishment of a Framework Agreement on Cooperation; and that the French Government has responded to these initiatives by the appointment of a Delegate responsible for Caribbean relations.

Much the same can be said of the role of, and CARICOM's relationship to, Puerto Rico, whose economic development proceeds within the framework set by its own relationship with the United States. And here too the OECS States are currently negotiating specific arrangements for cooperation with the Government of Puerto Rico.

Relations with Central and South America

As we have indicated earlier, a revival of interest in consolidating regional economic integration processes is currently characterising the South/Central American arena. These countries' activities would appear to have two objectives:

(a) to create economic spaces of substantial size which can serve as cost-effective production locations and zones of major purchasing power; and
(b) to create economic spaces which can be presented as zones for foreign investment, thus knitting the countries into the international trade and investment system.

The recent initiatives of the United States (NAFTA and EAI) have served to reinforce the perceptions in the South/Central American countries of the correctness of these strategies. Their objectives, following the current orientation of Mexico, would be to seek to achieve a certain level of integration with the United States economy itself in the hope of maximising, for their countries' development, the technological dynamism of that economy.

The relationship between the CARICOM countries and those states will, then, be determined within the parameters of these objectives and strategies, as the larger South American countries seek to ensure that they are not excluded from the emerging global trading and investment relationships.

It is probably the case that even the 'special relationships', born of geographical proximity, which the CARICOM States have had with the 'rim' countries of South/Central America, will be subordinated to these considerations. And it would certainly appear that the geopolitical and territorial controversies and disputes have been muted in recent years —such controversies having been the main focus of Caribbean/Latin America international relations in the post-independence period.

Still, a first consideration for CARICOM policy will now be how to transform geographical proximity into economic networking in spite of difficulties in trade and economic cooperation in the past. The first focus of CARICOM policy would obviously be on the 'rim' countries Venezuela, Columbia and Mexico, now characterised as the Group of 3 (G3), and which have shown renewed interest in devising systems of economic networking with the Caribbean and Brazil in terms of geographical relationship with Guyana and incipient economic relationships with Trinidad and Tobago. Most of these countries are now engaged in extensive economic liberalisation processes, involving, in particular, reduction of tariffs and removal of non-tariff barriers which have always been salient aspects of their economic development and effective impediments to regional trade.

The recent Venezuelan initiative in the direction of economic integration with the Caribbean Common Market matches, in fact, that country's extensive interest in the political and security stability of the Caribbean which it has continually displayed at least since the early 1960s. And while the interest in extensive economic integration may vary with regime changes in Venezuela, it would certainly be in the interest of the CARICOM Countries to explore the parameters of an economic relationship with that country in the context of the offer of a one-way free trade area and the general liberalisation process in which that country is engaged, a process whose momentum will certainly increase.

At the same time as the Group of 3 and other South American countries seek to pursue further integration into the global economy and to achieve meaningful locations in the hemispheric economy dominated by the United States, they are currently seeking to build coalitions capable of effective negotiation in both the political and economic arenas in the hemisphere. The CARICOM countries have only incipiently begun to involve themselves in issues arising in these arenas, and mainly as these arise in the OAS framework. In effect, the diplomatic presence of CARICOM in South America has low visibility and still minimal participation in the discussions of emerging trends and policies on the continent.

An effective diplomatic relationship of a deliberately long term nature with the Group of 3 could constitute for CARICOM an entry into the diplomatic and economic dialogue in South America, thus providing also linkages to countries such as Argentina and Chile which are likely to play leading roles in the evolution of the Enterprise for the Americas Initiative. The importance of the G 3 forum for exploring the long-term implications for CARICOM of Mexico's integration into NAFTA also cannot be under-rated.

A further objective of CARICOM policy must be the exploration of possible levels of economic relationships with the Central American countries. Extensive military conflict in recent years has tended to obscure the significant advantage which some Central American countries have taken of the Caribbean Basin Initiative. Further, all indications are that the United States will adopt a similar 'Caribbean Basin' approach to the EAI, thus grouping the CARICOM countries along with Central American states in terms of access to the United States market and the related provisions of the EAI.

Here, in fact, are the makings of a system of competition between the two sub-groupings of the Caribbean Basin born of what might be called 'comparative advantage competition,' in industrial and agricultural exports. The political and diplomatic distance between the CARICOM and Central American groupings, reinforced by the Guatemala-Belize dispute, has hitherto hindered exploration of the various aspects of this 'comparative advantage competition.' The current formalising of a Caribbean-Central American forum should now serve to approach this matter.

In this regard, the post-independence diplomatic interests of Jamaica in attempting to consolidate relationships with Central American countries, particularly Mexico, should be utilized by other CARICOM Governments; so too should the location and necessary interest in close relationships on the part of Belize. CARICOM Governments should, as it were, allocate lead roles to these two countries in elaborating a series of networks through the creation of joint teams in a variety of subject areas, thus building up a formal system for discussion, negotiation and implementation of programmes of cooperation.

This methodology would have the additional advantage, too, of drawing Belize more closely into an active relationship with other Member States of the Caribbean Community, thus reinforcing the coherence of the Community.

Again, the widening of the European Community and the evolution of the single European market are impacting on the CARICOM-Central American relationship; raising as they do the interest of Central American states (through the medium of the transnational corporations) in maximising banana sales throughout the Single Market. In addition, the Central American countries with, now, a 'metropole' —Spain —in that Community, are themselves being encouraged to explore the potential for aid, trade and investment with that Community. A gathering coincidence of interest therefore impels the CARICOM countries to, as suggested above, seek to institutionalise its diplomatic intercourse with the Central American states.

Finally, we have earlier noted the post-independence interest of Guyana in developing and consolidating institutionalised relationships with mainland countries on the South American continent such as Venezuela and Brazil. Trinidad and Tobago's geopolitical and commercial interests in deepening ties with these countries has also been noted; as too, the complementary interest of Venezuela in establishing close diplomatic and other relations with the countries of the Eastern Caribbean.

We believe that, for the future, it will be important for CARICOM to seek to strengthen relationships with Brazil. Its location, the ethnic make-up of the country's population and its rising status as a rapidly industrializing state all point to advantages for us in pursuing this orientation.

Again, Guyana and Trinidad and Tobago might for the Caribbean Community be allocated lead roles in the development of this relationship, allowing the building over time of diplomatic and negotiating teams and networks drawn from the Member States of the Community, and permitting Member States to gradually identify and exploit particular areas of cooperation with Brazil.

The limited financial and human resources available for diplomatic activity in the broad sense of that term requires for CARICOM that those states with special interests in particular geographical areas of particular states outside of the Community be permitted to take the lead in consolidating relationships, incorporating the interests and participation of other Member States on the basis of guidelines agreed by the Community as a whole. All of this will become more functionally coordinated and regionalised through the roles envisaged for the CARICOM Commission in the next Chapter on 'Structures of Unity'.

3. INTERNATIONAL RELATIONS TOWARD THE METROPOLES: EEC AND NAFTA

North America and the United Kingdom have been the two historical focal points of the external relations of the CARICOM States. This situation continued into the first phase of the post-independence period; and, as we have suggested, earlier attempts at diversification of relations in the 1970s have proven not to have been particularly successful. Links with the 'ethnic mother countries' of India and Africa have largely been maintained for cultural and psychological reasons.

With the entry of the United Kingdom into the EEC, the CARICOM States, as with other Commonwealth countries, quickly perceived that there was a danger of their being relegated to a status less than that of inclusion within the preferential systems which they had hitherto enjoyed. The response of the CARICOM States was to seek what were referred to as 'bankable assurances' that their access to the United Kingdom market would be maintained.

The long period of persistent integration of the United Kingdom into Europe since the 1970s to the present, culminating in her adherence to the single European market, can be seen in terms of CARICOM Governments continuing this diplomacy of 'bankable assurances' even as it was becoming apparent that the liberalisation implicit in the single market process might well impede the long-term implementation of the assurances received under the Lomé Convention with respect to trade. A close look at the declining trade relationship between the United Kingdom and an another Commonwealth Country, New Zealand, would also have indicated that, as far as the European Community was concerned, historical and cultural relationships would be gradually subordinated to market relationships and a renewed geopolitical interest in strengthening the system of cooperation of European states.

A second perception of CARICOM Governments over the period would also have been that Europe as a whole, rather than the United Kingdom, would quite quickly become the focal point of their international relationships in that part of the globe. The advent of the

Single Market would then have simply reinforced this perception.

The difficulty with proposing policy recommendations from these perceptions was that the CARICOM States had little presence or visibility on the European Continent, and certainly in respect of leading states like Germany, which has been a strong advocate of free market rather than preferential economic relationships. In addition, European Community Governments were progressively tending over the period to allocate responsibility for trade negotiations to the Community System as a whole through the European Commission, while on the other hand there were no systematic attempts on the part of the CARICOM countries to reciprocally treat the matter in this way —apart from periodic negotiations concerning the Lomé Convention. The CARICOM system has therefore shown little institutional coherence in the face of increasing institutional coherence on the part of the European Community.

Until, then, the recent flurry of activity in respect of protection of preferential arrangements for banana exports, Europe's perception of the Caribbean may well have been one of increasing political and economic distance. While the widening of the European Community to include both Spain and Portugal has in fact tended to give European diplomacy a wider Hemispheric vision, rather than one concerned with the ex-colonial zone of states in the Caribbean part of the Hemisphere.

Yet, as we have earlier suggested, the fact that some European States (France, the Netherlands) have maintained minor possessions in the Caribbean Region, will have given some of the CARICOM States in proximity to those possessions some hope of European interest in maintaining an overall framework of regional stability. The interest of France, for example, in seeking to ensure that her Overseas Departments have some part in the general implementation of the Lomé Convention, may be indicative of this. Initial attempts by some Eastern Caribbean States to elaborate a framework of cooperation with neighbouring Overseas Departments will indicate the possibilities inherent in exploiting France's interest.

In the wake then of the European Community's own evolution, what can be said to constitute Caribbean Community interests in the New Europe? In the short-term it will surely be the case that the central interest will focus on maintenance in some form of the preferential relationship by emphasising the agreements reached under the Lomé Convention. Since, however, non-adherents to Lomé of some significance, like India and other Asian states, as well as certain Latin American countries, will surely in the future be pressing the European Community to convert the special arrangements applying to the ACP countries into general arrangements relating to most developing states, the CARICOM countries will have to fashion a joint response to any such development with a view to maintaining their present advantages.

The question which arises in this context is what institutional linkages CARICOM States, as small entities, can establish for themselves with the European Community. It is already being suggested that so severe are the developmental problems in Africa that special arrangements, more substantial than the Lomé Aid arrangements will have to be made for them through the multilateral aid system rather than by any single economic or political bloc.

It is difficult to perceive how bilateral relationships between CARICOM States and Europe can assure the establishment and continuity of such linkages. And, further, even a CARICOM initiative in this regard will probably be met by the suggestion that the complete Caribbean Archipelago should form the basis of any institutionalised system of arrangements between Europe and this Region. Thus again the probability that future diplomacy will need to focus on the question of the diplomatic redefinition of the Caribbean Region.

We therefore stress here the importance of the Caribbean Community adopting an holistic approach to this problem of effective representation and presence in the European Community. CARICOM should agree on a number of sectoral areas — financial, trade, investment, technology transfer, tertiary education — in which it is necessary to establish, under the aegis of the Lomé Convention, close and continuing cooperative relationships with the European Community or particular member-states of the Community. The Caribbean Community should then seek to develop negotiating teams of some permanence for the purpose of pursuing in depth Caribbean Community and State interests in the various sectoral areas, and establishing firm networks with institutions and personnel in the European Community. These teams, co-ordinated and given

Relations toward the Metropoles

coherence by the CARICOM Commission referred to later, should have representatives from relevant private sector interests.

Such an approach should reduce the ad hoc and reactive nature of contemporary Caribbean diplomacy towards the European Community and towards non-Anglophone Caribbean and Central American states now seeking to pursue closer relationships with Europe. In this way, too, the widening political and economic distance between Europe and CARICOM, in the face of other European interests in the Hemisphere, can be bridged over time.

Such an approach requires, however, clear agreements on the part of CARICOM States on a long-term orientation to Europe; a firm belief that a collective approach will maximise the use of limited financial and human resources available for such tasks; and a firm commitment of monetary resources to underpin the work of the established teams.

The two countries on the North American Continent, the USA and Canada, have been historically the object of large migrations by Caribbean peoples. In more recent times, with a decline in United Kingdom investment in CARICOM, substantial shifts in trade patterns have taken place, including major investments from both the United States and Canada in the mineral, manufacturing and tourism sectors. It is probably fair to say that, in the first decade or so of Caribbean independence (the 1960s), trade and investment relationships predominated over aid relationships as far as the United States was concerned. On the other hand, the historic Canadian willingness to make major allocations of aid, particularly in infrastructural sectors has been maintained. Canada in fact has in recent years defined CARICOM as an area of special interest as far as economic and technical assistance is concerned.

In spite of the substantial economic interest of the United States in the CARICOM Region, it could be said that, certainly up to the end of the 1970s, the CARICOM Region has remained largely unaffected by the historically intense strategic interest which the United States has had in the wider Caribbean area. The general exception to this in historical terms would be periods of global war.

This generally benign strategic interest has, of course, partly been the result of the American sense of assurance that the United Kingdom and other European powers would seek to ensure the security and stability of the countries and geopolitical zones in the Caribbean in which they had particular interest. In fact this has generally been the case, the major exception to this generalisation being the relatively recent American intervention in Grenada — a situation in which there appeared to be some hesitancy on the part of both European and larger CARICOM States.

Given the absence now of any Soviet presence in or threat to the Caribbean area as defined by the United States, it is likely, following the Grenada intervention, that the CARICOM sub-sector will return to relative quiescence and minimal interest on the part of the United States as far as protection of her security interests are concerned.

But the major change in the hemisphere from the point of view of countries of the CARICOM system is not the absence of a Communist threat, since in large measure this has not been a central aspect of CARICOM concerns. It is, rather, the current attempts at rearrangement of the framework of hemispheric economic relations which constitutes the contemporary revolution in the system of relations to which CARICOM countries had become accustomed. CARICOM countries had already been concerned that NAFTA would remove such advantages in trade in investment as they were able to derive from both the CBI and CARIBCAN. Added to this now is the strategic decision of Mexico to establish free trade relations with the United States and Canada in a system characterised by reciprocity. The question arising then is whether the terms agreed in the future between Mexico and the North American states will set precedents for the adherence of other hemispheric states irrespective of differences in level of development.

In this context it will be incumbent on CARICOM Governments not only to seek a negotiating instrument with the United States as is being attempted in the establishment of the Council on Trade and Investment. It will also be necessary to arrange for detailed discussions with Mexico as the negotiations for and implementation of the free trade system proceed.

In respect of Canada-West Indies relations which have had an historic specificity, CARICOM Governments should, it would seem, seek to reinforce the Canadian interest, though now in an era of more limited resources devoted to aid, in assisting in higher education, infrastructural development, particularly in the area of transportation, and in the appropriate exploitation and conservation of the marine environment.

In respect finally of both Canada and the United States, it would appear that CARICOM Governments have not yet found ways of utilising the diverse skills and competences of the now large West Indian populations which exist in those countries. While many persons of West Indian origin are now nationals of Canada and the US, we have perceived a willingness on the part of many of them to make a contribution to the development of the Region. Caribbean Governments need to more actively identify our compatriots in the occupational locations in which they now exist, and seek to define ways in which they can be of assistance to us.

In summary, two questions arise for CARICOM Governments in relating to the metropoles of North America and Europe. The first is whether their own negotiations towards establishment of a CARICOM Single Market, will lead to development of a sufficient integration instrument directing local (regional) factors of production, so as to present an economic space attractive to capital investment similar to (though smaller than) those economic spaces being constructed in various sectors of the Hemisphere. For it is the character of the regional economic space that will shape the potential for participation in the relations of the wider space of the hemisphere. The Commission's research and findings, as already indicated in a previous Chapter, conclude that the larger market of CARICOM is indeed adequate economic space to begin the building of our production base, the development of the professional service sectors, as well as franchise type operations.

And the second question concerns whether the co-operative approach co-ordinated by a central CARICOM facility, as discussed later, can be developed and sustained by CARICOM Governments, giving to the European and North American spheres an appropriate sense of the continuity of CARICOM diplomacy and of effective, even though small, presences in their centres.

4. RELATIONSHIPS IN OTHER AREAS

CARICOM Governments since their independence have all assumed membership in the Commonwealth and in the United Nations. The Commonwealth they have been able to utilise, first, as a source of relatively easily negotiated technical assistance with limited conditionalities. But secondly, and as importantly, they have sought, and have been able, to utilise the Commonwealth as a conduit to establishing continuing relationships with both developing and developed states in which they have not (for reasons of limited resources) been able to have diplomatic presences.

CARICOM Governments have also been able to utilise the United Nations system in much the same way. Both the Commonwealth and the UN have too, permitted the consolidation of relationships with countries which can be said to be the ethnic or cultural 'kith and kin' of the Caribbean countries — in particular India and countries on the African continent.

We believe it to be important that small countries such as ours continue to utilise those institutions as media for reinforcing these bonds, and also for establishing bonds with small like-minded states in regions sometimes too distant for us to sustain institutionalised bilateral relations.

In addition, as global political arrangements dramatically change and affect the *modus operandi* of international institutions like the UN and the international financial institutions, it will be important that the Caribbean Community seeks to form long-term diplomatic and negotiating alliances with other selected developing countries and with small and medium-sized developed states, in order to ensure that, in the re-orientation of global institutions, its interests and objectives are given some place of prominence.

CARICOM Governments must, therefore, given their limited resources, seek to construct an effective division of labour and allocation of roles and responsibilities, in order to ensure a sustained collective, *Community* orientation to the central debates in the international institutions; and in order to give themselves visibility *vis-à-vis* particular countries whose interests they wish, for cultural or economic reasons, to attract and maintain.

What we say here, in relation to the Commonwealth and the UN, applies to other institutions with which the Caribbean has been perhaps less familiar, but which in their spheres of activity have importance for us: for example GATT and the Organization of American States. And the Caribbean Community needs to develop a consensus on how to relate to existing, basically Latin American, institutions like SELA which have sought to attract its Member States to effective membership for some time.

5. COMPULSIONS FOR WIDENING INTEGRATION

In the next Chapter we address the central question of deepening the CARICOM integration process; but we have never had far from our thoughts the related matter of widening the process of regional integration.

'What Caribbean?'

In our Progress Report we raised the question 'What Caribbean?' and in this Chapter we have explored various aspects of our relationships in Latin America and the hemisphere, and in the wider world. What we said in our Progress Report remains valid. We explained how CARICOM has spent many years in intellectual discourse about the 'widening' and the 'deepening' of integration. They were understandable contentions for the time through which we had passed — the first, fragile, formative stages of the evolution of the economic Community. Now, however, it profits us little to pursue these dialectics as threshold questions — as if what is involved are competing alternatives between which we must make a definitive choice. The two are not necessarily irreconcilable. The West Indies must both deepen the process of integration to which it has set its hand and reach out to a wider Caribbean at appropriate levels of cooperation.

As we go down both tracks, however, those earlier questions

443

continue to have relevance — but as principles that help to shape the pace and character of our progress in each direction; not as barriers to action altogether. We need a more positive mindset which does not ignore that too rapid a widening of the Community could slow down the deepening of the integration process and overwhelm CARICOM itself yet recognises as well that the widening of integration in the Caribbean is necessary, both in itself and for enlarging the gains of integration. Such a start with a widening process may well spur us to action in strengthening the integration bonds between our founding West Indian partners. Our Region keeps on affirming that this is our intent; but we fulfil it at a pace so halting that it almost resembles retrogression. A decade of deferment of the CET is a reminder of how easy it is to put off widening until we deepen, but never deepen and so never widen.

The dual track approach may produce differing levels of integration within the Caribbean; it may produce circles of association that start with the intimate West Indian family and others that encompass an extended family of the non-English speaking islands of the Caribbean, and a still larger circle of closer relations with countries of the Caribbean Basin that includes territories of the South and Central American littoral. We believe that we have to be confident of both our identity and our capacities, and be ready to take a lead in the creation of a real Community of the entire Caribbean.

For all the reasons we have given earlier in this Chapter, we simply have to widen our horizons as we look to the twenty-first century. As the world has grown smaller with the communications revolution and the compulsions of interdependence, those already small are in danger of being miniaturised. It is a danger that will continue. In the process, individually small West Indian countries become depreciated in the global balance sheet. Time was when Caribbean Islands held high value in metropolitan scales — higher than the 'icy wastes' of Canada or the small outpost of Manhattan. That time is gone. Regionalism, however, can be our essential value added; but regionalism in CARICOM terms alone is no longer enough. Altogether, we are a market of five and a half million, smaller than any but the very smallest economy of Latin America. The wider Caribbean — including Cuba in the North and Suriname in the South — is a market of 32 million: still not a giant in the world economy with which we must interact, but with a better chance of survival. The region of the Caribbean Basin, including Venezuela, Colombia and Central America, is a community of 112 million; with Mexico, almost 200 million.

In this wider market we have important advantages, including among them larger opportunities for trade and investment that become open to our fast developing indigenous business community. Already, the Region as a whole has produced entrepreneurs who hold their own internationally. Some of them are beginning to move into the wider Caribbean area. On our visit to Cuba, we were proud to see the part Jamaican entrepreneurs are playing in the dynamic opening up of the tourist industry there. It should be a purpose of regional policy to give that process every encouragement.

CARICOM the 'Inner Core'

We have had consultations in the wider Caribbean at a variety of levels. Along the way we have had points of contact in many countries of the Region with individuals and sometimes Governments. We have held a special symposium in Venezuela on CARICOM/Latin America relations and made visits to Cuba, Curacao, the Dominican Republic, Martinique, Puerto Rico and the US Virgin Islands, either as a Commission or as individual Commissioners. We have followed closely the path-breaking discussions between CARICOM and Central American countries at San Pedro Sula in 1992. There could not, of course, be anything in the nature of even a pre-negotiation of specific proposals. Such a process was not open to us. Our conversations were exploratory and in the nature of a learning process. But two factors emerging from them are pertinent. First, our consultations have confirmed our earlier perceptions as set out in the Progress Report; secondly, they suggest to us the existence of a climate in the Caribbean propitious to the approach we there sketched out. Now, we must be more specific.

A word, first of all, about the concept of 'widening'. We are firmly of the view that the widening of CARICOM's relations into the entire Caribbean must be an essential part of the way forward. But we believe it would be a mistake to see that process of widening simply in terms of enlarging CARICOM's membership. There are important factors to be balanced. On the economic side, we have to feel our way in enlarging the CARICOM market so that we make progress in that direction without being overwhelmed by new members and end up being lost within our own widened Community. Yet, there are political compulsions as well as economic ones for regional cohesion, including specific proposals for membership from, for example, the Dominican Republic and Venezuela, as well as an external environment that increasingly looks to, and sometimes demands, dealing with larger units than CARICOM. So, how do we widen? Our view is that CARICOM should remain the inner core of our relationships in the Region, and that we should consciously create space beyond membership of CARICOM for development of CARICOM's integrationist relationships with Caribbean countries from Central America to Suriname, from Cuba to Venezuela.

An Association of Caribbean States

What we see and propose is a new Association of Caribbean States — the ACS — anchored on CARICOM and promoted by CARICOM. As the largest integration movement in the Caribbean, we have a responsibility to take the initiative. In CARICOM, we have already begun to integrate 13 Caribbean countries. It is for us to take the lead in going further. Moreover, if we do not create the new space, CARICOM will be the only vehicle for the association of other Caribbean countries with us. CARICOM itself is not in all respects the most appropriate vehicle for those relationships, which will need to be tailored to a great variety of situations. The CARICOM Commission which we propose in the next Chapter for a central role in our own Community should be the spearhead of this initiative and the instrument of CARICOM action within it. In doing so, the Commission will emphasize CARICOM's unity within the wider association of Caribbean states, though it will remain important for CARICOM countries to be individual Member States of the new Association.

We see this Association of Caribbean States as being functionally active in an integration sense — not a mere symbol of Caribbean aspiration for unity. We believe that it should be the means of our creating within the wider Caribbean special trading and functional cooperation arrangements on terms to be negotiated — terms which will recognise the relative weakness of CARICOM economies in relation to some of the larger partners like Cuba and the Dominican Republic, Puerto Rico and Venezuela.

Starting with working out the details of the offer of the one-way free trade area which has already been made, the Association of Caribbean States (ACS) could be the vehicle through which other special arrangements could be promoted for the expanding of trade between CARICOM and other countries, or cooperating groups of countries, in the wider Caribbean including the littoral. In regard to specific external initiatives which are now being negotiated, for instance, NAFTA and EAI, ACS countries would develop arrangements for regular consultation and evolve concerted approaches to negotiations. The CARICOM Commission which is proposed in the following Chapter could take the lead in systematising such discussions and developing common positions.

There is a wide area of functional cooperation which could be developed within the Association of Caribbean States as a precursor to deeper relations among Member Countries, joint ventures between and among ACS countries and the widening of air, sea and telecommunication links covering the entire Caribbean and the littoral area among them, but so too are others in a variety of fields.

A start has already been made in tourism, with the decision taken at the level of the Caribbean Tourism Organisation to market the Caribbean as a Region with multiple destinations. We were glad to assist as a Commission in resolving difficulties over Cuba's recognition of Grenada and its membership of the CTO, in the spirit of that new Caribbean-wide harmony that must be both the beginning and the end of this effort to integrate the Region of the Caribbean Sea.

Many of the Caribbean countries now participate in the meetings of CARICOM Ministers of Health and are also members of the Caribbean Epidemiological Institute (CAREC). There is a major area for cooperation in protecting, mapping and harvesting the resources of the Caribbean Sea, much of which now formally falls within the collective Exclusive Economic Zones of the several countries. Equally, the entire Region needs to apply its collective efforts in the area of control over the spread of communicable diseases, the curbing of drug trafficking and the prevention of other anti-social activities. There is, moreover, a pressing imperative to develop cooperation among the Universities in the Region, focussing on student and faculty interchange, research and development, and the upgrading of science and technology in the wider Caribbean.

This network of cooperative activity, when it is effected, will narrow the divide which now separates CARICOM from its neighbours in the wider Caribbean and the littoral — indeed separates the non-CARICOM states one from another, and brings within reach the eventual unification of the Caribbean.

We were specially glad for the opportunity the Commission was afforded, through the good offices of the Ambassadors of CARICOM countries to the Organisation of American States, to address the Permanent Council of the Organisation on 27 March 1992, during our visit to the diaspora in the United States. The Commission took the opportunity to share with the Permanent Council our vision of a wider Community of Caribbean States beyond the English-speaking countries, and left with the impression that it is a vision likely to be shared in the hemispheric family and an initiative likely to be welcomed. The following is an extract from the Chairman's address to the Permanent Council on that significant occasion:

> Let me end, therefore, on a note which looks beyond the West Indian community, looks beyond CARICOM, to our wider Caribbean community of which many of your countries are a part. Our history of colonialism has reinforced the separateness of a dividing sea, and Caribbean people have grown up largely as strangers looking more to our respective metropoles than to each other: neighbours, each looking beyond our Caribbean neighbourhood... The Caribbean Basin was the crucible of the encounter between Europe and the first people of the Americas. 500 years later it could be the crucible for welding together the states and peoples that to a peculiarly significant degree are the product of that encounter.

The Wider Vision

There will be many aspects of the new Association of Caribbean States to be developed, elaborated and negotiated. That is a necessary process; but we believe it to be important at the outset to outline the vision towards which CARICOM should reach. Put simply, the peoples of CARICOM and their Governments must no longer think in narrow terms merely of 'the Commonwealth Caribbean,' but in wider terms of a 'Caribbean Commonwealth' — and must work to fulfil this larger ambition. The ambition itself must encompass, besides the 13 CARICOM Countries, all the countries of the Caribbean Basin. It must reach out, therefore, to all the independent island states of the Caribbean Sea and the Latin American countries of Central and South America whose shores are washed by it. And it must be open as well to the Commonwealth of Puerto Rico, the island communities of the French West Indies, the Dutch islands of Aruba and the Netherlands Antilles, the US Virgin Islands and the remaining British dependencies.

That wider Caribbean is our natural community as a sub-region of Latin America. It lacks the cultural bedrock of CARICOM; but has a cultural dynamic of its own. It lacks the linguistic homogeneity of CARICOM; but increasingly we speak the language of the Sea that is our cradle — the common voice a shared geo-political and ecological environment requires of us. It lacks the commonality of CARICOM's political culture; but it aspires to common democratic norms and can only strengthen their fulfilment by association. There is already enough of the raw material of oneness — so supremely demonstrated at CARIFESTA — from which to mould the Association of Caribbean States. And if we start with practical measures and workable arrangements that contribute concretely to the development of its constituent parts — and from our point of view, of course, to the economic development of CARICOM countries — we shall build surely in this wider Caribbean: even as we strengthen CARICOM in our more closely integrated Community.

The vision of the future must be one of widening circles of integration starting with our circle of CARICOM kinship and broadening out to our extended Caribbean family. It may be that not all Caribbean Basin countries will be ready to pursue this vision from the outset. That should not deter us. And the conception should be clear: the architecture must provide for all, and its integrity must not be compromised. None must be excluded *ab initio*.

An Early Ambition

We do not advance these proposals for widening the integration process by means other than enlarging CARICOM's membership in a defensive mode. We believe that the concept of an Association of Caribbean States is one that should have taken root already in our Region. It is, indeed, a concept as indigenous to our Region as was the related concept of an Association of South-East Nations to the ASEAN region. A decade before President Reagan launched his Caribbean Basin Initiative, the idea of an association of Caribbean Basin countries had actually been raised within the region — and by CARICOM countries.

It is not without significance that from the Inaugural Meeting of the CARICOM Heads of Government Conference held in St Lucia in 1974, the then still six independent Member States authorised consultation throughout the Region on a Guyana proposal to convene a meeting of the Heads of State and Governments of the countries of the Caribbean Basin: consultation between the political leadership of the free, independent, developing states of the Caribbean Basin — with the intent of formulating 'a concept of the Caribbean Basin as an area of tranquillity, of justice and of progress'. The Government of Trinidad and Tobago offered to host the Summit meeting. In due course, the Government of Venezuela offered to host the Preparatory Ministerial Meeting. A special meeting of Caribbean Basin Foreign Ministers discussed the proposal during the 1974 General Assembly in New York: so substantial was the support for the idea. Regrettably, those early proposals were never carried forward as they should have been, and the initial impetus faded only to be replaced by discontinuities within the Region. From the outset, however, CARICOM was looking beyond itself to its destiny in the wider Caribbean.

The time has come for an invigorated CARICOM to take the lead anew. We recommend that CARICOM take the initiative in advancing the specific idea of an Association of Caribbean States and in developing it in regard to both economic relations and functional cooperation. The time to act is now. The leadership space will not be ours to occupy if we let the moment pass.

We were asked specifically to advise on the proposal from the Dominican Republic for membership of CARICOM and there is now the Venezuela one-way free trade proposal. We believe both should be taken up in the context of our proposal for an Association of Caribbean States. Indeed, this clear expression of integrationist interest from two major partners in the wider Caribbean could provide a foundation for developing concrete proposals for the new Association of Caribbean States.

Non-independent and Caribbean countries

A word should be said about two sub-sets of the wider Caribbean region: the non-independent countries and the wider group of Caribbean ACP countries. As regards the former, there was a time, close to our own independence in the 60s and 70s, when we were disdainful, and somewhat arrogant, about others not yet independent. Times have changed, however. We have learned the limits of independence and that they do not justify superior airs. But there have been changes as well in the roles of the metropoles in relation to more autonomous Caribbean countries. We do not believe that our vision of an Association of Caribbean States can exclude them — once they are allowed to participate in their own right and wish to do so — any more than CARICOM has excluded Montserrat. There must be a place for them all in the Association of Caribbean States — and a welcome for all who wish to occupy it. But there are other possibilities. We refer later, for example, to our keeping an open mind about their direct relationship with CARICOM.

But there is another point of linkage and it relates to the second category: the independent Caribbean countries not part of CARICOM that are now members of the African, Caribbean and Pacific Group (ACP) associated within the framework of the Lomé Convention. They are the Dominican Republic, Haiti and Suriname. As we explained earlier, we come together with them, and the European Community countries, in the Caribbean Forum which is, therefore, an existing institution for sub-regional cooperation. At the moment, it functions essentially in a Lomé context. Is it capable of broadening into a forum for exploring deeper cooperation with European Community countries — even beyond Lomé arrangements — and one which draws into the process the non-independent Dutch and French Caribbean territories whose status is one of substantial autonomy? There seem to us to be many possibilities here, both in terms of wider Caribbean cooperation and larger cooperation with Europe. The CARICOM Commission can follow up these opportunities even as it goes forward with the central mission of establishing the Association of Caribbean States.

Windows on the World

Multiple Entry Points

As we develop the structures of unity responsive to the need to both deepen the CARICOM integration process and widen Caribbean regional integration, one matter of fundamental importance needs to be emphasized. The processes of deepening and widening we have described will preoccupy us; but, it is not our intention, it is not our proposal, that they should be our exclusive pursuits. CARICOM's structures of unity must not constitute a prison. They must have windows on the wider world and pathways that lead outward. West Indian Governments and people must consciously maximise every advantage and potential that history and geography have bequeathed us. It is a feature of that legacy that CARICOM has multiple entry points to the world. Those entry points may be more the result of cruel history than careful planning; but they are, in the result, a precious heritage.

As we have made clear, we have entry points to Europe; to Africa and Asia; to Canada; to the United States; to the Commonwealth; to Latin America; the Lomé Convention; our cultural bedrock; our roles in the old Non-Aligned Movement and whatever succeeds it in a post-Cold War world; CARIBCAN and our 'special relationship with Canada'; the CBI, the Enterprise for the Americas Initiative (EAI) and the potential of NAFTA; Commonwealth functional cooperation, including the CFTC and Commonwealth political links; our work in the Latin American group at the United Nations and our membership of the OAS — are all elements of those multiple entry points. We must preserve them all, and consolidate them, simultaneously with deepening CARICOM and developing our Association of Caribbean States.

The 'co-ordination of foreign policies' is already one of the objectives of CARICOM as expressed in the Treaty of Chaguaramas and the Committee of Foreign Ministers has been one of the more purposeful arms of CARICOM. The CARICOM Commission which we are proposing will give this aspect of the Community's work added vigour — quite apart from the development of the Association of Caribbean States. It is one of the reasons why the 'external affairs' unit of the Secretariat might well be located close to the Commission's Headquarters.

Hemispheric Links

The Association of Caribbean States must stand by itself as the major thrust of CARICOM in our wider Caribbean Basin; but we must have no illusions of exclusivity or compartmentalisation in our external relations — and nowhere more so than in the hemisphere. We shall have to go down several avenues to progress and they will often intersect across the course, and not always with symmetry or certainty. Our relations with the United States will always be a major dimension of our economic and political life; we are already actively engaged with US-led initiatives which present opportunities and challenges in equal measure.

Earlier in this Chapter we set out what we feel should be the strategy for CARICOM in relation to some of these initiatives: the United States-Canada Free Trade Agreement, the wider North American Free Trade Area negotiations involving Mexico (NAFTA) and the Enterprise for the Americas Initiative (EAI). We have recommended that we continue to pursue the last of these — the Enterprise of the Americas Initiative, for which the Region (as CARICOM) has already concluded a Framework Agreement. We must also follow assiduously (and with all the partners) progress in relation to NAFTA in particular. We are also involved in the CARICOM-Central America dialogue begun at the San Pedro Sula encounter. Jamaica represents CARICOM on the Latin American Group of 9 (the Rio Group) in relation to a wide range of Hemispheric issues. All this must continue with the CARICOM Commission acting as our coordinator and interlocutor in close consultation with CARICOM Governments.

The burdens on us are staggering. We were told in Washington that some 300 professionals had been ear-marked for the NAFTA negotiations with Mexico. There will be a tendency to produce from those negotiations a template for etching out similar agreements with other countries or groups of countries. We might well be seen as being among the latter. But that is altogether taking us too much for granted; we shall have to be defending our corner and insisting on our special interests — such as retention of CBI preferences and 'non-reciprocity' — at every turn. There is really no time to lose.

Strengthening Ties with Canada

A good example of exploring our entry points is the value we see in deepening our special relationship with Canada. We believe that the Canada/West Indies link offers special potential for strengthening. Together, we are the Commonwealth countries of the hemisphere. That shared history has forged strong ties over the years and provides a natural bond. The West Indian diaspora in Canada is further strengthening those ties. Canada's tradition of internationalism makes it a partner in the developed world with whom partnership does not imply hegemony. In the world that is evolving, CARICOM will have need of partners and special relations which are not counter-productive.

In the realm of higher education, a central aim of Canadian aid might be to assist in building long-term relationships between Canadian and Caribbean intellectual and research institutions, to permit the continuity of scientific and intellectual work in the Caribbean environment whose Caribbean resources may not be sufficient for this. The long-term aim would be the continued development of the human and social resources of the Region.

Canadian assistance in the development of the infrastructure of transportation is a major underpinning for the revival and development of a dynamic trade and investment relationship. In addition, Canadian expertise in the technology of satellite communication for education and for the data services industry would be specially valued. But helping CARICOM's integration process through enhancing communications via a CARIBCAN satellite would be a contribution of immeasurable value.

Finally, the exploitation of the Caribbean marine area is still not highly developed, while at the same time effective access to the 200-mile Exclusive Economic Zone provides the Caribbean public and private sectors with a major challenge. An effort should be made by Caribbean Governments therefore, to ensure that this area remains a priority for Canadian cooperative assistance. For it is limited not only to fisheries and mineral development, but to tourism and the important issue of the conservation of the marine environment in the course of economic development.

We believe, therefore, that as we approach the twenty-first century particular attention should be given to strengthening this special relationship — and not only at the level of Canada as a donor country. Might it not be, for example, to our mutual advantage as part of that relationship to work out special possibilities that enable, even induce, Canadian retirees to reside in the Caribbean — their rather special place in the sun. And why shouldn't we, with Canadian help, be for them their sun-belt in the context of tourism and tropical fruit production — much as Florida is in this respect to the rest of the US.

There is much that Canada can do to help us face the future including, for example, special assistance in human resource development over and above conventional arrangements and special mechanisms that facilitate West Indian Canadians contributing their skills in CARICOM's development. When we address later the question of the Assembly of Caribbean Parliamentarians we will explain how we see the Assembly furthering this special relationship through joint periodic sittings with Parliamentarians from Canada, including Parliamentarians from the legislatures of the Provinces. Beyond that, the periodic meetings at Summit level of Canada and the Commonwealth Caribbean, and the existing instrument of the Canada/CARICOM Joint Trade and Economic Committee, which can meet flexibly at either Ministerial or technical levels, present us with tools that can be applied purposively and with resolution to the achievement of these objectives.

In the chart opposite we seek to illustrate CARICOM's points of entry to the world and the concept of multiple relationships by which we feel policy should be guided — with appropriate adjustments in the light of changing circumstances. We emphasise that these relationships are not all on the same footing or of equal importance to CARICOM.

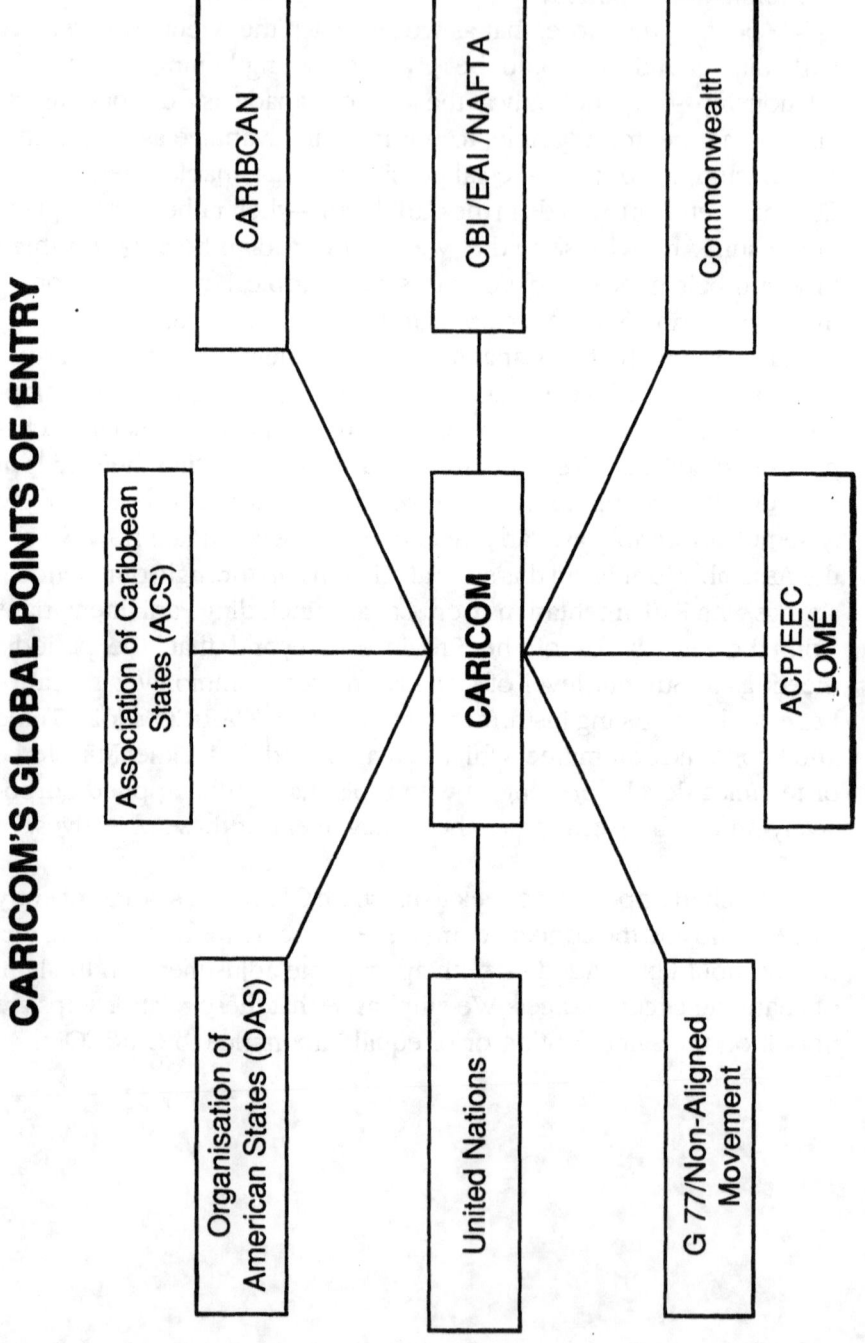

Recommendations

1. that CARICOM bridge the divide between its Member States and other states and territories of the Caribbean and Latin America, recognising the advent of an increasingly "Caribbean Basin" approach to international negotiations and development issues, as well as the changes within and among Latin American countries;

2. that CARICOM countries adopt a collective approach to current and potential changes in the international community, including international political and financial institutions, and reflect this approach in common arrangements for international economic negotiations and diplomatic representation;

3. that, in the context of its unique place within the wider Caribbean, CARICOM play a distinct role in assisting the process of normalising Cuba's relations in the Hemisphere;

4. that CARICOM Member States continuously reaffirm their solidarity with the people of Haiti, and collectively mobilise diplomatic and financial resources, within the limits of their capacity, to provide support, directly and through regional and international bodies, for the resolution of the Haitian crisis;

5. that, looking beyond the Caribbean Community, CARICOM seek to strengthen relations with Brazil;

6. that CARICOM's relations with the wider Caribbean not be restricted to membership of, or association with, CARICOM itself which should be the core family of the Caribbean integration process;

7. that the possibility be left open for membership of, or a special form of relationship with, Suriname, as well as the smaller British, Netherlands, French and US territories;

8. that CARICOM initiate proposals for the establishment of an Association of Caribbean States directed to both economic integration and functional cooperation with the other Caribbean Basin countries;

9. that the ACS be open to all CARICOM Member States, the other island states of the Caribbean and the Latin American countries of the Caribbean littoral; the ACS should allow for a variety of arrangements appropriate to its membership;

10. that CARICOM, the Dominican Republic, Haiti and Suriname collaborate in strengthening the Caribbean Forum within the Lomé Convention as a mechanism directed to both economic integration and functional cooperation and for achieving greater cooperation in the fields of external trade, investment and development assistance between themselves and the European Community;

11. that, beyond the deepening of CARICOM and establishment of the ACS, CARICOM countries consolidate and strengthen their relations with countries beyond the Caribbean — which relations are part of CARICOM's historical inheritance: Europe (Lomé), the Commonwealth (CFTC, etc.), Canada (CARIBCAN), Africa and Asia (G77 and the Non-Aligned Movement), Latin America (OAS), and the United States (CBI, the EAI and NAFTA);

12. that, in the context of a changing hemisphere, Caribbean countries pursue as a matter of high priority and with a sense of urgency the possibility of negotiating as a group a commom position for entry into NAFTA under arrangements whereby the benefits under the CBI are maintained, as recommended in Chapter V.

13. that a particular effort be made to give greater content to the 'special relationship' with Canada;

PART III

TIME FOR ACTION

CHAPTER XII

DEFINING A STRONG COMMUNITY

In the preceding part of this Report (Chapters IV-XI) we have laid out the challenges and opportunities which these extraordinary times present to the West Indies. In doing so, we have drawn attention to a variety of policies which our Region might adopt and pursue and a number of specific actions which it ought to take, ranging from approaches to development, special economic, social and cultural issues that demand attention, potential strengths that remain unused and our posture in the wider Caribbean, the hemisphere and the world. In at least some respects, these matters have to be addressed at a national level. But, together, they bear on the regional environment; and many, if not indeed all, require action at the regional level — much of it urgent action to define a strong and enduring West Indian society. It is with that action that this remaining part of our Report is concerned. What is the way forward for CARICOM as a Community?

1. THE DEEPENING OF CARICOM

Commitment to CARICOM

We look, first of all, at CARICOM as a Community committed to the goal of integration. As we pointed out in our Progress Report, our mandate takes its starting point from the Treaty of Chaguaramas. But the Treaty was itself a beginning, not an end: the beginning of the process of Caribbean integration through the Economic Community and Common Market. That beginning was made possible by the political decision reached earlier in 1973 after rigorous discussion and negotiation that culminated in the Georgetown Accord. It is essential to recognise that the aims of our leaders as elaborated in the Accord and later in the Treaty go beyond the enhancement of trade. They have continuing life and validity, and have remained present in our minds throughout our work. Common to both was the primary 'determination to consolidate and strengthen the bonds which have historically existed among their peoples'.

We believe that determination to be as firm now among CARICOM Governments as it was in 1974, and that it reflects a yearning that is widespread among West Indians everywhere. It is the driving force of regional ambition, and the Commission's quintessential mandate. The Treaty of Chaguaramas sought to give it fulfilment through processes of regional integration.

In the first part of this Report (Chapters I-III) we outlined the commitment of the Region to a far-reaching process of integration, to a Single Market and Economy, to wide-ranging cooperation in external relations, to functional cooperation across the board. Had the Region not committed itself to such a process, we would certainly have urged it as the necessary response to both the challenges and the opportunities of the time at hand and ahead. As it is, we need only, first of all, underscore the wisdom and timeliness of these political decisions and commitments. West Indian Governments have identified the right way forward. What remains to be done is to ensure that, as a Region, we make progress along that way — with all the deliberate speed that our situation demands. That means, pre-eminently, developing machinery for implementation.

Implementation: the 'Achilles Heel'

From all we have said before in this Report, and as we foreshadowed in our Progress Report, implementation has been the 'Achilles heel' of the integration movement. What we said in that Report bears restating for its centrality to our recommendations:

> The virtual absence of effective machinery for implementing regional decisions has become a major impediment to the progress of the integration movement. It has generated a degree of scepticism, if not of inertia, among important sectors in the Region. This is damaging to the credibility and effectiveness of the regional process. The most cynical commentators portray the situation as one where Governments attend regional meetings, take decisions and then turn their backs on them, leaving them to gather dust in the files of the CARICOM Secretariat.

This is a rather extreme presentation of the matter. Particularly within recent years the Caribbean Heads of Government Conference — as the highest organ of the Caribbean Community and Common Market — has been an effective instrument of decision making. Even the 'unanimity rule', which the Mills Report has rightly highlighted as a matter for modification in the interest of effective action, has not prevented the annual CARICOM Summit from reaching conclusions on a wide range of important matters both in relation to Common Market issues and to functional co-operation. Consensus has been possible at the Summit to a truly remarkable degree. Caribbean leaders have been at their best in terms of regional commitments when they have been together at the Summit. And their collective commitments have encouraged West Indian publics to believe that real progress is being made in many directions relevant to their lives, and in particular to their livelihoods. Expectations have been raised to a high level; but the sad reality is that more often than not performance has failed to follow promise. The reason is not hard to find.

... (it) lies substantially with national Governments and the absence of machinery that leaves implementation at the mercy of political, administrative and legislative processes in thirteen Capitals.

If the integration movement is to be strengthened, if it is to recover lost ground and respond to the demands of the present and the future, the West Indies must put in place machinery that overcomes this weakness. The weakness itself should not surprise us; it is not that the regional machinery for implementation has broken down or is otherwise inadequate to its task; it is simply non-existent. It was never put in place. Perhaps, in the beginning, that was a tolerable omission. Such decisions as needed implementation could be left to action in national capitals. However, the experience of 25 years since Dickenson Bay, and more particularly of 19 years since Chaguaramas, has demonstrated beyond serious argument that regional integration requires regional machinery endowed with the capacity to make integration effective.

New Machinery for Action

From the outset, there has been regional machinery in the form of a central Secretariat, first under the CARIFTA Agreement then under the Treaty of Chaguaramas. As a Commission, we have had the good fortune of having in our membership three of its Secretaries-General whose service together spans some 17 years. We know the Secretariat's strengths and its weaknesses, its successes and its failures, its ambitions and its frustrations. Without doubt, it has served the Region well, served it against great odds; sometimes, as in the 7-year period when Heads of Government did not meet in Conference, it held the Region together beyond the call of duty, certainly beyond the expectations of the Treaty. It has shown a high level of dedication to regional goals and, over the years, it has brokered compromises and negotiations that called for indefatigable commitment.

But neither the CARIFTA nor the CARICOM Secretariat was designed or empowered as machinery for implementation of the innumerable decisions that are the bedrock of integration. In the end, to borrow T.S. Eliot's famous lines: 'between the idea and the reality, between the motion and the action, between the conception and the creation, between the emotion and the response — falls the shadow'. It was, in fact, no single shadow: sometimes inertia, sometimes regional commitment overtaken by national preoccupation, sometimes the sheer burden of over-stretched bureaucracies, sometimes an unravelling of regional consensus under pressure of local interests. But, invariably, it was a shadow that delayed, and often indefinitely deferred, action which the process of integration required and which political decision had actually decreed. It was not a shadow the Secretariat could prevent; and not one it could lift once it had fallen.

CARICOM leaders and the Secretariat have been aware that problems with machinery were frustrating progress. The Pollard Report in 1985 addressed the related question of decision-making; the Mills Report, a substantial study commissioned from a group of eminent West Indians specially versed in matters of administration, was a comprehensive analysis of Secretariat machinery. Both called for changes. We have been asked specifically to take into account those aspects of the Mills proposals that touch on matters within our mandate, and we do so later in this Chapter. The point is, however, that earlier studies and reports have been constrained by the institutional arrangements provided for in the Treaty of Chaguaramas. We have no such constraint, and we have no hesitation whatever in saying that an adequate response to the need to accelerate implementation of integration decisions is not to be found in tinkering with the Secretariat or in changing its administrative and technocratic roles, but in supplementing it with new machinery equipped to perform a new and necessary function.

If we are serious about integration, we have at least to be certain that there are West Indians charged with the task and endowed with authority to make integration work. They have to be engaged upon that task exclusively: 24 hours a day, 7 days a week. And they have to be drawn from the public and political community of the Region, for theirs is not a bureaucratic function: they must initiate and mobilise, facilitate and secure action. The need should be obvious. If, when the European Community was established by the Treaty of Rome, the countries of Europe had contented themselves with establishing the European Summit and a Council of Ministers and did nothing about establishing the European Commission, where would Europe have been today? Almost certainly, the integration process would have proceeded at the pace of the slowest, and integration itself would not have made the progress it has made — to the advancement of the interest of member countries of the Community and the betterment of the lives of its people. What we have to do is develop structures of unity relevant to our circumstances and our needs and, in doing so, be ready to depart from models elsewhere, discarding what is not appropriate but benefitting, as other integration movements have done, from experience. What must emerge is a truly Caribbean model of machinery for action.

A Community of Sovereign States

There is an important practical and political reason why the route outlined above is the one we should go. The alternative routes of a federal system or one of closer political unity are not options now open to CARICOM as a whole. We are too close to the federal experiment that raised so many hopes, yet failed at its first major political hurdle. We do not recommend federation, federal structures or federal concepts as the way forward for CARICOM. It is important that these exclusions be fully understood, not only to avoid misunderstandings, misinterpretations and misrepresentations, but also because of the importance of the conceptual basis of the alternative we are proposing. Both federalism and other forms of political union involve the surrender of sovereignty, in part or in whole, to a federal or unitary government. If there is a powerful and enduring political will to accept that transfer, strong arguments can be developed for these systems. But neither is viable if the political climate for it does not exist, either at the level of Governments or people. Particularly as regards Governments, we do not believe that this is the case across the board in the Region, and in public consultations — even when, as was the case occasionally, we were encouraged to return to federalism — we made it clear that we were not advancing proposals along these lines. We believe that at this time most West Indians would agree that we are right.

Our proposals are rooted instead in the concept of CARICOM as a Community of sovereign states who by treaty agree to the pooling of certain of their sovereignties and to exercising them collectively in very specific respects. It is the sharing of the exercise of sovereignty, not a transfer of it, that is involved in the integration process. Sovereignty for Caribbean countries is admittedly less than substantial. Our condition is more one of powerlessness than of power; more of a contraction of choice than of a profusion of options — even for the largest, the most stable or the most resource endowed among us. But that is not to say that sovereignty is meaningless. The need is to recognise the limitations of our situation and to augment such national powers as now exist by exercising them collectively in a CARICOM context on a more systematic and effective basis in areas where their real potential can be enhanced by regional action. In terms of sovereignty, integration is a strengthening process, not one which weakens or diminishes its participating states.

No one has expressed better the concept of integration at the heart of the Commission's recommendations for the immediate future than Prime Minister Erskine Sandiford of Barbados when he said at the opening of the eleventh Summit in 1990:

For me, the Caribbean Community, the Integrated States of the Caribbean of which I have spoken, is much more than the efforts to secure free internal trade, or a common external tariff, or the harmonization of fiscal incentives or a common industrial, agricultural or transportation policy, or the establishment of a common market, or even the formation of a full economic union. For me, the Caribbean Community is nothing more and nothing less than the efforts of the Caribbean people to create a new and unique political entity that respects the national sovereignty of each individual territory, while at the same time pooling aspects of that sovereignty and pooling aspects of their resources in order to promote and preserve peace, promote and preserve democracy, promote and preserve fundamental human rights and the rule of law, and promote and preserve economic and social development among Caribbean people.

Making a Reality of Community

Sovereignty is one thing; contractual obligation is another. We cannot agree to act together in particular ways and remain free to act as we please or as every passing advantage induces us. If integration is to work to the long term advantage of the Region and all its Member States, CARICOM commitments must be binding commitments — morally, functionally, legally. They must be taken seriously by Governments and people, by the business community, by organised labour, by non-governmental actors. CARICOM must command our collective loyalty. Unless it does, all the machinery we devise will not suffice to make it work optimally. That will mean giving up insular prejudices and broadening our perceptions from a focus on what we lose to what we gain — for each must give so all may have a better chance to prosper. But, most of all, it requires us to accept that each of us belongs both to our own country and to our wider West Indian nation. It is admittedly not a nation with a flag or an anthem, a constitution or a government; but it is a nation in the wider sense of being our single West Indian homeland : the heartland of our kinship. That sense of belonging to CARICOM and of CARICOM belonging to us must be the underpinning of all the institutions and structures and machinery we develop to make the integration process work. CARICOM is not something on the side; it has to be a dimension of ourselves — each and every one of us.

We do well to remember the opening words of the eleven-year-old report of the 'Wise Men's' Commission entitled *The Caribbean Community in the 1980s*:

> The Roots of the Caribbean Community are not buried in doctrines of integration economics. CARICOM is not just the product of economic regional planning. Responsive as it is to the economic and political realities of the post-war world, Caribbean regionalism is the outgrowth of more than 300 years of West Indian kinship — the vagaries of the socio-economic political history of transplanted people from which is evolving a Caribbean identity. Without that element of West Indian identity a Community of the Caribbean would be mere markings on parchment — a Community without a soul, without vision of a shared destiny, without the will to persist and survive. It is not without significance that in the very first words of the Treaty of Chaguaramas, the Heads of Government of the Region expressed their determination 'to consolidate and strengthen the bonds which have historically existed among their people'.

The fact of our being a Community of sovereign states must not detract from our need to be a 'community' first and foremost — for it is the reality of community that enlarges our prospects as sovereign states. Keeping a sense of community to the fore calls for more than structures of unity. It will avail us nothing to gear up for the world of market economies and liberal democracy and simultaneously gear down by clinging to old habits of self-centredness. There is no magic in the symbols of 'community'; they must be reflected in our way of life.

That was why in our Progress Report we stressed the need for mobility of people within CARICOM: the free movement of skills, beginning with West Indian graduates of UWI and other accredited institutions and with West Indian media personnel. It was why we stressed as well the fundamental need for hassle-free travel for the people of CARICOM. The spontaneous, irrepressible and highly successful activity of our 'informal commercial sector' — our hucksters and higglers — has demonstrated that there are substantial gains for all in such mobility. It needs to be fostered and facilitated — not as a tolerable exception in hard times; but as a normal expression of West Indian entrepreneurship and inventiveness. CARICOM Heads of Government acknowledged this at Basseterre in specifically identifying this sector in the context of promoting mobility. But that, in itself, made a point: these informal traders had not waited for Governments; they had moved to occupy economic space created by the contraction of foreign exchange for traditional imports, and traditional ways of importing.

There is other economic space that the reality of CARICOM creates; space that will be similarly occupied by West Indians to the benefit of the Region's economic health once they are given the chance. But we have to think regionally if we are to act regionally. We have — Governments most of all — to overcome 'littleness'. That, for the most part, we are so small in size and so limited in resources compels us to be big in our minds if we are to reach beyond these limitations in a world that shows every disposition to ignore the small and the weak. All this is implicit in the goal of a 'Single Market and Economy' which the Region's political leadership has already adopted. We will not reach that goal, however, if we do not shift gear mentally and attitudinally as we climb towards the broad regional plateau.

We cannot, for example, journey to a Single Market and Economy with a mindset that looks askance at investment that comes from other parts of CARICOM; or, worse still, impedes it because it isn't 'local'. We cannot talk 'community' and treat community partners as 'foreigners'. The Treaty of Chaguaramas tells us they are not; but performance has to begin in our minds before it is reflected in policy and practice.

In the course of our consultations, we frequently introduced ourselves without any reference to the various parts of the Region from which we each came. We explained this by telling our audience that it was a deliberate omission reflecting our view that it simply did not matter who came from where. We were trying to make a point. The encouraging thing is that on every occasion that explanation drew spontaneous applause. West Indians will respond to leadership that opens up regional horizons. Like the hucksters and higglers, the people of the Region have actually begun the journey toward them.

Leaving Space for Unity Within

Those are powerful realities of 'oneness'. It follows that in choosing now the path of integration, rather than federation or closer political union, the Region must leave space for intra-CARICOM political groupings where parts of the Community feel able to integrate more closely than the whole — under the CARICOM roof. As the Commission has been at work, for example, the Windward Islands have been exploring proposals for political union. We made it clear at all stages that the Commission did not see these efforts as being in any way inconsistent with the wider goals of regional integration: provided, of course, that the efforts themselves were conceived, as we understand them to be conceived, within the CARICOM framework of regional integration. There could be other groupings, or enlargement of the Windward Islands Scheme to embrace others.

We recognise that the situation, the potential, the capacities of CARICOM Member States vary greatly, and that CARICOM arrangements must accommodate these special needs. The Treaty of Chaguaramas did so in relation to what were described at that time as the 'LDCs'; so did the negotiations for the Common External Tariff under the Treaty. The LDCs of 1973 were to become in the 1980s, as OECS member countries, the most economically stable CARICOM countries, with sustained growth rates in CARICOM exceeded only by Barbados. They remain, however, small and highly vulnerable Member States. They are particularly disadvantaged in having to provide infra-structure not much below that of larger societies. They need the benefit of special consideration under the Treaty; but that is the point. All integration processes must make some such allowance for weaker members. Europe's Single Market in 1993 will provide for special arrangements to meet the particular vulnerabilities of, for example, Spain and Portugal and of depressed areas within other member states. That is the way for CARICOM too — and the Treaty of Chaguaramas already allows for it in appropriate cases. It may be felt by some that 'LDCs' may no longer be an apt description. We have no hesitation, however, in acknowledging that for the foreseeable future CARICOM will have to respond in particular ways to the special needs and requirements of the relatively smaller societies of the OECS countries.

A Place for Small States

In the previous Chapter we explained our view that the widening process does not have to be seen simply in relation to enlarging the membership of CARICOM. However, we feel we should make a special point here about just that possibility in relation to some of the smaller countries of the Region with population numbers and economies closer to the scale of our own. We refer to the American, British, Dutch and French Islands and Suriname — that have shared with us a recent history of relations with European metropoles and many of whom still have those relations. We believe there may be a special niche in CARICOM itself for these countries and that their continuing relations with the United States or Britain or Holland or France should not be seen as an insurmountable hurdle once the countries themselves are allowed to participate in CARICOM — and wish to do so — in their own right. Martinique and Guadeloupe are close neighbours of Dominica and Saint Lucia. The US Virgin islands are 'West Indian Islands' and of course West Indians have played important roles in the development of Curacao and Aruba. Suriname is Guyana's neighbour; as an already independent country it is specially well positioned for membership of CARICOM. As our concept of a Community of Caribbean States unfolds, it will become clearer where these countries fit most naturally and beneficially and how they themselves see their relations with us developing. The point we make here is that we should not close our minds to their playing roles within CARICOM itself, if that is the path they prefer.

Security

We are addressing Heads of Government separately on questions of security which are in any event under consideration by an intergovernmental committee — chaired by Prime Minister Sandiford. We were able to facilitate meetings of regional security chiefs — both army and police — and they have given us insights into the opportunities as well as the difficulties of more coordinated action on the security front. Here we wish to raise only a few issues.

The first is the obvious need for pooling resources in appropriate cases. These will range from disaster relief to attempted *coups d'état*; what is 'appropriate' must be a matter for ad hoc decision-making by Heads of Government — certainly at this stage. But even within those parameters much can be done in advance by way of political guidelines for regional responses and practical arrangements to ensure swift decision-making and implementation.

The second is a point we make elsewhere in the context of unified services. We believe that in an effectively integrated Community there can, and should, be greater interchangeability among offices of the security forces. There is now some regional recruitment, especially in police forces. However, we believe the time has come to explore a regional security service in the form of an officer corps whose members can expect to be moved to forces within the Region — overcoming in the process the frustrations of limited career opportunities and enlarging the independence of officers from even the appearance of political favouritism on the one hand or political victimisation on the other.

Finally, we believe that the time is at hand for creative thinking in relation to the security vulnerabilities of small states. In a new era of global governance, countries like ours should be able to dispense with the need for significant military expenditure, mindful of the reliance we can place in a global '999' emergency system under genuine United Nations control. Such ideas are being explored in several quarters. We should be in the forefront of this search for new ways to guarantee real security. Our memorandum to Heads of Government will deal with these and other issues.

2. STRUCTURES OF UNITY

Central to the deepening of CARICOM in the manner described above is the establishment of the CARICOM Single Market and Economy as already agreed by Heads of Government. At the heart of our task, therefore, has been enquiry as to the structures necessary to achievement of these goals. In that context, we see the structures of unity for which a revised Treaty of Chaguaramas must provide as being as follows:

- The Conference of Heads of Government;
- The Council of Ministers;
- The CARICOM Commission;
- The CARICOM Assembly;
- The CARICOM Charter of Civil Society
- The CARICOM Supreme Court; and
- The CARICOM Secretariat.

Except for the Conference of Heads of Government for which the Treaty provides, we shall deal with each in turn; but we emphasise at the outset that we envisage them as an integrated whole and recommend them as such. To remove or significantly modify any part is to weaken the overall structure and render it less capable of serving the goals of the Treaty. But that does not mean that they have all to be assembled at once. As we explain later (see '4. Transitional Arrangements' below), if a start is made with the CARICOM Commission, machinery will have been put in place for erecting the remaining structures of unity in a methodical manner and on a negotiated basis consistent with the needs of Community.

The Council of Ministers

One of the ways in which institutional arrangements can help to encourage attitudinal change is by reflecting at ministerial level in every CARICOM country political responsibility for CARICOM affairs. We strongly urge that this be done, though not necessarily by its being a singular ministerial portfolio; some of our Cabinets are necessarily so small that multiple portfolios are inevitable. We are sure, however, that making the furtherance of the goal of the Treaty of Chaguaramas the responsibility of a specific Minister (with appropriate departmental support) in each member state of CARICOM would be a gain both in psychological and practical respects. There must be in each Cabinet a Minister whose role is to call attention to the obligations and opportunities deriving from CARICOM: to be, as it were, a custodian of Community purposes — which are national purposes too. A constituency supportive of CARICOM exists among the people of the Region; we need to demonstrate that one exists as well at the level of Governments.

At the Community level, these Ministers will invariably be the ones who sit on the Council of Ministers of the Community; a Council we see playing a substantial role in the Community's structures of unity. It would not displace specialist ministerial consultations, like those of Ministers of Foreign Affairs or of Health or of Education. But, in the revised Treaty of Chaguaramas, we recommend that the Council of Ministers be authorised to act in regional decision-making across a wider band of issues than those that now fall to be considered and resolved by the Common Market Council.

We see the Council of Ministers as occupying a central place in CARICOM's structures of unity and, in that process, relieving the Conference of Heads of Government as the supreme organ of the Community in many matters that now overwhelm Summit agendas. The Commission will initiate many matters requiring inter-governmental approach with the Council and, with Ministers representing their Heads of Government, carry them to decision in the Council. Additionally, we envisage the Commission developing a process of closed sessions with the Council, at which issues can be aired in an informal manner as part of a streamlined process of consultation leading to decision-making and the implementation of decisions.

The CARICOM Commission

Since we are not proposing federation or political union for the 13 CARICOM countries, the thrust of our proposal is how to make CARICOM more effective — not how to remake it or how to replace it. But it is important that this too is not misunderstood for either marking time or mere tinkering with the status quo. Indeed, the very fact that we do not go for radical restructuring of political organisation in the Region, means that we face a highly demanding challenge to imagination and creativity in making regional integration a more effective vehicle for the realisation of the hopes and ambitions of our people. This is why, for example, we do not believe that the way forward lies merely in 'strengthening' the CARICOM Secretariat. It is entirely illusory to expect the Secretariat, however enhanced, to by itself fill the serious gaps that now exist in the machinery of regional integration and, as we have seen, even moreso for developing CARICOM's place in the wider Caribbean area. One can, of course, restructure the existing machinery so fundamentally that it changes its basic character from being an inter-governmental bureaucracy to an executive authority drawn from persons with extensive political experience. But to do that and imply that the way forward lies in 'strengthening' the Secretariat is to be disingenuous. Besides, the Secretariat, as an inter-governmental bureaucracy, CARICOM's 'administrative organ', has a place in the integration process — an important place — and it can and should be strengthened as such in the ways we shall come to.

In making a reality of integration, we feel strongly that there needs to be a central directorate deriving its authority from the decisions of CARICOM Governments taken collectively and itself drawn from persons with high level experience in the public and political life of the Region. If CARICOM is to go forward, if the many advances that are needed regionally are to be made in trade, in production, in communications, in building on the cultural bedrock, in mobilising for CARICOM's external relations, there is no substitute for that central directorate drawn from the Region's public and political culture. If the Commission was in any doubt about this, the experience of the implementation of our own interim Programme for Immediate Action would have confirmed our judgement. The CARICOM Secretariat could not have secured the implementation of those proposals. Implementation called for political action and it was eventually the initiative, sometimes unilateral, of the political leaders who were given the portfolio responsibilities for the particular items that made progress possible; that and the pressure of public opinion exerted through the media.

The fact that progress remains delayed in some countries is a pointer to the need for a central authority, freed of national, domestic responsibilities and allegiances, and appropriately empowered to implement CARICOM's decisions. Had there been that facility at the centre, the proposals which the Commission put forward in our Progress Report would have come from it, and once (as happened) CARICOM Heads of Government had adopted them, their implementation would have been accelerated by the interposition of the authority, both at the level of initiation and mobilisation and of implementation. This gap in the integration process has to be filled by what we would describe as the Commission of the Caribbean Community — the 'CARICOM Commission' — drawn, we emphasize, from within the ranks of the Region's public and political community. We do not see this as a large body. In fact, we believe that a start should be made with a Commission of three, a President of the Commission and two other Commissioners — plus the Secretary-General of CARICOM who, we propose, should be an ex-officio member.

Guiding Principles of the Commission

A number of questions arise in relation to the establishment, functioning and authority of the Commission, and we have given some attention to them. It would be tempting to elaborate a detailed structure. We believe, however, that the development of the structure is a matter that can best evolve, on the basis of inter-governmental discussions, with the aid of the Commissioners themselves. In short, our proposal is that Heads of Government should identify the team that will take on the central task and that they should themselves have a hand in shaping the authority and functioning of the Commission.

CARICOM has neither the time nor the multiplicity of human resources to indulge in anything like the protracted exercise that preceded the Federation in terms of inter-governmental committees and preparatory processes. Nor does that overall experience encourage the belief that in that way we necessarily get it right. We have to begin to occupy the dwelling as we build it. What is important is to agree upon the architecture, and it is to this that we address our proposals. If these proposals find favour with Caribbean Governments and people, we would recommend that they be put into operation straightaway. January 1, 1993, is not too soon for us to have appointed the President of the CARICOM Commission and his two other colleagues.

In that context of urgency we propose that the following principles should guide the establishment of the Commission:

- that the Commission be initially limited to a President and two Commissioners appointed by CARICOM Heads of Government by consensus for a period of 5 years, renewable only once for a further period, from among persons with high-level public and political experience in the Region. The President shall be appointed by the Heads of Government and the other Commissioners appointed by them in consultation with the President. The Secretary-General of CARICOM should be an ex-officio member;

- that the Commission should have two principal mandates, namely:

  (i) to further the process of integration among the members of CARICOM: that is, the mandate to deepen the process of integration, and
  (ii) to develop relations between CARICOM and the wider community of Caribbean countries: that is, the mandate to widen the process of integration;

- that, in fulfilling its mandates, the Commission will work within the parameters of policy decisions taken by CARICOM Heads of Government or under their authority in relation to the CARICOM Single Market and Economy, CARICOM's functional cooperation programmes and CARICOM's external relations;

- that the Commission will be empowered to put forward proposals for approval and to implement decisions taken by CARICOM Heads of Government or under their authority within the ambit of the Commission's mandate and in conformity with procedures that recognise the sovereign authority of Member States of CARICOM;

- that the Commission and the Secretariat will be financed under a formula of automatic transfers to be agreed upon by member Governments;

- that the CARICOM Secretariat should be the Secretariat of the Commission, and should be appropriately streamlined, and in part relocated, to fulfil its separate functions in relation to the CARICOM Commission, the CARICOM Single Market, CARICOM functional cooperation and CARICOM external relations.

If these principles are accepted and the members of the Commission designated, we would propose that advances be made by Member States to cover the first year's budget of the Commission, reimbursable from the sums automatically provided under the formula to be agreed; and that an inter-governmental task force be established to work with the Commissioners and their immediate staff and the Secretariat in developing the formal modalities for the Commission, including an appropriate revision of the Treaty of Chaguaramas. These modalities will inevitably involve an elaboration of the six principles above, as well as other matters related to them. It might be helpful, therefore, if we were also to make a few observations with respect to that process.

Bridging the Implementation Gap

A central element of the Commission's rationale is its facilitation of the implementation of Community decisions. We need to say a word about how this is to be accomplished through the operation of the Commission.

Essentially, we have to devise machinery by which CARICOM decisions can be translated into action with a minimum of delay. Some decisions can be implemented by administrative action as, for example, the recommendation we made in our Progress Report for CARICOM citizens to enter CARICOM countries through the line reserved for nationals and for a sign at airport immigration counters to denote this. The CARICOM decision to do so involved both physical arrangements and administrative instructions to immigration officers. Others, however, will require a combination of administrative and legislative action. This may be the case in some countries with regard to our other recommendation, also adopted by CARICOM Heads, that CARICOM countries should no longer require work permits for CARICOM nationals who are graduates of UWI — and other accredited institutions — or duly accredited media workers. Even where actual changes in the law are not required to give effect to this decision, policy instructions would be involved in relation to the exercise of existing statutory powers. There will be other cases still, as in our third recommendation, regarding the establishment of the Caribbean Investment Fund, where legislative action, even if only of a 'subsidiary legislation' kind, would be required to put in place the agreed exemptions and other arrangements to facilitate the operations of the Fund.

Innumerable decisions will require implementation through one or other of these methods. Since we are not proposing an authority with supra-national power, it becomes both more necessary and more complicated to devise appropriate arrangements for uniform and expeditious implementation. We believe, however, that this can be achieved.

We propose that the revised Treaty of Chaguaramas should recognise the evolution of a body of Community law deriving from decisions of CARICOM Heads of Government, and other instrumentalities, taken in pursuance of the Treaty. Members should agree under the Treaty to give effect to rights and duties within their states arising under Community law. For the most part, those rights and duties will be as set out in Instruments of Implementation drawn up by the CARICOM Commission and themselves approved by CARICOM Heads of Government or by the Council.

These Instruments of Implementation should be the subject of close prior consultation between the Commission and Governments. The absence sometimes of full prior consultation before decision-making was one of the basic flaws pointed out in the Pollard Study on Decision-Making in CARICOM and a contributory factor to non-implementation of decisions. Such consultation must be in good faith; it should not be made a substitute for non-implementation; but Capitals (including relevant interest groups where appropriate) must at least have an opportunity to comment. Such prior consultation is the surest way of avoiding problems at a later stage and should become routine in the working of the Community. Sometimes decisions can be taken on the basis of draft Instruments of Implementation; at other times, in more complex matters, the decision may be taken in principle and the draft Instrument to give effect to it prepared for further consultation. In both cases consultation on the draft Instrument is essential. In thus streamlining the decision-making process, we would be greatly assisting implementation.

The Instrument of Implementation will be declaratory, not statutory. It will enunciate the decision in terms that are operational; but it will not itself have the force of law. However, the revised Treaty should stipulate that where a decision is duly taken, either by the Heads of Government Conference or by the Council, Member States accept an obligation to give legal effect to it under their domestic law. The basic national CARICOM Act giving effect to the revised Treaty should desirably provide for this to be accomplished by local regulations (made and published by the national CARICOM Minister) in terms consonant with the relevant Instrument of Implementation.

The revised Treaty and relevant legislation should also provide that rights and duties stipulated under an Instrument of Implementation can be the subject of an Implementation Order made by the CARICOM Supreme Court in exercise of its original jurisdiction (as proposed later) at the instance of any CARICOM citizen (individual or corporate) or of the CARICOM Commission or a member State. Such an Implementation Order will be limited to clarifying Community law and requiring Member States to give effect to it by appropriate action. Similarly, where issues involving the interpretation or application of the Treaty arise, provision should be made for their preliminary reference to the CARICOM Supreme Court. It will be the duty of the Commission to report to CARICOM Heads of Government any failure on the part of a member State to give effect to an Implementation Order of the Court in breach of its Treaty obligations. This system for the enforcement of Community decisions will be authorised by both the revised Treaty and the Agreement and legislation establishing the CARICOM Court. It will provide for sanctions by the Conference of Heads of Government or the Council — like the suspension of area treatment — in appropriate cases.

We believe that such a system will allow the Commission to play a catalytic role in moving action from decision to implementation. Many decisions may require administrative action only; but even where legislative action is required at the level of Member States, the Commission (through the system of Instruments of Implementation) can play a major role in securing expeditious uniform action. This system will require, of course, the goodwill of Member States. If we do not create a governmental apparatus at the centre, with power to override national action — and we are not proposing this — we must proceed on a consensual basis, and that must imply that member states will respect and cooperate in giving fulfilment to decisions taken in CARICOM by due process. In the last resort, CARICOM cannot prevail against a member State whose Government defies Community law by reneging on a decision properly taken and basically breaching its Treaty obligations. In that situation the ultimate sanction will have to be a political one. We cannot avoid this situation without departing from our fundamental premise that CARICOM is a Community of sovereign states. We do not believe that we should strain that foundation by trying to guard against a breach of Treaty obligations. CARICOM must proceed on an assumption of the readiness of member countries to discharge Treaty obligations in the utmost good faith. To question the validity of such an assumption is to conclude that CARICOM cannot aspire to being more than an 'anancy-style' organisation which elevates West Indian '*picong*', '*mamaguy*' and '*mauvais langue*' to a regional credo. We do not accept so caustic a judgement. We are sure we can do better.

The system proposed above is operationally feasible and could facilitate timely implementation of determinations of the organs of CARICOM. It may be implemented in Member Countries by Acts of Parliament without the need for constitutional amendment, and will ensure the desired certainty and uniformity in the application of the relevant law. It involves no derogation from national sovereignty and does not confer supranational competence on CARICOM organs. However, its successful implementation will depend, in the final analysis, on the willingness of Member Countries to discharge their Treaty obligations. It will depend, in other words, on the seriousness of all CARICOM Governments that the integration process should work.

Given that seriousness, which must be our basic assumption, what the system recommended does is to provide machinery to fill the implementation gap that has to date frustrated much CARICOM action. It is the very least that CARICOM can put in place if the integration process is to go forward.

A Method of Financing

We propose that the Commission be financed by a form of automatic transfers agreed to by Member States and embodied in the Treaty of Chaguaramas. It is self-evident that the Commission must function on a basis of independence if it is to discharge its functions as the executive arm of CARICOM. It will derive its mission from decisions taken by member Governments, but in the execution of that mission it must not live a hand to mouth existence dependent on financial support from Capitals voted, or not voted, by Parliaments. Apart from questions of principle, there is also the practical consideration that public and political figures in the Community of the seniority we look for on the Commission are unlikely to commit themselves to such service except in the context of an assured base of financial support for the budget of the Commission. How do we provide that assured base?

In February 1991, CARICOM Heads of Government, at their Second Intersessional Meeting in Trinidad and Tobago, mandated the Secretariat to mobilise a Working Group of Senior Officials of Member States to examine the question of a source of financing for the Secretariat which would not depend on releases of funds by Member States to finance the operating costs of the Secretariat. The Secretariat's budget would continue to be subjected to scrutiny and subsequent approval by the Council of Ministers, but the sources of financing would be predetermined.

This question of an independent source of financing was raised prior to 1991; indeed in 1984, the Seventeenth meeting of the Standing Committee of Ministers responsible for Finance had given preliminary consideration to a proposal for such an independent source, but the matter was not definitely concluded.

The need for an independent source of financing for the activities which the Secretariat was mandated to undertake arose because several Member States had accumulated large arrears in their assessed contribution to the agreed Secretariat's budget. This made it difficult for the Secretariat to organise and implement its allotted tasks with efficiency and dispatch.

The problem of the arrears of assessed contributions to the Secretariat's budget in past years will have to be addressed as a separate issue, since overdraft financing has had to be used to meet the operations costs of the Secretariat. But it is clear that if, in the future, the Commission is to be able to discharge the enlarged mandate which we propose and, in particular, to deepen and enlarge CARICOM while developing durable bases for long-term cooperation between CARICOM and the rest of the Caribbean and with the countries in the littoral of the Caribbean Sea, it must be assured that it will have the quantum of resources which Heads of Government agree is necessary for the task.

Unless this is done, it will not be possible to recruit the quality of the personnel required. This therefore, requires us to consider as a priority matter, the question of an independent source of finance for the activities of the Commission.

The Working Group of Senior Finance Officials referred to above, in their Report, made the following principal recommendations:

(i) the new method (of financing) should be an import tax levied on extra-regional imports, excluding commodities subject to special contractual arrangements relating to the imposition of import duties;

(ii) provision should be made for the supplementing of these resources through the possibility of "calling-up" funds and continuing access to an overdraft facility;

(iii) the tax should be the property of the Community to be used initially for the execution of the Work Programme of the Secretariat, as approved each year;

(iv) the level of the tax should be set initially at approximately 0.125 per cent for all Member States except The Bahamas, for which it would be 0.02 per cent.

The computation which the Senior Officials made showed that, based on certain assumptions of extra-regional import growth, the imports referred to at (iv) above would have generated revenues of approximately EC$16m in 1991, a level which would have been adequate to finance the operational needs of the Secretariat. The widened mandate which we propose for the Commission will require a modest increase in the projected operating costs of the Commission. There will also be certain one-off start-up costs which will have to be met, e.g., transport facilities and office space and equipment.

In order to accommodate these costs, we propose that the import tax on extra-regional imports should be fixed initially at 0.15 per cent of extra-regional imports for Member States and 0.025 per cent for The Bahamas. Using the assumptions which the Senior Officials made, the import tax at these levels will generate revenues of about EC$18.9m per year (taking into account the reduction mentioned below). The rates should be reviewed every five years and any surpluses, over and above the sums required for the operations of the Commission and for a reserve fund to be decided by Heads of Government, would be dealt with in a manner which the Heads will also decide.

A residual question remains; this is the matter of ensuring that the proceeds of the import tax do not form part of the Consolidated Fund of the individual Governments and, therefore, require the appropriation of the amounts by the parliaments of Member States. To obviate this need, we propose that the matter be dealt with through the sale of CARICOM stamps. In brief, each Customs administration in Member States will sell importers CARICOM stamps to be affixed on Customs Entry documents before they are processed by the Customs. The administration, custody, sale and accounting for such stamps will require the Customs administrations to incur additional costs for which they must be reimbursed. We propose that the reimbursement be 10 per cent of the sale of stamps. In short, our proposal is the following:

(i) CARICOM will issue stamps to the individual Customs Administrations;

(ii) the individual Customs Administrations will sell the stamps to importers who import goods which fall within the eligible categories. Eligible importers will be required to affix stamps to a value equivalent to 0.15 per cent of the value of the imports, except that in the case of The Bahamas, the impost will be 0.025 per cent of the value of the imports;

(iii) the Customs Administrations will put into a special account the proceeds of sale of stamps, less the agreed amount to reimburse the Customs Administrations for the additional costs which they will incur; we propose that the reimbursement charge should be 10 per cent of the sale of stamps;

(iv) the CARICOM Commission and the individual Custom administrations will agree on the measures of financial control and audit of the sale of stamps;

(v) where necessary, requiring the affixation of CARICOM stamps should be made enforceable through legislation; and

(vi) the CARICOM Commission would be authorized by the individual Exchange Control authorities to maintain external accounts in each country and have the right of conversion of the net proceeds of the sale of stamps into such foreign currencies as its operations require.

The CARICOM Assembly

We applaud the initiative that has led to the Agreement for the establishment of the 'Assembly of Caribbean Community Parliamentarians'. We see the Assembly as an important component of CARICOM'S structures of unity. Certainly, there is a manifest need for a regional forum that can deliberate on Community matters. National Parliaments have little inclination to do so, although we believe more can be done in this direction: for example, by Governments reporting to their Parliaments on regional developments. All too often members of national Parliaments, including Government members, hear of regional affairs from the media. Even the conclusions of Heads of Government Conferences are not formally reported to all but a few Parliaments; and, with even rarer exceptions, almost never to the people directly, for example, through radio broadcasts or press conferences at home. This is part of the wider problem of the flawed working of the parliamentary system on which we commented in our Progress Report and which we raise again below. It has a special relevance in relation to integration matters.

Broader Participation

Integration inevitably involves inter-governmental negotiation and decision-making; but it is not the preserve of Governments alone. People need to be drawn into the process, and parliamentarians are not the sole 'representatives' of people. They are their representatives in Parliament, not in every aspect of civic life — even less in every aspect of regional affairs. We are disappointed, therefore, that these first welcome steps to constitute a regional forum should have been so hobbled. We would have preferred to see the Assembly developed as an Assembly of the people of CARICOM; not just of its parliamentarians. That could have been achieved while leaving room for the inclusion of parliamentarians in the Assembly's membership. It would have been better to have started the Assembly as a forum of CARICOM'S social partners — something closer to the Regional Economic Conference that was held in Port-of-Spain in 1991, though with a wider agenda.

It may still be possible to establish a 'CARICOM Assembly' constituted to attract membership from within and outside Parliaments. It is surely a good thing for our Region that there should be a place in CARICOM'S structures of unity for non-governmental actors: NGOs, the private sector, the labour movement, the academic community, even representatives of the West Indian diaspora. National political structures tend in practice to exclude them all, and while this development is understandable and was perhaps inevitable as domestic politics developed, we live in a new era in which 'empowerment' cannot be written off simply as a 'buzz' word, but needs to be understood as requiring us to go beyond conventional forms of 'representation'. Our first preference and recommendation, therefore, is to see the Assembly of Caribbean Community Parliamentarians recast as the CARICOM Assembly, with Parliaments being required to elect to the Assembly a mix of parliamentarians and non-parliamentarians, and for conventions of consultation to be inaugurated whereby the involvement of social partners in the Assembly can be assured.

Observers

A second-best alternative would be to revise the Agreement to ensure that observers may be invited to participate in the deliberations of the Assembly from among the people of CARICOM. We understand that this was initially contemplated. It is a pity it was abandoned. As the Agreement now stands, observers can be invited from non-CARICOM countries — and not solely from the parliamentarians of those countries — but not from the people of CARICOM. This is perhaps another example of the syndrome we have evolved in the Region of believing that once an election has been held only elected representatives have a right to be involved in decision-making. We believe this to be a too restricted and somewhat old-fashioned concept. It has certainly had a cramping effect in relation to an otherwise admirable scheme for the development of a deliberative regional forum. If the Assembly's basic conception is not modified, however, we strongly urge that at the very least the observer provision be liberated to allow the Assembly itself to invite the social partners to share in the deliberations of the Assembly along with other observers from beyond the Community. Among them could be, following the example of the Windward Island Constituent Assembly, young people, farmers, religious groups, women, labour and business.

Joint Sessions

Yet another approach would be for the Assembly itself to be empowered to develop a structure of meetings in the nature of specially enlarged forums. We mentioned earlier, for example, the importance we attach to strengthening the special relationship with Canada. We believe that joint meetings of the CARICOM Assembly and Canadian representatives, including Provincial representatives, would be a major contribution to that strengthening process. An annual CARICOM-Canada Forum would considerably enlarge the potential of CARIBCAN. Another joint forum might be one that brought together CARICOM and the wider Caribbean. As the intergovernmental process regarding a 'Community of Caribbean States' moves forward, much might be accomplished by periodic deliberative occasions with the countries of the Caribbean Basin organised around the CARICOM Assembly.

In short, we are anxious to see the Assembly as an effective, flexible and credible forum in CARICOM'S structures of unity. The Agreement has not yet been signed by all Member States. This is the time to modify it; and the necessary revision of the Treaty of Chaguaramas provides an appropriate basis for doing so. Indeed, if our proposals for the establishment of the CARICOM Commission are accepted, we would urge modification of the Agreement to permit the Assembly to invite the President of the Commission to participate in its proceedings — for example, through the President presenting an annual report on the state of CARICOM — a presentation which may come in time to provide a valued opportunity for debate of regional goals and their achievement. We would go further, however; we believe there should be an opportunity for Commissioners to answer questions in the Assembly. This will serve two purposes. The first, to develop more openness in Community affairs; the second, of course, to increase the accountability of the Commission. That accountability will in turn enhance the Commission's authority.

Fulfilling the Assembly's Objectives

We feel obliged to comment on another aspect of the Agreement for the Assembly of Caribbean Community Parliamentarians. The Agreement provides, explicitly and unexceptionably, that the Assembly's 'objectives' shall be, inter alia:

> ... to promote greater understanding among Member States and Associate Members for the purpose of realising and safeguarding the ideals and principles of democratic Governments in the Community and facilitating the economic and social advancements of their peoples;

> ... to encourage the adoption by the Governments of Member States of the Community of a common policy on economic, social, cultural, scientific and legal matters deliberated upon by the Assembly.

These are laudable objectives for the CARICOM Assembly — even one with the restricted membership presently contemplated. An Assembly that strives to fulfil them will contribute in a major way to fulfilling the goals of the Treaty of Chaguaramas itself. But we fear that the Assembly's fulfilment of its stated objectives could be seriously jeopardised by the provisions of Article 5.4 of the Agreement to the following effect:

> It shall not be competent for the Assembly to discuss or adopt any resolution on any matter which is exclusively within the domestic jurisdiction of a Member State or Associate Member of the Community and any question whether any matter is within the competence of the Assembly for the purposes of this paragraph shall be decided by the Speaker of the Assembly.

We do not believe it could be the intent to curb the Assembly in deliberating on virtually anything to which a Member Government of CARICOM objects.

Certainly the people of CARICOM will see a regional forum, if we are to strengthen civil society in CARICOM and improve the quality of governance, as precisely the place to discuss matters of concern to the vitality of CARICOM as a community: matters which cannot wholly be divorced from the health of the constituent parts. They will have been discussed freely virtually everywhere else: in the regional media, at regional street corners, in extra-regional institutions.

As the late Sir Arthur Lewis rightly urged 30 years ago, opening regional windows on aberrations within our Region is precisely one of the values of unity. Nothing less would be consistent with our concept of civil society in CARICOM. The Assembly will, we trust, be left free to deliberate all matters properly within the purview of its objectives as already set out in the Agreement. Those objectives are not an invitation for the regional Assembly to meddle in national politics; but discussion of matters arising under the Treaty in relation to the Single Market and Economy, or functional cooperation, or CARICOM's external relations, or under the Charter of Civil Society, should not be narrowly circumscribed.

Additionally, in all these areas, we would recommend that the Assembly should have the right, either in plenary session or through Committees, to hold public hearings to which persons can be invited to provide views and advice. Like its deliberative function, such hearings would carry no executive authority, but they would likewise provide for an airing of regional issues.

A CARICOM Charter of Civil Society

In our Progress Report we reflected on the need for a normative structure of 'Community' in CARICOM in terms which we repeat:

> The time is at hand when the Region must reflect the reality of 'Community' beyond structures of economic integration. That was always implicit in the Treaty of Chaguaramas and explicit in its provisions for functional co-operation. Experience has shown that in some fundamental respects there must be an ethos of Community that reflects itself in civil and political norms no less than in those that come naturally at the economic, social and cultural levels. We envisage, therefore, a normative structure of the Community through which member countries commit themselves to respect for the fundamental elements of civil society like free elections and functional systems of democratic governance, and social and economic justice.
>
> We have been encouraged to believe that agreed processes of electoral reform in Guyana are likely to remove one major area of concern in this regard. We look forward to the consolidation of those processes which we acknowledge to be a matter of legitimate interest to the entire Region.
>
> But there is room for disquiet in other respects right across the Region. One such concern derives from the increasing incidence of corruption in public life and the particular contribution of the illicit drug trade to this process. We are fully conscious of the degree to which the Caribbean can be made a pawn in a larger process of wrong doing. But that cannot blind us to the enormous damage that can result to civil administration in our Region from even these secondary roles. The magnitude of financial inducements is such that they endanger on a large scale systems of public administration of which the Caribbean had every reason to be proud — deficiencies and derogations not withstanding.
>
> There are other developments, it is true, that give us

encouragement for civil society — like the proposal just discussed for the establishment of an Assembly of Caribbean Parliamentarians. Similarly, we have been greatly encouraged by the emergence of non-governmental organisations to a position of prominence and respect in public life — nowhere better demonstrated than at the Regional Economic Conference earlier this year in Port of Spain when Caribbean NGOs gave ample proof of their right to be heard and our need to listen to them at the level of regional decision-making.

Even as we were conducting our consultations and receiving with renewed insistence complaints about the quality of governance of the kind we signalled in the Progress Report, the then Prime Minister of Jamaica appointed a Committee of Advisers on Government Structures in Jamaica: so current and critical is this crisis in governance. The Jamaica Committee was chaired by one of our members, Professor Rex Nettleford, and two others, Sir Alister McIntyre and Dr Marshall Hall, were members of the Committee. The principal item of the Committee's terms of reference was as follows:

> There has been little fundamental change from the Colonial period in the role and organisation of Government when Jamaica achieved its independence and the basic structure has remained virtually the same since. With the rapid movement to a market-based economy brought about by liberalization and deregulation and changes in the world environment, the Group of Experts has as its main task to provide answers to the question of what should now be the appropriate role of Government in this new environment.
>
> What functions should it undertake and how should it organise itself to deliver the maximum benefit to the population at large, while ensuring that the most vulnerable groups are protected, that the social sectors are supported and economic growth achieved.

The preliminary report of the Jamaica Committee was given to Prime Minister Manley on 26 March 1992. It is concerned, of course, with governance issues in Jamaica; but the issues themselves do not pertain to Jamaica alone. They arise, in varying degrees of intensity, in all CARICOM Countries. Accordingly, the conclusions of the Committee and their recommendations for Jamaica have relevance to the entire Region. It is yet another example of our underlying commonalities. The following findings, for example, are pertinent to CARICOM as a whole:

- Today, there is considerable disquiet about the failure so far of the economy to return to a path of robust and sustained growth; about the negative economic and social impact of current stabilization and adjustment programmes; and about the intractability of social problems such as unemployment, crime, drug abuse and trafficking. All of them raise the call for improving the quality and performance of Government.

- There are many proponents of the view that the Government should be down-sized and its role minimised, because of inefficiency, and insignificant responsiveness to the needs of the public, especially those of the business community. This is essentially a negative approach to the problem. Because of the national and global considerations, a more positive approach would be to restructure and reform the Government in all of its component parts, to make it leaner, more cost effective, more facilitative, and supportive of the development process.

- There is a clear need for Government to be put in perspective. There is need to ensure that the Government and people regard themselves as different but complementary parts of the same whole; that Government and its supporting bureaucracy are not seen as millstones around the necks of a powerless citizenry; that Government is not encouraged to continue projecting itself as sole Provider and Deliverer in a messianic dispensation of a saviour one week and his crucifixion the next; that distrust, disintegrative tension, and cynicism do not continue to inform the relationship between the governors and the governed; that the citizenry does not feel deliberately deprived in the world at large and to the ability for the individual to cope with the deep social forces operative in a society. The mass of the population has historically suffered economic disabilities and harbours to this day a particular sense of being deprived and wronged. This in turn leads to an endemic commitment to 'beating the system' (presided over by Government) or to making things not work.

- Apart from the traditional functions of law and order, defence, security and foreign affairs, we envisage new nuances with respect to the role of Government in the economy. The establishment of market economies and the globalization of production do not, however, imply a shift to a system of *laisser-faire*. What it does imply is not necessarily less government, but different and better government.

- The Government should conceive of itself as the hub of a network of social partners engaged in a process of continuing interaction for the purpose of policy formulation and implementation. Efforts should be made to reach a common understanding among political parties, the business community, trade unions, NGOs, and other bodies on the broad goals of economic and social development, and on the policy framework through which rules will be established for the management of the economy, and the respective roles of each partner in management would be delineated. The Government could function as strategic broker in trying to reconcile different interests among the partners, and to facilitate the effective discharge of their respective responsibilities.

Disaffection with Governance

It is now all too evident that tension between economic distress and democratic governance could be the major destabilising factor of the future in developing countries. Social discontent in the wake of structural adjustment programmes forced forward at an inhuman pace could make nonsense of the democratic traditions West Indian societies have zealously cultivated. Events in Trinidad and Tobago, and later Venezuela, carry their own confirmation of the dangers that could lie ahead. West Indian societies need each other more and more and West Indian political leadership — of all parties — acknowledges this. We need to reduce that tension both by development that removes a sense of inequity and by enhancing public confidence in governance — questions of the kind the Jamaica Committee addressed.

On the governance front, it was frequently brought to our attention, for example, that in some, by no means all, Member States there was a marked infrequency of sittings of Parliament; statistics we have been supplied by Parliaments have borne this out. The statistics speak for themselves.

NUMBER OF SITTINGS OF PARLIAMENTS IN CARICOM MEMBER STATES
JANUARY – DECEMBER 1990

Antigua and Barbuda	6	Guyana	36
The Bahamas	53	Jamaica	51
Barbados	42	Montserrat	10
Belize	6	St. Kitts and Nevis	3
Dominica	8	Saint Lucia	21
Grenada	21	St. Vincent and the Grenadines	8
		Trinidad and Tobago	44

Statistics are for the elected Chambers — supplied by Clerks of Parliament.

It is not surprising then that there has been so much complaint to the Commission of decline in standards of governance and erosion of the quality of civil society — again, not everywhere, but in too many parts of the Region for us not to detect an unhealthy trend.

A paper prepared for the Commission on 'Governance and Democracy' in CARICOM has brought out a number of other issues, some of which were identified in the course of our consultations. They include matters relating to the electoral system, the functioning of Parliament, the rôle of the Leader of the Opposition, the Public Service and local government. They deserve discussion in the Region in the process, which is clearly under way and deserves to be encouraged, of re-appraising issues of governance after between 15 and 30 years of independence. Separately, these issues arise at a national level; together, they bear on the quality of governance in the

Community and are the concern of our entire Region. Certainly, they are on the minds of the Region's people. They are not criticisms of any particular Governments or any single Party; indeed, many of the existing arrangements have all-Party support. They suggest that it is time to ask whether we are going into the twenty-first century on the best possible basis of governance.

We believe, however, that we can now go further in elevating some of these matters to the level of principles and precepts to which member Governments of CARICOM give clear commitment. Such matters as a free press, a fair and open democratic process, the effective functioning of the parliamentary system, the absence of corruption from public life, respect for the rights of women and children, the right of association, freedom from political victimisation, respect for religious and cultural diversity, greater accountability and transparency in Government, greater public access to information — and there are others — do not turn on the state of economic development. It is within the competence of CARICOM societies to make them part of the national ethos.

There are other issues, like a commitment to the goal of health and education and employment opportunity for all CARICOM citizens, that depend in large measure on the availability of resources, but which need to be the fundamental underpinning of development goals. There are others still, like prison conditions, that are influenced by resources but can be significantly improved by enhanced effort. Reform of prison conditions — which are notoriously bad throughout the Region — is in fact a good example of an area in which the very processes of developing the Charter can be a factor in mobilising action for change.

In all these areas, which together constitute the elements of civil society in CARICOM Countries, there is room for clearer norms. There is too much evidence of shortcoming in all these areas for us to accept complacently that these are all goals to which all CARICOM Governments and societies are committed. Something more is needed to underline that commitment and to be a point of reference for calling defaulters to book where performance falters.

We recommend, therefore, that as CARICOM goes forward to a deepened level of integration Member Governments, in the name of the people of the Region, should subscribe to a CARICOM Charter of Civil Society elevating these goals and commitments to guiding principles of the Community.

There will be some respects in which relevant rights and freedoms are already safeguarded by national Constitutions. So much the better; but what is needed in a Community context is a clear political statement of the standards of civil society which the people of CARICOM can be confident will be respected as part of the political ethos of CARICOM. As we have said, many of those norms are respected and promoted by some Governments within CARICOM; in those cases, the Charter will serve as reinforcement of prevailing practice.

We do not consider that at this stage the Charter provisions can be made enforceable on Member Governments; but we see no overriding difficulty in allowing for a system under which an advisory opinion may be sought from the CARICOM Supreme Court on non-compliance with the provisions of the Charter. Such a possibility will enhance the status of the Charter and respect for its principles and precepts. It will be another building block of civil society in our Region.

We recommend that the CARICOM Commission should put in hand the preparation and negotiation of the Charter of Civil Society, along with the revision of the Treaty of Chaguaramas, so that the structures of unity we recommend may be assembled in an integrated manner. The content of the Charter is a matter for negotiation between Member Countries. It is uniquely one to which the citizenry of the Region can make a particular contribution.

We attach much importance to this proposal for a Charter of Civil Society. CARICOM needs normative moorings; we have found widespread yearning for giving the 'Community' a qualitative character — values beyond the routine of integration arrangements; indeed, standards by which these arrangements themselves can be judged and to which they can be made to conform. The Charter can become the soul of the Community, which needs a soul if it is to command the loyalty of the people of CARICOM.

The Charter is particularly relevant to our concept of a Community in which the social partners play a more fundamentally involved role. We are evolving in the Region a political ethic which acknowledges that all sectors of society have a contribution to make, and a right to make it. We have not worked out just how this is to be translated into practice; but of course it will only be translated into practice if the acknowledgement goes deep. If it is superficial it will be transient and will not endure, and our communities will be the worse for that. Involving social partners more functionally does produce its own tensions: but, they can be creative tensions with partners themselves recognising their obligations as constructive players and the limits of their roles. We hope the Charter of Civil Society will help to provide a framework of such a genuinely participatory political environment in CARICOM. That framework has to be developed by a process of discussion and negotiation; which is why we have done no more than indicate an outline of the Charter. We make it clear, however, that none of this implies a diminution of the authority of Government to govern. What is needed is an environment propitious to genuine consultation in the processes of governance — not a substitute for constitutional government. This may be too elementary to need asserting; but we would not want any misunderstandings on this score.

The CARICOM Supreme Court

The Time Has Come

The question of the establishment of a Caribbean Court of Appeal as a final court of appeal from the domestic jurisdictions of CARICOM Member Countries, replacing, where they still exist, appeals to the Judicial Committee of the Privy Council, has been the subject of discussion in CARICOM for over twenty years. In 1988 a decision was taken by the Conference of Heads of Government to proceed to the establishment of the Court, and the Government of Trinidad and Tobago offered facilities for it to be headquartered in Port of Spain. To date the Governments of Barbados and Trinidad and Tobago have indicated support, but the Court has not yet been established. We do not need to recapitulate the long discussion that occupied CARICOM at the level of Attorneys General, Law Ministers and Heads of Government in this matter; but we do need to address some questions.

First of all, we believe that the time is at hand for establishing the Caribbean Court of Appeal — what in an integration context we would prefer to call the CARICOM Supreme Court. We do not wish to minimise the issues which have characterised the discussion; indeed, we shall address some of them; but we are strongly of the view that we cannot, like characters in a Chekhov play, go on sitting around tables forever discussing the pros and cons of action and in the process forever deferring it. We believe the CARICOM decision was the right one, even in the context of an appellate jurisdiction alone; but the case for the CARICOM Supreme Court, with both a general appellate jurisdiction and an original regional one, is now overwhelming — indeed it is fundamental to the process of integration itself.

The Privy Council Dimension

On the general issue of the need for a regional court of appeal it is sometimes inferred that, based on the limited number of appeals which go to the Privy Council — an average of some 15 a year over the period 1982 to 1988 — there is unlikely to be enough appellate work to justify establishing the court. We believe that these figures tell a different tale: one of an appellate process beyond the reach of most; one limited largely in practice to criminal cases involving the death penalty or civil appeals using the process as a delaying tactic. The abolition of the death penalty will severely reduce appeals to the Privy Council. The case for a reachable regional Court of Appeal rests instead on the number of appealable cases that have nowhere in practice to go. It also rests on the development of our systems of law that are now deprived of the quality jurisprudence generated by a final court of appeal located in the Region and staffed by the very best of our lawyers — who are less and less being attracted to the highest judicial offices in local jurisdictions.

We suspect that there is sometimes an unspoken question. Can the West Indies produce a Court that will function with the independence and the erudition of the Judicial Committee of the Privy Council? We have not the slightest hesitation in answering that question in the affirmative; indeed, we go further. As CARICOM Countries come to grips with the post independence development of our societies, with issues like those pertaining to governance and the securing of civil society everywhere, it must be to a local, not an external, court that we must look for the sensitive and courageous development of the law. In that time, the case for a Caribbean Court will rest on its being a tribunal of superior credentials to the Judicial Committee. On the matter of judicial talent for staffing the Court, there can be no room for doubt. Some of our own highest judicial officers have sat on the Privy Council itself; the Caribbean has now provided a judge of the world's highest judicial tribunal — the International Court of Justice at the Hague; several of our lawyers have been in demand as Chief Justices and Judges of Courts of Appeal in jurisdictions like The Bahamas, Bermuda, the Seychelles and several countries of continental Africa. When Commonwealth countries look for legal talent, it is often to the Caribbean that they turn. What ails us that we lack the confidence to go forward?

We believe that a Caribbean Supreme Court manned by distinguished West Indian jurists and in which litigants have confidence, is likely to attract a larger number of appeals from countries of the Region than the Privy Council now does. Its knowledge and understanding of regional problems, language, and culture, coupled with its identification with the very ethos of the Caribbean Community, at once invests it with intrinsic qualities which the Privy Council, despite its great learning, does not and can never hope to possess. The importance of these attributes in the judicial law-making process is not to be overlooked or underestimated.

It should also be borne in mind that the cost of appealing to a Caribbean Court of Appeal is almost certain to be less than the costs that would be involved in appealing to the Privy Council. This factor will undoubtedly encourage the fairly large number of dissatisfied litigants, who currently refrain from pursuing rights of appeal to the Privy Council because of the attendant expense, to take their cases to the Caribbean Court. This is bound to result in a larger volume of appellate work from countries within the Region than presently obtains. In addition, the existence of a Caribbean Court of Appeal, despite the acknowledged problems of the law's delays, should certainly guarantee to litigants greater expedition in the hearing and determination of appeals than the Privy Council, overburdened as it is with appeals from many other Commonwealth countries, is capable of achieving.

The Integration Need

But there is now another reason for establishing a court of high authority in the Region, and that is the process of integration itself. Integration in its broadest economic sense — involving a Single CARICOM Market, monetary union, the movement of capital and labour and goods, and functional cooperation in a multiplicity of fields — must have the underpinning of Community law. Integration rests on rights and duties; it requires the support of the rule of law applied regionally and uniformly. A CARICOM Supreme Court interpreting the *Treaty of Chaguaramas*, resolving disputes arising under it, including disputes between Governments parties to the Treaty, declaring and enforcing Community law, interpreting the Charter of Civil Society — all by way of the exercise of an original jurisdiction — is absolutely essential to the integration process. It represents in our recommendations one of the pillars of the CARICOM structures of unity.

Essentially, our recommendation is that the Court should have an original jurisdiction in matters arising under the Treaty of Chaguaramas (as revised) and that any CARICOM citizen (individual or corporate) and any Government of a member State of the Community or the CARICOM Commission itself, should have the competence to apply for a ruling of the Court in a matter arising under the Treaty. This will include, perhaps prominently so, matters in dispute between Member States in relation to obligations under the Treaty, particularly under the Single Market regime; but it will also provide for the clarification of Community law as it develops pursuant to decisions taken within the CARICOM process. As already indicated, we envisage that that original jurisdiction should also be exercisable to a limited degree in the context of the CARICOM Charter of Civil Society which we have separately recommended.

Developing Community Law

We believe the arguments for the Court to be unassailable. It needs only to be added as an important footnote to what we have said about the establishment of the CARICOM Supreme Court that the process of development of Community law in the future will be part of the equally necessary evolution of reform of our legal systems themselves. The point we make here is that we can now look for return on the investment the Region has made in the development of law as a major discipline in the University of the West Indies. Our academic lawyers are a resource on which we can expect to draw in all these fields of CARICOM endeavour. Certainly the new Court will be able to function in a regional legal environment that lends it the intellectual support of the Faculty of Law and the Law Schools. We feel confident in urging the Region to take this necessary next step.

We should say a word about cost, for this is a material consideration. A CARICOM Supreme Court will require the provision of resources but, in one sense, this is like straining at a gnat when we have already swallowed a camel in terms of national expenditure on the judicial system. Even so, we should find ways of reducing costs. One way, we feel, is to locate the Court in one place. We have already referred to the generous offer by Trinidad and Tobago; that is a great help. Another device might be to allow some of the members of the Court to remain in their home locations — other perhaps than the Chief Justice. Communications have improved so greatly, both physical communications and telecommunications, that savings can be explored in new and imaginative ways. Where the resources will be most needed will be in attracting and retaining the very best of our judicial talent for service on the Court. On this we cannot skimp; but it will be one of the most productive investments the Region can make in the interest of making CARICOM work and in the wider cause of civil society throughout our Region.

The CARICOM Secretariat

CARICOM'S Administrative Organ

Under the Treaty of Chaguaramas, the CARICOM Secretariat is the 'administrative organ' of the Community. Under our proposals it will remain so. However, with the establishment of the CARICOM Commission as the 'executive organ' of the Community it is specially important that an effective inter-locking relationship be established between the Commission and the Secretariat. The Commission will require its own modest Headquarters Staff, appointed in consultation with the Commission itself; but they will be a unit of the Secretariat which, in an overall sense, will service the Commission under the functional authority of the Secretary-General — who we recommend be accorded the honorary title of Ambassador.

But more is required if we are to minimise costs and maximise the use of resources. We could propose elaborate self- standing machinery with separate lines of authority and rigid distinctions between Community and inter-governmental institutions. This is the route that leads to Brussels. A case can be made for it on grounds of theory and symmetry; but it ends up being an indulgence we cannot afford. We have to rely, instead, on a style of collaborative administration with all the crew pulling together to a common beat.

Servicing the Commission

The Secretariat will be a substantial resource of the new Commission. Only the Commission will bring forward proposals; but the proposals the Commission initiates and ultimately places before Community organs, including the Conference of Heads of Government, will have been developed with the assistance of the Secretariat. As the administrative organ of the Community the Secretariat will continue to service such meetings. Given the interposition of the Commission's executive authority, however, it is important that a bridge be built at the highest level. We believe this is best done by having the Secretary-General play a full part in the work of the Commission in his official capacity as Head of the Secretariat. For this reason we propose that the CARICOM Secretary-General be an ex officio member of the Commission. At an appropriate time — perhaps in five to seven years — these arrangements can be reviewed in the light of experience. For the time being, however, we strongly recommend this pragmatic approach in the interest of cost-effectiveness, relevance and a smooth evolution to this next stage in the integration process.

The Mills Report

We have been asked specifically to take into account those aspects of the recommendations of the Review on CARICOM Regional Programmes and Organisations (the Mills Report) which have a close bearing on our mandate. In one sense, that could cover the entire Report; but we know that was not intended. We feel that six areas of the Mills recommendations come in the category we should address and we set them out below together with our comments as requested:

1. Decision-making

In addressing the need to expedite the decision-making process in CARICOM, the Mills Report concluded that this would essentially entail review of the unanimity rule. It strongly supported the proposals made by a group of regional officials and experts at the request of the Conference of Heads of Government (1984) and submitted to the Conference in June 1985. In essence, these recommendations involved construction of a hierarchy of levels of decisions, some of which would be taken by simple majority, others by two-thirds majority, and the most critical, via the unanimity rule.

We agree essentially with the Mills recommendations, though we believe that the defect it seeks to remedy in the CARICOM process may be alleviated by the recommendation we have made for the CARICOM Commission process and our particular emphasis on pre-negotiation of proposals in a constant process of consensus building. We made the point in our Progress Report that in fact the unanimity rule had not been responsible for frustrating action in so far as decisions tended to be reached by consensus. We believe that is the right approach, whatever the rule on decision-making; and we will expect the basic practice to continue. But even the process of consensus building can be helped if the unanimity rule was relaxed save for cases where it was considered essential. We, therefore, support the Mills Report in commending the 1984 proposals described above and would urge that they be considered for incorporation in the revised Treaty of Chaguaramas. In that context, we attach much importance to CARICOM's decision-making process being so constructed that it does not impede the progress of those parties who feel they can proceed towards the goals of integration at a faster pace.

2. Decision-Implementation and Monitoring

The Mills Report stressed the need for introduction of mechanisms for overseeing and monitoring the effective and expeditious implementation of decisions by Member States.

We have in our Report agreed whole-heartedly with this view, and the main heads of our recommendations on the structures of unity are directed to this end. The CARICOM Commission is primarily intended to meet the meet the need the Mills Report highlighted and which we fully endorse.

3. Settlement of Disputes

The Mills Report supported the recommendations made by a group of experts in January 1981 for a three-stage process which would involve efforts to settle through the 'good offices' function of the Secretary-General; followed, if necessary, by a process of conciliation by an eminent individual selected by a panel; in the event of failure, recourse to a Tribunal, as provided by Articles 11 and 12 of the Annex to the Treaty.In addition the Report recommended that any settlement agreed on in complying with any of these procedures should be binding and implemented without delay. The Mills Report acknowledged that their proposals would require review and amendment of the Treaty.

We fully agree with the principle of this recommendation. We would see the CARICOM Commission being a further step in this 'good offices' process and as being responsible for the conciliation process. We envisage that the original jurisdiction of the CARICOM Supreme Court would replace the Ad Hoc Tribunal now provided for in the Treaty of Chaguaramas — though it will always remain open to the parties to a dispute to agree on formal Arbitration rather than recourse to the Court.

4. Public Awareness and Participation

The Mills Report stressed the importance of increased and improved information flows between the Secretariat and Member States, dissemination of educational and cultural programmes to sensitise the peoples of the Community, widening the range of participation, and greater personal contact among the peoples. They concluded, however, that while these imperatives are applicable generally across the Region, they need particular emphasis in relation to The Bahamas and Belize — with additional focus on improved air and sea links.

The Report also highlighted the importance of regional organisations and Governments involving the private sector and NGOs where feasible, in planning, implementing and evaluating activities.

We have spent much time in our Report amplifying these ideas and putting forward a variety of recommendations to respond to the need to which the Mills Report alluded. We have dealt specifically with the issue of 'remoteness' of Belize and The Bahamas and with the need to involve the social partners more fully in CARICOM activities at all levels. Our specific proposals on the CARICOM Assembly and the Charter of Civil Society are of direct relevance.

5. Funding

The Mills Report called for strong and determined efforts on the part of many Governments to bring their contributions to the Regional Organisations up-to-date; and for quinquennial review of the contribution formula for every organisation, together with the organisation itself. In addition, consideration should be given to the suggestion made by the late Prime Minister J.M.G. Adams of Barbados that an independent source of income be provided for the Secretariat and other regional institutions.

We have gone further in proposing that both for the budget of the CARICOM Commission and that of the Secretariat, a system of automatic funding of the budgets agreed by CARICOM Governments be put in place. We regard this matter as of critical importance if the integration process is to be the essential part in the life of our Region that all are agreed it should.

6. The Widening of CARICOM

In recognition of the fact that CARICOM contains only 15 per cent of total Caribbean population, the Mills Report concluded as follows:

> ... the perpetuation of a concept of 'Caribbean Community', confined to roughly one-half of the number of the countries and territories entitled to the description 'Caribbean', and representing an even smaller proportion of the total number of persons who could legitimately claim to be 'Caribbean people', is not only a travesty of Caribbean history. It is also a prescription for certain failure of such a Caribbean in an emergent 21st century. There are already clear signs that that century will be characterised by the efforts of four or five major global groupings of countries to establish a *modus vivendi* for economic co-existence.

Our Report provides a substantial and supportive response to these observations and offers concrete recommendations to the Region for giving effect to the widening of the integration process to embrace all 'Caribbean people' while deepening the integration process on which CARICOM has already embarked.

In general terms, therefore, our Report supports the primary proposals of the Mills Report that bear on our mandate. To some extent we have taken them further in that our specific recommendations provide for their implementation. What remain are political decisions on both Reports.

Recommendations

1. that CARICOM's overall structure be that of a Community of Sovereign States;

2. that the Community allow for closer groupings among its Member States provided those groupings are consistent with overall CARICOM commitments;

3. that the leadership of CARICOM recognise its fundamental responsibility to respond to contemporary challenges and opportunities and to rapidly deepen the process of integration between Member States under a revised Treaty of Chaguaramas;

4. that the deepening process aim at establishing a Single Market and Economy (already agreed by CARICOM Heads)

within the shortest possible time, and enlarging the range of functional cooperation within the Community;

5. that there be 'Ministers for CARICOM Affairs' in all Member States, and a wider role for the Council of Ministers on which they will sit than is now exercised by the Common Market Council;

6. that the essential reform of the CARICOM structure required to achieve these goals be the creation of an executive authority — the CARICOM Commission — with competence to initiate proposals, update consensus, mobilise action and secure the implementation of CARICOM decisions in an expeditious and informed manner;

7. that the Commission be drawn from CARICOM's public and political community, be limited initially to a President of the Commission and two other Commissioners, and that the Secretary-General of CARICOM be an ex-officio member of the Commission;

8. that the mandate of the Commission place emphasis on both the deepening of integration through building the structures of unity proposed and the widening of integration in the Caribbean through the proposed Association of Caribbean States;

9. that the Commission be serviced by the CARICOM Secretariat, which should provide the Commission Headquarters staff, and be appropriately decentralised for that purpose;

10. that the Commission and the Secretariat be directly financed by an agreed percentage of regional import duties;

11. that the agreement for a CARICOM Assembly of Parliamentarians be revised to permit the participation of other social partners, preferably as members, but certainly under arrangements which allow for an enlarged forum free to deliberate on matters pertinent to the quality of CARICOM as a community;

12. that, as a necessary element of deepened integration, there be a CARICOM Supreme Court, with original jurisdiction in matters arising under the revised Treaty of Chaguaramas, including the authority to issue orders enforcing the implementation of CARICOM decisions; and with an appellate jurisdiction from the Courts of Member States. The Court's jurisdiction should be designed to assist the evolution of CARICOM law and its uniform enforcement;

13. that a CARICOM Charter of Civil Society be developed as an element of the Community's structure of unity with competence in the CARICOM Supreme Court to issue declaratory judgments and advisory opinions on matters relating to the Charter's provisions. The Charter should deal with such specific matters as a free press, a fair and open democratic process, the effective functioning of the parliamentary system, the absence of corruption from public life, respect for the rights of women and children, the right of association and freedom from political victimisation, respect for religious and cultural diversity, greater accountability and transparency in governance and greater public access to information;

14. that the first step in implementing the core recommendations on CARICOM structures, if agreed by CARICOM Governments, be the appointment, by 1 January 1993 of the CARICOM Commission whose initial task should be to coordinate the building of the structures through revision of the Treaty of Chaguaramas and related negotiations;

15. that transitional arrangements be agreed to permit the Commission to function with appropriate authority until the remaining structures, including the overall legal structures, are in place following an inter-governmental process with which the Commission and Secretariat are associated.

3. THE PUBLIC SERVICE

The public services of the Region in the post-Independence period have not escaped the difficulties experienced by many of their counterparts in the Third World. In the initial period after Independence a small core of indigenous senior civil servants have had to face a multiplicity of new tasks for which they had been barely prepared as new policy activities were imposed upon Governments. Then in order to meet these tasks many of the public services underwent fairly rapid expansion, bringing into the institutions many who, while fully certificated, had not necessarily been socialised into the norms of the public service.

While Governments were fairly quick to introduce training schemes designed to upgrade the administrative efficiency and responsive capacity of the public services, it took some time for new systems of assessment and monitoring to be put into effect. At the same time, in response to the expansion of the private sector in most of the countries, many experienced and innovative public servants were drawn away from the services, leaving, often, glaring gaps in seniority, administrative experience, and maturity in decision-making and implementation.

The severe economic difficulties which many of the countries of the Region have undergone in the late 70s and 80s have now severely compounded the problems which the public services have faced. Many indeed have been ravaged as inadequate facilities, declining rates of remuneration in the face of devaluation and inflation, and consequent lowering of morale have become the order of the day. Public servants who have, more often than not, had the responsibility for implementing programmes of inflation and structural adjustment have themselves been victims of it, as deep cuts in public expenditure have affected the personal and public standards to which they had become accustomed.

In addition, in some countries, many senior civil servants, accustomed to norms of behaviour deriving from the Westminster system, have found themselves increasingly bewildered as the line between political responsibility and public service responsibility became increasingly blurred. They have found themselves forced to undertake virtual political functions. The politicisation of the public services, often under the weight of particular political ideologies, has not, it is now agreed, done anything to sustain the efficiency or the long-term morale of Caribbean public services. And it is not surprising that in recent years the combination of acutely declining remuneration and politicisation has led to accusations of corruption creeping into certain areas of the public services.

In many of the smaller islands of the Region, too, limited governmental capacity for adequate remuneration has tended to lead to rapid turnover of senior level staff, as they have been attracted to other spheres, or have migrated to better prospects in other countries.

As the sphere of regional integration has widened, the public services have found themselves not only having to cope with the severe circumstances of local situations, but with coordinating the implementation of a larger and increasingly diverse number of decisions taken at the regional level. It is not, in that context, surprising that a fair portion of the blame for the lack of implementation of decisions taken by Ministers at regional levels has been placed on the lack of capacity or dynamism of the national public services. Many will in fact argue that some of the blame should well be attributed to lack of will and attention on the part of the political directorate as they have absorbed themselves in local matters after regional meetings.

But it can, too, be argued that present arrangements for necessary linkages between the regional bureaucracies and the national public servants charged with implementation of decisions, often requiring local and external actions, are not appropriate; and secondly, that the internal arrangements of the public services do not match the interdepartmental coordination requirements that many regional decisions necessitate. The result has often been late or lagging implementation of these decisions.

The deepening of the integration process and the need to develop new structures of unity as the Region seeks to respond to the dynamics of internal and external imperatives provide the opportunity to examine afresh the need to overhaul, restructure and reform the public service of the Region if all efforts at progress are not to be frustrated. Time and again elsewhere in this Report it has been stated and demonstrated that *"we do it better when we do it together".* The critically important area of the public service is no exception to this general rule.

Accordingly, short of political unity which it is agreed is not being contemplated at this time, the concept of the collective exercise of sovereignty as between the Member States of CARICOM cannot be restricted to the level of the political directorate, but should equally be applied at the level of the civil service of the Region. There is no doubt that the answer to many of the ills besetting public administration in the West Indies today lies in closer cooperation and more effective collaboration at the level of the civil service.

Following a CARICOM Ministerial Roundtable on Public Management in February 1992, the Executive Secretary of the Caribbean Centre for Development Administration (CARICAD), in a submission to the West Indian Commission, made the following observation —

> The new demands of governance require the management of the state with skill, learning, experience and innovativeness that will certainly prove beyond the reach of any of our member countries as singular entities, despite the extraordinary gifts with which our societies have been so richly endowed.
>
> The management of the business of governance cannot be approached, in the 21st century, as an undertaking by individual member countries of CARICOM without recourse to the collective benefits of our most talented, richly experienced and highly trained sons and daughters confronting our common problems and designing creative solutions, in so far as may be possible. By force of circumstances, if not by conscious policy, the case for the pooling of talent and experience, in an attempt to stave off the high-cost demands of rapid technological changes and increasingly harsh competition for access to goods and services in a world of global markets, is irrefutable.

Action is needed now to offer civil servants a wider field for ambition and to make available to the Region a deeper pool of human resources in the public sector. The search for mechanisms to address this need go no further than agreement for early implementation of a system of secondment and/or transferability throughout the Region, due regard being paid to protection of pension rights and other benefits. To move in this direction is nothing new, as CARICOM Heads had many years ago approved an intra-regional technical cooperation scheme which, had it not been allowed to fall into disuse, would by now have effectively secured the objectives which are now being somewhat belatedly addressed. This action should be complemented by harmonisation of the curricula for in-service training and sharing of such public service training facilities as already exist throughout the Region.

The positive gains to be derived from implementation of the proposed programme include:

- greater opportunities for hands-on experience in, and familiarisation with, parts of the Region other than the officer's country of origin;

- the benefits from close interpersonal contacts throughout the civil services of the Region;

- a better understanding of the peculiar problems of countries, or groupings of countries, within the Region;

- an opportunity to widen the field of selection for important and sensitive appointments, including instances in which absence of any previous relationship with the host society could be an important asset;

- the facilitation of exchange of experience and expertise, obviating the necessity to waste time in re-inventing the wheel;

- according preference to intra-regional personnel, a logical corollary to the action now underway to encourage the movement of skilled and qualified personnel throughout the Region, and to retain such human resources within the Region.

This list of potential positive gains is by no means exhaustive, and what is proposed for the home or central civil service hold no less true for the foreign services of the Region. In this latter area, the impact of structural adjustment and administrative reform is already resulting in reduction of the foreign service personnel of CARICOM Member States and the closing of overseas missions.

Shared overseas diplomatic representation would undoubtedly be far more cost-effective and permit a wider deployment of the Region's representational presence globally. Complementing joint representation in some missions could be a structured programme of representing the interests of each other in countries and organisations. The Treaty of Chaguaramas anticipated even closer coordination of external policies and action. To move in the direction proposed would constitute a significant step towards achieving this objective.

At this time, given the realities of the Region, there could perhaps be no greater motivational force for West Indian public servants than that which would be provided by a clearly defensible and well-defined role within a process of integration to which the Governments of the Region are fully committed.

Joint External Representation

Article 17 of the Treaty of Chaguaramas commits CARICOM Member States to aim at the fullest possible coordination of their foreign policies. Likewise, Article 39 of the Common Market Annex to the Treaty requires, *inter alia*, that Member States should also seek as far as practicable to coordinate their positions and presentations at all international economic, financial and trade meetings at which they are represented. As far back as the pre-independence period, the Region recognised the need for a joint approach to negotiations with the outside world, whether in relation to other states or within the context of specific trade and commodity agreements. Post-independence, the validity of this approach has been conclusively demonstrated in the successful negotiation of the Lomé Convention, CARIBCAN, and successive CBI Agreements.

However, as the economies of the Member States of CARICOM come increasingly under pressure, the need to adopt structural adjustment programmes, including drastic reductions in the public service establishment, has brought with it a new urgency which, *inter alia*, points clearly in the direction of joint overseas representation.

The Commission is aware that under the auspices of the Standing

Committee of Ministers responsible for Foreign Affairs (SCMFA) a Working Group of Joint/Coordinated External Representation has been at work and has put to the ministerial body various options including joint external representation, closer coordination of representational activities among separate overseas missions, and the possibility of establishing either a CARICOM office on its own or a CARICOM presence within the context of joint representation in certain strategic locations.

While valuable work has been done by the Working Group, the fact is that even as the work proceeds it is being rapidly overtaken by the realities of our time. Increasingly, CARICOM Member States have been unilaterally reducing the establishment of their foreign service in response to the need to cut back in budgetary terms and in particular in terms of foreign exchange expenditure. This has meant not only the drastic reduction of staff in several overseas missions of CARICOM Member States but also in some instances the closure of missions. The danger here is that such a reactive approach on the part of some CARICOM Member States is in all probability leading to piecemeal action which, while meeting budgetary constraints, could well be counterproductive in terms of attaining the objectives set out in the Treaty of Chaguaramas.

During the course of our consultations with the West Indian communities in the United Kingdom, Canada and the United States, the Commission was greatly impressed with the extent to which High Commissions, Embassies and Consulates-General were able to work together as a team to ensure the effectiveness and success of the Commission's programme. This demonstration of the potential of joint representation was not lost on the West Indian communities concerned. On several occasions their umbrella organisations reiterated the call for joint representation as a way of more effectively representing the needs of the Region in diplomatic terms and meeting the needs of the West Indian communities in consular terms.

As the Commission moved from country to country and city to city in the course of its consultations with the West Indian diaspora, we were made aware not only of action already in train to effect drastic reductions to the staffs of Embassies, High Commissions and Consulates but also of an on-going effort to relocate these offices in less expensive premises.

To continue to examine the matter of joint representation on the basis of the foreign exchange arithmetic of the several Member States could well, in the final analysis, prove to be an exercise in futility as the rate of exchange of CARICOM currencies and the availability of foreign exchange continues generally to deteriorate.

In the light of its recent observations and available information, the Commission strongly recommends a proactive rather than a reactive approach to the matter of joint representation. The commitment of the CARICOM Heads of Government to the establishment of a Single Market and Economy by 1994 reinforces the validity of the objectives enshrined in the Treaty of Chaguaramas. This implies that CARICOM States should now look to joint representation rather than to the half-way house of coordination of external representation and that, within the context of joint representation, the element of CARICOM as CARICOM could, as appropriate, be worked into the overall matrix. In this direction would undoubtedly lie both greater cost effectiveness and enhanced performance.

In the light of all the foregoing the Commission suggests that, taking the lead of the Organisation of East Caribbean States (OECS), and mindful of the objectives of the Treaty of Chaguaramas, the SCMFA should mandate a Working Group on joint external representation to commence work immediately, with a view to submitting to CARICOM Heads of Government as early as possible a comprehensive proposal and implementation programme for joint representation in capitals in which CARICOM countries require diplomatic and consular representation, and in areas in which representation is required at international organisations of critical importance to the Region. Indeed, the following objectives, as already developed by the SCMFA in August 1991, constitute the objectives of an effective programme of action:

- joint diplomatic missions or joint trade and investment promotion offices in foreign capitals;
- shared facilities in selected capitals of strategic interest to the Community;
- representation at meetings or international organisations;
- representation at meetings or international organisations and other international conferences;
- representation on the governing bodies of international organisations;

- adequate representation of CARICOM nationals at senior levels in international organisations; and
- rationalised consular services.

To the foregoing proposals the Commission would however add one further suggestion. Now that CARICOM is moving rapidly towards a Single Market and Economy and in the light of all the integration processes at work in the political, social, economic and cultural spheres of regional activity, the need for CARICOM Member States to maintain High Commissions in each other's capitals would no longer seem to exist. As the concept of the West Indian homeland, albeit comprising several sovereign states, is developed, the Commission is of the view that, in the age of the telephone and the fax machine, the needs of inter-governmental communications are well served. Indeed, there have already been, progressively, closures of missions intra-regionally — the most recent case being the Barbados High Commission in Trinidad and Tobago, followed by that of the Trinidad and Tobago High Commission in Barbados. Again, this *ad hoc* approach, while reactive to economic and budgetary constraints, unnecessarily gives rise to speculation in the popular press regarding the possible 'tit-for-tat' nature of these decisions. Now that the Region is committed to freedom of movement of CARICOM nationals, another reason for CARICOM States having diplomatic and consular missions throughout the Region no longer holds good.

In summary, therefore, the Commission proposes that, with immediate effect, CARICOM Governments should take the decision to implement in a rational, effective and orderly way a programme of joint representation overseas; and we propose that this action should be synchronised with the move towards a Single Market and Economy. The Commission is in no doubt that by adopting this approach the Region would at one and the same time effect considerable budgetary and foreign exchange savings and put in the field a much enhanced diplomatic and consular service better equipped to meet the demands of the decade of the '90s and the challenges of the rapidly approaching 21st century.

4. TRANSITIONAL ARRANGEMENTS

Earlier in this Chapter we proposed that if CARICOM Heads of Government agreed with the thrust of our recommendations and, in particular, with the need to establish the CARICOM Commission, it should be designated and made operational under interim arrangements and that the Commission, assisted by the Secretariat, should be engaged in an inter-governmental process for refining and elaborating CARICOM's structures of unity using the recommendations as a basis. It is out of such a process that will come the revised Treaty of Chaguaramas and the ultimate form of such institutions as the CARICOM Supreme Court and the CARICOM Assembly, and the CARICOM Charter of Civil Society. Our Commission would have discharged its basic mandate. We believe, however, that resources would be available through technical assistance programmes to support that work of implementation in its initial stages.

If CARICOM leaders, with the support of West Indian publics, accept the broad thrust of our recommendations, the single most important decision needed now is for the establishment of the CARICOM Commission. The Commission, then will be responsible for developing and refining — and bringing to Heads of Government for specific approval — the other elements of our recommendations. The Commission will be providing the architectural drawings without which we cannot build; but unless we take this first step, we will not build at all.

On the next page is a chart illustrating CARICOM's structures of unity as we envisage them under a revised Treaty of Chaguaramas.

5. FORWARD: THE ONLY WAY

The history of West Indian efforts at unity in the administrative, political and economic spheres does not inspire hope, much less confidence. We believe, however, that the burden of failed effort

Time for Action

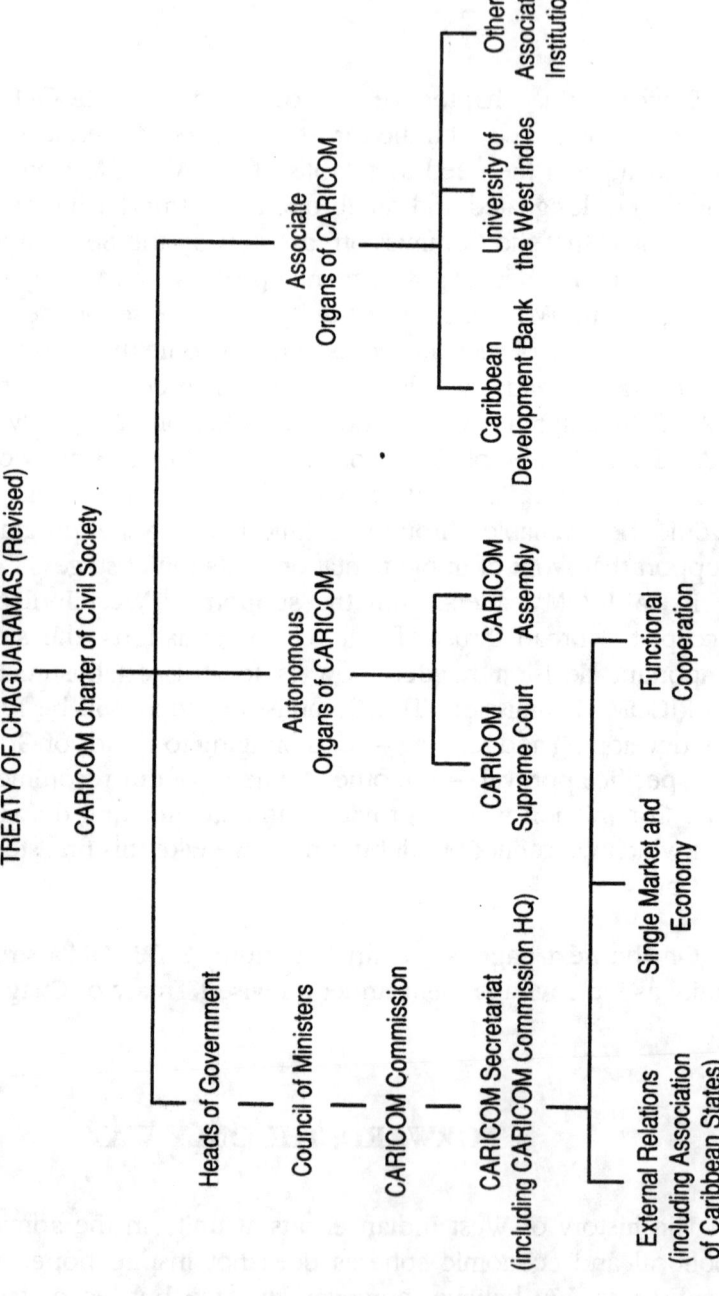

rests not so much on West Indian people as on West Indian decision-makers over centuries of such efforts. In the beginning it was the old plantocracies guarding fiefdoms, then established interests of a later period protecting enclaves of social, economic and political influence. Today's political directorate — of all parties — is tempted in the same direction under the pressures of domestic politics; but times and generations have changed. Political survival in small societies turns, even more conclusively than in large ones, on the economic state of the country. In CARICOM, it turns specifically on the capacity of Governments to deliver standards of living consistent with the aspirations of West Indian societies hyped up by proximity and openness to North America. In this situation, it is no longer the case that political power is best guaranteed by refusing to share any part of it. On the contrary, contemporary realities argue strongly for enlarging economic options by enlarging unity. That is what has led to economic integration in Europe, in North America, in South-East Asia, and is leading to similar movement elsewhere, including Latin America. If history alone were to be our guide the odds should have been heavily tilted against unity in Europe; more heavily tilted than in the West Indies or the wider Caribbean. Integration does not guarantee economic prosperity; but for all the reasons we have advanced in this Report it significantly improves our prospects — and that means political prospects as well.

But something else has changed, or at least has matured. The West Indian people have not waited on Governments; they have integrated — in their own informal but highly effective way. Indeed, through culture and sport and non-governmental activity of every kind, they have been steadily building structures of unity of their own. They are more than ready to occupy formal structures of unity that the political establishment builds. We have no wish to offer the West Indian people on the eve of the twentyfirst century a re-run of an old movie of unity. We do not believe that we are doing so. We believe the scene has changed in fundamental ways and that the prospects for unity are better — essentially because the compulsions are stronger. From time to time, we have no doubt, old instincts will re-emerge; there will be new temptations to return to old insularities. But, they will increasingly run counter to the tide of unity and need not turn us back if we keep faith with our goals and our belief in their attainment. Most of all, in times when any waver we must insist, not just as a matter of agreement but as a matter of conviction, on a mathematics of unity which asserts that one from any number leaves that number less one.

We mentioned earlier in this chapter the need to leave space for intra-CARICOM political groupings where parts of the Community feel able to integrate more closely than the whole — under the CARICOM roof. Once such closer coming together of parts of the integration movement does not reflect a weakening of commitment to the wider CARICOM process — and this is an essential premise — such unification could in fact be a strengthening factor, or at the very least, a neutral one, in relation to integration. But we underline that basic premise: a primary overarching commitment to the CARICOM integration process. If a coming together of some CARICOM partners reflects a slackening of commitment to regional integration, then it must be clear that that coming together is in a context of falling apart. We do not believe that can be good for any of the CARICOM partners or for the CARICOM partnership as a whole.

It is one thing, however, for parts of the Community to develop closer ties than the norm of community relations; it is quite another to develop sub-communities whose regional relations fall below that norm. In that direction lies disintegration. The concept of 'a community of communities' is almost a contradiction in terms to the extent that it implies clusters of Member States with diminishing commitment to the CARICOM process.

But there is a final, very practical, reason for us to go forward together. As we approach the twentyfirst century we dare not turn aside from each other. Local identities may be in vogue; but we do well to remember that they are invariably being indulged under the roof of regional homes — in both Western and Eastern Europe. We began to build our regional home a long time ago. Dismantling it would be a malign act. And it is dismantling that we will face if integration is not perfected but allowed to begin the inevitable alternative process of unravelling. There is no way for us but forward. It should be for us the natural way. It is for us the best way.

This is not to say that we envisage no opposition to the main body of our recommendations. What is evident to us may not be evident to all; there is always room for legitimate disagreement. But there is more besides. The reason for CARICOM's slow progress has not always been due to a lack of political will or simple inertia. Behind bureaucratic delays, for example, too often lay bureaucratic resistance to change: a lack of enthusiasm for new approaches. This is not an indictment of all the Region's bureaucrats, many of whom have been in the front rank of technical work to advance regionalism. But systemic resistance has been real. The same will be true of the efforts to move CARICOM along towards deeper integration; and resistance may come from other quarters. Vested personal interest in the status quo seldom presents itself as such; but it remains a powerful impediment to progress. The West Indies cannot afford to be held back by either faintheartedness or the perceived self-interest of key players in the political, bureaucratic, business or other sectors.

To take a specific example: we have proposed that efforts be made to explore 'unified' West Indian teams in major world sporting events like the Olympic Games or World Cup Football or Davis Cup Tennis. We are sure there is wide regional support for this at the level of the public. We believe it will have the support of very many of the Region's sports people. We are less than sure of its welcome by all sports administrators, some of whom owe their offices to the prevailing system of separate teams. If the proposal is otherwise valid and has the support of West Indian publics, these personal resistances must be overcome; but because such objections are likely to make an appeal to national sentiment, it will take a strong political commitment to 'community' to overcome them. When they are overcome — and West Indian sports men and women (as teams) place us in the front rank of world sports — we will ask ourselves with justifiable pride why we had not unified our teams long ago. It could be the same with the CARICOM Commission or, for example, the CARICOM Assembly. The point we are making is that we must expect some resistance to change; but that, since no progress is ever made without overcoming doubt, those who support change must be prepared to argue for it.

We are mindful too that there will be some voices urging that we have not gone far enough. In our public hearings some claims were made for political unity beyond integration. They reflect a valid sentiment, and will be raised again. We have explained our reason for not pursuing that path for the Region as a whole. What we must guard against, however, is a siren song of larger unity which, though it does not say so, and may not mean to, makes the best the enemy of the good. We are particularly prone in the Region to such philosophical meandering which in the end only brings us back to the point from which we started. That, too, is an indulgence we cannot afford, and must be on guard against. Our proposals trace a path between a standstill scenario and an idealistic odyssey. But times may change; what seems idealistic now may become attainable tomorrow. If it does, the Region itself will review what is in place. Our own proposals will unquestionably require refinement as we go down the path of change; but we have no doubt that they map out the direction we need to travel now — a conviction rooted, not in any conceit of our own, but in the consultative process with the people of the Region that has brought us to our recommendations.

This Report is our principal means of communicating our findings and arguing for change. In the time available to us before the Report is considered by Heads of Government, we will help to clarify our proposals and explain our recommendations. Beyond that, however, it is the people of the Region and West Indians everywhere who must exercise their influence for securing action — if that action seems to be right for our Region as a whole. CARICOM's political leadership will be looking for such indications of support.

After initial, and understandable, scepticism the Region's media have played a major role in supporting the Commission's work. It can play a decisive one in giving voice to the sentiments of West Indian people on the Commission's Report: a voice which we believe will be supportive of change in most of the basic ways we have proposed. In our work, as the Grand Anse Declaration required, we did 'let all ideas contend'; they will continue to do so; that is both right and natural. But there must be, ultimately, an end to contention. There comes a time for decision; for us now, that time cannot be long deferred. Our situation in the Caribbean does not allow us the indulgence of perpetual debate.

Preparing CARICOM for the tewntyfirst century, as envisaged in the Grand Anse Declaration of 1989, is a wide-ranging challenge, but one within the competence of West Indian people and critical to our future.

APPENDICES

APPENDIX "A"

GRAND ANSE DECLARATION AND WORK PROGRAMME FOR THE ADVANCEMENT OF THE INTEGRATION MOVEMENT

Issued at the Tenth Meeting of the Conference of Heads of Government of the Caribbean Community, Grand Anse, Grenada —July 1989

At this our Tenth Meeting here in Grenada, we, the Heads of Government of the Caribbean Community inspired by the spirit of cooperation and solidarity among us are moved by the need to work expeditiously together to deepen the integration process and strengthen the Caribbean Community in all of its dimensions to respond to the challenges and opportunities presented by the changes in the global economy. Accordingly, we set out a work programme and specific initiatives to be implemented over the next four years.

The Common Market

We are determined to work towards the establishment, in the shortest possible time, of a single market and economy for the Caribbean Community. To that end, we shall ensure that the following steps are taken not later than 4 July 1993, taking into account the need for the continuance of Special Measures for the LDCs:

1. the three Common Market Instruments required by the Treaty of Chaguaramas — the Common External Tariff, the Rules of Origin, and a Harmonised Scheme of Fiscal Incentives — fully revised, agreed and effective by January 1991;

2. customs co-operation and our Customs Administrations strengthened to prepare ourselves for movement towards a Customs Union;

3. the signature by all of us to the Agreement establishing the CARICOM Industrial Programming Scheme (CIPS) by September 30, 1989;

4. the enactment, by January, 1990 of the legislation required to give effect to CIPS and the CARICOM Enterprise Regime (CER);

5. a scheme for the movement of capital introduced by 1993 starting with the cross-listing and trading of securities on existing stock exchange;

525

6. technical work to commence immediately on the establishment of a regional Equity/Venture Capital Fund;
7. the CARICOM Multilateral Clearing Facility strengthened and re-established for current and capital transactions by December 1990;
8. further arrangements for intensifying consultation and co-operation on monetary, financial and exchange rate policies by July 1990;
9. the removal of all remaining barriers to trade by July 1991;
10. immediate activation of Article 39 of the Annex to the Treaty of Chaguaramas in order to promote consultation, co-operation and co-ordination of policies at the macro-economic, sectoral and project levels;
11. arrangements by January, 1991 for the free movement of skilled and professional personnel as well as for contract workers on a seasonal or project basis;
12. immediate and continuing action to develop, by. 4 July 1992, a regional system of air and sea transportation including the pooling of resources by existing air and sea carriers conscious that such a system is indispensable to the development of a Single Market and Community;
13. greater collective effort for joint representation in international economic negotiations and the sharing of facilities and offices to this end, with immediate effect.

Development Issues

In examining the longer term prospects for development, we recognize the primary importance of Human Resource Development and the expansion of scientific and technological capability to the modernization of the regional economy.

Accordingly, we adopted the resolution in Annex I on Human Resource Development and the University of the West Indies (UWI) which among other things recognizes the pivotal role of the UWI and enshrines our commitment that it shall continue indefinitely as a regional institute.

Human Resource Development is of special value in the exploitation of new opportunities arising in the services sector through the development of information technology. We consider these possibilities to hold significant potential for economic growth and development. Accordingly, we shall initiate immediately, consultations with the private sector, trade unions and education institutions to determine the specific strategies for taking full advantage of these opportunities.

We are conscious that people, rather than institutions, are the creators and producers of development. We acknowledge the special roles of the private sector, the trade union movement, the regional universities, the religious organizations, women and youth organizations and people of all walks and conditions of life in moving CARICOM forward.

In this connection, we agree to take the following steps:

(i) The establishment of an Assembly of Caribbean Community Parliamentarians and of a Ministerial group to work out the modalities;

(ii) The establishment of an Independent West Indian Commission for Advancing the Goals of the Treaty of Chaguaramas as agreed in the Resolution at Annex II;

(iii) The convening of a Caribbean Economic conference as agreed in the Resolution at Annex III;

(iv) The elimination, by December 1990, of the requirement for passports for CARICOM nationals travelling to other CARICOM countries;

(v) The elimination of the requirement for work permits for CARICOM nationals beginning with the visual and performing arts, sports and the media travelling to CARICOM countries for specific regional events;

(vi) The organizing of a series of events around 1992 to highlight our achievements in the areas of sports, the performing arts, literature and other areas of cultural endeavour, business and commerce and education. The series will commence with the staging of CARIFESTA in 991 and include a major Trade fair early in 1992 in Trinidad and Tobago.

We are acutely aware of the fragility of the environment on which our economies rest and of the myriad threats to that environment from internal and external actions and activities. To protect our environment, we support all international initiatives to safeguard the global environment and strongly endorse the Port- of-Spain Accord on the Management and Conservation of the Caribbean Environment by our own Ministers responsible for conservation of the Environment.

Machinery for Intergovernmental Consultations

In order to ensure the full and timely implementation of the programme set out above, we shall intensify and make more frequent the contact and consultations among ourselves. We shall meet as often as necessary to advance the decision making and the implementation of this programme.

ANNEX II
GRAND ANSE RESOLUTION ON PREPARING THE PEOPLES OF THE WEST INDIES FOR THE TWENTY-FIRST CENTURY

Heads of Government:

Fully supported the idea of maximizing the opportunities of CARIFESTA (1991) and the Quincentennial celebrations (1992) for the expression of the creative genius of the Caribbean people, for promotion of awareness of common history, identity and common destiny, and for projection achievements in the Region in the fields of literature, the creative arts, sports, culture, politics, economic and human development;

Accepted the proposal for the establishment of a commission of eminent West Indians to promote the purposes outlined in the paper with special emphasis on the process of public consultation and involvement of the peoples of CARICOM through leaders, teachers, writers, intellectuals, creative artistes, businessmen, sportsmen, trade unionists, churches and other community organizations.

Further agreed as follows:

1. that no later than October 1, 1989, the Commission be established as an **Independent West Indian Commission for Advancing the Goals of the Treaty of Chaguaramas** and report to Heads of Government prior to their meeting in 1992;

2. that the Chairman of the Commission be Sir Shridath Ramphal;

3. that the Secretary-General of CARICOM and the Director-General of OECS be ex-officio members of the Commission;

4. that the Chairman of the Commission should consult with heads of Government of Member States with a view to appointing the other members of the Commission as soon as possible; and

5. that the Commission should establish a budget for its work and be empowered to seek contributions to its budget from Member States and external sources.

APPENDIX "B"

THE WEST INDIAN COMMISSION

Patron
Dame Nita Barrow, Governor-General of Barbados

Chairman
Shridath Ramphal, Chancellor, University of the West Indies; University of Guyana; Warwick University, Britain; President, World Conservation Union (ICUN); Advisor, United Nations Conference on the Environment; First Executive President, Willy Brandt International Foundation; Secretary-General of the Commonwealth of Nations (1975–1990); Member, South Commission (1987–1989); Member, World Commission on Development and Environment (1984–1987); Chairman, United Nations Committee on Development Planning (1975–1977); Served as Vice-President, United Nations General Assembly; Minister of Justice, Guyana (1973–1975); Minister of Foreign Affairs (1972–1975); Attorney General (1966–1972)

Vice-Chairman
Alister McIntyre, Vice-Chancellor, University of the West Indies; Chairman, International Forum on Debt and Development, The Netherlands; Personal Representative, of the Secretary-General, United Nations, on the Guyana/Venezuela Border Controversy; Member, Committee to Review the Structure of Government, Jamaica (1990); Member, Group of Caribbean Experts on "The Caribbean Community in the 1980s" (1982) Member, Governing Body, Institute of Development Studies, Sussex (1984–1991); Assistant-Secretary United Nations Conference on Trade & Development (UNCTAD)(1988); Deputy Secretary General, (1982–1987); Chairman, Commonwealth Group of Experts on New International Economic Order (1975– 1977); Member, United Nations Committee on Development Planning, (1975–1977); Secretary General of the Caribbean Community (1974–1977); Director, Institute for Social & Economic Research (ISER), University of the West Indies (1967–1974)

Appendices

Members

Leonard Archer, Secretary-General, Commonwealth of the Bahamas Trade Union Congress; Founding Member and Director, Teachers and Salaried Workers Cooperative Credit Union Limited, Bahamas; Member, General Council, Administrative Committee, Caribbean Congress of Labour; First Alternate Member for the Caribbean, Executive Board, International Confederation of Free Trade Unions (ICFTU) (1985); President, Caribbean Congress of Labour (1983–1986); Principal, Nassau High Schools, (1971–1983)

William Demas, Governor, Central Bank of Trinidad & Tobago; President, Caribbean Development Bank (1974–1988); Chairman, Expert Group on Caribbean Integration in the 1980's (1981); Secretary-General, Caribbean Free Trade Association (CARIFTA) & Caribbean Community and Common Market (CARICOM) (1970–1974); Former Chairman, United Nations Committee on Development Planning; Member, Group of Commonwealth Experts on Reform of the International Monetary, Financial and Trading System (1983); Chairman, Ministerial Commission to Review Functioning of the East African Community (1975); Permanent Secretary, Ministry of Planning and Development, Trinidad & Tobago (1967–1968)

Howard Fergus, Writer, Senior Lecturer/Resident Tutor, University of the West Indies, Montserrat; Speaker, Legislative Council; Chairman, Education Advisory Committee; Chairman, CARICOM Foundation of Arts and Culture; Chairman, Project Advisory Committee Canada/UWI Strengthening Project; Member, Board of Directors, West Indies School of Theology; (1982–1988); Member, History Panel, Caribbean Education Council (CXC) (1979–1985); Acts as Governor of Montserrat 1976 to present; Chief Education Officer (1970–1974)

Marshall Hall, Group Managing Director, Jamaica Banana Producers; Chairman, Jamaica Mutual Life Assurance Society; Member, Caribbean Banana Exporters Association; Member, Board of Directors, Guardian Life of the Caribbean, Trinidad; Management Consultant; Chairman, Chief Executive, Jamaica Public Service Company Limited (1975–1979); Professor/Chairman, Department of Management Studies, University of the West Indies (1971–1975); Visiting Professor, Makerere University (1970–1971)

F. Allan Kirton, Minister of Religion; International Church Person In Residence, Mission Resource Center, Emory University, Atlanta; General Secretary, Caribbean Conference of Churches (1983–1991); Methodist Pastorates — St. Vincent, Trinidad, Haiti, Barbados (1966–1982); University Chaplain, University of the West Indies/Lecturer, Codrington Theological College, Barbados (1972–1975); District Christian Education Secretary, South Caribbean District (1967–1970)

Vaughan Lewis, Director-General, Organisation of Eastern Caribbean States; Chairman, Board of Governors, Sir Arthur Lewis Community College, St. Lucia; Consultant to UNITAR — Training of Diplomats in the Caribbean LDCs; Director, Institute of Social and Economic Research, UWI, Jamaica (1977–1982); Member, Expert Group on Caribbean Integration in the 1980's (1981); Ford Foundation Visiting Fellow, Concilium on International Studies, Yale University (1981); Visiting Professor, Department of International Relations, Florida International University (1980); Lecturer, Department of Government, University of the West Indies, (1968–1972)

Sandra Mason, Senior Magistrate with Additional Responsibility for Juvenile and Family Courts, Barbados; Member, United Nations Committee on the Rights of the Child; Chairman, National Committee, International Year of the Family; Deputy Chairman, Child Care Board; Chairman, Advisory Board, School of Continuing Studies, U.W.I.; Member, Advisory Board, Barbados Youth Council; Chairman, Executive Council, Boy Scouts; Member, Board of Directors, Young Men's Christian Association

Gillian Nanton, Senior Economist; Government of St. Vincent and the Grenadines (1983–1989); Represented the Government on several Boards including the St. Vincent Banana Growers Association and the St. Vincent Marketing Corporation; Director, Eastern Caribbean Central Bank (1986–1989); Presently Assistant to Executive Director, Canada/Caribbean, International Monetary Fund, Washington, DC

Phillip Nassief, Chairman, Chief Executive, Dominica Coconut Products; Chairman, Fort Young (1986) Limited; Member Board of Trustees, Caribbean Central American Action Group; Member, Caribbean Association of Industry and Commerce (Director — 1987–1990); Chairman, National Development Foundation of Dominica (1981–1984); President, Dominica Association of Industry and Commerce (1977–1979)

Rex Nettleford, Professor, Director School of Continuing Studies, Pro-Vice Chancellor, Director of Studies, Trade Union Education Institute, University of the West Indies; Editor, *Caribbean Quarterly*; Founder/Artistic Director, National Dance Theatre Company of Jamaica; Member, Executive Board, UNESCO; Member, ILO Team of Independent Experts Monitoring Implementation of Sanctions Against Apartheid; Governor, NEWSCONCERN International, London; Member Board of Trustees of AFS International, New York; Member, Academic Council for Latin American and Caribbean Studies, Wilson Center, Washington D.C.; Consultant on Culture to UNESCO and OAS; Founding Governor, International Development Research Centre (IDRC), Ottawa; Chairman, Commonwealth Arts Organisation, Sydney, London (1980–1987); Chairman, Committee to review the Structure of Government, Jamaica (1992); Cultural Advisor to the Government of Jamaica; Fellow Institute of Jamaica; Living Legend Awardee National Black Arts Festival, Atlanta, (1990)

Roderick Rainford, Secretary-General, Caribbean Community & Common Market (CARICOM) since 1983; Deputy Secretary-General (1980–1983); Provided Planning and Advisory Services in the Fields of Trade and Industrial Development in senior positions in the Govenment Service of Jamaica (1973–1980); Research Fellow and Tutor in International Relations, University of the West Indies and University of Toronto (1970–1973); Resident Tutor, Extra-Mural Department, University of Zambia (1967–1970).

Frank Rampersad, Coordinator, University Centre Project; Chairman,University of the West Indies Advisory Committee; Member, National Economic Advisory Committee, Trinidad & Tobago; Chairman, Technical Committee On Caribbean Basin Initiative (CBI); Chairman Technical Committee on Regional Air Transportation Services; Deputy Chairman and Chief Financial Officer, Amar Group of Companies (1990–1992) President, National Insititute of Higher Education (Research, Science and Technology) Trinidad, (1978–1990); Coordinator Regional Economic Conference (1990); Chairman, British West Indian Airways (BWIA) Ltd.(1981–1986); Chairman, UNCTAD Expert Group on Special Arrangements for Least Developed Countries (1983); Member, Commonwealth Expert Group on Venture Capital Fund (1982); Director, Economic Affairs, Commonwealth Secretariat, London (1976–1978); Permanent Secretary, Ministry of Finance, Trinidad & Tobago (1965–1975).

Neville Trotz, Science Advisor to Commonwealth Secretary General; Secretary, Commonwealth Science Council; Secretary-General, National Science Research Council (1984–1991); Director, Institute of Applied Science and Technology, Guyana (1979–1991); Member, Executive Committee Commonwealth Science Council for Biennium (1988–1990); Member, Guyana

National Commission for UNESCO (1980-1991) Dean, Faculty of Natural Sciences, University of Guyana (1976-1979); Head, Department of Chemistry, University of Guyana (1974-1976)

Director-General
Donald Brice

Senior Staff
Sheila Chan, Project Coordinator (Conference Services)
Irma Graham, Project Coordinator (Documentation)
Sandra Grant, Project Coordinator (Administration)
Gladstone Pollard, Office Manager
Janet Singh, Head, Chairman's Office

Meetings/Consultations Staff
Sandra Granger (Research Officer/Rapporteur)
Anne Simpson (Research Officer/Rapporteur)

General Services & Support Staff
Victor Best
Brenda Howell
Marvelle Jordan
Melinda Mills

Consultants/Advisors
Sandra Baptiste/George John, Communications Consultants
Ian McDonald, Editoral Consultant
Delisle Worrell, Director of Studies

Appendix "C"
Meetings and Workshops

The Commission held 13 meetings:

First meeting, Wildey, St. Michael, Barbados, 9–11 April, 1990

Second meeting, St. Vincent & the Grenadines, 30th September, 1990

Third meeting, Antigua & Barbuda, 16th December, 1990

Fourth meeting, Kingston & Montego Bay, Jamaica, 13–15 March, 1991

Fifth meeting, WIC London Office, 19th April, 1991

Sixth meeting, Christ Church, Barbados, 24–25 May, 1991

Seventh meeting, Nassau, The Bahamas, 15–16 June, 1991

Eighth meeting, Mona, Jamaica, 12–13 October, 1991

Ninth meeting, Toronto, Canada, 9 December, 1991

Tenth meeting, Port-of-Spain, Trinidad, 28 January, 1992

Eleventh meeting, Kingston, Jamaica, 21 February, 1992

Twelfth meeting, Washington, U.S.A., 28–29 March, 1992

Thirteenth meeting, Barbados, 10–13 May, 1992

Two special core group meetings were also held at the Secretariat offices, Barbados, on 3rd September, 1990, and 7th September, 1991, respectively.

To assist the Commission in its work, a number of technical workshops/symposia on selected topics were convened.

Workshops

A Common Currency for the Caribbean	—	Barbados February 22–23, 1991
Tourism	—	Jamaica February 16, 1992
Information	—	Barbados March 9, 1992
Human Resource Development	—	Jamaica March 14, 1992
Investment, Trade and Development	—	Trinidad March 20, 1992
Challenges Facing Caribbean Youth	—	St. Kitts and Nevis May 6, 1992

Symposium

CARICOM, the Wider Caribbean and Latin America	—	Caracas, Venezuela April 27–28, 1992

Appendix "D"

ITINERARY AND CONSULTATIONS

The Programme below sets out the itinerary and consultations undertaken by the Commission. References to 'sectoral groups' include: academicians, business (including small business), labour/trade unions, non-governmental organizations (NGO's), practitioners of art and culture (including entertainers), professionals, religious organizations, service clubs, university and sixth-form students, women's organizations, youth and sporting bodies.

ANTIGUA AND BARBUDA

December 17-18, 1990
St. John's: Prime Minister and Cabinet, Opposition and other political parties, media representatives and sectoral groups. Public Meeting.
Barbuda: Barbuda Council, other political parties. Public Meeting.

BAHAMAS

June 17-18, 1991
Nassau: Prime Minister and Cabinet, Opposition and other political parties, media representatives and sectoral groups. Public Meeting.
Freeport: Sectoral groups. Public Meeting.

BARBADOS

May 18-20, 1991
Bridgetown: Prime Minister and Cabinet, Opposition and other political parties, media representative, heads and senior officers of Caribbean regional organisations, sectoral groups. Faculty and students, UWI, Cave Hill. Public Meeting.
St. Peter: Public Meeting.
St. Philip: Public Meeting.

DOMINICA

May 26-28, 1991
Roseau: Prime Minister and Cabinet, Opposition and other political parties, media representatives, sectoral groups. Public Meeting.
Marigot: Carib Chief and Council. Public Meeting.
Portsmouth: Public Meeting.

BELIZE

June 12-14, 1991
Belize City: Media representatives, sectoral groups. Public Meeting.
Belmopan: Prime Minister and Cabinet, Opposition, Indigenous Groups (Maya, Mestizo, Garifuna), Public Service Union. Public Meeting.

GRENADA

September 28-29, 1990
St. George's: Prime Minister and Cabinet, Opposition and other political parties, media representatives, community development organizations and representatives of rural parishes, sectoral groups. Public Meeting.
Carriacou: Public Meeting.

GUYANA

July 21-24, 1990
Georgetown: President and Cabinet, Minority Leader, representatives of ruling party, the Peoples National Congress, and other political parties, media representatives, staff of the CARICOM Secretariat, sectoral groups. Public Meeting.
New Amsterdam: Public Meeting.
Linden: Public Meeting.

JAMAICA

March 11-16, 1991
Kingston: Prime Minister and Cabinet, Opposition, other Political parties, media representatives, sectoral groups. Faculty and students, UWI, Mona. Public Meeting.
Port Antonio: Public Meeting.

Mandeville: Public Meeting.
Montego Bay: media representatives and sectoral groups. Public Meeting.

February 20-21, 1992
Kingston: Public Meeting

MONTSERRAT

December 14-15, 1990
Plymouth: Chief Minister and Cabinet, Opposition and other political parties, media representatives, sectoral groups. Public Meeting.

ST. KITTS/NEVIS

December 11-13, 1990
Basseterre: Prime Minister and Cabinet, the Opposition, Governor of the East Caribbean Central Bank, media representatives, sectoral groups. Public Meeting.
Saddlers Village: Public Meeting.
Nevis: Premier and Cabinet, Opposition Party. Public Meeting.

SAINT LUCIA

October 3-5, 1990
Castries: Prime Minister and Cabinet, Opposition, Committee for OECS Unity, media representatives, sectoral groups. Public Meeting.

ST. VINCENT AND THE GRENADINES

October 1-2, 1990
Kingstown: Prime Minister and Cabinet, Opposition and other political parties; media representatives, sectoral groups. Public Meeting.
Barrouallie: Public Meeting.
Mesopotamia: Public Meeting.

Itinerary and Consultations

TRINIDAD & TOBAGO

July 25-28, 1990
Port-of-Spain: Prime Minister and Cabinet, Opposition and other political parties, media representatives, sectoral groups.
Tobago: Public Meeting.

January 27-28, 1992
Port of Spain: Prime Minister and Ministers, Sixth form students. Public Meeting.
San Fernando: Public Meeting.

WEST INDIAN DIASPORA

UNITED KINGDOM

April 15-19, 1991
London: CARICOM High Commissioners and senior staff, representatives of the West India Committee; Minister for Overseas Development and Minister responsible for Caribbean Affairs, Foreign and Commonwealth Office; West Indian media, the cultural community, university students, sectoral groups, prominent West Indians. Public Meeting.
Birmingham: Public Meeting.

CANADA

December 4-10, 1991
Montreal: Public Meeting.
Ottawa: CARICOM High Commissioners and senior staff; Secretary of State for External Affairs, Minister of Multi-Culturalism, Vice President and representatives of both CIDA and IDRC, Canadian Government officials, sectoral groups. Public Meeting.
Toronto: CARICOM Consular representatives and senior staff; W.I. sectoral groups and students; Public Meeting.

U.S.A.

March 26-31, 1992
Washington: CARICOM Ambassadors and senior staff. Caribbean media representatives and members of Caribbean community

organisations, representatives of the International Affairs Division of the Department of the Treasury, members of the U.S. Congressional Black Caucus, and with representatives of the Carnegie Endowment for International Peace (Think Tanks). Roundtable discussion with the Deputy Assistant Administrator for the Bureau of Latin America and the Caribbean at USAID, and other State Department officials.

Officials of international funding agencies as follows: Vice-President, World Bank; President, Inter-American Development Bank; Acting Managing Director, Director, Western Hemisphere Department and Executive Director, Caribbean Region, International Monetary Fund; also Permanent Council of the Organization of American States and Department of US Trade representatives. Dialogue with Caribbean international professionals organised by the Washington DC Chapter of the University of the West Indies Guild of Graduates on the topic, Caribbean Development Issues. Public Meeting.

New York: Caribbean Community Ambassadors to the United Nations, diplomatic representatives and members of the Consular corps; Caribbean professionals and businessmen comprising members of the Caribbean American Chamber of Commerce and Industry, the Caribbean Research Center and Caribbean Action Lobby; also Caribbean staff members of the United Nations. Discussions with Caribbean and other media representatives Interviewed on WLIB radio. Talks with representatives of United Nations agencies as follows: Associate Director and Chief, Division III – Caribbean, United Nations Development Programme (UNDP); Executive Director and Deputy Director, Latin America and Caribbean Division, United Nations Fund for Population Activities (UNFPA); Deputy Director, Programmes, United Nations Children's Fund (UNICEF). Public Meeting.

Appendix "E"

Submissions to the Commission

The Commission wishes to express its sincere appreciation and gratitude to all those individuals, organisations and institutions, many of whom are listed below, who spared the time to take part in its consultations or to submit memoranda for its use. Without their participation, support and advice the Commission would not have been able to fulfil its mandate. A list of those who submitted written memoranda follows. (The list was prepared from information on the Secretariat's files. It is possible, however, that some submissions may not have reached the Secretariat and the Commission apologizes for any omissions.)

Abbott, Diane, M.P., U.K.
Abbott, George C., Department of Political Economy, University of Glasgow, U.K.
Abdulah, David, Trinidad & Tobago.
Afro-Canadian Newspaper, Montreal, Canada.
Aird, Eve, University of Belize.
Alcena, Kevin J., Nassau, The Bahamas.
Ali, Haseeb, Manager, Guyana Islamic Trust, Georgetown, Guyana.
Allen, Oscar, St. Vincent.
Allsopp, Dr. Richard, UWI, Cave Hill, Barbados.
Alumni Association of the Consortium Graduate School of Social Sciences, U.W.I., Mona, Jamaica.
Alves, Kester, Director, Information Services, Guyana Public Communications Agency, Guyana.
Anderson, Roy K., 4041 Baychester Avenue, Bronx, N.Y. 10466, U.S.A.
Anderson, Prof. Wolseley, York University, Ontario, Canada.
Andrews, Vernon E., Seventh-Day Adventist Church, Trinidad & Tobago.
Angoy, Wilton A., St. Michael, Barbados.
Antigua and Barbuda Nationals Association of Greater Washington D.C., U.S.A.
Antigua Chamber of Commerce Limited, St. John's, Antigua.
Antigua Girls' High School.
Azeez, Moulvi Abdool, Executive Member, Guyana Human Rights Association and Member, Steering Committee, Guyana Action for Reform and Democracy.

Appendices

Bacchus-Gill, Kay R.A., LL.B. (Hons), St. Vincent.
Bahá'í Community, Barbados.
Bahá'í Women's Group of Barbados.
Bahá'í Community in St. Kitts.
Bahá'ís, National Spiritual Assembly, Dominica.
Bahá'ís, National Spiritual Assembly, Grenada.
Bahá'ís, National Spiritual Assembly, Guyana.
Bahá'ís, National Spiritual Assembly, Jamaica.
Bahá'ís of the Leeward Islands, St. John's, Antigua.
Bahá'ís, Spiritual Assembly, Plymouth, Montserrat.
Baldeo, Dawn, Caricom Secretariat, Guyana.
Baptiste, Colin Oliver, Dominica.
Barbados Agricultural Society.
Barbados Agro-Processing Company Limited.
Barbados Boy Scouts Association, Barbados.
Barbados Chamber of Commerce and Industry.
Barbados Employers' Confederation.
Barbados Labour Party Women's League.
Barbados Methodist Council, Office of Chairman.
Barbados National Association of of Washington, D.C., U.S.A.
Barbados Youth Council.
Barnes, O.A., CARICOM Secretariat, Guyana.
Barrow, E.H.E., Lincolnshire, U.K.
Basir, Isahak, Vice-President R.P.A.-G.A.P.A., Essequibo Coast, Guyana.
Beckles, W.W., Registrar, Caribbean Examinations Council, Barbados.
Beddoe, I.B., Petit Valley, Diego Martin, Trinidad.
Belize Bahá'í Community.
Belize Bank Limited, Belize City, Belize.
Belize Chamber of Commerce and Industry.
Belize National Teachers' Union, Belize City, Belize.
Belize Sugar Industries Limited.
Belize Sugar Industries Limited, Marketing Agents, U.K.
Bellot, Parry, Parbel Enterprises, Roseau, Dominica.
Benjamin, Colin, Willowdale, Ontario, Canada.
Blackett, Fr. Harcourt, Barbados.
Blackman, Dr. Courtney N., International Business Consultant, Bradenton, Florida, U.S.A.
Boland, Herbert, Willowdale, Ontario, Canada.
Bonnick, G.G., Washington D.C., U.S.A.
Bramble, P. Austin, O.B.E., J.P., former Chief Minister of Montserrat.
British Caribbean Junior Chamber of Commerce, London, U.K.

Browne, Chedmond, Plymouth, Montserrat.
Burke, Victor, Toronto, Canada.
Buxo, C.A., Grenada.

Cacho, Cornelius P., Florida, U.S.A.
Callender, Lorna A., Basseterre Junior High School, St. Kitts.
Caribbean Academy of Sciences, Prof. R. Saunders, President, Trinidad & Tobago.
Caribbean Action Lobby, Eastern Parkway, Brooklyn, N.Y., U.S.A.
Caribbean-American Community Comprehensive Center, New York, U.S.A.
Caribbean Association of Industry and Commerce, Bridgetown, Barbados.
Caribbean Association of Nutritionists and Dietitians, Jamaica.
Caribbean Banana Exporters' Association, London, U.K.
Caribbean Broadcasting Union, Barbados.
Caribbean Catholic, London, U.K.
Caribbean Centre for Development Administration (CARICAD), St. Michael, Barbados.
Caribbean Community Advisory Task Force on Education, Georgetown, Guyana.
Caribbean Confederation of Credit Unions, Barbados.
Caribbean Congress of Labour, Barbados.
Caribbean Council of Prince George's County, Maryland 20775, U.S.A.
Caribbean Development Bank, Barbados.
Caribbean Food and Nutrition Institute, Jamaica Centre, UWI Campus, Kingston, Jamaica.
Caribbean Food and Nutrition Institute, Trinidad Centre, St. Augustine, Trinidad.
Caribbean Heritage Group, Washington D.C., U.S.A.
Caribbean Integration Movement, Barbados.
Caribbean News Agency, St. Michael, Barbados.
Caribbean Organszation of Indigenous Peoples, COIP Secretariat, Belize.
Caribbean Research Center, Medgar Evers College Auditorium, Brooklyn, New York, U.S.A.
Caribbean Rights, St. Michael, Barbados.
Caribbean Tourism Organisation, Barbados.
Caribbean Union Conference of Seventh-Day Adventists, Barbados.
Caribbean Union of Teachers, Castries, St. Lucia.
Caribbean Women's Health Association, Inc., 2725 Church Avenue, Brooklyn, N.Y., 11226, U.S.A.
Caribbean Youth Conference, St. Lucia.

Appendices

Carr, Wilfred I., (Guyanese), Toronto, Canada.
Carrington, His Excellency Dr. Edwin, High Commissioner to Guyana, Trinidad & Tobago.
Caswell, Gracelyn, Librarian, Public Library, Plymouth, Montserrat.
CASWIG, Guyana.
Catholic Bishops, Dominica.
Catholic Bishops, Grenada.
CCC Antigua Programme Centre, St. John's, Antigua.
Chamber of Commerce and Industry, Belize.
Charles, Embert, Executive Director, Folk Research Centre, St. Lucia.
Charles, Hubert J., Co-ordinator, Caribbean Network of Educational Innovation for Development (CARNEID), Barbados.
Christian, H.L., Goodwill, Dominica.
Church of God of Prophecy, St. John's, Antigua.
Clemetson, Marcia, Secretary, Institute of Divine Metaphysical Research, Inc., Kingston 11, Jamaica.
Collins, Aubrey, Georgetown, Guyana.
Collymore, Clinton, M.P., People's Progressive Party, Guyana.
Committee for a Preliminary Count, New Amsterdam, Guyana.
Commonwealth Liaison Unit of Barbados.
Conference of Caribbean Unity, Washington D.C., U.S.A.
Cornibert, Bernard, U.K. Representative, Windward Islands Banana Growers' Association, London, U.K.
Council of Caribbean Organizations, Inc., Washington D.C., U.S.A.
Council of Presidents of the Environment of Trinidad & Tobago, c/o Eve Anderson Associates, Port of Spain, Trinidad.
Cox, Eileen, President, Guyana Consumers' Association, Guyana.
Crosse, Leroy A., M.Sc., LL.B., Toronto, Canada.
Cupidon, Janet, Council of Voluntary Social Services, Jamaica.

D'Aguiar, St. Pius X Catholic Church, East La Penetence, Georgetown, Guyana.
Daniels, Mrs. Cecelia, Parent, Montserrat.
Darbyshire, Ann Glanville, Ottawa, Canada.
Dassrath, Romeo Suresh, c/o La Ramain P.O., Trinidad & Tobago.
David, Wilfred and Peggy, Washington D.C., U.S.A.
Dawson, Johnathan, West Midlands, U.K.
Depradine, Colin A., Caribbean Metereological Institute, Barbados.
Dental Council of Trinidad & Tobago.

Submissions to the Commission

Dick, Emmanuel, Federation of Trinidad & Tobago Organizations, Toronto, Canada.
Dominica Association of Disabled People.
Dominica Association of Industry and Commerce, Dominica.
Dominica Association of Washington, D.C., U.S.A.
Dominica Christian Council, Roseau, Dominica.
Dominica Cricket Association.
Dominica Overseas Nationals Association, London, U.K.
Duncan, Dr. Neville, Head, Government and Sociology Department, University of the West Indies, Cave Hill, Barbados.
Duncan, Richard, Grenada.
Dundas, Carl W., U.K.

Economic Affairs Secretariat, OECS, St. John's, Antigua & Barbuda.
Edgecombe, Hilton, Montserrat.
Edge Enterprises, Plymouth, Montserrat.
Elcock, L.D., LLM, Attorney-at-Law, Pt. Cumana, Trinidad & Tobago.
Elliot, Henson, North West District, Guyana.
Ellis, Clarence, Inter-American Development Bank, Washington DC, U.S.A.
Emmanuel, Trevor, Grenada.
Erskine, Douglas, Belize City, Belize.
Ethiopian Orthodox Church, Scarborough, Tobago.
Ethiopian World Federation, Inc., London, U.K.
Eudoxie, Ann, Castries, St. Lucia.
Evans, Ancella, a young person of the Caribbean, The Bahamas.

Federation of Independent Trade Unions of Guyana.
Felix, Andrew, Committee for Free and Fair Elections in Guyana, Washington, D.C., U.S.A.
Fenton, C.E.O., Bank of Montserrat Ltd.
Ferdinand, Garwin G., Hornsey, London, U.K.
Fevrier, Willie, Dominica Planned Parenthood Association.
Fontenelle, Valerie H., B.A.A. (National of St. Lucia), Canada.
Foote, Nelson N., Mill Valley, California, U.S.A.
Forbes-Davies, C.T. (Mrs.), U.K.
Forde, Hon. H. DeB.,Q.C., M.P., Leader of the Opposition and Chairman of the Barbados Labour Party.
Forde, Kenneth, Chaguanas, Trinidad & Tobago.

Appendices

Forde, Margaret M.J., Washington D.C., U.S.A.
Forte, Dianne, National Black Women's Health Project, Atlanta, Georgia, United States.
Forrester, Fr. Kenneth M., St. David's Rectory, Plymouth, Tobago.
France-Carbonneau, Faustina, President, Minority Business and Professional Network Forum.
Francis, Ambassador E. Frank, Kingston, Jamaica.
Francis, Jennifer, Dip. CAM, MIPR, International Communications Management Strategist, London, U.K.
Francis, J.P., Coordinator, Pan African Secretariat, Jamaica.
Francois, Walter F., M.A. Econ. (National of St. Lucia), Canada.
French, Joan, Coordinator, Caribbean (NGO) Policy Development Centre, Barbados.

George, Novack S., San Fernando, Trinidad.
George, McChesney D.B., Anguilla.
Gibson, Rev. Dr. Ashton, Bridgetown, Barbados.
Gibson, Clint, Scarborough, Ontario, Canada.
Gilkes, U.M. (National of Montserrat), Montreal, Quebec, Canada.
Girvan, Norman P., President, Kingston 7, Jamaica.
Glinton, Maurice, Freeport, The Bahamas.
G.N.L.Y.C., S. Padmore, Secretary, Guyana.
Goddard, Joseph R., General Secretary, National Union of Public Workers, Barbados.
Goddard, Philip C., Barbados.
Gomez, The Right Rev. D.W., Bishop of Barbados.
Gonzalez, Dr. R.M., National Science Council, St. Michael, Barbados.
Government of Grenada, Carriacou and Petite Martinique.
Government of Montserrat.
Governor of Montserrat.
Grace Kennedy Foundation, Kingston, Jamaica.
Graham, Loretta A., Red River Community College, Winnipeg, Canada.
Grand Bahamas Human Rights Association, Freeport, The Bahamas.
Greaves, Stanley, St.Michael, Barbados.
Grenada Association of Toronto, Subcommittee, Canada.
Grenada Civic Awareness Organization.
Grenada Popular Theatre Organisation.
Grenada United Associations of New York, Barbey Street, Brooklyn, New York.
Guild of Undergraduates, U.W.I., Montserrat.

Submissions to the Commission

Guyana Bar Association.
Guyana Council of Churches.
Guyana United Sad'r Islamic Anjuman.

Habibulla, A.K., M.P., Vice-Chairman, Religious Advisory Committee to His Excellency, The President, Guyana.
Hall, Herman, Publisher, Everybody's Magazine, Brooklyn, New York, U.S.A.
Harper, Nigel, Barbados High Commission, Canada.
Hastick, Hon. Roy A., President/Founder/CEO, Caribbean American Chamber of Commerce, New York, U.S.A.
Headley, Oliver St. C., Head, Department of Chemistry, University of the West Indies, St. Augustine, and Chairperson, Caribbean Solar Energy Society, Trinidad & Tobago.
Henry, Esco, Crown Counsel, Montserrat.
Henry, Desmond, U.S.A.
Hinds, Cora, Associate Professor, University of Ottawa, Canada.
Hofius Limited, Belize City, Belize.
Homer, Floyd, President, Trinidad & Tobago Biological Society.
Hope, Hallam R., Journalist, Barbados.
Hosein, H.R., Ontario, Canada.
Houston, Thomas P., St. Michael, Barbados.
Howard University School of Business, Washington/New York, U.S.A.
Hoyos, Patrick, President, Caribbean Publishing and Broadcasting Association.
Hunte, Julien R., St. Lucia Labour Party.
Hunte, Sir Keith D., UWI, Cave Hill Campus, Barbados.

Ingraham, Hubert A., Leader of the Opposition, Nassau, The Bahamas.
Insurance Corporation of Barbados.
Institute of Chartered Accountants of Trinidad & Tobago.
Insurance Association of the Caribbean, Barbados.
Isaiah Morter Harambee Association, Dangriga, Belize.
Iseard, Dr. Barry S., Freeport Industrial Development Associates, Freeport, The Bahamas.

Jacobs, Carlton, President, Antigua & Barbuda National Association, Essex, U.K.
Jagan, Dr. Cheddi, Leader of the Minority, Guyana.

Appendices

Jamaica Support Foundation, Washington D.C., U.S.A.
Jamaicans living in Canada: Alwyn Spence, Keith Barrett, William Harrison.
James, Winford, Teacher, Trinidad & Tobago.
Jeffrey, Dr. Henry B., Dean, Faculty of Social Sciences, University of Guyana.
Joda Productions, Barbados.
Johnson, Peter B., Executive Director, Caribbean/Latin American Action, Washington D.C., U.S.A.
Joint Workers' Council, St. Vincent.
Jones, Edward P.,Head, Meteorological Services Division, Central Administrative Services, Tobago.
Jones, Frederick N., Middlesex, National of St. Kitts-Nevis, U.K.
Jordan, Alma, Valsayn Park, Trinidad & Tobago.
Jordan, Robert J., CCH, Georgetown, Guyana.
Joseph, Lucian, U.W.P.Y.A., St. Lucia.

Khenti, Akwatu, Federation of Trinidad & Tobago Organizations, Toronto, Canada.
KIMIT, Montserrat Historical Society, Plymouth, Montserrat.
Kirby, Rev. Ermal, Coordinating Secretary Public Affairs, The Council of Churches for Britain and Ireland, Inter-Church House, London, U.K.
Kinton, Charles T., Montserrat.
Kokoram, Richard, Hillview College, Trinidad & Tobago.

Lambey, Pablo, President, National Garifuna Council, Belize.
Labour Party Black Section Arm, National Executive Committee, U.K.
Lang, Alan G., Ajax, Ontario, Canada.
La Touche, C. Nikita, Barbados.
Lestrade, Star S., Dominica.
Lewis, Dr. Lowell, PPH, FRCS, Director of Health Services, Montserrat.
Lewis, Valerie I., Montserrat.
Lynch, Dr. Acklyn R., University of Maryland, Baltimore, Maryland, U.S.A.
Lynch, Sir Douglas P., Bridgetown, Barbados.

McDonald, Vincent R., Professor, Department of Economics, Howard University, Washington, D.C., U.S.A.

Submissions to the Commission

McDougall, Lorna, Ag. Executive Director, Breast is Best League, Belize City, Belize.
MacFarlane, Anthony L., MD, Ontario, Canada.
McIntosh, Cecil D., Bequia, Grenadines, St. Vincent.
McIntosh, Simeon, Professor of Law, Howard University Law School, Washington, D.C., U.S.A.
Maragh, Michael, Faculty of Education, U.W.I., Mona, Jamaica.
Marcelle, Gillian M., Diego Martin, Trinidad.
Marco, Guy, Special Student/Studio Assistant, University of Guyana.
Mark, Randolph, The Grenada National Farmers' Association.
Martin, Allan, University Negro Improvement Association, Kingston, Jamaica.
Mascoll, Felix O., (Barbadian) Ontario, Canada.
Mason, Trevor D., Sir Arthur Lewis Community College, Morne Fortune, St. Lucia.
Maurice Bishop Patriotic Movement, Grenada.
Media Practitioners, Concerned Group, Dominica.
Michael, Franklyn, Director of Agriculture, Montserrat.
Mills, John, Canada.
Milne, Anthony, Journalist, U.K.
Ministry of Planning, Personnel, Establishment and Training, St. Lucia.
Mitchell, Fred, Leader, People's Democratic Force, Nassau, Bahamas.
Montreal Council of Caribbean Associations, Inc., Quebec, Canada.
Montserrat Chamber of Commerce and Industry.
Moore, Colin A., Esq., Chairman, Marcus Garvey Independent Democratic Club, New York, U.S.A.
Morris, V.A. and Company, Jamaica.
Murray, Lascelles, Retired Teacher.

National Advisory Committee on Political Union of the East Caribbean, Kingstown, St. Vincent.
National Council of Women, Kingstown, St. Vincent.
National Development Party, Montserrat.
National Trade Union Congress of Belize.
National Consultative Committee, Dominica.
Neil, Dr. Dwain A., Chester, England.
New Democratic Party, c/o Hon. Stuart Nanton, Kingstown, St. Vincent.
New Life Organization, Palmiste, St. John's, Grenada.
New National Party, Grenada.
Noel, Jim (T & T National), Toronto, Ontario.

Appendices

Noguera, Felipe, Secretary-General, CANTO, Trinidad & Tobago.

O'Gorman, Pamela, Jamaica.
Okuboh, Ervine S., Director, Chapeltown Business Centre, U.K.
Ollivierre, E. Maxwell, York University, Toronto, Canada.
Organisation of Eastern Caribbean States Secretariat, St. Lucia.
Osbourne, E. Karney, M.B.E., Montserrat.

Palmer, Ransford W., Ph.D., Howard University, Washington, D.C., U.S.A.
Pan African Movement.
Parris, L.A., M.B.E., J.P., Nevis, St. Kitts-Nevis.
Pastakia, Christopher M.R., Environmental Specialist, West Coast Berbice, Guyana.
Patrick, Nesta, Trinidad.
Pentecostal Assemblies of the West Indies, Barbados.
People's Democratic Movement, Guyana.
People's National Congress, Guyana.
Perkins, Edrisse Anita, Montserrat.
Persaud, Bishnodath, Commonwealth Secretariat, London, U.K.
Philbert, Franklyn, St. Patricks, Grenada.
Phillips, Sir Fred, Barbados.
Phillips, Jeffrey M.P., Ontario, Canada.
Phillips, W., Grenada.
Pierre, Laureen (Amerindian), Guyana.
Pierre, Lauton J., D.D.S..Washington, D.C., U.S.A.
Pilgrim, R. Ferdinand, U.S.A.
Pinelands Creative Workshop, Barbados.
Pompey, Rawlston B., Inspector of Police, Antigua and Barbuda.
Press Association of Jamaica.
Private Sector Organization of Jamaica.
Progressive Labour Movement, Antigua.
Public Service Union of Belize.
P.U.P. Secretariat, Belize.

Queen's College, Barbados.
Queen's Royal College/Bishop Anstey High School Alumni Association of Ontario, Canada.

Submissions to the Commission

Rabess, Gregory, Roseau, Dominica.
Rahat, Dr. M.J., Doctor of Natural Therapeutics, Guyana.
Ramnarine, Deo, Caribbean Telecommunication Union, Port of Spain, Trinidad.
Ramsammy, Dr. Leslie, President, United Republican Party, Guyana.
Red Thread Women's Development Project, Georgetown, Guyana.
Redhead, Wildred A., Grenada.
Reece, Most Rev. Donald J., D.D., Bishop of St. John's-Basseterre, Antigua.
Reid, Howard N., St. Catherine, Jamaica.
Rickinson, Peggy, Barbados.
Riley, Seymour D., Temple of Light Church of Religious Science, Jamaica.
Roach, Victor, President, B.H.S., Barbados.
Rodway, John, Surrey, U.K.
Rotary Club of Grenada.
Rothwell, Miles A., Engineer, Barbados.
Rowe, Owen, Montreal, Canada.
Rudder, Michael F.C., Christ Church, Barbados.
Ryan, Rueben E., Accountant, Plymouth, Montserrat.

St. Clair, Gandolph (St. Lucia), Toronto, Canada.
St. Christopher Heritage Society, Basseterre, St. Kitts.
St. Hill, Leonard Earl, Barbados.
St. Kitts-Nevis Labour Party.
St. Kitts-Nevis Trades and Labour Union.
St. Lucia Media Workers Association.
St. Omer, Prof. V., Director of School of Veterinary Medicine, Faculty of Medical Sciences, University of the West Indies, Trinidad & Tobago.
St. Vincent & Grenadines Association of Edmonton, Alberta, Canada.
St. Vincent & The Grenadines Association of Montreal, Inc., Quebec, Canada.
St. Vincent & The Grenadines Association, Toronto, Canada.
St. Vincent & The Grenadines Chamber of Industry and Commerce.
St. Vincent & The Grenadines Christian Council.
St. Vincent & The Grenadines Human Rights Association, c/o Victor Cuffy, President.
Saunders, Maurice C., Esq., LL.B, U.W.I., Mona, Jamaica.
'Save the Children Fund', Dominica.
San Fernando Rehabilitation Centre Limited, Trinidad & Tobago.

Scott, Yvonne Glasford, Caricom Secretariat, Guyana.
Seaga, Rt. Hon. Edward, P.C., M.P., Jamaica.
Sebastian, Caril T., Student, Antigua.
Sibblies, Langston, Toronto, Canada.
Sir Arthur Lewis Community College, St. Lucia.
Sirju-Charran, Dr. Grace, Coordinator, Women and Development Studies Group, St. Augustine, Trinidad & Tobago.
Skeete, Angela, St. Michael, Barbados.
Small Projects Assistance Team Limited, Dominica.
Smith, Selwyn P., Executive Secretary, Caribbean Centre for Development Administration, Barbados.
Soroptimist International of Antigua.
Springer, Charles R.C., O.B.E., J.P., St. Thomas, Barbados.
Stanislaus, Dr. Lamuel A., Grenada's Former Ambassador, Permanent Representative to the U.N., New York, N.Y., U.S.A.
Stevens, Christopher, Overseas Development Institute, Regents College, Inner Circle, Regents Park, London, U.K.
Sutherland, W., Belize City, Belize.

Taylor, Cherrie, Independent Observer, Montserrat.
Tertullien, Mispah, Nassau Guardian Newspaper, The Bahamas.
Thomas, Chantal, Black Students' Network, McGill University, Montreal, Quebec, Canada.
Thomas, Vereen, Montserrat Allied Workers' Union, Plymouth, Montserrat.
Thompson A., Grenada.
Thompson, P.A., CAIC, Barbados.
Thorndike, Tony, Professor of International Relations, Staffordshire Polytechnic, U.K.
Thwaites, Peter J.C., Jamaica.
Tiwari, Rampersaud, Scarborough, Ontario, Canada.
Trinidad & Tobago Association, Washington, D.C., U.S.A.
Trinidad & Tobago Institute of Architects.
Trinidad & Tobago National Library Information and Archive Service.

UNESCO, Washington, D.C., U.S.A.
United National Democratic Party of Antigua/Barbuda.
University of Belize.
University of the West Indies, Faculty of Agriculture.
University of the West Indies Medical Alumni Association, Canada.

Venton, R..G., Guyana.
Vidale, James C., President, Trinidad and Tobago Association, Washington, D.C, U.S.A.

Wadsworth, Marc, Thames Television, U.K.
Watts, Raymond J., 555 Sherbourne Street, Toronto, Ontario.
Watty, Erickson, Dominica.
Watty, William, The Methodist Church, South Caribbean District, Trinidad & Tobago.
West India Committee, Commonwealth House, London, U.K.
White-Davis, Hope P., 4433 Carpenter Ave., Bronx, New York, U.S.A.
Whitehorne, Pat, BBC Caribbean Service, U.K.
West Indian Association of Guyana.
Wickham, Peter W., St. Michael, Barbados.
Widmer, Edward, Chairman, National Spiritual Assembly of the Bahá'ís of Guyana.
Wilkin, Charles, St. Kitts.
Williams, Hubert S., Journalist, Barbados.
Williams, Rolston E., Nevis, St. Kitts-Nevis.
Williams, Wilbert W., Arima, Trinidad.
Wills, Vibart J., Nassau, The Bahamas.
Women's Revolutionary Socialist Movement, Guyana.
Working People's Alliance, Guyana.

Xavier, Llewellyn, Artist, St. Lucia.
Xunantunich Organisation for Mayan Culture Preservation and Development for Women's Affairs.

Appendix "F"

COMMISSION PUBLICATIONS

The Commission published an information booklet, six Occasional Papers and an Interim Report. These are:

Let All Ideas Contend: A Framework for the Participation of the West Indian People in the work of the West Indian Commission

Occasional Paper No. 1
Towards West Indian Survival — An Essay by William G. Demas;

Occasional Paper No. 2
Reaching for the Future — A Timely Trilogy
Statements by the Prime Ministers of Barbados, Jamaica and Saint Vincent and the Grenadines;

Occasional Paper No. 3
To be a Canoe — Presentation by the Chairman of the West Indian Commission to the Twelfth Meeting of the Conference of Heads of Government of the Caribbean Community, Basseterre, 2 July 1991;

Occasional Paper No. 4
A Common Currency for the Caribbean — A Study by Dr. Delisle Worrell

Occasional Paper No. 5
Whither Caribbean Health — A Study by Professor Sir George Alleyne and Miss Karen Sealy

Occasional Paper No. 6
Compulsions of Integration by Dr. Vaughan Lewis, Director-General, Organisation of Eastern Caribbean States Secretariat, St. Lucia.

Towards a Vision of the Future — Progress Report on the Work of the Independent West Indian Commission.

Papers Prepared for the Commission

The Commission benefited from a number of commissioned studies and technical papers prepared by experts from within the region, on a number of major issues which it was felt required in-depth analysis and careful examination of options for action. They are listed below:

ALLEYNE, Prof. Sir George /SEALY, Karen	Social Issues: Whither Caribbean Health
ALLEYNE, Prof. Mervyn	Cultural Dimensions of West Indian Development: Language and Communication
ANTROBUS, Peggy	Towards a Vision of the Future: Gender Issues in Regional Integration
BANNISTER, Yolande	A Social Charter for the Caribbean
BECKLES, Dr. Hilary	Cultural Dimensions of West Indian Development: Ethnicity and the Creolisation Process
BISNAUTH, Dr. Dale	Cultural Dimensions of West Indian Development: Religion and Philosphy
CAMPBELL, Frank	Canada and the Caribbean Community — the Nature and Future Direction of the Special Relationship
CARICOM SECRETARIAT	Agricultural Development within the Caribbean Community and Common Market — A Review and Issues to be considered for Future Development.
	Issues in Regional Air Transportation
CHARLES, EMBERT	Cultural Dimensions of West Indian Development: Cultural Penetration

Appendices

CHARLES, Hollis	Human Resources Development: Science and Technology Resources — Infrastructure and Policies in the Commonwealth Caribbean
CRAIG, Jerry	Cultural Dimensions of West Indian Development: Indigenous Cultural Mechanisms for Economic Survival
CROPPER, Dr. Angela	The Environment and Development in the Caribbean
EMMANUEL, Dr. Patrick	Governance and Democracy in the Commonwealth Caribbean
FERGUS, Dr. Howard	Cultural Dimensions of West Indian Development: The Arts in Education: A Caribbean Perspective
GILL, Henry	CARICOM, the Wider Caribbean and Latin America
McINTYRE, Dr. Arnold	Investment, Trade and Development in the Caribbean
JAMES-BRYAN, Merryl	Challenges Facing Caribbean Youth as the Region Aproaches the Twenty-first Century — Survival or Destruction
JEFFREY, Dr. Henry	Sports and West Indian Integration
McDONALD, Ian	Cultural Dimensions of West Indian Development: Bedrock of a Nation — Cultural Foundations of West Indian Integration — An Agenda for the '90s — An Essay
MORDECAI, Martin	Preparing for the Information Society: Communications in the West Indies in the 1990s
PAYNE, Dr. Anthony & SUTTON, Dr. Paul	Caribbean International Relations beyond 1992: Between Europe and North America?

PALACIO, Dr. Joseph PIERRE, Laureen	A Study of the Aboriginal Peoples of the Caribbean
POON, Dr. Auliana	Tourism as an Axial Product — Potential for Linkages and Development of Services
ST. CYR, Dr. Eric	Strengthening Financial Institutions in the Caribbean
SANGSTER, Dr. Alfred & GLASGOW, Sandra	Learning to Earn: A Basis for National Survival
SEARWAR, Lloyd and GONZALES, Dr. Anthony	Structures of Unity for the Caribbean Community
WILSON, Dr. Donald/ MORRISEY, Michael	Human Resources Development: Cooperating for Quality: An Agenda for Education in the Caribbean
WILTSHIRE, Dr. Rosina	Caribbean Regional Population Movements: Towards Freedom of Movement within CARICOM
WORRELL, Dr. Delisle	Common Currency Arrangements for the Caribbean

Special Reports

Report of Conference of Commonwealth Caribbean Military Commanders — June, 1991.

Policing the Region — 1992 and Beyond — Association of Caribbean Commissioners of Police — April, 1992

Women's Organisations in Barbados and Regional Integration — A Survey — Women and Development Studies Unit, UWI, Cave Hill Campus.

APPENDIX "G"

SELECT ANNOTATED BIBLIOGRAPHY
ON CARIBBEAN REGIONAL INTEGRATION

AER LINGUS
Study of the feasibility of establishing a multinational air carrier for the Eastern Caribbean and Guyana : final report. - [Dublin] : Aer Lingus, 1990. – iv,90,[86],55p.
Report financed by Commission of the European Communities on behalf of the Caribbean Community Secretariat.

ANTROBUS, Peggy
Gender and human resources development in the Caribbean in the year 2000. - St. Augustine : U.W.I. Institute of Social and Economic Research, 1990. - 12p.
Presented at the 15th Annual Conference of the Caribbean Studies Association, Trinidad and Tobago, May 22-26, 1990.

ANTROBUS, Peggy
Women and human development. In Rethinking Caribbean development edited by George W. Schuyler and Henry Veltmeyer. - Halifax: International Education Centre, 1988. - p.159-168.

AXLINE, W. Andrew
Caribbean integration : the politics of regionalism. - London : Francis Pinter, 1979. - 233p.

BACCUS, Earl
Review and update of the scheme for harmonisation of fiscal incentives to industry : final report. - [Georgetown] : CARICOM Secretariat, 1987.

BARBADOS CONSENSUS on development of local and regional entrepreneurship and skills in the member states of the Caribbean Community. - [Georgetown : CARICOM Secretariat], 1985. - 3p.
Statement agreed on at the Sixth Conference of Heads of Government of the Caribbean Community, Bridgetown, Barbados, 4th July 1985.

BENNETT, Karl M.
Caribbean experience with floating and managed floating exchange rates. - Waterloo : University of Waterloo, 1988. - 40p.

BENNETT, Karl M.
Monetary integration in CARICOM. - [S.l. : s.n.], 1990. - 11p.
Sixth Adlith Brown Memorial Lecture presented at the Regional Programme of Monetary Studies, Guyana, 1990

BERIFF, Jorge Rodriguez, FIGUEROA, J. Peter and GREENE, J. Edward eds.
Conflict, peace and development in the Caribbean. - London : Macmillan Press, 1991.

BIRD, V.C.
Address ... at official opening ceremony of the Third Meeting of the Conference of Heads of Government of the Caribbean Community, Ocho Rios, 1982. - 5p.

BLAKE, Byron W.
The International Monetary Fund and the structural adjustment process in small open economies. - [S.l. : s.n.], 1984. - 23,3p.
Paper presented to the Conference on the Trade Unions and the International Monetary Fund, sponsored by the Caribbean Congress of Labour and the American Institute for Free Labour Development, Barbados, 27-29 August 1984.

BLAKE, Byron W.
The role of small businesses in the Caribbean economy : address ... - [Georgetown : CARICOM Secretariat], 1988. - 14,[4]p.
Presented at Second Annual International Small Business Convention on Mobilizing Finance for Small Businesses, August 22-24, 1988, Kingston, Jamaica.

BLAKE, Byron and SANATAN, Roderick eds.
Profile of Caribbean services for international trade. - Georgetown : CARICOM Secretariat, 1991. - x,294p.

BOOZ, ALLEN & HAMILTON INC.
Export-oriented industries for the Caribbean Community : final report. - New York : Booz, Allen & Hamilton, 1985. - 3v.

BOURNE, Compton
Caribbean development to the year 2000 : challenges, prospects and policies. - London : Commonwealth Secretariat, 1988. - xi,218p.
Prepared for the Caribbean Community Secretariat with the assistance of an Advisory Group from the Commonwealth Caribbean.

BRATHWAITE, Nicolas
Opening address ... In Conference of Heads of Government of the Caribbean Community Meeting (11th : 1990 : Kingston, Jamaica). Communique and addresses. - [Georgetown : CARICOM Secretariat, 1990]. - p.11-14.

BREWSTER, Havelock and THOMAS, Clive Y.
The dynamics of West Indian economic integration. - Mona : UWI, Institute of Social and Economic Research, 1967.

BRODBER, Erna
Perceptions of Caribbean women : towards a documentation of stereotypes. - Cave Hill : UWI. Institute of Social and Economic Research 1982. - 62p.

BRYAN, Anthony T. and BOISSIERE, Noel
National commercial policies and intra-regional trade flows : a study of the OECS-CARICOM relationships, 1981-1984. - Buenos Aires: BID/INTAL, 1986. - 109,[19]p.

BRYAN, Anthony T., GREEN, J. Edward, and SHAW, Timothy M. eds.
Peace, development and security in the Caribbean : perspectives to the year 2000. - London : Macmillan, 1990. - xix,332p.

BURNHAM, L.F.S.
Response ... at the opening ceremony of the Third Meeting of the Conference of Heads of Government ... Ocho Rios, 1982. - [S.l. : s.n.], 1982, 9p.

BUSTAMANTE INSTITUTE OF PUBLIC AND INTERNATIONAL AFFAIRS
USA, USSR and the Caribbean - the new realities. - Kingston, Jamaica : The Institute, 1991. - 90p.
Proceedings of a symposium held in association with the Press Association of Jamaica, July 19-20, 1990.

CARIBBEAN COMMUNITY. Working Party on the Harmonisation of Company Law in the Caribbean Community
Report ... - [Georgetown : CARICOM Secretariat], 1981.

Select Bibliography

CARIBBEAN COMMUNITY SECRETARIAT
Caribbean Community Programme for Agricultural Development. - Georgetown : CARICOM Secretariat, 1989. - 193p.

CARIBBEAN COMMUNITY SECRETARIAT
External debt of the Caribbean Community. - Georgetown : Caribbean Community Secretariat, 1989. - 15p.
Paper presented at the 25th Regular Meeting of the Latin American Council, Cartagena de Indias, Columbia, July 25 to August 10, 1989.

CARIBBEAN COMMUNITY SECRETARIAT
Programme for agro-industry development/diversification in the Caribbean Common Market. - Georgetown : CARICOM Secretariat, 1989. - 80p.

CARIBBEAN COMMUNITY SECRETARIAT
Regional programme on drug abuse abatement and control : CARICOM countries and Suriname. - Georgetown : CARICOM Secretariat, 1987. - 1v.(various pagings)

CARIBBEAN COMMUNITY SECRETARIAT
Technical assistance guide to West Indian human resources on the environment. - Georgetown : CARICOM Secretariat, 1990. - vi,162,39,4p.

CARIBBEAN COMMUNITY SECRETARIAT. Statistics Section
CARICOM statistics digest 1970-1981. - Georgetown : CARICOM Secretariat, 1984. - iii,199p.

CARIBBEAN DEVELOPMENT BANK
Measures for structural adjustment in the member states of the Caribbean Community. - Wildey, Barbados : CDB, 1984. - 194p.
Study requested by the Conference of Heads of Government of the Caribbean Community.

CARIBBEAN LINE LIMITED
Annex to final report of the feasibility study on a Caribbean Shipping Service. - Port of Spain : Caribbean Line Ltd., 1990. - 1v. (various pagings).
Prepared for the Caribbean Community Secretariat.

CARIBBEAN LINE LIMITED
Final report of the feasibility study on a Caribbean Shipping Service. - Port of Spain : Caribbean Line Ltd., 1990. - 1v. (various pagings).
Prepared for the Caribbean Community Secretariat.

CARIBBEAN POLICY DEVELOPMENT CENTRE
Challenges in Caribbean Development : Interventions of Non-Governmental Organisations at the CARICOM Regional Economic Conference, Trinidad, February 1991. Compiled by Joan French, 1992. In Press.

CARIBBEAN RIGHTS and PENAL REFORM INTERNATIONAL
Improving Prison Conditions in the Caribbean – Report and Papers from a Conference – December 1991 – 144 p.

CARIBBEAN ROUND TABLE ON STRUCTURAL ADJUSTMENT AND EMPLOYMENT ISSUES (1991 : Port-of-Spain, Trinidad and Tobago)
Papers ... - Port-of-Spain : ILO, 1991.

CARIBBEAN SYMPOSIUM ON EXCHANGE RATE MANAGEMENT (1988 : Trinidad and Tobago)
Management on exchange rates in the Caribbean : summary of conclusions of the Symposium. - London : Commonwealth Secretariat, 1988. - 7p.

CARRINGTON, E.W.
Practical agenda for revitalizing the Caribbean Community. - Brussels, Belgium : ACP Secretariat, 1986. - 31p.

CARRINGTON, Edwin W.
Mutual interaction for economic integration in the Caribbean. - [Georgetown : CARICOM Secretariat], 1975. - 15p.
Prepared for the Commonwealth Foundation Seminar on the Professions, Universities and Civil Service, Kingston, Jamaica, 13 - 18 January, 1975.

CARRINGTON, Edwin W.
The Caribbean and Europe in the 1990s. - Mona : UWI. Institute of Social and Economic Research, 1989. - 24p.
Fourth Adlith Brown memorial lecture.

CEGIR
Study on regional industrial programming in the CARICOM countries : executive summary. - [Montreal : CEGIR], 1980. - 3v.

CHERNICK, Sidney E.
The Commonwealth Caribbean : the integration experience. - Baltimore : published for the World Bank [by] The Johns Hopkins University Press, c1978.

CONFERENCE OF HEADS OF GOVERNMENT OF THE CARIBBEAN COMMUNITY (10th: 1989 : Grande Anse, Grenada)
Development of a regional capital market. - Georgetown : CARICOM Secretariat, 1989. - 9p.

CONFERENCE OF HEADS OF GOVERNMENT OF THE CARIBBEAN COMMUNITY. Inter-Sessional Meeting (1991 : Port-of-Spain, Trinidad and Tobago)
[Communique]. - [Georgetown : CARICOM Secretariat], 1991. - 4p.

CONFERENCE ON ALTERNATIVES FOR THE 1990S CARIBBEAN (1991 : London)
Papers. - [London : University of London?], 1991.
Conference sponsored by the University of London. Institute of Commonwealth Studies; University of London. Institute of Latin American Studies.

CONFERENCE ON FINANCING DEVELOPMENT IN THE CARIBBEAN (1989 : Barbados)
Papers... - Cave Hill, Barbados : UWI. Institute of Social and Economic Research, 1989.

DAVID JONES AND ASSOCIATES
Market development programme for non-traditional agricultural products from the countries of CARICOM : final report. - Middlesex, England : David Jones and Associates, 1988. - ii,230p.

DELOITTE HASKINS AND SELLS MANAGEMENT CONSULTANTS
Export market orientation programme for selected Caribbean countries. - [S.l.] : Deloitte Haskins and Sells, 1988. - 92p.

DEMAS, William G.
Consolidating our Independence : the major challenge for the West Indies. - St. Augustine : UWI. Institute of International Relations, 1986. - 33p.
Distinguished lecturer series 1986.

DEMAS, William G.
Essays on Caribbean integration and development. - Mona : UWI. Institute of Social and Economic Research, 1976.

DEMAS, William G.
Perspectives on the future of the Caribbean in the world economy. -Port-of-Spain : Central Bank of Trinidad and Tobago, 1988. - 30p. -Includes bibliographical references.

DEMAS, William G.
The economics of development in small countries with special reference to the Caribbean. - Montreal : McGill University Press for the Centre for Developing Area Studies, 1965. - 150p.

DEMAS, William G.
Towards West Indian survival. - St. James, Barbados : West Indian Commission Secretariat, 1990. - 74.p.

DEMAS, William G.
West Indian nationhood and Caribbean integration : a collection of papers. - [Bridgetown, Barbados] : CCC Publishing House, 1974.

DURRANT, Fay
Regional information system strategy for the Caribbean to the year 2000. - Port-of-Spain : UN. ECLAC, 1987. - 123p.
Paper presented at the Meeting on Regional Information System Strategy for the Caribbean, Trinidad and Tobago, May 27-29, 1987.

EMMANUEL, Patrick
Approaches to Caribbean political integration. - Cave Hill, Barbados : UWI. Institute of Social and Economic Research 1987. - vi,94p.

FARRELL, Terrence W. and CHRISTOPHER, Janice
Macro/monetary relationships in the Caribbean : an eclectic review of literature. - Kingston : Institute of Social and Economic Research, 1986. - 44p. - Bibliography : p.36-44.
Paper presented at the 18th Regional Monetary Studies Conference, Basseterre, November 5-7, 1986.

FIELD-RIDLEY, D.
Towards a CARICOM single market and economy. - Georgetown : CARICOM Secretariat, 1991. - 139p.

FRANCIS, Fitzgerald A.
Some fundamental issues associated with the implementation of fiscal policy in CARICOM member states. - St. John's, Antigua : OECS. Economic Affairs Secretariat, 1985. - 36p.
Paper presented at the Seminar on National Economic Management in the Caribbean Region, Barbados, February 11-15, 1985.

GARCIA NUNEZ, Humberto
Boots, boots, boots : intervention, regional security and militarisation in the Caribbean. - Puerto Rico : Projecto Caribeno de Justicia y Paz, 1986.

GEISER, Hans J., ALLEYNE, Pamela and GAJRAJ, Carroll
Legal problems of Caribbean integration : a study on the legal aspects of CARICOM. - Leyden: Sijthoff; St. Augustine : UWI. Institute of International Relations, 1976.

GEORGETOWN Declaration on the deepening and widening of CARICOM. - [Georgetown : CARICOM Secretariat], 1986. - 2p.
Statement issued by the 7th Conference of Heads of Government of the Caribbean Community, Georgetown, Guyana, 1986.

GILL, Henry S.
Economic implications for Latin America and the Caribbean of changes in Eastern Europe. - St Augustine : UWI, 1990. - 58p.
Presented at "Crisis in Eastern Europe : the Emerging New World Order and its Implications for the Third World", Trinidad and Tobago, May 9-20, 1990.

GIRVAN, Norman
Reflections on regional integration and disintegration. In Integration and participatory development : selected papers and proceedings of the 2nd Conference of Caribbean Economists / edited by Judith Wedderburn. - Kingston : Friedrich Ebert Stiftung, 1990. - p.1-6.

GIRVAN, Norman and BECKFORD, George eds.
Development in suspense : selected papers and proceedingss of the first conference of Caribbean economists. - Kingston : Friedrich Ebert Stiftung; Association of Caribbean Economists, 1989. - xx,366p.

GONZALES, Anthony P.
Trade diplomacy and export development in a protectionist world : challenges and strategies for Caribbean states. - St. Augustine : Institute of International Relations, 1984. - 80p.

GREEN, Cecelia
The world market factory : a study of enclave industrialization in the Eastern Caribbean and its impact on women workers. - Kingston : CARIPEDA, 1990. - 219p.

GROUP OF CARIBBEAN EXPERTS
The Caribbean Community in the 1980s: report by a group of Caribbean experts... Georgetown : CARICOM Secretariat, 1981.

HAMELINK, Cees J.
Telecommunications policy in the Caribbean region : report of a policy workshop. - The Hague, Netherlands : Institute of Social Studies, 1985.

HARKER, Trevor
Caribbean Integration in the Changing Global Context. – Port-of-Spain : ECLAC/CCDC, 1991. – 21p.

HEINE, Jorge and MAINGOT, Leslie F. eds.
Caribbean and world politics : cross currents and cleavages. - New York : Holmes and Meier, 1988. - 400p.

HENRY, Ralph
The basic situation in manpower planning in Caribbean countries. - Port-of-Spain : UNECLAC, 1981. - 106p.

HOSTEN-CRAIG, Jennifer
The Effect of a North American Free Trade Agreement on the Commonwealth Caribbean – The Edwin Meller Press, 1992. – 141p.

HOYTE, Harold
Influence of foreign television on Caribbean people. - Christ Church, Barbados : Caribbean Publishing and Broadcasting Association, 1986. - 11,[9]p. : ill.

HOYTE, Hugh Desmond
CARICOM - alive and vigorous. - Georgetown : Office of the President, 1987. - 19p.
Address by the President of Guyana.

INAUGURAL SEMINAR OF THE UNIVERSITY OF THE WEST INDIES WOMEN AND DEVELOPMENT STUDIES PROJECT
Gender in Caribbean development : papers presented at the Inaugural Seminar ... / edited by Patricia Mohammed and Catherine Shepherd. - Mona : UWI. Women and Development Studies Project, 1988. - xvii,372p. - Includes bibliography.

INCE, Basil ed.
Contemporary international relations of the Caribbean. - St. Augustine : UWI, Institute of International Relations, 1979.

INTEGRACION Latinoamericana. Special English issue, October 1987. - Buenos Aires : INTAL, 1976-

INTERNATIONAL BANK FOR RECONSTRUCTION AND DEVELOPMENT
Caribbean Common Market : trade policies and regional integration in the 1990s. - Washington, D.S. : World Bank, 1990. - 251p.

INTERNATIONAL BANK FOR RECONSTRUCTION AND DEVELOPMENT
The Caribbean : export preferences and performance. - Washington, D.C. : World Bank, 1988. - xiii,75p.

JACKSON, Rashleigh E.
The diplomatic role of CARICOM and CARICOM/Latin American relations : speech ... - [Georgetown : Ministry of Foreign Affairs, 1986]. -23p.
Delivered at Caribbean Conference on Development and Regional Cooperation organized by the Commonwealth Institute, London, on March 7, 1986.

JAMES-BRYAN, Meryl
Human resources development : the Caribbean challenge of the nineties. - St. Michael, Barbados : UWI. Women and Development Unit, 1990.

LALTA, Stanley
Some fundamental issues related to fiscal harmonisation in the Caribbean Community. - Georgetown : CARICOM Secretariat, 1987. - 16p.

LAYNG, Anthony
Creole culture and economic change : a dynamic relationship. - St. Augustine : UWI. Institute of Social and Economic Research, 1990. - 6p.
Presented at the 15th Annual Conference of the Caribbean Studies Association, Trinidad and Tobago, May 22-26, 1990 .

LENT, John A.
Mass communications in the Caribbean. - Ames : Iowa State University Press, 1990. - 398p. : ill.

LESTRADE, Swinburne A.
CARICOM's Less Developed Countries : a review of the progress of the LDCs under the CARICOM arrangements. - Cave Hill, Barbados : UWI. Institute of Social and Economic Research, 1981. - ix,85p.

LESTRADE, Swinburne A.
Review of the performance of ECIPS and alternative scenarios regarding overseas investment promotion arrangements for the OECS countries. - Washington, D.C. : Eastern Caribbean Investment Promotion Service, 1989. - 26p.

LESTRADE, SWINBURNE A.
The LDCs in CARICOM : a review of the Special Regime for CARICOM LDCs. - Georgetown : CARICOM Secretariat, 1979.

LEWIS, J. O'Neil
Some thoughts on Caribbean integration : past and present. In *Caribbean Affairs*, 2(3), July-September 1989, p.42-61.

LEWIS, Vaughan
Some perspectives on Caribbean Community integration. In *Caribbean Affairs*, 1(1), 1988, p.85-100.

LEWIS, Vaughan A. ed.
Size self-determination and international relations : the Caribbean. - Mona : UWI, Institute of Social and Economic Research, 1976.

MANLEY, Michael
A history of West Indies cricket. - London : Andre Deutsch, 1988. -575p.

MANLEY, Michael
Opening address ... - In Conference of Heads of Government of the Caribbean Community Meeting (10th : 1989 : Grand Anse, Grenada). Opening addresses and communique. - [Georgetown : CARICOM Secretariat, 1989. - p.6-7.

MC DONALD, Ian
To be a West Indian : a personal view of the integration movement : address ... - Georgetown : I. McDonald, 1990. - 25p.
Presented at the University of the West Indies (St. Augustine), 29th March, 1990

MC INTYRE, Alister
Caribbean after Grenada : four challenges facing the regional movement. In Caribbean regionalism : challenges and options. - St. Augustine : Institute of International Relations, 1987. - 89p.
One of three contributions in the Distinguished Lecturer series by A. McIntyre, S. Ramphal and W. Demas.

MC INTYRE, Alister
Current problems of economic integration : the effects of reverse preferences on trade among developing countries. - New York : United Nations, 1974.

MC INTYRE, M.A.
Human resources development : its relevance to Jamaica and the Caribbean. - Kingston : Grace Kennedy Foundation, 1990. - 35p.
Grace Kennedy Foundation Lecture, 1990.

MILLET, Richard and WILL, W. Marvin eds.
The restless Caribbean : changing patterns of international relations. - New York : Praeger, 1979.

MILLS, D.O. and LEWIS, Vaughan A.
Caribbean/Latin American relations. - 1982. Unpublished.
Study prepared for the United Nations Commission for Latin America (Office for the Caribbean) and the Caribbean Community Secretariat.

MILLS, Gladstone E., BURTON, Sir Carlisle, LEWIS, J. O'Neil and SORHAINDO, Crispin
Report on a comprehensive review of the programmes, institutions and organizations of the Caribbean Community. - Georgetown : Caribbean Community Secretariat, 1990. - 121,42p.

MITCHELL, James F.
Two decades of Caribbean unity. - Kingstown, St. Vincent : Government Printing Office, 1987. - 25p.

NASSAU Understanding : structural adjustment and closer integration for accelerated development in the Caribbean Community. - [Georgetown : CARICOM Secretariat], 1984. - 7p.
Policy statement issued by the Fifth Conference of Heads of Government of the Caribbean Community, Nassau, The Bahamas, July 7, 1984.

NETTLEFORD, Rex
Caribbean identity in the world of ideas. - London : Commonwealth Secretariat, 1986. - 23p. - Includes bibliographical references.

NETTLEFORD, Rex
Caribbean Cultural Identity: The Case of Jamaica. - Kingston : Institute of Jamaica and Los Angeles, UCLA, 1979.

1992 AND THE CARIBBEAN [CONFERENCE] (1989 : Barbados)
1992 and the Caribbean : issues and opportunities : Lomé IV and beyond. - London : West India Committee, 1989. - 239p.
Sponsored by the West India Committee, Commonwealth Secretariat and CARICOM.

OCHO Rios Declaration. - [Georgetown : CARICOM Secretariat, 1975]. - [4]p.
Statement issued by the 3rd Conference of Heads of Government of the Caribbean Community, Jamaica, 1975.

PARSAN, Elizabeth
Trade and production cooperation between Caribbean and Latin American countries. - [S.l. : s.n.], 1990. - [3],51p.
Report commissioned by the Caribbean Community Secretariat for the CARICOM Export Development Project.

PAYNE, Anthony
The politics of the Caribbean Community 1961-79 : regional integration amongst new states. - Manchester, England : Manchester University Press, 1980. - xi,299p.

PAYNE, Anthony and SUTTON, Paul eds.
Dependency under challenge : the political economy of the Commonwealth Caribbean. - Manchester, England : Manchester University Press, 1984. - xi,295p.

POLLARD, Duke E.
Decision-making in the Caribbean Community : a preliminary report. - Georgetown : Caribbean Community Secretariat, - 1985. - 102p.

POLLARD, Duke E.
Institutional and legal aspects of the Caribbean Community. In Caribbean studies, 14(1), 1974, p.39-74.

POLLARD, Duke
Problems of drug abuse in Commonwealth Caribbean countries. - Georgetown : CARICOM Secretariat, 1987. - 28p.

PORT OF SPAIN ACCORD on the management and conservation of the Caribbean environment. - Georgetown : CARICOM Secretariat, 1989. - [3]p. Issued by the First CARICOM Ministerial Conference on the Environment, Port of Spain, Trinidad and Tobago, 31 May-2 June 1989.

PORT OF SPAIN CONSENSUS of the Regional Economic Conference : securing Caribbean development to the year 2000 and beyond. - Port-of-Spain : [s.n.], 1991. - 4p.

RAINFORD, Roderick G.
Address ... [at] Symposium marking the twenty-fifth anniversary of the Bank of Guyana. - [Georgetown : CARICOM Secretariat], 1990. - 16p.

RAINFORD, Roderick
Caribbean focus : development and regional cooperation in CARICOM. - Georgetown : Caribbean Community Secretariat, 1986. - 19p.
Paper presented at the Conference on Development and Problems of Regional Integration at the Commonwealth Institute's "Focus on the Caribbean" in Britain on March 6, 1986.

RAINFORD, Roderick G.
Caribbean integration : business and economic opportunities : an overview. - [Georgetown : CARICOM Secretariat], 1991. - 19p.
Paper presented at a workshop organised by the Mona Institute of Business, UWI, Kingston, Jamaica.

RAINFORD, Roderick G.
Options and strategies for a Caribbean development agenda for the 1990s. - Georgetown : CARICOM Secretariat, 1989. - 21p.
Paper prepared for the Congressional Study Mission and Consultation, Jamaica, November 2-4, 1989.

RAINFORD, Roderick
Regional economic planning and development for the Caribbean : the management imperative. - St. Augustine : UWI. Management Studies Department, 1987.
Paper presented at the Management Conference, Trinidad and Tobago, March 1987.

RAINFORD, Roderick G.
Towards an integrated single market in the Caribbean Community. - Georgetown : CARICOM Secretariat, 1989. - 15p.
Address to the South Trinidad Chamber of Commerce.

RAMPHAL, Sir Shridath
A time to close ranks : opening address ... - [St. Michael, Barbados : West Indian Commission], 1992.
Presented to Trincom/92 : Caribbean media and telecommunications in the information age.

RAMPHAL, Shridath S.
Options for the Caribbean : the lure of real politik. In Caribbean regionalism : challenges and options. - St. Augustine : Institute of International Relations, 1987.
One of three contributions in the Distinguished Lecture series by A. McIntyre, S. Ramphal and W. Demas.

RAMPHAL, Shridath S.
No island is an island. - London : Commonwealth Secretariat, 1988. - 14p.

RAMPHAL, Shridath S.
To care for CARICOM : the need for an ethos of Community. - [Georgetown : Caribbean Community Secretariat], 1975. - 14p.

RAMSARRAN, Ramesh
Capital movements : the experience of Commonwealth Caribbean countries, 1970-1984. - St. Augustine : UWI. Institute of International Relations, 1986. Paper presented at the 18th Regional Monetary Studies Conference, St. Kitts/Nevis, November 5-7, 1986.

RAMSARRAN, Ramesh F.
Commonwealth Caribbean in the world economy. - London : Macmillan, 1989. - xvi,294p.

REPORT on the further development of the origin system for the Caribbean Common Market. - Georgetown : CARICOM Secretariat, 1985. - 136p.

ROBINSON, A.N.R.
Opening address ... In Conference of Heads of Government of the Caribbean Community Meeting (10th : 1989 : Grand Anse, Grenada). Opening addresses and communique. - [Georgetown : CARICOM Secretariat, 1989]. - p.10-12.

ROLE of the Caribbean in the global information village. - Port-of-Spain : Inprint Caribbean, 1990. - 141p.
Paper presented at TRINCOM 90, jointly sponsored by the Trinidad Express Newspapers Ltd., the Caribbean Association of National Telecommunication Organizations (CANTO) and LATCOM Inc. of Miami.

SANATAN, Roderick and WILLIAMS, Franklyn S.M. eds.
Telecommunications for Caribbean development : proceedings of the CARICOM Telecommunications Symposium 1989. - Nassau : Bahamas Telecommunications Corporation, 1990. - iv,201p. : ill. - Includes bibliographies.

SANDERS, Ron
Narcotics and Corruption. In *Caribbean Affairs*, First Quarter 1990

SANDERS, Ron
Stringent Measures in Illegal Drugs. In *Caribbean Affairs*, Third Quarter 1990

SANDIFORD, L. Erskine
Opening address ... In Conference of Heads of Government of the Caribbean Community Meeting (11th : 1990 : Kingston, Jamaica). Communique and addresses. - [Georgetown : CARICOM Secretariat], 1990. - p.5-9.

SARGENT, Leslie
Regional communication in the Caribbean. - Paris : UNESCO, 1982. - ii,126p.
Mission undertaken for UNESCO, May 23-July 17, 1982.

SEARWAR, Lloyd
Foreign policy decision-making in the Commonwealth Caribbean. In *Caribbean Affairs*, 1(1), 1988, p.59-84.

SEARWAR, Lloyd
The dilemmas of being small : some thoughts on the CARICOM approach to the North Americas Initiative. - Georgetown : L. Searwar, 1991. - 34,2p.

SEARWAR, Lloyd
The superpowers and conflict in the Caribbean Basin. - Georgetown: L. Searwar, 1991. - 41,5p.

STEVENS, Christopher
The Single European Market : implications for Caribbean agricultural exports. - [S.l. : s.n.], 1988.
Paper presented at the "1992 and the Caribbean" Conference organized by the West India Committee, London, September 30-October 1, 1988.

SUTTON, Paul ed.
Europe and the Caribbean. - London : Macmillan, 1991. - xii,260p.

TEN YEARS OF CARICOM : papers presented at a Seminar on Economic Integration in the Caribbean held in Bridgetown, Barbados, July 1983. - Washington, D.C. : IDB, 1984. - 351P.
Seminar sponsored by the Inter-American Development Bank.

TENNYSON, Brian Douglas ed.
Canadian-Caribbean relations : aspects of a relationship. - Sydney, Nova Scotia : University College of Cape Breton. Centre for International Studies, 1990. - vii,379p.

THOMAS, Clive Yolande
The poor and the powerless : economic policy and change in the Caribbean. - New York : Monthly Review Press, 1987. - xv,396p. - Bibliography : p.379-388.

UNIVERSITY OF THE WEST INDIES. Institute of International Relations
Issues in the preparation of small states for the conduct of foreign relations
: papers for seminars in the LDCs of the Commonwealth Caribbean. - St.
Augustine : UWI, Institute of International Relations, 1979.

WEDDERBURN, Judith
Integration and participatory development : selected papers and proceedings
of the 2nd Conference of Caribbean Economists. - Kingston : Friedrich
Ebert Stiftung, 1990.

WILTSHIRE-BRODBER, R.
Caribbean integration : performance and promise. - Paris : OECD
Development Centre, 1986. - 61p.

WORKSHOP ON REGIONAL CURRENCY ARRANGEMENT AND
STRENGTHENING FINANCIAL INSTITUTIONS IN THE CARIBBEAN (1991
: Barbados)
Papers... - St. James, Barbados : West Indian Commission Secretariat, 1991.

WORRELL, DeLisle
Harmonization of exchange rates in the Commonwealth Caribbean. -
Bridgetown : Central Bank of Barbados, 1987. - 17p.

WORRELL, DeLisle
Common exchange rate strategies for the CARICOM region. - Bridgetown :
Central Bank of Barbados, 1985. - 13p.

WORRELL, DeLisle
Exchange rate strategies in the CARICOM region. - Bridgetown, Barbados :
[D. Worrell], 1986. - 22p.
Address to CAIC Workshop in Antigua, on April 23, 1986.

APPENDIX "H"

LIST OF REGIONAL ORGANISATIONS/ASSOCIATIONS/INSTITUTIONS

ADVISORY COMMITTEE FOR HIGHER
EDUCATION IN LATIN AMERICA AND
THE CARIBBEAN (CRESALC)
University of the West Indies
Mona, Kingston 7
JAMAICA

ARAWAK CEMENT CO. LTD.
Checker Hall
St. Lucy
BARBADOS

ASSOCIATION CARIBBEAN D'ETUDES
ET DE RECHERCHES EN TRADITIONS
ORALE (ACERTO)
The Ministry of Culture
Roseau
DOMINICA

ASSOCIATION FOR CARIBBEAN
TRANSFORMATION (ACT) LTD
3 Pelham Street
Belmont
Port of Spain
TRINIDAD AND TOBAGO

ASSOCIATION FOR COOPERATION IN
BANANA RESEARCH IN THE
CARIBBEAN AND CENTRAL AMERICA
(ACORBAT)
Fort de France
MARTINIQUE

ASSOCIATION OF ARCHITECTURAL
SOCIETIES AND INSTITUTES IN THE
WEST INDIES
c/o Barbados Institute of Architects
P.O. Box 9B
Bridgetown
BARBADOS

ASSOCIATION OF CARIBBEAN
ECONOMISTS
President 1992:
Miguel Ceara Hatton
CIECA
Santo Domingo
DOMINICAN REPUBLIC

ASSOCIATION OF CARIBBEAN
HISTORIANS
c/o D. Gail Saunders
Department of Archives
P.O. Box SS6341, Nassau
BAHAMAS

ASSOCIATION OF CARIBBEAN
UNIVERSITIES AND RESEARCH
INSTITUTES (UNICA)
P.O. Box 11532
Caparra Heights Station
San Juan
PUERTO RICO 00922

ASSOCIATION OF CARIBBEAN
UNIVERSITY RESEARCH AND
INSTITUTIONAL LIBRARIES (ACURIL)
SECRETARIAT
P.O. Box 5
University of Puerto Rico
San Juan
PUERTO RICO 00931

ASSOCIATION OF COMMONWEALTH
ARCHITECTS IN THE CARIBBEAN
c/o Caribbean Planning Associates
22 Trafalgar Road
Kingston 10
JAMAICA

BAR ASSOCIATION OF THE
ORGANISATION OF THE EASTERN
CARIBBEAN STATES
7 High Street
P.O. Box 629
Castries
SAINT LUCIA

BARBADOS MUTUAL LIFE INSURANCE
SOCIETY
Collymore Rock
St. Michael
BARBADOS

BIBLE SOCIETY IN THE EASTERN
CARIBBEAN
P.O. Box 36B
Brittons Hill, St. Michael
BARBADOS

BIBLE SOCIETY OF THE WEST INDIES
24 Hagley Park Plaza
Kingston 10
JAMAICA

BRITISH CARIBBEAN CITRUS
ASSOCIATION
c/o CCGA of T & T Ltd.
Eastern Main Road
Laventille
TRINIDAD & TOBAGO

CARIBBEAN AGRICULTURAL AND
RURAL DEVELOPMENT ADVISORY
AND TRAINING SERVICE (CARDATS)
Lowthers Lane
P.O. Box 270
St. George's
GRENADA

CARIBBEAN AGRICULTURAL
RESEARCH AND DEVELOPMENT
INSTITUTE (CARDI)
University Campus
St. Augustine
TRINIDAD & TOBAGO

CARIBBEAN AGRICULTURAL
TRADING COMPANY (CATCO) LTD
Old Terminal Building
Grantley Adams Airport
Bridgetown
BARBADOS

CARIBBEAN AGRO-ECONOMIC
SOCIETY
The Secretariat
Department of Agricultural Economics
and Farm Management
University of the West Indies
St. Augustine
TRINIDAD & TOBAGO

CARIBBEAN AIR CARGO LIMITED
Old Terminal Building
Grantley Adams International Airport
Christ Church
BARBADOS

CARIBBEAN AMERICAN
INTERCULTURAL ORGANIZATION
(CAIO)
Suite 114
1629 Columbia Road, N.W.
Washington, D.C. 20009
UNITED STATES OF AMERICA

CARIBBEAN AREA SQUASH RACKETS
ASSOCIATION
P.O. Box 387
Bridgetown
BARBADOS

CARIBBEAN ARCHIVES ASSOCIATION
c/o National Archives of Trinidad &
Tobago
P.O. Box 763
Port of Spain
TRINIDAD & TOBAGO

CARIBBEAN ASSOCIATION FOR
FEMINIST RESEARCH AND ACTION
(CAFRA)
P.O. Box 442
Tunapuna Post Office
Tunapuna
TRINIDAD AND TOBAGO

CARIBBEAN ASSOCIATION FOR THE
REHABILITATION OF THE DISABLED
c/o Trinidad and Tobago Society of
Rehabilitation and Disabled
721 New Street
Port of Spain
TRINIDAD & TOBAGO

CARIBBEAN ASSOCIATION OF
CRIMINOLOGY
Faculty of Law, UWI
Cave Hill Campus
BARBADOS

CARIBBEAN ASSOCIATION OF
ENVIRONMENTAL HEALTH OFFICERS
Dalkeith
St. Michael
BARBADOS

CARIBBEAN ASSOCIATION OF HOME
ECONOMISTS
c/o Ms. Zola Holder
Education Officer, Home Economics
Ministry of Education
Alexandra Street
St. Clair
TRINIDAD & TOBAGO

CARIBBEAN ASSOCIATION OF
INDUSTRY AND COMMERCE, INC.
P.O. Box 259
2nd Floor, Musson Building
Lower Hincks Street
Bridgetown
BARBADOS

CARIBBEAN ASSOCIATION OF LAW
LIBRARIANS (CARALL)
P.O. Box 231
Kingston 7
JAMAICA

CARIBBEAN ASSOCIATION OF MEDIA
WORKERS (CAMWORK)
c/o Rickey Singh
Donwyne, Strathclyde Drive
Bank Hall
St. Michael
BARBADOS

CARIBBEAN ASSOCIATION OF
MEDICAL TECHNOLOGISTS
c/o Pathology Dept.
Queen Elizabeth Hospital
Martindale's Rode
St. Michael
BARBADOS

CARIBBEAN ASSOCIATION OF
NATIONAL TELECOMMUNICATION
ORGANISATIONS (CANTO)
35 Independence Square
Port of Spain
TRINIDAD & TOBAGO

CARIBBEAN ASSOCIATION OF
NUTRITIONISTS AND DIETICIANS
c/o Caribbean Food and Nutrition
Institute (CFNI)
UWI Campus, St. Augustine
TRINIDAD & TOBAGO

CARIBBEAN ASSOCIATION OF
PHARMACISTS
P.O. Box 203
22 Dunrobin Avenue
Kingston 10
JAMAICA

CARIBBEAN ASSOCIATION OF
POLITICAL ECONOMISTS (CAPE)
SECRETARIAT
Plas Bureau
Paramaribo
SURINAME

CARIBBEAN ASSOCIATION OF
PROFESSIONAL SECRETARIES
P.O. Box 141
Montego Bay
JAMAICA, W.I.

CARIBBEAN ASSOCIATON OF PUBLIC
HEALTH OFFICERS
San Juan
TRINIDAD

CARIBBEAN ASSOCIATION OF PUBLIC
RELATIONS CONSULTANTS
6 Kings Way
Kingston 10
JAMAICA

CARIBBEAN ASSOCIATION OF
REHABILITATION THERAPISTS (CART)
The Senior Physiotherapist
Georgetown Hospital
Georgetown
GUYANA

CARIBBEAN ASSOCIATION OF SUGAR
TECHNOLOGISTS
80 Abercromby Street, P.O. Box 230
Port of Spain
TRINIDAD & TOBAGO

CARIBBEAN ASSOCIATION OF
MENTAL RETARDATION
P.O. Box 792
San German
PUERTO RICO 00753

CARIBBEAN BROADCASTING UNION
(CBU)
Corner Wanderers Gap
Dayrells Road
St. Michael
BARBADOS

CARIBBEAN CANE FARMERS'
ASSOCIATION
4 North Avenue
Kingston 4
JAMAICA

CARIBBEAN CENTRE FOR
DEVELOPMENT ADMINISTRATION
(CARICAD)
27 Block 'C'
The Garrison
St. Michael
BARBADOS

CARIBBEAN COMMON MARKET
STANDARDS COUNCIL
c/o Caribbean Community Secretariat
Bank of Guyana Building
P.O. Box 10827
Georgetown
GUYANA

CARIBBEAN COMMUNITY AND
COMMON MARKET (CARICOM)
SECRETARIAT
Bank of Guyana Building
P.O. Box 10827
Georgetown
GUYANA

CARIBBEAN CONFEDERATION OF
CREDIT UNIONS
'Roseville'
Maxwell, Christ Church
BARBADOS

Appendices

CARIBBEAN CONFEDERATION OF
SHIPPERS' COUNCILS
15 Dominica Drive
Kingston 5
JAMAICA

CARIBBEAN CONFERENCE OF
CHURCHES
George Street & Collymore Rock
P.O. Box 616
Bridgetown
BARBADOS

P.O. Box 911
St. John's
ANTIGUA & BARBUDA

P.O. Box 527
Jingston
JAMAICA

P.O. Box 876
Port of Spain
TRINIDAD & TOBAGO

CARIBBEAN CONGRESS OF LABOUR
The National Union of Public
Workers Bldg.
Dalkeith Road
St. Michael
BARBADOS

CARIBBEAN CONSERVATION
ASSOCIATION
Savannah Lodge
The Garrison
St. Michael
BARBADOS

CARIBBEAN COUNCIL FOR THE
BLIND (CCB)
Newgate House
Newgate Street
St. John's
ANTIGUA & BARBUDA

CARIBBEAN DEVELOPMENT AND
COOPERATION COMMITTEE (CDCC)
ECLAC
P.O. Box 1113
Port of Spain
TRINIDAD & TOBAGO

CARIBBEAN DEVELOPMENT BANK
P.O. Box 408, Wildey
St. Michael
BARBADOS

CARIBBEAN ELECTRICAL UTILITIES
SERVICES CORPORATION (CARILEC)
c/o Mr. H.S. Jabbal
Dominica Electricity Services Ltd.
Castle Street, P.O. Box 13
Roseau
DOMINICA

CARIBBEAN EMPLOYERS'
CONFEDERATION
43 Dundonald Street, P.O. Box 911
Port of Spain
TRINIDAD & TOBAGO

CARIBBEAN ENVIRONMENTAL
HEALTH INSTITUTE
P.O. Box 1111
Morne Fortune
Castries
SAINT LUCIA

CARIBBEAN EPIDEMIOLOGY CENTRE
(CAREC)
Federation Park
P.O. Box 164
Port of Spain
TRINIDAD & TOBAGO

CARIBBEAN EVANGELICAL
THEOLOGICAL ASSOCIATION
P.O. Box 121
14 West Avenue
Constant Spring, Kingston 8
JAMAICA

Regional Organisations

CARIBBEAN EXAMINATIONS
COUNCIL
Block A, The Garrison
St. Michael
BARBADOS

CARIBBEAN FAMILY PLANNING
AFFILIATION (CFPA) LTD
Factory Road, P.O. Box 419
St. John's
ANTIGUA & BARBUDA

CARIBBEAN FARMERS DEVELOPMENT
COMPANY (CFDC)
P.O. Box 1223
Castries
SAINT LUCIA

CARIBBEAN FEDERATION FOR
MENTAL HEALTH
P.O. Box 1322
Port of Spain
TRINIDAD & TOBAGO

CARIBBEAN FEDERATION OF YOUTH
P.O. Box 1230
Castries
SAINT LUCIA

CARIBBEAN FINANCIAL SERVICES
CORPORATION (CFSC)
Chapel Street
Bridgetown
BARBADOS

CARIBBEAN FISHERIES TRAINING
AND DEVELOPMENT INSTITUTE
Chaguaramas
TRINIDAD & TOBAGO

CARIBBEAN FOOD AND NUTRITION
INSTITUTE
P.O. Box 140
Kingston 7
JAMAICA

CARIBBEAN FOOD CORPORATION
30 Queen's Park West
P.O. Bag 264
Port of Spain
TRINIDAD & TOBAGO

CARIBBEAN FOOD CROPS SOCIETY
College of the Virgin Islands
Kingshill
U.S. VIRGIN ISLANDS 00820

CARIBBEAN FOOTBALL UNION
119 Edward Street
Port of Spain
TRINIDAD & TOBAGO

CARIBBEAN GRADUATE SCHOOL OF
THEOLOGY
14 West Avenue
P.O. Box 121
Constant Spring
Kingston 8
JAMAICA

CARIBBEAN GENERAL & MARINE
INSURANCE BROKERS LTD. (CGM)
Lower Collymore Rock
St. Michael
BARBADOS

CARIBBEAN HISTORICAL SOCIETY
17 School Road
Point Fortin
TRINIDAD

CARIBBEAN HOCKEY ASSOCIATION
c/o Ms. Maureen Yard
"Bert Ville", 1st Avenue
Rockley
Christ Church
BARBADOS

CARIBBEAN HOME INSURANCE CO.
LTD.
201 & 302 1st Floor, Kays House
Roebuck Street & Magazine Lane
Bridgetown
BARBADOS

Appendices

CARIBBEAN HOTEL ASSOCIATION
18 Marseilles Street, Suite 2B
Santurce
PUERTO RICO 00907

CARIBBEAN HOTEL TRAINING
INSTITUTE
18 Marseilles
Santurce
PUERTO RICO 00907

CARIBBEAN HOTELS ADVISORY
COUNCIL
Caribbean Hotel Training Institute
18 Marseilles
Santurce
PUERTO RICO 00907

CARIBBEAN INDUSTRIAL RESEARCH
INSTITUTE (CARIRI)
Tunapuna Post Office
TRINIDAD & TOBAGO

CARIBBEAN INSTITUTE FOR SOCIAL
FORMATION (CARISFORM)
UTAL, CLAT's Headquarters
P.O. Box 6681, Caracas 1010-A
VENEZUELA

CARIBBEAN INSTITUTE FOR THE
PROMOTION OF HUMAN RIGHTS
(CARICARE)
45 Eastern Main Road
Curepe
TRINIDAD AND TOBAGO

CARIBBEAN INSTITUTE OF MASS
COMMUNICATIONS (CARIMAC)
University of the West Indies
Mona, Kingston 7
JAMAICA

CARIBBEAN INSTITUTE ON MENTAL
RETARDATION & DEVELOPMENTAL
DISABILITIES (CIMRDD)
94C Old Hope Road
Kingston 10
JAMAICA

CARIBBEAN LABOUR
ADMINISTRATION CENTRE (CLAC)
Verona House, Bank Hall
St. Michael
BARBADOS

CARIBBEAN LAW INSTITUTE
University of the West Indies
Faculty of Law
P.O. Box 64, Bridgetown
BARBADOS

CARIBBEAN MEDICAL COUNCIL
10 Caledonia Avenue
Kingston 5
JAMAICA

CARIBBEAN METEOROLOGICAL
INSTITUTE/CARIBBEAN
OPERATIONAL HYDROLOGY
INSTITUTE
P.O. Box 130
Bridgetown
BARBADOS

CARIBBEAN METEOROLOGICAL
ORGANISATION
P.O. Box 461
St. Ann's Avenue
St. Ann's
Port of Spain
TRINIDAD & TOBAGO

CARIBBEAN NATURAL RESOURCES
INSTITUTE (CANARI)
Clarke Street
Vieux Fort
ST. LUCIA

Regional Organisations

CARIBBEAN NETWORK FOR
INTEGRATED RURAL DEVELOPMENT
(CNIRD)
#40, Eastern Main Road
St. Augustine
TRINIDAD & TOBAGO

CARIBBEAN NETWORK OF
EDUCATIONAL INNOVATION FOR
DEVELOPMENT (CARNEID)
CARNEID Coordinating Centre
P.O. Box 423
No. 7, Garrison
Bridgetown
BARBADOS

CARIBBEAN NEWS AGENCY
Culloden View
Beckles Road
St. Michael
BARBADOS

CARIBBEAN NURSES ORGANIZATION
P.O. Box 583
Christiansted
St. Croix 00820
U.S. VIRGIN ISLANDS

CARIBBEAN ORGANIZATION OF TAX
ADMINISTRATORS
c/o CARICOM Secretariat
Bank of Guyana Building
P.O. Box 10827
Georgetown
GUYANA

CARIBBEAN PEOPLE'S DEVELOPMENT
AGENCY (CARIPEDA)
Tyrell Street
P.O. Box 1132
Kingstown
ST. VINCENT & THE GRENADINES

CARIBBEAN PLANNING ASSOCIATION
22 Trafalgar Road
Kingston
JAMAICA

CARIBBEAN PRESS COUNCIL (CPC)
c/o CARIMAC
University of the West Indies
Mona, Kingston 7
JAMAICA

CARIBBEAN PROJECT DEVELOPMENT
FACILITIES (CPDF)
2nd Floor, Musson Bldg.
Hincks Street
Bridgetown
BARBADOS

CARIBBEAN PUBLIC SERVICES
ASSOCIATION (CPSA)
Dalkeith, Dalkeith Road
St. Michael
BARBADOS

CARIBBEAN PUBLISHING AND
BROADCASTING ASSOCIATION
Dayrells Road
Christ Church
BARBADOS

CARIBBEAN PUBLISHING COMPANY
LTD.
Compass Bldg.
Box 1365
Crewe Road
GRAND CAYMAN

CARIBBEAN REGIONAL COMMUNITY
EDUCATION CENTRE
Patricia Charles, SLACE
c/o Caribbean Research Centre
P.O. Box 1097, Castries
SAINT LUCIA

Appendices

CARIBBEAN REGIONAL COUNCIL FOR
ADULT EDUCATION (CARCAE)
P.O. Box 1810
St. John's
ANTIGUA AND BARBUDA

CARIBBEAN REGIONAL DRUG
TESTING LABORATORY
c/o Government Chemist's Department
Hope, Kingston 6
JAMAICA

CARIBBEAN RESEARCH CENTRE
P.O. Box 1097
Castries
SAINT LUCIA

CARIBBEAN RESOURCES
DEVELOPMENT FOUNDATION
(CARDEV)
c/o Mr. Aaron Matalon
7-9 Harbour Street
Kingston
JAMAICA

CARIBBEAN RIGHTS
5 Third Avenue
Belleville
St. Michael
BARBADOS

CARIBBEAN SHIPPING ASSOCIATION
5-7 King Street
P.O. Box 40
Kingston 15
JAMAICA

CARIBBEAN SOCIETY OF
EDUCATIONAL ADMINISTRATORS
(CARSEA)
c/o School of Education
University of the West Indies
Mona
Kingston 7
JAMAICA

CARIBBEAN SOCIETY OF HOTEL
ASSOCIATION EXECUTIVES (CSHAE)
18 Marseilles Street, Suite 2B
Santurce
PUERTO RICO 00907

CARIBBEAN SPORT CULTURE
ENTERTAINMENT PHYSICAL
TRAINING AND RECREATION
EXCHANGE (CARISCEPTRE)
Suite 2, Bay Cottage
Beckles Hill, St. Michael
P.O. Box 57B, Bridgetown
BARBADOS

CARIBBEAN STANDARDS
INFORMATION EXCHANGE SERVICE
(SCIES)
Guyana National Bureau of Standards
77 W1/2 Hadfield Street
Werk-en-Rust
Georgetown
GUYANA

CARIBBEAN STUDIES ASSOCIATION
Interamerican University of Puerto Rico
P.O. Box 3682
San German
PUERTO RICO 00753

CARIBBEAN TELECOMMUNICATIONS
UNION (CTU)
17 Queen's Park West
Port of Spain
TRINIDAD & TOBAGO

CARIBBEAN TERTIARY ASSOCIATION
c/o University of the West Indies
Mona
Kingston 7
JAMAICA

CARIBBEAN TOURISM
ORGANISATION (CTO)
"Mer Vue"
Marine Gardens, Christ Church
BARBADOS

Regional Organisations

CARIBBEAN UNION CONFERENCE OF
SEVENTH DAY ADVENTISTS
Mango Lane
Speighstown
St. Peter
BARBADOS

CARIBBEAN UNION OF TEACHERS
P.O. Box 262
Bridgetown
BARBADOS

CARIBBEAN VETERINARY
ASSOCIATION
c/o Ministry of Agriculture
Animal Health Division
St. Clair
Port of Spain
TRINIDAD & TOBAGO

CARIBBEAN WOMEN'S ASSOCIATION
(CARIWA)
Hillcrest, Factory Road
St. John's
ANTIGUA & BARBUDA

CARIBBEAN WOMEN'S CRICKET
FEDERATION
c/o Jean Carmino
Diego Martin Main Road
New Lalta, Diego Martin
TRINIDAD & TOBAGO

CARIBBEAN WOMEN'S LEAGUE
c/o Mrs. Leotta Burke
Brittons Cross Road
St. Michael
BARBADOS

CARIBBEAN YOUTH CONFERENCE
P.O. Box 1550
Castries
SAINT LUCIA

CENTRO REGIONAL PARA EL
FOMENTO DEL LIBRO EN AMERICA
LATINA Y EL CARIBE (CERLALC)
Calle 70 No.7-52
Apartado Aero 57348
Bogota
COLOMBIA

CHRISTIAN CHILDREN'S FUND OF
THE CARIBBEAN REGION (CCFCR)
P.O. Box
St. John's
ANTIGUA & BARBUDA

CHRISTIAN LITERATURE CRUSADE
P.O. Box 239
Bridgetown
BARBADOS

COMMONWEALTH CARIBBEAN
ASSOCIATION OF YOUTH/
COMMUNITY WORKERS
Secretary
Stubbs P.O.
ST. VINCENT

COMMONWEALTH CARIBBEAN LAWN
TENNIS ASSOCIATION (CCLTA)
P.O. Box N10169
Nassau
BAHAMAS

COMMONWEALTH CARIBBEAN
MEDICAL RESEARCH COUNCIL
Tropical Metabolism Research Unit
University of the West Indies
Mona, Kingston 7
JAMAICA

COMMONWEALTH YOUTH
PROGRAMME
Caribbean Centre
6/7 Duncan Street
P.O. Box 101063
Georgetown
GUYANA

Appendices

CONFERENCE OF MINISTERS
REPONSIBLE FOR HEALTH
Caribbean Community Secretariat
Bank of Guyana Building
P.O. Box 10827
Georgetown
GUYANA

COORDINORA REGIONAL DE
INVESTIGACIONES ECONOMICAS Y
SOCIALES (CRIES)
Managua
NICARAGUA

COUNCIL OF CARIBBEAN
ENGINEERING ORGANIZATIONS
Faculty of Engineering
UWI, P.O. Box 1118
St. Augustine
TRINIDAD & TOBAGO

COUNCIL OF CARIBBEAN
INSTITUTIONS FOR DEVELOPMENT
(COUNCARID)
P.O. Box 1097
Castries
SAINT LUCIA

COUNCIL OF LEGAL EDUCATION
Norman Manley Law School
P.O. Box 231
Kingston 7
JAMAICA

EAST CARIBBEAN CONFERENCE OF
S.D.A.
Education Department
P.O. Box 723
Kingstown
ST. VINCENT & THE GRENADINES

EAST CARIBBEAN ORGANISATION OF
DEVELOPMENT FOUNDATIONS
(ECODEF)
c/o NDF Dominica
P.O. Box 313, 28 Kennedy Avenue
Roseau
DOMINICA

EAST CARIBBEAN SAFE DIVING
ASSOCIATION
P.O. Box 86
Welches Road
St. Michael
Barbados

EASTERN CARIBBEAN CENTRAL BANK
Church Street
P.O. Box 89, Basseterre
ST. KITTS

EASTERN CARIBBEAN INVESTMENT
PROMOTION SERVICE (ECIPS)
1730 M Street, N.W., Suite 901
Washington, D.C. 20036
UNITED STATES OF AMERICA

EASTERN CARIBBEAN INSTITUTE FOR
DEMOCRACY
Hanover Street
P.O. Box 252
Roseau
DOMINICA

EASTERN CARIBBEAN STATES
EXPORT DEVELOPMENT AGENCY
(ECSEDA)
Old Street
Box 371
Roseau
DOMINICA

EASTERN CARIBBEAN INSTITUTE OF
AGRICULTURE AND FORESTRY
Centeno
via Arima P.O.
TRINIDAD, W.I.

Regional Organisations

FAMILY NURSING EDUCATION
PROGRAMMES/PAHO/WHO
P.O. Box 877
Kingstown
ST. VINCENT & THE GRENADINES

GROUP OF LATIN AMERICAN AND
CARIBBEAN SUGAR EXPORTING
COUNTRIES (GEPLACEA)
Av. Ejercito Nacional 373
1er Piso
Col. Granada 11520 D.F.
MEXICO

GUILD OF GRADUATES OF THE
UNIVERSITY OF THE WEST INDIES
c/o University of the West Indies
Mona, Kingston
JAMAICA

GULF AND CARIBBEAN FISHERIES
INSTITUTE
University of Miami
4600 Rickenbacker Causeway
Miami, Florida 33149
UNITED STATES OF AMERICA

INSTITUTE OF CARIBBEAN STUDIES
P.O. Box 22361
University Station
Rio Pedras
PUERTO RICO 00931

INSTITUTO CARIBE DE
ANTROPOLOGIA Y SOCIOLOGIA
Fundacion La Salle de Ciencias
Naturales
Apartado Postal 8150
Caracas
VENEZUELA

INSURANCE ASSOCIATION OF THE
CARIBBEAN, INC.
1AC Building
Collymore Rock, St. Michael
BARBADOS

INTERAMERICAN INSTITUTE FOR
COOPERATION IN AGRICULTURE
(IICA)
P.O. Box 55-2200
Coronado
COSTA RICA, C.A.

INTERGOVERNMENTAL
OCEANOGRAPHIC COMMISSION
ASSOCIATION FOR THE CARIBBEAN
AND ADJACENT REGIONS (IOCARIBE)
UNESCO-ROSTLAC
Casilla de Correo 859
Montevideo
URUGUAY

ISLAND RESOURCES FOUNDATION
Red Hook Centre
Box 33
St. Thomas
U.S. VIRGIN ISLANDS 00802

LATIN AMERICAN AND CARIBBEAN
FEDERATION OF THE SOCIAL
ECONOMY SECTOR FOR TRADE
(FENLACES)
Candela-Nigaragua
De la Rotondo de Bello
Horizonte 2 Cuadras Arriba
5 al sur 1 Abajo
Barrio Bello Horizonte
Managua
NICARAGUA

LATIN AMERICAN AND CARIBBEAN
WOMEN'S HEALTH NETWORK
Isis International
Casilla 2067
Correo Central
Santiago
CHILE

Appendices

LEEWARD ISLANDS CRICKET
ASSOCIATION
c/o Mr. Richard Aspin
Montserrat Technical College
Plymouth
MONTSERRAT

LIAT (1974) LTD.
Monplaisir Bldg.
Brazil Street
Castries
SAINT LUCIA

MUSEUMS ASSOCIATION OF THE
CARIBBEAN (MAC)
P.O. Box 112, GPO
Bridgetown
BARBADOS

NATIONAL CHILDREN'S HOME
Caribbean Regional Office
'Dumfries', Henry's Lane
P.O. Box 83 B.H.
St. Michael
BARBADOS

ORGANISATION OF EASTERN
CARIBBEAN STATES (OECS)
Central Secretariat
The Morne, Castries
SAINT LUCIA

ORGANISATION OF EASTERN
CARIBBEAN STATES
Economic Affairs Secretariat
P.O. Box 822
St. John's
ANTIGUA & BARBUDA

ORGANISATION OF THE
COMMONWEALTH BAR
ASSOCIATIONS (OCCBA)
P.O. Box 551, Chambers
Corn Alley, St. John's
ANTIGUA AND BARBUDA

PARTNERS OF THE AMERICAS
(CARIBBEAN REGIONAL OFFICE)
Lambert House
Probyn Square
Bridgetown
BARBADOS

PENTECOSTAL ASSEMBLIES OF THE
WEST INDIES
P.O. Box 100
Port of Spain
TRINIDAD & TOBAGO

REGIONAL EDUCATIONAL
PROGRAMME FOR ANIMAL HEALTH
ASSISTANTS (REPAHA)
P.O. Box 10814
Mon Repos
East Coast Demerara
GUYANA

REGIONAL NURSING BODY
CARICOM Secretariat
Bank of Guyana Building
P.O. Box 10827, Georgetown
GUYANA

SOCIETY FOR CARIBBEAN
LINGUISTICS
c/o Department of Linguistics & Use of
English
University of the West Indies
Mona, Kingston 7
JAMAICA

STANDING COMMITTEE OF
COMMONWEALTH CARIBBEAN
STATISTICIANS
Caribbean Community Secretariat
P.O. Box 10827, Georgetown
GUYANA

STANDING COMMITTEE OF
MINISTERS RESPONSIBLE FOR
AGRICULTURE
Caribbean Community Secretariat
Bank of Guyana Building
P.O. Box 10827
Georgetown
GUYANA

STANDING COMMITTEE OF
MINISTERS RESPONSIBLE FOR
EDUCATION
Caribbean Community Secretariat
Bank of Guyana Building
P.O. Box 10827
Georgetown
GUYANA

STANDING COMMITTEE OF
MINISTERS RESPONSIBLE FOR
ENERGY, MINES AND NATURAL
RESOURCES
Caribbean Community Secretariat
Bank of Guyana Building
P.O. Box 10827, Georgetown
GUYANA

STANDING COMMITTEE OF
MINISTERS RESPONSIBLE FOR
FINANCE
Caribbean Community Secretariat
Bank of Guyana Building
P.O. Box 10827
Georgetown
GUYANA

STANDING COMMITTEE OF
MINISTERS RESPONSIBLE FOR
FOREIGN AFFAIRS
Caribbean Community Secretariat
Bank of Guyana Building
P.O. Box 10827
Georgetown
GUYANA

STANDING COMMITTEE OF
MINISTERS RESPONSIBLE FOR
INDUSTRY
Caribbean Community Secretariat
Bank of Guyana Building
P.O. Box 10827
Georgetown
GUYANA

STANDING COMMITTEE OF
MINISTERS RESPONSIBLE FOR
LABOUR
Caribbean Community Secretariat
Bank of Guyana Building
P.O. Box 10827
Georgetown
GUYANA

STANDING COMMITTEE OF
MINISTERS RESPONSIBLE FOR LEGAL
AFFAIRS
Caribbean Community Secretariat
Bank of Guyana Building
P.O. Box 10827
Georgetown
GUYANA

STANDING COMMITTEE OF
MINISTERS RESPONSIBLE FOR
SCIENCE AND TECHNOLOGY
Caribbean Community Secretariat
Bank of Guyana Building
P.O. Box 10827
Georgetown
GUYANA

STANDING COMMITTEE OF
MINISTERS RESPONSIBLE FOR
TOURISM
Caribbean Community Secretariat
Bank of Guyana Building
P.O. Box 10827
Georgetown
GUYANA

Appendices

STANDING COMMITTEE OF
MINISTERS RESPONSIBLE FOR
TRANSPORT
Caribbean Community Secretariat
Bank of Guyana Building
P.O. Box 10827, Georgetown
GUYANA

STANDING CONFERENCE OF
POPULAR DEMOCRATIC PARTIES IN
EAST CARIBBEAN STATES (SCOPE)
c/o Julian Hunte
St. Lucia Labour Party
Castries
SAINT LUCIA

SUGAR ASSOCIATION OF THE
CARIBBEAN INC.
c/o Sugar Manufacturer's Association
80 Abercromby Street
P.O. Box 230
Port of Spain
TRINIDAD & TOBAGO

UNEP's REGIONAL OFFICE FOR LATIN
AMERICA AND THE CARIBBEAN
(ROLAC)
Edificio Naciones Unidas
Presidente Masaryk 29
Apartado Postal 6-718
Mexico 5. DF
MEXICO

UNESCO/CARNEID COORDINATING
CENTRE
No. 7 Garrison
P.O. Box 423
St. Michael
BARBADOS

UNITED NATIONS ECONOMIC
COMMISSION FOR LATIN AMERICA
AND THE CARIBBEAN, SUBREGIONAL
HEADQUARTERS FOR THE
CARIBBEAN/CARIBBEAN
DEVELOPMENT AND COOPERATION
COMMITTEE (ECLAC/CDCC)
22-24 St. Vincent Street
P.O. Box 1113
Port of Spain
TRINIDAD AND TOBAGO

UNIVERSITY OF THE WEST INDIES
(UWI)
Cave Hill Campus
Cave Hill
Bridgetown
BARBADOS

Mona Campus
Mona
Kingston 7
JAMAICA

St. Augustine Campus
St. Augustine
TRINIDAD & TOBAGO

UNIVERSITY OF THE WEST INDIES
(UWI)
Institute of International Relations (IIR)
University of the West Indies
St. Augustine
TRINIDAD & TOBAGO

Institute of Social and Economic
Research (ISER)
Cave Hill
Bridgetown
BARBADOS

Institute of Social and Economic
Research (ISER)
Mona
Kingston 7
JAMAICA

Regional Organisations

Institute of Social and Economic
Research (ISER)
St. Augustine
TRINIDAD & TOBAGO

WEST INDIA RUM REFINERY LTD.
Brighton
Black Rock, St. Michael
BARBADOS

WEST INDIAN ASSOCIATION FOR
COMMONWEALTH LITERATURE AND
LANGUAGE STUDIES (West Indian
ACLALS)
c/o Prof. Edward Baugh
English Department
University of the West Indies
Mona, Kingston 7
JAMAICA

WEST INDIAN LIMES ASSOCIATION
INC.
c/o 2 Pasea Street
St. Augustine
TRINIDAD & TOBAGO

WEST INDIES AGRICULTURAL
ECONOMICS ASSOCIATION
c/o Caribbean Development Bank
Wildey
St. Michael
BARBADOS

WEST INDIES CENTRAL SUGAR CANE
BREEDING STATION
Groves
St. George
BARBADOS

WEST INDIES CRICKET BOARD OF
CONTROL
Kensington Oval
Fontabelle
St. Michael
BARBADOS

WEST INDIES GROUP OF UNIVERSITY
TEACHERS (WIGUT)
University of the West Indies
Mona, Kingston 7
JAMAICA

WEST INDIES JAYCEES
8 Melville Lane
Port of Spain
TRINIDAD & TOBAGO

WEST INDIES RUM AND SPIRITS
PRODUCERS ASSOCIATION
P.O. Box 170
Bridgetown
BARBADOS

WEST INDIES SCHOOL OF
THEOLOGY
#4 Bridge
Maracas Royal Road
Maracas, Curepe
TRINIDAD

WEST INDIES SHIPPING
CORPORATION (WISCO)
48-50 Sackville Street
Port of Spain
TRINIDAD & TOBAGO

WINDWARD ISLANDS BANANA
GROWERS' ASSOCIATION (WINBAN)
Wm Peter Boulevard
P.O. Box 115
Castries
SAINT LUCIA

WINDWARD ISLANDS FARMERS
ASSOCIATION (WINFA)
P.O. Box 817, Paul's Avenue
Kingstown
ST. VINCENT & THE GRENADINES

WOMEN & DEVELOPMENT UNIT
(WAND)
Extra-Mural Department, UWI
The Pine
St. Michael
BARBADOS

Y.W.C.A. CARIBBEAN AREA
COMMITTEE
21 Hope Road
Kingston 10
JAMAICA

www.ingramcontent.com/pod-product-compliance
Lightning Source LLC
Chambersburg PA
CBHW060747230426
43667CB00010B/1471